T0386228

# THE LION
## — AND —
# THE ROSE

# THE LION
# — AND —
# THE ROSE

## THE 4TH BATTALION OF THE KING'S OWN
## ROYAL LANCASTER REGIMENT
## 1914-1919

## KEVIN SHANNON

FONTHILL

*This book is dedicated to the memory of those men who served in the battalion between 4 August 1914 and 11 November 1918, and especially to the grandfather I never knew.*

*It is also dedicated to the memory of the grandsons of that generation, who served and died for their country; in particular to Ade, Jock, Terry, and Lenny, who gave everything; and to Tojo and Dave, two great comrades sadly missed.*

Fonthill Media Limited
Fonthill Media LLC
www.fonthillmedia.com
office@fonthillmedia.com

First published in the United Kingdom
and the United States of America 2015

British Library Cataloguing in Publication Data:
A catalogue record for this book is available from the British Library

ISBN 978-1-78155-438-8

Typeset in 9.5pt on 13pt Minion Pro
Printed and bound by CPI Group (UK) Ltd, Croydon, CR0 4YY

# Contents

# Acknowledgements

This book would not have been possible without the help and patience of my wife, Glynis, whose assistance with research, photography, and proof-reading was crucial to its completion. I'd also like to thank the staff at the Barrow and Blackburn Libraries for their help accessing newspaper reports and original editions; Liverpool Record Office for their great help in locating various primary sources and their kind permission to use some as illustrations in the book; Peter Donnelly from the King's Own Royal Regiment Museum in Lancaster, whose earlier work in collecting information together about the battalion made my research so much easier. This work would also have been much more difficult without the knowledge and expertise of the many contributors from the Great War Forum, who answered those obscure queries, enabling me to add that extra detail into my narratives: in particular, Andy Moss for his in-depth knowledge of the battalion and great collection of photographs; and Ian Riley and Ken Lees for their knowledge about 55 Division. Thanks are due to Graham Lindow for his photographs of Samuel Oliver; John Jackson and the Clark family for the photographs of William Clark and Tom Mayson; and Ivor Holden for the photograph of Joseph Steele. Thanks too to my old comrade Steven Kippax, for his trips to the National Archives to dig out those files I'd forgotten about. Heartfelt thanks are also due to Jay Slater and the staff at Fonthill Media for their help in producing this volume.

# Glossary

| | |
|---|---|
| *ADS* | Advanced Dressing Station |
| *ASC* | Army Service Corps |
| *B CdG* | Belgian Croix de Guerre |
| *BMV* | Italian Bronze Medal for Military Valour |
| *Bn* | Battalion |
| *CCS* | Casualty Clearing Station |
| *CdG* | French Croix de Guerre |
| *Cheshires* | Cheshire Regiment |
| *CLLE* | Charger Loading Lee-Enfield |
| *Coy* | Company |
| *CRA* | Commander Royal Artillery |
| *CWGC* | Commonwealth War Graves Commission |
| *D* | died |
| *DCLI* | Duke of Cornwall's Light Infantry |
| *DCM* | Distinguished Conduct Medal |
| *Deliberate attack* | a pre-planned and coordinated use of firepower and maneuver to carry out an attack |
| *DG* | Dragoon Guards |
| *Div TC* | divisional Tunnelling Company |
| *DLOY* | Duke of Lancasters Own Yeomanry |
| *DOW* | died of wounds |
| *DSO* | Distinguished Service Order |
| *E. Kent* | East Kent Regiment |
| *E. Lancs* | East Lancashire Regiment |
| *E. Surreys* | East Surrey Regiment |
| *Effective fire* | enemy fire which begins to cause casualties among one's own troops |
| *FGCM* | Field General Court Martial |
| *GCM* | General Court Martial |
| *Gds* | Guards |
| *Glam. Yeo.* | Glamorgan Yeomanry |
| *Glasshouse, the* | British Army military prison |
| *Glosters* | Gloucestershire Regiment |

| | |
|---|---|
| *GS wagon* | general service wagon |
| *H* | Home Service Only |
| *HE* | high explosive |
| *IBD* | Infantry Base Depot, or the 'Bull Ring' |
| *ICT* | Inflammation of the Connective Tissue, or Internal Cruciate Tear |
| *IR* | Infantry Regiment (German) |
| *KAR* | King's African Rifles |
| *KIA* | killed in action |
| *KLR* | King's Liverpool Regiment |
| *KORL* | King's Own Royal Lancaster Regiment |
| *KRRC or KRR* | King's Royal Rifle Corps |
| *KSLI* | King's Shropshire Light Infantry |
| *LC* | Labour Corps |
| *Leic. Yeo.* | Leicestershire Yeomanry |
| *Leics* | Leicestershire Regiment |
| *LF* | Lancashire Fusiliers |
| *Light Rwy Op Coy* | branch of RE who built and ran the narrow gauge railways |
| *Lincs* | Lincolnshire Regiment |
| *LNL or LN* | Loyal North Lancashire Regiment |
| *MC* | Military Cross |
| *MCR* | Manchester Regiment |
| *MGC* | Machine Gun Corps |
| *MiD* | Mentioned in Dispatches. |
| *Mil Foot Police* | Military Foot Police |
| *MM* | Military Medal |
| *MO* | Medical Officer |
| *Monmouths* | Monmouthshire regiment |
| *MORC* | Medical Officers' Reserve Corps (US Army) |
| *MSM* | Meritorious Services Medal |
| *N. Staffs* | North Staffordshire Regiment |
| *Northampt. Yeo.* | Northamptonshire Yeomanry |
| *NVS* | brought to the Notice of the Secretary of State for Valuable Services rendered |
| *OP* | Observation Post |
| *OR* | other rank |
| *Ptn* | Platoon |
| *R CdG* | Romanian Croix de Guerre |
| *RA* | Royal Artillery |
| *RAMC* | Royal Army Medical Corps |
| *RAP* | Regimental Aid Post |
| *RCM* | Regimental Court Martial |
| *RDC* | Royal Defence Corps |
| *RE* | Royal Engineers |

| | |
|---|---|
| *RE* | Royal Engineers |
| *RFA* | Royal Field Artillfery |
| *RFC* | Royal Flying Corps |
| *Rgt* | Regiment |
| *RIR* | Reserve Infantry Regiment (German) |
| *RN* | Royal Navy |
| *RR* | Reserve Regiment (German) |
| *RSAF Enfield* | Royal Small Arms Factory in Enfield |
| *RWF* | Royal Welsh Fusiliers (they did not become 'Welch' until 1920) |
| *Rwy Op Div* | Railway Operating Division |
| *S. Lancs* | South Lancashire Regiment |
| *Sherwoods* | Sherwood Foresters |
| *SMLE* | Short Magazine Lee-Enfield |
| *SWB* | Silver War Badge |
| *TEWT* | Tactical Exercise Without Troops |
| *TMB* | Trench Mortar Battery |
| *VC* | Victoria Cross |
| *W. Surreys* | West Surrey Regiment |
| *WIA* | wounded in action |
| *Yeo.* | Yeomanry |
| *Yorks and Lancs* | Yorkshire and Lancashire Regiment |

# Foreword

In my spare room was a cardboard box containing papers and other items I had cleared from my mother's house after her death, but hadn't yet examined. An inspection revealed an old pencil case containing a number of postcards of her father in uniform, a broken pocket watch, his cap badge, a Silver War Badge still sealed in its box, and a few forms concerning his medical discharge in 1917. This rekindled the desire to find out about the grandfather I never knew, and from this small collection I was furnished with his regiment, battalion, and regimental number.

Sadly, his and somewhere between 70 to 80 per cent of all service records from the Great War were destroyed in the Blitz, and many of those that remain were badly damaged by fire, water, and mould. I decided that the only way I could discover more about where he had served and what had happened to him was to find out as much as I could about those he served with, and from the details of their war try to reconstruct as much as possible about his. This meant that I had to start by finding out their names.

No complete roll survives for any of the territorial battalions of the King's Own. It's possible that one was never compiled in the first place, as a battalion would only maintain lists of those men currently serving with them. However, the Regimental Museum in Lancaster published the Medal Rolls for all the King's Own (Royal Lancaster) and it was to these that I turned to in an attempt to produce a roll for 1/4th King's Own. Unfortunately, these don't give the full story, since those who were discharged either for medical reasons or to munitions work before the battalion's deployment to France in May 1915 don't appear on any medal roll, and many of those who went to France but were later transferred are not in the King's Own rolls either. Paradoxically, the Medal Rolls show war service with the King's Own for many men who never actually fought with them in France, having been transferred to another unit before leaving Étaples or Rouen, or brought in after the fighting had ended, so all these had to be weeded out. I now had the biggest jigsaw puzzle in the world, with all the pieces around the edges missing and no picture on the box! Luckily other sources, such as newspapers and histories, provided hints as to who some of these missing people were, and perusals through the medal index cards, archives, military records, and Silver War Badge records all helped to add men to the list (or indeed remove them). The 'Battalion Roll' in Appendix 4 is not complete, but it is certainly the most complete one compiled to date. The ranks given in the narrative are the ranks held at the time the events took place, whereas the ranks in the appendices are those ranks held when the individual left the battalion, or the war ended. Any promotions that took place between the end of the war and discharge in 1919 (or later) have not been applied. It is inevitable that I should make a few errors in these, and for that I apologise in advance. The numbers men held were 'battalion' and not 'army' numbers, as these were only introduced some years later. Numbers in the Territorial Force (TF) ran from 1 to 9999, but it became clear that these were inadequate due to the high volume of casualties and transfers: men who were transferred in got a new number; in March 1917, all men in the battalion were given a new six-figure number; and men posted 'missing' were rarely declared 'killed in action' until the passage of approximately a year, so men who went missing in mid-1916 were allocated six-figure numbers, even if it was later decided that they had indeed been killed. Regular soldiers continued to hold four-figure numbers, and from the beginning of the war, men who joined 'service' battalions or were later conscripted held five-figure numbers. The numbers given in the narrative and appendices are the later numbers, if these were allocated.

One of the problems with war histories is that they tend to break war up into a series of 'events'—they jump from one major incident to the next, as if absolutely nothing happened in between. Yet, 43 per cent of this battalion's fatalities did not occur in 'set-piece' battles. War diaries reinforce this interpretation, as the poor overworked adjutant sitting in his dugout, pencil in hand, trying to complete the form by the flickering light of a candle, frequently had tasks he considered far more important to the winning of the war than writing an essay on 'Army Form C. 2118' (the war diary form). Very rarely were 'other ranks' mentioned by name, so I have tried to fill in these gaps and tell the story of the battalion and the men who served in it for the entire period of the war, and in some cases for the years afterwards.

The battalion's actions are better understood walking the actual ground where they unfolded, but as most readers are unlikely to be able to do this, I have used overlays of original trench maps to calculate the *approximate* coordinates of positions, which can be entered as 'placemarks' on Google Earth. A combination of this and Google Street-View add a dimension to these events that a paper map cannot offer. I have also included sketch maps for most of the front-line locations the battalion served in, and having a photocopy of these handy would help readers to better follow the narrative. These maps are only roughly to scale, drawn using information gleaned from the combined and often conflicting evidence of original trench maps, sketch maps (in official, divisional, and regimental histories), modern maps, aerial photographs, and written accounts; however, these sketch maps do show the relationship of various positions to one another. What maps don't easily show are fields of fire; having walked the ground myself, I have used a 'soldier's eye' to comment on these when appropriate.

In the minds of the public, the Great War can be summarised in the first day of the Somme, or Passchendaele: an epic tale of brave men led by 'donkeys', going needlessly to their deaths by the thousand. If a theatre of war other than the Western Front is mentioned, it tends to be Gallipoli, and then only in passing. The war is typically recounted as four and a half years of constant suffering and misery—a simplistic and stereotypical view encouraged by anti-establishment perspectives from the second half of the twentieth century. Sadly, British attitudes to the Great War owe more to 'Oh What a Lovely War' and 'Blackadder' than they do to historical reality, and I suspect that the recent series of 100th anniversaries will do little to challenge them. When the politicians' promises of 'homes fit for heroes' turned into mass unemployment and the Great Depression, veterans were left embittered. Many remained so for their entire lives, and their perceptions of the sacrifices they'd made changed.

War is bloody. War is bloody awful. But war can be bloody marvellous, too, in the eyes of some participants. While this book does feed into the Great War's mythology—as the story of men's struggles and sufferings, and sufferings there were—there is and was far more to war service than that. For some of the malnourished and feeble teenagers joining the colours, this was their first experience of three meals a day, free clothes, and free dental and medical care; many of the surviving medical records show how youngsters blossomed under the military regime. War was not all death, disease, and labour, though we concentrate on these aspects the most. Men laughed and joked with each other, especially when things were tough, and sports and theatrical entertainments punctuated long periods of frightfulness and boredom. Men who had held menial jobs when they enlisted learned skills and trades which led to better employment after the war. Soldiers took pride in themselves and their units as they do today, and this pride does not suddenly evaporate upon discharge. Men were nourished by the comradeship that military service provided; Old Comrades associations met for many years after the war had ended. Quite a few must have missed the life, since they re-enlisted in the TF after the war, some even joining the regular Army. It is difficult to describe to a civilian just how intense the feelings of comradery after combat can be: phrases along the lines of 'band of brothers' may seem terribly clichéd, but they are rooted in reality. Nothing reinforces the joys of life more than nearly losing it. Combat can be intensely exhilarating and exciting, and some men enjoyed it. I suspect that for many ex-soldiers, adjusting to and dealing with the banality of life in 'Civvie Street' was not easy. For many, the war would never leave them, especially as they got older.

# August 1914 – 2 May 1915
# Your King and Country Need You

Until 1908, the Home Defence was supplemented by a number of locally organised, part-time militia and volunteer units. With the exception of some who had provided 'service' companies or squadrons in Egypt in 1882 (postal units), the Sudan in 1885 (postal, telegraphy, and engineer units), and the Boer War from 1899 to 1902 (infantry and cavalry), supplements to the Home Defence had not served overseas.[1] Realising that political changes and military lessons learned during the Boer War required a number of Army reforms, the Secretary of State for War in the 1906 Liberal Government, Richard Haldane, introduced a series of wide-sweeping measures in 1907. As late as 1870, the French were viewed as the 'enemy', but the last thirty years of the nineteenth century saw a gradual thaw in relations, and with the signing of the Entente Cordiale in 1904, a recognition that cooperation would be mutually beneficial. Haldane was well aware of the Foreign Secretary's private agreement to come to France's aid in Europe should it be attacked, and that if this were to happen, modernisation and reorganisation of the British Army was imperative. Some historians have argued that the need for an expeditionary force was not quite as clear cut in 1906, as Haldane and other politicians of the day would later claim. Peter Simpkins argues that this recognition was more a gradual process that developed between 1906 and 1912.[2] A series of changes to the Home Defence establishment, training, tactics, and administration addressed Haldane's concerns, but with the regular Army overseas engaged in a continental role, the defence of Britain remained in question. The 1907 Territorial and Reserve Forces Act provided the machinery to settle the matter.

Under this act, the volunteer, yeomanry, and militia units were disbanded and their place taken by the Territorial Force (TF) and Special Reserve. The latter was loosely based on the old militia and destined for soldiers who had not served with the regular forces, however agreed to serve overseas in the event of war. The former consisted of fourteen divisions of locally raised and funded men; each division of three infantry brigades; and each infantry brigade of four battalions and attached arms of cavalry, engineers, artillery, transport, and medical services. There was no obligation for the TF to serve overseas, but men from these units could, if they wished, volunteer for service abroad. For most infantry volunteer units, there was little change other than in the designation of their unit, and for the men of the 4th King's Own (Royal Lancaster) this was the case, continuity being otherwise maintained. When the TF officially began on 1 April 1908, the 1st Volunteer Battalion of the King's Own was re-designated the 4th, and the 2nd Volunteer Battalion the 5th. Regular infantry regiments designated their two regular battalions the 1st and 2nd, with one home-based and the other usually on garrison duties abroad (in the case of the King's Own, the 1st was at Dover and the 2nd in India). The 3rd battalion of an infantry regiment was the designation for the Special Reserve Battalion. In the case of the King's Own, the 4th (militia) Battalion was disbanded and the 3rd (militia) Battalion re-designated the 3rd Service Battalion. The nomenclature of these battalions remained thus until they went overseas and their second-line battalions were formed, upon which the foreign service battalion were designated the 1/4th or 1/5th and the home-based unit the 2/4th or 2/5th. When the 2/5th went to France in February 1917 their home-based unit became the 3/5th.

In 1914, the 4th was comprised of eight companies and had headquarters in Ulverston. In the days before private transportation was common, men had to live locally to their nearest TF unit: A Company was at Ulverston, with a drill station in Grange Over Sands; B Company, also at Ulverston, had drill stations at Greenodd, Haverthwaite, and Lakeside; C, D, E, and F Company were all based in Barrow; G Company at Dalton, with a drill station at Askam; and finally H Company at Millom, with drill stations at Broughton-in-Furness, Coniston, and Hawkshead. In January 1915, a general reorganisation of TF infantry condensed the eight companies into four. The tragic local consequences of creating Pals battalions in the Great War are well known, and although the 4th was not technically a service or pals' battalion, its men did come from geographically concentrated areas. Many of the 4th worked together in the shipyards and ironworks of Barrow, or in the mines of the Furness District; and many were also related to each other, with brothers, in-laws, uncles, fathers, and sons all serving in the same place at the same time. Men from local industries joined in their droves, anxious to supplement their wages and put a bit of adventure into their young lives. The men of Ireleth even took their vicar to war when they mobilised, as Rev. Edward Ridley was also a sergeant in the battalion! These close relationships and familial ties would help sustain the men in times of need, but equally amplified the war's horror, at home and on the battlefield.

Recruits to the TF infantry had to be at least seventeen years old, and no older than thirty-five; at least 5 foot 2 inches tall; and with an acceptable chest measurement, depending on age and weight. Oddly enough, the minimum heights for the Army Postal Service (TF) were greater! A lad of fourteen could enlist in both the TF and regular forces, providing the consent of a parent or guardian had been obtained; but service overseas would be at the discretion of the CO, and thus it was expected that the lad would be kept out of harm's way. Each battalion usually had sixteen fourteen-to-seventeen-year-olds, but a discretionary maximum of one extra per company was allowed to form an absolute maximum of twenty-four. The total establishment of a TF infantry battalion was set at 1,009 of all ranks, twenty-nine of whom were officers, including the regular officer attached to the battalion as adjutant. Recruits enlisted for a maximum of four years, though there was an option to re-enlist at the end of this period. At any time during this service a soldier could, if he gave three months' written notice, resign. With service permissible from fourteen it was actually quite unusual for a recruit to lie about their age before the outbreak of the war, though there were a small number who did. One such guilty individual was Robert Elborough, who enlisted on 15 June 1914: although the age he gave is unfortunately no longer on record, he was foolish enough to feature in *The Barrow News* of 16 October 1915 with the heading, 'Called up at thirteen and a half—Barrow's Youngest Soldier.' Thankfully, he was serving at home at the time and not with the rest of the battalion in France, and since just about every soldier from Barrow either bought this paper or had their families post it to them, it didn't take too long for this news to filter back to his unit. Once the Army had verified the story, the coding on his medal index card reveals that he was discharged for 'having made a mis-statement as to age on enlistment'.

After the war had begun, underage enlistment became endemic, as young men assured that the war would be 'over by Christmas' desperately tried to get involved. Men were urgently needed, so overworked recruiters would take a likely looking lad's word for it if he said he was nineteen. No statistics can verify just how many underage soldiers fought with the 1/4th in their first two years of overseas deployment, though it's fair to say that numbers must have been considerable, as more than a dozen soldiers aged seventeen or younger were killed in France and Flanders, or died at home from wounds received there. It's quite clear that no official policy condoned underage recruitment, as records show many young soldiers from the 1/4th had their military careers cut short and were sent home from France and Flanders when the Army realised their age. Underage soldiers in the training system were similarly dispensed with. But it wasn't just the very young who lied about their age—a considerable number of older men made the necessary subtraction to their years in order to be accepted. The Military Service (or Conscription) Act of January 1916 put a stop to these deceptions, for no one underage could be sent call-up papers.

Every man was expected to attend for a minimum of forty days in the first year of enlistment, twenty of which had to be completed before the fortnight-long annual camp held every August, and also the recruits' musketry course. Subsequently, the requirement became a minimum of ten days prior to the annual camp, the camp itself and the annual musketry course. The Army was fully aware that,

> In the limited time available for the Territorial Force in peace it is not to be expected that, as a whole, it can be trained up to the standard of regular troops. The training should be directed towards laying the foundation on which more extended training can be based, and should be wholly confined to such elements as are essential to success in war.[3]

In November 1906, Haldane stated that the primary role of the TF battalions was to provide the 'main means of home defence on the outbreak of war, both for coast defence strictly and for repelling possible raids.'[4] The expectation was that by the time they were needed to bolster the regulars, the territorials could be brought up to the same standard as their regular counterparts, and the men of the National Reserve used to replace casualties in regular units.

To begin with, recruits would be taught basic drill and care and presentation of uniform. The lessons of the Boer War were still fresh in the minds of the military, and physical fitness and musketry were also high on the agenda. Many of the recruits during the Boer War had been turned down due to poor physical condition and once in South Africa, the difference between the marksmanship of the irregular Boers and the regular British Army had come as something of a shock. Consequently, a massive emphasis was thereafter placed on musketry, and by 1914, the regular British Army was probably the finest in the world at this discipline. The TF infantry spent as much time as possible on the range and was expected to pass the same stringent marksmanship tests as the regulars. Expectations in 1914 may come as a shock to today's generation of soldiers, who almost never engage targets beyond 300 m with a rifle: the *Field Service Regulations of 1909* described ranges of up to 600 yards as 'close'; 600 to 1,400 yards as 'effective'; and between 1,400 and 2,000 yards as 'long'. All soldiers, from cooks to clerks, were expected to achieve a minimum of fifteen hits on the standard silhouette target at 200 yards in one minute—and woe betide any commanding officer whose men achieved no better than this minimum standard. The annual qualification shoot for a trained soldier comprised 250 rounds, between the ranges of 100 and 600 yards, standing, kneeling, and lying; sometimes with the bayonet fixed, and sometimes without. Perhaps the most famous element of the qualification shoot was the 'mad minute', when a soldier fired fifteen-rounds in one minute, into a target 300 yards away. Soldiers would also learn how to allow for crosswinds when aiming, how to judge distances, and how to zero their own rifles. The rifle used by the 4th in 1914 was the Charger Loading Lee-Enfield (CLLE), since the Short Magazine Lee-Enfield (SMLE)—introduced to regular units in 1907—had not by then filtered down to TF units. For the first couple of years of the war, rifles were is such short supply that many new recruits never even held an Enfield until they got to France, having carried out their basic training with the Japanese Arisaka rifle, of which 150,000 had been purchased from the Japanese Government in late 1914. Recruits joining the 4th were luckier, as photographic evidence clearly shows that they were issued with the CLLE. While never achieving the standard of a regular unit, the shooting proficiency of men of the 4th in 1914 was well above that of regular battalions later in the war.

Physical training was covered by regular sessions of callisthenic exercises, cross-country runs, football, rugby, and most of all frequent route marches. The Army of 1914 marched almost everywhere, alternative transport being extremely rare unless long distances needed to be covered, so marches of 10 to 15 miles were routine. Falling out of the line of march without permission was judged a heinous crime by both officers and senior NCOs, who saw this as a poor reflection of the unit.

The 980 men of a battalion establishment were not all 'rifle and bayonet'. Each battalion had two Maxim guns, requiring one sergeant, one corporal, twelve men, and two drivers to attend to them. A further twenty-eight drivers were required for the battalion's horse-drawn transport—each battalion was allowed eighteen horses, two general service wagons, and an MG transport. Specialist sergeants were also needed to fill the roles of farrier; battalion cook; pioneer; saddler; shoemaker; armourer; and QM. A further fourteen men attached from the regular Army fulfilled the duties of drivers and medics, but after war was declared these returned to their parent units and the posts had to be filled internally. Once a battalion was mobilised, just two GS wagons were not nearly enough and more transport had to be sourced as a matter of urgency. The requirements of this extra transport also drew on the manpower available to fighting companies.

On Sunday 2 August 1914, the 4th mobilised for their seventh annual camp at Kirkby Lonsdale, in spite of the rumours of impending war which had been circulating. Upon arrival there the brigade commander, Col. G. L. Hibbert DSO, issued a warning not to make arrangements for a long stay as orders had been received to hold the troop trains in readiness at Kirkby Lonsdale, and further orders were expected to send troops to their peace stations. In the early hours of the next day, orders were received for the battalion to return; once the detachments had reached their various headquarters, the men were dismissed to their homes with a warning that mobilisation may be imminent. This in fact began when the telegram reached Barrow HQ at 6 p.m. on 4 August. At 5 a.m. the next day, medical inspections began, and by 7 a.m. the HQ companies had been inspected and tasked to guard the Kent and Leven Viaducts and the Millom detachment sent to guard the Duddon Viaduct. Under orders of the OC Barrow Coast Defences, the battalion took over the protection of the Vickers works and the harbour and docks of the Furness Railway Company. HQ was then established in the Holker Street Schools and surplus men not on guard duty were billeted there.

This may seem like over-reaction to a modern reader, but it was believed that saboteurs were a real threat to these vital strategic industries. And although Germany did not land parties of saboteurs or attempt what would later be called 'commando' raids, it certainly had the capability to do so, especially in those days, long before radar, when the chances of intercepting hostile vessels were much fewer. There were those at the time who ridiculed this concern, to which Kitchener repeatedly replied, 'I am only prepared to rule out the feasibility of an invasion if I can learn that the Germans regard it as an impossible operation.'[5] Although German raids did not occur, German naval bombardments of Hartlepool and Scarborough demonstrated the vulnerability of British shores. Popular fiction of the day—such as in Erskine Childers's *Riddle of the Sands* or the figure of Conan Doyle's villain Oberstein—all portrayed Germany as the enemy, desperate to either steal British secrets or invade. While a full-scale invasion was highly improbable, a raid on one strategic target close to the sea or sabotage act by an individual was not, and the Government would have been culpable not to take precautions. There was a general air of anti-German hysteria, much evident in the newspapers, and foreigners of all nations ran the risk of being arrested as German spies, purely because they were not British. *The Barrow News* of 8 August 1914 published a story about of one Fred Appel, who was arrested on the first day of the war as a spy, although the case was dismissed for lack of evidence. He was, however, immediately re-arrested as he stepped from the dock, to the apparent satisfaction of the reporter, and sent to prison to await deportation as an undesirable alien. Another story from the same issue can only be from the realms of the imagination— either the journalist's or more probably that of two Territorials writing anonymously to impress their fathers. In any case, it can be safely filed into the 'utter codswallop' drawer. Headlined 'Austrian Water Poisoner' on 8 August 1914, *The Barrow News* article reports on a letter sent to the father of one of these soldiers. The two men,

> [...] were on duty guarding the waterworks of an English town when an Austrian crept up and seized his companion from behind, holding a pistol to his head.

The letter continues,

> I prodded him with my bayonet. As I expected, he turned round, dropped his pistol and closed with me. I tackled low and we soon had him '*hors de combat*' ... we took him to the guardroom and searched him. He had three test-tubes filled with typhoid germs with which to contaminate the water ... the man was court-martialled today and is to be shot tomorrow.

Other precautions had more basis in common sense. *The Barrow Gazette* of Thursday 15 October published the details of new measures to improve national security. These included the following prohibitions:

> [...] the storage of celluloid or cinema film beyond the prescribed amount; impose on all persons landing or embarking in the United Kingdom a declaration as to whether they are carrying letters for delivery or to be posted and they may be asked to produce such letters. Prohibit the sale of wireless telegraphy equipment ... give power to stop persons about to board any ship who may be suspected of leaving with the purpose of communicating with the enemy.

Readers were also informed that communication with people of any nationality resident in Germany or Austria, or with Germans or Austrians resident in Britain, was by any means other than postal services now illegal. Regulations also came into force about the storage of petroleum and other inflammable spirits; and, just in time for Guy Fawkes Night, the lighting of bonfires and fireworks within defended harbours and proclaimed areas was made illegal. This last prohibition was not meant solely to prevent fires destroying strategic installations and supplies: it also addressed concerns that enemy agents may use fires in these areas to delineate them as targets for an air raid by Zeppelins. Alarms sounded for the first air raid scare on 6 August.

For the QM, Lt James Crossley, this was a period of intense activity. Billets and rations had to be found; stores, ammunition, and equipment procured; and transport for any order to move at short notice secured. A selection of transportation was requisitioned, including a motor lorry and a milk float, and water carts were procured from the local authority. To pull this selection, a miscellany of horses ranging from Clydesdales to polo ponies were requisitioned from civilian sources. On 8 August, an advance party was ordered to Liverpool in anticipation of a move to Ireland, where the battalion expected to relieve a regular regiment of its duties while it went to the Front. However, later that day they were recalled, as the move had been cancelled. This was indeed a period when the great military game of 'hurry up and wait' (still popular with the forces today!) was played out to its fullest. Still, behind the scenes cogs were actually turning, and on 10 August the Barrow defences were taken over by another unit, and the next day the battalion moved to Ulverston and billeted in the Victoria Grammar and Dale Street Schools.

It wasn't until 2.45 a.m. on the 15 August that orders were received to move to Slough to guard the main line of the GWR between Paddington and Maidenhead. The numbers of men and the amount of equipment to be moved required two trains: the first, packed with men, left Ulverston at 10.30 a.m.; the second, also carrying the battalion's transport, followed an hour and a half later. The first train arrived without incident at Slough at 7.30 p.m., but the second was delayed after one of the horse boxes disintegrated at Crewe, injuring one horse so severely that it had to be shot. As before, the battalion was billeted in various schools for the night.

On Sunday 16 August, the battalion was given the duty of protecting the line between Paddington and Twyford, and companies allotted sectors along this stretch. HQ was established at Slough, where fortunately a large empty house nicknamed 'Black Lead Castle' served admirably as a headquarters. Every bridge, crossing, and station along the line was to be guarded twenty-four hours a day. For the detachments at the various stations, the accommodation was somewhat less salubrious. Officers and men were lodged in waiting rooms without furniture, bedding, or any other domestic comforts for the three months that this duty would continue. True to the customs of soldiers since the dawn of time, individual detachments 'acquired' various items to make life more amenable. For example, the Millom detachment at Langley Park managed to erect a kitchen using advertisement hoardings and wagon sheets, and then equip it with every utensil a cook could wish for. Also in keeping with soldiering tendencies, the battalion adopted animals: cats and dogs were added to the ration strength, or in the case of the Millom detachment—who always liked to go one better—a tame fox and an Airedale terrier, which surprisingly became the best of pals. In a letter to a Barrow newspaper, one Hanwell resident praised the men for their cheery and friendly nature, adding that local vocabulary had been enhanced by the addition of 'champion' to describe something wonderful. He also noted how the detachment guarding the Greenford Avenue bridge, had once organised a railwayman's' hut under canvas, and that at night a fire burned constantly, a dixy of stew suspended over it for the men coming off duty.[6] Football matches were organised against local teams and photographs illustrate that bottled beer donated by the locals found its way to the isolated detachments more than once! One part of the aforementioned letter probably did not go down well among the girlfriends left behind in Barrow.

> The Hanwell Territorials have gone to Gibraltar, leaving their girls behind them disconsolate, so the Lancashire boys, chivalrous as all Lancashire boys are, have 'taken them on' for the time being.

The people of Barrow had not forgotten their men, and as winter approached appeals were made for socks, gloves, balaclavas, and blankets. Once the battalion was deployed overseas, the aptly named Mayor of Barrow, Alfred Barrow, organised a 'Cigarettes for the 4th King's Own' appeal in conjunction with two local newspapers—much to the satisfaction of the men. Army-issue cigarettes were universally considered vile, and the battalion was keen to show its appreciation with letters of thanks from the Front. Pte Sam Eagers, killed as a sergeant in 1917, wrote:

> Just a few lines on behalf of my comrades and myself thanking you for the cigarettes which you have been kind enough to send out here to us. They were very scarce before you commenced your fund, but now though with the help of you and others we can gladly say we are now well supplied. As you know we have been in the trenches and I can safely say we received the cigarettes whilst we were there. I dare say they were partly supplied by your fund. I thank you and the people of Barrow who are doing their best.[7]

Soldiering in peacetime could be a dangerous occupation, and the multitude of battle casualties during war tends to distract from those who died on home service. Soldiers whose weapon-handling focused far more on shooting the enemy rather than not shooting each other, live ammunition, and excited fears of German spies and saboteurs, proved a dangerous combination. Add a close and unfamiliar proximity to fast moving trains into the mix, and it was less than twenty four hours before tragedy struck. The first fatality was twenty-two-year-old Sgt James Tindall from Ulverston, oldest son of Inspector James Tindall of the North Lonsdale Constabulary. Company commander Capt. Nicholas Barnes, a friend of the family, had warned his sergeant about the dangers of the line, instructing him that routine crossings had to be made via the footbridge. Anyone tasked with inspecting the track was cautioned to take extreme care. Around 11 p.m. that same night, Sgt Tindall was struck by a train and died shortly thereafter. Three days later in Paddington, Pte William Long, a member of the sergeant's platoon and a key witness to the accident, gave his account at the inquest, reported in *The Barrow News* of 22 August 1914.

> He last saw him about 11 o'clock, about 150 yards away from the end of the platform, when Tindall was crossing the rails. As the latter had crossed one set of rails, the witness shouted to him that a train was coming. This was an electric train leaving Royal Oak for Westbourne Park but there was also another train coming in the opposite direction. Tindall stood erect between the two sets of rails. As the trains passed each other the witness lost sight of his companion, who was eventually found some distance away, lying on his face in the six foot way.

A verdict of 'death by misadventure' was given. That Thursday, James Tindall received a military funeral in Ulverston, the route of the cortège lined with locals, flags on all public buildings at half-mast.

By the end of November, another five had died on the railway: on 9 September, a popular eighteen-year-old from Millom, Pte Harry Kendall; and on 26 September, another Millom man, Pte William Martindale. Three weeks later, nineteen-year-old Pte Charlie Keith from Lindale became the fourth to fatally misjudge the speed of trains. At 9 a.m. on 19 November, twenty-year-old Pte John Singleton went on duty at the viaduct near Hanwell Station and ten minutes later, just after the Reading express had passed, was discovered by another sentry lying in the middle of the line. At the inquest on 21 November, the driver of the express train stated that he had seen the deceased, who had been walking along the opposite line, when he suddenly crossed the 6-foot way and stepped in front of the engine. Another witness confirmed that the driver had been blowing the whistle as he approached. A verdict of 'accidental death' was returned.

The first accidental shooting happened just ten days after the battalion first deployed along the railway, though fortunately, no one was killed. A careless sentry discharged his rifle, the round passing through the roof of the hut used by the off duty guard as their sleeping quarters. The bullet must have struck something solid on the way through, such as a bolt, for it fragmented and only lightly wounded two Dalton men, Gerard Huck and William Templeton (who only needed a number of stitches on his brow). The next incident, a few days later, was much more serious. At 9.20 p.m., nineteen-year-old Pte Fred Benson from Broughton-in-Cartmel was on duty at the bridge between Slough and Burnham Beeches, when he saw a figure approaching through the darkness and gave the challenge, which went unanswered, as did a further two challenges. Benson fired one round, which dropped the approaching man. When he went to investigate, he saw to his absolute horror that the person he had just shot was his guard commander and friend, L/Cpl Thomas Ward. The bullet passed through Ward's stomach, just above the belt buckle, and exited through the lance corporal's back to strike the bridge support. The twenty-eight-year-old gardener from Temple Sowerby died minutes later. After hearing evidence from Pte Benson and a civilian witness who had heard the sentry challenge three times, the coroner passed a verdict of 'justifiable homicide'. As is the case when one friend shoots another, the effects on the man pulling the trigger were considerable. Fred Benson was inconsolable and in deep shock, which developed into epilepsy and led to his medical discharge.

The next serious incident followed less than two months later on 18 October, and resulted in the death of seventeen-year-old Pte John Bett from Barrow. This young man had been something of a local celebrity, when as a Boy Scout he had saved a young boy from drowning in the tidal channel between Walney Island and the mainland. One sentry, a Pte Clucas, had been posted to guard an iron bridge near the creosoting works, with Pte Bett posted 300 yards away at a culvert under the line. Around 9 p.m. and contrary to orders, Bett left his post to go and chat with Clucas. Forty-five minutes later, upon hearing the approach of two civilians, Pte Clucas swung round to issue the challenge: as he did so, his rifle discharged, and the bullet hit Bett in the head. Clucas claimed that the safety catch must have dropped as he swung round, the trigger snagging his greatcoat, although in my opinion it's much more plausible that the safety catch was never applied in the first place and he had his finger on the trigger! A third soldier, Pte William Edmondson, who had been guarding a post further up the line, ran down upon hearing the shot, arriving just before Bett expired. Although the inquest delivered a verdict of 'accidental death', the jury was quite critical of the battalion and added to the verdict the rider, 'Did not consider that proper supervision was displayed by officers and NCOs and that discipline was very lax indeed.'[8]

The foreman of the jury, an ex-regular soldier, had doggedly interrogated the witnesses. He believed that the soldiers had been distracted by talking to two girls another witness had seen on the footpath earlier, and mentioned that he had even heard of girls being in the soldiers' shelters at night time. The coroner agreed to the request and the rider was forwarded to the War Office. Surviving records do not show what happened to Clucas, though he will not have got off lightly, the typical punishment for accidentally killing a comrade being six months' detention and then a transfer to another battalion or, more commonly, another regiment. What can be said with certainty is that this particular Clucas—and this is if the surname was spelled correctly by the newspapers in the first place—did not see service abroad with any battalion of the King's Own.

Three weeks later, *The Barrow News* of 7 November reported an incident which took place on Tuesday the 3rd, involving Pte William (Wilf) Ely from Dalton. It was late at night and the soldier challenged a man approaching him through the fog. The challenge was ignored, so Ely fired one round at the man, who drew a revolver and fired back, the bullet piercing the private's cap. Two signal wires were found to have been cut, and a search of the local woods, fields, and roads involving forty policemen and many soldiers failed to find any trace of the assailant. Thankfully, no one was injured in this incident, though the story as it is reported does seem somewhat unbelievable. On 8 January 1915, Pte Geoffrey Cockshott was wounded in the left forearm by a negligent comrade and did not go overseas with the rest of the battalion that May. He was then claimed for munitions work, even though he had agreed to serve overseas.

Perhaps one of the saddest accidents took place a year after the battalion had deployed to France. It involved two soldiers who had been with the battalion in England in 1914. As he was still only fourteen, Drummer George Lovell was left behind to serve as a bugler with the reserve battalion. The men were guarding various locations in the Margate area and on 30 May 1916, Pte Stephen Boundy was messing about with his rifle in the guardroom when he accidentally fired the weapon. The shot ricocheted off the stove, fatally wounding then fifteen-year-old George Lovell in the stomach. Boundy was court-martialled and sentenced to six months' detention, although the charges of loading his rifle without authority was dropped during the trial. This was the last of the accidental shootings on the Home Front concerning men who served with the battalion before their deployment overseas, but certainly not the last when it came to the Front—poor weapon-handling led to further and unnecessary calamities in France and Belgium.

The early months of mobilisation were a time for the battalion to weed out men whose fitness levels were not up to the rigors of active service, and to get rid of those whose attitude was proving to be a menace. In the initial rush to enlist in August and September 1914, it was not uncommon for a recruiting station to enlist several hundred men on a single day. Coupled with the fact that the doctor attending only got paid for the number of men accepted (rather than the number of men examined), this led to some highly suspect enlistments. A completely random sample of fifteen men discharged in their very early days certainly casts doubt on the competence or indeed honesty of some of these doctors. Since none of these men were ever integrated into the battalion, I haven't included them in the Roll. Of these fifteen, one was discharged as a result of a fractured femur in the first few days of training. Another was discharged on the grounds of 'services no longer required', as he was being held by civilian authorities for 'housebreaking' and was sent to a reformatory. Five were discharged for making a false declaration as to age, with four aged fifteen or under and one in his late fifties. One man was judged 'mentally deficient' and 'incapable of understanding even the simplest of instructions'. One was so under-developed that he could not lift his pack, and six were discharged for a variety of pre-existing medical conditions. One of these had suffered from chronic bronchitis since childhood; another had 'hammer toe' so severe that no boots could be found to fit him. One man had been injured some years earlier and walked with a noticeable limp, since his thigh muscle had wasted away; another had suffered an accident at the age of ten, which had left his right hand so deformed that he could not reach the trigger of a rifle! Another recruit was suffering the effects of TNT (trinitrotoluene) poisoning from his work in the munitions industry, while the final man had suffered a weak bladder all his life, and needed the toilet every thirty minutes.

In the months before the battalion's deployment abroad, a number of keen and effective soldiers were lost to sickness. The first to receive a medical discharge was seventeen-year-old Pte James Caddy, the youngest of three brothers in the battalion. Pte Herbert Tomlinson was discharged less than a week later, on 22 October, followed on 5 December by Pte John Baynes from Barrow, who had developed epilepsy. In the weeks before Christmas, another three men would also be given their papers: Thomas Holmes from Barrow, and shortly afterwards Thomas White from Barrow and Herbert Redpath from Ulverston for previously unknown heart conditions and, in the case of the latter, also defective teeth. Dental problems were common before free dental care, and although imperfect teeth may not seem to affect the performance of a soldier, it must be remembered that in the field men may have to survive on iron rations, a mainstay of which was the infamous biscuit. This biscuit may on paper have been full of necessary protein, but was harder to eat than a lump of wood! Nearly 100 years later, many examples of 'trench art' chiselled from this 'foodstuff' survive, as it was a popular raw material for carving small picture frames. When forced to eat it, men needed to soak the biscuit for some time before it became soft enough to chew, and even then only a good set of gnashers would do the job! One recipe to break up the monotony of bully beef was to put biscuit inside a piece of cloth, attack the bundle violently with a hammer until the biscuit was smashed into powder, mix this with bully beef, and then cook this mixture as rissoles.

With marching such a vital skill, men's feet had to be up for the mark, too. The flat feet of Barrow boilermaker, Pte James Billingham, were cause enough for his discharge. Also discharged with flat feet, hammer toes, and varicose veins was thirty-six-year-old Barrow resident Alfred Brown. Forty-three-year-old Millom miner L/Cpl William Armstrong was discharged because of bunions on the day the rest of the battalion sailed for France; he surely must have been torn between the relief of no longer having to undergo punishingly long marches, and the frustration at seeing his mates off to war without him. Twenty-two-year-old Pte James Inman was another who found the long marches a torment: he'd suffered a foot injury some time before enlistment and this constant exercise so aggravated the injury that his foot became deformed. His discharge on medical grounds must have been a bitter disappointment, especially since he saw his two brothers, also in the battalion, go off to France without him. How he must have felt when he received the news of their deaths can only be imagined. It wasn't just good feet that an infantry soldier needed, but first-class hearing and eyesight, too. On 25 March 1915, twenty-one-year-old L/Cpl Reginald Hawksby from Barrow was discharged because he was so deaf that he could not hear orders, while twenty-three-year-old Pte Robert Howie's myopia had deteriorated to the extent that he could not see the targets on the range. Unable to pass the musketry test, the latter was discharged on 19 March, returning to his job at Vickers. All these men had joined to serve their King and Country, become an integral cog in the battalion machine, and made the kind of friendships that they might otherwise not have found in civvie life. To be told that they were no longer needed would have been devastating for most. Among those to go was twenty-one-year-old Pte Osborne Longworth from Chorley, discharged on 28 November because of defective teeth and his malnourished appearance. However, Longworth was made of stronger stuff than they had given him credit for. He was back in the recruiting office five months later, passed as fit, and a mere five months after their arrival in France, he re-joined the battalion that had earlier spurned him. He was later promoted to corporal and served in the trenches until invalided back to Britain with a wounded knee in April 1918. Osborne Longworth was just one of a cluster of men to be discharged for medical reasons in the run up to overseas deployment, but he was the only one to make his way back into the ranks. Health problems did not only result in discharge: a number of men died from illness and disease before the battalion had even left for France. The first, on 18 September, was L/Sgt Leonard Atkinson, a twenty-nine-year-old from Barrow. He was followed by another three, all within a month of each other: seventeen-year-old Pte John Wilkinson on 12 January; twenty-five-year-old Pte William Bayliff from Ulverston on 4 February, as a result of inflammation of the kidneys and meningitis; and four days later, another Barrow man, forty-seven-year-old Pte Henry McDonald.

Months of railway guard were difficult: not only was the battalion scattered along 30 miles of railway, but it also had to siphon off experienced NCOs to train the heavy influx of new recruits. This left many sections with a less than ideal level of supervision for young soldiers, who were in the close proximity of friendly girls and frequent gifts of food and drink from a well-meaning civilian populace. It must be remembered that the men of the battalion were in essence civilians: while many had been with the TF for years and mastered the skill of looking like a soldier, they were still 'civilian'-minded, as a steady stream of disciplinary charges testified. But once the battalion was reunited in November, the regime toughened up considerably. At this stage of the war, an officer commanding a TF battalion had the authority to discharge soldiers whose behaviour and attitude he considered unsuitable.

The first discharge on grounds of misconduct occurred twenty days after mobilisation. Nineteen-year-old Pte William Small from Barrow had been with the TF since March 1912, so was no green recruit. A mere ten days after war was declared, he'd been ordered by Cpl Bainbridge to pick up a piece of paper, and refused. His punishment was one day's detention—a sentence far more lenient than would be awarded for disobedience later in the war. His attitude problem must have continued, for a mere ten days later he was discharged for 'unsatisfactory conduct'. Another experienced soldier to be sent packing was thirty-five-year-old Dalton miner, Pte James Grenfell, a veteran of the Boer War. After his third charge of drunkenness, he was discharged on 28 October for 'unsatisfactory conduct'. Yet another to kick against the system was twenty-one-year-old riveter, Joseph Allington, who after his third arrest for drunkenness attempted to strike an NCO—he was discharged on 13 November. Allington was a confirmed hell-raiser: he was conscripted into the RAMC later in the war, and charged on various occasions with another four counts of drunkenness, violently resisting arrest (twice), causing a disturbance, being absent without leave, using obscene language when addressing an NCO, creating a disturbance in barracks, creating a disturbance in a hospital ward, drunkenness on duty in a hospital ward, leaving his post when on duty in a hospital ward, neglect of duty when on night duty, losing 7 pints and 14 ounces of brandy and 1 pint and 6½ ounces of whiskey worth £3 15s 5½d—not hard to guess where that went! To crown it all, Allington even managed to be charged with wearing a 'good conduct stripe to which he was not entitled'! Twenty-year-old Pte Francis Stark from Barrow fell afoul of Military Law when he was found sleeping on sentry on 12 October. As this was only three days after his being charged with 'inattention on sentry duty', the book was thrown at him and he was put before a District Court Martial and sentenced to twenty-one days' detention. To the civilian mind this may not seem a serious crime, but from a military standpoint it's one of the worst, for an inattentive sentry could cause the deaths of many. The maximum penalty while on active service was death by firing squad, and had Stark been found asleep on duty overseas, it's unlikely that the sentence would have been less than six months' detention. There were, however, two cases in Mesopotamia when soldiers were shot for this offence. The young Stark did his time, but was discharged because of a severe stammer soon after his release. It is to be hoped that this was an existing affliction, and not one brought about by the harsh regime of a military prison! His sentence no doubt served as a 'shot across the bows' to other trouble-makers in the battalion, but it remained difficult to keep soldiers under supervision until the battalion was reunited in November.

Military law and retribution could be the subject of a book in its own right, but offences were judged at a number of levels, and justice meted out accordingly. For the pettiest of offences, NCOs would hand out extra duties, or allocate the most unpleasant fatigues to the guilty, such as 'shit wallah' for the day (the individual responsible for emptying the latrine buckets). Offences could be as minor as dirty boots, or a pocket not fastened. Again, to the civilian mind these seem petty in the extreme, but to the military a vital piece of equipment, i.e. the boot, was in a condition that may have rendered it ineffective, and a pocket left undone was a pocket that may allow important items to fall out and be lost. Unless this type of offence was repeated, or took place before a more senior rank on parade, the offence would probably not get as far as a charge sheet. A company commander could hand out punishments such as confinement to barracks or loss of a day's pay. One charge commonly featuring on conduct sheets was that of 'insolence to an NCO'. This was a 'catch-all' charge and though the 'crime' may have been answering back, it might just have been 'for looking at me in a funny way' and an NCO's favourite for the surly and uncooperative. The next level of offence was dealt with by the CO, who could hand out minor punishments without redress to court martial, though minor offences rarely reached the CO, having been dealt with at company level. A CO was able to sentence men with up to twenty-eight days' detention, twenty-eight days' field punishment, or twenty-eight days' loss of pay. In this last category, the soldier would be given the option of accepting the CO's punishment or opting for a court martial before the sentence was announced. It was a very foolish soldier who chose the second alternative, for the punishment meted out by a court martial was invariably stricter than the CO's. The most serious of offences would land a soldier in front of a court martial, made up of between two and nine officers. The FGCM could hand out a sentence of death, but these would have to be confirmed by the GOC, and for the vast majority of crimes that did not receive the death penalty in a civilian court, the sentence was commuted to hard labour. Exceptions to this system of justice were officers and NCOs above the substantive rank of corporal, both of whom could only be tried by District Court Martial or higher, as thirty-three-year-old Sgt James Cook discovered on 4 March, when a he was reduced to corporal for being drunk. (The soldierly qualities of this Liverpool-born clerk for Barrow Council would shine through again later.)

Fines were also used for an assortment of military offences, particularly in the field. Pte James Moore discovered as much on 3 June 1915, when he was fined two days' pay for 'speaking improperly to an NCO'. The harshness of the fine increased with the severity with which each battalion might judge an offense; thus Pte William Scott lost five days' pay for not wearing his helmet in the trenches, and Pte John Waites lost the same for not wearing his smoke helmet (an early gas mask). These were deemed serious offences because they may have resulted in the individual becoming a casualty, and as such needed a punishment that not only disciplined the individuals concerned, but deterred others from doing the same. The sentence most frequently handed out was to be 'Confined to Barracks'. Although this sounds like 'grounding' a naughty teenager, it's worse than this, as the unlucky soldier was not just barred from leaving the barracks or entering any canteen in the perimeter, but had to parade in full equipment at various times throughout the day and get 'beasted' round the parade square by an NCO. All this would take place in addition to any military tasks the man had to perform as part of his ordinary military duties and meant the soldier got no free time whatsoever. The next stage of punishment was Field Punishment No. 1. This was usually supervised at brigade or divisional level by the Provost Staff, and the prisoner would spend at least two hours in every twenty-four tied or shackled to an immoveable object, such as the wheel of a wagon. The prisoner was only allowed to spend three in four days bound up, and was not to be sentenced for more than twenty-one days in total. In between the periods spent shackled, the prisoner would be given hard physical labour. This punishment was universally hated by soldiers because of the humiliation of being shackled up like an animal. Far more common was Field Punishment No. 2—identical to No. 1, with the exception that the prisoner was never shackled. The surviving records for men who served with the 1/4th show that some generalities may be made as to what sort of soldier committed which sort of offence. Insolence, refusal, or hesitation to obey orders and drunkenness seem mostly committed by either the very young or conversely the much older ex-soldiers recalled to the colours. The majority of married men seem to have displayed more maturity and discipline, though there were naturally exceptions. The main offence committed by married men was that of willingly returning late from leave, the scarcity of which, particularly once the battalion had moved overseas, makes their disobedience easy to understand. The records for married men whose conduct sheets did not include the above are actually in a minority; most men probably reckoned that it was worth taking the punishment in return for a little extra time with their families. Company commanders obviously understood this too, as NCOs guilty of returning late usually got a severe telling off but kept their rank; privates seem to have been docked the same number of days' pay as they were absent for, or confined to barracks for that amount of time.

Apart from the previously mentioned 'death by firing squad', a court martial could hand out long prison sentences. A sentence of up to two years' hard labour would be served in a military prison, and conditions in the 'Glasshouse' could make or break any individual. For longer sentences, the guilty would be sent to a civilian prison; some, such as Liverpool Prison, even had military sections. Records of men from the 1/4th sentenced to long periods of detention show that very few actually served their complete sentence. Most had their sentence commuted and returned to active service and, if good behaviour ensued, the remainder of the sentence was quashed.

The battalion received a severe blow to their deployment prospects in February 1915, when several hundred men were recalled to return to their civilian employments in the shipyards and steelworks of Barrow. Later in the war, the iron ore mines would also demand—and get—their men back. This was particularly damaging as these were fully trained soldiers almost to a man, some of them competent NCOs, too. Most of the service records for this initial batch of men have been destroyed, but out of the sixty-one that survive, every man had signed the form agreeing to be deployed overseas. Initially, the authorities asked them to volunteer for service abroad with regular battalions, but they had shown no interest in this suggestion—they had joined a local unit with their mates, and they were going to war as part of the same! It was therefore decided to ask TF battalions to serve overseas as complete units, and men wholeheartedly signed up for this. In the case of some of those returned for munitions work, the battalion were probably not too disappointed to be losing them. For example, Glasgow-born Pte Thomas Donald was returned to his civilian employment as an iron moulder in Barrow towards the end of October, having been charged twice in two weeks for 'improper conduct as a sentry'—both parties probably breathed a sigh of relief at the parting of ways. Sgt Braithwaite, too, probably allowed himself a little smile when Pte William Caddy was discharged to civil employment shortly before the battalion deployed overseas, for at times the private had been the bane of his life. Caddy had been caught asleep on duty in late August, and just five weeks later, Sgt Braithwaite had discovered the private absent from his post while he was doing his rounds of sentries; then, to cap it all, he had suffered the humiliation of having to declare 'One man absent' to the inspecting officer one morning parade in February, because Caddy was still in bed. Considering that the punishment for all three offences amounted to fifteen days' confinement to barracks, and that he was no raw recruit (having enlisted in March 1911), the twenty-one-year-old had got off extremely lightly. By contrast, the brother with whom he had enlisted was a model soldier, and when he was killed on a daring trench raid two days before Christmas 1916, held the rank of L/Sgt. His loss to the battalion was great enough to be mentioned in the QM's memoirs, something few ORs achieved.[9]

The return to civilian employment was often the last thing soldiers wanted. They had signed up to go to war, and didn't see why they should be left at home while their pals went off to France. None of these men were discharged from the Army, however, and their civil employment continued to count for 'military duty'. Nineteen-year-old Pte Joseph Jones was so fed up with this that he deserted the Vickers shipyard in September 1915 and joined the artillery. He deliberately failed to inform the Army about his previous service, and it was some time before his sins were found out. Making a false statement on enlistment was a serious offence, and the young soldier could easily have been imprisoned for it. However, he must have made all the right impressions, for his records contain a series of correspondence between army records and his current OC, who did not want to lose this efficient soldier. In the end, the OC won and Joseph Jones continued to serve in the RFA, the charge of 'false enlistment' dropped. Pte Herbert Carter joined the RN as soon as his TF term of service expired in 1917, and after the war re-joined the King's Own. Steel moulder Sgt Henry Hughes was another who missed the camaraderie of the forces, and as soon as he was discharged from his civil occupation, voluntarily joined the RFC as a mechanic. After 1916, the terms of the Military Service Act meant that TF men discharged to civil employment under 'Class W' and whose agreed service period had terminated were liable to be called up once the munitions industry no longer required their services. The terms of this law gave the RN priority over any recruits who opted to serve with them, and was one way to avoid the horrors and discomfort of trench warfare—although an unlucky man may have found himself serving on a naval infantry unit in the trenches! The surviving records show that, out of these, only two were actually called up: Pte Ben Priestley was one of the unlucky pair, conscripted into the Coldstream Guards in April 1918; the other was Cpl David Mulholland, conscripted into the London Regiment in September 1917. Both men survived the war. In late 1915 to early 1916, there were quite a number of men whose term of enlistment expired, and as this was before conscription, they were sent home and discharged. However, these men knew that conscription was imminent, and that when called up they would have to serve wherever the Army wanted. With this in mind, many of them voluntarily extended their service, preferring to stay with their unit and take the month's leave (offered as an incentive to re-enlist). By and large, those who didn't extend their term were men employed in the munitions industry, or whose health had deteriorated.

In addition to providing detachments to protect the railway, the battalion was also faced with the problem of training hundreds of new recruits. Within the first weeks of conflict, Lancashire men had volunteered to serve in droves, and a significant number wanted to be in the King's Own. Numbers issued by the 4th Battalion between 4 August and 31 October suggest that around 280 new men volunteered to serve with them in these three months. The first wartime recruit appears to be Thomas Edmondson from Ulverston, who had previously served with the battalion and re-enlisted on 7 August. As a Sergeant, he would be killed in action in November 1916. Others who volunteered had also served with the battalion before. One of these, twenty-eight-year-old Barrow grocer, William Clark, had risen to the rank of sergeant before his period of engagement had ended. Cheerfully beginning again from the bottom rung as a private, he was placed into the QM's stores.

Apart from the rudimentary medical, minimum height requirements were sometimes blatantly ignored: two of the later recruits were only 4 foot 10 inches, well short (pardon the pun) of the 5-foot-2-inch minimum. Most men were around the 5-foot-5-inch mark, but some were much taller. Ulverston labourer Pte Henry Bertram, who enlisted on 31 August 1914, was an astounding 6 foot 3 inches and weighed in at 202 lb—a stark contrast to Bolton clog maker Pte Walter Farrell, at 4 foot 10 inches and 89 lb. Extreme variations such as these made the job of the CQMS a trying one when it came to finding boots and uniforms to fit them! Recruits for the 4th were in a better position than those volunteering for service battalions, because, as a TF battalion, the 4th had a good supply of uniforms and boots; and even if the 4th had the same 'one-size-fits-all' clothing policy as everyone else, the battalion tailor could alter uniforms. A more vital problem was the correct fitting of boots, given the sheer amount of marching the men were submitted to. Uniform-fitting was not a one-off exercise: many of the men, particularly some of the younger ones, filled out and grew as physical exercise and three meals a day began to take their effect. It was still common to find recruits from poorer backgrounds malnourished, particularly from the cities, and military service actually led to health improvements for them. For those who had held sedentary occupations before the war—such as hairdressers, or shop and office workers—the physical demands of basic training must have come as a shock to their systems. One forty-year-old butcher earned seven days' Field Punishment No. 2 for insolence to an NCO when, on being told to march faster, he remarked in exasperation, 'I will if you give me a new pair of legs.'

There is no simple answer as to why men volunteered; often, theirs was a combination of reasons. By the first Saturday after the declaration of war, *The Barrow News* was already running advertisements from Kitchener's campaign, appealing for 100,000 volunteers who were, 'immediately necessary in the present grave National Emergency.'[10] Telling men that their King and Country needed them plucked at the patriotic conviction that ran deep through almost all in the nation. The same edition has photographs of streets crowded with people cheering on the 4th as they mobilised, capturing an almost carnival-like atmosphere about the town. There was also genuine anger at Germany's treatment of 'tiny' Belgium; propaganda stories of German atrocities and the sufferings of the BEF in the retreat from Mons all fuelled the recruiting drive. Some men signed up out of local pride, wanting to show that their town could do more for their country than other places; some signed up because their friends or members of their family had; some thought it would impress the girls. Just about everybody believed the war would be over in a matter of months, and those who joined the enlistment queue didn't want to miss their chance to play their part in this great historical event. Luckily, one to recognise that this would be a long war was Kitchener himself.[11] To say that men volunteered because their lives were boring is to judge the past through a twenty-first-century lens. People didn't miss what they didn't know about, and expectations were vastly different to what they are today. However, it would be challenging to argue that adventure was not a major incitement for the young to enlist in their droves.

The 4th faced a far worse recruiting problem than many areas, not because men were reluctant to enlist, but because the largest employers in their recruiting area were strategic munitions industries. After the initial rush, these employers realised that they needed the men themselves and it became obvious to the 4th that recruits had to come from elsewhere. Consequently, recruiting parties moved further south to the areas around Preston, Chorley, and Adlington. Unfortunately, this coincided with the national downturn in recruiting in early 1915, so although the Derby Scheme provided them with a steady trickle of replacements, numbers continued to be made up of volunteers from 2/5th King's Own, the second-line battalion of the 5th, who recruited from Lancaster, Morecambe, Fleetwood, and Blackpool areas. The Derby Scheme, initiated in October 1915 by the Director General of Recruiting, Lord Derby, was a last call for men to volunteer before a scheme for national conscription was introduced. It was hoped that this would bring in many of the single men who so far had not volunteered, but in fact drew more married men, due to a promise that they would not be called upon until the single men had been mobilised.[12] Men were allocated into a number of groups dependent on age and marital status, and told that they would be called upon by group number. Men who volunteered under the Scheme could also choose which regiment they went to, being warned that should they delay their enlistment until conscription, this choice would be made by the Army. In the drive to recruit from a wider area, the 4th did not forget their traditional home; 5 April saw a recruiting party under the leadership of Capt. W. Hibbert visit the Millom, Bootle, and Broughton districts. In an interview with the newspapers, Hibbert warned that unless enough people volunteered, conscription would come into force, accusing those who hesitated of prolonging the war and telling them that they would bear responsibility for the consequences.[13] The pressures on single civilians were further bolstered by the newspapers; letters such as the following, sent by Pte Albert Ashburn to his parents, quickly found their way into the papers.

> If you were out here you would see some sights. I came through a town and it is nothing but ruins. If the boys of Barrow were able to see the sights that we have seen they would not hide behind the shipyard. They would join the Army at once and come out here, and pay the Huns back in their own coin. Let the men with wives and kiddies stop behind in the yard.[14]

Such arm-twisting did not produce much in the way of results, for just about all those willing to volunteer had already done so, or were employed in strategic work and unable to leave. Conversely, the same paper also published a story about a person who should not have been wearing a uniform at all. A woman was arrested and appeared in the Barrow Police Court on the morning of 5 January, still dressed in uniform. Luckily for the soldier whose mother this was, she remained anonymous.

She was charged with 'wearing the uniform of the King's Own Regiment in such a manner as to bring His Majesty's uniform into contempt'. She explained that this was not her intention, but that she was seeking her husband, who had been 'scandalised by a woman', and whom she believed would be easier to find 'in places a woman would be unable to look for him'. With this intent she had returned home and donned her son's uniform, a member of the 4th recalled to munitions work. Thankfully, common sense prevailed and the case was dismissed with a financial penalty.

Some women thought that they should be able do far more than knit socks, collect blankets and cigarettes, and hand out the odd white feather. In the wonderfully ambiguous headline, 'Famous Woman Shot', *The Barrow News* published a plea from a Miss Gladys Davidson.[15] The subheading 'Anxious to serve as a Sniper on the Battlefield' possibly reassured those who had imagined some ghastly local murder—or perhaps not! This was a plea from a well-known female marksman from Lancashire, who had recently beaten the American sharpshooter 'Miss Cody' in a competition at Accrington and was begging to be allowed to form a 'women's regiment of snipers'. Nothing came of this suggestion, and the idea was hurriedly brushed under the carpet. Had Miss Davidson been born twenty years later and lived in Russia, her pleas would no doubt have been gratefully received; however, British society still widely resisted women leaving the home. Given that the Suffragettes scared the establishment rigid, the apoplectic reaction to the idea of issuing women with rifles would have been a sight to behold!

Training for the new recruits at Slough would have begun with drill, that mainstay of the British Army. The original motives behind drill—that of manoeuvring bodies of men around the battlefield, or demonstrating the available numbers of a regiment to those clutching the purse strings—had disappeared with the advent of the rifle and smokeless propellant. These had been replaced by an understanding that drill teaches men to obey orders without hesitation, and instils in them group cohesion and pride in their appearance and skills—in short, that drill turns a bunch of civilians into soldiers! Of equal importance in the Slough recruits' training was, once more, physical fitness: a soldier who could not complete a twenty-mile march and then fight at the end of it was no use to anyone. To this end, they were given daily PT and route marches, building up to longer distances each week. Musketry was obviously taught, though the level of competence didn't reach anything like the excellence of pre-war days, as there were neither time nor range facilities to reach earlier standards, and infantry tactics were mainly left for soldiers to pick up when they reached their platoons. One skill both cheap and easy to train men in was bayonet fighting. Certainly, its combat effectiveness during the war continues to be questioned today, but as a way to imbue recruits with aggression, it was (and remains) second to none. There is something about the command, 'Fix … Bayonets!' that sets the pulse racing and focuses the mind. These recruits were keen to learn and the battalion had some excellent NCOs, both involved in the basic training and at platoon level; for this reason, the accelerated basic training bore fruit.

In October, the 4th Battalion was asked by the War Office whether it would like to go to Egypt to join the East Lancashire Brigade. Tempting though the offer was, it replied that it would rather remain with the West Lancashire Brigade. Nevertheless, orders were later issued by the War Office to nominate two companies to go to Egypt. Protests were made about breaking up the battalion, but these companies were withdrawn from their tasks and equipped for warmer climes. Much to the relief of Lt-Col. Wadham, this order was rescinded at the last minute and their place taken by two companies from a different regiment. Change seemed to be in the air when, on 9 November, all companies except the Paddington detachment were withdrawn from their railway-guarding duties. No doubt this came as a great relief to those responsible for discipline and training. Much work still needed to be done with regards to infantry tactics and deployment, which couldn't be accomplished while the battalion was spread along the GWR. On 26 November, the battalion moved to Sevenoaks to join the rest of the brigade. The 4th was billeted in unfurnished houses and lacked any structure large enough to use as a drill hall or for social events. But at least battalion training was now possible, even if the 4th also had to send off detachments to guard TNT store in the caves at Chiselhurst.

With Christmas approaching and few facilities available, it was a shame that no leave was allowed. Shortly before Christmas, the battalion was split into two, with one half undergoing intensive musketry training and practice at Sandwich, while the other half trained or guarded the TNT store. Everyone made the most of their first Christmas away from home, and local residents did what they could to make it as pleasant as possible for them, though many must have been terribly homesick (many of the battalion were aged only just sixteen or seventeen at the time). The people of the Furness District did what they could by sending parcels and foodstuffs. At New Year's Eve, the men would have enjoyed a beer with their comrades, and perhaps wondered how many of them would be celebrating the next together! For one soldier, New Year's Eve was a day to forget: eighteen-year-old Pte Herbert Newsham from Dalton spent it sitting in a hospital ward nursing a fractured collarbone, after the horse he had been exercising near the railway station had shied and thrown him onto the cobbles. Lack of leave remained a sore issue, and a letter to the newspapers by an anonymous soldier early in February 1915 tells of the men's chagrin.

Sir—Will you allow me a little space in your valuable paper just to say a little more concerning the leave and railways expenses of the 4th Battalion King's Own (RL) Regiment training at Sevenoaks. We have been mobilized now nearly six months, and have had no leave. I can assure you that the majority of us would be only too glad to get back to Barrow again, but as we all know, it is no use thinking of Barrow altogether while there is such a great stake at hand; but when you are not accustomed to the experiences of being away from home so long, one cannot help thinking a little about it, and I am sure a little leave would help to break the monotony of our daily training.... The fare is over £2 and you have nearly twenty four hours travelling, and if you are really fortunate enough to get leave, it is only four days. What is the use of four days leave when you have all this inconvenience to contend with. There has already been a few of our battalion home on leave, and the majority of them have had their fares sent to them from home. Otherwise I am afraid they would not have got home, because it wants a little studying how to save £2 out of seven shillings per week, out of which you have all necessaries to buy, washing and mending to pay for, and then a little of it goes towards extras in the food line.... Other battalions can get seven days free leave, in fact most battalions have already received seven days free leave, while we must have some particular business to attend to, and then perhaps we will get four days leave with all the above inconvenience. Is it fair that we fellows who were serving the colours before the commencement of the war should not be considered, while those who have joined since the commencement of the war should get seven days free leave without the slightest inconvenience? Perhaps some prominent gentleman in Barrow will consider my statement and add a few words that may bring to me and my fellow comrades that little pleasure to which we are all anxiously awaiting. I am yours *etc.*, A Private. Sevenoaks.[16]

Sadly, the plea for 'free leave' went unanswered. On 22 February, the half of the battalion not at Shoreham on musketry moved to Margate into some excellent billets in Westcliff—although a guard still needed to be mounted at Chiselhurst to protect the TNT, the men appreciated the change. This move only lasted just over a week: on 1 March, the battalion was moved on to Tonbridge and billeted in the south end of the town. It remained there, training hard until 18 April, although it was still called upon to provide guard detachments at Dungeness, the Birling Gap, and Cuckmere Haven. While at Birling Camp, Lt Henry Huthwaite and twenty-three-year-old Sgt John Brockbank got more excitement than they bargained for. A sentry reported that a trawler had run onto rocks about 50 yards from the beach, and the lieutenant took a squad of men to see if they could assist. As he was trying to communicate with the trawler crew, Brockbank lost his footing on the slimy rocks and fell into the sea. It was only with great difficulty that the squad managed to rescue their sergeant from the turbulent waters. Much of their training was based on the *Field Service Handbook of 1909*—since the lessons of the Western Front had not yet trickled back to the TF in Britain—and while this guide did make mention of trench warfare, its intricacies within the current conflict were unknown to the officers and NCOs. Their training was more relevant to a colonial infantry force, and included such things as the manufacture of makeshift rafts to cross rivers.

It had proven impossible to field 55 West Lancashire Division as a complete unit, mainly as a result of men's return to munitions work. The War Office therefore decided to split the division and field individual battalions into the fray, as reinforcements for other divisions. On 14 April, the 4th was warned that it would be joining 51 Division as part of its Lancashire Brigade. The four battalions of the Lancashire Brigade were 1/4th King's Own, 1/8th King's Liverpool (simply known as 'King's'), 1/4th Loyal North Lancashire, and 2/5th Lancashire Fusiliers. On 28 April, the battalion moved to Bedford to meet up with its new division and re-equip there with new clothing, vehicles, and fresh horses for the transport.

Such was the shortage of SMLEs that some units did not receive them until 1916, and the battalion was almost certainly still armed with the CLLE when it was deployed. It probably did not get the SMLE until late 1915 or early 1916, and during a period when it was out of the line and could retrain, zero, and familiarise themselves with the new rifle. They were, however, issued with Mark VII 'foreign service' ammunition to replace the older Mark VI with its lower velocity. The CLLE needed alterations to both rear sight and magazine to accurately fire and feed the Mark VII round, and factories such as RSAF Enfield were working flat out to modify CLLEs accordingly. In February 1915, this factory modified nearly 28,000 rifles for issue to troops deploying abroad. It is reasonable to presume that the 'refitting' described by Wadham includes a 'one-for-one' exchange of old CLLEs for modified ones.[17] There were a few instances of units deploying with unmodified CLLEs, but as this generated much criticism in their war diaries and no such mention is made by the 1/4th, we can assume that they were unaffected by the new ammunition issue.

Even though they would soon be deploying overseas, 51 Division had no opportunity to train as an ensemble, though the 4th carried out a long route march in full kit on 2 May. There was little rest after this march, as stores had to be collected from the depot and dispatched to the Channel ports. Not all the men had been involved, for on the previous day three officers and 100 men had loaded the battalion's transport and made their way to Southampton docks. From there they sailed ahead of the rest as an advance party and landed in Le Havre. They would be reunited with the remainder of the battalion later.

# 2

# 3 May 1915 – 20 July 1915
# The Apprenticeship

The 1/4th Battalion of the King's Own moved to Folkestone by train on 3 May, embarking after dark and crossing the Channel to Boulogne soon afterwards. This was a voyage that almost no one in the battalion would have experienced before, since holidays on the continent were then the preserve of the rich. The cattle boats used as military transports were hardly the height of luxury, however, and in many cases still carried evidence of their prior use! It was 11 p.m. when the 1/4th arrived at Boulogne; almost as if to better acclimatise the men, the rain poured down in sheets and made the 2-mile march up the steep hill to the temporary arrivals camp a miserable one. The rest of the night was spent in leaky tents on top of a windswept hill. Few were sorry to see dawn. The first loss to the battalion did not fall prey to disease, accident, or enemy fire, but to a posting. Twenty-one-year-old Flookburgh market-gardener Pte Robert Nelson was posted away to become 'batman' to Brig.-Gen. Herbert, never to return to the 1/4th; such were the intricacies of his travels to various theatres of war, that even Infantry Records lost track of him.

At 9 a.m. on 4 May, the battalion paraded and marched to the station at Pont de Briques. There they met up with their transport, already on the train that took them on to Berguette, after which followed a march to Ham-en-Artois to join the rest of the brigade. They only remained in these billets for a day, for on 6 May, the brigade began a long, miserable march through the wet night until it reached Calonne-sur-la-Lys, where it was to be part of the divisional reserve. At this early stage, new sights and smells helped to steer the soldiers' minds away from their discomfort, and the arrival of the Meerut Division, possibly the first non-white people most of the men had ever seen, gave an impression of great adventure. At night, the rumble and flash of the big guns lit the sky to the east, and sleep was a long time in coming.

According to the battalion's *War Diary*, heavy bombardment was heard south-east of its position at 4 a.m. on 9 May, although this differs by one hour from Edmonds's *Official History*, which notes 5 a.m.[1] This was the start of the preliminary bombardment for the British attack at Aubers Ridge. The battalion had previously been warned to expect a move at very short notice, and was parading, wagons loaded, by 6 a.m. The first gas helmets were issued, and although primitive, were better than nothing at all! The battalion was also given a Vermorel sprayer, which was similar to the garden pump used in the battle against the greenfly, only larger. They were meant to spray anti-gas agents on pockets of gas, but found alternative uses spraying defoliants to keep the area around the wire clear of vegetation, or disseminating pesticide to clear dugouts of infestation. Also issued was one shotgun, though as there are no further references to this weapon, it must be presumed that it was never used. One item which was put to work and of which there was never adequate supply was the ubiquitous sandbag. Outside of its primary function, it was invaluable as a carrier for rations and all sorts of stores; as another layer of outer covering for boots and puttees; and small strips of the Hessian cloth soaked in fat and placed in the bottom of an empty tin made a workable cooker. At 5 p.m., the battalion received notice that the attack was unsuccessful and that another was due later, though road congestion prevented fresh troops getting on location in time for it to go ahead. According to the *Official History*, an attack the next day was called off as High Command realised that supplies of artillery ammunition were insufficient. Ammunition shortages occurred partly because munitions factories were not yet developed enough to supply the demands of the Front, though output was many times greater than pre-1914. Shortages were compounded by the poor quality of the fuses in many of the HE rounds—which at times didn't explode at all in the soft ground—unreliable ammunition and the worn barrels on many guns—which caused shells to drop short of their intended target, often killing British troops. These shortages were not helped by an order from the War Office demanding that 22,000 shells be sent from stocks in France for use in the Dardanelles.[2] Demand for ammunition always tended to outstrip supply throughout the war, among the French and German armies too; and yet, they frequently managed to provide their soldiers with effective artillery support, whereas the British seemed incapable of doing so. It's probably fair to comment that major problems lay more with the number of guns allocated to each area of front, something much improved upon later in 1916; the obsolete design of much of the artillery; and the way that the artillery interacted (or didn't!) with infantry during an attack. The casualties were abundant, and although the shortage of effective artillery fire may be seen as the greatest factor, there was also the difficulty of directing fire on German MGs, which were very well concealed and in many cases only discovered once they had begun to mow down the attacking infantry. The types of shell available also played their part, as the lighter guns—the majority of artillery support—were only capable of firing shrapnel, which did not destroy breastworks or wire.

At 10 a.m. on 10 May, the 4th was placed on two hours' notice-to-move, and while they waited for orders, the day was spent on musketry practice. At 4 a.m., orders were updated and reduced the notice-to-move to one hour, a state of readiness that was not relaxed until 10.30 p.m. the next day. On 12 May, the designation of the division changed to 51 (Highland) Division, of which the 1/4th was now part of 154 Brigade.

On the evening of 18 May, the battalion made another long and wet march to La Prayer, near Estaires. The CO commented that their overcrowded billets in a disused convent were the filthiest yet encountered in France; the floors were inches deep in mud, and seemed to have been used as the town rubbish dump.[3] They were not there for long: on 20 May, they moved further south to Locon, acting as the reserve while 152 and 153 Brigade manned the trenches. The filthy conditions did not help in the battle to keep men fit and healthy: minor cuts and grazes often turned septic, and a slow trickle of soldiers joined the sick list. One such on 21 May was twenty-year-old Pte William Ferguson from Ulverston. He had cut his hand some days earlier, but the wound had turned septic and although the Highland Casualty Clearing Station (CCS) in Lillers and No. 3 General Hospital in Rouen had both done their best, he ended up being transferred home for treatment and did not return until 25 November.

On 23 May, the battalion was warned that they were likely to go into the trenches on either the 25th or 26th, and one officer and twelve ORs from the Leicestershire Regiment were attached to impart the knowledge they had already acquired. Before the huge training camps had been set up in Étaples and Rouen, fresh battalions got scant tuition in trench warfare prior to actually experiencing it. Trench design differed depending on soil, terrain, the depth of the water table, and when it was built, as trench warfare was a constantly-evolving science. On the Festubert front, the water table was very close to the surface, and it was only possible to dig down a couple of feet before the excavation began to fill with water. Consequently, trenches here were breastworks with a raised parapet of sandbags, which gave far less protection than those dug deeper. Breastworks were a much easier target for artillery and at the very minimum, sandbags needed to be forty inches thick at the top just to stop a bullet. German machine-gunners were very good at aiming at a fixed point on a parapet and using their fire to 'erode' away the outer layers of sandbags, thus leaving anyone behind this section vulnerable to small arms' fire. Breastworks were also more susceptible to the ravages of weather and tended to rot and settle after constant rain. This was particularly dangerous for taller men, as a trench where previously they may have been able to walk through with impunity, now left the tops of their heads dangerously exposed. Sandbags also needed to be constructed at the correct angle of slope, a job ideally done from the German side of the breastworks. Fully aware of this, German gunners fired speculative bursts at the front of the breastworks at regular intervals throughout the night, knowing that the opposing infantry would be hard at work repairing the devastation from daylight shelling. A hit by HE from either artillery or trench mortar could completely obliterate the breastwork, often burying the defenders under a pile of sandbags and frequently carving out a crater a couple of feet deep, which then filled with water. Troops spent night after exhausting night at repairs, which were promptly demolished during the day by just a few minutes of bombardment.

The inability to dig down because of the high water table prevented effective overhead cover for the men, and in the pre-Brodie helmet days of the soft field service cap, many head wounds ensued. Even the best cover was no match against a direct hit from an HE shell, and it wasn't until later in the war that better dugouts would be developed. In the early days, primitive concrete bunkers were sunk into the trench line, but these always suffered from the damp. One bunker in the division's sector had filled to such a depth of water that a doctor fresh out from Britain, believing that this was actually a cistern for the storage of drinking water, tested the water quality and then marked it with the notice, 'For ablution purposes only, not for drinking'. Some well-intentioned but dim individual had knocked a hole in the base 'to let the water drain out': water began to seep into the bottom of the bunker, finally rising to the level of the water table.[4] In this sector of the Front, the high water table also meant that deep communication trenches were not viable and re-supply and troop movements had to take place across the open at night in the most discrete location possible—though German observation was pretty comprehensive!

Fresh battalions suffered higher casualties, while the men of more seasoned units knew when and where to keep their heads down. The curiosity of 51 Division's men to see what was over the other side of the breastwork cost them dearly. An analysis of casualties based on the records of the 1/4th shows that over half of casualties were wounded, or killed, within three months of arriving at the Front. After making it through this period, the odds of becoming a casualty dropped considerably. (See Appendix 1)

The difficulty of movement to the front line during daylight hours hindered officers, NCOs, and others such as runners from learning their way around between the rear and the front line: this meant that night working parties got lost, wasting much time and energy. The short interval between landing in France and being deployed into the trenches meant that it was very much a case on learning on the job. So when the 1/4th entered the line for the first time at 2.30 a.m. on 26 May, it was a tense yet exciting experience for all. Their preparation for the trenches had consisted of one day of lectures on the 24th and a demonstration of grenade-throwing, although the company officers had missed even this, as they were being shown around the trenches they were to take over from 1/7th Gordons. The battalion marched and reached Le Touret at 7 p.m. on the 25th, but were held up there for two hours during a heavy bombardment of the Rue de L'Epinette at Richebourg. Fortunately, their guides met them at 10 p.m. as planned, and the relief went smoothly without casualties.

The trenches taken over by the division were opposite the Ferme-du-Bois, and had been recently seized from the Germans by a Canadian division. As such, they were not yet fully consolidated and in a parlous state, with no covered approaches, poorly constructed breastworks, and no arrangements for either cooking or sanitation. It was obvious that there was a great deal of work required to make them habitable. For men just out from England, this was a herculean task, particularly for the junior officers and NCOs in charge especially as it had to be done in the dark.[5] Not only were large working parties needed to repair the breastworks, dig communication trenches, and carry supplies forward to the men in the front line, but evidence of the recent battle littered the area and had to be cleared. The bodies and body parts of those killed in the fight for the trench lay strewn across the area, and the stench of decomposing flesh stuck in the throats of all. Apart from the immediate unpleasantness of hundreds of decomposing corpses in close vicinity, there were the obvious dangers to health and morale to consider: burying them under cover of darkness became a matter of high priority. The battlefield was also scattered with discarded equipment which needed to be to be salvaged before it was ruined. And if this wasn't enough, daylight saw the enemy do his very best to destroy each night's work. The 1/4th may have had a quiet start to their first day in the trenches, but towards the evening, the Germans began to increase the frequency of their shelling.

Around midday on 27 May the trenches were heavily shelled, and the battalion suffered its first battle casualties of the war. Three were killed outright in this bombardment, the youngest among them the eighteen-year-old Pte John Atkinson, originally from Askam, who was struck in the neck by a shell splinter. His family had migrated to South Africa before the war and he had returned to Britain to enlist. Only slightly older was Liverpool-born Pte George Tyer, a nineteen-year-old who had moved to Ulverston for work and enlisted pre-war. The oldest of the fatalities that day was one of the stretcher-bearers and another Ulverston native, twenty-four-year-old Pte Edward Fisher; he was a married man with a young baby. Edward Fisher had been wounded by one of the first shells to land, but when he saw that his friend George Tyer was hit, he ignored his own injury, grabbed a medical kit, and went to his assistance. As he was treating him another shell screamed in, killing both men outright. Ten men were wounded besides, and although twenty-two-year-old L/Cpl James Smith's wound was on this occasion superficial, he would soon be less lucky. Twenty-nine-year-old married man, Pte Edward Worth received a wound to his finger troublesome enough for him to be evacuated home for treatment, though he made a full recovery and returned in September 1916. Twenty-seven-year-old Pte William Jeffrey, from Backbarrow, was wounded in the head, back, and thigh by shrapnel, and treated at No. 4 Stationary Hospital at St Omer, as was twenty-year-old Pte Edward Whiteley, wounded in a leg and foot. Pte David Craig, a popular seventeen-year-old from Barrow, was among the casualties, and died from his wounds the next day. Twenty-nine-year-old Pte John Fell from Barrow got his Blighty wound brewing tea: the kindling he used for the fire contained ammunition which exploded, badly damaging his fingers. Upon his eventual recovery almost a year later, he was transferred to the RE.

Relieved by 1/8th King's, the battalion moved back about half a mile to the Rue de L'Epinette Redoubt. The shelling continued and as the transport was bringing up the rations around midday, a barrage dropped around them at 'Windy Corner' (50° 34′ 31.40″ N, 2° 45′ 16.23″ E). One shell killed CQMS Hubert Page instantly. The thirty-seven-year-old from Barrow had been an engineering draughtsman with Vickers, was a veteran of twenty years' service with the Volunteers and TF, and was a serious loss to the battalion. His first child was born after mobilisation, and he had only spent forty-eight hours with his new baby. Pte John Scott wrote to his mother about this bombardment.

A shell burst about twenty yards in front of me and flew over me and our Jack. [Three of his brothers also served in the battalion] Their shells began to burst again and Quartermaster-Sergeant Page of Barrow was killed outright. I was blown off my horse into a ditch. When I got up I was with Cook-Sergeant Collinson, who was also in the ditch, he also having been blown off his horse. We were, however, no worse, thank God! It was quite an hour and a half when another shell came and dropped about ten yards from my cart. Our Jim, Creighton [Pte William Creighton] and Billy Ranger dived under it, and Ranger, although only having a leg out, was hit and taken away to hospital. He is not badly wounded. Soon after I dived into a dugout when a shell was coming and a chap called Leviston dived on top of me. He was hit in the back.[6]

Pte William Ranger was evacuated to England, later transferred to the Royal Fusiliers and then the MGC. The shrapnel that hit twenty-three-year-old Pte Arthur Leviston in the back was travelling in a steep downwards trajectory and caused a wound from which he died soon after reaching the RAP. (Sources use a number of terms for this facility, frequently omitting 'regimental', and sometimes calling it the 'dressing station'; for the sake of continuity, I will use the modern abbreviation of 'RAP' in future references to it.) (This 'Windy Corner' is at the crossroads of Rue des Charbonniers and Rue des Haies in Richebourg, and not the same 'Windy Corner' of Givenchy-lès-la-Bassée.)

Later on the night of 27 May, a working party of four officers and 200 men carried supplies to the front line, but returned without casualties at 3 a.m. The battalion then left for the billets at Le Touret and spent the next six days out of the line, though they were hardly safe. On the 30th the next day, working parties from all four companies went back to the front at 9 p.m. Just after midnight, the parties from A and D Company returned, having been sent back on account of heavy bombardment of their intended working area. Of B and C Company there was no news until two hours later, when both returned reporting that they had come under shellfire and a number of men were missing—seven from C and thirty from B. Fortunately, all but five had returned by 6 a.m. Of those five, Pte Thomas Baxter from Barrow had been killed outright, and L/Cpl James Smith, slightly wounded just three days earlier, had a compound fracture of the femur—he died from shock after his leg was amputated on 6 June. Twenty-three-year-old Pte Thomas Preston from Newton in Cartmel was also very badly wounded, and he too succumbed to his injuries, dying on 8 June. Pte Thomas Athersmith from Ulverston was wounded in both back and hip, evacuated home and given a medical discharge in January 1917. The last of those who went missing was twenty-one-year-old L/Cpl Thomas Knipe, from Hawkshead. Apart from shell shock, he suffered shrapnel wounds to an ankle, and this, like many wounds, went septic. His treatment at the base hospital at St Omer lasted for six weeks and from there he was posted on to the base staff at Étaples; he did not return to the battalion until October. Another man wounded, though returned with the rest of the party, was twenty-one-year-old Pte Alfred Fullard from Askam. The injury to his right hand was minor, and he was treated at No. 7 CCS at Merville and returned to the battalion two weeks later. One of that working party, Pte Joseph Hackett, wrote home:

I am lucky to be able to write to you, for I had one of the narrowest escapes of my life on Sunday last. Our platoon was sent to build trenches between the first and second lines of trenches and we had hardly started when snipers got to work against us. But that wasn't the worst by a long way. Shortly after midnight our lot started shelling the German lines and the Germans fired back. We were right in amongst it and shrapnel fell like rain, and we were in a direct line with it. Men were wounded on each side of me; one was killed within four yards of me [Thomas Baxter]. There we lay, cramped in a little narrow communication trench for three quarters of an hour. Then I made a dash for it and got in a dugout in the third line of reserve, and there I lay till our party sadly depleted, passed by and a private of the Loyal North Lancs woke me up and I joined my party. We passed down the shell swept road to our windowless barn where we slept the sleep of nearly the dead.[7]

On 30 May, twenty-three-year-old Pte Gerard Huck wrote home to his mother,

We have just come out of the trenches, after being in four days and five nights. I am sorry to say that we have suffered a big loss in our company. It is really a pity to see such fine fellows going down without a minute's notice. It is too difficult for me to tell you exactly what it is like. But one thing I know is it is like hell on earth. The last time we were in they shelled us for seven hours. The shells seemed to come from nowhere. We were in the Battle of Festubert. You will see the picture in the 'Sunday Herald,' of June 6th. Dear mother, J. Tyson, of the Lots, Askam, and myself have been recommended by the lieutenant of our company for bringing in a 'dixy' of tea for the wounded men in our trench. We had to go 200 yards in the open for it, and we got back safe with a bit of luck, because we had three shells right near us. You must excuse scribbling this time, as I am tired and my nerves are not as well as I would like them to be.

Gerard Huck, wounded for the first time before the battalion had even left England, was discharged medically unfit on 1 September 1916 after exposure to gas affected his lungs too badly for him to soldier on. He died in Westmoreland Consumption Sanatorium on 10 March 1917, but wasn't recognised by the Commonwealth War Graves Commission (CWGC) as dying as a result of his wounds until well into the twenty-first century. (This recognition was brought about thanks to the hard work and dedication of Andy Moss, who also provided the information from the letter above.)

Having been transferred to IV Corps on 30 May, 51 Division was relieved by the Indian Corps, and at 5 p.m. on the evening of the 31st, the battalion moved out of its billets at Le Touret to a nearby field. It then set off at 10 p.m. for the five-hour march to new billets at Le Cornet Malo, near Locon. It had been a tough introduction to trench warfare, especially for the men who had lost good pals, and there could not have been a man among them unhappy to be heading away from the artillery now bombarding their old trenches as they began their march—yet morale remained high. The men were still healthy, in spite of a measles' outbreak out which would no doubt claim those who were not immune. Proximity in the trenches meant that infectious diseases spread rapidly. Today in the UK, measles are not seen as a killer. Sadly, an epidemic which hit 51 Division during its stay at Bedford in the winter of 1914 killed sixty-five men, 10.8 per cent of all who caught it.[8] The four days at Le Cornet Malo provided much needed rest and the battalion was able to bathe in the nearby Canal d'Aire—perhaps not the apex of ablutionary indulgence, but better than nothing.

At 1 a.m. on 6 June, officers went forward to reconnoitre the trenches the battalion would be moving to later that day. By 2 p.m., D Company had manned the front-line trench with B and C in support and A back in reserve. Despite his demotion in March, Cpl James Cook was too good an NCO to stay at that rank for long and was promoted back to sergeant once the battalion had settled in the trenches. Surprisingly, there was no shelling at all until 10 a.m. on the 8th, when British guns began a bombardment to cut German wire. Fearing an imminent attack, the German guns responded with a heavy bombardment of D Company's trench, killing ten and wounding twelve. Two of the men killed, Privates Thomas Crossman from Whitbeck and James Hoggarth from Sawrey, were only seventeen years of age. Some of the wounded, such as Pte Benjamin Moore who was medically discharged that November, were amongst the longest-serving members of the battalion, and the loss of experienced soldiers was felt keenly. Privates John Barrow, James Hoggarth, William Knipe, John Bennett, and Cpl William Milton were all killed by one shell that landed inside the trench where they stood. John Bennett was a veteran of the Boer War, married with one child, and a first-class soldier. In a letter to his wife, company commander Capt. William Barratt reported that the five had been buried together just behind the front-line trench and a wooden cross planted on their grave. All the men are commemorated on the Le Touret Memorial, their graves lost in the fighting that continued in the area until almost the end of the war. Pte John Edgar's wound was only slight, but as he was also suffering from trench nephritis, he was evacuated home and it was eighteen months before he returned. One lucky soldier, twenty-three-year-old Pte Thomas Hodgson from Cartmel Fell, missed all this action, for he was dispatched to hospital by the MO shortly before the bombardment began, and there diagnosed with German measles.

### Killed or died from wounds from the bombardment on 8 June 1915

| Pte John Jarvis Barrow | 2509 | KIA-8/6 | Pte John Bennett | 2507 | KIA-8/6 |
|---|---|---|---|---|---|
| Sgt Frederick James Burn | 1417 | KIA-8/6 | Pte Thomas Crossman | 2262 | KIA-8/6 |
| Pte John Fitzwilliam | 1567 | KIA-8/6 | Pte James Hoggarth | 2485 | KIA-8/6 |
| Pte William Myles Holmes | 1864 | DOW-9/6 | Pte William Knipe | 2487 | KIA-8/6 |
| Pte John William Lister | 2045 | KIA-8/6 | Cpl William Henry Milton | 1203 | KIA-8/6 |
| Pte Joseph Swindlehurst | 1873 | KIA-8/6 | | | |

### Those known to have been wounded on 8 June 1915

| Pte Frank Burns | 2017 | WIA-8/6 | Pte Sidney Dickinson | 200301 | WIA-8/6 |
|---|---|---|---|---|---|
| Pte Harry Greenhow | 2698 | WIA-8/6 | Pte Thomas Hodgson | 2729 | WIA-8/6 |
| Pte Alfred Johns | 200384 | WIA-8/6 | Pte Alfred Paully Johnson | 2177 | WIA-8/6 |
| Pte William Newton | 200541 | WIA-8/6 | Sgt Charles Gott Woolcock | 200488 | WIA-8/6 |
| Pte Benjamin Atkinson Moore | 1017 | WIA-8/6 | | | |

The battalion was relieved by a combined force of 1/4th Loyals and 1/8th King's on the night of 9–10 June and back in billets by 3 a.m. Twelve hours later, it moved again to fresh billets west of Locon. Because of losses sustained by D Company, reorganisation was necessary and one officer and fifty-three men were transferred over from B Company to fill the gaps. The CO had been ill for some time, and at the insistence of the MO reported to hospital, was sent back to England, and upon his recovery in December posted to command 3/4th Battalion in Blackpool. Maj. Thompson assumed command of the 1/4th. The battalion remained in billets for four days, and when a second smoke helmet was issued on 12 June, and the British preliminary bombardment began on the 13th, the men realised that it would not be long before they were in the thick of it again.

On 12 June, orders were issued to 51 Division for an attack on the German positions on 'Rue d'Ouvert', just over a mile from Festubert. 154 Brigade was detailed for the attack scheduled for the 15th. Rue d'Ouvert itself was and is a hamlet, stretching like a ribbon along the road of the same name; the German trench that went by that name ran parallel to and some 100 to 200 m west of the road. 51 Division's target was a salient known as 'Sap L8', (50° 32′ 34.90″ N, 2° 45′ 40.91″ E) 300 m deep by 200 m wide, which jutted out at a corner of the Rue d'Ouvert trench where the road turned sharply to the north-east. It was defended by the II and III Battalions of 134 IR (Infantry Regiment) from Saxony. The divisional objectives were the houses—used as strong points to the rear of the salient—marked on the maps as L11, L12, L13, and K7. K7 was about 400 m to the right of the salient and a divisional boundary where they would link up with 7 Division. On 13 June, British artillery targeted the wire around the sap; the sound of the guns could clearly heard by the men in their billets at Locon, though they did not begin their move forward until 7 p.m. on the 14th. Despite considerable congestion on the road at Le Touret, they were only held up for an hour, and by 11.30 p.m. all the companies were squeezed into an old British trench with 1/6th Scottish Rifles. The Rifles were supposed to have been in another trench and there was not space for both battalions, so when at 1.30 a.m. of the 15th room was made in the reserve trench at Point M4, B Company moved into that. The initial wave of the attack was to be made by 1/4th Loyals to the right of the salient and 1/6th Scottish Rifles to the left. The King's Own were to follow up the first wave if the attack showed signs of success. Maj. Thompson's plan was for A Company, currently short of two platoons (who were at Lt Gardner's disposal as runners in the event of communication failure), to hold Sap L8; B and C Company would support the first wave, while D Company would be in reserve in the fire trench. Fifteen minutes before the attack began, the companies moved up to their allotted positions. One soldier's letter to his mother was anonymously published by the local paper.

> We had always been talking for weeks past about what it would be like to go over the trench top in the open. The time drew near and at half past five o'clock, we got the order to advance to the firing line. An artillery bombardment was raging at this time, the shells bursting over the top of us. A few were hit before we reached our place in the line.[9]

For at least an hour before the projected attack time, the British barrage on the German lines can best be described as desultory. Only a few random shells were sent over, giving the defenders ample time to climb up from their dugouts and prepare. According to the *Divisional History*, it was obvious that the Germans were fully aware of the forthcoming attack.

On the 15th we had a most uncomfortable day. The Boche rose early, having apparently known our plans. In fact, some of them were heard to call across No Man's Land, 'Come along, Jocks; we're waiting for you.' And undoubtedly they were. From early morning we were subject to continual shellfire, causing many casualties to us.[10]

When the first wave went over the top at 6 p.m., it was met by withering fire from rifles, MGs, and artillery—many were killed before they had even cleared the parapet. Ten minutes later, B Company moved into the trenches just vacated by the first wave, and C and D took over the support trench shortly before 7 p.m. The wounded retrieved from the attack began to filter their way back through their trench, and soon afterwards, word was sent back by runner to bring A Company forward to the fire trench.

German artillery did not ignore the battalion's jumping-off trenches, and for nearly two hours the men crouched in the shallow trenches, as the number of casualties from this and rifle and MG fire rose steadily. In a letter home, nineteen-year-old Pte Norman Palmer from Walney described the effect of the bombardment: 'A lot of the men went mad before even a move was made, in consequence of the noise; others were struck dumb.'[11] For all soldiers, the waiting is usually far worse than the actual 'doing', as once things begin to happen the training kicks in; but for men who had never been 'over the top' before, watching the first wave go forward into the concentrated fire and then spending two hours helplessly absorbing the German artillery must have been torturous. A letter home published by a local paper gives some idea of how the men coped.

> The Scotch and Lancashires had gone over by this time, and the noise of the machine gun fire and rifle fire was terrific, and the wounded started to file past us. Seeing so many for the first time gave us a queer feeling, but after telling one another that 'we were too small to be hit', and passing one or two jokes about coming VC's, we recovered our nerve.[12]

Among those in the jumping-off trench wounded by the bombardment was twenty-two-year-old Pte William Sykes, whose leg was badly shattered by a shell. Another was the popular 2Lt George Bigland from B Company, listed in the *War Diary* as 'wounded and missing'. It is probable that 2Lt Bigland, who had only just got married before leaving for France, was killed outright. Local legend around Ulverston suggests that he was shot in the temple by the sniper he had peered over the parapet to try and locate, in spite of a warning from his platoon sergeant. Neither his nor William Sykes's bodies were ever seen again; both were likely buried by the heavy shelling.

In 1915, the use of the grenade was a specialist job, and given the primitive nature of British grenades at the time, this was no bad thing. Grenades were the weapon of the volunteers in the bombing squads; each company had a squad of about twenty men tasked as 'bombers', while the rest would attack with rifle and bayonet. At 8 p.m., B and C Company were ordered over the top to support the first wave, but due to delays caused by a broken bridge in No. 1 Communication Trench, A Company had still not arrived, so D Company was ordered to support the Loyals to the right. When the whistles blew to signal the attack, Maj. Thompson was the first to clear the parapet. The companies to the left found themselves in that worst of situations faced by any attacker: that of uncut wire. Fortunately, the wire in the centre section of the salient was then cut by the bombardment, and the attackers were able to progress through this gap, though it had the grave disadvantage of bunching the attackers to the benefit of the German machine-gunners. The soldier whose letter was published in the paper continued his story.

At last the order came 'Over the top King's Own.' We went over with a willingness. We had no thought of being hit. The first thing we ran into was a deep ditch full of mud [a formidable obstacle that can still be found in the fields to the west of the road] and we were up to our waist, but we soon scrambled out and made a dash for the German line. The wounded men lying about made one forget everything. Our only determination was to get near enough to have a shot into the Germans. We reached the first trench and got over that, and proceeded across the open to the second trench, which the Scotch and Lancs were holding against the enemy. I will never forget the sight in that trench. Germans were lying all over the place dead. We had to walk all over them as they were blocking the place up. Then what proved to be the worst time for the 4th King's Own came. That was when they were ordered to get over the trench and advance in the open, and then dig themselves in. This is done by laying in the open field, and with a small [entrenching] tool digging into the soil and banking it up in front. At this time the shells were bursting amongst us and the bullets ripped over our backs like hailstones. Many a good man cried out in agony as a bullet struck him. Others were hit never to rise again, but we continued to dig deeper.[13]

Some men did not make it as far as the second trench. One of the officers hit on the way across gave his revolver to a passing soldier, urging him, 'Never mind me, make the best use of it you can'. The letter does not identify this officer, but it was either the Adjutant Lt Ernest Hewitt, or Lt George Walker, neither of whom were ever seen again. Another soldier told his story in a letter home, which was again passed on to the local paper.[14]

It was just getting dark and I could not see the Germans, but I kept on advancing with my mates, and I was wounded half way between the German trenches and our own. I lay on the ground until it was dark and sneaked back to our trenches the best way I could. Indeed I was not sure whether I was going back to our own trenches or the Germans. I had been shot through the right hand. When I got to the trench I met another poor chap—a Scotsman, who was seriously wounded, and I attended to him, and stood by him until an officer came and relieved me, and told me to go and get my hand bandaged. I ran down the communication trench and met my own doctor, Dr Rutherford of Barrow, who bandaged my hand and told me to get to the nearest ambulance station. I got into a motor car and they took me to a hospital. I was there all night, and then I was taken next morning to another hospital. It was not until the next morning when I was tightening my belt that I discovered that I had been hit with another bullet, which had pierced the leather watch pocket and smashed a small looking-glass inside. I thought I was lucky to escape that one, but I did not know I had been struck there.[15]

The torn belt and the shrapnel ball extracted from the soldier's hand were put on display at Parnell's Hairdressers in Hindpool Road, Barrow. Other men did not get much further. Sgt Leslie Taylor reached the end of the second trench only to be hit by a shell and buried, as seventeen-year-old Pte John Hughes recounted in a letter to his mother.

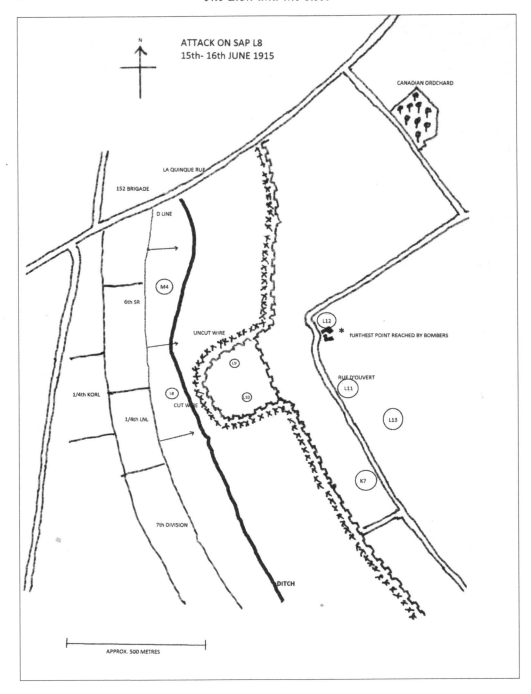

ATTACK ON SAP L8
15th- 16th JUNE 1915

CANADIAN ORDCHARD

LA QUINQUE RUE

152 BRIGADE

D LINE

M4

6th SR

UNCUT WIRE

L12

* fURTHEST POINT REACHED BY BOMBERS

L9

RUE D'OUVERT

L11

1/4th KORL

L8

CUT WIRE

1/4th LNL

L10

L13

7th DIVISION

K7

DITCH

APPROX. 500 METRES

When we got to the end of the trench we found it blocked and Sergeant Leslie Taylor buried. We dug him out and it took us half an hour, immediately afterwards a shell burst and buried Sergeant Taylor and myself. We have been dug out and brought to some hospital.[16]

Twenty-one-year-old Taylor's back had been torn apart by shrapnel, and despite the best efforts of the doctors, he died from his injuries on 2 July. Pte John Hughes recovered from his wounds, which were minor, but didn't return to the 1/4th—possibly someone discovered his true age? Whatever the circumstances, Hughes returned to active service in 1917 and was killed while serving with 1/ King's Own in May 1917.

Pte Norman Palmer was another to fall in this offensive. When a first shell buried him, he managed to struggle his way out of the soil; but shortly after, a second shell burst gave him a scalp wound and a bullet simultaneously hit him in the palm of his left hand, blowing out a large portion of the back of his hand and mangling his fingers. As he remarked laconically in a letter to his mother, 'I think it will be a long time before I swing a hammer again'. Palmer lost some of his fingers, and was medically discharged in March 1916.

The bombing squad in Capt. Pearson's B Company was led by Lt Geoffrey Taylor, with twenty-three-year-old Sgt William Farish as his second in command. Farish was shot in the buttock in the third line of the German trenches, the shock of which rendered him unconscious. When he came to, he was all alone, but managed to crawl down the steps of a German dugout before passing out again. Drifting in and out of consciousness and losing blood, it was late on the 16th when he finally heard English voices outside the dugout; these turned out to belong to a platoon of one of the Guards regiments. The officer in charge sent for a stretcher party, but when it arrived it had neither stretcher nor water, which Farish desperately needed. He then crawled for over half a mile along a narrow communication trench where he found another stretcher party, who luckily had a stretcher with them.[17] Farish was awarded the DCM for his gallantry in leading the bombing squad deep into German lines, and was discharged as time-served on 23 December 1915; he went back to Vickers as a riveter. Of the twenty men from B Company's bombing squad, only Lt Taylor and three other men returned.

Within five minutes of the first wave going over the top, shellfire had severed all phone lines between battalion and brigade headquarters, so the backup plan to use the two A Company platoons to carry messages between the attacking waves and headquarters was brought into play and worked very efficiently. It still took time to pass messages on, and at 9.30 p.m. a desperate plea arrived from Lt Taylor for more grenades and support from MGs. Although the battalion had penetrated the third German line, it was on a narrow front and totally unsupported on both flanks, as those attacks had also met uncut wire. Neither of the two German battalions defending Sap L8 had suffered many casualties in the British bombardment: backed up by a plentiful supply of grenades, they were putting up a stout resistance. British grenades were in short supply due to a direct hit by a shell on the advanced ammunition store and forward supply parties took heavy casualties. The battalion's MG officer, Lt Alexander Wright, was ordered to move his guns from Point M4. Finding the narrow trench they had to move along choked with dead and wounded, and knowing that the attackers depended on him providing supporting fire as quickly as possible, twenty-year-old Sgt John Owen ordered his gun teams to proceed along the parados (opposite the parapet of the trench), exposing themselves to the enemy fire. An accurate salvo of shells dropping around them forced them back into the trench, which was less congested at this point, and they paused briefly to regain their breath. It was here that the man carrying the tripod suffered a breakdown; Wright ordered Owen to relieve the disabled soldier of his burden, and they resumed their approach. Wright had gone on ahead to a gap in the parapet, to see if he could spot where the German communication trench was, when a 'Jack Johnson' high explosive struck the trench just in front of the party. In a later interview, Sgt Owen recalled,

> I was half buried and at the time I had the tripod. As soon as I pulled myself out, a little to the right, there was one of our men, but I could see nothing of him; he was buried. I just saw a part of the gun which he was carrying protruding from the earth. We got it cleared and the fellow shouted from underneath. If there had not been someone there, it would have been all up with him. I got him out.[18]

Shells continued to fall around the group as Owen dug out the casualty. One landed less than 10 yards away and might have killed all of them, had it not turned out to be a dud. The Maxims and gunners had been buried by the explosion, and Sgt Owen recovered the pair of guns and their equipment, and freed all his men. The young NCO received the DCM, and when interviewed modestly replied that every one of his men in the MG section had acted like a hero that day. Owen had only left his job at Vickers to enlist in late August 1914, and was typical of the outstanding young NCOs the battalion was fortunate to have. He was later transferred to the MGC, awarded the MM in addition to his DCM, and rose to the rank of RSM.

A retreat was ordered at 10 p.m., but this was two hours before D Company could establish contact with the Grenadiers on their right and coordinate the move. The forward troops consolidated their defences in the remains of the German breastworks to the best of their ability, but were only able to put up a slender breastwork to protect themselves against a German counter-attack. This came at 12.30 a.m., and the defenders found themselves assailed from the front and both sides by a vastly superior force; short of ammunition and grenades exhausted, it was clear that their position was untenable and a fighting withdrawal commenced. Artillery support was inhibited by the lack of communications—no-one in the rear knew which positions were British and which were held by the Germans. For some of the battalion, withdrawal was easier said than done; CSM Roger Horne and Capt. Pearson found themselves isolated.

> Finally when the big counter-attack came and our troops had to retire I got left among the wretched Germans with Captain Pearson. Oh my stars, what a time we had; tried all sorts of dodges for breaking through to our own line, but always got nabbed by the German patrol, and they gave us it every time. Finally just as day was breaking, we worked along outside the back of their trenches and barbed wire until we came to a ridge which had been captured by the Grenadiers the night before. There the last German batch twigged us and loosed off freely at fifteen yards range. Captain Pearson never rose again. We had arranged our directions and I had to go in the opposite direction. Wasn't I glad to reach our lines again with only one bullet in me out of the scores that were intended for my carcase. From there I had to hobble to the reserve. I got my leg dressed and they carted me off to the rear.[19]

Horne's thigh wound meant time in England, but he made a full recovery. He later served with 12/ King's Own and was subsequently commissioned into the Royal Welsh Fusiliers, rising to the rank of Captain. Capt. Pearson was less fortunate: his wound was serious, and he was captured and repatriated for medical reasons in September 1917.

Several men behaved with great gallantry on this retreat. Twenty-seven-year-old married man Pte Horace Barker was one of the bombers, and nearly made it back to safety in the trench when he stopped to help a wounded officer. As he was carrying the casualty a shell landed, killing the officer and wounding Barker in several places. He was rescued by others from the battalion and taken to the dressing station, where he died from his wounds on 20 June. Maj. Thompson recommended him for a decoration, but he received nothing. Others, too, braved the heavy MG fire in No Man's Land in their search for the battalion's wounded: Sgt William Bell and twenty-nine-year-old Cpl Thomas Dixon from Dalton went out time and again. For his courage Bell received the MC, a rare distinction for a sergeant. As was so often the case, Thomas Dixon got no medal at all, but four days later was promoted to Sergeant, taking over the platoon of his old comrade, the late Sgt Barker Clarke.

The attack on Sap L8 had cost the battalion dearly. Casualties came to 152 of all ranks, fifty-nine of whom were killed or died later from their wounds, while others were lost to the battalion through injuries that precluded further military service. One of these was twenty-three-year-old Pte Thomas Hodgson from Cartmel Fell. He was hit in the arm, leg, and foot, as well as burned in the face by a shrapnel shell which exploded nearby. Although he was lucky to survive at all, his injuries were severe and long-term, bringing about his medical discharge in May 1916. Sgt Fred Rose was wounded in the leg, thigh, and both arms; he received his medical discharge in April 1916. CSM William Winder, a forearm and ankle shattered by bullets, got his in March 1916. The battalion paid a high price in senior NCOs. Young soldiers had also suffered, three of which to die were Pte Robert Oversby and Pte Frederick Williams from Ulverston, and Pte James Saville of Waberthwaite—all only seventeen years of age. Neither were men safe behind the lines, as twenty-one-year-old Cpl Thomas Tickle discovered when he was having a minor wound cared for at the RAP. A shell landed close by and blew him into the air, causing several days' loss of memory from concussion. For most of the dead, there is no known grave; their names were simply recorded on the Le Touret Memorial. For the families of men posted 'missing', there were months of worry and heartache: well into 1916, photographs of the missing appeared in the papers alongside pleas from anxious mothers for information. The attack must have been a particularly miserable occasion for twenty-year-old Pte Thomas Pugh from Ulverston, as not only was he in peril from the German shells and fire, but also suffering from German measles! He was packed off to hospital for two weeks upon returning from the attack.

Although a further offensive had been planned for 17 to 18 June, this was cancelled because it was felt that any gains made would be insufficient to justify the losses in men and expenditure in munitions.[20] The *Divisional History* apportions blame for the failure of these attacks to,

[...] the inadequacy of the artillery preparation. Subsequent battles proved that the number of guns and the allotment of ammunition per gun required is far in excess of those allotted to the Division for the Battle of Festubert, if infantry are to have a reasonable chance of success in attacking organised resistance, protected by strong wire entanglements. In addition, the inadequacy in the number of the guns, the 15-pounders again proved themselves highly unsatisfactory. As evidence of the unreliability of their ammunition, it is worth recording that Captain Duncan of the 8th

Argyll and Sutherland Highlanders had an eye knocked out by a (British) shrapnel bullet half a mile behind the British line.[21]

The artillery failed to cut all the wire across the attack front, cause casualty to the German defenders, or even keep them in their dugouts when the attackers went forward. This is not a criticism of the gunners themselves, for they did their best with what was available. The Germans knew about the attack in advance from observing British preparations from the higher ground on which they were located, or possibly intercepting British field telephone conversations. This was a very ambitious plan of attack for inexperienced troops, and was, but for the first stage, to be carried out in darkness. The attackers may well have held the ground had the attacks on each flank succeeded, but the gains were on too narrow a front to hold with both flanks 'in the air'. Lack of effective ammunition resupply played its part, particularly with grenades, though the inadequacy of the bomb used by the battalion at this time—compared to the German stick grenade—made this less of a factor. Probably of greater significance was the difficulty in consolidating captured breastworks before the Germans mounted counter-attacks. The enemy often withdrew most of its men from the first-line defences when facing an attack, reducing casualties from bombardment and relying on enfilade fire from flanking positions and MGs placed in depth between second and third trench lines to cut attackers' numbers down. They would then counter-attack with rapid momentum, using specially trained units over ground they knew well, aware that the reduced number of opponents would not be able to consolidate its gains in time.

Killed or died from wounds from 15 to 16 June 1915

| | | | | | |
|---|---|---|---|---|---|
| Pte Horace Edward Barker | 1236 | DOW-20/6 | Pte William Beckett | 2905 | KIA-15/6 |
| Pte Addison Bell | 2700 | KIA-15/6 | Pte Tom Bell | 3019 | KIA-15/6 |
| 2Lt George Bradyll Bigland | | KIA-15/6 | Pte Thomas Patrick Blake | 200016 | KIA-15/6 |
| L/Sgt John Ephraim Brockbank | 2239 | KIA-15/6 | Pte John Thomas Brocklebank | 1881 | DOW-24/6 |
| Pte John Thomas Brocklebank | 2560 | KIA-15/6 | Pte Edward Norman Burn | 2276 | DOW-20/6 |
| Pte Wilfred Clark | 2316 | KIA-16/5 | Sgt Barker H. Clarke | 812 | KIA-15/6 |
| Pte Jacob Cubitt | 2538 | KIA-15/6 | Pte Ernest Curwen | 2562 | KIA-15/6 |
| Pte Samuel Date | 2801 | KIA-15/6 | Pte George Henry Durham | 1853 | KIA-15/6 |
| Pte John Edward Fawcett | 2557 | KIA-15/6 | Pte Andrew Fox | 2938 | KIA-15/6 |
| Pte John Henry Frawley | 1863 | KIA-15/6 | Pte Robert Garnett | 1057 | KIA-15/6 |
| Pte Edward Greenhow | 2699 | DOW-30/6 | Pte Mark Grigg | 2719 | KIA-15/6 |
| Pte Ernest Hadwin | 2604 | KIA-15/6 | Pte Joseph Hillyard Hall | 3049 | KIA-15/6 |
| Pte William Harrison (POW) | 2723 | DOW-7/7 | Pte Isaac Ernest Harrison | 2773 | KIA-15/6 |
| Lt Ernest Henry Hewitt | | KIA-16/5 | Pte John Hartley | 2689 | KIA-15/6 |
| Pte Robert Horne | 1474 | KIA-15/6 | Pte Christopher Johnson | 2627 | KIA-15/6 |
| Pte William Leviston | 2620 | KIA-15/6 | Pte John Logan | 2598 | KIA-15/6 |
| Pte John Loraine | 1852 | KIA-15/6 | Pte William John Lowther | 2134 | KIA-15/6 |
| Pte Edward John Metters | 2657 | KIA-15/6 | Pte James Mitchell | 1290 | KIA-15/6 |

| | | | | | | |
|---|---|---|---|---|---|---|
| Pte Thomas Mitchell | 2668 | KIA-15/6 | | Pte Moses Newby (POW) | 2691 | DOW-2/8 |
| Pte Randolph Newsham | 2267 | KIA-15/6 | | Pte Richard Newsham | 2543 | KIA-15/6 |
| L/Cpl Robert Oversby | 2628 | KIA-15/6 | | Pte George Edward Park | 2666 | DOW-18/6 |
| Sgt Frank Postlethwaite | 736 | KIA-15/6 | | Pte Richard Henry Prisk | 2633 | KIA-15/6 |
| Pte Philip Connolly Roberts | 2163 | KIA-15/6 | | Pte James Terrell Rowse | 1883 | KIA-15/6 |
| Pte George Warrior Ryland | 2058 | DOW-16/6 | | Pte James Henry Saville | 2015 | KIA-15/6 |
| Pte Ernest Henry Shelton | 2328 | KIA-15/6 | | Pte Henry Sprout | 200698 | KIA-16/5 |
| Pte James Sprout | 2947 | DOW-3/7 | | Pte William Sykes | 2066 | KIA-15/6 |
| Sgt Leslie Clifford Taylor | 1439 | DOW-2/7 | | Cpl Nat Humphries Taylor | 2388 | KIA-15/6 |
| Lt George Henry Walker | | KIA-16/5 | | Pte Robert Wallace | 1805 | DOW-2/7 |
| Pte Frederick Williams | 2069 | KIA-15/6 | | Pte Stephen Williams | 200555 | KIA-15/6 |
| Pte John J. Wilshaw | 2955 | KIA-15/6 | | | | |

## Known to have been wounded on 15 or 16 June 1915

| | | | | | | |
|---|---|---|---|---|---|---|
| A/Cpl Thomas Atkinson | 200141 | WIA-15/6 | | Pte Joseph Balderston | 1922 | WIA-15/6 |
| Pte Fred Barrow | 1416 | WIA-15/6 | | Pte Fred Berry | 2624 | WIA-15/6 |
| | | | | A/Sgt Francis William Canby | 200298 | POW-15/6 |
| Pte Edward Bevins | 265626 | WIA-15/6 | | | | |
| Pte Fred Casson | 1689 | WIA-15/6 | | Pte Edward Cornthwaite | 2753 | WIA-15/6 |
| L/Cpl James Coupland | 200480 | WIA-15/6 | | Pte James Howson Edwards | 200427 | WIA-15/6 |
| Sgt William Henry Farish | 1281 | WIA-15/6 | | Pte Leonard Fox | 200333 | POW-15/6 |
| Pte William France | 1321 | WIA-15/6 | | Pte Tom Gendle | 200581 | WIA-15/6 |
| Pte George Graveson | 200525 | WIA-15/6 | | Pte Harry Greenhow | 2698 | WIA-15/6 |
| Pte George Grosvenor | 200560 | WIA-15/6 | | Sgt Frederick L. Gott | 2026 | WIA-15/6 |
| Pte John William Harrall | 200497 | POW-15/6 | | Cpl William George Hinds | 200117 | WIA-15/6 |
| Cpl Tom Hird | 200532 | POW-15/6 | | Pte Thomas Hodgson | 2729 | WIA-15/6 |
| Pte Charles Holyday | 1098 | WIA-15/6 | | CSM Roger Hallewell Horne | 495 | WIA-16/6 |
| Pte Joseph Hoskin | 2754 | WIA-15/6 | | Pte John Robinson Hughes | 200274 | WIA-15/6 |
| Pte Albert Johnson | 2140 | WIA-15/6 | | Pte Thomas Leck | 200599 | POW-15/6 |
| L/Cpl Frederick Marwood | 200385 | POW-15/6 | | Pte Josiah Boase Mitchell | 1166 | WIA-15/6 |
| Sgt John S. Owen | 2340 | WIA-15/6 | | Pte John Morgan | 200499 | WIA-15/6 |
| Pte John Edward Parker | 200386 | WIA-15/6 | | Pte Norman Palmer | 1494 | WIA-15/6 |
| Pte Gilbert Quigley | 1749 | WIA-15/6 | | Capt. William G. Pearson | | WIA-16/6 |
| Sgt Frederick Robertson | 1506 | WIA-15/6 | | Pte Peter Quinn | 200143 | WIA-15/6 |
| Pte Fred Walter Saunders | 200193 | WIA-15/6 | | Cpl Pearson Singleton | 200176 | WIA-15/6 |
| Sgt Fred Rose | 1721 | WIA-15/6 | | Pte Thomas Smith | 200206 | POW-15/6 |
| Cpl Joseph Downham Smith | 1740 | WIA-15/6 | | L/Sgt Thomas E. Thompson | 200199 | WIA-15/6 |
| Pte Walter Stone | 200192 | WIA-15/6 | | Pte William Tomlinson | 200537 | POW-15/6 |
| Cpl Thomas Tickle | 1470 | WIA-16/6 | | CSM William Henry Winder | 118 | WIA-15/6 |
| Pte William Williamson | 1479 | WIA-15/6 | | | | |

At 1.45 a.m. on 16 June, 1/8th King's took over the fire trench while the exhausted survivors of the 1/4th made their way back, assembling in Le Touret at 10 a.m. and onwards to billets at Pacaut, where they rested on the 17th. The brigade commander sent the following message that day:

> The Brigadier has received personal instructions from Lieutenant General Sir H. Rawlinson, Commanding IV Corps to convey to the Brigade his appreciation of the gallantry shown by all ranks in the attacks of the 15th and 16th instant under very trying circumstances. The Brigadier wishes to add on his own behalf his appreciation of the pluck and spirit evinced by all and while he deplores the heavy losses incurred congratulates the brigade on the fine fighting qualities displayed.[22]

The next four days were a time of reorganisation and training. Much needed to be done, with some platoons virtually wiped out and a number of vital promotions to be decided upon to replace the fallen senior NCOs. There were heavy casualties amongst the specialist bombers, so men were sent away to the Divisional Bombing School for training on the Béthune bomb. Much equipment had been damaged, lost to enemy action, or just plain lost, and all this had to be replaced. Working parties were also needed to ferry supplies to the Front, but it was not until 22 June that the demands for labour really took a toll on the survivors, when 360 men and nine officers were dispatched to Le Touret on just one working party. Had the battalion been up to strength, this duty would have claimed just over one man in three, but given the casualties over the last month, this took up almost the entire battalion.

When Edward Whiteley re-joined the battalion on 20 June after hospital treatment for wounds received on 27 May, he must have been devastated to discover the absence of so many of his friends, even if rumours had reached him in hospital. History doesn't recall how he felt when he returned to the trenches as part of a working party on the 24th, but he must have been nervous. He was detailed to repair the wire in front of the British trench line with others from his platoon when German shells dropped all around them. A shell splinter struck him on the front of his left leg below the knee, shattering the bone to pieces. His comrades were able to stop the bleeding and carried him back to the RAP. Fifteen months later, after four operations to remove fragments of steel and dead bone, he was discharged as 'no longer medically fit'—a phrase which offers little detail. His service record, on the other hand, gives an insight into the impact this injury had on this previously active twenty-year-old.

> Tibia bent inwards, necessitating walking on the outside of his foot. Can only walk with the help of a stick. Cannot walk half a mile without pain. He will never be capable of performing the duties of a soldier.

For this the Medical Board awarded Whiteley a 75-per-cent pension for one year, to be reduced to a paltry 25 per cent thereafter.

While Whiteley was being evacuated, the rest of the battalion was on the move again, first to Estaires and the next day further north. No one was disappointed to be leaving the Festubert sector and its dreadful conditions. Rumours of a move north to Armentières had been circulating for the last couple of days and one, no doubt based on a misheard conversation between senior officers, was for a move to India, an idea which filled the men with enthusiasm. However, the move north stopped short of Armentières, as 51 Division were to re-join the Indian Corps and take over the trenches from the Lahore Division just south of Laventie—a far cry from actually going to India! If anything, this was 'out of the frying pan and into the fire'. These trenches were breastworks too, and although they were in a better state of repair than the ones they'd just left, the defences themselves were much weaker because the fighting had been less intense here. The front line was a single chain of breastworks, with 200 to 400 m to the rear, and a series of detached supporting outposts every 300 to 500 m along the length of the line. The reserve line was a similarly spaced series of outposts, 1,000 to 1,500 m back from the support line. Communication trenches linking the front line and the outposts were almost non-existent, and the German trenches on the lower slopes of the Aubers Ridge overlooked the complete British trench system. These outposts had an added disadvantage, as not only did they stand out distinctly from the soggy plain to German artillery observers, but they also concentrated the defenders into small areas, meaning shellfire caused more casualties than it would otherwise have done in an extended line of defence. One particularly unpopular section was known as 'Red Lamp Corner'. The trench line was discontinuous, so the ends of the trench sections were not always a similar distance from the enemy front line, and Red Lamp Corner was where the trench stopped abruptly in a section about 100 m away from the German front line. The next section of British line continued 300 m distant from the German lines and the two butt-ends were joined by a fire-stepped communication trench, constantly enfiladed by close-range rifle and MG fire. Because of this alignment, the right hand edge of the foremost section of trenches was directly in front of the rearmost section, and to avoid friendly fire incidents in the dark, a red lamp was lit, only visible from the rear, to demarcate the left hand limit of the arc of fire for the rearmost trench.

After dark on 27 June, the battalion moved forward to relieve the Liverpool Irish in the trenches. Its sector ran from Fauquissart in a roughly southerly direction to Neuve Chappelle, a distance of 1½ miles. No trench maps had been issued to the battalion, so it was a relief when it found its trenches without trouble. Another deficiency that concerned the 1/4th more was a complete lack of periscopes: with German trenches only 100 m away in some stretches, this would prove a deadly omission. This period was one of unending hard work for the men, as divisional commander Maj.-Gen. Bannatyne-Allason was extremely unhappy with the state of the defences.[23] Every available man was set to work extending the support lines to make them continuous, or digging communication trenches to connect the various lines. After dark, everyone was involved in strengthening the defences in their own section of trench, and out of the line they worked on the support lines and communication trenches. There seemed no end to their labours. This would have been onerous enough with a full strength battalion, but by 28 June the 1/4th's fighting strength was a mere 398 men, and they were stretched very thinly.

Being without periscopes was beginning to have its effect, as an increasing number of men fell victim to German snipers. On 1 July, Pte Albert Phizacklea and Sgt Robert Pickin were both wounded by sniper fire—neither man would return to combat. Albert Phizacklea was discharged as 'time-served' in May 1916, and Sgt Pickin was commissioned into the RE. The sniping the next day was worse, with Sgt Frederick Clampitt wounded and Privates James Dodd and Reginald Tyson killed. Clampitt had a very lucky escape when a bullet only grazed his face, but he was back with his platoon four days later. That night, the bodies of Dodd and Tyson were carried back behind the lines and given a proper burial. Today they rest as they served, next to each other in the Aubers Ridge British Cemetery. A temporary relief from the constant sniping ensued on 3 May when the battalion moved to billets in Laventie. Although well out of the range of small arms, the billets were shelled at regular intervals, fortunately without success for the enemy.

In early July, the GSO1 of 51 Division, Col. Ian Stewart, decided that the division needed to revise its grenade training policy and that every soldier needed to know how to use them.[24] Though every rifleman had carried grenades, these weren't for his use but were to be passed on to the dedicated bombers when they ran short. This way of operating had a number of obvious disadvantages, for example if the men nominated as bombers became casualties, the ordinary soldier unfamiliar with the grenades of the day, was almost as likely to blow himself up as he was to kill the enemy should he try to use them. And when the man on the spot would find himself in a situation where the immediate use of grenades to clear an enemy from a position was the best way forward, having to wait for a suitable bomber to come along was not ideal. Basic bombing training was carried out with all men, while dedicated bombers went through a much more intensive and up-to-date course. When battalions came out of the line, as many as possible were passed through a much more intensive course. The division was using the Béthune, or Battye Bomb. This weapon had been designed by Capt. B. C. Battye of the RE and was made in the Béthune Ironworks, hence its name, and consisted of a cast-iron cylinder filled with explosive. The open end of the cylinder was sealed with a wooden plug through which protruded a length of Bickford safety fuse. The fuse was either lit with a match or cigarette, or had a Nobel fuse lighter crimped to the end of it. To use the Nobel fuse lighter, the soldier had to grip the grenade tightly with his throwing hand, tear off the tape, and then pull out the safety pin with the other hand. He then needed to press down hard on the outer cap of the fuse lighter and twist in either a clockwise or anticlockwise motion, not forgetting to throw the grenade immediately.[25] The Battye bomb was never available in the quantities soldiers needed and was a vastly inferior design to the German stick grenade, though preferable to other British designs around and certainly better than the No. 1 grenade to cause such tragedy to the 1/4th later that year.

On 4 July, thirty lucky men went off to bomb school, while 300 less fortunate men joined a working party for the 'sanitary improvement of billets'. On the same day, twenty-one-year-old Pte Samuel Bagot probably became the envy of the entire battalion when he fell off the cook limber while preparing the men's meal, breaking his left wrist—the dream Blighty wound. He was sent to work in a blast furnace once his wrist had healed and did not see any more active service. The hard work was obviously taking a toll: on 5 July, the battalion was granted special dispensation to field a working party of only fifty men for the night. Frequently, the parties would return with losses due to enemy action. For example, on the 6th, only forty-eight men returned from the overnight party, two being wounded by shellfire. One of these was twenty-four-year-old Pte William Watson from Millom, who was wounded in the back by shrapnel and would never return to the battalion, recalled to employment in the iron ore mines. The break from working parties was brief and in the following days men were again deployed in their hundreds on working parties, or covering parties for those in No Man's Land. The type of work done always resulted in the men getting covered in mud by the end of the task and keeping clean was impossible. Initially, all ranks were expected to bathe in local streams and when Gen. Sir James Wilcocks, commander of the Indian Corps, inspected the battalion on the 5th, minor miracles were performed in order to look presentable. So it was that on the 7th, the battalion was able to send the men off, one company at a time, to the new bathing facility at La Gorgue. A brewery there had been converted into a bathhouse, with the huge brewing vats serving as communal tubs. The men handed in their muddy, lice-ridden underwear and shirts before they climbed into the vats and received a clean set upon leaving. The morale boost procured by something so simple was immense, and the men sang happily all the way back to Laventie. Their move back into the support line on the 9th must have come as some sort of mixed blessing, as at least they wouldn't have to tramp for miles before starting work!

On 13 July, the battalion received the first batch of reinforcements for some time when twenty of their men returned from spells in hospital. This now brought the battalion strength up to twenty-two officers and 563 men, still well below establishment. For some time, the battalion had been training up snipers, and these now began to even up the score that enemy snipers had claimed upon the battalion. One German sniper wounded nineteen-year-old Pte William Walker from Barrow, but the battalion's snipers managed to kill two of the enemy. Both British and German artillery continued to be quiet, but the front-line soldiers were jumpy and frequent outbreaks of rifle and MG fire, triggered off by both sides punctuated the nights. This resulted in three wounded when they moved forward to take over the breastworks at 10.45 p.m. on the 15th. It is during this period that one of the strangest entries can be found in the *War Diary*, probably attributable to nerves: on the evening of the 17th, the sighting of 'civilian snipers' seen behind the front line was reported and an immediate hunt for them launched. Nothing was found, either that evening or the next day; in all probability, the sighting was merely either of British troops or local Frenchmen taking a walk.

The British lagged behind the enemy in the development of both trench mortars and rifle grenades, to which front-line soldiers of 51 Division had no means of retaliation. In an ingenious attempt to close the range gap, the division drew from history and the battalion was issued with a catapult capable of throwing a round bomb on a high trajectory into the German trenches. Whether it was the Leach catapult—a scaled-up version of the traditional Y-shaped catapult, powered by rubber cords and wound back by a winch—or the West Spring Gun—powered by steel springs—records do not show. An obvious advantage of the catapult was the lack of muzzle flash or loud bang to give away its location, such that the intended target received no warning to take cover. Though there were drawbacks and neither weapon was particularly accurate, the rubber of the Leach tended to lose its bounce as time and weather wore upon it, and the West had the nasty habit of removing the fingers of its operators, including those of its inventor when he first demonstrated the weapon! Whichever one it was, experiments with this new weapon obviously annoyed the enemy, as on the 19th, they retaliated with a trench mortar on A Company's position, slightly wounding twenty-seven-year-old Sgt Robert Bray from Millom. Snipers were still active, and when A Company's Pte Arthur Chadwick from Ulverston chanced a look over the parapet, he was hit in the head. Although the twenty-three-year-old was still alive when his comrades carried him to the RAP, he died shortly afterwards without regaining consciousness. Trench mortar retaliation continued the following day, and twenty-nine-year-old Sgt Jack Reid from Barrow was killed outright, and twenty-two-year-old Ulverston man Pte Joseph Clayton wounded so badly that he died two days later.

The catapult was not the only unconventional weapon the 1/4th was given. On 21 July, the *War Diary* mentions an 'unsatisfactory test of cartridge guns covering front.'[26] Exactly what form this weapon took we do not know, as its very lack of success has ensured its erasure from records. The 'cartridge gun' may not have lived up to its inventor's dreams, but the battalion snipers more than made up for this lack of success, with five hits over this and the next day, and the battalion suffering only one man injured with a minor wound to the hand. This was the last time the battalion would man these trenches, as 51 Division had received orders to move south.

# 27 July 1915 – 2 January 1916
# Pastures New

After a brief stay in billets at Estaires, the battalion marched to Berguette on 27 July, then moved by train, via Calais, to Ribemont-sur-Ancre. As the men climbed down stiffly from the overcrowded wagons to which they had been confined for the last twelve hours, the fresh air of this unspoilt region in the grey light of dawn struck a huge contrast to the cloying stench of the front line. Billets had been found for them in Bouzincourt, and the sunny, 6-mile march was a mere saunter through the countryside to these men. The roads of Furness tend to meander their way around various obstacles, so the arrow-straight roads, rolling hills, and open countryside of these chalk lands were a new experience. If you take the modern D119 to Laviéville, then the Rue Grenet to Millencourt, and the Rue Thenette to Bouzincourt, you will be following their footsteps through scenery that has since changed very little. In July 1915, the British soldier was still a rare sight here, and the locals paused in their work to watch the battalions marching past, the kilts of the Scottish battalions arousing particular interest. After that month's rigours, a period of routine work felt like a holiday and some men relaxed a bit too much! The locals made sure that there were plenty of ways that the soldiers could spend their pay, be it food, drink, or souvenirs; but for twenty-four-year-old Pte John Waites from Millom, the temptations of the estaminets would have to wait, as the day they arrived in Estaires he was fined five days' pay for not wearing his smoke helmet in the trenches. The next to feel the wrath of authority was twenty-five-year-old Ulverston tailor Pte Thomas Wilcock. He was caught in one of the estaminets at 2.45 p.m., when he should have been working, and also fined five days' pay. Just one day later, twenty-four-year-old Pte Edwin Newton from Barrow was given a ferocious twenty-eight days' Field Punishment No. 1 for being drunk, a punishment designed to send a message to the others. There was obviously a stamp-down on alcohol, as the day after, thirty-two-year-old Pte Joshua Nowell from Dalton was given two days' Field Punishment No. 1 for having intoxicating liquor in his billet.

The trenches the battalion took over from 1/8th King's on 7 August had been manned by the Bretons of the 22 Division of the XI Corps of the French Army until 51 Division arrived. These were a wonder to behold to the men of the battalion, used to the muddy breastworks further north. The trenches were deep and dry and accessed by meandering communication trenches. Initially, navigation was confusing: there seemed no logic behind the twists and turns of their layout, and although they were all named after French military heroes, it wasn't long before more familiar names began to replace these. Less than 2 miles north from the centre of Albert was the village of Aveluy, just behind the front line, where, despite sporadic German shelling, some French inhabitants still remained. The trenches held by the battalion opposed the German line from slightly north of their stronghold at Ovillers, to just north of heavily-fortified La Boiselle. In between these two German-

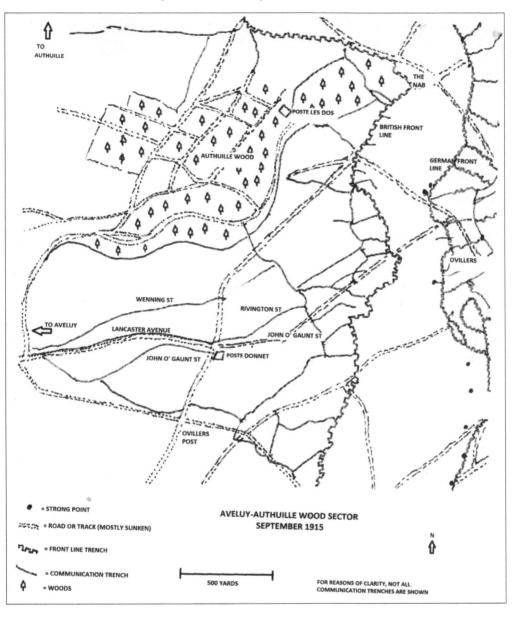

TO
AUTHUILLE

THE
NAB

POSTE LES DOS

BRITISH FRONT
LINE

AUTHUILLE WOOD

GERMAN FRONT
LINE

OVILLERS

WENNING ST

RIVINGTON ST

TO AVELUY

LANCASTER AVENUE

JOHN O' GAUNT ST

JOHN O' GAUNT ST    POSTE DONNET

OVILLERS
POST

= STRONG POINT

= ROAD OR TRACK (MOSTLY SUNKEN)

= FRONT LINE TRENCH

= COMMUNICATION TRENCH

= WOODS

AVELUY-AUTHUILLE WOOD SECTOR
SEPTEMBER 1915

N

500 YARDS

FOR REASONS OF CLARITY, NOT ALL
COMMUNICATION TRENCHES ARE SHOWN

held villages was a narrow valley, named 'Mash Valley' to accompany the neighbouring valley to the south of La Boiselle, itself named 'Sausage Valley' after the German observation balloon positioned there.

After five months on the Western Front, the battalion was regarded as an experienced unit, so men from both the Royal Berkshire and the Norfolk Regiments spent time in the trenches under the 1/4th's tuition. Although their first day in the trenches was quiet, there was intermittent shelling around 6.30 p.m., though no casualties ensued. During the night of 9 August, rifle and MG fire drove off two German working parties in No Man's Land, the enemy retaliating the next day by shelling C and D Company to the left of the battalion's line. D Company in particular seemed to have been singled out for retribution, and just after noon, eighteen-year-old John Hillen from Millom was killed. That night, his comrades carried his body back three miles behind the lines for burial.[1] A talented singer and teller of jokes, Hillen had been popular and several of his comrades wrote to his mother sending their condolences. He had an older brother, Edward, who had been seriously wounded earlier in the year, and his parents were visiting him in hospital in London when they received the news of the death of their youngest son. The next three days were quiet in the front trenches, but the peace did not last long; shelling resumed on 14 August, killing twenty-four-year-old Pte Myles Burton from Cartmel.

Although these defences were better than the breastworks of Festubert, they still required a lot of labour to bring them up to the required standard. Trenches needed to be deepened and widened, and parapets strengthened. Loopholes had to be incorporated into the parapets to give sentries protection against sniper fire, though it was vital to build these so that someone peering through the loophole was not silhouetted, alerting a sniper of its use. Listening posts were established in No Man's Land and manned under cover of darkness. These could be in a small trench, a 'shell scrape', or just a convenient shell hole holding a couple of men, and gave a vital few seconds' warning of an enemy raid or working party.

In the afternoon of the 16 August, British heavy artillery targeted La Boiselle, and as could be expected, German artillery answered in kind, though work on strengthening the parapet continued between shells. At 10 p.m., C Company sent a working party out in front of the trench line, but this was spotted and driven back by hostile artillery, sustaining just one casualty—twenty-five-year-old Pte Shepherd Dixon from Ulverston, wounded by shrapnel in the hip and left knee. The wounds required long-term treatment and proved serious enough for him to be medically discharged in May 1916. He was only capable of light work after the war, and shrapnel remained embedded in his femur. Work on the parapet continued the next day, despite light shelling, but it was dangerous labour as German snipers lay in wait for one of the workers to get careless. When L/Cpl Richard Woodward from Barrow exposed his head above the parapet, one was ready, and the B Company NCO was killed by a single shot.

The men were quickly exhausted after a long stretch in the trenches, for nights were mostly taken up by heavy manual work, patrols, raiding parties, or sentry duty. In the morning they got little sleep, curled up on the fire-step or sleeping in the cramped holes dug into the side of the trench, frequently disturbed by shellfire and constant movement around the trench. After eleven straight days in the trenches, lack of sleep was beginning to tell, and when an NCO crawled out to check one of the listening posts and found twenty-three-year-old Pte Thomas New and twenty-one-year-old

Pte John Tyson both fast asleep, there was trouble! The pair, former workmates at the Hodbarrow Mining Company, were put on CO's Orders and sentenced to twenty-eight days' Field Punishment No. 1, a serious punishment, but a mere fraction of what they would have received from a court martial (the usual destination for those accused of this offence). The CO evidently understood how tired they were. In any case, both would be recalled to work in the mines before the year was out. Another soldier, twenty-year-old Pte Edward Rushton from Ulverston, was sent before a FGCM at Aveluy. No record remains of the charge made, but the *War Diary* records that he was found 'not guilty'. Replacements arrived during this period, though the battalion was still vastly under strength; the men were nevertheless allowed to go on leave in groups of seven at a time.

At 7 p.m. on 19 August, a mine was detonated in front of the German positions at La Boiselle, followed up by howitzer shells from the British heavy artillery. Possibly expecting an attack or maybe just out of pique, the Germans retaliated with a heavy bombardment of the front line from both artillery and trench mortars. The communication trenches and Aveluy were also shelled by German medium artillery in an attempt to break up any concentration of troops in case an attack was imminent. The only casualty from all this expenditure of ammunition was seventeen-year-old Pte Gilbert Rorison, grazed in the face by a shrapnel ball. It wasn't until 8.15 p.m. on 21 August that the battalion was relieved and pulled back to a support line at Poste Donnet (50° 1′ 38.80″ N, 2° 40′ 42.27″ E). Twelve days had been the longest stretch they'd done at the front so far, but luckily the good weather, decent trenches and lack of serious aggression from German artillery had made the time bearable. Tiredness was the major issue facing the battalion, as on the 20th another three men went before a Field General Court Martial (FGCM), all charged with sleeping on sentry duty. It must have come as a relief to all to be pulled back to support duty on the night of the 21st, and although this did not mean that their labours would end, it did give the men a chance to sleep. The old French communication trenches were shallow and narrow, and were difficult to navigate, so it was decided that it would be easier to simply dig new ones rather than embarking on laborious modifications. On the 22nd, German artillery fired shrapnel shells at Post Louis, where a working party was labouring away, and also fired at various other parts of the support line; no casualties occurred, however, despite a direct hit on A Company's latrine by an HE shell on the 23rd. Possibly the biggest irritation for the men over this period was not having received their mail on the 23rd, a result of the Channel being closed to shipping for fear of German naval activity.

On 26 August, one sergeant and twenty-six men were detached to join the divisional mining company, 179 Tunnelling Company of the RE, working opposite La Boiselle. These men, who included L/Cpls John Jackson and John Riley and Pte Harold Puckley, were all skilled hard-rock miners from the Hodbarrow Mining Company, and provided much muscle and know-how to the newly established company. 179 Tunnelling Company had arrived at the division on 22 August only 300-men strong, so each infantry brigade was ordered to supplement it with an attachment of sixty men who had been miners in civilian life.[2] The tunnelling war was a particularly nasty one, with both sides trying to intercept each other's tunnels, destroying them and their tunnellers by the careful placement of directional charges known as 'camouflets'. Occasionally, troops would break through into the enemy's tunnel and have no choice but to engage in vicious hand-to-hand combat.

The use of mines, or 'saps', was unpopular with the ordinary soldier. The knowledge that the enemy was digging away below one's feet with the intention of blowing the whole section of trench sky high was not a thought that contributed to peace of mind. Working parties from the infantry had to carry spoil away from the sap, and in chalky areas such as the Somme, this glaring white chalk had to be disposed of miles back and disguised from enemy aerial reconnaissance. Work like this was both dangerous and hard graft, in addition to which the chalk leached through the sandbags and made the uniforms of the men carrying them filthy. Sometimes the explosions of heavy shells near the shaft caused roof collapse, and on 5 September, Pte John Riley received a certificate and MiD for helping to rescue two men who had been injured in just such an incident.[3] Cpl Alfred Graves, a thirty-one-year-old miner from Millom, received the DCM for this; his citation reads, 'he assisted for four hours, under fire from enemy trenches only twenty 5 yards distant, in the operations for rescuing two entombed miners at shaft head.'[4] Alfred Graves was one of fourteen soldiers who left the trenches for good on 6 October, when the Hodbarrow Mining Company succeeded in claiming back some of its former employees. John Riley had a different fate in store.

At Midnight on 28 August, the battalion was relieved and marched to billets in Martinsart. Although the weather was foul—the rain torrential and the roads muddy—the men were happy to be leaving, a chance to get clean again and enjoy some rest, or at least as much of it as training and working parties allowed! However, they were disappointed to find the billets surrounded by a sea of mud, dilapidated, and in a filthy condition. It wasn't just the men who suffered; the battalion's horses and mules were, in the only place available to picket them, up to their fetlocks in mud. The men from transport may not have had to dig new trenches or carry away mine spoil, but they had more than their fair share of toil trying to keep the animals clean, fit, and healthy, maintaining the limbers and wagons, and delivering supplies to the front trenches. Neither was this a safe job, as German artillery always tried to target transport when it brought rations and supplies forward.

There was plenty to occupy the men at Martinsart, as 100 went to the Divisional Bombing School—the machine-gunners were finally issued with two new Vickers guns to replace their battered Maxims and needed to re-train with these. It wasn't just the machine-gunners who had new equipment, for at long last the obsolete 15-lb field guns of the divisional artillery were replaced by the 18-pounder—good news for everyone in the division. The 15-lb ammunition had been restrictive, and what had been available was so erratic that it was almost as dangerous to friendly troops as it was to the enemy.[5] Large working parties were called upon to assist the RE each day, for instance on 31 August. On this day, the battalion strength was twenty-three officers and 543 men. However, sickness, men away on detachment to 179 Tunnelling Company, the requirements of training for the MG section, and duties behind the lines (such as the transport) meant that the actual number of men available to man the trenches was a mere 374—a far cry from the nominal 1,000—and this at a time when the sickness rate was in fact low. Reduced numbers of available men meant that rest was a rare treat and that fatigue parties were larger, so only forty-nine men from the battalion were not on fatigues or at the Bombing School. The battalion suffered no fatal casualties for two weeks, but this run of luck came to an end on 31 August, when Pte Henry Mason from Egremont was killed by shellfire while attached to the RE.

Though chalk uplands tend to be well drained, the geology of this sector of the Somme region was a source of strain for working parties because of the thick layer of clay overlying the chalk. When it had been wet for some time, as was the case in August 1915, the mud became particularly tenacious, and the constant movement of men and vehicles churned this up into a morass in places.

At times men sunk past their knees, and every step made was a step in boots three times the weight and size due to the clinging mud. The soil was hard to dig, as the clay stuck to the shovel and usually needed to be scraped off to clear it from the blade. Although 1 September was one of the few days on which it did not rain, the ground was still sodden, so when Pte George Huddleston received a slight wound to the shoulder from a shrapnel ball, the couple of days in the hospital away from the mud and toil would have felt like a godsend. The only casualty from this period of 'rest' referred to in the *War Diary* was twenty-year-old L/Cpl Mark Drinkall from Grange-over-Sands. He was badly injured in his knee by a piece of shrapnel on 4 September, when at 10 a.m. the Germans sent ten heavy shells into the billeting area of Martinsart. This wound exerted long-term effects, and he was invalided out in May 1916. Although surviving records are vague and incomplete, it seems probable that another man, twenty-nine-year-old Pte Charles Marr from Millom, was hit in the left hand by shrapnel at the same time—Marr's surviving records show that the timing of his journey home match Drinkall's. Marr returned in April 1916, but was posted back to England again four months later, and nine months afterwards discharged to munitions work in the iron ore mines, no doubt to the great relief of his wife and four young children. Marr was wounded again in 1921: he had joined the Defence Force and was practising skirmishing at Flookburgh when he tripped and stabbed himself with his own bayonet, though luckily the wound was minor! Probably almost as painful was Sgt Ernest Clarke's transfer to England, who, with a crop of boils to the neck, needed three months' hospital care. As his eight years of service were due to end just after he was cured, he was not sent back to France and instead discharged on 23 April 1916. In civilian life, the twenty-seven-year-old father of two had been a furnaceman at the Millom Ironworks and his skills were needed there; he did not re-join the King's Own until after the end of the war, whereupon he re-enlisted. By 9.15 p.m. that night, the battalion were back in the front line. One man to miss all this was twenty-six-year-old Pte Ernest Twidale, as the day before the billets were shelled he was detailed to escort a prisoner back to Étaples, a round trip that took him six days!

At 8 p.m. on 6 September, B Company sent a reconnaissance patrol out in front of the enemy's wire, which returned safely some hours later with useful information about the enemy's defences and dispositions. German working parties were out in force on the nights of both the 7 and 8 September, and were every time spotted by sentries and artillery fire directed onto them, with mixed results. In the early hours of 9 September, nineteen-year-old L/Cpl Harold Martin from Millom and Pte John Carrick were in a listening post to the left of the sector, forward of their own wire. On their own in No Man's Land, the D Company pair were fully alert and silently scanned the ground all around them. Out of the dark, Harold Martin spotted a small German patrol working their way along the front of the British wire; waiting until they were almost on top of him, he sprang up and shouted, 'Hands Up!' One officer and two men immediately surrendered. Seeing that there was a fourth German, the L/Cpl instructed the officer to order the other man's surrender, which he did. When a squad had escorted the prisoners back to the battalion's trenches, he gathered up the enemies' weapons and he and Pte Carrick returned to their listening post—a fine piece of soldiering from both young men. Each received the DCM and promotion to corporal. Later that same day, around 7.30 p.m., the enemy began to target the parapet with rifle fire—possibly trying to screen a working party—and then sent over a dozen small-calibre shells, attempting to locate the listening post, though without success.

On 11 September, the CO and half the officers and NCOs of newly arrived 9/ East Lancashires visited the battalion to get their first taste of trench life. It was a warm and sunny day, and although the *War Diary* tells us all was quiet, twenty-four-year-old Pte James Smith (713) from Barrow, was wounded by shrapnel in the right thigh and evacuated home—regrettably not his last experience as a casualty, either. Around 7.30 p.m., the Germans again swept the parapet with rifle and MG fire, and although no one was hit, this was an inconvenience to the men trying to work on the parapet. On 14 September, Poste Donnet was shelled, slightly wounding twenty-eight-year-old Pte Albert Gillbanks and thirty-two-year-old Pte Soloman Richardson, both from Millom.

The next day, two companies of 9/ East Lancashires arrived in the trenches for instruction and German MG fire caused three casualties, two from direct hits and another when a rifle was struck sending a splinter into a man. One of the wounded was eighteen-year-old Pte George Smith from Barrow, a member of the pre-war battalion. His wound necessitated evacuation home for treatment and once he recovered he was promoted to Lance Corporal and posted to Oswestry. Depot soldiering obviously didn't agree with him as he was demoted shortly thereafter for 'being drunk and incapable,' and three months later charged for 'striking an NCO', for which he received fourteen days' detention—quite a light sentence, upon reflection. Less than two months later, he was in trouble again, this time for being 'absent from parade': this must have been the final straw for Lt-Col. Wadham, his former CO from the 1/4th and now CO at Oswestry, because he then posted Smith back to the battalion in France.

While Pte Smith was being stretchered away from the trenches, Pte Richard Grimshaw, a twenty-five-year-old from Barrow, was up in front of the CO, Lt-Col. Thompson, charged with failing to fall-in for the routine stand-to between 4 to 5 a.m. As usual, the sentence reflected how heinous the crime was considered, and he was given twenty-one days' Field Punishment No. 1. On 17 September, the day before the battalion moved back to the support line, it manned Poste Les Dos (50° 2′ 17.1″ N, 2° 40′ 55.70″ E) in Authuille Wood (marked on most trench maps as 'Wood Post') and Poste Donnet. A and B Company areas received shellfire from 11 a.m. to 1.30 p.m., but no casualties occurred, save for one man in C Company wounded by shrapnel.

At 10 p.m. on 21 September, the battalion marched out to billets at Hénencourt and as usual, the time was spent on kit inspection, making up deficiencies, parades, route marches, and yet more working parties. Disciplinary charges were heard, although Pte Tom Muckalt's offence was serious enough for a FGCM, and he was transferred to the Worcesters after serving his sentence. Pte John Waites was up before the CO again, this time for 'gambling in an estaminet', for which he got seven days' Field Punishment No. 2. The next day it was the turn of newly-married Pte Joseph Greenhow from Keswick. He had fallen out of the line of march without permission, a serious infraction in the eyes of his seniors. Being an infantryman is a young man's game and at thirty-four, Joseph was past his prime. He had just spent two weeks in hospital after a cut to the foot had turned septic, and to be awarded seven days' Field Punishment No. 1 for falling out on the march must have seemed a tad unfair! The same night, while on a working party to the front, eighteen-year-old Pte Joseph Barnes was wounded by shellfire, and evacuated back to England, though he would return.

Because of the planned offensive at Loos further to the north, the number of working parties between 20 and 25 September multiplied. Although the Third Army was not involved in the actual offensive, it was ordered to make it look as though an attack was also planned for the Aveluy sector.

Consequently, artillery was active in targeting the German wire and unprecedented numbers of shells were supplied to the division, with 1,800 rounds for the 18-lb guns issued in just three days.[6] Any cutting of German wire or pulverising of trenches was mostly down to the division's artillery, as the supply of trench mortars was most unsatisfactory. The division had one 1½-inch mortar battery and one 4-inch mortar battery, both with limited ammunition supplies. On 2 September a 2-inch mortar battery joined the division, but no ammunition for it was supplied until 7 October.[7] The Germans, on the other hand, possessed a plentiful supply of both mortars and ammunition. Towards the end of August, frequent bombardments of the British trenches were launched from these weapons, and although the largest commonly seen was nicknamed the 'oil can' or 'rum jar' by the men, the weapon was not particularly accurate; it devastated whatever it hit, sometimes flattening whole sections of trench. This projectile was time-fused, however, and its slow flight gave its intended victims a chance to run for cover, as sentries watching its flight shouted warnings and directions. A second type described in the *Divisional History* is referred to as the 'aerial torpedo,' which, although smaller, was far more accurate. When the ammunition for the 2-inch mortar did arrive, it was nicknamed 'the plum pudding' or 'toffee apple' by the men of Lancashire in reference to its shape, though the Scotsmen—who comprised the majority of the division—named it the 'Donald Dinnie,' after the famous Scottish hammer-thrower from the Highland Games. This projectile had a long iron handle, 2-inch diameter, and large football-shaped warhead affixed on top. The division sometimes suffered casualties when this handle was blown back into the British trenches upon the round exploding in the German trench.[8]

Upon the battalion's return to the support line on 26 September, the weather deteriorated further, adding wet and cold to life's routine discomfort. German machine-gunners paid particular attention to Poste Les Dos and scored a high-value hit when they wounded Brig.-Gen. Hibbert in the shoulder upon his visit there. It is an enduring myth that top brass sat out the Great War secure in the luxury of chateaux miles behind the lines, while their men toiled and died in the mud. In fact, locating divisional or corps HQs in chateaus made absolute sense, as the large staffs had to be housed. Besides, generals did visit the Front, as casualty rates for men of this rank show, and probably too often! In *Tommy* (2005), Richard Holmes lists a total of fifty-eight general officers killed on the Western Front and suggests the figure for wounded probably exceeded 300.[9] Only 28 per cent of fatalities among ordinary soldiers were caused by small arms fire, compared to 38 per cent among the generals—not a likely fate in a chateau, all those miles behind the lines! By contrast, only one brigade commander was killed in Western Europe in the Second World War. Enemy MGs were so active that, the very next day, twenty-three-year-old Dalton man Pte Henry Gilbert was shot through the lower right jaw at Poste Les Dos, possibly by the same gunner who wounded his brigade commander. Although he survived the wound, the injury was enough to end of his soldiering days; he was demobilised to munitions work in August 1916, receiving a medical discharge at the end of the war.

Unfortunately, the liberal supplies of ammunition to the artillery dried up once the push at Loos had finished, and despite HQ being targeted by thirty shells, there was insufficient ammunition to reply shell for shell. The policy of 'artillery retaliation'—whereby a bombardment of division trenches, especially by trench mortars, would be answered by a set number of shells—had been quite effective in reducing the number of times that the Germans used trench mortars in the sector.[10] Despite the relative inaction of the battalion, the strength was actually forty less than it had been a month earlier, bringing it to exactly 50 per cent of their original establishment: reinforcements were of the essence. How galling it must have been for Lt-Col. Thompson to receive an order to send a further fourteen men back to the iron ore mines! Among them were Cpl Alfred Graves DCM, and Privates William Rigg, John Coward, John William Coward, Henry Date, John Hughes, Thomas Radcliffe, and William Sharpe. All fourteen were dispatched to the Channel ports as soon as the battalion left the line on 3 October.

The battalion returned to the front line on 8 October to relieve the Liverpool Irish, though there was a problem with the handover when discrepancies were discovered between the amounts of ammunition and equipment in the trench stores and that detailed in the paperwork. Handover of a section of trenches was not just a simple matter of moving one group of personnel in and another out. The day before a move back into a trench line, a reconnaissance of the trench was always undertaken by battalion officers and senior NCOs. It also became practise for battalion snipers to occupy the new trenches twenty-four hours before the rest of the battalion, and they would liaise with the snipers of the outgoing battalion as to best procedures for that sector. Conversely, the machine-gunners of the outgoing battalion would remain for at least another twenty-four hours before relief by the incoming battalion's gunners. On their reconnaissance, officers would establish the condition of the wire and parapets and any work in progress upon these. A trench 'log book' was kept daily and passed over to the new unit, which helped considerably with continuity of effort.[11] Arcs of fire and the position of enemy MGs and snipers would be ascertained and any particularly dangerous areas of the trench line highlighted. The position of existing listening posts would be passed on, though battalions often preferred to establish their own because they took for granted that the enemy already knew the position of existing ones. This was a particularly difficult task for any unit, as all viable positions had probably been used before and snipers faced similar problems when it came to choice of lair. The position of the small arms ammunition store, the bomb store, and the general trench store, and a list of all contained within, had to be obtained from the outgoing battalion. When it came to checking actual stores against the paperwork, officers on take-over had to be particularly vigilant, as it was not unusual for outgoing units to try to pass deficiencies on to a naive relief.

Once in a new trench, officers and NCOs needed to pass on all relevant information to every soldier: methods of communications with the artillery, both by phone and by visual signals such as rockets, needed to be shared; procedures to follow in the case of heavy bombardment, or in an attack or counter-attack, passed on. The QM needed to know the route for his transport to deliver rations and supplies and the drop-off points for these. Of routine but vital importance were the locations of latrines, water supplies, and any cooking arrangements available. All officers needed to know the position of HQs, and be able to brief their company runners accurately enough for them to find it too. As can be imagined, taking over a system of unfamiliar trenches was challenging! Each man carried 120 rounds of .303 ammunition in his pouches, but an additional supply equivalent to 120-rounds-per-man was kept in the trenches and another 10 to 20,000 rounds of .303 stored at battalion HQ.[12] Reserve ammunition, stored in a dry place in the trench line, was not supposed to be opened unless there was an attack. Each morning, it was the responsibility of every platoon commander to check to see if the lids on the boxes opened freely and that the tin sheet which weatherproofed the ammunition was still unbroken. Any box that had been opened was to be used to top up the men's ammunition pouches and then returned to battalion stores where it would be exchanged for a new box.[13]. Apart from the grenades in the bomb store, a number of 'ready-use' grenades were kept in the trenches, and their condition needed monitoring.

The next three days were fairly quiet, with tit-for-tat shelling, night patrols into No Man's Land to disrupt German working parties, and several reconnaissance patrols near the German wire. Pte Walker from B Company was slightly wounded on 12 October. At 4 p.m. the next day, Lt-Col. Thompson was visiting the fire trench when a German shrapnel shell burst directly overhead, wounding him in the shoulder. The CO was evacuated to the CCS, Maj. Nicholas Barnes assuming command. Also wounded was twenty-eight-year-old Pte John McMaster from Barrow, though his wound was severe enough to warrant evacuation home; he was yet another to be redeployed to munitions work upon recovery. The 14th saw more shellfire on Poste Donnet, and in retaliation brigade artillery targeted enemy transport in Ovillers. There was also continued activity from the German front trench with frequent outbreaks of rifle fire and shouts. The 15th was foggy, and despite the terse comment in the *War Diary* of 'little to report', the battalion had its first fatal casualty in six weeks, when twenty-two-year-old Sgt James Charnock from Dalton was wounded and died before reaching the CCS. His platoon commander, Lt Amos Beardsley, wrote to his mother: 'He was very much liked and respected by all the platoon and, in fact by the whole company ... his death was a great blow to us all'.[14]

The fog carried on into 15 and 16 October, yet the Germans dropped three 77-mm shells accurately onto Lower Donnet, one of which wounded Ulverston quarryman Pte Harry Greenhow in the left thigh. The twenty-one-year-old had already been wounded once during the attack of 8 June, neither would this be the last time he was stretchered off. He was sent home to recover and never returned to the battalion, posted instead to the MGC upon his recovery in October 1917. Sentries reported that British aircraft were circling over German lines, occasionally firing bursts of MG at the ground, which led the battalion officers to wonder if they were trying to signal that the Germans were concentrating forces for an attack, although nothing ensued. On the 17th, German artillery again demonstrated their accurate registration of the British network when a shell dropped straight out of the fog and exploded directly over the trench, wounding three men from A Company. One of these was L/Cpl David Sandwell, who was evacuated home, his right hand punctured by shrapnel. He too was transferred to munitions work upon his recovery. Another of the wounded was thirty-two-year-old married man L/Cpl Albert Garnett, who died from his wounds three days later. Just before dusk on 20 October, German artillery sent fifty shells into D Company's positions on the left of the trench line, which despite blowing in the parapet in three places caused no casualties.

The next day, the battalion were relieved in the trenches and moved back to support, with HQ, A, and D Company in Lower Poste Donnet and B, and C in Poste Les Dos. As previously, the enemy shelled these positions sporadically and working parties filled the night hours. It was on this day that the divisional commander decided that the entire division needed better dugout accommodation.[15] The dugouts inherited from the French appeared decent, but a number of incidents had shown that they were in fact death traps. Having only 3 to 4 feet of top cover, a direct hit by a shell, particularly from the larger trench mortars, would collapse the lot onto the occupants with invariably fatal results. The Tunnelling Company was too busy mining in front of La Boiselle to assist, so the job was given to the Divisional Pioneers, 8/ Royal Scots, with assistance from skilled miners from the infantry battalions. The new shelters gave up to 12 feet of top cover, a massive improvement. The additional work carrying away the spoil from these added further burden to the already overworked infantry, but the visible rewards meant they took to it stoically. On 24 October, one of the runners took advantage of the mist to leave the communication trenches and take a short cut between Preston and Lancaster Avenues, where he was surprised to see an unexploded 6-inch shell lying in the open, a find he reported to the artillery. The following day, the battalion received reinforcements for the first time in ages, comprising three NCOs and nineteen men from the depot. On the same day, three of the wounded also returned. However, orders were also received to send another eight men back to the Hodbarrow mines, one of them thirty-four-year-old Pte William Allen from Millom. Truly a case of 'the Lord giveth and the Lord taketh'! One who probably wasn't nearly as pleased as the rest of the battalion to move back to billets on the 28th was Henry Rigg from Ulverston. The twenty-seven-year-old had been awarded seven days' Field Punishment No. 1 for being drunk in the billets the last time they were there and his punishment would begin as soon as the battalion were back in Aveluy.

The break from the front line was much shorter than the men had been hoping for, as the on 29 October, a working party of 130 men was sent to trudge through the pouring rain back up to the line to help 1/4th Loyals repair a fire trench damaged by trench mortar and artillery fire that morning. One of them, twenty-one-year-old Pte Jeremiah Clarke, was slightly wounded by shrapnel. The next day, German artillery extended their barrage to include the billets in Aveluy and about fifty shells of various calibres landed in the village. As soon as it was dark, another working party of 100 men set out again to help the Loyals rebuild their trench. Enemy shelling resumed in the early hours when at around 2 a.m. of the 31st, thirty howitzer shells landed in the village, though fortunately, most were duds. Sadly the working party in the trench line were not so fortunate, and C Company's eighteen-year-old Pte James Vincent from Barrow was killed outright, while D Company's Sgt John Wells and A Company's L/Cpl George Holmes were both wounded. Thirty-four-year-old Holmes from Ulverston was one of the longest serving members of the battalion, having joined in 1908. With a compound fracture to his hand caused by a shrapnel ball, he was evacuated home. This was the last the battalion saw of this experienced NCO, as he was posted to 8/ King's Own when he returned to France in September 1917.

The rain continued unabated into November and it was now that problems in the construction of the old French trenches began to materialise—a situation made worse by the new dugouts and mining operations' high demands on manpower, for they limited the strength available for trench maintenance.[16] Whereas British trenches had an outwards slope, the sides of French trenches were cut vertically. Because of the layer of clay overlying the chalk, the sides of the trenches still subsided, bending and breaking the wooden revetments, however much was tried in the way of revetting. Dams had to be constructed at the entrances of dugouts to prevent rivers of mud and water flowing down the steps and flooding them. Large areas of fire trench in C and D Companies' positions had collapsed and the two main communication trenches, Rivington Street and John O' Gaunt Street, were all but impassable. It wasn't just the British who suffered from the weather, as the Germans were heard pumping out their trenches on 3 November. Fortunately, there were still large numbers of skilled miners in D Company and their artistry with the shovel helped the battalion deliver excellent results in trench repairs. Such was the scale of the problem that large working parties from other units were pulled off shelter construction and called in to help clear the communication trenches. The 1/4th was lucky: some of the other battalions lost men when older trench shelters collapsed and suffocated the occupants. Conditions were temporarily eased when the first frosts came, but the change in weather actually worsened the problem once it began to thaw. The frost in the wet chalk had accelerated freeze-thaw weathering and made it crumbly, so that when it thawed this too began to collapse into the bottom of the trenches.[17]

German artillery may have been quiet at this time, but British guns weren't. German MG positions and saps to the battalion's front received special attention from 18-pounders and howitzers. The discomfort faced in these conditions was near intolerable. Heavy rain fell most days and the wind, either from the north or the east, was bitterly cold. To compound this, men were fouled in mud from head to toe; merely walking over the slippery morass became an ordeal, especially when laden with heavy burdens, and contributed to the sick list with injuries to muscles, tendons, and ligaments. Despite the twice-daily inspections, it was difficult to keep weapons free from mud and rust; mud-free pieces of rag, or—rarest of all—pieces of the precious 'four-by-two' to pull through the rifle barrels, were zealously guarded. The French dugouts were a big improvement on the small 'dog kennels' of the breastworks, but this was not saying much! What did improve the lives of the men was the steady trickle of comforts from home, collected after campaigns in the local papers. Tobacco and cigarettes, woollen underwear, scarves, gloves, and balaclavas all helped make life that little bit more bearable.

Although there had been little enemy activity in the dreadful conditions, British aggression had not gone totally unanswered. Dalton man, twenty-one-year-old Pte William Kewley was wounded by a shrapnel ball to shoulder. On the bright side, he did get just over three weeks in a clean hospital bed, though he must have been somewhat disappointed not to have been sent back to Blighty! In a little over five months, he would be discharged at the end of his period of engagement and return to his job as a joiner with the Lindal Iron Mining Company. The battalion were due to be relieved in the late afternoon of 7 November by the Argylls, so D Company planned a special patrol for 7.30 a.m. The rear of the German wire had a large board affixed to it, containing a taunting comment towards the French who had occupied the line prior to 51 Division's arrival. The patrol crawled forward and stole this board, bringing it back to the British trenches and also located the position of an enemy listening post, all without the Germans being aware of anything amiss. Though this may seem like a pointless act of bravado, it was all about 'dominating' No Man's Land and taking the initiative. That British soldiers had been able to get to the rear of their wire and remove such a large board without discovery must no doubt have preyed on the minds of German sentries at night.

The battalion rested in the billets in Hénencourt until 17 November, suffering only one casualty of enemy action from all the men dispatched on working parties. The unfortunate soldier, hit in the thumb by a shrapnel ball on the 16th, was a twenty-six-year-old from Barrow, Cpl Thomas Edmondson, who had been the first man to enlist after war was declared. There were also casualties from sickness and injury, some of whom were lost to the battalion forever. On the 14th, Pte Charles Woodhead was evacuated back to England suffering from otitis media (inflammation of the middle ear) and upon return to France in June 1916, was transferred to the Manchesters. On the 16th, Pte James Marriott of A Company was evacuated to England to undergo a hernia operation, and upon his return in August 1917 was posted to the 1/5th. On the 18th, Pte William Carey, a twenty-one-year-old from Ulverston, slipped and fell while repairing the trench parapet and injured his shoulder, side, and hip when he landed on equipment. Although described in the accident report—all non-combat wounds or injuries had to be investigated—as injuries which were 'not of a serious nature,' they were bad enough for him to be evacuated to England, where once recovered he was posted into the regimental police in Oswestry and later transferred to the Military Foot Police (MFP). But the event with the biggest impact on the battalion was the arrival of a new CO on 10 November. Lt-Col. Frederick Carleton DSO was a regular officer from the King's Own and had previously served with the 4th as its regular Adjutant. A veteran of the Nile, South, and West African campaigns, he took a long, hard look around and decided that there was much to be improved upon. In the words of the QM,

> Almost at once the battalion began to feel the influence of a new personality. This influence had the qualities of an east wind, and, with all its tonic properties, the battalion felt impelled to brace itself unwontedly to meet its cutting edge. Our education was not yet complete.[18]

When the battalion moved to trenches on 17 November, it was to a new location for them. This time they were further north into the Authuille sector, the northernmost boundary marked where Thiepval Avenue met the front line (50° 3′ 0.86″ N, 2° 40′ 51.35″ E) and the southernmost where Campbell Avenue met it (50° 2′ 35.10″ N, 2° 40′ 44.49″ E). Thiepval Avenue followed the modern-day D151 from Authuille to Thiepval, and the front line stood just under 500 m short of the turn off for the Thiepval Memorial car park.

This was one of the quietest trench postings the battalion would ever see in the war; apart from one private wounded on 22 November, enemy action caused no casualties. The sludgy conditions were hard on the men, and on the animals too. Horses and mules struggled with their loads in the deeply rutted mud tracks between transport lines and the front line. Not only did they cart food, ammunition, and military supplies, but also copious quantities of coal, coke, and charcoal to warm the trenches. On one occasion, Pte Dixon loaded his limber with two and a half tonnes of coal in Martinsart and his two mules pulled the load magnificently until they reached Aveluy Wood, where the track crossed a shallow depression filled with 18 inches of mud. The limber stuck fast and no amount of persuasion could get the mules moving again.[19]

Soldiers returning after wounds, injury, or sickness frequently found that they were posted away from their units to a bunch of complete strangers. For both the men and their original units, this was a source of irritation; it took time for a man to acclimatise himself to the ways of a unit or sub-unit, and the chances of becoming a casualty were much higher for men new to a platoon, even if they were experienced soldiers. It was common for entire drafts of men fresh out of training in England and proudly displaying their new cap badges to be transferred *en masse* to a regiment which had recently suffered heavy casualties. Much sickness was weather-related; nineteen-year-old Pte Arthur Dickinson's trench foot was so severe that he was sent home for treatment, and it was April 1917 before he was fit to return, assigned to the battalion's transport rather than the trenches. Twenty-three-year-old Pte Thomas Fell's rheumatism had deteriorated, and he too was invalided home and discharged as medically unfit in June the following year. One of the 1/4th's sick did return, however: twenty-four-year-old farmer Pte Tom Mayson from Silecroft, after treatment for rheumatic fever. This exceptional soldier, known as 'Tickler' to his chums—possibly because of a fondness for the jam of the same name—would achieve great things in 1917. One man with mixed feelings about the return to billets on the 28th was Pte Hugh McIlheron, who had mislaid his rifle and was sentenced to pay for a new one. As rifles cost £3 5s (about forty-three days' pay), the ubiquitous ham, egg, and chips with beer or wine in local estaminets were out of the question on this and the following periods of 'rest', unless some of his comrades took pity on him. Although the battalion received a draft of forty-four men on the 25th, some of them familiar faces, more men left for the Millom mines on the 27th. These included Cpl Harold Binns and Privates Thomas Fell, Clarence Bosanko, Frederick Giles, Matthew Lee, William Pearson, and Walter Warren.

One new arrival on 25 October probably should not even have been in the Army. Twenty-six-year-old former Millom miner, Richard Penaluna had been with the 4th pre-war, but was discharged as time-served. Working in Ireland when war began, he had gone to his local recruiting office and signed up with the Royal Dublin Fusiliers. Two months later, they discharged him as medically unfit, as he had a deformed toe and found marching difficult. Obviously unhappy with the Army's verdict, he returned to his native Cumberland and a week later entered the recruiting office in Ulverston, omitted to tell them that he had just been discharged and after passing the rudimentary medical entered the training system. The irony of a Millom miner arriving at the battalion at exactly the same time that soldiers were doing the reverse was probably not lost on those in charge. Sadly for Penaluna and many of his old pre-war comrades, their war ended prematurely at a place called Guillemont.

The battalion moved back into the line on 5 December, to its original location opposite Aveluy. The weather continued to play havoc: thick, clinging mud making some areas impassable; trench sides continually collapsed; some flooded to such an extent that it became impossible to maintain an unbroken front line in the divisional sector, especially as the trench in the middle of the sector had been smashed by a recent bombardment. The length held by the 1/4th was split into three detached sectors, each held by a single company with the fourth back in support. The area in-between these was deep slough, dotted with fetid pools of water. The *War Diary* has little to say about 8 December, although German 77-mm's dropped around the railway bridge in Aveluy wounded a man and the battalion lost two men in an accident at the Brigade Bombing School. Twenty-four-year-old Pte Charles Birch was only lightly injured and able to re-join the battalion soon afterwards, but for Pte Henry Rigg, the grenade fragments which penetrated his left thigh meant a transfer home for treatment. Only five ORs were wounded by enemy action during the whole of December, one of whom, Pte Edward Davis from Millom, was hit in the hand by a fragment of a hand grenade. Another was twenty-four-year-old James Bamber from Ulverston, whose wrist was smashed by a shrapnel ball and earned him an evacuation home.

Despite a relaxation in German activity, the battalion continued to patrol and probe enemy positions. On 15 December, twenty-year-old L/Cpl Obadiah Bates from Barrow led a patrol out once darkness fell and succeeded in getting right up to the German wire without being detected. Another patrol reported deep mud between the trenches in front of P 134 (a sector of enemy trenches). It is likely that hostilities decreased as a result of both sides putting so much effort into keeping their trenches intact and their men dry. Between 8 and 15 December, the number of cases of trench foot that demanded hospital attention was on the rise. Twenty-two-year-old Pte Thomas Fish ended his eight days with the battalion when he was hospitalised for a gastric ulcer and returned to England. Upon his recovery eight months later, he was posted to 8/ King's Own and medically discharged with the same complaint less than a year later. The conditions even led to the MO Maj. Rutherford being incapacitated, for whom Capt. John St Andrew Titmas of the RAMC temporarily stepped in. Trench foot was particularly prevalent in the winter and spring months of the early years of the war, before strategies to prevent its onset were properly in place. This painful and potentially crippling condition led to about 2.5 per cent of the 1/4th spending time in hospital. The symptoms were numbness, swelling, and pain and if untreated, the foot could turn gangrenous, leaving little alternative but amputation. Thirty-four-year-old Pte Hartley Marsden from Preston had a big toe amputated because of trench foot and was given a medical discharge in May 1916. Medical services quickly identified the causes as circulatory: constant immersion in cold water and pressure upon the feet as they swelled inside the boots, restricting blood flow. The QM's records show that, from 1916 onward, a battalion would use over 30 gallons of whale oil per month in preventative measures, with a noticeable drop in the number of cases of trench foot from this time on. The men were required to rub their feet daily with this evil-smelling substance; it gave their feet some degree of protection, though they rarely had a chance to get dry in this sector's communication trenches (where the mud was frequently over knee-level).

Surviving medical records for the 1/4th reveal that another major cause of hospitalisation was ICT, which harvested 4.8 per cent of the men, many of whom were labelled as 'ICT-knee'. Unfortunately, 'ICT-knee' can mean either 'inflamed connective tissue' of the knee (swollen knee), or 'internal cruciate tear' of the ligaments in the knee (the symptoms of which are, again, swollen knee!). Whichever was the case, it required treatment in England. Moreover, those afflicted were often reposted elsewhere upon recovery, such as for twenty-two-year-old Pte Edward Walsh—evacuated back to England with 'ICT-knee' in December and then posted to 1/ King's Own. Another man lost through ICT was eighteen-year-old Pte Norman Barnett from Barrow; his ICT an infection to the hand after it was injured on 8 September, and when he recovered he was reclaimed by Vickers. While it was common to empty wards in France of minor cases prior to a battle, or just afterward when wards were overcrowded, most of the ICT evacuation cases in the 1/4th seem to have been at quiet times on the Western Front.

On 16 December, the battalion marched back to billets at Hénencourt, anticipating a well-earned break from the trenches. But training had to continue, and on the 18th twenty-year-old Lt John Ward from Lytham was detailed to give a lecture on the No. 1 grenade. As he was demonstrating its use, calamity struck. How or why the safety pin was removed is no longer on record, as all copies of the enquiry have been destroyed. Whether or not Lt Ward thought this was a drill grenade and demonstrated how it was detonated by banging it against a table, or whether it was just dropped or knocked accidentally, is unknown. A sergeant major from another regiment once gave a safety lecture with one, warning the men about the dangers of catching a hard object with the end, and struck a table in demonstration, with predictably lethal consequences. Ward was mortally wounded upon the grenade's detonation, and eighteen-year-old James McQuade from Belfast killed outright. Thirteen other men were wounded, one of whom was Pte William Hoggarth, who was medically discharged in April 1916. One of the most seriously wounded was Sgt William Kirkby, who was blinded by the accident and medically discharged the next year. One of the local papers ran the story of his injury.

Sergeant William Kirkby is the first of the King's Own Royal Lancasters to lose his sight in this terrible conflict. He is now at his home, 13, Cobden-street, Dalton, and when a '*Guardian*' reporter saw him last Tuesday he was agreeably surprised to find Sergeant Kirkby in a particularly happy frame of mind, and quite cheerful. There was nothing dull or pessimistic about this gallant fellow, who will carry his reminder of the great European war to the end of his days. He said he had been in the war zone nine months before the explosion of a bomb on December 18th, which caused such serious injuries that at first his life was despaired of. He remembers being struck in the right eye and on putting his hand to the place the eye dropped into the palm. He ran some hundreds of yards in that state until he fell through exhaustion. He also had a wound in the head, from which the doctors took a piece of shrapnel. He was removed to hospital, and though receiving every skilled attention the sight of the left eye gradually waned and left him sightless ... His cheerfulness can be exemplified in his remark: 'Well, I'm not so bad as thousands of my comrades. I am glad I'm alive. I have every opportunity for getting on in the world. I am going training to the Blind Institute at St. Dunstan's, Regent's Park, London, and hope soon to pick up a trade.' Mrs. Kirkby, who is delighted to have her husband home again, showed me a piece of shrapnel which had gone through Sergeant Kirkby's clothing, past 30 rounds of ammunition, pierced through his infantry training book, his prayer book, and map, and lodged in his pocket wallet, going through letters and papers in the wallet, making a hole in the forehead of his brother's photograph, also through the bust of his father's photograph.[20]

The hole in Kirkby's photograph was a chilling portent of what was to come, for his brother Cpl Ben Kirkby was indeed among those killed at Guillemont in August 1916. The day of the No. 1 grenade demonstration was incidentally Capt. Titmas's last with the battalion; his duties were taken over by Belfast-born doctor Lt James Gatchell RAMC, who prior to the war had worked as a missionary doctor in Africa. This accident was neither the welcome, nor the farewell either might have expected.

The next day, forty reinforcements arrived, twenty-eight of whom were new to the battalion. They didn't have long to adjust themselves to their platoons, as the battalion was back into the trenches at Authuille on 21 December. C Company manned Mound Keep, which turned out to be a hot location—the Germans firing thirty-two shells at it between 10.30 and 11 a.m. on the 23rd. It was believed that their target had been McMahon's Blockhouse, but not one shell struck it. The period between Christmas and New Year was fairly peaceful in the trenches; the main activity from the German side was the firing of large trench mortar rounds, most of them duds. On New Year's Eve, twenty-five-year-old Lt Edward Spearing was wounded in the shoulder by a fragment from a rifle grenade. The only fatality in the battalion during this period was one of the mules, killed by shellfire on Christmas Day when the Germans rather un-sportingly shelled the billets in reprisal to 51 Division's equally un-festive rebuffs. The *Divisional History* rather dryly describes the exchange of greetings.

On Christmas Eve he [the Germans] sang carols; this was at once stopped by the Divisional Artillery. He then came out of his trenches to fraternise; this was also stopped by the Divisional Artillery. He retaliated by shelling Albert; the Division on the right immediately shelled Courcelette. The enemy then shelled Aveluy; the gunners replied by shelling Pozières. The enemy had the last word, for he then shelled Martinsart, where he hit a horse, a mule [belonging to the 1/4th] and a limber loaded with grenades, which fortunately did not burst.[21]

In 1915, Christmas Day was business as usual at the Front. Sickness continued to send men to hospital and, in many cases, home. It was during these few days that the battalion lost thirty-seven-year-old Maj. Robert Little, not to return, and A/CQSM John Sandham, hospitalised with German measles!

# 3 January 1916 – 20 July 1916
# Old Friends, New Places

January 1916 was a time of great, but not unwelcome change. On the 3rd, the battalion set off on a series of marches that lasted until the 7th, at Longprés-Les-Corps-Saints. No longer in 51 Division, 1/4th King's Own joined its former comrades from 55 (West Lancashire) Division there, now reformed with its original component units. The 1/4th became a part of 164 Infantry Brigade, along with the 1/8th King's Liverpools, 1/4th Loyal North Lancashires, and 2/5th Lancashire Fusiliers.

Despite no longer being in the line in this much drier location, sickness, injury, and accident still took their usual toll. The first fatal casualty of the year was Dalton-born Fred Graham, who succumbed to the cumulative effects of wounds received and died at home on the 4th. A few days later, thirty-five-year-old married father of six from Rochdale and resident of Preston Pte Hartley Marsden was admitted to hospital suffering from both trench fever and trench foot. Although the trench fever was cured after a couple of weeks, his trench foot was severe enough to necessitate the amputation of his big toe and subsequent discharge. The battalion tailor, thirty-year-old Sgt Harold Dawson from Coniston, was posted to the divisional tailors' shop, a posting he must have relished for its comfort and security. As battalion tailor, Dawson would rarely have ventured into the front-line trenches, but his existence had still been dangerous and uncomfortable, as the battalion HQ and stores were always within German artillery range and a prime shellfire or air raid target. Divisional HQ was further back from the front, and it was less customary for these to be hit by gunfire, even if they were a much sought-after target in an air raid. Joining Dawson at divisional HQ was twenty-nine-year-old Pte Henry Bertram from Ulverston. The tallest man in the battalion at 6 foot 3 inches, he'd been selected to work as a groom in the divisional stables, a far safer posting than his previous one with the TMB!

The battalion was disenchanted by the state of the billets and the locals, who were actively hostile. Their antipathy had its roots in the behaviour of a previous battalion, whose men had caused a lot of damage and ill-feeling; it was some time before cordial relations could be restored.[1] On 9 January, sixty-three new men arrived from England, followed by another forty on the 27th. This may have been the largest draft of replacements yet seen, but the battalion was still woefully under strength.

Sgt William Maden, who arrived on the 9th, was actually fortunate to be there in the first place, let alone as a sergeant! He had been in both the TF and Special Reserve of the Lancashire Fusiliers, and as a corporal in their 4th Battalion, fallen foul of authority in December 1914 and been 'busted' back down to Private. Unhappy with this outcome, he deserted in January 1915 and joined the King's Own. His soldiering qualities were obvious and by April 1915, he'd been promoted to sergeant, whereupon he'd confessed all to his new CO. Fraudulent enlistment and desertion were serious offences and could have led to imprisonment. However, common sense was frequently used and if the soldier fitted in well

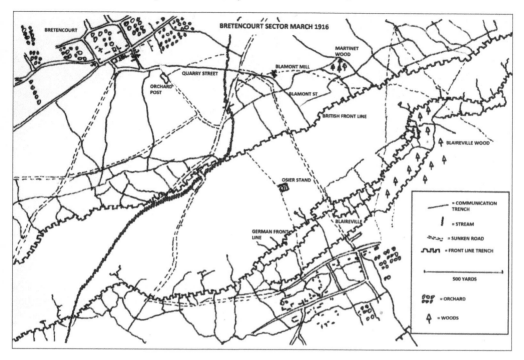

with his new unit, then matters were sorted out and the soldier remained where he was without further punishment. It turned out to be the right decision: Sgt Maden was an asset to the battalion. He was, however, later lost to the battalion after receiving a gunshot wound to the jaw and suffering from trench fever, both of which led to his home posting and eventual medical discharge in 1919.

January was a month of training and reconstruction, interspersed with parades and any fun that could be had. Officers went riding, or in the case of some of the 'newer gentlemen' learnt to, to the amusement of all. This was not without its dangers, as twenty-three-year-old 2Lt Harold Hodkinson discovered. His horse stumbled, unseating him and dragging him for some distance with his foot caught in the stirrup. The injuries were bad enough to give the young officer from Wigan a spell in hospital.

The battalion arrived in Candas on 1 February and immediately took over fatigue duties from 9/Inniskilling Fusiliers. They were tasked with providing the manpower for 112 (Railway) Company, RE, who were building a light railway line between Candas and Puchevillers. The men would march out to the railhead early in the morning, returning each night to billets. Two weeks later they were on the move again: on the 15th they marched 11 miles to an overnight halt at Thieures, before continuing the next day for Sombrin. Although only a five-hour march, the journey was notable for the appalling weather (torrential rain and gale force winds) and it took the men most of the next day to get clean, dry, and ready for an inspection. Training intensified and specialists such as signallers, snipers, and bombers attended training schools at brigade and division, and then practised their arts in conjunction with the whole battalion. Drafts of replacements continued to arrive, much to the relief of officers. One of these new men, bespectacled nineteen-year-old Pte Albert Taylor from Preston, would mature into a very fine soldier indeed.

Beyond basic training, it took many additional months to actually get a man to act like a soldier. To the uninitiated, the job of an infantryman appears fairly simple—something along the lines of standing up, looking fierce, and heading straight for the enemy. In reality, it takes a great deal of experience before a squad can move cohesively and the survival chances of everyone in the squad are enhanced once this has been achieved. Soldiers need to know their different formations and arcs of fire; this may be straightforward enough when static, but once the squad are in 'section attack', can only attained by practice. The procedure of bombing along a trench also took a lot of training if the inexperienced were not to blunder forward into their own grenades, or fail to give their comrades proper cover. This training needed to be engrained in each man, so that, exhausted and under stress, they could put it into action without thinking—and it was this intensity of training that was so difficult to imbue in wartime. The cold and heavy snow blocking many of the roads did not help the progress of the training agenda, either.

It wasn't until 3 p.m. on 25 February that the battalion began the 6-mile march to the trenches at Monchiet. A short distance for the men normally, but a nightmare in the blizzard that greeted them. The wind blew snow directly into their faces, and deep snow made every step laborious for those at the front, trampling the snow flat, and awkward for those behind, slithering and sliding in their hob-nailed boots over frozen *pavés*. The battalion transport struggled on every incline, their heavy loads taxing the willpower of the mules and horses pulling them; a number of wagons were unable to make any headway at all. The battalion arrived at its destination shortly after dark, and for some there was no rest, as the stranded transport left behind needed rescuing. The next day, the battalion moved into the line, holding the Blamont and Ravine Trenches in front of Bretencourt, part of the series of defences protecting Arras. Snow continued to fall.

One man who missed this hellish journey was battalion master-cook Sgt Henry Rayment. The twenty-three-year-old returned home to Ulverston upon 'termination of engagement' on 23 February. Although he had declined to re-engage, he was conscripted that August and, complete with a new tattoo on his right forearm (of clasped hands bearing the name 'Rachel'), he was posted to 9/ King's Own in Salonika as a private. Dangerously wounded in April 1917 by a shrapnel ball to the head which fractured his skull, he was evacuated to Malta, where he died of meningitis on 10 November 1917. In his will he decreed, 'to my best ... [word missing due to damage] Rachel [...] my box of small silver coins and the four gold pieces, and I leave the remaining money and effects to my mother.' We do not know whether Rachel received his bequest, for his service record yields no more information on the subject. Rayment's Rachel eventually married in 1926 and died at the grand old age of ninety-six. As the Conscription Acts were not yet fully in force, February saw many a long-serving man discharged upon expiry of his period of engagement. Like Rayment, very few of them extended their service to remain with the battalion, a sign of just how foul the conditions faced by the men were, for after nearly a year of fighting together, the decision to leave one's comrades and friends would not have been a light one. However, the lure of life back home was too great a temptation to refuse. Most of the returned resumed employment in strategic industries, so few of them were later conscripted, although a few did re-enlist of their own volition.

In the twenty-first century, popular perception of No Man's Land is of a landscape resembling the surface of the moon; of deep, water-filled craters overlapping each other; of earth churned up and slick with muck. In places this description would be apt, but not for Bretencourt in early 1916. The opposing front lines were anywhere between 200 to 500 m apart, and long grass covered No Man's Land, although it was all snowed under at this time. About half way across No Man's Land was a thick cluster of osier (willow) trees (50° 13′ 29.17″ N, 2° 42′ 37.34″ E) which provided cover for the various aggressive patrolling activities from both sides. For the battlefield tourist, this sector is quite a difficult one to visualise today: some of the roads on the trench maps between Bretencourt and Blaireville have been moved, or no longer exist. Where the end of the Blamont Street communication trench met the front line and became Blamont Trench, can be found at 50° 13′ 46.06″N, 2°42′ 43.39″ E. The D34 road from Bretencourt to Blaireville, known today as 'Le Blanc Mont', follows the old road quite closely, and the end of Blamont Street is about 120 m to the left of this road, at the point where it crosses the old front line. The old front line crossed the modern D34 about 530 m after the modern-day crossroads with the D3. The stream shown on the sketch map appears to seriously hinder movement, but in reality is little more than a ditch and can easily be cleared.

Although February was 'quiet' as regards action, the constant shovelling of mud and snow in an effort to keep trenches and roads clear ensured that the men got little rest. Meanwhile, new recruit Albert Taylor was already making his mark. This was his first time in the trenches, and by the end of the month he was recommended for and received the MM.[2]

On 1 March, heavy rain turned the snow into slush. Overnight temperatures dropped again and heavy snow began to fall at 8 p.m. on the 2nd. To compound the miserable weather, German shells targeted the trenches, and L/Cpl Herbert Sadler was wounded in the left shoulder by shrapnel and evacuated home. He did not re-join the battalion after leaving hospital, but returned to his job with Vickers in October. That night, they were relieved by the Liverpool Irish and marched back to billets at Monchiet. Incessant work and poor weather had taken their toll and the QM noted that the men were struggling on this march.[3] Rest was allowed on the 3rd, although equipment still needed to be cleaned and a draft of twenty men arrived (only nine of these were new, the remainder being men on the sick list returning to duty). That night, the snow resumed and fell heavily all night and for the next couple of days. Despite the conditions and when not engaged in road-clearing, training continued, with specialists departing for training at brigade and all men practising for gas attacks. It was at this time that the battalion received the Lewis gun and 2Lt Lesley Bowman from Ulverston went off with seven men to Wisques to learn about this new weapon. With the concentration of Vickers guns into brigade MG companies and later to the MGC, it was clear that battalions needed their own, portable firepower: the Lewis filled this gap nicely, and further still offered the opportunity to rewrite infantry tactics. At just under 30 lb, it was hardly light; the 47-round drum magazines were both heavy and bulky, and required a team of four to operate and carry ammunition, at least two of whom would have to have been Lewis-trained. Like most weapons, the Lewis was prone to stoppages with the ingress of dirt and needed to be kept clean if it was to function reliably. With the right team, it was an extremely effective addition to a platoon's firepower. The allocation of Lewis guns was initially one per company, but by the end of the war every platoon had at least two.

At 9.20 p.m. on 8 March, the battalion returned to the trenches and made progress clearing the trenches of mud and slush, or as Lancastrians would say, 'slutch'. After dark, working parties quietly made their way forward to the belt of wire in front of their own trench, men carrying heavy coils of wire, wooden stakes, and other tools necessary to reinforce this vital defence. The wonderfully silent screw picket was not to make its appearance in British use until some months later, so the men muffled the tops of stakes and even the sledge hammer with Hessian, taking absolute care not to make any noise or knock one metallic object against another. Less than 200 m away, German sentries in front-line trenches would be alert and listening for just such a warning to send up a flare. Men had learned that any movement after a flare went up was fatal. The trick was to freeze, despite the feeling of total exposure in the flare's bright light, and hope that their silhouettes would blend into the broken background of uneven shapes and shadows. The flicker of movement from a man who lost his nerve and dived for cover would bring immediate retribution in the form of MG fire, which swept backwards and forwards inches above the ground, and a barrage of shrapnel from artillery. Inevitably, men whose feet seldom had a chance to dry continued to suffer from trench foot and on the 14th, one of the draft from the end of January, twenty-six-year-old Pte William Penny, was admitted to hospital.

The transition into spring may have made life less miserable in the trenches, but it also prompted increased enemy artillery fire and sniping. On 13 March, just a moment's exposure gave one of these snipers a high-value target. CSM Harold Gendle from Millom was shot in the head and carried back to the RAP. He died of the wound on 15 March, the only casualty from this tour of the front line. Despite the shortfall in numbers, men continued to be discharged once their term of engagement ended, and as these were often NCOs, the repercussions were considerable. For example, in just one week, the battalion waved goodbye to CQMS John Kay, C/Sgt James Walker, Sgt William Kirkby, Sgt John Garnett, and a number of junior NOCs and privates. Promotions had to be made, though fortunately for the battalion, some outstanding junior NCOs were waiting in the wings.

The weather improved in April and the battalion were able to continue to enhance the trenches. Despite the better weather, the sector remained calm, though the battalion continually patrolled No Man's Land at night around the osiers and as far as the German wire, sometimes clashing with enemy patrols similarly intent. The CO, Lt-Col. Carleton DSO, was foremost in tasking and indeed leading these patrols, much to the unease of his officers, who felt that lieutenant-colonels should not be crawling around No Man's Land every night. Yet this was typical of the CO, an officer who led by example and understood how important it was for his battalion to continually take the initiative rather than just react to German moves. It was also a good opportunity for him to get to know the men and their capabilities, and allowed the men to take inspiration from a leader who was not afraid of getting his hands dirty. Carleton recognised the value of self-confidence and aggression in trench warfare, and dominating No Man's Land was the best way to show the men that they were superior to the enemy. These operations weren't without danger, and on 3 April, twenty-three-year-old Pte Joseph Gaskarth from Grange-over-Sands was wounded in the right knee. Gaskarth's comrades succeeded in bringing him back to their lines, but the wound was serious enough to prevent him returning to infantry. Around this time, another officer became the unlikely star of the night patrol. Capt. James Augustine Tolming 'Jat' Clarke was thirty-nine years old, married, and although born in Ulverston, was working as a loom engineer in Bolton when the war began. He was commissioned in 1914 and served as a captain with 3/ King's Own. Posted to the 1/4th in mid-December 1915, he had reverted to Lieutenant, but his abilities and maturity soon saw him promoted back to Captain. Older than most of the 'temporary gentlemen' (who also tended to be single), 'Jat' and his right-hand-man Pte 'Jerry' Holmes (possibly James Holmes) became an essential element to any successful raiding party.[4] It was not just officers who impressed on these patrols, for on 24 April, Sgt William Hayhurst from Ulverston received a MiD, as did Sgt Richard Jackson on the 30th. For reasons unknown, Hayhurst reverted to Corporal at his own request a month later.

As might be expected, the handling of weaponry by drained and inexperienced soldiers had unfortunate consequences. At 6.45 p.m. on 19 April, newly-married Pte Joseph Royle from Blackpool was cleaning his rifle in Liverpool Sap. On duty with him at the time were Privates George Gill and Alfred Pilkington. Their platoon sergeant, Millom blacksmith Sgt Elvy Brooks, entered the sap and walked to where Gill was observing No Man's Land through the periscope. Brooks picked up the flare pistol and discovered that it was in a rusty condition. Gill reported to his Sergeant that it was loaded, but when the latter opened it and tried to extract the flare cartridge he discovered that it had swollen and jammed in the breech. Noticing that Royle had now finished cleaning his rifle, Sgt Brooks passed him the flare gun and ordered him to clean the outside to get rid of the rust. He omitted to warn the private that the pistol was loaded, taking it for granted that he would know this, and inexperienced as he was, Royle did not think to check. Brooks had walked back about 15 yards around the corner of the sap when he heard a loud report and returned quickly to find Royle nursing an injured hand, shot by the flare gun as he cleaned it. Stretcher bearers were called and Pte William Nicholson attended, bandaging Royle's hand and helping him to the RAP.

On 3 May, twenty-two-year-old sniper Sgt John Brewer from Ulverston was hit by an enemy sniper and lost an eye; he died from infection of the wound over a year later, while instructing at Oswestry. It might be expected that a shot through the eye would be immediately fatal, but it's likely that the round itself did not actually hit him. Many of the observation points and snipers' positions were protected by a heavy steel shield, with a swinging plate covering an aperture large enough to sight a rifle through. German snipers were well aware of the positions of these, and often kept sighted in on them, waiting for signs of movement. They had discovered, as had their British counterparts, that if a bullet was carefully removed from the cartridge case and then inserted back into the case facing the opposite way, that this projectile would penetrate the shield. When this round struck the steel, it would send out fragments of steel spall, one or more of which could easily penetrate an eyeball, blinding the victim. Even a round that struck close to the face and sent ordinary debris such as sand or grit into the eye could cause blindness, and pieces of foreign matter left behind after medical treatment easily led to infection. Brewer's injury had apparently healed and he had continued to instruct up until a week before his death, only being admitted to hospital after complaining of headaches.

More activity in No Man's Land meant an escalation of casualties. On the night of 7 May, a reconnaissance patrol led by 2Lt Bowman was spotted by a German sentry and he and three of his men were wounded by MG fire. Bowman was only slightly injured and returned to the battalion on the 12th. On 10 May, another Ulverston man, twenty-five-year-old William Postlethwaite, was killed in action, and three days later twenty-one-year-old Pte Samuel Barnett succumbed to wounds received on the 7th. Despite these casualties, patrolling continued and towards the end of the month, Capt. 'Jat' Clarke succeeded in establishing an outpost in the osiers. This infuriated the Germans, who tried on both 27 and 28 May to oust them. The latter attack was driven off by a combination of fire from the battalion's snipers, a Lewis gun team and some very carefully coordinated fire support from British artillery. During these attacks, twenty-year-old Privates Percival Pimm from Garstang and George Brown from Millom were killed. Pimm's nineteen-year-old younger brother, who was also serving with the battalion, was killed in action less than a month later. Among those who distinguished themselves in these actions was thirty-three-year-old Sgt Richard Jackson from Ulverston, awarded a MM for his patrol work during this period.[5] A moment's inattention was particularly hazardous in daylight, as twenty-two-year-old Ebenezer Eaton discovered on 28 May, when a sniper put a bullet through his right shoulder. He must have reflected on his luck as he boarded the hospital ship for home, for the round could so easily have been fatal; he did not return to the battalion, but was later claimed instead by his old employer at the iron works. Although shelling was infrequent, it still made itself felt by the shrapnel it sent flying; on the last day of May, twenty-eight-year-old Preston bargeman Pte George Ashcroft was lightly wounded in the side and arm, and nineteen-year-old Ulverston man Pte J. Harry Wilson was wounded much more seriously, dying on 2 June; another, twenty-year-old Pte Thomas Noble from Dalton, died from his wounds on 17 June. The 12th saw another big upheaval in battalion life, as Lt-Col Carleton was promoted to Brigadier-General and went off to command 98 Brigade. Maj. Balfour was given temporary command until the appointment of Lt-Col. Joseph Swainson DSO of the DCLI as the new CO.

One unusual occurrence concerned twenty-three-year-old Lt Amos Beardsley, an articled clerk in Grange-over-Sands before the war. On 5 June he relinquished his commission and returned to England. He appears to have upset Lt-Col. Carleton, who reported that he was, '[…] incapable of exacting discipline and imposing his will on those over whom he is supposed to exercise command.'[6] In a letter to the War Office asking to be employed in any commissioned post suitable, Beardsley explained that he had been an officer with the battalion for three years and that during that time—including thirteen months at the front—he had not received a single adverse report prior to his sacking. Nevertheless, he was forced to resign his commission, as the War Office declined to offer him any other employment as an officer. Weeks later, he was conscripted into the Tank Corps as a Private, and remained thus until 9 September 1918. On that day, his tank received a direct hit near Bellenglise, killing three of the crew outright. Beardsley remained in the tank until it received another direct hit, which this time killed the commander and seriously wounded a gunner. Beardsley helped the wounded gunner to a ditch and stayed with him until he died, whereupon he returned to the tank—now under heavy artillery and MG fire—rescued the wounded driver, and brought him out to a place of safety in a trench before returning again to the tank, remaining with it until relieved. For his devotion to duty under trying circumstances he was awarded the MM and promoted to corporal. Another of the battalion's subalterns also departed a few weeks later: Lesley Bowman transferred to the RFC to train as a pilot. Returning to France just before Christmas 1916, he joined No. 53 Squadron, flying Royal Aircraft Factory R.E.8s on artillery observation. He was slightly wounded on 10 June 1917 at 6.40 p.m. On 25 June, just five days after recovering from this wound, he and his observer 2Lt James E. Power-Clutterbuck became Baron von Richthofen's fifty-sixth victims. The German's fire set the R.E.8 ablaze and it fell to earth near Le Bizet, its wings broken off. Although sources suggest both bodies were recovered, Bowman has no known grave, but is simply commemorated on the Arras Memorial.[7]

The battalion received a number of drafts and steadily began to approach proper manning levels, but it was noticeable to old hands that the character of the battalion was changing, as the familiar faces from the Furness District thinned out. One new recruit was a twenty-four-year-old from Fleetwood, Pte Leslie Bebbington. His service records show him to be a single man with no relatives, who on the day before he left Étaples wrote his will on a scrap of paper, leaving half his worldly belongings to his landlady, a Mrs Brown, and the other half to his best pal from training, Pte Robert Merrett. Both men survived the war.

One new soldier, who arrived at the battalion on 4 May, was John Sloan. He spent a total of eight days in the trenches at a time when hardly any shelling occurred, then returned to billets with the battalion. He and fifteen other recent arrivals were sent to the Bombing School at Rivière on 18 May and on arrival, Sloan dumped his equipment, telling the others he was going to find the latrines—and that was the last they saw of him! He was arrested nearly 100 miles away four days later, attempting to board an England-bound ship in Rouen and returned under escort. Sloan was tried on 29 June and found guilty of a clear case of desertion. He was sentenced to death and shot on the morning of 16 July. Much controversy still surrounds those shot at dawn, and I for one have no intention of adding to it by using modern values to judge those of nearly 100 years ago. At the time, there was some measure of disquiet over the penalty for desertion, though many soldiers of the day did not have any such reservations—if they stuck it out, why shouldn't others? A deserter had, furthermore, not only abandoned his duty, but his comrades in arms.

In fact, only a small percentage of those sentenced to be shot were actually executed, so Sloan was an unlucky exception. Most of those shot were serial deserters, whereas this had been Sloan's first offence. Often, battalion officers could give extenuating evidence to the court martial as to the bravery shown by the accused on previous occasions, or medical evidence of previous trauma, but Sloan was a total newcomer, with no combat experience. Moreover, his trial took place shortly after the first day of the Somme, a time when senior commanders were concerned that any weakness may lead to mass desertion. It's even debatable whether Sloan should have been serving in the first place—his is the only service record I've seen (out of over 4,000) from the King's Own where the recruit has signed his attestation papers, 'X'. His records signal that he spent an unusually long time in basic training and his instructors were obviously worried about his progress, as he was brought before a travelling medical board in August 1915 and graded, 'Unfit for any military duty'. Though this had been on the grounds of an 'inferior physique' rather than lack of mental acuity, it appears that his extended training was because of his malnourishment. His lack of education, coupled with Lt-Col. Swainson DSO's court martial estimation that he did 'not appear to be either capable or willing to learn his duties,' suggests that Sloan possibly wasn't capable of understanding what he had got himself into. There is even debate as to where Sloan actually came from, and his name appears with different spellings in various documents (sometimes as 'Sloane'), the confusion no doubt arising from his illiteracy. In one book, the author records that he was born in 1895 and came from Preston, though other evidence casts doubt over this assertion.[8] Sloan's service record survives and from this it can be calculated that he was born on or around 9 September 1891. There seems no reason why this date should not correct, as lying about the finer details of a date of birth prior to 1895 would have been pointless. He was, in any case, living in Workington with his aunt Sarah Sloan, whom he gave as next of kin. Another researcher has suggested to me the possibility that he was born in the North East, where his personal effects were sent to a Mrs Elizabeth Ann Fleming of Hebburn Colliery, probably his mother, who is believed to have remarried. There have also been suggestions that he was from Ireland. Sloan was not the first to desert and certainly not the last, but he was the only one from 1/4th King's Own to pay the maximum penalty.

Not so for twenty-year-old Pte John Neville from Ulverston, who was attached to 164 MG Company. Just after midnight on the night of 8 to 9 August 1916, he deserted the trenches at Guillemont. He was arrested at 9 a.m. the following morning, court-martialled on 17 August, found guilty of desertion, and sentenced to five years' penal servitude. In September that year, this sentence was commuted to two years' hard labour, and within eleven months he was released from No. 1 Military Prison at Rouen under suspension of sentence. The Army allowed him leave in Britain, where he promptly disappeared again, this time awol for nineteen days before re-arrest. At this court martial, he was sentenced to six months' hard labour, to run concurrently with his previous sentence. He was released early from No. 10 Military Prison in Dunkirk and returned to the battalion on 16 June 1918, his only misdemeanour after this being 'inattention on parade' on 20 December 1918, for which he was confined to barracks for seven days—at least he was able to celebrate New Year! The different treatment of the two Johns, both deserters around the same time, probably stems from the Army's perception of each man's history.

John Neville had been out with the battalion since the beginning, through Festubert and trench foot and hospital, a faultless soldier right up to the point where he couldn't take any more, at the end of one of the battalion's most traumatic days in the entire war. John Sloan hadn't.

On 19 June, the battalion moved four miles further north into trenches near Agny. This sector was more active than Bretencourt and over the following fortnight, German artillery and trench mortar fire caused significant damage. The battalion spent much time repairing the trenches, only for the opposition to destroy all their hard work with a few well-aimed hits. Although casualties were moderate, a constant trickle of them was stretchered off to the RAP. On 22 June, the only casualty was 2Lt Stanley Voyle, a twenty-six-year-old from Pembrokeshire who was shot through the left leg. The *War Diary* attributes this to an accidental wounding, his service record only elucidating as far as 'gunshot wound in action'.[9] Voyle eventually recovered and returned to active service. A closer examination of the details in his records rule out a shrapnel ball or a gunshot from the front, as the round penetrated the lower third of the calf muscle on the inside of the left leg and exited through the upper third on the outer. The most likely scenario is that he was accidentally shot from behind by one of his men, while both were in the prone position out in No Man's Land. On 23 June, Sgt Thomas Cheeseman was hit in the arm and elbow by shrapnel, wounds which led to his medical discharge in 1917. Also hit was thirty-year-old Pte Alfred Wright from Ulverston, struck in both head and arm, though not as seriously as his Sergeant. Although not hit by shrapnel or splinters, Pte George Gill was partially buried by a trench mortar shell and then taken back to the RAP suffering from shell shock. The next day, D Company's woes did not relent, as trench mortar fire wounded Cpl Roger Hartley and Privates John Duke and Arthur White. Twenty-four-year-old Pte Joseph Harris was also partially buried by one of the large trench mortar projectiles and sent back to the RAP to be treated for the trauma. For these men, many of whom had spent their civilian lives toiling in the mines, being buried alive was a fate viewed with unique horror.

Maj. (and soon to be Lt-Col) Joseph Swainson DSO of the DCLI assumed command on 25 June, and received a very warm welcome from the enemy, who seemed to have it in for D Company. That day two of the battalion were killed, the only fatalities from this tour of the front. The first was Joseph Royle, only just back from hospital after his accident with the Very pistol. The second, nineteen-year-old Pte William Pimm, was the younger brother of the pre-deceased Percy (thankfully, neither of the other Pimm sons were old enough to serve in the war). Although the intensity of German fire lessened on the next day, HQ joined their target list and twenty-four-year-old Pte John Smith 468 was wounded.

That night, 2Lt John Johnstone took a patrol of two men into No Man's Land and after a short firefight against a patrol from 6/ Bavarian RR (Reserve Regiment), captured two and brought them back to the battalion lines. As dawn broke on the next day, they saw that they had also killed one of the German patrol, whose body was clearly visible on the battalion wire where he had fallen after being shot. Emboldened by that success, Johnstone took another patrol out the next night, but this had a tragic conclusion. As they made their way back to their own lines, one of the sentries mistook them for enemy raiders and opened fire. Johnstone was slightly wounded, but L/Cpl Frederick Holme and Pte John Rodgerson both received bullets to the hip and Cpl Richard Slater a bullet through the knee, an injury which led to him being discharged to munitions work after leaving hospital. Twenty-one-year-old Pte William Wilkinson also had a lucky escape that day, when a splinter from a trench mortar round grazed his face and thigh, which, although minor, resulted in four days at the ADS. His face wound continued to get infected, so he was evacuated home at the beginning of August and transferred to the RE upon his recovery. The remaining days of the month saw unremitting trench mortar activity, as both sides matched each other shell for shell. The brigade's mortars concentrated on trying to destroy the wire in front of the German trenches, and possibly thinking that there was an attack impending, the enemy concentrated their fire on the British trenches. Casualties were few, though eighteen-year-old Pte Wilfred Mylchreest from Dalton, nineteen-year-old Pte William Lunt from Barrow, and twenty-year-old Cpl Walter Donaghy from Barrow were all wounded in this exchange.

Disease was an ever-present companion. Conditions included decomposing flesh in No Man's Land, latrine buckets, all kinds of waste and rubbish; and although the battalion tried its best to keep the trenches themselves as clean as possible, the exposed areas outside them were a feasting ground for the flies and rats. The MO made frequent inspections of the trenches and as far as the health of the battalion was concerned, one of the most important individuals was the sanitary corporal responsible for the latrines. Any soldier caught peeing anywhere but in the allocated bucket would invoke the full wrath of the military—typically, a week to ten days' Field Punishment for 'Committing a nuisance'. Men became verminous; despite their very best efforts, it was impossible to keep clean. Any infectious skin complaint was bound to spread, but two diseases in particular took a sizeable bite out of the available manpower. The first was scabies, which, painful and unpleasant as it was, was nothing new and easily treatable. It did, however, cause manpower shortages that the battalion could have done without, putting 7.7 per cent of the battalion in hospital for approximately two weeks per man. The second and most prevalent was trench fever, first encountered during the summer of 1915. Symptoms included headache, dizziness, severe lumbago, stiffness in the front of the thighs, and pain in the legs (chiefly in the shins), the symptoms often reappearing in a series of cycles. No cure for trench fever was found, however it was eventually recognised that lice were responsible for its transmission, and as the use of chemical disinfectant cumulated, the incidence of trench fever declined. While no accurate figures for the number of British troops affected exist, it is estimated at around 500,000.[10] Eight per cent of the 1/4th were admitted to hospital on account of trench fever, making this the single biggest cause of sickness-related hospitalisation.

Another disease of concern to medical services was trench nephritis, the main symptoms of which were breathlessness, the swelling of the face or legs, headaches, and a sore throat. The disease attacked the kidneys, was extremely debilitating, and claimed the lives of 400 men of the BEF during the war. No definite cause was ever discovered, although cold, exposure, contamination of water by rat urine, and lead poisoning were all considered. Approximately 35,000 men suffered from trench nephritis during the war.[11] It landed just over 1 per cent of the 1/4th in hospital, so was not as devastating as other diseases in the grand scheme of things, though for an individual soldier it was frequently life-changing. For example, thirty-four-year-old Pte George Thistleton from Longridge was invalided back to England on 5 May and discharged as no longer fit. The surviving records of those who suffered from trench nephritis tend to demonstrate a more serious long-term effect on those over the age of thirty, though a broader study would need to confirm this.

The men of 55 Division could not have failed to realise that something big was happening a mere 12 miles to their south, as the week-long artillery bombardment prepared the ground for the Somme offensive. The huge mine detonated under the Hawthorn Redoubt at 7.20 a.m. on 1 July—the first of seventeen mines detonated in the initial phase of the attack—would also have been clearly audible to them. Their attention focused further south, so there was little German activity around Bretencourt that day, although occasional shell fire gave twenty-nine-year-old Pte John Parsons from Ulverston a minor wound to the knee, which was treated at the CCS. Cpl William Hayhurst, who had received a MiD for his work in April, was wounded in the head by shrapnel, evacuated home, and transferred to the MGC upon recovery; L/Cpl Herbert Phillips also suffered a wound. On 4 July, further casualties ensued when the enemy shelled the rear and eighteen-year-old Ulverston man William Barrow received a wound to the head which fractured his skull. He had only arrived with the battalion on 9 January that year, and although the medics did what they could for him, he died while being transported from the ADS of 2/1 West Lancashire Field Ambulance to 37 CCS. Also a victim was twenty-six-year-old Pte William Penny, who had only returned from a two-month stay in the base hospital at Rouen a fortnight earlier. Wounded in both arm and leg by shell splinters, he travelled with his comrade to 37 CCS, where he died the next day. As the barrage crashed down around the battalion cookhouse, nineteen-year-old Ulverston grocer Pte Fred Werry became another casualty. Dashing to the deep cellar used as a shelter and accessed by a 9-foot-deep trench, he mistimed his jump, caught his foot on the edge, and fell into the trench, badly twisting his knee as he landed. This injury led to his evacuation home at the end of the month. He was posted to Oswestry as an instructor and on 14 February 1917 suffered an almost identical accident, when he fell into a deep trench on the assault course. He ended up with a 30-per-cent pension for the damage to his knee.

Though hostile activity in the battalion's own line was minimal over the following day, many men were tasked to provide working parties for a New Zealand Tunnelling Company. Working parties were always hazardous; any movement of large detachments of men during daylight hours was bound to bring artillery fire down if they were seen by enemy observation posts. At night, the men could escape direct observation, but the Germans had all supply routes and communication trenches registered by their artillery, and would drop speculative barrages on these locations at various times during the night. One of those unlucky enough to be caught by this tactic had already been wounded once just over a week earlier, but this time Pte Wilfred Mylchreest was transferred to the Labour Corps upon his recovery, though he was transferred back to the battalion again on the day after the attack on Givenchy in April 1918. On 8 July, a shell killed Pte Arthur McDowell outright. The eighteen-year-old American-born was a British citizen and in July 1915 had crossed the Atlantic from his home in Pittsburgh to serve at just seventeen (he simply told everyone he was nineteen and no one questioned him). The other casualty of the day was twenty-eight-year-old John Singleton from Haverigg, whose brother Pearson had been wounded and invalided out after the attack on Sap L8. Yet it was not the Germans who were responsible for his injury, but one of the battalion's mules. Though not as destructive as a HE shell, the mules could (and did) bite and kick with devastating accuracy. While watering them at Simencourt, one of the ill-tempered animals took offence to Singleton's presence and made its feelings known by delivering a mighty kick to the private's leg. His fibula fractured, he was evacuated to England and did not return until 1917. The following night saw another fatality from shellfire, when twenty-three-year-old Pte Richard Nelson from Grange was caught behind the lines as he was returning to HQ. Richard Nelson had jokingly been nicknamed 'Lucky' by others in the battalion due to a plethora of close escapes, but on that night his luck ran out.[12] Wounded on the same day was twenty-year-old Cpl Walter Donaghy, whose injuries this time were severe enough for his medical discharge; he eventually recovered, re-joined the 4th after the war and rose to the rank of CSM. The final casualty before the battalion left the sector on 20 July was Pte Walter Wooff from Barrow, who succumbed on the 19th to wounds received earlier that month. After being on the receiving end of a heavy bombardment all night at Bretencourt, the 4th left for Simencourt the next morning without further loss.

# 21 July 1916 – 30 September 1916
# Into the Cauldron

For over a week the men had suspected that the battalion was to take part in an offensive. Training had stepped up, particularly in section attacks, and it didn't take much imagination to guess sights were set on the Somme, where the battle still raged. The fine weather of the beginning of July was still evident and the march westward to Sombrin on the 21st was hot, dusty, and tiring—though for old hands, the direction and diminishing volume of duelling artillery was welcome. The battalion spent the night at Sombrin and on Saturday morning split from the transport, which proceeded independently to Berneuil at a slow pace while the men travelled by double-decker bus, a happy departure from marching. Now a part of the Fourth Army, the 1/4th spent Monday practising section attacks once more. At 3 a.m. that night, it began the 5-mile march to Candas and entrained for Méricourt, before marching onwards to Méaulte. Billets were extremely hard to come by in the crowded village, and at 4 p.m. the next day began the short march to Happy Valley, approximately half way between Méaulte and Bray (the men bivouacked there under less congested circumstances). After the sweat and grime of the dusty marches and several days' training, 29 July was set aside for bathing; company by company, the men made their way south to the Somme at Bray, grateful for a chance to wash off the chalky dust and get some clean clothes.

Two new items had been issued since the battalion had first deployed to Bretencourt, both of which greatly improved survival and fighting capabilities. The first was the steel helmet, issued to all ranks: initially unpopular because of its discomfort and impairment of hearing, its qualities were soon made apparent by a reduction in head wounds. The second innovation was the Mills No. 5 grenade, which was infinitely superior to its predecessors; time-fused—rather than percussion-fused—it was more reliable, safer, and had a much greater zone of lethality. It wasn't perfect and manufacturing errors, poor storage, but mainly plain clumsiness led to accidents; soldiers were prone to crimping the split pin too hard to ease the force needed to pull it out. It also took more work to bring to readiness, as it was supplied without the detonator and fuse, which came in a separate tin for safety reasons. Its pros far outweighed its cons, however, and a slightly modified version was still in use with the British Army as late as the 1970s.

Sunday 30 July was a day of mixed fortune. The sounds of war had been heard all night, as British guns prepared the ground for an assault by 30 Division on Guillemont; even the soundest sleepers could not have missed the detonation of an ammunition dump at the Briqueterie (50° 0′ 5.66″ N, 2° 47′ 28.06″ E) south of Bernafay Wood, a bare 5 miles away from them, by a German counter-bombardment at 3 a.m. A thick fog lay over the dawn, pierced by the sounds of rifle and MG fire from the attack which began at 4.45 a.m. After church parade in the morning, decorations earned by men during their service at Bretencourt were presented by Brig.-Gen. G. T. G. Edwards, OC 164 Brigade. Later that day, German aircraft bombed Happy Valley and although no casualties were suffered by the 1/4th, other units bivouacked there were not so fortunate. There was bad news from 164 MG Company at Bray, 3 miles to the south-east.

One of the 1/4th serving with 164 MG Company was twenty-year-old Pte Albert Brown from Preston. He and his comrades were taking advantage of the glorious weather and their bathing time in the River Somme. The current can be strong here, and Brown was swept away, his body never recovered (or identified, if it ever was recovered later); he is commemorated on the Thiepval Memorial. It later transpired that the youngster's name was in fact Harold Brierley, and that he was barely sixteen years old. The only boy and youngest of four children, he enlisted under a false name, gave a false name for his next-of-kin, and his non-existent home address was actually a gap in a row of houses near the grocers where he worked. The local postman must have been 'in the know', as the casualty notification reached Samuel Brierley, Harold's father, and an annotation on a page of his record shows his real next-of-kin's name, although the majority of records weren't amended. The CWGC nevertheless commemorated him on the Thiepval Memorial as Albert Brown, unaware of this addition, or his true identity.

That night on 30 July, the battalion left its bivouacs and marched to the front, where it relieved men of 89 Brigade, 30 Division. They had fought tooth and nail the previous day to capture and hold the trenches near Maltz Horn Farm, the only gains from the unsuccessful attack on Guillemont. The British front line ran south from between Trones Wood and Guillemont, crossing the road just to the west of what is now Guillemont Road War Cemetery, through the eastern edge of Arrow Head

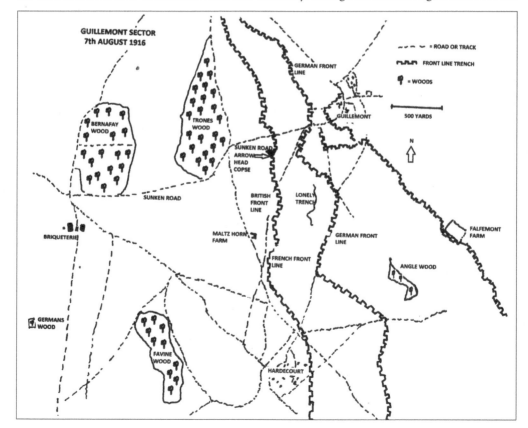

Copse, then due south just to the east of Maltz Horn Farm, where it became the French sector. The approach was along the sunken road which passed along the southern edges of Bernafay Wood and Trones Wood, but as the men made their way down a communication trench near their destination, a devastating salvo of artillery dropped around them. Thirty-five-year-old 2Lt Charles Lincey from Cleveland, twenty-two-year-old L/Sgt William Inman from Ulverston, and twenty-year-old Pte Thomas Bowron from Barrow, who had only been with the battalion for two weeks, were all killed instantly. William's older brother L/Cpl George Inman wrote to their mother,

> I am sorry to say I have bad news for you at this time. William was killed on Monday morning about four o' clock. Death was instantaneous. We were going to the trenches along a communication trench when a shell burst close to him. Two or three more were knocked out by the same shell. He was buried alongside some of his comrades. I would have written before but we were in the trenches and we had a rough time of it. I can tell you. I am myself quite well.[1]

Twenty-four-year-old Pte George Poskitt from Ulverston was critically wounded and died soon after reaching the RAP. The battalion felt his loss especially, for he had been recommended for the MM for trench raids in May and June—though those higher up the chain of command had chosen not to award it. Among the other eleven wounded was twenty-year-old Ulverston fitter Pte Joseph Hurst, hit in the chest and evacuated home to complete his recovery. He was not to return to the battalion, transferring instead to the RE in February 1917 and with whom he was wounded for a second time in October 1917. He never served on the Western Front again, although he was posted to Russia in September 1918.

The trenches at Maltz Horn Farm were newly captured, so the battalion had its work cut out if it was to consolidate the position. Indeed, while still in German hands these had received the full attention of British artillery prior to the attack on the 30th, and the battalion set to work reversing the fire positions and replacing sandbags. German shelling of both the rear and front line continued throughout the night of the 30th. The battalion's Pioneer Sergeant, twenty-five-year-old Sgt Roger Steel from Ulverston, was killed instantly when a shell landed in the shell hole he was sleeping in.

The battalion transport was bivouacked in the former German lines near Carnoy, and when daylight broke on the morning of the 31st, QM Lt James Crossley was astounded at the destruction that British guns had wrought.

> A giant of steel seemed to have ridden over the proud German defences. Villages were wiped completely out of existence—Fricourt, Mametz, Carnoy, Maricourt, Montaubin, all a tumbled heap of rubble; woods were laid waste. Saddest of all there was not a blade of green grass visible. Trenches were everywhere blown out of recognition. In every direction disused gun pits with piles of empty shell cases showed how the artillery had advanced. Disrupted sandbags littered the broken earth. A poignant reminder that victory is not purchased without cost lay in the newly-delved earth, where blue flags were fluttering over the dead.[2]

From his location Crossley could observe the Mametz Road, its edges littered with the remnants of destroyed transport and dead horses, and the never-ending streams of traffic passing to and from the Front. 'Up roads' and 'down roads' were organised to limit congestion. Supplies travelled east, while lines of exhausted men rotating from the Front headed in the opposite direction; ambulances, empty wagons, and limbers rattled alongside them. The enemy perpetually shelled this road, but as soon as it was damaged either from shellfire or from erosion from the sheer volume of its thoroughfare, the men of the Labour Corps would be called in with their picks and shovels. They and the transport drivers were rewarded with scant recognition by the press, but in this maelstrom of hot steel carried out this highly dangerous, vital job, day after day.

Although greatly enhanced, British artillery was still far from ideal. The supply of ammunition was much improved as a result of Government efforts to increase capacity in the munitions industry, though the quality of ammunition, particularly with regards to fusing, left much to be desired. It has since been widely acknowledged that as many as one third of the shells expended in the week leading up to the first day of the Somme failed to explode. The manufacture of artillery shells is not something that can be dramatically increased overnight: it requires new plants to be built and workers to be trained—and most skilled workers were now in khaki! Lloyd George's Munitions Committee did their best, but Haig was less than impressed when during a visit to his HQ in July 1915, a member let slip his impression that the shells were the same solid cast iron cannonballs as in Wellington's army.[3] Possibly the artillery's greatest material weakness was its dependence on shrapnel firing 18-pounders to destroy wire, and its overreliance on too small a supply of heavy guns to pulverise enemy defences. It was not until the development of the graze fuse in 1917 that the 18-pounder became an effective solution to wire.

Back to 31 July, British guns continued to bombard enemy lines and German artillery replied in kind. The men spent the day digging in and consolidating, fully aware that their own safety depended on the thoroughness of their work. The Liverpool Irish held the northernmost stretch of the sector to the 1/4th's left, and to the 1/4th's right near Maltz Horn Farm was the 156 Infantry Regiment of the French Army. Suspecting further attacks, the Germans did not interrupt their shelling of the front line and supply routes. There were numerous wounded on 1 August, but the only fatalities that day were twenty-two-year-old Liverpool-born Pte Henry Atkinson and eighteen-year-old Pte John Perry from Ulverston. Perry was another soldier who had lied about his age, and was still only seventeen when he had joined the battalion the previous November. Twenty-two-year-old Dalton miner L/Cpl Tom Crossley received a wound to the leg that confined him to hospital in England for the next four months, as did nineteen-year-old Pte Alexander Saunders from Ulverston, though it would be ten months before he was fit enough to return. Twenty-year-old Lewis-gunner L/Cpl George Simpson from Dalton was also wounded, and after treatment in hospitals in Croydon and Birmingham was posted to Oswestry as a Lewis gun instructor for the remainder of the war, rising to Sergeant before his discharge. Twenty-five-year-old married father of one Pte Frank Nolan from Ulverston had been with the battalion for less than a month. He suffered the first of two Blighty wounds that eventually led to his discharge and a disability pension. Another casualty from that draft was the thirty-two-year-old mill worker from Bolton, Pte Henry Howarth, whose wound would also send him home. Twenty-one-year-old Glasson-Dock-born Vickers worker L/Cpl William Lamb, and twenty-year-old Pte Harry Derbyshire, twenty-year-old Pte Henry Heaton, and twenty-five-year-old Frederick Hanley from Preston, joined them on the hospital ship home, though the men were sent to different institutions after landing. The wound of Ulverston blacksmith's mate Pte Andrew Rowe, one of the older men in the battalion at thirty-eight years of age, was also serious enough to warrant evacuation, and he never returned. The Army recognised that his civilian skills were of more benefit to the RE than to the infantry, so transferred him there in January 1917.

Some soldiers in the battalion went through the entire war without a scratch, while others seem to have been inherently unlucky (what today's squaddies darkly refer to as 'bullet magnets'). Twenty-three-year-old Dalton man Pte George Thompson could quite accurately be described as a 'shell magnet': 1 August was the first of five such encounters, each increasing in severity. Dazed and shocked by a near miss, he was led away to the RAP and admitted that same day to No. 12 General Hospital in Rouen for shell shock treatment; the speed of his evacuation through the chain of the RAP, the CCS, and beyond demonstrates the efficiency with which the medical system operated when not overwhelmed by mass casualties. After ten days' treatment, he was fed back into the system via the 'Bull Ring' of 23 IBD at Étaples, and returned to the battalion nineteen days after leaving it. Not all the casualties that day were infantrymen in the trenches. Thirty-two-year-old Pte Robert Weaver from Leyland, a cold-shoer with transport, received a minor shrapnel wound to his left wrist on the supply run to the lines and was sent back to No. 3 General Hospital at Rouen. Upon his recovery two weeks later, he was reposted to 7/ King's Own. On 2 August, twenty-one-year-old Pte William Crowther from Millom was sent back down the line with shell shock to join Thompson. Thirty-four-year-old Pte Robert Armstrong from Walton-le-Dale was wounded in the head by shrapnel and evacuated home, eventually to be posted to the 1/5th in March 1917.

The battalion still intended to control No Man's Land. Through periscopes the Germans were observed to set up an advanced position between the lines, and the CO decided to make this untenable for them. Although the *War Diary* does not elucidate the exact position, the Germans had probably advanced to the stretch of trench later named 'Lonely Trench' (50° 0′ 17.70″ N, 2° 49′ 16.07″ E). Just over 100 m from the battalion's trench and only slightly less from the German front line, it was a target too tempting to ignore. At 8.30 p.m. on 2 August, a single platoon from B Company led by twenty-six-year-old 2Lt Joseph Rudduck from Dromana (Australia) climbed the parapet and dashed across No Man's Land—but in vain. They got hung up by the wire and were met by a devastating barrage, forcing them to retire. Among the wounded was Rudduck himself, hit while leading the attack; twenty-year-old Cpl Edward Hodgson from Ulverston, too, was shot through both arms; and twenty-year-old Millom engine-cleaner Cpl Edward Savage. Hodgson and Savage were destined for a hospital ship back to England. Only three weeks with the battalion, Pte Edward Lenaughan from Bolton suffered a minor wound to the thigh, giving him ten days in hospital before the Bull Ring and his return. Unfortunately, the bodies of the two men killed had to be left behind, the surviving attackers having had their hands full rescuing the wounded. Both were from Preston: thirty-one-year-old Cpl William Stewart, father of two young children, and twenty-six-year-old Pte John Strickland, father of one. Two of the wounded died over the next couple of days: twenty-three-year-old Pte Joseph Coombe from Millom, and twenty-one-year-old L/Cpl Norman McKenzie, who had travelled all the way from his home in Washington (USA) to enlist. Determined not to fail, the brigade's trench mortars opened up accurate and lethal fire on the isolated trench, forcing German withdrawal, and at 8.47 p.m. 2Lt Albert Brockman led another platoon over the parapet. This time there was total success, and the position was taken without loss. German casualties were severe for they had been amassing in the front trenches for an attack on the British positions and the mortar rounds had hit them in their tight concentrations. Not surprisingly, German artillery replied in kind and less than an hour later, all phone communication to the rear was lost. Later that night they were relieved by 1/4th Loyals and moved into reserve in the Dublin and Casement Trenches in front of Maricourt (49° 59′ 52.70″ N, 2° 47′ 20.45″ E).

The enemy shelled the left flank of the trench line, and although there was no damage to the actual trench structure, shrapnel was deadly to anyone in its path. A Company suffered particularly badly; of the seven men killed on 3 August, the youngest was seventeen-year-old Pte James Hems from Barrow, who had added three years to his age in order to enlist. Also killed and not much older were eighteen-year-old Pte George Robinson (080), nineteen-year-old Harry Parker, and twenty-year-old Pte Charles Davies. L/Cpl Percy Smith and Privates Jonathan Miles and George Moses died too, and although all seven were properly buried behind the lines, their graves were lost in the chaos of shelling that ensued on the Somme for another three and a half months. All seven were subsequently commemorated on the Thiepval Memorial.

Of the wounded, twenty-year-old Pte Stephen Nelson from Carnforth got off comparatively lightly with a wound to his thumb from a shrapnel ball, though the concussion of the shells and the trauma of seeing his platoon decimated also left him shell-shocked. Twenty-year-old Pte Thomas Parkinson was hit in the thigh by a shell splinter, a wound that was frequently fatal. Although the introduction of the Thomas Splint saved countless lives, it needed to be applied as quickly as possible to be effective, something not always possible amid the chaos of the trenches. Parkinson's life was saved, but his military involvement was over, as subsequent operations left one leg shorter than the other, and he was medically discharged in October 1917. The Thomas Splint is still in use and holds the leg in a fixed position to the torso, preventing the splintered ends of bone from causing further damage to blood vessels and thus reducing blood loss and trauma. Although most shells were either shrapnel or HE, it was common for gas shells to be mixed in with them, which often caught out the unwary or those with faulty smoke helmets. One such unfortunate was Pte Henry Courtnell from Barrow, who was exposed to enough gas to warrant his evacuation home. He returned in April the next year and served with the TMB for two months before being posted back to England for munitions work at Vickers. Twenty-seven-year-old Pte John Steel from Thwaite Head received multiple shrapnel wounds to his face, left shoulder, arm, and side, though none of them life-threatening. He was evacuated to Alexandria Hospital in London and it was a while before he re-joined the battalion, only to be killed in July 1917.

On 4 August, two working parties of sixty men each were detailed to go to the front-line trenches and, as usual, this meant more casualties, though none of them fatal. Twenty-year-old Pte Alfred Wright from Barrow received his second wound of the war and was evacuated home. He would never re-join the battalion, posted instead to 1/ King's Own on his recovery and wounded for the third and final time with them in May 1917. After this he was transferred to munitions work, his skills as a blast-furnaceman being much in demand. That night, the battalion went into bivouacs near Carnoy.

Lustrous summer weather prevailed and after a battalion inspection on 5 August the men went bathing. The next day, each company held its own inspection, followed by bayonet practice and PT before allowing the men to bathe again in the afternoon. Not everyone had been able to sample the cooling waters of the Somme on such a fine day, as the men from transport were still busy looking after wagons, horses, and mules, all of which was very time-consuming. Also detached from the battalion were the men of 164 MG Company and 164 TMB, who had their own independent schemes of rotation from the Front. They lost two men from the 1/4th that day: twenty-one-year-old Pte Robert Young from Millom took a shrapnel ball to the head and was evacuated home in a seriously ill condition. The wound prompted the onset of epilepsy, yet he recovered, and was posted to 1/ King's Own in March 1917, only to be wounded again two weeks later and this time transferred to munitions work upon his recovery. The other victim of this shell burst, seventeen-year-old Pte Fred Bellamy from Barrow, was killed instantly; another soldier who had added three years to his age at enlistment, he nonetheless lies in Bernafay Wood Cemetery alongside four of his comrades.

For some time it had been obvious that training had a specific purpose, and at 8.15 p.m. on 7 August, the battalion moved out from their bivouacs and marched to the Front. For once the battalion suffered no casualties in the move into the front line. The sector occupied by the 1/4th lay to the south of the modern-day road from Guillemont to Montauban, just east of Arrow Head Copse, although any evidence of a copse in that location has long since vanished. Anyone wishing to find the battalion's position on 8 August should stand with their back to the entrance of the Guillemont Road Cemetery, facing across the road. The centre of Arrow Head Copse, which was only about 40 m wide, will be 140 m ahead of you (50° 0′ 33.00″ N, 2° 48′ 58.11″ E). The British front line will have been about 20 m to your left, running more or less due south until it will have met the sunken track from Guillemont to Maltz Horn Farm. To find the assault line of 8 August, move a couple of m past the end of the cemetery nearest to Guillemont and face across the road. The four companies of the battalion were spread along a line of about 250 m from the far edge of the road directly in front of you; the left flank of C Company will have been level with the edge of the road today, while the other three companies will have extended away from you.

By August 1916, Guillemont had long ceased to be a recognisable village, reduced to piles of rubble, and each mound converted into heavily fortified positions by German defenders. In addition, the defensive area was peppered with deep dugouts that had multiple exits. The 'village' was partially protected by belts of wire up to 5 m thick, all covered by robust trenches; and to the south-west, the direction from which the King's Own would be attacking, were three lines of trenches, each protected by wire. Guillemont's location made it a strategic asset, for it commanded superb fields of fire. Although positions to either side of the village could provide enfilading cover for its defence, the layout of the defences of Guillemont itself meant that an attack from any direction was also vulnerable to fire from within. Guillemont's operational value was equally enhanced by its proximity to the boundary between British and French sectors; its capture was crucial to any French advance, and to any British advance further north, for that matter.

Several attacks on Guillemont had previously seen little success. The 19/ Manchesters had actually penetrated Guillemont on 23 July, but their limited number had been unable to hold back German counter-attacks. Just a week later, another attempt was made but failed with heavy casualties, the only gain being Arrow Head Copse. Part of the problem in taking Guillemont was down to the difficulty in communication between the attackers at the front and the artillery at the rear, as gunners unsure of exactly how far attacking troops had got were reluctant to drop shells near the target, for fear of hitting their own men. This allowed German troops to regroup for counter-attacks without interference. Runners frequently failed to survive the trip back across open land and any telephone wires were soon cut. Shiny metal triangles worn on the backs of attacking troops could not be seen in the smoke and dust, or in the case of the attack on the 23rd, fog. Ground panels, mirrors, lamps, and flares carried by officers and NCOs were frequently invisible for exactly the same reason, or were just as frequently never deployed as the men carrying them were dead. Low-flying aircraft tried to spot where the attackers had reached, but again fog, smoke, and dust tended to obscure everything. In 2006, Walter Reid even cited dogs as a means of ferrying messages around the battlefield, and photographs of dogs bearing drums of field telephone cable on their backs survive—the idea being that they would run to advance posts, laying out the cables as they progressed. Fear of the British public's reaction to this meant any mention of the use of dogs in correspondence was strictly censored, and there is still little public awareness of their involvement in the Great War to this day.[4] After the second failure to secure Guillemont, commanders realised that any attack from the west stood little chance of success due to its complete lack of cover, and that an attack to the south-west had to be supported by an attack by the French across the Maurepas Ravine.[5]

In a communication to the Army groups on the Somme on 3 August, Haig stressed the need for thorough preparation in both attack and consolidation for counter-attack. He warned commanders that this phase of the Battle should be treated as a 'wearing out' battle, and that 'economy of men and material' had to be maintained in order that Britain should outlast the Germans. Haig also brought home that the capture of Guillemont, Falfemont Farm, and Ginchy were priorities in his eyes, while instructing that no attacks be launched until 'the responsible commanders on the spot are satisfied that everything possible has been done to ensure success.'[6] It was initially planned to begin the attack on Guillemont on 7 August in conjunction with a French attack on Hems, a considerable distance to the south, and a further French move in the Maurepas Ravine on the 11th. The attack at Hems went ahead as scheduled, though the British postponed their assault until the 8th due to delays caused by heavy German bombardment (particularly on the advanced trenches to be used as jumping-off points). Earlier consideration of the necessity of a coordinated move against Guillemont and the Maurepas Ravine seems to have been brushed aside.

On the 7th, a series of 'Chinese attacks' were launched on the Guillemont front. These were a series of heavy, concentrated barrages on the German front line in which the fire lifted and moved back to reserve trenches and lines of communication, thus trying to draw the enemy out of their bunkers and into the front line. The deception was further embellished by lifting dummy attackers over the British parapets. After the lapse of a suitable length of time, the artillery suddenly switched back onto the German front trenches. More than simply killing the Germans lured into the front line, these Chinese attacks also aimed to lull the enemy into ignoring the real attack scheduled for 4.20 a.m. the next day. Complex and varied systems of communication were once again the order of the day, and a wireless station was established in a trench between Favière Wood and Maltz Horn Farm. And, once again, the view of the battle was obscured when a brisk easterly wind blew smoke and dust back into British lines and—as might have been expected—runners in the open suffered the consequences. In a nutshell, the attack plan for 8 August was no different to the ones that had failed in July. That an attack needed to be coordinated with French advance immediately south of Guillemont, the hard-learned lesson of the previous month, fell by the wayside. Drawing some of the fire away from the Liverpool Irish (who were to attack to the north of the Trones Wood–Guillemont Road), the area between Waterlot Farm and the northern edge of the village was to be simultaneously attacked by 2 Division. However, this drew away none of the fire directed at the 1/4th attacking from the south-west or the 1/5th King's attacking to their right, for whom the situation was even worse.

It's all too easy to criticise the 'donkeys' responsible for planning these attacks with the gift of hindsight. The very term 'donkey' owes more to the political chicanery, back-stabbing, and cult of the Great War than it does to reality. It must be remembered that, unlike the Navy, the British Army prior to the Great War was in reality a small force trained to fight colonial wars, and not a major player on the 'world stage'. Limited technology and inexperience, particularly in the use of artillery as a shield for infantry, combined with the limitations of existing infantry tactics offered no real alternative to the methods turned to in August 1916. But lessons from the Battle of the Somme and subsequent campaigns were later brilliantly applied, radically changing the way the world perceived the British Army.

Merely holding the line was simply not an option, either militarily or politically. The French needed pressure at Verdun relieved, the loss of which would otherwise have had dire consequences, and this pressure could only be slackened by a British offensive. In addition, Haig was aware of the events on the Eastern Front and the importance of preventing German troops from leaving the Western Front to boost the Austrians facing Brusilov's offensive.[7] As to location, Haig's desire to make the attack further north at Ypres had been overruled, and the Somme was not his first choice. He had also by the beginning of August accepted that a breakthrough and subsequent collapse of the enemy's fighting capability was a mere pipedream; capturing objectives bit by bit was the only way forward.[8]

Had Haig got his way and attacked further north, he may have achieved a limited breakthrough, for the German defences around the Salient were then a mere shadow of the ones that faced his army a year later. Haig believed that an attack in Flanders leading to the capture of the German rail hub at Roulers would have a significant impact on Germany's ability to deploy men and supplies across the northern part of the Western Front.[9] Possibly the factor most responsible for the war's persistence was the railway, which allowed the rapid mobilisation of masses of troops, supplies, and ammunition to areas of concern, and sustained armies in the field over winter—something that was not possible before the railway age. Both sides were just too strong for a single thrust to deal a final blow, and the ability to deploy barbed wire and MGs swiftly with artillery cover made short work of any attack that got beyond the supporting distance of its own guns and supply capability. To many minds educated in the *Blackadder* school of history, it was the attritional nature of the Great War which ultimately caused the callous annihilation of a generation. Yet according to William Philpott, this is just another myth to add to the collection: casualty rates were higher in the mobile phases of the war in 1914 and 1918, both due to the lack of trench protection and the increased scale and intensity of the fighting.[10] Neither does an overall death rate of 16 per cent of those who served constitute 'the death of a generation', as horrific as this was.

The efficacy of logistics is an often overlooked facet of warfare. Soldiers cannot fight—or live—without ammunition, water, or food. Vast quantities of supplies had to be collected in the rear without alerting enemy reconnaissance planes to their scale and position. They then had to be brought forward into divisional and brigade munitions and RE supply dumps, the majority lugged by overworked infantry. Divisional records show that in addition to the normal supplies held in brigade, battalion, and trench stores, for the attack on 8 August the advance dumps of 55 Division stockpiled 400,000 rounds of .303 ammunition; 40,000 No. 5 grenades; 4,000 rifle grenades; 9,000 rounds of 3-inch Stokes mortar ammunition; 2,000 rounds of 2-inch Stokes mortar ammunition; 800 white rockets; 1,400 water tins; 11,000 day rations; 3,800 1-inch Very cartridges; 1,900 1½-inch Very cartridges; and 900 green flares. The RE stores also requisitioned the following (incomplete) list: 24,000 sandbags, 3,900 coils of barbed wire, 1,400 pickaxes, 2,800 shovels, and 4,000 5-foot-long wooden stakes. These were just some of the items that were collected together and carried forward to the front stores.

The battalion's battle plan organised the four companies left to right across the line of attack in the following order: C, B, A, and D. Two platoons from each company occupied the advanced trench, while the rest remained in the front-line trench. At 3.45 a.m., the men in the advanced trench crawled forward into No Man's Land, allowing the other half to take their place. At 4.10 a.m., the first line crawled further forward, while the second line took up the position that had just been vacated 20 yards to the rear of the first line. These were immediately followed by two platoons from 1/4th Loyals, the carrying party of all that would be needed for the immediate consolidation of any gains. So far, the whole of the battalion was now lying in No Man's Land and the Germans seemed none the wiser. But barely a minute after the second line had crawled forward, a massive bombardment of shrapnel fell on the British front-line trench, forcing both lines of attackers to crawl up closer to German lines.

At 4.20 a.m., the first wave leapt to their feet and rushed forward, only to have their progress completely blocked by two unexpected rows of concertina and barbed wire. As they reached them a volley of grenades exploded in their midst, killing and wounding many. One soldier, nineteen-year-old Cpl George Bell, was seriously hurt almost as soon as he rose to his feet; his comrades placed him in a shell hole for protection while they continued the attack, and he was never seen again. The German stick grenade could be thrown further than the British Mills bomb, and the defenders of Guillemont had perfectly judged the placement of the wire fixed there overnight; whereas British attackers were within the range of the German trenches, the latter were just that bit too far out for British grenades to reach. There is also evidence that the Germans had placed small teams of bombers in shell holes forward of their lines in anticipation.

The second wave now moved forward, and was swept with a storm of rifle and MG fire from both its immediate front and the southernmost trench of the outer defence works. With further advance looking impossible, the men retired out of grenade range and began to dig in 50 yards to the front of their start position, all the while taking casualties. One particularly troublesome MG was situated just behind the first line of enemy trenches, on a small mound directly to the front of Arrow Head Copse; from this slightly elevated position, its gunner was able to pour fire onto the attackers at a range of about 100 m. So effective was this fire—which was enfilading for the two left-hand companies—that it pushed both to their left, and the left flank of C Company was forced over to the other side of the Trones Wood–Guillemont Road. The position of the German gunner can best be appreciated by walking along the first track on the right between the Cemetery and Guillemont. About 200 m from the junction with the main road, climb up the embankment and look back towards the start positions. The field of fire this gunner enjoyed was so good, it is a miracle was that any of the attackers survived!

Communication to the rear was hindered by smoke, dust, and the constant rain of shrapnel, meaning runners stood little chance. The surviving officers attempted to maintain the attack, but were cut down as soon as they exposed themselves. Lt-Col. Swainson DSO had tried to rally his men and lay grievously wounded out in the open. Two men from the battalion and a sergeant from 2/2 West Lancashire Field Company, RE, had tried one at a time to rescue him, but each had been shot and killed, their bodies lying in No Man's Land near the CO. Tragically, the names of these brave men were never recorded. Two minutes after the start of the attack, 2Lt Gabriel Coury from 3/ South Lancashires, with two platoons of his pioneers from 1/4th South Lancashires, had begun to dig a communication trench towards the attacking waves. When he reached the attackers he realised that all their officers were casualties and rallied them, preventing their withdrawal. Observing that Swainson was still alive and fully conscious of the fate of the previous would-be rescuers, Coury left the trench and in full view of the enemy hoisted Swainson onto his shoulders. Seeing that he was struggling under the load, a Pte Haworth also went forward and assisted him and the wounded officer

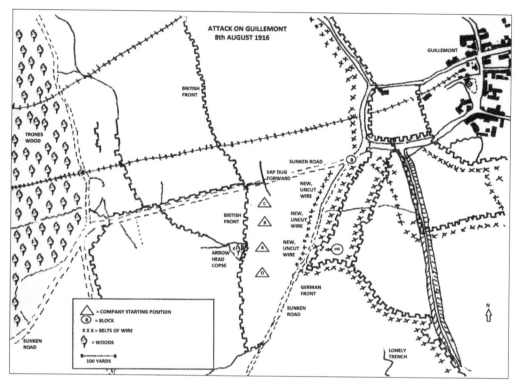

back to the trench. For this valiant act, Coury was awarded the VC. Unfortunately; Pte Haworth, on the other hand, did not even receive a MiD (there were a number of 'Haworths' in the battalion, but it was either Albert or George Haworth who performed this feat). The sacrifice of those who died trying to rescue Swainson was of no avail, for he died from his wounds the next day. There were numerous acts of valour that day: many witnessed by officers were rewarded; others got nothing.

Although the battalion had stalled in front of the German wire, it attempted to find ways around the problem. With all the officers on the left rendered casualties, this flank was commanded by B Company CSM William Bell. The only officer left on his feet in the forward area was twenty-six-year-old Capt. Henry Huthwaite, who despite leading his company in the charge, remained unwounded and now had the considerable task of reorganising the battalion and continuing the attack. Predictably, all telephone wires save for one company's had been broken by shellfire, and the only means of communication was by runner. All contact with the Liverpool Irish on the left had been lost, but when word eventually reached the battalion that the attackers were actually inside Guillemont, it was decided to try to blast a way through the barricade in the road at the edge of the German defences (probably where the main Montauban–Guillemont Road meets the sunken track to Maltz Horn Farm, though some sources suggest it was further up this track). After much delay caused by communication difficulties, a Stokes mortar and ammunition were brought forward to the new trench and targeted on the barricade. But the barricade remained intact, so orders came from the rear to send a grenade party forward at noon to assault it; fortunately for all concerned, this plan was abandoned, as it was to all intents and purposes suicidal.

British artillery had been shelling German positions intermittently throughout the morning but, as was so often the case, many of the shells dropped short and British artillery caused the battalion many losses. This was not so much incompetence on the part of the gunners as a consequence of the parlous state of the guns themselves. Although British artillery had improved out of all recognition since the early days, many guns had for weeks been in constant action and were worn out, hence many rounds dropped short. Communication difficulties also hindered attempts to inform the artillery that they were shelling their own side. Initial plans to dig a fresh trench in front of the barricade held by the battalion on the Montauban–Guillemont Road were shelved when it was realised that the Germans already had a strong fighting patrol out, and bombing parties established in shell holes close to the route of the intended trench made the operation unviable. The men were exhausted after a day's heavy fighting and much reduced in numbers, but the OC was determined to end the day with them in control of No Man's Land. Once dark had fallen, a strong fighting patrol was made up from the fittest men and sent out to disrupt German activities, driving off their patrols and bombers lurking in shell holes. In charge was CSM Bell, who continued to lead and inspire despite a wound to his neck. Bell received the DCM for this and within the week was being treated in Manchester for his wound; he was posted to 1/ King's Own upon his recovery. Capt. Huthwaite received the MC for his 'most conspicuous gallantry and devotion to duty'.[12] For the moment, battalion command had fallen to twenty-seven-year-old Capt. Harold Brocklebank, who had been with the rear party and moved forward when news reached him that the CO had fallen.

Another hero of Festubert, Sgt John Owen DCM, also received recognition for the attack on Guillemont. In a letter home he wrote,

> I have been awarded the Military Medal and have been presented with the ribbon by the General. I was awarded it for taking command of my section in the last attack we made, also killing a few Germans who tried to bomb my gun and men.[13]

When all the machine-gunners were transferred into the MGC, Owen went with them, rising to the rank of RSM by the end of the war. No doubt keen to avenge the death of his older brother, Sgt Wallace Chadwick fought like a demon and was awarded the MM. for his courage. Severely wounded by shrapnel to shoulder and head, he was evacuated to England and posted to the depot after leaving hospital, receiving a 20-per-cent pension for these injuries when he was demobilised.

With No Man's Land to itself, the battalion spent the hours of darkness trying to bring in as many of the wounded as possible from the shell-torn mess, and strengthening their new trench line. Former Barrow policeman, thirty-seven-year-old Cpl Matthew Porter was the MO's orderly and, as darkness fell, went out into No Man's Land repeatedly. Paying scant heed to his own wellbeing, he searched the ground for his comrades amid heavy shelling and brought in any wounded he could find. After Festubert, Porter had been recommended for the DCM for similar actions but received nothing; this time, his courage was rewarded with the MM.[14] Another to confront the horrors of No Man's Land that night was stretcher-bearer Pte Charles Milton; the nineteen-year-old from Barrow was awarded a DCM for bringing back many wounded with complete disregard for his own safety, while under fire from both shrapnel and MGs.[15] How distressing scouring No Man's Land for the wounded must have been can only be imagined: 107 comrades lay dead in an area little bigger than a football field, each casualty needing to be checked for signs of life. One hundred and two lie there still.

The contrasting nature of an infantry battalion in the Great War is superbly illustrated in the difference in the ages of those killed at Guillemont. Three of the men—Pte James Kelly from Bolton, Pte Joseph Dyson resident in Barrow, and Pte Francis Walpole from Preston—were forty six years old, a ridiculous age for any infantryman. In sharp contrast, newly arrived Pte William Liptrot from Bolton was only seventeen, four years younger than his stated age, and Pte William Henry Nicholson from Dalton had only just turned seventeen. Also a mere seventeen years old was D Company's Pte Cyril Settle from Bolton. None of these soldiers' true ages came to light until after they were killed.

Among the dead lying out in No Man's Land was eighteen-year-old Samuel Oliver from Blawith. The young private from 'B' Company had added two years to his age when he signed up. While in basic training, six suspiciously young-looking recruits had lined up for the photographer, Oliver smiling proudly towards the camera (second from the right, as pictured on the front cover). Oliver pencilled his name over his head on his copy of the picture and posted it home. One of the wounded brought back to the lines was also only seventeen: Pte Andrew Lowther from Ireleth, hit in the head by shrapnel as he advanced. He was evacuated to England and transferred to the Labour Corps when he left hospital. Nineteen-year-old L/ Cpl Clarence Tyson from Coniston was also carried in from No Man's Land, and ended up in a hospital in Largs in Scotland; he was later posted to 1/ King's Own and killed with them in May 1917.

Of the Liverpool Irish surrounded in Guillemont, only two men made their way back; when their ammunition ran out, the remainder were either killed or captured and marched into captivity up the slope to Ginchy, in full view of British lines. 55 Division's only gains had been on the right abutting the French sector, where 1/5th King's pushed the line forwards about 200 m and seized part of Cochrane Alley, where sappers from 1/1 West Lancashire Field Company blocked it with explosives half way along its length.

At 3.55 a.m. on 9 August, the battalion was relieved by the Liverpool Scottish and marched to bivouacs south-west of Carnoy. Apart from a roll call confirming just how bloody the previous day had been (271 officers and men killed, wounded, or missing), the men were rested. Out of the 107 killed in the attack, only five and an additional eleven who died later from their wounds have a known grave. For the families of many of those killed there would be no information beyond the notification 'missing', and for months afterwards, their local papers published their pleas for more information. For some families, the news was worse than they could have imagined: in Dalton, the Nicholson family received word that both their sons were dead. Twenty-nine-year-old Edward was immediately declared killed in action, and his seventeen-year-old brother, William Henry Nicholson, though initially reported wounded, was in fact also killed. Edward had been with transport, but had volunteered to move to a fighting company to keep an eye on his younger brother.[16] They were not the only pair of brothers killed that day: twenty-four-year-old L/Cpl John Cloudsdale and twenty-seven-year-old Pte Thomas Cloudsdale from Ulverston knew the same fate.

For the families of those men who died from wounds there were sometimes words of comfort from a friend or relative in the battalion, or sometimes the overworked nursing sisters and chaplains from the casualty stations and hospitals took the time to write to relatives. Having myself read quite a few of these letters, one thing they all have in common is the dubious assertion that the wounded soldier passed away peacefully, without pain or fear. The descriptions of wounds in these letters seem to have very little to do with the horrific reality of injuries caused by explosive and high velocity bullets; yet who can criticise the authors of these letters for trying to give some measure of comfort to the bereaved? I can personally vouch that describing the death on active service of an only son to distraught parents is highly distressing, an ordeal faced by many who returned home with their lives. The family of nineteen-year-old Pte William Norman Nicholson received two letters.[17] The first was from the sister in charge of the 21 CCS:

> Your son was admitted into this hospital yesterday suffering from wounds to the back and body. He was very ill and gradually got worse. I regret to say that he passed away at 2.40 pm this afternoon. He did not speak of anyone or leave a message. He will be buried in the cemetery attached to the hospital.

The hospital chaplain, Rev. J. M. S. Walker, wrote to the late private's sister:

> Now as you know he passed away from the World of strife and weariness into the Peace of Paradise. I am glad to tell you that he prepared for and received Holy Communion before he passed away. I buried his body this afternoon in the peaceful hospital ground amid the ripening cornfield and 'neath the shade of the poplar tree.

The parents of nineteen-year-old Pte James Whiteway from Ulverston found out their son had been killed before the official notification arrived, when they received a letter from his friend, Pte William Bevins, mourning 'one of the best pals a fellow ever had'.[18] Some of the wounded were captured and after recovery put to work. One of these was twenty-year-old Pte James Clegg from Preston. His was put into forced labour in a coal mine near Munster, where on Christmas Eve 1916 a roof collapse crushed his left leg. He still had trouble walking after his repatriation at the conclusion of the war, and was awarded a small pension.

No doubt questions were asked at the time as to why this attack had failed. The unexpected rows of wire between the sunken road and the jumping-off positions, coupled with the lack of a supporting attack by the French against the Maurepas Ravine, must have been discussed. Unbroken wire was far from uncommon in the early stages of the war, and although the 18-lb shrapnel shell was liable to contribute little to destroying wire, the howitzers certainly could. An intriguing clue as to a major flaw in the plan of this attack rests in the archives of 55 Division.[19] The 'Heavy Artillery Objectives and Barrages' map does not even feature the first line of enemy trenches facing the 1/4th, the closest heavy shells targeted being some 500 yards to the rear of the section that A and D Company attacked. C Company was slightly more fortunate, as the barrage only fell a mere 100 yards behind the enemy on their flank. The map of 18-pounders, while illustrating the genesis of the 'creeping barrage', also places the first phase of bombardment from these batteries some 500 yards behind the German front line—though at least this map has the first line of enemy trenches marked on it! A look at the timings shows that the barrage facing the King's Own was due to lift at zero hour, from what was in reality the enemy's second line of defence, and then lift from their third line of defence a mere ten minutes later, an advance that no infantry could possibly have made in the time allowed! This evidence suggests that the only shellfire to actually hit the defences that the 1/4th were assaulting were British rounds that fell short—this goes a long way towards explaining why the battalion faced such a rapid response from the German defenders as they stood up to attack. Rather than sheltering in their dugouts, these defenders were already lined up and ready to repel the assault.

The next day, the men paraded for company inspection as a prelude to a visit from Maj.-Gen. Jeudwine that afternoon. Although the inspection went well, it was probably a good thing that the

General had not arrived early, as twenty-year-old Pte John Roskell from Preston managed to garner an injury from a refuse incinerator, which exploded as he passed it. Morale was boosted by a series of concerts, though working parties still had to be found. On the night of the 11 to 12th, one officer and seventy men were sent to dig forward communication trenches; they were heavily shelled, with two wounded. Those fortunate enough to miss this working party found, to their disgust, that they were to provide the labour force for one of the tunnelling companies instead; their day was made more interesting when one of the captive observation balloons broke away from its mooring and its observer escaped by parachute—a rare sight at the time. For one young soldier, this would be his last bit of excitement while serving with the battalion, for someone back home had discovered that Belfast-born Pte Francis Brown was only in fact only seventeen. He was immediately sent to Calais and put on the first available transport home, and discharged on the 16th. Brown was subsequently called up under the Conscription Act in May the next year and served in the Labour Corps; however, his posting to Scotland obviously didn't suit him because he deserted in January 1918, and was arrested on the Springfield Road in his native Belfast; he was sentenced to fifty-six days' detention.

Killed or died of wounds received in the attack on Guillemont of 8 August 1916

| | | | | | |
|---|---|---|---|---|---|
| Pte Robert Abbott | 3427 | DOW-9/9 | Pte John Charles Anson | 201351 | KIA-8/8 |
| Pte James Ashworth | 200735 | KIA-8/8 | Pte Nelson Athersmith | 201099 | KIA-8/8 |
| Pte James Boardman Atherton | 201421 | KIA-8/8 | Pte Arthur Atkinson | 1975 | DOW-30/8 |
| Pte Isaac Atkinson | 200697 | KIA-8/8 | Cpl Joseph Balderston | 1922 | DOW-1/9 |
| Cpl George Bell | 200273 | KIA-8/8 | Pte Thomas Blezard | 200627 | KIA-8/8 |
| Pte Fred Briggs | 201005 | KIA-8/8 | 2Lt Albert John Brockman | | KIA-8/8 |
| Pte John Burrow | 200759 | KIA-8/8 | Pte George Caton | 200957 | KIA-8/8 |
| Pte Thomas Clark | 201311 | KIA-8/8 | L/Cpl John Cloudsdale | 1829 | KIA-8/8 |
| Pte Thomas Cloudsdale | 2469 | KIA-8/8 | Pte John Clough | 201341 | KIA-8/8 |
| Pte Thomas Robert Corlett | 3032 | DOW-12/8 | Pte William Cottam | 1895 | KIA-8/8 |
| Pte Andrew Coulter | 2797 | KIA-8/8 | Pte John Cowell | 200926 | KIA-8/8 |
| Pte William Burn Cowper | 201103 | KIA-8/8 | Pte Alexander Crabb | 201363 | KIA-8/8 |
| Pte James Craig | 200492 | KIA-8/8 | Pte Benjamin Crispe | 2145 | KIA-8/8 |
| Pte Harry Currie | 3128 | KIA-8/8 | Pte William Dean | 4049 | KIA-8/8 |
| Pte Ben Dixon | 200692 | KIA-8/8 | Pte Robert Donovan | 200919 | KIA-8/8 |
| | | | Cpl William Albert | | |
| Pte James Downham | 201126 | KIA-8/8 | Downham | 1979 | KIA-8/8 |
| Pte John Duckworth | 4187 | KIA-8/8 | Pte Joseph Dunn | 201373 | KIA-8/8 |
| Pte Joseph Dyson | 2335 | DOW-1/9 | Pte Andrew Evans | 1622 | DOW-18/8 |
| | | | Pte Charles Watson | | |
| Pte Thomas Ford | 4142 | KIA-8/8 | Frearson | 200025 | KIA-8/8 |
| Pte William Kenneth Gentles | 200821 | KIA-8/8 | Pte John Edward Gill | 1524 | KIA-8/8 |
| Pte Walter Glover | 1636 | KIA-8/8 | Pte James Greenhalgh | 4092 | KIA-8/8 |
| Pte Edgar Hall | 3760 | KIA-8/8 | Pte Joseph Henry Hartley | 201325 | KIA-8/8 |

| Name | Number | Status |
|---|---|---|
| Pte Harry Ashley Hatton | 201349 | KIA-8/8 |
| Pte Ernest Haythornthwaite | 3254 | KIA-8/8 |
| Cpl Norman Hill | 200640 | KIA-8/8 |
| 2Lt Harold Hale Hodkinson | | KIA-8/8 |
| Pte Thomas Howcroft | 200966 | KIA-8/8 |
| Pte Robert Hughes | 3265 | KIA-8/8 |
| Pte George James | 200687 | KIA-8/8 |
| Pte Ambrose Kelly | 2364 | KIA-8/8 |
| Cpl Benjamin Atkinson Kirkby | 201062 | KIA-8/8 |
| 2Lt Joseph Percy Lawson | | KIA-8/8 |
| Pte William Liptrot | 4076 | KIA-8/8 |
| L/Cpl Alfred Loftus | 200846 | KIA-8/8 |
| Pte Arthur Leo Macdonald | 200609 | KIA-8/8 |
| Pte Walter Mason | 3657 | KIA-8/8 |
| Pte William Matthews | 3213 | KIA-8/8 |
| 2Lt Lister Metcalf | | KIA-8/8 |
| Cpl John Miller | 200300 | KIA-8/8 |
| L/Sgt Charles Morris | 3130 | DOW-12/8 |
| Pte John Nelson | 200881 | KIA-8/8 |
| Pte William Henry Nicholson | 200655 | KIA-8/8 |
| Pte Samuel Oliver | 3478 | KIA-8/8 |
| Pte Richard Penaluna | 2969 | KIA-8/8 |
| Pte Thomas Raven | 2264 | KIA-8/8 |
| Pte Joseph Remington | 200720 | KIA-8/8 |
| Pte Frank Pearson Rigg | 3792 | KIA-8/8 |
| L/Cpl Soloman Robinson | 3583 | KIA-8/8 |
| Pte James Schofield | 201359 | KIA-8/8 |
| Pte Robert Shaw | 201402 | KIA-8/8 |
| Pte William Smith | 201375 | KIA-8/8 |
| Pte William James Sprout | 200681 | KIA-8/8 |
| Lt-Col. Joseph Leonard Swainson | | DOW-9/8 |
| Pte Thomas Turner | 200786 | KIA-8/8 |
| CQMS Richard Usher | 2410 | KIA-8/8 |
| L/Cpl William Hudson Haythorn | 3379 | KIA-8/8 |
| Pte Peter Higson | 4093 | DOW-16/8 |
| 2Lt George Hilton | | KIA-8/8 |
| Pte Thomas Hodson | 3314 | KIA-8/8 |
| Pte Thomas W. Huck | 200108 | KIA-8/8 |
| Pte Joseph William Ireland | 200806 | KIA-8/8 |
| Pte Neil Jamieson | 1790 | KIA-8/8 |
| Pte James Kelly | 4154 | DOW-10/8 |
| Pte Arthur Lancaster | 3281 | KIA-8/8 |
| Cpl Charles Norman Lewis | 1797 | KIA-8/8 |
| L/Cpl John Lockhead | 2226 | KIA-8/8 |
| Pte William Lowe | 201014 | KIA-8/8 |
| Pte Thomas Martin | 200674 | KIA-8/8 |
| Pte Joseph Mather | 4218 | KIA-8/8 |
| Pte William John McKay | 3047 | KIA-8/8 |
| Sgt John Miles | 2946 | KIA-8/8 |
| Capt. Ralph D'Albin Morrell | | KIA-8/8 |
| Pte Daniel Muncaster | 2986 | DOW-11/8 |
| Pte Edward Nicholson | 809 | KIA-8/8 |
| Pte William Norman Nicholson | 3690 | KIA-8/8 |
| Pte John James Parsons | 3470 | KIA-8/8 |
| Pte Fred Porter | 201348 | KIA-8/8 |
| Pte William Henry Rawsthorne | 3655 | KIA-8/8 |
| Cpl Stanley Richardson | 2194 | KIA-8/8 |
| Sgt George Robinson | 1577 | KIA-8/8 |
| L/Cpl Joseph Sandilands | 2863 | KIA-8/8 |
| Pte Cyril Settle | 4064 | KIA-8/8 |
| Cpl Albert Singleton | 3416 | KIA-8/8 |
| Pte Henry John Snaith | 200411 | KIA-8/8 |
| Pte William Henry Steenson | 200982 | KIA-8/8 |
| Pte Thomas Swainson | 201504 | KIA-8/8 |
| Pte William Unsworth | 4166 | KIA-8/8 |
| Pte Francis Arthur Walpole | 200975 | KIA-8/8 |

| | | | | | | |
|---|---|---|---|---|---|---|
| Pte Robert M. Walters | 2378 | KIA-8/8 | | Pte James Whiteway | 3640 | KIA-8/8 |
| Pte Tom Wilkinson | 200036 | KIA-8/8 | | Pte Thomas Williams | 200694 | KIA-8/8 |
| Pte Joseph Wilson | 201049 | KIA-8/8 | | Pte Philip Wood | 201397 | KIA-8/8 |
| | | | | Capt. Alexander Allen | | |
| Pte Edgar Woodburn | 200088 | KIA-8/8 | | Wright | | KIA-8/8 |

## Known to have been wounded in the attack on Guillemont of 8 August 1916

| | | | | | | |
|---|---|---|---|---|---|---|
| Pte William Allen | 200577 | WIA-8/8 | | Pte Henry Thomas Ashmore | 201429 | WIA-8/8 |
| Pte John Backhouse | 2392 | WIA-8/8 | | A/CSM William Bell | 200086 | WIA-8/8 |
| Pte Thomas E. Bewsher | 201140 | WIA-8/8 | | Pte George William Caine | 3158 | WIA-8/8 |
| Pte John Capstick | 200701 | WIA-8/8 | | Sgt Wallace Chadwick | 200120 | WIA-8/8 |
| Lt Alfred Matthews Clark | | WIA-8/8 | | Pte James Clegg | 202013 | POW-8/8 |
| Pte Richard Clegg | 200320 | WIA-8/8 | | Sgt Jonathan Coward | 200252 | WIA-8/8 |
| Pte Thomas Conroy | 200659 | WIA-8/8 | | Pte William Cryan | 201357 | WIA-8/8 |
| Pte Stanley Darby | 3552 | WIA-8/8 | | Cpl Thomas Dumphey | 200948 | WIA-8/8 |
| Pte James Edmonson | 200132 | WIA-8/8 | | Pte Hugh Edmondson | 2391 | WIA-8/8 |
| 2Lt George Hubert Ferns | | WIA-8/8 | | Pte Harold Fullard | 3618 | WIA-8/8 |
| Pte James Greenhill | 200665 | WIA-8/8 | | Pte Albert Gunning | 200610 | WIA-8/8 |
| L/Cpl John Edward Haslam | 4195 | WIA-8/8 | | Pte Robert Henderson | 200418 | WIA-8/8 |
| Pte William Hodgson | 200716 | WIA-8/8 | | Pte Randolph Houghton | 4139 | WIA-8/8 |
| Pte Robert A. Hughes | 200653 | WIA-8/8 | | 2Lt John Jackson | | WIA-8/8 |
| Pte William Stephen Jackson | 3571 | WIA-8/8 | | Pte Robert Johnson | 200642 | WIA-8/8 |
| Cpl Matthew Keelan | 200932 | WIA-8/8 | | Cpl Harry Herbert Kitchen | 200267 | WIA-8/8 |
| Pte Andrew Lowther | 3617 | WIA-8/8 | | Pte James W. Marshall | 1759 | WIA-8/8 |
| Pte Robert McKeron | 200662 | WIA-8/8 | | L/Cpl James Ivan Menzies | 200745 | WIA-8/8 |
| 2Lt Rolland Garratt Metcalfe | | WIA-8/8 | | Pte John Percy Murphy | 200812 | WIA-8/8 |
| Capt. William Campbell Neill | | WIA-8/8 | | Pte Richard Noble | 2960 | WIA-8/8 |
| Pte Joseph Tyson Palmer | 200247 | WIA-8/8 | | L/Cpl Harry Parnell | 200481 | WIA-8/8 |
| Sgt Francis Arthur Redman | 1674 | POW-8/8 | | Pte Henry Rigg | 200598 | POW-8/8 |
| Pte William Rimmer | 3493 | WIA-8/8 | | Sgt Henry Robinson | 200686 | POW-8/8 |
| Pte William Rushton | 200277 | WIA-8/8 | | Sgt Harry Smith | 200604 | WIA-8/8 |
| Pte Frank Thompson | 200410 | WIA-8/8 | | Cpl William Thompson | 200125 | WIA-8/8 |
| L/Cpl Clarence Tyson | 200791 | WIA-8/8 | | 2Lt Sidney Frederick Walker | | WIA-8/8 |
| 2Lt John Welch | | WIA-8/8 | | L/Cpl Richard A. Whiteman | 200568 | WIA-8/8 |
| Pte Jackson Whittam | 3308 | WIA-8/8 | | Pte Reuben Whittle | 200874 | WIA-8/8 |
| 2Lt Joseph Mark Wilcock | | WIA-8/8 | | 2Lt Charles Elisha Withey | | WIA-8/8 |
| Pte Ernest M. Woodhouse | 200523 | WIA-8/8 | | Pte John Woodruff | 200847 | WIA-8/8 |

On 14 August, the battalion marched to billets at Méricourt for an interval of rest, reorganisation, and training. The first reinforcements arrived on the 16th, when a party of 100 men from 3/10th

Manchesters were transferred *en masse* to the battalion straight from Étaples. The next day, eight men returned from hospital and nine from Oswestry, having also passed though the Bull Ring. Among this first batch to pass through Oswestry were Privates Saul Cohen and Arthur Hammond. Cohen had clearly shown promise there, having been promoted to Lance Corporal; but he had obviously overdone things when celebrating his twentieth birthday, for he was swiftly demoted back to Private for insolence towards and threatening to strike an NCO. Arthur Hammond was, at thirty-six, older than most infantrymen, but of a strong build and 6 foot 2 inches besides; he had worked outside all his life, initially as a farmhand in Rivington, and latterly as a gardener for Lord Lever.

18 August was the battalion's last night at Méricourt for a while yet. Their last day of hard training there during the heat wave was rewarded with the luxury of a hot bath at Ville-sur-Ancre. The *War Diary* of the 1/4th imparts the impression that the four days at Méricourt were spent in drill and training, away from the dangers of the trenches; however, individual service records show that this was not the whole story. The machine of war still had to be fed, and men behind the lines were the only available stokers. On the 16th, John Roskell returned to the CCS he'd not long left after his accident with the incinerator, this time after sustaining shrapnel wounds to his forearm which necessitated evacuation home. Upon his eventual recovery in July 1917, he was posted to 2/5th King's Own. Another casualty was Pte Henry Beck from Millom, who was also put on a hospital ship for England, but upon his recovery was claimed for munitions work and saw no more active service.

At 4 a.m. on 19 August, the battalion paraded at Méricourt Station and, once entrained, began the journey westward to Abbeville—a trip of about 40 miles as the crow flies, but took six hours to complete. Once there, the battalion marched to billets at Lambercourt. The move ushered in a period of intensive training at both platoon and company levels, including an 8-mile route march in torrential rain on 25 August. The next day's training was supervised by Maj.-Gen. Jeudwine, and in the evening another draft of twenty-nine men arrived, while two officers and fifty-eight of the longest-serving men left for the coast at St Valery-sur-Somme for a seaside holiday. Not only did new techniques need teaching, but the high turnover of men and officers meant that, even if a particular battalion had historically practised a certain skill many times over, the men belonging to this battalion could still be relative beginners. Consequently, the battalion spent the 28th and 29th building a strongpoint at Cahon. Upon its completion, the men marched back to Lambercourt, loaded a convoy of lorries with large bags and company kit, and at 11.15 p.m. made their way eastwards along the southern side of the River Somme in 'Light Marching Order', arriving at the station at Pont Remy at 5 a.m. They departed at 8 a.m. and arrived back at Méricourt four hours later. The battalion then marched north and spent a very wet night bivouacking in a cornfield outside Dernancourt before moving to billets in huts and tents near the Albert–Corbie Road the next day.

The first week of September was devoted to training in old front-line trenches, but this time the training environment expanded to brigade level, in imitation of holding the actual front. Battalion routine went undisturbed; men came and went. George Hosking, a twenty-one year old from Barrow, was promoted to Corporal on 2 September, only to be evacuated to England a week later suffering from shell shock after a bombardment on the southern edge of Delville Wood. On the same day of Hosking's promotion, Pte John Duerden, supposedly nineteen years old, was sent on his way home. Orphaned in 1910, he'd only joined the battalion a month earlier, and when he was posted overseas, his horrified grandmother had informed the Army of his true date of birth (April 1900).

He was later conscripted into the Manchesters and appears to have survived the war. A piece of news that must have relieved the old hands was the capture of Guillemont on the 3rd, which meant that they would not have to face that daunting task again. Experienced infantry officers who survived the war with hindsight expressed the opinion, that at no time in the war did the Germans fight better than at Guillemont and Ginchy.[20]

Just after 10 a.m. on 6 September, the battalion arrived at the divisional reserve bivouac a little under a mile south-west of Fricourt. From there, they moved up to the reserve trenches at Montauban Alley on the 8th, a long communication trench running in a north-easterly direction just north of Montauban. A myriad of carrying and working parties were required to carry stores forward to maintain communication trenches, and battalion officers and SNCOs reconnoitred the forward positions. The front line at Delville Wood was utterly devastated: blasted stumps dotted the shell-cratered mud, and the craters themselves were filled with water. The heat wave of July and early August had been on the decline since 10 August, after which most days had seen rain of varying degrees of heaviness. The wood had been the scene of desperate fighting since 14 July, but the Germans still held about 20 yards of the north-eastern sector of the wood, having pulled off a successful counter-attack on 31 August. Both sides rained constant and heavy artillery on each other, and the areas outside the trenches were littered with the unburied and decomposing remains of human wreckage. On 7 September, two companies of 2/ Queen's tried and failed to take this area back from the Germans; it was this battalion that the 1/4th would be relieving.

Delville Wood, aptly nicknamed 'Devil's Wood' by the British, occupied an important strategic position. German strongpoints—of which Delville, Guillemont, and Ginchy were just three—cannot be viewed in isolation. The geography of the Somme and its long vistas meant that their fields of fire were interconnected, so that if one was attacked, it could be supported by fire from its neighbours.

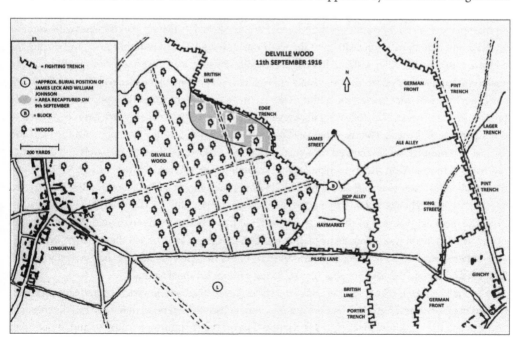

Guillemont had been a vital position because it not only controlled the route of British advances, but also prevented French advances from its position on the boundary of Franco-British sectors. One reason why Guillemont had taken so long to capture was enfilading fire from Ginchy. To advance further, the British needed to take the latter, but its left flank was dominated by the German positions around the north-east corner of Delville Wood. A visitor to Delville today should take a short stroll along the road from the memorial in the direction of Ginchy, first to the water tower at the corner of the wood, and then along its outer boundary and down the first curve to the left. Pause for a moment here; turn around towards Ginchy, and you will see the field of fire the German machine-gunners enjoyed at this point. Now continue along the path until about 50 m short of the next curve, where Hop Alley met Delville Wood (50° 1′ 36.27″ N, 2° 49′ 12.47″ E). Continue on to the corner, where Ale Alley joined the wood (50° 1′ 38.63″ N, 2° 49′ 12.82″ E). Look both ways, and you will appreciate how this position could enfilade attacks to both the Switch Line to the north-west and Ginchy to the south-east.

Now that Guillemont had fallen, plans to drive enemy lines back in a coordinated attack across the Delville–Ginchy sector crystallised. This had to be a broad attack, if the effectiveness of enfilading fire from any one position was to be reduced. 16 Division of XV Corps would assault Ginchy to the right of 55 Division, and 1 Division of III Corps from the left. Firstly, 1/4th Loyals and 2/5th Lancashire Fusiliers of 55 Division would take a line of trenches which roughly ran from the western edge of Ginchy to the eastern edge of Delville Wood; next, they would take possession of Hop Alley as far as the outskirts of Ginchy, and Ale Alley right up to its junction with Pint Trench (50° 1′ 41.80″ N, 2° 49′ 45.84″ E). Both Hop and Ale Alley ran at right angles to the British front line. At 3 a.m. on 9 September, the King's Own received the order for their role in the attack, and at 5.45 p.m. the battalion moved further forward and occupied the support trenches of Crucifix Alley (approx. 50° 1′ 9.96″ N, 2° 47′ 49.58″ E), minus one company which was detached to support 1/8th King's.

British artillery had been bombarding German positions and batteries since 7 a.m. In retaliation and an attempt to nip an obvious attack in the bud, enemy guns shelled British support trenches with shrapnel and HE, and battery positions with gas. The 1/4th was moving forward into this mess, and during the advance into Crucifix Alley suffered five casualties, four of which were diagnosed with shell shock. An analysis of battalion service records show that approximately 4 per cent of the men were hospitalised with shell shock at least once during their time at the front—a lower percentage than popular myth would propound—but this and the following days resulted in a distinct rise in shell shock cases compared to other periods of the war. Twenty-three-year-old Bolton man Pte Edward Bennett, with the battalion for just two months, was evacuated with shell shock, as was George Thompson, barely ten days after returning to the battalion after treatment for the same condition. William Crowther had been back with the battalion just over two weeks after his initial bout of shell shock, and this bombardment triggered another, for which he got another two weeks in hospital, the last until his capture at Givenchy in April 1918. The most experienced of the four shell shock victims was twenty-five-year-old Pte James Lamb from Barrow. He too was granted a fortnight's rest in hospital and returned to the battalion. Nineteen-year-old Preston weaver Pte Harry Fryer was the only one of these five casualties to be physically injured; he spent four days in the field hospital after receiving a minor shrapnel wound.

When it became clear that 55 Division's attacks had failed, the battalion was ordered forward again to hold the front line. Hop Alley had proved much more heavily defended than was initially thought, and a previously unknown trench (later named 'Haymarket') running parallel to and about 50 m south of Hop Alley had delayed the attack with disastrous consequences. The attacks had not been total failures, since 48 and 49 Brigade had captured Ginchy to 55 Division's right and held it in spite of multiple German counter-attacks that evening; furthermore, the Germans had finally relinquished their hold on the north-eastern edge of Delville Wood. The companies of the 1/4th were split up along the brigade front, and it became all but impossible for HQ to keep abreast of the situation. German artillery pummelled the forward and communication lines relentlessly, cutting telephone cables and hitting runners. And to compound this, many men held positions in shell craters forward of the original line, and in daylight their movement was impossible.

Six men were killed. Pte Henry Dobson from Ulverston was one, and nineteen-year-old Blackburn miner James Brownlow, who had only joined the battalion the day before, was another. Also only nineteen was Pte William Johnson from Millom. Twenty-six-year-old Pte James Leck from Greenodd was initially posted as missing, but his and Johnson's bodies were found three days later by one of the chaplains from 14 Division and buried approximately half way between the edge of Delville Wood and Waterlot Farm [see previous map, Delville Wood on 11 September 1916], along with the bodies of two men from the South Lancashires. Judging by their initial burial site, it is probable that they were either runners, or were killed as they moved up to the front line, as this position is part way between Crucifix Alley and the front-line position. Leck's body was only rediscovered in the 1940s and reburied in London Cemetery.[21] Edward Lenaughan, only back with the battalion for two weeks after his previous injury, was also killed, and the only one of these six with no known grave. The last of the six to die was twenty-year-old 2 Lt Wilfred Leah, who'd held his commission for less than two months. A life-insurance clerk in Manchester in civilian life, he'd joined the army as a ranker and served with the Manchesters before being commissioned.[21]

Service records show that at least six men had to be treated for shell shock after the battalion's move to the front line. That some of them—Cpl George Hosking, L/Cpl James Smith (713), and L/Cpl John Wilson—had been out with the battalion for sixteen months, and were therefore no strangers to artillery fire, is a testament to the bombardment's ferocity. Sometimes the effects of shell shock were fairly short-lived, and more akin to concussion from a nearby burst; such was the case for twenty-six-year-old Joseph Barrow from Broughton-in-Furness, who was able to re-join the battalion the next day, or twenty-seven-year-old Pte James Young from Chadderton, who returned after a couple of weeks. On the other hand, its effects could last for years; these were severe in the case of George Hosking, though an accident led to his partial recovery.

> Corporal Geo. Hosking [...] has just recovered the power of speech after being dumb for five months as the result of shell-shock. The manner in which his speech has returned has been something of a miracle. The Corporal was proceeding up a flight of stairs when he fell and rolled to bottom. He was unconscious for several hours, but on regaining his senses discovered to his great joy that he could speak again. He could hardly realise the fact after his five months of awful silence. The fact that Corporal Hosking was unable to converse with his friends was having a prejudicial effect on his mind and health, but it is hoped now that he has overcome this great affliction he will soon regain his bodily strength.[22]

He was not returned to the battalion, but transferred to munitions work at Vickers in November 1917 with a pension for shell shock and tuberculosis. Another old hand to experience shell shock on this occasion was newly promoted Cpl Gilbert Rorison, his face still scarred from a wound of almost a year earlier. Only just eighteen years old, he was still too young to legally be at the Front. For those whose first exposure to shellfire this was, such as twenty-six-year-old Chadderton man Pte James Young, the experience must have been unspeakable. The last of those known to have gone down with shell shock that day was Pte Ernest Grey from Failsworth. Like James Brownlow, he'd only joined the battalion the previous day, but was a more experienced soldier. A married man of thirty-two with four children, he'd been a lance corporal with 10/ Manchesters in England, but in February that year had forged his OC's signature on a leave warrant and was arrested by railway officials while travelling home to see his family. Charged with this and absence without leave, he'd been demoted, sentenced to ninety days' detention, and transferred to the King's Own some months after his release. Grey never saw his family again.

At 6 p.m. on 10 September, word was passed down that the battalion would carry out a surprise attack on Hop and Ale Alley the next morning at 5.15 a.m. This was hardly good news—it had been raining solidly, and the men had not rested for the past four days, struggling along communication lines with heavy loads. Since moving into position in the front line in the early hours, most of the battalion had been lying in sodden craters seeking what shelter they could. Ration supply was near impossible, and as soon as dark had fallen, HQ was faced with the monumental problem of locating the scattered companies and briefing junior officers and men about the attack at 5.15 a.m. Not the best circumstances in which to launch an attack!

All four fighting companies were to take part: D on the left, A and B in the centre, and C to the right. It was decided that no preliminary bombardment should take place so as not to alert the Germans, so German trenches were fully manned and protected by unbroken wire when, slipping and sliding through the muck, the men left their shell holes to advance. They were met by a fusillade of rifle and MG fire from Hop and Ale Alley, and as Pint Trench and Lager Trench (a strongly held German trench parallel to Ale Alley, which led eastwards off Pint Trench, just to the south of its junction with Ale Alley). As soon as fire opened, most took cover; it was obvious to even the least experienced among them that this attack could not proceed without artillery support. Dog-tired and dispirited, the men crawled back to their own line. British artillery remained silent while German guns pounded the battalion's front line for the next forty-eight hours.

Casualties on the 11th were not heavy compared to the toll sustained at Guillemont, but there were significant losses to officers and NCOs, who accounted for nine of the sixteen dead. Twenty-one-year-old 2Lt George Glenie, the Lewis gun officer, and twenty-six-year-old Lt Edward Spearing, who had commanded D Company in the attack, both failed to return to the trenches. No one saw either of them fall and their bodies were never recovered; they are commemorated on the Thiepval Memorial. Twenty-four-year-old L/Cpl Arthur Diggle from Bolton was killed, as was twenty-year-old L/Cpl Joseph Jarvis from Oldham, who had been with the battalion for exactly one month. Twenty-year-old Pte William Rimmer from Barrow, who had only just returned from hospital after being wounded in the face at Guillemont, was seen to be killed, though his body was never recovered; neither was that of Sgt Robert Robinson. Also freshly recovered from his wounds at Guillemont and killed that day was L/Cpl John Haslam from Bolton, a recent transfer from the Loyals. The youngest to die on the 11th was Ulverston painter Pte William Fell, yet another young man to have lied about his age upon enlistment and only just eighteen when he was killed. Of the last two who fell in the attack, the first was Pte Robert Lovell, born in London but working in Ulverston when he enlisted, who was reported hit by his comrades upon their return. The second was twenty-one-year-old L/Sgt Charles Shaw from Coniston, recently promoted to replace his friend Sgt Richard Usher, who'd died at his side at Guillemont.[23]

Not all the men killed on the 11th were cut down in the open. Pte Joseph 'Fred' Newby was positioned in a shell hole with his Lewis gun team when a shell exploded next to him. The popular twenty-year-old from Barrow took the full force of the blast and was killed outright. His brother Tom witnessed the whole incident from his position, less than 100 yards away.[24] Twenty-year-old L/Cpl Robert Dixon from Dalton, who was attached to the TMB and in the support line as the attack commenced, was also killed by a shell. His friend Pte Nicholson wrote to his parents:

Just a line to tell you of the deep regret and sympathy that is felt in all the battery through the loss of your son, Bob. He was well liked and respected by all of us and he had only recently received promotion, and no doubt he would have worked his way up to Sergeant if he had lived longer. I was an old friend of his. I was with him for over twelve months in England, and came over to France with the same draft as him, and joined the Trench Mortar Battery with him, and I can say I never met a better hearted lad. He was killed instantly with a large shell. He did not have a moment's pain. He was hit as he was crossing a corner of the trench. The trench was blocked with wounded at this corner and he could not get past without inconvenience to the wounded, so he went across the top and was caught by the shell. It was just the sort of thing he would do. Much as his loss is to us, it cannot be compared to yours. I got his letters and photos out of his pocket and will send them on. He died a glorious death for his King and Country and we are proud of him.[25]

The last sentence is interesting in that it shows the attitudes of men in September 1916 towards the war, sentiments that can be found in so many of the letters of condolence and very much at odds with the views held by most people today about war in general and the Great War in particular.

Once back in their front line, the men were not safe; the bombardment continued, and a further five men were killed instantly or died from their wounds shortly afterwards. Twenty-one-year-old Pte Frank Webster from Flookburgh had been wounded previously, but this time was killed outright by a shell burst; his remains were laid to rest in what is now the Delville Wood Cemetery, close to his comrade from the same company, Pte Percy Johnson. Twenty-one-year-old Pte William Phillip was hit on the 12th, a pre-war member of the battalion, and succumbed to his wounds the next day. The last of those to die in that punishing bombardment was Sgt John Williams, an electrician born in Widnes but working in Ulverston. Twenty-four-year-old Pte William Phillip, terribly damaged by shrapnel, clung on to life until the 15th. Only five service records of the men wounded on these two days survive, but if we were to hazard an estimation by applying the usual ratio of killed to injured, around forty men were wounded on 11 September. Some, such as CSM Thomas Braithwaite, were lost to the battalion: the thirty-two-year-old senior NCO, who had enlisted in February 1913, was precluded from any further service abroad by the wound to his left arm. Another NCO with an arm wound was twenty-two-year-old Sgt Albert Jackson, who spent the rest of the war as an instructor at Oswestry. Initially declared missing, nineteen-year-old Pte Alfred Downham from Morecambe had only joined the battalion two days earlier, and had been evacuated with a minor wound—a new man, no one had recognised him, and it wasn't until his return a few days later that the ensuing paperwork caught up with him. The bombardment of the 11th also resulted in many a shell shock victim, for instance twenty-seven-year-old Pte John Hornby from

Horwich. Like Downham, he'd only arrived at the battalion two days earlier, and in keeping with policy, neither man had been committed to battle until they'd got a bit more experience. But German artillery were not in on this arrangement, and heavy shelling of his location in the support trenches resulted in two days at the CCS for him and Pte William Waters, a twenty one year old from Barrow also suffering from shell shock. Upon his return, Hornby was attached to 177 Tunnelling Company. There was one final casualty of the attacks on Hop and Ale Alley, 164 Brigade commander Brig.-Gen. Edwards. His failures at Guillemont and Delville Wood were unacceptable to Jeudwine, and he was sacked. His replacement, Brig.-Gen C. I. Stockwell, was cast from an altogether different mould!

It must have been a great relief to the 1/4th King's Own when 8/ King's Royal Rifles took over the line on the night of 12 September, and it was able to march back to and bivouac at Bécordel-Bécourt. On the 13th, they marched to Ribemont and bivouacked under canvas, remaining there for three days. It was a time of reorganisation and refitting; of bayonet and musketry practice; and PT and drill under the RSM. There was time for more pleasant activities, too, chiefly bathing and rugby—the battalion's team demolished the South Lancashires in a match on the evening of the 15th, though some missed out on the occasion when 2Lt Richard Bradley was tasked to take 120 men to help guard German POWs at Mametz. On the 16th, the RSM's parade was brought to an unexpected stop by sudden orders to move to Buire; two and a half hours later, the battalion were established in well-appointed billets there, delighted by the improvement in their living quarters and also by the sight of a long column of nearly 900 German prisoners being marched under escort through the village. To widespread dismay, this comfortable stay didn't last long, for by 2 p.m. the next day they were on the road again, back to the bivouacs at Bécordel-Bécourt; they passed several battalions *en route*, marching in the opposite direction, before arriving at 6 p.m.

Suspecting an early move the next day, the men retired early, but the order did not come until much later. It wasn't until 3.30 p.m. on 18 September that they moved off in torrential rain to occupy York Trench, just south-west of Longueval. Evry man was issued with grenades and ammunition and the guard party under Lt Bradley re-joined them. At midnight, they moved again, but not forwards to the front line; instead, they were split into working parties and acted as mud-mules again before being returned the way they had come to Bécordel-Bécourt. They stopped short of their destination to bivouac in torrential rain near the POW cage at Mametz. It must have been galling for these 120 men, who had only just marched all the way from this very location to York Trench, and now had had to march straight back again. The old tune, 'Grand Old Duke of York', must have been summoned to mind, though history does not record whether anyone was bold enough to voice it!

This had not been a straightforward move, as most of the men in their detached working parties arrived at Mametz caked in mud, tired, and hungry, only to find nothing there for them. Their bivouac for the night consisted of a bemired field littered with tangles of brushwood and slit trenches, the locations of which only became obvious in the dark night when some unfortunate soldier fell into one. The night was punctuated with outbursts of loud and violent swearing, as men struggled unsuccessfully to keep their footing and avoid the gashes in the ground. A lucky few 'acquired' scraps of canvas for a makeshift shelter, but for most there was no relief to their misery. These were ideal conditions for sickness, for which rank was no prevention. Maj. Balfour, A/CO since the death of Lt-Col. Swainson DSO, wound up in hospital at this time, for example. Conversely, there only seems to have been one battle casualty from the working parties, L/Cpl Thomas Edmondson from Dalton. He was evacuated to England and eventually discharged as no longer fit in April 1917.

On 19 September, the rain stopped as the sun rose weakly above the men; they began to dry themselves and clear themselves and their equipment of as much mud as possible. The first priority were the weapons; even though the breeches of the rifles were protected by canvas sleeves, the rest of the firearm was not, and nothing was more dangerous than attempting to fire a rifle with a mud-blocked muzzle. Not that this was the men's prime motivation—their soldiering had by now become more professional, and a rifle well looked after was a mark of pride just as much as the opposite was an object of apoplectic fury to the platoon sergeant! None must have kept this more vividly in mind than Cpl Tom Mayson. As a private, on 2 June 1916, the day after his return to the battalion after treatment for rheumatic fever in England, he was awarded ten days' Field Punishment No. 1 for having a dirty rifle and telling the inspecting officer that he had cleaned it. This cannot have been held over his head for too long, however, since he was promoted to Lance Corporal just over a month later, and full Corporal after Guillemont. Just to add a little incentive to their efforts at Mametz, the men were told that they would be inspected by the RSM the next day on the 20th. In any British Army unit, then and now, the RSM is a mighty individual, answerable only to God and the Colonel, and woe betide any man or junior officer who upset him—captains and majors know better! More bivouac materials arrived and the QM was able to scrounge a few tents. The OC, who had been warned that the battalion's next move would likely be an attack at Flers, sent a reconnaissance party of officers to examine the approach to Flers from Mametz. Heavy bombardment interrupted the mission and the officers had to return, but they were able to complete it the following day.

21 September saw 600 men, virtually the entire strength of the battalion, engaged in working parties either in the communication trenches or carrying stores forward. The next day, another similarly sized working party was sent to Longueval, but as there was no requirement for a night-time carrying party, the OC authorised a generous rum ration for all ranks. It was delivered in distinctive jars bearing the initials 'SRD', which men joked stood for 'Seldom Reaches Destination', and was one of the war's great comforts. Issued at the discretion of the commanding officer, it was the great panacea for cold, aching, and fed-up troops, although some teetotal commanders withheld it from their men—luckily, these were the exception. The next morning, after they had recovered from the previous night's rum, the men were paraded and their smoke helmets checked. With the increased use of both poison and lachrymatory gas, this was a vital precaution, and helmets found lacking in effectiveness were swiftly replaced. Further training in the use of both Lewis guns and grenades was carried out in the knowledge of their importance in the forthcoming attack. Even during this time of need for experienced soldiers, the battalion was still losing men to munitions work, and on the 22nd, thirty-year-old Millom ironworker Sgt Thomas Crellin was claimed by his civilian employers and left France to return to his wife and two young children.

Battle casualties, sickness, and recalls to munitions work had taken their toll, such that there were no longer enough men to field four fighting companies. Consequently, on 24 September, the battalion was reorganised into just two companies, No. 1 and No. 2. At 5 p.m. they left one half company at a time to take over the reserve trenches, and by 11 p.m. were established. No. 2 Company was positioned in King's Walk and No. 1 in Green Trench, both a couple 100 m north-east of Delville Wood. Tanks had been deployed there for the first time ten days earlier, and had assisted a considerable advance of the forward line; the German front line now ran roughly along the line of the road from Miraumont to Warlencourt and Le Barque. As usual, reserve trenches did not fail to attract German artillery and No. 2 Company, in the foremost of the battalion's two trenches, suffered most of the casualties the next day. Nineteen-year-old Pte William Carradus died from his wounds a couple of days later, and twenty-five-year-old Pte

Alfred Burns—a pre-war member from Ulverston, who was to spend six months in hospital before his eventual recovery—was subsequently commissioned into the Labour Corps. Also lost to the battalion was thirty-one-year-old Bernard Winstanley, shot through both thighs by a shrapnel ball. The former warehouse clerk from Lancaster received a medical discharge and a 30-per-cent pension after the end of the war. While both companies manned the reserve trenches, some platoon commanders went forward to reconnoitre the lines of approach to Flers, just under a mile to the north. The reconnaissance had gone smoothly until, just as they got back into the support trenches, a bursting shell wounded thirty-four-year-old 2Lt Tom Beazley so severely that he would still be in a convalescent home for officers three years later.

55 Division was back on the offensive as part of a general offensive by the Fourth Army along its whole front. The division had two objectives on 25 September.[26] Firstly, to take Gird Trench and Gird Support Trench from south of Guedecourt, where they were cut by the sunken road from Flers to Guedecourt called 'Pilgrims' Way' (50° 3′ 16.52″ N, 2° 50′ 21.85″ E); and then northwards to their junction with another sunken road running north from Factory Corner, a stretch of about 1 mile (50° 3′ 57.25″ N, 2° 49′ 38.93″ E) [Points 'A' to 'B' on Guedecourt Sector map below]. Factory Corner itself (50° 3′ 43.83″ N, 2° 49′ 29.05″ E) was to be captured by 1/ Canterbury Regiment of the New Zealand Division, to 55 Division's left. The second objective for the day was to wheel to the right and then seize the sunken road between the divisional boundary to the west of Guedecourt as far as, but not including, Factory Corner [Points 'C' to 'D' on Guedecourt Sector map below]. The attack, carried out by three of the King's Liverpool battalions of 165 Brigade, was a great success. The men had kept so close to the creeping barrage that the Germans were caught in their dugouts before they were able to deploy their MGs. By 6.30 p.m., it was realised that 21 Division (to 55 Division's right) had not been able to capture Guedecourt, which left 55's flank exposed, forcing 1/7th King's to build strongpoints. They and 1/6th King's received reinforcements from their reserve battalion, 1/5 King's.

The 26th was dedicated to consolidating gains and keeping the enemy on the back foot. Developments to 55 Division's right that day show just how far British infantry tactics had advanced since 1915. Bombers and two companies of 7/ Leicestershires from 110 Brigade moved up Pilgrim Way and then along Gird Trench in a southerly direction, supporting a single tank which drove along the edge of the trench, driving the Germans before it. As the enemy fled across open ground a British observation aircraft called in accurate artillery fire, and after signalling to the artillery to cease, flew low along the ranks of the Germans, raking then with MG fire, whereupon 370 of them promptly surrendered. British casualties amounted to five. This type of inter-arm cooperation would be further evolved by the end of the war.

On 26 September, the German bombardment intensified and two men, twenty-year-old Pte Harry Evans from Barrow and previously shell-shocked Pte Ernest Grey, were both killed instantly. Pte Thomas Varcoe from Dalton received multiple shrapnel wounds and was taken to 31 CCS, where he died two days later. The eighteen-year-old had nearly been posted to 8/ King's Own six days earlier, but the move had been cancelled at the last moment and he had remained with the battalion. Surviving records show that four other soldiers were wounded that day, though there were almost certainly more. Cpl Tom Mayson was hit in the hand by a shrapnel ball and spent three weeks in hospital before re-joining. Twenty-four-year-old Pte Percy Miller from Blackpool received minor wounds, but was patched up and back in the trenches less than two weeks later, although—and most unusually for someone with no mining background—he was this time attached to 177 Tunnelling Company.

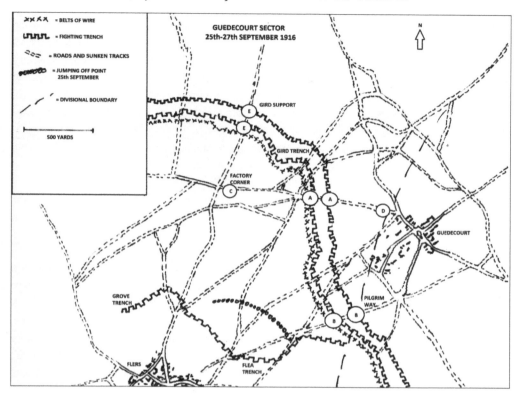

Fortunately for the battalion, this excellent soldier returned to them in December of that year. Twenty-five-year-old Ulverston blacksmith Pte George Gill, one of the witnesses to Pte Joseph Royle's accident, was evacuated with shell shock for the second time in three months and also attached to 177 Tunnelling Company upon his recovery. Another shell shock casualty for the second time was Pte William Waters, though he too would recover after a week's rest and soldier on in the trenches for the rest of the war; he became a sniper in January 1917, rising to Corporal and post-war to Sergeant.

27 September saw a renewal of the attack as Gen. Rawlinson, Commander of the Fourth Army, was anxious to exploit the previous day's advantage. In conjunction with the New Zealand Division, 164 Brigade was to take the Gird trenches northwards from Factory Corner, to where they were cut by the Ligny–Tilloy Road. (Points 'A' to 'E' on the sketch map.) The 1/4th was tasked with the fifth wave of this attack and at 9.45 p.m. on the 26th was ordered forwards, with Maj. Balfour back in command after his stay in hospital. Three platoons of No. 1 Company occupied the strongpoints at the end of Grove Alley, 600 metres north-west of Flers, and No 2. Company plus one platoon from No. 1 Company occupied Smoke Trench, east of Grove Alley—well-positioned to act in support against a German counter-attack on any gains made. Grove Alley was still choked with Germans killed in the day's preliminary bombardment or by grenades and bayonets when 1/9th King's stormed the trench. The men of the 1/4th had no choice but to clamber over the corpses to reach their position. But they needn't have worried; the expected counter-attacks never materialised, as the Germans were facing severe shortages of manpower and had no spare troops to make another play for control (either west of Guedecourt or further south at Lesboeufs).

As it turned out, the Liverpool Irish captured their objective without difficulty. In the morning of the 27th, 110 men and three officers from 1/4th King's Own carried stores forward for the RE to construct strongpoints in Gird Support Trench. This was completed successfully without a single casualty. At 2.30 p.m., these men were again detached and placed in a position to the right of the battalion at Factory Corner. The Germans may not have had the men to counter-attack, but their artillery was still a force to be reckoned with and the trenches the battalion occupied came under heavy and sustained bombardment. Eight men were killed outright by the shellfire, including young Pte Alfred Downham who had had such a narrow escape two days after joining the battalion earlier that month. Luck also ran out for Pte Harry Fryer, another of the casualties from earlier that month; he is the only one killed that day who has a known grave. The other fatalities were Cpl Thomas Balderson from Barrow, Pte John Griffiths from Hollinwood, Pte John Hodgson from Ulverston, Pte Samuel Hough from Bolton, Pte James McGowan from Oldham, and Pte Randolph Houghton from Bolton, not long recovered from his wounds from Guillemont. They are all commemorated on the Thiepval Memorial. Arthur White, promoted to Corporal after returning from hospital after his previous wound, had another lucky escape when a shrapnel ball wounded him in the right eyelid, narrowly missing the eyeball and resulting in a fortnight's stay in hospital. With shrapnel piercing his left wrist and acute shell shock, twenty-year-old Pte Thomas Ashton from Barrow was evacuated home and upon his return to fitness went back to Vickers for the duration of the war. Another of the wounded, Pte Edward Wright, was also claimed back by the munitions industry upon his recovery; he returned to the Barrow Haematite Mines after recuperating from a shrapnel wound to the buttocks. Former Cook-Sergeant, but now Private in a Lewis Gun team, twenty-seven-year-old married man from Preston Robert Fenton was another shell shock victim, fatally wounded the next day either at the ADS or on his way back to the battalion (his records show he never reached the battalion). He died from a shrapnel wound to the thigh at 26 General Hospital, Étaples, on 26 October. Twenty-three-year-old Pte Harry Garstang from Barrow received multiple shrapnel wounds and after his eventual recovery in England was transferred to the RE. Twenty-eight-year-old Cpl William Hinds was wounded in the left hand by shrapnel, but fortunately for the 1/4th was back within two days; this mature and experienced soldier was to prove a strength in months to come.

At 2 a.m. on 28 September, the battalion moved forward to take over Gird Trench and Gird Support Trench from the Liverpool Irish and spent the day under heavy bombardment again. A German working party was spotted in the early hours, and three patrols armed with Lewis guns were sent into No Man's Land in the hope of harassing them—without success, as the enemy returned to their own lines by the time the patrols got out. One of the Lewis-gunners, twenty-three-year-old Pte Phillip Baines, impressed his commanders and was given a MiD for his ability and resourcefulness in handling his gun on the 27th and 28th, as well as for his work on patrols and raids. Baines was in fact recommended for the DCM, but this was not awarded, so the MiD in the King's Birthday Honours was a form of consolation. Possibly more rewarding for the young private was the extra pay that he received with his first stripe.[27]

Between 2 a.m. on the 28th and 2 a.m. on the 29th (when the battalion was relieved by the Royal West Surreys), thirteen of its men were killed by shellfire and a further five would die over the following days and weeks from wounds received in that twenty-four-hour period. There is only one surviving service record for men wounded on this day—that of twenty-eight-year-old Arthur Parkinson from Lancaster, who had joined the battalion nineteen days earlier. He was hit in the buttocks by shrapnel and evacuated home; another who would never return to the Front, he was transferred to an Agricultural Company of the Labour Corps after his convalescence. One of those killed in the shelling was L/Cpl John Riley, who had been awarded the MC for helping to save men trapped in a collapsed tunnel a year earlier. Around midnight on the 28th, the battalion sent a small raiding party out to bomb the enemy front trenches. Two brothers, John and Robert Postlethwaite were part of this group, but when they returned, twenty-seven-year-old L/Cpl Robert Postlethwaite wasn't with them. He was never seen again.

If the wartime overall 2.3:1 ratio of wounded to killed were to be made, it's possible to estimate casualties for this one day 'holding the line', as just over sixty men from a battalion that was under half strength to begin with—quite a price to pay. The wounded all needed to be looked after, and the MO continued to treat them as shells rocked the RAP.[28] Stretcher bearers who braved the fire to bring in the wounded, like twenty-three-year-old Pte James Kitchin, were much appreciated by their patients. He and battalion runner twenty-one-year-old L/Cpl Thomas Jackson were both honoured for their devotion to duty and coolness under fire with a MiD in the King's Birthday Honours for 1917.[29] Only one of them would return home at the end of the war.

Killed or died from wounds received on 28 and 29 September 1916

| Pte Percy Allen | 201688 | KIA-29/9 | Cpl Edward Wilson Barrow | 200618 | KIA-28/9 |
|---|---|---|---|---|---|
| Pte Fred Fittes | 200761 | DOW-28/9 | Pte Robert Edward Fenton | 3269 | DOW-19/10 |
| Pte Thomas Hesketh | 4936 | KIA-28/9 | Pte William Hutton | 3093 | DOW-11/10 |
| Pte George Liddell | 201295 | KIA-29/9 | Pte Richard Noble | 2960 | KIA-28/9 |
| L/Cpl Robert Francis Postlethwaite | 201675 | KIA-28/9 | | 2188 | DOW-29/9 |
| | | | L/Cpl John Riley | | |
| Pte William Rowlandson | 2897 | DOW-2/10 | Pte James Simm | 201655 | KIA-28/9 |
| Pte Harry Smith | 4978 | DOW-30/9 | L/Cpl William John Strode | 201650 | KIA-28/9 |
| Pte William Swarbrick | 201694 | KIA-29/9 | Pte Herbert Burrow Symons | 3002 | DOW-14/10 |
| Pte John Walmsley | 5027 | KIA-28/9 | Pte Allen Gordon Wilson | 200626 | KIA-28/9 |
| L/Cpl John Wilson | 3003 | KIA-28/9 | | | |

The relief of leaving the trench line will have been tempered by arduous marches through liquid communication trenches, and thence over ground either churned up by shells or trampled into a slippery quagmire by millions of marching feet. On top of this, the men knew only too well that the German guns had all the lines of march well-registered and shelled these as a matter of routine by night. Still, the further away from the Front they got, the safer they were. The route to their allotted billets in Mametz took them past the shattered stumps of Delville Wood, and through the smear of brick-coloured sludge that was once the village of Longueval. Once on the roads, the going was easier but much more congested, and the battalion was soon strung out in the traffic over a considerable distance. Their transport had gone ahead to Mametz and the QM Lt Crossley was delighted when he was allocated a tented bivouac for the battalion, for these were deemed a rare indulgence at the time. Consider his consternation when a battalion of New Zealand infantry decided that they were going to usurp this bivouac, totally ignoring his protests. They descended upon him, 'like the Assyrians of old, or the plague of locusts, and take possession,' he fumes in his memoirs; 'Protests from a mere Quartermaster of infantry were met with airy nonchalance.'[30]

Fortunately, Crossley was made of more determined stuff than the Kiwis took him for and, leaping astride his trusty steed 'Olivette', he galloped off to brigade HQ to summon the cavalry. A short time later, he was heartily glad to see the intruders march out of the bivouac in one direction as the 1/4th marched in from the other, blissfully unaware of the narrow escape they'd had and desperate for rest and sleep. Exactly twelve hours after they'd left the trenches, they were on the march again, this time back to Dernancourt, where four hours later, they were squeezed into densely crowded billets. The 30th was spent cleaning up and the men's kit was inspected, after which orders arrived for a move by train away from the Somme! At this point, many who had been sick but had clung on in the trenches for the sake of their pals or their men reported to the MO and were sent to hospital—including Capt. Brocklebank and Lt Albert Park. The last two months had dealt the battalion serious casualties, with a total of 588 men killed, wounded, or missing in action, plus a further nine accidentally wounded— and this without taking into account those ailing from sickness. The 1/4th, however, was not the worst off in the brigade—this solemn credential fell to the Liverpool Irish, who had 1,195 casualties. In total, 164 Brigade suffered 3,167 casualties, and 55 Division as a whole 7,836.[31]

As always, lessons learned in battle and potential tweaks to divisional efficiency were assessed, and unlike the vast majority of military paperwork around these events, documents from a divisional conference held after the fighting in the Somme have survived.[32] Training was high on Maj.-Gen. Jeudwine's agenda; he recognised that much still needed to be done to improve the fighting efficiency of his troops. It was debated whether instructional schools ought to be set up at brigade or divisional level (or both) for bombing, signalling, sniping, and trench mortars. The ongoing training of officers was seen as a task for individual COs, though COs were sounded out as to whether an instructional school for young officers was desirable at both army and divisional level. Infantry fighting was discussed, and COs were reminded that the rifle and bayonet were the infantryman's primary weapons, though the continuing emphasis placed on bayonet training was questioned. Marksmanship was still thought to need constant practice; to develop a better standard of rapid and accurate fire, every battalion was urged to construct a thirty-yard range where soldiers could practise while standing in a trench. There was a suggestion that the snipers regularly competed against each other as a way to raise the standards. The use of indirect fire by Lewis guns was brought up, as was the desirability of training to fight in the open and not just from trenches. There had been issues in the recent battles derived from the troops' inexperience in attacking while wearing their smoke helmets, and this had to be rectified. The difficulties of maintaining communications between attacking infantry and artillery was also a pressing topic, as was the need to practise signalling both in the trenches and when battalions were on the move. Procedures for affiliation with both artillery and RE were to be honed, and further instruction to transport officers provided.

Various elements of life in the trenches came under scrutiny at the Mametz assessment. Maj.-Gen. Jeudwine was obviously unhappy with the quality of the barbed wire defences and the thickness of parapets, which was no doubt brought up in the face of an impending move back to breastworks. Officers were to be given training in the supervision of working parties, and the hours worked and weights carried by men on these was from now on to be strictly regulated. Officers would also get training in trench engineering by the divisional commander of the RE. The welfare of the men both in and out of the line was not neglected, and every soldier's feet were examined daily in the billets, and not just when they were in the line. The importance of baths, recreation room, canteens, and coffee bars in billets was emphasized; the morale-boosting properties of battalion bands and the divisional theatre company stressed.

# 6

# 1 October 1916 – 30 June 1916
# The Salient

At 1.30 p.m. on 1 October, the battalion entrained for Longpré-les-Corps-Saints; on the next evening, onwards to Hopoutre, where they arrived at 6.30 a.m. on the 3rd, and were immediately marched to billets in Poperinghe for baths and a general clean-up. Nine hours later, they were joined by the 100 men unlucky enough to have been in the fatigue party detailed to load the brigade equipment into a train at Longpré. Hopoutre was a railway siding for men and supplies bound for Poperinghe, built when it was decided that using Poperinghe Station for the movement of large numbers of troops and munitions was too dangerous, as it was a well-registered target for German long-range artillery. Hopoutre ('hop out!') was jestingly given a faux-Flemish, in the same vein as Bandaginghem, Mendinghem, and Dosinghem, three famous military hospitals in the Salient. Although nothing remains of Hopoutre, the site may be found approximately 0.6 miles along the N333 from the roundabout with the N38 after leaving Poperinghe (50° 50′ 24.73″ N, 2° 42′ 17.68″ E).

At noon on 4 October, the whole battalion was marched off to O Camp (50° 51′ 58.97″ N, 2° 47′ 13.67″ E), about 2 miles north-east of Poperinghe, which was to be its home for the next ten days. O Camp's virtually new wooden huts were a major improvement in accommodation standards for men who had been roughing it for months. They trained, built strongpoints, and revetted trenches, though there were also the inevitable inspections, drills, route marches, and PT to go through; and on the nights of both the 7th and the 8th, up to 200 men were requisitioned as digging parties at the Front. From the scores of boards warning either 'Wind Dangerous' or 'Wind Safe', it was clear that gas was a greater element of danger here than they had previously experienced, and the necessary training was not omitted.

Although some replacements had been allocated to the 1/4th, it had not yet recovered its full capacity, particularly with regard to junior officers, and preserved its organisation into two companies. When not occupied with military duties, officers visited Poperinghe, enjoying the facilities of the Toc H Club, or for the younger officers, Skindle's and Kiki's restaurants, where the atmosphere was altogether livelier and the fresh seafood a sumptuous treat after two years of Army fare. For their entertainment, ORs sought out the numerous estaminets and cafes. The off-duty venues of officers and men were strictly segregated, the only two exceptions being the Toc H itself and official leisure activities organised by battalion or division, such as 55 Division's Concert Party, which performed in Poperinghe every night while the brigade was there and was much acclaimed by all ranks.

This could not last, however. At 5.15 p.m. on 14 October, the battalion marched the mile to Brandhoek Station and entrained for Ypres, arriving at 7.30 p.m., whereupon No. 1 Company was billeted in the Ramparts and No. 2 in the School (50° 50′ 57.75″ N, 2° 54′ 6.91″ E), about half way

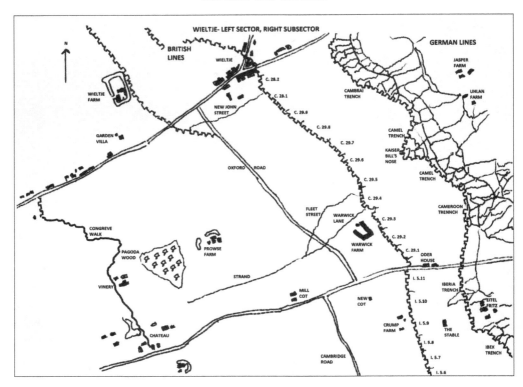

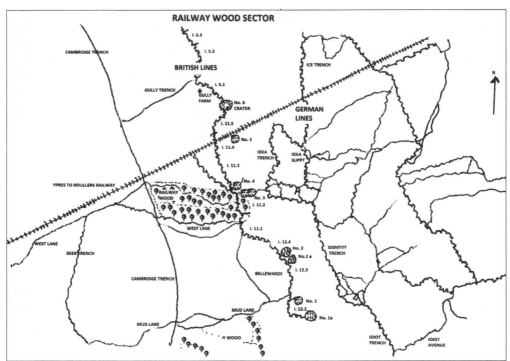

between the Menin Gate and Hellfire Corner (50° 50′ 54.46″ N, 2° 55′ 1.22″ E). The devastation of this once impressive town made its mark on members of the battalion, not least the QM:

> Of all the ghostly and melancholy ruins along the Western Front Ypres stands out almost unchallenged.... The deplorable ruin of its once beautiful structure bore evidence of the cost of its retention.... I have known no more eerie feeling than that experienced when crossing this desolate square on a quiet night.[1]

At 6.30 p.m. the next day, the battalion moved off one platoon at a time; No. 1 Company was to take over the trenches in the left sub-sector of the right sector (Railway Wood, 50° 51′ 12.92″ N, 2° 56′ 6.27″ E), while one half of No. 2 was in support and the other half in reserve. This was a far from ideal situation, but numbers were still so low in the front line that there was no choice but to draw men from No. 2 Company to man it effectively. In places such as the eastern tip of Railway Wood, the trenches there were less than 25 yards apart and men from both sides kept quiet for fear of drawing fire. To the battalion's right was a large gap. The last connected outpost was in the British-held No. 1a Crater (50° 51′ 3.95″ N, 2° 56′ 16.73″ E). The line continued to the south of the Ypres–Hooge Road, some 700 yards away, where the trenches were held by New Zealanders. In this gap, a series of small posts known as the 'Grouse Butts' were patrolled by sections and manned by Lewis teams at night. As with any position, these posts needed to be regularly visited by the duty officer, a hazardous task; Capt. Gardner had one such close call when he was 'captured' by the battalion on the right flank, and had to be taken back to their HQ so that his credentials could be checked. Fortunately for him, the patrol had asked questions before opening fire.

Despite a dozen trench mortar rounds hitting the trenches on 16 October, there were no casualties, and at 6.30 p.m. the next day the companies exchanged places. A combination of the previous day's mortar fire and heavy rain since that morning meant that men from neither company got much rest, the trenches being in such a state of disrepair. Although the morning of 18 October started off quietly, more enemy trench mortars smashed the trench in three different locations, possibly in retaliation for the battalion snipers' three hits the previous day. One of the company cookhouses took a direct hit from a trench mortar round. Twenty-eight-year-old Grange grocer Pte Joseph Gibson was killed instantly, and another soldier wounded. One of his NCOs wrote to Gibson's mother,

> Your son Joe was killed about 5 p.m. on October 18th. I was with him at the time and had a narrow escape myself. He has been my chum for a long time out here and I have never had a better. He has always been as a brother to me. There was not a better soldier in the battalion and everybody feels his loss. A piece of trench mortar struck his shoulder and must have touched his heart, as he was killed outright and suffered no pain and was not disfigured in any way.[2]

After another day of heavy rain on the 19th, the battalion was relieved and returned to its billets between the Menin Gate and Hellfire Corner, to be welcomed there by that great delight of the British soldier, a steaming hot mug of tea. Although it spent the next three days out of the line, the entire battalion was on working parties, leaving no time for training even though twelve new officers had joined. The front-line trenches and the dugouts at Railway Wood were in need of constant repair, and the awkward and laden journeys there and back hellish for troops. A long communication trench, West Lane (50° 51′ 1.45″ N, 2° 54′ 27.83″ E), began a mere ¼ mile from the School Billet and meandered its way eastwards until it joined the front line at Railway Wood. For the southern part of this sector, about 200 m from Railway Wood, a turning to the right was made into Beek Trench (50° 51′ 5.88″ N, 2° 56′ 13.52″ E), which worked its way around a natural rise in the ground before becoming Mud Lane and Mud Trench and ½ mile later ending at the extreme right section of front-line trench. Beek Trench had been Mud Trench, but was renamed so as not to demoralise new arrivals to the sector! For once, no one in the working parties was killed or wounded, though news filtered through of the death of one of their sergeants wounded at an earlier date. Twenty-two-year-old Sgt Francis Redman from Ulverston had received light wounds when the rifle he had been holding was blown to pieces at Guillemont, but had then been wounded again, possibly on 28 September, and died in hospital in Étaples on 23 October.[3] On their last day out of the line, the battalion was once again divided into four companies, and half the battalion and HQ moved to billets in Ypres Prison, which although clean and dry was also freezing (50° 51′ 8.11″ N, 2° 52′ 42.08″ E).

For their next spell at the front beginning on 23 October, the battalion occupied the trenches in the right sub-sector of the left sector. This stretch ran from Wieltje (50° 52′ 17.64″ N, 2° 55′ 14.02″ E) across the Ypres–Verlorenhoek Road (50° 51′ 51.28″ N, 2° 55′ 45.39″ E) until it met up with the trenches of Railway Wood. Although the approaches to this trench line were marginally better than the right sector, the trenches themselves were in a dismal condition. A and B Company manned the forward trenches, while C was divided between a number of posts. The water had risen over the level of the trench boards, so everyone wore gumboots; the trenches had to be deepened and the water pumped out; and establishing a drainage system became a priority. The high water table in the Salient meant that trenches could not be dug to the depth that the battalion had enjoyed on the Somme, so a shallow trench was augmented by breastworks of sandbags similar to the defences at Estaires. The excavated area of these trenches still needed timber supports and the revetting in them strengthening to prevent further subsidence. D Company, which occupied the support line, was delegated as the 'carrying company', and thus bore the brunt of the backbreaking work involved in trench improvement; it carried timber, nails, wire, rations, and other supplies to the line. After dark, working parties crept out into No Man's Land and reinforced the barbed wire defences. Patrols went out into No Man's Land each night, though no enemy patrols were encountered on these excursions.

German artillery frequently shelled either the front or support lines, mostly without effect, but on 25 October, a bombardment which began at 9.30 a.m. and lasted until 1 p.m. wounded five, one of whom was gravely hit in the head by shrapnel. Twenty-one-year-old Pte James Rowell from Barrow was evacuated to No. 3 Canadian CCS in Lijssenthoek, but died from the resulting infection exactly a month later. In the days before antibiotics, a penetrating wound often attracted infection and was dealt with by amputation; however, this was no option for wounds to the head, so these were often fatal. The filthy conditions at the Front; the time it took to actually get the casualty to a CCS, which in mid-battle was sometimes days and long after septicaemia or gangrene had set in; and the difficulty of actually cleaning out the interior of certain wounds—all of these factors, in spite of the best attentions of medical staff, resulted in copious deaths and amputations. Twenty-four-year-old Pte John Robinson from Caton was evacuated home with shrapnel wounds to his left arm, and although his arm recovered, he had been suffering from trench nephritis at the time of injury. This occasioned his medical discharge in April 1917, the deterioration of his health thereafter, and his eventual death on 27 September 1921—just missing the cut-off point for recognition by the CWGC by four weeks.

By 8.15 p.m. on 27 October, the battalion had been relieved; conditions were so bad that men came out of the line still wearing their gumboots for the march back to their billets in the Ypres Prison. On the 30th, the men marched to Elverdinghe, where C and D Company were billeted at the chateau, and A and B occupied three of the defensive 'L' Posts (L2, L4 and L8) west of the town. Until the entire battalion moved back to Ypres on 7 November, companies rotated between the three L posts and worked around the chateau. Much sweat was expended by working parties involved in the detested task of scraping mud off the roads, yet the battalion still managed to find time to train. Elverdinghe was within range of German heavy artillery, but even though a few rounds landed around the chateau during their stay, the battalion remained casualty-free. At 5.15 p.m. on 8 November, it relieved the Liverpool Irish near Railway Wood. D Company was positioned to the left of the firing line and C to the right; A and B were in support; and one platoon of B occupied the Grouse Butts.

On the morning of 9 November, about fifty trench mortar and 77-mm shells fell along the line, blowing in the parapet in half a dozen places, but remarkably causing no casualties. West Lane was hit by a rapid barrage of a dozen 77-mms, all concentrated on a small area about half way along its route through Railway Wood. Fortunately, no one was traversing the trench when this occurred! Things relaxed the next day, and the men were able to repair the damaged parapets without interference, despite a few 5.9s hit between the start of Junction Trench and Section I 11.1 (50° 51′ 11.81″ N, 2° 56′ 6.37″ E), where the front line exited Railway Wood. Trench sections in the Salient were given a number to help reference their location based on their large grid square—in this case, 'I'—the sub-square—in this case, '11' —and then individually numbered—in this case, '1'. A trench map reveals that the shells on the 9th all landed within a ten yard radius of the above position (50° 51′ 11.67″ N, 2° 56′ 6.40″ E).

On 11 November, the Germans targeted Section I 11.1 once more. Trench mortars blew in the parapet in two places, and almost completely flattened the 100-m stretch between I 11.1 and Crater No. 2, the nearest of the four British-held craters south of the wood. The mortaring did stop once British howitzers targeted their firing positions, a tactic that both sides employed effectively and one reason why the trench mortars of one's own side were almost as unpopular with the infantry as the enemy's mortars! In the early hours of the morning, C and D Company sent patrols out to reconnoitre the German saps which projected into No Man's Land. These patrols got close enough to see torches flashing, hear working parties in the saps, and, still unobserved, retire back their own lines to report.

On 12 November, the battalion was relieved by the Loyals and marched back to billets in Ypres—A and B Company in the Ramparts, C in the School, and D in a billet new to the battalion, one of the four Hornworks. The 1/4th remained in Ypres until 18 November, but all the men were most days on working parties at some point. On the 17th, twenty-five-year-old Pte James Holgate was wounded by shrapnel in the left knee on one such working party, and evacuated home. After leaving hospital he was posted to 1/ King's Own and killed with them in September 1918. At 5.15 p.m. on 18 November, the battalion began the trudge back up to the line to relieve 1/5th South Lancashires. With each half-company spaced 100 yards apart, passing through the Menin Gate was a tense operation; this was a regular target for German artillery, a choke point, but it could not easily be avoided. But on that evening, 'Lady Luck' favoured the battalion. It made it through, and was again deployed south of Wieltje, with 7/ King's in Railway Wood and the Liverpool Irish to their left.

Unsurprisingly, the men were put straight onto trench repair, building 'U' frames and strengthening the sandbag revetting. There was some artillery activity by both sides and on 21 November three British shells landed directly in the German held Camel Trench, where it jutted out into No Man's Land opposite C 29.6., a position known as 'Kaiser Bill's Nose' (50° 52′ 6.26″ N, 2° 55′ 43.39″ E). Working on the trenches in daylight was extremely dangerous, as just a moment's carelessness could give a German sniper all the opportunity he needed and exactly this fate was suffered by twenty-seven-year-old married man, Sgt Thomas Edmondson. He was working in front of Crump Farm (50° 51′ 44.49″ N, 2° 55′ 46.81″ E) when a sniper thought to be located in Eitel Fritz (50° 51′ 45.17″ N, 2° 56′ 2.22″ E) killed him outright from a range of just over 300 m. Although Sgt Edmondson was the only sniper casualty that afternoon, others had close calls. Considering the shelling and constant patrol activity at night, there were few casualties during this period. One of these on 24 November was Capt. Frederick Slater, B Company's OC, who ended up in hospital badly bruised after being crushed by sandbags, when his HQ was destroyed by a trench mortar round at noon. Five hours later, the battalion was relieved and returned to billets in Ypres. Although they were out of the front line, aggressive actions continued and at 11.30 that night, the battalion sent out a patrol into No Man's Land. It encountered a strong German patrol; two men were wounded and another two missing. One of the wounded was twenty-three-year-old Pte William Fallows from Barrow, who with a gunshot wound to the abdomen was extremely lucky to survive; he played no further part in the war, receiving a medical discharge in 1918. Both of the missing, one of whom was twenty-one-year-old Pte Ernest Rimmer from Barrow, survived having been captured by the enemy patrol. Although the *War Diary* does not record this information, the patrol destination may have been Oder House, a ruined house half way between both lines regularly patrolled by both sides (50° 51′ 52.24″ N, 2° 55′ 52.01″ E).

On Saturday 25 November, 206 men were detailed to form a working party to bury cable near Machine Gun Farm (50° 51′ 16.80″ N, 2° 52′ 6.41″ E). Field telephones were the best method of communication between front and rear, but the cable was vulnerable to damage from shellfire, the movements of men, and wheeled traffic. The best way to protect this valuable resource was by burying it as deep as possible, sometimes 6 to 8 feet down. To give an understanding of just how demanding of labour this activity was, in 1917 alone the British buried 80,000 miles of field telephone cable.[4] Those not chosen for this detail were employed in a general clean-up. The next evening, the battalion entrained for Brandhoek then made the one-mile march back to the huts at O Camp, a welcome change from the billets in Ypres. Monday was spent cleaning equipment, themselves, and their billets prior to Tuesday's inspection by the CO, which was followed by musketry practice, drill, and specialist officer training from bombers or Lewis-gunners. At 7.15 a.m. on a cold and foggy Wednesday morning, the entire battalion paraded for PT; with Brig.-Gen. Stockwell due to inspect the billets at 9.15 a.m., I suspect many of the NCOs thought the time prior to this could have been better spent, especially as he was due to return the following day. After the inspection, the remainder of the morning was occupied by drill and saluting practice. The men were then allowed to watch the football match against a team from 1/4th Loyals in the afternoon, the first in a series of matches against other divisional units, although some forty men under Capt. 'Jat' Clarke were detached for a special task.

A large raid was planned for 23 December, and Clarke was to lead it. Preparations were meticulous: this working party would spend six out of the next seven days constructing a mock-up of their objective and the area of No Man's Land between it and their jumping-off point, a ditch running in a north–south direction next to Oder House. In places they dug actual trenches, though mostly just marked an area with white tape. The day before the intended raid, all the men involved would be rested, but the two days preceding this would be taken up with intensive rehearsals. Their target was from the northern tip of the Iberia trench system (50° 51′ 50.53″ N, 2° 55′ 56.21″ E) northwards for 300 yards into Cameroon Trench (50° 51′ 59.04″ N, 2° 55′ 57.02″ E) and the Cameroon Support Trench. The objective was to kill as many Germans as possible, capture prisoners, and identify the German units holding this trench. Artillery cooperation had been just as carefully arranged, with a complex system of coordination. Their task was to cut the wire in front of Cameroon and Cameroon Support Trench, and damage and destroy Cameroon Trench and Cameroon Reserve.[5]

Most of the nineteen days out of the line had been spent in rigorous training and the skills of the men, recent replacements in particular, had been considerably enhanced, in that non-specialists nonetheless received bomber and Lewis gun instruction. As might be expected, the training was in addition to, and not instead of, working parties. No fatalities occurred on these working parties, but some men were wounded. Pte William Robinson from Barrow was hit (for the third time) on 2 December in the arm, leg, and side by shrapnel, and evacuated home on 5 January. On 14 December, the battalion returned to Railway Wood to relieve the Loyals.

December in the Salient was usually wet and cold and this year was no different. Torrential rain made conditions in the trenches miserable and in places the forward trenches were all but impassable. As ever, the men were constantly occupied, repairing 'U' frames and rebuilding sagging sandbag parapets. The worst trench section was a 100-yard stretch that connected the southern edge of Railway Wood to Crater No. 2, a section regularly targeted by the enemy and prone to flooding. At night, wiring parties crept out into No Man's Land and got through sixty-three coils in just two days. Throughout the day of the 15th, artillery plagued the battalion, and HQ was on the receiving end of much of it, one shell landing next to the cookhouse and wounded two of the officers' servants. At around 4 p.m., the front line was battered by mortars, and British artillery (including a 12-inch gun) and the brigade TMB retaliated immediately. Shortly before 4.30 p.m., a red SOS rocket was fired from the battalion's right, and both sides' artillery worked to a crescendo, only ceasing at 5.20 p.m. This exchange of steel caused further damage to the trench line and Mud Lane was blown in for about 30 yards. Crater No. 1 also received a number of direct hits, in which two men were wounded: one was twenty-seven-year-old Pte John Clough from Lancaster, with the battalion for only nine days; the other man suffered shell shock.

Conditions in the trenches were especially tough on some of the battalion's older members, as records of those evacuated for rheumatism, myalgia, or heart complaints indicate. The battalion tried to put such men into jobs which were kinder on them. One such was Pte William Birch, a miner and father of four from Chorley who lied about his age upon enlistment, and was actually approaching his forty-fourth birthday when they sent him away onto a cooking course on 18 December—you've got to hope that he at least got a good Christmas dinner! Shortly after his return in January, he was posted to divisional road control and remained there until December 1918.[6] Not even the young were exempt, however, and the winter of 1916 saw a peak in sickness from all ages. More men on the sick list meant that more pressure on those still fit, which in turn led to more sickness—and thus went on this vicious circle. Concern that soldiers ending up in hospital may be posted elsewhere upon their recovery did not ease the strain, either. Saul Cohen was posted to 8/ King's Own when he left hospital and severely injured by multiple shrapnel wounds to jaw, left wrist, and both feet in May 1917. The young soldier was treated in the same Manchester hospital he'd worked at as a civilian, and underwent the amputation of one of his feet and partial amputation of the other.[7] After the previous day's hectic artillery exchanges, 16 December was much calmer. The men set about trench repairs and revetting, as well as a new dugout and cookhouse in the support lines to replace those destroyed.

There was considerable mining activity around Railway Wood, and seven craters in the 500-m stretch of trenches between the northern tip of Railway Wood and Crater No. 2a. (A later trench map shows no fewer than eighteen!) These had been occupied by one side or the other, and subsequently integrated into their trench system as advanced though somewhat vulnerable positions jutting into No Man's Land. Getting to a new crater first was always crucial, as the lip nearest to the opposition often gave a superior tactical position, and good infantry units in the trenches always had a consolidation party on alert for such an occurrence. At 5.55 a.m. on 17 December, the Germans exploded a small mine near the entrance to Crater No. 2a, partially burying the personnel from No. 3 Lewis team. The OC immediately called out the consolidation party and secured the crater, freeing the partially buried men and gun. The Germans had made no effort to occupy this and the charge—little bigger than a mortar round—suggested an endeavour to kill and demoralise, rather than an attempt to make any serious territorial or tactical gains. The damage was still considerable and in the early hours of the 18th, an additional sixty men were drawn from support companies to help repair it and further strengthen the wire in front of the crater. By 8 p.m. on the 18th, the battalion were back in billets in Ypres, having been relieved by 1/5th King's. Patrol activity was maintained, and on the night of the 18th to 19th, 2Lt Tom Holdsworth's patrol came into contact with the enemy; he and one of his men were wounded.

For the officers and 200 men of the raiding party, these four days out of the line were occupied with rehearsals. Capt. 'Jat' Clarke had been given a free hand to select those going on the raid and picked the best men available. Every man from the remainder of the battalion was working at either the Potijze Château Dump (50° 51′ 42.88″ N, 2° 54′ 57.89″ E) or at 'X' Lines. After the final rehearsal on 20 December, the raiding party was inspected by none other than FM Sir Douglas Haig himself, and although the next day was supposed to be one of rest, sixty were claimed for a working party. Later that night, a special meal was laid out for the raiders in the large dining hall of the Prison, and after a couple of hours' sleep, they were woken at 1.30 a.m. of the 23rd and inspected. Unlike most military inspections, the inspecting officer was not on this occasion looking for shine—quite the opposite! The men blackened their hands and faces, removed badges, and no doubt underwent the 'rattle test' (being made to jump up and down to check that none of their equipment made a noise). Instead of rifles, they were armed with grenades, pistols, clubs, or bayonets, save for those acting as 'covering party', who had rifles and Lewis guns. In anticipation of casualties and their quickest possible treatment, the MO brought the RAP forward to the front line dugouts in C.29.2.

At 3.15 a.m., the men left in small groups for the ditch near Oder House and advanced once the barrage lifted at 5.25 a.m. to form a protective box around the target trenches. The raiders entered their respective objectives only to find them deserted. The bombardment had devastated the German trenches, but there was no one to capture, and no dead Germans to secure identification from. Their objectives unattainable, they began to fall back to British lines. Although the German trenches had been evacuated, the reaction from German defences was immediate. German in-depth defence allowed effective fire on No Man's Land from MG positions to the rear and sides, and German artillery responded, such that the raiders had to cross this maelstrom in both directions. The first groups came back at about 6. 45 a.m. and were treated to hot baths, clean uniforms, a good breakfast, and the rest of the day off, while the rest of the battalion worked in fatigue parties under the town-major. According to the *War Diary*, when the roll was called, two men were declared killed, another three missing (other records actually show six men noted killed in action), and thirty men wounded, five of whom later died from their wounds. Among the wounded were subalterns Henry Hart and Frederick Smith. It had been a costly morning, many of the best in the battalion now incapacitated. Pte Arthur Akred from Barrow, hit in the abdomen, died from his wounds at the CCS at Lijssenthoek on Christmas Day. The twenty-six-year-old father of three young children had been wounded on no less than four previous occasions and each time insisted on returning to his platoon.[8] Sgt Matthew Caddy, one of the battalion snipers, had got through up until then without a scratch, but that night a shell landed next to him, killing the young NCO outright (two weeks after his twenty-second birthday). His platoon commander, 2Lt George Topham, wrote to his parents: 'He was one of my best non-commissioned officers, had been promoted to sergeant because of his good work, and was held in great esteem by his men.'[9] Another to fall was twenty-four-year-old Pte Thomas Newby, whose younger brother Fred had been killed that September. Newby left a wife and a young child at home in order to join the colours. His platoon commander, 2Lt Harold Lauder, wrote,

A short time ago he came under my command as a sniper, and I am proud to tell you that he was one of the truest, most enduring and bravest fellows in the battalion. It is with such feelings as these that I write and ask you to mix with your grief the pride that only by such men as your husband has the British Army won such respect, not to say fear from the enemy.

His company commander, Capt. Alfred Procter, contributed his own condolences, too.

His loss is greatly regretted by his comrades and by the officers under whom he served, for he was a sterling good fellow, devoted to his duty and a splendid example to all. I personally feel his loss very deeply as I had marked him out for promotion. Only two nights before his loss, when I had a most dangerous patrol to do, I was delighted to have him with me as a sound, reliable man.[10]

One of the more seriously wounded was twenty-two-year-old L/Cpl James Little from Millom. He was shot in the left side of the abdomen and lay helpless in No Man's Land. His friend from Ulverston, Pte Cuthbert Whalley, had been the first man to reach the German trench, but was hit in the neck and thigh by shrapnel as he climbed the parapet. Undaunted, he refused help and encouraged the others on with shouts of 'Come on the Lions', before limping back towards British lines. Midway across No Man's Land, he found Little, heaved him onto his shoulders, and carried him back to British lines where stretcher-bearers took over. Only then did he accept treatment for his wounds. His friend died at Lijssenthoek the next day. For his courage, Whalley was recommended for—though did not receive—the MM. He had been part of a tightly knit Lewis gun team and had refused promotion several times, preferring to remain with his pals. He had been wounded three times previously, and had survived a number of close calls. Once, just after being sent forward to man a listening post, a shell landed on his gun team, who had remained behind, killing them all. He had become equally attached to his new team, who had gone over on the raid with him; when he left hospital in England, he refused the offer of the position as a Sergeant instructor at Oswestry in order to return to his team at the Front. Tragically, he was not posted back to his pals in the 1/4th, but diverted straight from Étaples to 8/ King's Own, killed in action with them two days after joining, on 12 May 1917.[11]

Twenty-one-year-old Pte Thomas Ashton from Ashton-under-Lyne was hit in the side. He had only been with the battalion for three months, but was obviously considered a decent soldier as he was included in the raiding party. The wound was fatal and he died at Lijssenthoek on Boxing Day. Cpl Fred Baxter from Ulverston was the last of the wounded to die. His right knee was smashed by a bullet, infection set in, and despite the amputation of his leg at No. 13 General Hospital in Boulogne, it spread too far and he died on the 8 January 1917. Although the raiders were able to take shelter as soon as they returned to British lines, the stretcher-bearers were not so fortunate. Theirs was an example of the utmost courage and sacrifice, as they searched No Man's Land time after time for the fallen. Carrying a wounded man on a stretcher over hard and level ground is no easy task, but doing this through deep mud while under fire takes gargantuan effort. Stretcher bearer Cpl Matthew Porter was recommended for a bar for the MM he had won at Guillemont, for once again repeatedly risking his life to save the wounded—it wasn't approved.[12] While his dugout shuddered under the concussion from enemy artillery, the MO had continued to work on the wounded, his coolness and courage an inspiration to all. For his work here and at Guedecourt on 27 and 28 September, he was awarded the MC.[13]

Nineteen-year-old Barrow riveter, Pte William Lunt was posted to 7/King's Own on his return to France and then transferred on to the RE. Another Barrow man, twenty-nine-year-old Pte Robert McKeron, was wounded for the third time, this time by shrapnel in his hand and posted to 8/ King's Own on his recovery, being wounded a further three times! Sgt Ernest Newham was evacuated to England with a wound to the back. The shrapnel ball was found to be lodged close to his heart and the surgeon advised against its removal. Ernest Newham recovered, but was posted to Africa to serve on attachment to the King's African Rifles. One of the wounded who did return after treatment in hospital in Edinburgh, was L/Cpl Gilbert Rorison. The eighteen-year-old had been wounded by a shrapnel ball which passed through his left arm, just missing the bone. This was his third wound and thankfully, his last.

Killed or died from wounds as a result of 23 December 1916

| Pte Arthur Akred | 2783 | DOW-25/12 | Pte Thomas Ashton | 4900 | DOW-26/12 |
|---|---|---|---|---|---|
| Cpl Fred Baxter | 3659 | DOW-8/1 | Sgt Matthew Caddy | 200124 | KIA-23/12 |
| Pte John Henry Clarke | 4062 | DOW-23/12 | L/Cpl William Douglas | 200438 | KIA-23/12 |
| Pte Walter Finch | 201388 | KIA-23/12 | Pte John Halligan | 200080 | KIA-23/12 |
| L/Cpl James Little | 2658 | DOW-24/12 | Pte James Millington | 201042 | KIA-23/12 |
| L/Cpl Thomas Henry Newby | 200719 | KIA-23/12 | | | |

Known to have been wounded on the 23 December 1916

| | | | | | | |
|---|---|---|---|---|---|---|
| Pte Joseph Atherton | 200855 | WIA-23/12 | | Cpl Robert Bell | 200707 | WIA-23/12 |
| 2Lt Henry Royston Hart | | WIA-23/12 | | Pte William J. Lunt | 201004 | WIA-23/12 |
| Pte Robert McKeron | 200662 | WIA-23/12 | | Sgt Ernest Lascelles Newham | 200945 | WIA-23/12 |
| L/Cpl Gilbert Rorison | 200337 | WIA-23/12 | | 2Lt Frederick James Smith | | WIA-23/12 |
| Pte Cuthbert Whalley | 200607 | WIA-23/12 | | | | |

Through no fault of the battalion's, the raid had failed. Later deliberation by Command decided that the enemy, alerted by the preliminary bombardment which had begun a week before the raid was due, had pulled their personnel back from the front line. Later raids would be more successful when guns fired a short, but devastating bombardment shortly before the raiders attacked, a tactic that was made possible because of changes in artillery procedure. Registered fire was when each individual gun fired single rounds until their shots landed on the target, and was very different from 'morning hate', which was when guns indiscriminately blasted the general area. So clearly distinguishable was gun registration that it was akin to sending an invitation to the enemy to join in the next attack! In early 1917, artillery developed methods for 'predicted fire' and also used 'offset registration', whereby a gun registered a nearby target and the necessary corrections were applied on the day—though this did give some measure of warning to the enemy and also betrayed the positions of guns to possible counter-battery fire.

At 7 p.m. on Christmas Eve, the battalion moved back into the front line near Potijze, with A Company holding the right of the line and B the left. The other two companies were further back, with C in Congreve Walk and D in 'X' Line. While there was no truce on Christmas Day, neither was there any hostile activity, and the day was spent raising the parapets and strengthening the weaker areas of the sandbag wall. The festive spirit did not last beyond Boxing Day, whereupon the Germans sent a few shells over, one of which wounded twenty-year-old Pte Thomas Bowes. The former shipyard worker from Barrow was evacuated home for treatment. Taking advantage of the low level of enemy activity, the work on strengthening the trenches and fire bays continued and dugouts were cleared of mud and generally improved. B Company also built a new company HQ in section C 29.5 (50° 52′ 3.08″ N, 2° 55′ 35.09″ E). In the five days spent at the front, the men had added considerable barbed wire in front of their positions, using 200 coils in just two sections of their line, C 29.1 and C 29.2. Once relieved by 1/5th South Lancashires, 1/4th King's Own marched back through Ypres to the Asylum and boarded a train to Brandhoek; they arrived there at 9. 30 p.m., then marched back to billets at O Camp.

29 December was spent cleaning and catching up with the various administrative tasks left to one side until the battalion was out of the line. One man who wasn't going to enjoy this period much was twenty-three-year-old Pte Ernest Preston from Barrow. He had incurred the wrath of authority for disobedience of an order and Lt-Col. Balfour sentenced him to twenty-one days' Field Punishment No. 1. The usual training and series of inspections took place over the next few days and on New Year's Eve a series of church parades for the various denominations were organised. Some were nevertheless selected for that day's working party, burying telephone cable at Vlamertinghe, for which all four company commanders and 200 men had been required.

1 January 1917 was that precious rarity for the battalion in billets—a holiday! Not so for those attached to the TMB. Two men from the King's Own were still in the thick of it. A trench mortar duel had broken out and the brigade's TMB was under heavy and constant fire. The OC of 164 TMB was Capt. Ernest Myatt, and one of the Stokes mortar commanders Sgt Robert Adamson, both from the 1/4th. Their coolness, courage, and skill inspired the men under their command and the award of the MC to Myatt, whose leadership in November 1916 was also commended, and the DCM to Adamson, soon to be promoted to CSM, were the first medals of the New Year.[14]

On 2 January, any residual effects from the alcohol were banished when each company took part in a 6-mile route march, remaining within an hour's march of O Camp in case of sudden deployment. On the march the men practised 'rapid solution problems', for example, the company commander would alert his officers to an attack from the right, and then watch to see how they controlled the situation. Two hundred men were needed for cable-laying at Vlamertinghe on the 3rd, but otherwise, up to the evening of 7 January, this was a period of training and equipment checks. Although most of the training was practical, officers and men also attended a series of lectures on military topics and skills. There was so much deep snow and ice that on the 4th, a planned inspection by the brigade commander was cancelled and that day's training carried out in the relative warmth of the huts. With conditions ideal for both frostbite and trench foot, the MO supervised the men applying whale oil to their feet before their departure to Ypres on the 7th.

Though not in the front line, the regularly shelled town of Ypres was well within range of German artillery and therefore just as dangerous. 8 January was no different, and one barrage wounded five men caught in the open. The worst of these was L/Cpl Joseph Brooks; the twenty-three-year-old married man from Bolton died on the way to the RAP. In a separate incident, runner Pte Edward Carton was hit in the chest by a shell splinter as he carried a message back to B Company from brigade HQ. Although now nineteen, he had deployed to France as a seventeen-year-old and survived both Festubert and the Somme. Despite his wound, Edward Carton continued to company HQ with the message, collapsing only after he had delivered it. The wound proved fatal and he died at Vlamertinghe on 10 January. He was awarded the MM, which was presented to his proud but grieving father in Barrow on 23 June 1917.[15] Training continued apace in Ypres whenever the requirements of working parties did not interfere. The cold added to this burden, as additional supplies of coal and coke needed to be delivered to the men shivering in the trenches, and though the extreme cold froze the mud hard, it also made the ground and duckboards treacherous for heavily laden men.

It wasn't until 12 January 1917 that the battalion moved back into the front line, relieving the Loyals near Railway Wood. Battalion numbers were still not up to scale, so one company of the Loyals was required to remain at the Front, accommodated in Beek Trench. What these men thought of this arrangement is not recorded, but they were probably less than enthusiastic! D Company occupied the left of the line, with C to its right. A, B, and the Loyals made up the reserve and support. The Germans shelled both Mud Lane and West Lane for three days, but no further casualties ensued and a battalion of the Sussex Regiment relieved them in the evening of the 16th. They marched back to new billets in Ypres, and then on to new billets in D Camp (50° 52′ 4.54″ N, 2° 47′ 9.11″ E), just over the road from O Camp. As no train was available, they had to march all the way there, only arriving at 4 a.m. on the 17th. The usual routine (training, parades, and inspections) kept all ranks busy there.

On 23 January, the battalion moved to P Camp (50° 52′ 55.02″ N, 2° 44′ 49.52″ E). Due to fears that the enemy may take advantage of the ice to attack across the frozen canal, A and B Company were detached and billeted at Canal Bank in Ypres, as part of the reserve for 38 Division. Two thirds of 55 Division had left for their spell of rest in the rear, but 164 Brigade were kept near Ypres in case of a German offensive. The two companies sent to Ypres ended up on countless working parties—fifty men per day sent to help A & B Company—while the remainder of the 1/4th trained back at the billets in ether P Camp or D Camp. The battalion moved back again to D Camp on the 27th, so this series of moves seemed pretty pointless. There was only one fatality amid the working parties, when on 31 January thirty-four-year-old Pte William Bradley, a married man from Lancaster, was killed. Twenty-one-year-old Pte David Bell from Millom ended up with five weeks in hospital after burning his leg on a fire, though luckily for him, rather than being farmed out to another unit, he was posted back to the battalion after completing refresher training at Étaples.

One of the men was in very serious trouble. Pte John Duke, a twenty-nine-year old married man from Dalton, had been wounded in April 1916. In November of that year he had been sent home sick and then posted back to the battalion on 6 January 1917. He deserted from Étaples and was picked up by the military police shortly afterwards and faced court martial on 26 January. His previous good service must have been taken into consideration as his sentence was a lenient two years' imprisonment with hard labour. He was freed from No. 1 Military Prison in Rouen a year later under a form of parole, the 1915 Suspension of Sentences Act, and returned to the battalion. 'I have remitted the sentence in this case,' reads a letter from Brig.-Gen. C. I. Stockwell in May 1918, 'on the grounds of the good work done by this man during the last few months'.[16]

The comradeship of one's unit may have helped sustain a man away from his wife and family; but I have yet to read a single positive account of the morale-sapping experience of the Bull Ring at Étaples. Also under a cloud was one of the sergeants, Charles Cooper, who was arrested a few days later for being drunk on duty—so much so that he was admitted into 1/3 West Lancashire Field Hospital for two days as a result! His FGCM on 9 February reduced him to Private. The drop in pay would have a big impact on the allowance paid to his wife in Dundee, and I suspect the former gardener from Ulverston received some fairly terse letters from home! However, Cooper had not reached the rank of Sergeant for nothing, and he would indeed prove his worth again.

The beginning of February saw a change of routine when the brigade was pulled back out of the line. On 3 February, 1/5th King's Own relieved C and D Company and battalion HQ at D Camp (A and B Company were still in Ypres and followed next day). The men marched to the Cheese Market in Poperinghe, where they caught a train for Bollezeele in France, arriving there shortly before 11 p.m. At 1 p.m. the next day, the battalion received news that the enemy had attacked over a corps-wide front and that they were to be ready to march out in just ninety minutes. By 2.30 p.m., the entire brigade were on the move, but when they reached Esquelbecq 5 miles from their billets, they were halted and told to about-turn, as this had just been an exercise to see how quickly the brigade could react. Upon their return they discovered that A and B Company had joined them, and spent 5 February cleaning themselves, their uniforms, and equipment. Despite the full training schedule, time was set aside for entertainment and on 10 February a brigade boxing competition was held, with Maj.-Gen. Jeudwine presenting the prizes. Even at this stage of the war the battalion was losing men to the munitions industries, and on 9 February, twenty-two-year-old Dalton soldier Pte James

Dodgson was recalled to the iron ore mines. The cold and damp took their toll in chest complaints. For some such as thirty-year-old Pte Edwin Clegg from Brierfield, bronchitis would turn into pleurisy, a recurrent complication for men who soldiered on despite their illness. On 14 February, the married father of two was passed quickly through the medical system, initially to the RAP, then the CCS, and finally No. 13 General Hospital in Boulogne. He died of pneumonia ten days later.

Despite a move back to O Camp on 16 February, training continued unabated right up until 24 February. This preparation concentrated on day and night assaults at platoon, company, and full battalion level. The mythology of the Great War would have us envision infantrymen climbing out of their trenches and slowly walking shoulder to shoulder across No Man's Land into a storm of shell and MG fire. But this was never the case with trained troops, and variations of 'fire and movement' had been the procedure long before the war had begun. The methods of attack seen from some of the battalions at the Somme on 1 July 1916 were not typical of the Army as a whole, and the reasoning behind the choices made for that day had some merit, even if hindsight reveals them to be flawed. What had changed since 1914 were the weapons available to the infantry soldier, and a greater cooperation with other arms, such as artillery, tanks, and aircraft. Mills grenades, rifle grenades, and Lewis guns gave the infantry platoon firepower and flexibility far beyond that of 1914, but their proper use needed to be instilled in men by constant practice and refinement. The battalion had yet to make an attack behind a creeping barrage, or to work with tanks, and the timings and tactics necessary to operate to their best advantage had to be learned. By 1917, the average infantry officer was a much better leader and trainer of men than the keen but hastily trained and commissioned men thrown into office during the Army's great expansion in the early stages of the war; he was to play a much more prominent role in the training of his men. February's training encompassed all of this, and the ability of officers and NCOs to react and adapt to changing conditions and surprise was constantly tested, namely with the introduction of 'unexpected' circumstances into planned attacks. Although the battalion was out of the line, there were still losses: thirty-eight-year-old married man from Wrightington Pte John Fisher succumbed at Mendinghem to wounds received earlier that month.

On 25 February 1917, the last day before the move to the forward trenches, the battalion held an inter-company football competition at O Camp within range of German heavy artillery, who fortunately did not disrupt play. In the first round the 'Officers', with the CO in goal, met the 'HQ Staff', and were beaten 5–1. One man going by the pseudonym of 'Curly' sent a report on the tournament to the Barrow press!

> Some of the spectators were evidently impressed with the play of the Headquarters Team, as one Tommy was heard to say to his chum, 'Hi Jack, I'll bet thee my next pork and beans rations that Headquarters win the championship.'

B Company defeated C Company 3–1 in the next round, and D lost 5–1 to the Bombers. Curly continues,

> I enquired of one of my comrades who 'A' Company met in the first round and joyfully he replied, 'Sh! Sh! We are laffin we got a bye and go into the second round ready to meet ow't.' His joyfulness

soon ceased however, as whisper was wafted to his ears: 'Second Round, Headquarters v. 'A' Company.' Then he complained bitterly at the bad luck that dogged his Company's team in having to meet the team that had inflicted such a defeat on the Officers.

Curly's pal was right to be concerned, for HQ won that match 5–0! After the Bombers narrowly defeated B Company (the 'Busy Bees') 4–3, the final was played between HQ and the Bombers, and although kick-off was timed for 2. 30 p.m., it was nearly delayed due to the large crowd of spectators still winding their way through to the field. When the whistle blew for kick-off, Curly reported 3,000 onlookers from the armies of six nations.

Opinions differed as to who would be the ultimate winner of the Colonel's first prize. Good humoured chaif could be heard on all sides. One of the Bombers' staunch supporters carried a flag with the Bombers' War Badge artistically worked upon it. A brush pole and a manure sack had been commandeered from an adjoining estaminer, [sic] and Bomber Higginson, R.A. (Rotten Artist) had very ingeniously painted a bomb thereon, the colours used being jet black (pinched from a tar barrel) and nut brown. Another great attraction was the musical instruments which two of the 'Grenade Experts' had made out of empty biscuit tins. Splendid music poured forth at intervals, especially when the bombers scored.

Just before half-time, HQ gave away a penalty for handling the ball, but the shot taken by Cpl T. Bennett, a former Chorley player, went over the crossbar. Obviously, it's not just modern professional footballers who do this! A minute later, the Bombers did manage to put one in the net and at half-time they were leading 1–0. Spectators were entertained by a vocal quartet from the Bombers' supporters, led by Pte Sam Hughes singing 'Ah Oui' and a selection of tunes (allegedly!) from the biscuit tin band. The score at full-time was a 3–1 win for the Bombers, though the play was closer than this score would suggest. Both teams demonstrated sportsmanship, but it was a tough game. Curly remarked,

Geldart [Pte John Geldart from Kirkby] was inclined to play the man instead of the ball.... Tomlinson did his best on more than one occasion to bring down his opponents, but steadied up after receiving a mudbath at the hands of Corporal Bennett.

It seems fitting that Curly should also have the last say about the tournament:

On all sides could be heard the hope expressed that this would not be the last competition of this kind. By the time you get this, the battalion will be taking part in another match of a different character, and if they storm the Bosch trenches in the same manner as they did the goalmouth it will be NA-POO with the Huns—Curly.[17]

On 26 February, the battalion moved to Canal Bank in Ypres and on the following day took over a new section of trenches from the Welsh Regiment (not spelled 'Welch' until 1921) to the north of Wieltje, known as the Cross Roads Farm sector (50° 52′ 30.06″ N, 2° 54′ 42.19″ E). The four days spent in these trenches were quiet as far as enemy activity was concerned, but all the front and communication trenches needed much work because of the wet conditions. After four days back at the Canal Bank billets, despite constant demand for working parties, the battalion moved back into the line on the evening of 8 March. In the early hours of 11 March, a solitary figure, twenty-five-year-old Cpl Thomas Long from Millom, crawled out of D Company's trench and went forward to observe the enemy. His fate is recorded in surviving letters to his parents and sister. His company commander, Lt William Pattinson, wrote:

> It is with the very deepest sorrow that I have to tell you that your son was killed in action on the 11th March. He did a brave deed—went out by himself in the front of our line early in the morning to watch the enemy. In the evening he did not return, and a search party later found him near the German trenches, dead. It will be some comfort in your sorrow to know that he died painlessly and instantly.... Your son was a decent lad, well thought of by all his officers and popular with the men, and he is regretted very keenly by us all, and the Company wishes me to send their sympathy to you.[18]

Thomas Long was the second youngest of four brothers serving in the war; his older brother George, who was also in the 1/4th but serving with a different company, wrote to their sister, Bessie.

> It is with regret that I convey the sad news that Thomas was killed yesterday morning (Sunday). I saw him last night on the stretcher, they were carrying him by our place when they came in and asked us the way to the aid post. They told us who it was, and I went out and had a look at him. He will have a decent burial place. I don't know how you will let poor mother know about it. I have not written to her, so you will have to let her know. The Captain of his company has letters and everything out of his pockets. I hope you don't take this news too bad.[19]

Just after midnight on 13 March, a raiding party from 1/4th Loyals used the battalion's trenches for a raid on three of the dugouts in the German-held 'Canadian Trench' to their front. Although returning from a raid to another battalion's trench system was always risky, the raid passed without any 'friendly fire' incidents. 15 March saw the battalion back at Canal Bank, but not for long as they moved back to O Camp again the following day. D Company was detached to Proven for ten days, to provide working parties in the locality; the rest of the battalion spent its time either training or on working parties. Football was not forgotten, and on the afternoon of the 21st, the battalion defeated the Welsh Regiment 2–0; and the following afternoon, the ASC 2–0; and on the 23rd, the Liverpool Irish 6–2. Before enlistment, many of the men had played regularly for church and social clubs and mass enlistment had brought many semi- and professional footballers into the Army, so many battalions boasted teams of a high standard. The game was of such importance that a match always got a mention in the *War Diary*; so on the few occasions that a score went unreported, it must be presumed that the battalion lost!

Apart from poor D Company, who missed out on this entertainment, a number of other men departed this week for munitions work, though I suspect that they weren't too upset about making their way home. Those claimed were invariably among the most experienced soldiers and the hardest to replace. One of these was twenty-three-year-old Cpl Robert Phillipson from Dalton, who would re-join the battalion as soon as the war ended. His older brother, thirty-two-year-old Sgt Fred Phillipson, was another. Fred Phillipson had a chequered career with the battalion, and upset the 'powers to be' on a number of occasions, moving up and down the rank ladder like a yo-yo. Between October 1914 and February 1916, he'd been up before the CO and various company commanders charged with no less than fourteen offences, which included disobeying an order, breaking out of billets, drunkenness, and absence on parade. As a result, he had been given fourteen days confined to barracks, fourteen days' detention, thirty-one days' Field Punishment No. 1, and two fines. Despite all this, his abilities were such that he kept being promoted, and he was sadly missed.

When the battalion moved back into the line on 29 March, it was once again to the Cross Roads Farm sector. Although the *War Diary* reported that everything was quiet, at least one man was wounded: on 31 March, twenty-two-year-old Pte Norman Bullivant was hit in the arm by shrapnel and evacuated home. His recovery was limited and he was transferred to one of the agricultural companies of the Labour Corps in Wales, no longer 'infantry-fit'. The battalion continued to alternate between billets in the Canal Bank and the Cross Roads Farm sector until 16 April. Improving weather meant fewer sick, though the battalion did lose one very keen man in early April. Nineteen-year-old Pte Tom Gregory, a weaver from Clitheroe, had enlisted in the East Lancashires in March 1914 and gone to Egypt with 1/4th East Lancashires that September. There he had been diagnosed with a heart defect and was discharged as permanently unfit for military service. Undaunted by this rejection, he had waited a few months before enlisting in the King's Own, joining the 1/4th in the Salient in January 1917. Falling sick in April, he was sent to an English hospital and upon his recovery in June posted to 8/King's Own. The heavy burdens men carried for miles over poor terrain took their toll, and thirty-nine-year-old Burnley plasterer Pte Richard Blacklock returned to hospital in England with a hernia. At his eventual recovery the father of five was posted to 8/ King's Own and later transferred to the North Staffordshires in August 1918; he died of his wounds just five days before the war ended. Constant work and strain also damaged the health of another of the older members, namely QM Lt James Crossley. He too was posted home for a rest, and was replaced by Lt Phillip Powell, a former CSM with twenty-one years' service in the 1st and 4th Battalions.

The period between 17 April and 6 May was spent in billets in Herzeele, Buysscheure, and Moulle. For once there were no working parties and the battalion was able to concentrate on training, mainly in the attack and consolidation of captured trenches (though far more time was allocated on the range for riflemen and Lewis-gunners). For the first time since deploying to the Western Front, the battalion also took part in training for 'open warfare' at battalion and full brigade level, a measure of the hopes that commanders had for the forthcoming attacks in the Salient.

Platoon organisation was vastly different to 1915. Platoons were still organised into four sections, each under a corporal and one of which was the traditional rifle section, but here the similarities ended. In 1917, there was a Lewis section with just one gun, though later each would be allocated two. Another section was made up of rifle grenadiers, and the last of the four sections was made up of equal numbers of bombers and riflemen. Section sizes varied according to manning and equipment, but the rifle section frequently had as many as sixteen men. The Lewis section usually comprised an NCO and four men when the issue was one gun per platoon, though this increased when the platoon got its second gun. Training was restricted to the mornings, while afternoons were set aside for relaxation. Another inter-company football tournament was organised and all ranks enjoyed the estaminets, restaurants, and parks of nearby St Omer. Spring was well under way and the warm sunshine and green downs to the west of St Omer contrasted sharply with the torn earth and damp mists of the Salient. The concussion of shellfire and rattle of small arms fire replaced by the call of a myriad of birds in the hedgerows and fields, and on the clear, moonlit nights by the song of nightingales. It wasn't exactly a holiday, but a great tonic.

On 7 May, the battalion moved to A Camp near Vlamertinghe; their arrival was welcomed by German long range artillery, which caused casualties, though none fatal. The next day, the battalion took over the trenches near Railway Wood, and on the night of the 11th, battalions holding the line either side of the 1/4th raided all three German battalions, which prompted the German artillery's retribution. Twenty-one-year-old Pte Harry Bland from Heysham was killed outright by the bombardment and a number of men wounded. The most serious of these was twenty-year-old Pte Thomas Fox from Dolphinholme, who died shortly after reaching the RAP. Thirty-one-year-old Pte Daniel Washington from Alderley Edge received a minor shrapnel wound to the face, but was back with the battalion four days later, though his next wound would be more serious. Perhaps the greatest loss to the battalion that day was L/Cpl Albert Taylor, who got a Blighty wound to the leg; he had been awarded the MM for his gallantry in his very first month with the battalion, and recommended for a DCM in December 1916. Upon his return to fitness, he was transferred to the North Staffordshires and died from wounds in April 1918, a mere twenty days after joining his new unit. A single man whose parents were both dead, Taylor left his belongings to his sweetheart.

Two nights later, the battalion sent out a patrol of two officers and three men into No Man's Land, where they encountered a German patrol of fifteen to twenty men. Luck was on the side of the British, as they spotted the enemy first; a quick action ensued which resulted in the German patrol being driven off. It wasn't without cost: twenty-one-year-old Pte Andrew Dixon from Carlisle was wounded in the back by fragments from a German grenade. It was his second war wound, as in 7/ King's Own he had been wounded in the chest in November 1916, and posted to the 1/4th after his recovery. He was evacuated home and transferred to one of the agricultural companies when he left hospital. Returning to their old billets in the Ypres Prison on 14 May, the battalion spent the next five days in the usual pattern of training and working parties. Although there were no full-scale range facilities, the men were able to hone their musketry skills on a miniature range. There were the inevitable casualties in the working parties, though only one man, eighteen-year-old Pte Edward Monks from Lancaster, was killed, on 18 May. On 16 May, Cpl William Bray was wounded, for the second time, by shrapnel to the thigh, and after leaving hospital in England he returned to his civilian job in the Hodbarrow Mines.

From 20 to 26 May, the battalion were back in the Wieltje trenches where they had spent most of late 1916. The men were as busy as ever with patrols, repairing trenches, wiring parties, and collecting salvage. The collection and reconstitution of discarded equipment was an often overlooked, but vital part of the war effort; considerable savings were made in raw materials, manpower, and shipping resources by repairing rather than manufacturing afresh damaged equipment. For this to be effective, the material needed to be collected as soon as possible and infantry battalions were a ready source of labour for this task. On the evening of 23 May, the section of line held by the battalion was extended on the right as far south as Piccadilly (50° 51′ 32.81″ N, 2° 55′ 54.22″ E), giving the men a frontage of some 1,500 m. The only fatality during this time in the line was nineteen-year-old Pte

Fred Rogerson from Hooley Hill, who died from his wounds on the 24th. Twenty-three-year-old Sgt William Whiteside from Ulverston also received a minor shrapnel wound to the head on the 23rd, but was back a week later.

When the battalion came out of the line on 26 May, they were initially split between Post L8 and A Camp, constant demand for working parties affecting all. However, the last three days of May and first five of June saw the whole battalion building a new reserve trench, Cambridge Trench. Today, it can be traced along the minor road Begijnenbosstraat, which joins the N332 to the N37 just under a kilometre east of Potijze. The land slopes gently upwards towards the German lines so the work on Cambridge Trench was dangerously visible. Just how exposed they were can be appreciated by viewing this road from half way along Oude Bellewaerdestraat, which runs parallel to Begijnenbosstraat and close to the former German position Oskar Farm, part of the Ibex system.

The first of the casualties was L/Cpl Thomas Howarth, a twenty-seven-year-old miner from Westhoughton. On 31 May, a bursting shell badly wounded him in the shoulder and he was eventually discharged because of this and the resulting shell shock. The next day, twenty-four-year-old Pte Thomas Agar from Leigh was killed. On 3 June, two men were killed outright by shell fire and others wounded. The dead were twenty-five-year-old Edward Catterall from Blackburn and forty-one-year-old Pte Arthur Simpson from London. Simpson, a former regular soldier recalled to 1/ King's Own, had been injured just under a year earlier when a horse fell on him, breaking his leg. Once the fracture had healed he was posted to the 1/4th; he had only been with the battalion for three months when he was critically hit. He was carried to 2/1 Wessex Field Ambulance, but died there soon after. He left behind a wife and three young children.

Also very seriously wounded was twenty-two-year-old Pte William Clare from Chorley. This young soldier was evacuated home and had his left leg amputated at the thigh. Twenty-nine-year-old Pte Septimus Derdle, originally deployed to France with 1/5th Battalion, had already been wounded in the wrist in November 1916 and was posted to the 1/4th when he returned to France. Once more, he returned to England, this time with a head wound—and not for the last time, either! Twenty-four-year-old L/Cpl Joseph Armstrong from Newbiggin was bruised and shocked after being buried alive by a shell. His comrades were able to dig him out, but it would be two months before he was fit enough to re-join. The last of the men recorded wounded that day was Pte George Helme from Haverigg. The twenty-six-year-old was with the transport delivering supplies behind the lines when shrapnel hit his leg. He was probably not in a benevolent mood to begin with, as just two weeks previously he'd been fined five days' pay for a traffic violation while driving a horse-drawn wagon—a serious punishment for a married man, for his wife would lose her allowance for that period. The next day, another two men were killed: twenty-year-old Henry McGill from Preston and thirty-three-year-old Sgt James Mellon, a married father of four from Ulverston. Mellon's platoon commander, 2Lt Clement Ford, wrote to his wife:

> During the time he has been with the battalion out here, your husband has endeared himself to both officers and men by his soldier like […] and cheerfulness under most trying conditions. As his platoon officer I feel I have lost one of my finest NCOs and a true friend.[20]

Two months later, someone would be writing similar condolences to Ford's family.

The last reported wounded was twenty-two-year-old Pte Edward Motteram from Barrow, who spent just over a month in hospital for gas-poisoning. It's probable that the increase in casualties around this time was partly due to the deception tactics the battalion had been ordered to carry out. A major assault was planned for the Messines Ridge and it just was not possible to disguise the fact that a big push was about to begin. What was possible, though, was to mislead the enemy as to which part of the Salient the attack would take place at. The men were therefore ordered to use scaling ladders and helmets on sticks to mislead the Germans. When the attack did begin at 3.10 a.m. on 7 June, the sight, sound, and ground reverberations of the nineteen massive mines detonated under the Messines Ridge was awe-inspiring; unsurprisingly, the battalion had a quiet day, as German attention was focused elsewhere. The 8th saw another man killed, Pte Charles Kershaw from Preston, and on the next day another two, thirty-five-year-old L/Cpl John Nicholson from Lancaster and twenty-one-year-old Pte Leonard Wade from Armley. Wade had enlisted under an alias and was actually Leonard Jacobs.

For the first time in weeks, the score was not totally one-sided. On the evening of 9 June, the battalion sent a raiding party of thirty men led by Lt James Alexander into Ibex Trench (50° 51′ 39.46″ N, 2° 56′ 8.07″ E). The thirty-three-year-old Alexander led his men so close behind the barrage that complete surprise was achieved; they were able to get through the German wire even though this was uncut, and thence into the enemy's front trenches, utterly unobserved. This raid was a great success: all enemy dugouts in the section raided were cleared, three Germans were killed and another six captured, and the raiders suffered no losses. Two men, L/Cpl Charles Cooper and Pte James McAlarney, received the MM for their bravery, and Lt Alexander, who was on attachment from 7/ Lancashire Fusiliers, the MC. A key reason for their success was Cooper's detailed reconnaissance the previous night. On the way back from the raid, one of the men had got caught up in the German wire and the NCO went back to free him and then conducted the rest of the party back to friendly lines, too.[21] Cooper had to wait for his medal ceremony, as he had received a minor wound to the knee in the raid and when this became septic, he was evacuated to a hospital in Clacton and did not return to the battalion, being posted instead to the depot in Oswestry. McAlarney (spelled 'McAlerney' in some of his documents) had driven off a group of enemy who were bombing their way along the trench to support their raided comrades, driving them away with his grenades. Once the raiding party was back, he realised that one of their party was missing, and he returned to No Man's Land to find and return him to friendly lines.[22]

On the morning of 11 June, the battalion entrained at Esquelbecq and returned to billets in Bollezeele for three days before moving on to a combination of billets and bivouacs in Grand and Petit Difques, near Moringhem, to the west of St Omer. Although the battalion was well out of range of German guns, some men weren't. Thirty-year-old Sgt Henry Bradley from Barrow, attached to 422 Field Company RE, was admitted to hospital on 14 June and spent two weeks there recovering from the effects of a gas shell. The previous day, twenty-five-year-old Pte John Scargill from Halifax had been killed, and on the 15th and the 16th, a further two men died from wounds. Twenty-two-year-old Pte Anthony Solari is listed killed in action on the 15th in *Soldiers Died*, but the location of his burial supports the accreditation 'died from wounds' in the *Battalion History*.[23] On the 16th, twenty-year-old Pte James McMahon from Barrow died in hospital at Étaples from wounds received on the 11th while attached to the RE. That same week, Étaples played its part in the demise of another member of the battalion. Twenty-one-year-old Pte James Greenhill had only just returned to France after being wounded in the chest at Guillemont, and was being put through refresher training at the Bull Ring. He injured his hip in this training and less than two days after landing in France was heading back home on a hospital ship. He was posted to 2/ King's Own in Salonika upon his recovery. Another fatality out of the line was twenty-two-year-old Pte Arthur Dixon from Ulverston, who had been wounded some time earlier and died from wounds in hospital in Abbeville. A week before their return to the front, Pte William Butterworth from Brierfield reported sick with tonsillitis and, despite the seemingly trivial nature of this illness, he was sent back to hospital in England. The thirty-one-year-old died from complications during a fairly minor operation for an unrelated condition that August.

Training for the forthcoming attack was carried out over terrain similar to the objective's; all German positions were marked on the ground, and the men practised their timings and tactics again and again; the creeping barrage was simulated by drummers moving forward at a set pace. The battalion trained and held evening entertainments (football and boxing) until its return to Ypres on 1 July. Their intense preparations had alerted the enemy, however, and by early June, the Germans had moved eight out of twenty-three available reserve divisions to Flanders.[24]

# 7

# 1 July 1917 – 13 September 1917
# The Battle of Pilckem Ridge

When the battalion returned to the Front on 1 July 1917, it was initially billeted at Derby Camp (50° 51′ 27.76″ N, 2° 47′ 47.28″ E) and moved into its old positions near Railway Wood the next day. Their first two casualties occurred before they had reached the trenches: forty-one-year-old Pte James Curtis—a married father of six—from Fleetwood and thirty-five-year-old Pte John Singleton from Lytham were both killed by shell fire. If any of the men had doubts as to the imminence of the forthcoming offensive, the march forward from Derby Camp dispelled them, as the area was a mass of activity. New tracks to Ypres were being constructed through the countryside, new forward dumps and new gun positions were in evidence all over.

Once in the front line, work on strengthening trenches continued; wire had to be repaired and new dumps in the front-line trenches constructed, and at least one man, twenty-year-old Pte George Robinson (785), was wounded on 2 July. Although there were no fatalities when the trenches were bombarded on the 3rd in retaliation for a raid to the battalion's left, it all added to the labour required to repair the defences. On the 5th, one of the men attached to the TMB, thirty-six-year-old Pte Ernest Wiles from Barrow, was wounded in the scalp by shrapnel. On the 7th, Pte Harold Bayley from Bolton was killed by shellfire. The twenty-three-year-old had not been with the battalion for long, having been transferred from the DLOY in February for going absent without leave no less than nine-times, and notching up at least 130 days' Field Punishment in the process, though his record with the King's Own was impeccable! In the evening of the 9th, the battalion was relieved by the Loyals and moved back to Derby Camp. Although supposedly in billets, the actuality of their situation was far from restful. Capt. Robert Gardner, then OC of A Company, described the time between 9 and 19 July as 'a period of intense strain.'[1] Companies were housed in a series of dugouts and shelters spread along the route between Derby Camp and Ypres and as it grew dark, they would parade and move forward under the illusory cover of darkness, carrying supplies and munitions from dumps near Potijze and St Jean, and transferring them into forward dumps. Naturally, the Germans were doing their best to disrupt the preparations with gas, shrapnel and HE.

The constant use of gas meant that the men worked wearing their box respirators, an uncomfortable and restrictive burden, especially in hot weather. The Germans had developed mustard gas, but held back its use for what they viewed as a priority occasion so as not to diminish its effects. Unlike other forms of gas, mustard remained toxic in the long term, soaking into the soil and water-filled craters. Men who got this onto their skin soon suffered burns. The Yellow-X shells filled with mustard were mainly a hazard in and to the east of Ypres, but during daylight hours in the open country to the west, working parties were frequently attacked by MG from the air.

When the exhausted men returned to their dugouts at around 5 a.m., they were given breakfast then allowed to sleep until noon, whereupon a meal was provided and routine battalion tasks occupied the afternoon until their return to Ypres around 7 p.m. During the night, the devastated streets of Ypres were lit by the flames of dumps ablaze after hits from heavy artillery; and by day, clouds of smoke billowed into the sky. This increased exposure to fire heralded more casualties, the first, thirty-five-year-old Pte Edward Forster from Sunderland, killed on 10 July. On the following day, L/Cpl William Wood was evacuated home, severely wounded in the face. He was one of only two men from the battalion who received treatment from the pioneer of facial reconstruction surgery, Dr (later Sir) Harold Gillies at Queen's Hospital in Sidcup. On the 12th, twenty-one-year-old Pte David Bell from Millom was wounded in the left hand and spent two weeks in hospital before returning. On the 13th, Cpl William McDowell, one of the old hands from the MG section, was caught by gas and evacuated to England. McDowell's period of enlistment had ended in June of 1916, but he had immediately voluntarily re-enlisted and although this was into the MGC, he actually stayed where he was in 164 MG Company.

The CWGC and *Soldiers Died* note the death in action on 13 July of twenty-year-old 2Lt Percy Jolley from St Helens. A former sergeant from the South Lancashires, he was commissioned into the King's Own in 1917. Although multiple sources allocate him to the 1/4th, he doesn't appear in the list of officers joining the battalion, neither does his name appear on the lists of orderly officers, or in fact anywhere in the *War Diary*—which is unique.[2] The site of his burial in Louverval Military Cemetery is over 50 miles from the battalion's location, and it's almost certain that he was serving with 8/ King's Own and attached to them prior to ever reaching the 1/4th.

On 14 July, four men were killed and at least another four wounded. Twenty-four-year-old Pte John Barrow from Coniston was gassed, though fortunately not seriously. Thirty-three-year-old William Braithwaite from Barrow received his second face wound of the month, though this time it was more serious and he was transferred to the Labour Corps upon his recovery three months later. Thirty-eight-year-old Cpl William Masters was hit in the hand, legs, and face by shrapnel, and did not re-join until late September. Pte William Messham was lucky this time and only got a slight scalp wound from shrapnel; however it was only a matter of time before this twenty-one-year-old from Liverpool came to harm again. Pte William O'Neill from Fleetwood, who had received a MiD only that March, was killed outright by shell fire, as was twenty-two-year-old L/Cpl Joseph Collinson from Coniston. Thirty-one-year-old Cpl Arthur Jones from Chester and Pte John Kay from Blackpool were also killed.

It's understandable that Great War enthusiasts should frequently concentrate on the casualties; the majority of available information tends to relate to them, and it's the area that has the greatest impact on society. Perhaps this is a good opportunity to remind ourselves of just what this experience must have been like for those who soldiered on. Day after day, night after night, the men of British, Dominion, and Commonwealth forces placed themselves in harm's way. They were not 'superheroes', but ordinary men placed in extraordinary circumstances and a veritable cross-section of classes and backgrounds. Survival was a lottery, and no amount of fighting skill could defeat explosives in the wrong place! Each night, the battalion's familiar faces grew fewer and fewer. Yet the men persevered by way of comradeship, humour, fatalism, and pride. By now this must have seemed like a war without end; talk of it 'all being over by Christmas' had evaporated; and it was just a case of taking one day at a time.

For a minority of men, it was all too much. At 6.45 a. m. on 19 July, Pte John Crellin, a twenty-three-year-old from Manchester, was cleaning his rifle in his billet at 72 Rue D'Ypres in Poperinghe prior to going onto duty at the divisional baths. His section corporal, Benjamin Holman, reported the following to the court of enquiry.

> I was standing close by him and was also engaged in cleaning my own rifle. The accused was standing at the time. I did not notice the position of his safety catch. I cannot say whether the accused pulled the trigger. The rifle was fired and on examining it, I found an empty cartridge case in the chamber. The accused was wounded in the middle finger of the left hand. The accused ran out of the room shouting, 'Oh my hand, my hand. I am sorry I cleaned my rifle.' I followed him and assisted in bandaging his hand.[3]

The Army took an exceedingly dim view of self-inflicted injuries and Crellin would have faced a court martial for this had he not needed immediate medical attention. He was admitted to the 61 CCS at Dosinghem for treatment, pending his trial. On the night of 20 August, Dosinghem was bombed, causing sixty-eight casualties, fourteen of whom died. One of them to die of his wounds was Crellin. He had had what most infantrymen would call a 'cushy number', for he did not undertake the nightly walk towards the Front. Although Poperinghe was within range of heavy artillery and certainly in harm's way, it was considerably safer than anywhere further east! We'll never know why the strain was too much for young Crellin; perhaps he never experienced close comradeship in his infantry section, an environment where your mates usually got you through the bad times, and you did the same for them.

Another two men were killed on 15 July. Thirty-seven-year-old Pte Thomas Carr, a father of six from West Hartlepool, was killed outright. He had been with the battalion for less than three weeks. Also killed was twenty-seven-year-old Pte Joseph Folley from Middlesex. Wounded for the second time, though this time by the enemy, was Pte John Rodgerson, who was hit in forearm and finger by shrapnel. More seriously injured was twenty-eight-year-old Pte William Gilbert from Lancaster. A shrapnel shell bursting nearby hit him in the thighs, groin, and right forearm. Evacuated home, he was given a medical discharge and a pension.

Perils often went unseen in the dark. Old hands soon got to know if an incoming shell was worth ducking for by the sound it made, although the 77-mm 'whizz-bangs' tended to arrive too quickly for forethought. Gas shells made a distinctive sound and in daylight, if the sound of the shell was masked by other noises, the gas could be seen. At night, however, it was a different story. On the night of 16 July, as troops made their way forward carrying supplies, thirty-seven-year-old Leicester bootmaker Pte Harry Stevenson was caught by a whiff of gas before he had put his gas helmet on. Although not serious enough to kill or maim him, the dose did get him two weeks in hospital. More seriously affected by the gas was twenty-two-year-old Sgt Harry Parnell from Barrow. He was evacuated to England and treated in Manchester for mustard gas in his lungs, stomach, and eyes. Luckily for the battalion, though not for the enemy, he returned in May 1918. On the same night, twenty-three-year-old Pte Stephen Boundy received minor wounds to the wrist and finger by shrapnel—the first of three.

Wounds to hands and fingers were extremely common and it has been suggested by some, that men held their hands out from cover to deliberately get a minor wound. Whilst this may have occasionally taken place, the idea that this was common practice is unfounded and insulting. Be it 1914 or the present day, the natural instinct of a soldier under any sort of artillery fire is to make himself as small a target as possible; to put one's hands over one's head and face; to grip one's helmet to keep it in place. Because the blast from an explosion could catch the pronounced lip of the helmet, most soldiers did not wear the helmet chinstrap under the chin for fear of their necks being broken. Consequently, chinstraps were either worn with the strap just below the bottom lip—as required by divisional 'Standing Orders'—or around the back of the neck.

Even for men who had run the gauntlet in the forward area, the security of their shelters was purely illusory. On the morning of 18 July, a shell from a long-range gun scored a direct hit on a shelter shared by two men, both of whom were killed in their sleep. The first, thirty-four-year-old father of two Pte James Hopwood was a successful coal dealer and ironmonger from Lytham, originally from Stockport. The man beside him was twenty-one-year-old Pte Joseph Ribeiro, a single man from Stepney.

On 20 July, there was some respite as the battalion moved to a camp on the eastern edge of Poperinghe. Twenty-seven-year-old Pte Albert Johnson from Sedgefield was nevertheless wounded in the chest and right arm by shrapnel as they withdrew, and spent five weeks in hospital at Rouen before re-joining. The next day they moved to another camp near St Jean, though again there were casualties and twenty-three-year-old Pte Joseph Winder from Ulverston was killed outright. They spent four days here, devoting them to cleaning up after the rigours of the previous weeks and reorganising the platoons. On the 23rd, the brigade commander briefed officers and NCOs about the forthcoming offensive. On the 24th, their final day there, each company carried out a route march. The next day, another route march was completed and the battalion returned to the camp from five days earlier. On 26 July, the battalion was addressed by the CO and although there were no current casualties, two of the men wounded some time earlier succumbed to their injuries. Thirty-six-year-old Pte Jonathan Beaumont, a married man from Mossley, died at Lijssenthoek on the 26th, and twenty-nine-year-old Pte William Trewern, a married man and father of three from Cornwall, at Mendinghem on the 30th as a result of mustard gas-poisoning. Tragically for his widow Susannah, their youngest child was to also die that December. Another man who ended up in hospital was Cpl Albert Hodgson, accidentally burned in the face; he would not return to duty until mid-August. Twenty-one-year-old Pte William Scott's day did not go well either: he was up in front of the CO on a charge of failing to wear his helmet, and was fined five days' pay.

27 and 28 July were filled kitting out the men for the attack. Each man was issued with 120 rounds of .303, except for the signallers, scouts, runners, Lewis-gunners, bombers, and rifle grenadiers who only carried fifty rounds. In their pack men carried a towel, soap, a spare oil tin, holdall, iron and extra rations, an extra water bottle containing cold tea without sugar or milk, a groundsheet, and a mess tin. With the exception of the rifle grenadiers who had the No. 20 grenade, every man carried one No. 23 rifle grenade, complete with cartridge and rod in the top pocket of their jacket.

The No. 23 grenade was an adaptation of the No. 5 Mills grenade, with a longer time fuse and a different base plug into which the rod was screwed. This was when the magazine cut-off on the SMLE really came into use, as there was no need to remove the live rounds from the magazine: a special blank cartridge was placed in the breech, the grenade with rod attached was lowered into the barrel, and with the butt on the ground, the grenade was firmly gripped around the lever with one hand and the pin removed with the other. As soon as the spring-loaded lever flew off, a firing pin struck the detonator activating the time fuse in the grenade, so it was vital to fire it as soon as possible—quite a motivation to concentrate the mind! It was possible to arrange the grenade so that the bayonet held the lever in, but this was not fool-proof. The cup attachment carried by bombers and rifle grenadiers held the lever in position and allowed unlimited time in which to aim the shot, which could range out to 90 yards. The No. 20 grenade used by rifle grenadiers was a percussion grenade with a 10-inch long rod attached and, like the No. 23 grenade, was also propelled by a blank cartridge. The No. 20 grenade had a much longer range than the No. 23 and reliably reached 200 yards, with 250 yards not an unreasonable distance to aspire to. The higher breech and barrel pressure caused by the rod was pretty hard on the rifles, and grenadiers' weapons were bound with wire to strengthen them, though it didn't take long before even these rifles lost their accuracy.

Every man carried three empty sandbags under the braces of his pack, and in his right-hand jacket pocket a flare for signalling positions to aircraft (though only three SOS rockets were distributed per company). Every other man would also carry either a shovel or pick for the consolidation of captured trenches. One reason that orders specified the carrying locations of equipment was that if more were needed in a hurry, it was much quicker to source them from casualties, a practice still maintained today.

'Operational Order 44/A' dated 26 July 1917 goes into the preparation for the July 31st attack in elaborate depth, leaving nothing to chance. The timing and place of each phase of the operation is detailed, as are the kit and liaison points with other battalions. The locations of dumps and who was to provide carrying parties to maintain the forward dumps once the trenches were captured was also laid down (A Company). Procedures for mopping up strongpoints and the locations of enemy defences where valuable intelligence may be gained, such as HQ positions, were carefully mapped and squads allocated to each. The men tasked with mopping up and seizing enemy documents came from C Company, which had been training squads specifically for this purpose. They carried sandbags pre-marked with the labels 'Enemy Documents—Urgent', and men were to fill these with any written material discovered in the enemy positions.

A divisional POW cage was established north of Ypres (50° 51′ 50.18″ N, 2° 53′ 37.72″ E) and strict instructions as to what may be taken from the various prisoners and ranks laid down. For example, NCOs and men could only be searched for weapons, but all officers had to be thoroughly searched for documents. Officers were kept separate from their men on the march back to prevent them warning them about talking. Instructions were given that prisoners be martialled into large groups and that the escort should preferably consist of lightly wounded men not exceeding one tenth of the number of prisoners. Men were warned in no uncertain terms about collecting souvenirs during the attack, and a special squad was assigned for their later collection and fair distribution—a highly coveted mission, as certain souvenirs made for valuable barter!

Communications—the bane of many a past operation—were carefully planned, though their maintenance with the technology to hand was easier said than done! Cable-laying parties were detailed to lay telephone wire back from battalion HQ; and visual signalling stations were established at Jasper Farm (50° 52′ 17.16″ N, 2° 55′ 55.73″ E) and on Hill 35 (50° 52′ 33.13″ N, 2° 57′ 21.53″ E). Warnings were issued that visual signalling was only to be used when other options had run out, and that all messages had to be brief, for the poor signaller needed to be in the open if his light signals were to be spotted. Runner posts were established every 400 yards between the forward battalion HQ and Brigade HQ, for which each battalion within the brigade had to provide an extra six runners. All runners carried messages in their right-hand breast pocket; nothing else was to be carried here to aid the quick retrieval of messages from dead runners. No. 21 Squadron RFC would provide aircraft to monitor progress in the attack. Men were told that these aircraft could be identified by a 'rectangular attachment on right lower plane' and 'a white dumb bell on each side of the body'.[4] The plane would overfly the positions, sound a klaxon, then fire off a white flare. In response, the leading infantry position would fire an answering white flare and show the white and coloured sides of a Watson Fan, alternating them every thirty seconds. All signalling stations were marked with a blue and white board about 18-inches square, and all men, moppers-up in particular, were warned not to throw grenades into any dugouts where this was displayed. The day's SOS flares were rifle rockets, each bursting into two red and two green flares respectively. In the past, smoke and dust had made accurate observations difficult; but in the weeks leading up to the event, the soil was so hard that bullets ricocheted off it!

Communications were further complicated by the movement of HQ positions, which runners needed to be able to find. Initially, battalion HQ was to be in the mined dugout near the vinery in Congreve Walk (50° 51′ 47.95″ N, 2° 54′ 46.33″ E), but once the attack was under way, it moved 50 yards up behind A Company. Once Pommern Castle (50° 52′ 41.21″ N, 2° 57′ 1.03″ E) had been taken, it was planned to establish battalion HQ there. To ensure continuity of timings, signalling officer 2Lt Thomas Middleton was to report to battalion HQ at 2 a.m. on the day of attack, synchronise his watch with them, and then visit each company HQ to synchronise their watches to his. Middleton, a postal worker from Sparkbridge near Ulverston, had received the MM for his work between May and June 1916, and then been commissioned.

The MO would remain at the RAP at Potijze Château (50° 51′ 42.27″ N, 2° 54′ 55.97″ E) at zero hour, and only move forward as the advance progressed to re-establish the RAP at Pommern Castle. One NCO and four men from the Field Ambulance were attached to the RAP to assist the MO in communication between the RAP and ADS, initially situated at Canal Bank (50° 51′ 38.82″ N, 2° 52′ 59.73″ E). Collection posts for the wounded were established at St Jean (50° 51′ 53.39″ N, 2° 54′18.79″ E) and near Potijze (50° 51′ 30.69″ N, 2° 55′ 16.19″ E). A route to the rear was demarcated for all walking wounded to follow, taking them directly to the Mill at Vlamertinghe. At zero hour, two stretcher-bearers per company would leave Congreve Walk and follow the advance. The remaining eight bearers would remain and advance with battalion HQ. Once companies had achieved their objectives, one man from each platoon would be detached to act as an additional stretcher-bearer.

Three 'Straggler Posts' would round up any unwounded armed or unarmed soldiers moving to the rear through brigade lines. These were to be at the junctions of Potijze Road and Junction Road; Milner Trench and Junction Road; and St Jean Road and Junction Road. The last of these was to be manned by a detail from the Liverpool Irish—the first by Privates Geldart, John Bullock, and George Brindley and the second by Privates Tomlinson, John Watterson, and Timothy Benson. All three posts would be under the command of the battalion Provost Sergeant, George Frederick Jackson. Stragglers would be assembled into groups of ten and taken to the divisional straggler post near the canal in Ypres (50° 51′ 31.65″ N, 2° 53′ 0.53″ E); there they would be handed over to the Assistant Provost Marshal for redeployment or detention as he saw fit.

Twelve tanks from No. 16 Company of F Battalion, the Tank Corps, were to assist in the attack on the Green Line. Two sections comprising eight of the tanks were to attack in front of the leading company and the remaining section of four to advance at 'zero plus seven hours', with the purpose of clearing up any isolated pockets of resistance still holding out. Each section was given its objectives, which in many cases differed to the infantry's; to the usual system of coded discs and lights to signal their status to the rear were added one red and two green discs ('I have reached my objective'), three red ('I have broken down'), and one red and two white ('no enemy is in sight'). The weather in June and July had been perfect, so although the ground was pitted with shell craters, the terrain was not thought to be an issue by planners unfamiliar with the limited capabilities of tanks. Unfortunately, on Sunday 29th, a heavy thunderstorm had filled up many of these craters and turned the roads into a morass.[5] In the week before 31 July, the British had also fired 4,500,000 shells as preparatory bombardment, and these had finished off any residual drainage. And finally, the close proximity of the craters to each other presented a serious obstacle to the tanks.

The role of the pioneers and sappers was also planned in detail. These were tasked with making good the road between Wieltje and Gravenstafel to allow the movement of supplies along it. In addition to this road, they were to construct a number of tracks suitable for transport to move supplies around the front. One field company was to construct four strongpoints behind the Black and Green Lines, each to be garrisoned by half a platoon from the Liverpool Irish, and armed with one Vickers and one Lewis gun manned by men from 164 MG Company.

An offensive in the Salient had been on Haig's agenda in 1916; the Somme, however, had been forced upon him instead. It was also his chosen location for a 1917 offensive, but he was obliged by his political masters to support Nivelle's April and May offensive on the Aisne with diversionary attacks at Arras and Vimy. Haig was promised that, should Nivelle fail, he would get political support for an attack using the Salient as a springboard to clear the Belgium Channel ports of Oostende and Zeebrugge.[6] In May, British politicians had expressed views that there should be no offensive until American troops arrived in strength in 1918. However, the failure of the Nivelle Offensive, mutinies in the French Army, and increasingly tenuous situation in Russia (which freed growing numbers of German troops for the Western Front) fed concern that the Germans might win the war before the Americans arrived.[7] The First Sea Lord Adml Jellicoe also argued to the War Office that, in light of British shipping losses to Belgium-based U-boats and destroyers, the war could not continue into 1918. But Jellicoe's warning was unfounded, and even at the time that he voiced this opinion, the convoy system was starting to give results. According to Walter Reid, even Haig did not credit this fear: 'No one present shared Jellicoe's view, and all seemed satisfied that the food reserves in Great Britain are adequate'.[8] Haig's greatest worry was rather the fragility of the French Army, the collapse of which could have led to all-round defeat. In a private letter to Haig after the war, Marshal of the Royal Air Force Viscount Trenchard summarises of Passchendaele,

Tactically it was a failure, but strategically it was a success, and a brilliant success—in fact it saved the World. There is not the slightest doubt in my mind that France would have gone out of the war if Haig had not fought Passchendaele.[9]

Haig had only got tentative permission for preparation for the offensive, and formal permission only arrived six days before the attack began.[10] Haig had wanted to attack shortly after the success at

Messines, but was delayed by having to move men and heavy artillery from the Arras and Vimy sectors, where they had been to support Nivelle. The initial start date of 25 July also had to be postponed when Gen. Antoine, the French commander to the north, had asked for another three days to complete his counter-battery work.[11] The geography of the Salient also combined to cause delay. The German positions, set around the rim of a bowl and looking down as a far as seven miles behind British lines, gave German artillery observers unparalleled advantage. Because of the soft clay behind British positions, gun pits needed to be specially constructed and reinforced and any new position had to be built during the hours of darkness and successfully camouflaged before daybreak. Casualties among the RA were severe in the Salient. Poor flying visibility over a number of days also affected the results of the aerial reconnaissance that was so important to preliminary bombardment. All these delays had consequences for the eventual resumption on 31 July, when the weather turned two months earlier than was usual for the area.

To overcome the lack of ground observation, the British needed air superiority over the battlefield so as to allow reconnaissance aircraft to direct artillery fire and take photographs. The RFC strove to deny the enemy access to the key area stretching from the German lines to five miles to their rear, and in the last two weeks of July daily clashes between large groups of fighters were a daily spectacle. For example, on 26 July over Polygon Wood, ninety-four fighters battled for supremacy. The total of aircraft available would have been greater had not one squadron been ordered home to protect London after a German air raid on 7 July. By the end of the month, sufficient superiority was achieved. The RFC was also sending out bombers every night to strike German aerodromes and disrupt the strategically key railway facilities at Ghent, Thourout, and Courtrai; villages known to house enemy reserves; and the power stations at Bruges and Zeebrugge.[12]

Haig gave Gen. Gough, commander of the Fifth Army (of which 55 Division made up part of XIX Corps), two objectives: the first was to 'wear down the enemy', and the second to take the Passchendaele–Staden Ridge. Haig believed that the attacks might possibly break German resistance, so preparations were made for cavalry to be close enough to exploit any such breakthrough.[13]

As far as 55 Division were concerned, there were three main objectives for the attack, known as the 'Blue Line', 'Black Line', and 'Green Line'. The Blue Line was behind the German front and reserve trenches and ran roughly along the axis from Bossaert Farm (50° 52′ 37.92″ N, 2° 55′ 47.72″ E) to about 200 m to the rear of Grey Ruin (50° 52′ 8.73″ N, 2° 56′ 33.75″ E); the Black Line took a line from Spree Farm (50° 52′ 57.27″ N, 2° 56′ 35.94″ E) to just to the rear of Iberian (50° 52′ 39.52″ N, 2° 57′ 22.20″ E); and the Green Line ran along the start of the Gravenstafel Spur. The 1/4th would not be in the first wave of the attack, which would instead be launched by 166 Brigade on the left and 165 Brigade to the right. At zero hour, two battalions from each of these brigades would advance and capture enemy positions up to and including the Blue Line. Seventy-five minutes later, the remaining two battalions of 166 and 165 Brigade would move forward to take enemy positions up to the Black Line. These positions, known as the 'Stützpunkt Line', were basically a series of interlinked bunkers and shell holes. Following this, they were at 'zero plus three hours and thirty-three minutes' to move forward to capture Canvas and Capital Trenches (50° 53′ 10.37″ N, 2° 56′ 22.83″ E), if they were not yet in British hands.

The 1/4th and the rest of 164 Brigade would only begin to advance at 'zero plus six hours and twenty minutes'. They were to pass through the battalions of the other two brigades and take the

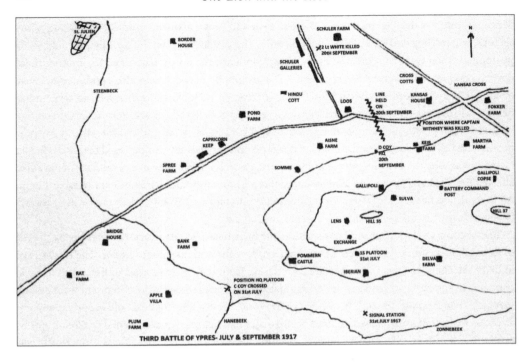

**THIRD BATTLE OF YPRES- JULY & SEPTEMBER 1917**

Green Line. Two companies of the 1/4th were to make up the attacking force, with D Company on the left and B Company to the right. C Company would supply the 'mopping-up' squads who would clear captured positions. C Company's targets were trenches to the north-west of Iberian and nearby dugouts; the Gallipoli Dugouts (50° 52′ 54.16″ N, 2° 57′ 26.40″ E) as far west as 50° 52′ 56.88″ N, 2° 57′ 3.86″ E, and the battalion boundary. A Company were to provide carrying parties and made up the seventh wave of the advance.

On the evening of 30 July, the battalion marched to the assembly point in Congreve Walk, the men quiet and pensive. Orders had besides been given to march silently, though quite how the Germans were likely to hear them above one of the biggest bombardments that the British had initiated so far in the war! No smoking or lights were allowed and the atmosphere was tense. For Pte Arthur Hammond, this march must have been miserable: he had been unwell for some time though not reported sick, and had a constant headache, sore throat, and swollen legs and face. As usual, a nucleus of the battalion known as the 'B Team' remained with transport in B Echelon, even though battalion strength was half of what it should have been. In case the attacking force was wiped out, withholding these men would facilitate the reconstitution the battalion. On the 31st, it was the CO who stayed behind, while the attacking force came under the command of Maj. Percival Robathan.

By 9 a.m., after five and a half hours of tough fighting, the attackers had captured both the Blue and Black lines. The 1/4th and the Loyals had begun their advance some forty minutes earlier, the distance from assembly trenches at Congreve Walk to the Black Line being of nearly 2 miles away. They passed through Pagoda Wood (50° 51′ 50.55″ N, 2° 54′ 58.44″ E) to the right of Prowse Farm (50° 51′ 54.31″ N, 2° 55′ 6.65″ E), and between Pagoda Street and the Strand to cross the German line at Kaiser Bill's Nose. The move forward from Congreve Walk was in artillery formation (single file). Although there was some shellfire from the enemy, the barrage was thought 'feeble' by 2Lt Charles Gribble of B Company, though to twenty-six-year-old Lt Charles Withey, the 'individual shells seemed more effective than usual'.[14] These barrages of mixed HE and shrapnel fell in three distinct places: the first just in front of Congreve Walk, the second to the rear of the enemy front line positions, and the third some 150 to 200 yards before the front of the Black Line. Despite having to walk the gauntlet of these three belts of artillery, battalion casualties were light. A Company suffered two men from 4 Platoon lightly wounded, as did 8 Platoon from B Company; C Company had three wounded; and D just one. The sub-unit to suffer the worst was actually battalion HQ and although Capt. Robathan's report did not specify the number, he described it as 'very slight'.[15]

Not all enemy positions between the Blue and Black lines were taken, and the brigade became involved in serious fighting to overwhelm these. Just to the left of the 1/4th's tactical bound was Spree Farm (50° 52′ 57.27″ N, 2° 56′ 35.94″ E), which was eventually overwhelmed by two platoons from 2/5th Lancashire Fusiliers.[16] In its capacity as 'moppers-up' for the Loyals, C Company was ahead of the rest of the battalion and just past Plum Farm (50° 52′ 25.76″ N, 2° 56′ 23.17″ E) came under heavy rifle and MG fire from the Bremen Redoubt on its flank. Because of the direction of fire, thirty-year-old company commander 2Lt Albert Ellwood ordered his HQ platoon to remain in single file, but to increase the distance between each man. This fire became heavier after they had passed Apple Villa, and at 9.40 a.m. it wounded three of his platoon (at 50° 52′ 33.22″ N, 2°56′ 46.49″ E). Ellwood left the stretcher-bearers to tend to these and pressed on, their advance covered by a convenient ditch until they reached the Steenbeck (at 50° 52′ 37.39″ N, 2° 56′ 45.78″ E), where they crossed amid a hail of small arms fire. Although 15-foot-wide at this point and extremely muddy, the stream was still fordable.

To Ellwood's left and tasked with clearing the 'Somme' stronghold and its surrounding dugouts was 10 Platoon under twenty-one-year-old 2Lt Charles Newbold.[17] Like HQ, this platoon had got off lightly in the walk up to the Black Line, with only one man wounded by shrapnel. Immediately after moving into extended file upon crossing the Black Line, it came under heavy MG fire from its left flank, though this gun was soon destroyed by troops to the left. The platoon was then engaged by another MG, this time directly in front of it, and promptly took cover and fired on the enemy position with rifles and Lewis guns. The platoon sergeant, twenty-eight-year-old Tom Mayson, began to work his way around the flank of the gun and was within 50 yards of it when a tank lumbered up and destroyed it. Within seconds, the tank itself was blasted by a direct hit from an anti-tank gun and the commander killed. Although Newbold records the number of this tank as F19 in his report, this cannot be correct, and it's probable that it was actually F13 'Falcon', commanded by thirty-two-year-old 2Lt Nathaniel Ready. What happened next is best told in Mayson's own words.

> Another gun however opened fire half left; so I crawled to a flank about for about 150 yards and got behind a mound and then found cover in a ditch. I approached to within about 20 yards of the gun when I threw a bomb; putting the gun out of action and wounded four of the team. The remainder of the team bolted into a dugout nearby. I went into the dugout after them; but found only three of them there; whom I slew with the bayonet.[18]

To the rear and about 500 yards to 10 Platoon's right, Ellwood's platoon made the next 200 yards in a series of dashes from cover to cover, half the men providing suppressive fire while the other half advanced. Just ten minutes after their first three casualties, they crossed the German defences close to Pommern Castle (at 50° 52′ 42.52″ N, 2° 56′ 55.27″ E). Although he found some men from 1/7th King's in the trench, Ellwood didn't realise that this was actually the Black Line, as according to the programme, this should have been about 300 yards further forward. At 9.58 a.m., Ellwood collected his men together behind the cover of some ruined outbuildings in Pommern Castle, finding that he was now reduced to a platoon of just six. Leaving them behind cover, he advanced alone to try to find the consolidated Black Line, but discovered no one, and returned. When he got back to Pommern Castle, he met an officer from another unit in the brigade, who told him that there was only one Lewis gun with five men forward of this position, so Ellwood gathered his men together and wait for their creeping barrage to begin. When it did at 10.12 a.m., Ellwood and his men advanced, Ellwood using his compass to maintain the 55-degree bearing needed to arrive at the objective. As a ranker with 1/5th King's Own before his commissioning, Ellwood was both an experienced and talented soldier, and knew just how easy it was to lose direction in an attack, especially when the terrain was as featureless as this! At this point, 12 Platoon under 2Lt Frederick Gilling was about 200 yards to their rear, however Ellwood was unaware of the locations of his other two platoons. Newbold's 10 Platoon was well in advance and to the left of the battalion's frontage, outside of Ellwood's field of view. And under 2Lt Arthur Latham 11 Platoon had been tasked with clearing Gallipoli, but had gone too far to the left and was hidden from view by the western slope of Hill 35.

In support of 3 Platoon from the Loyals (led by 2Lt Tyldesley), 11 Platoon had been unfortunate enough to have two men wounded within 50 yards of Congreve Walk, but remained further unscathed until it reached the Black Line at 9.50 a.m., whereupon it immediately came under heavy small arms fire. Taking cover behind a bank, 11 Platoon waited until the creeping barrage began and then fought its way from shell hole to shell hole, dealing with isolated pockets of resistance as it encountered them. The men cleared one dugout, sending six prisoners to the rear, and then took a 77-mm battery that had been giving the tanks problems. It was while it was thus engaged that 2Lt Latham lost touch with the Loyals and, as he later admitted, his own sense of direction.[19] Fully aware of the importance of pressing the enemy hard to prevent them reorganising, Latham pushed on, advancing to contact. L/Cpl James Topham took the one man remaining from his own section and cleared the enemy out from a position 'to a point on the left of Keir Farm' (50° 52′ 59.47″ N, 2° 57′ 33.58″ E);[20] they captured one Maxim, one officer, and twenty-five men, an action for which Topham was awarded the DCM.[21] Meanwhile, more troops moved through them towards the Green Line. Latham, who had now joined Topham, handed over command of his platoon to his Sergeant, ordering him to dig in and consolidate 300 yards to the front of these dugouts. Latham then took another of his section's lance corporals and advanced to reconnoitre its front, eventually finding his bearings when he was 200 yards south of Kansas Cross, probably near Martha House. Although Latham reported the 'left of Keir Farm' as the location of the enemy defences, Topham's report suggested Gallipoli as this location,[22] however both identifications are doubtful. Had Keir Farm been the correct position, repositioning forwards by 300 yards for consolidation would have brought these men level with the easily identifiable Kansas Cross. Upon his return to his platoon, Latham discovered that his sergeant had been sniped shortly after he had left and that Topham had taken command. Taking back control, Latham led the platoon towards what he now believed to be Gallipoli, only to be informed *en route* that this was in fact the dugouts to his right; he therefore took his platoon off on a tangent, only to discover that this location was actually Somme stronghold, where the brigade forward station was now located. This suggests that the actual position his platoon had captured earlier was Aisne Farm (50° 53′ 0.32″ N, 2° 57′ 9.98″ E), as a march from 300 yards forward of here in the direction of Gallipoli would put Somme to their right. Latham was still briefing the brigade major on what he knew about the positions on the Green Line when the enemy counter-attack began.

12 Platoon was following 15 Platoon from the Loyals under 2Lt Fullerton and sustained no casualties until it reached the Black Line. Although in extended order (line abreast), an MG to its front had dropped several men. Fortunately, a tank came up and knocked out this troublesome gun. In his report, L/Sgt Charles Brown gives it the serial 'A10', though this cannot be correct; the tank was probably F10, 'Feu d'Enfer', commanded by 2Lt Bertram Seymour and brought into action after F13 had been knocked out; it was later destroyed by a direct hit close to the company rallying point near Hill 35. Seymour was killed and most of his crew wounded.[23] By 10.30 a.m., the platoon had reached Iberian and found it was an unoccupied, shattered wreck—an untenable position, so the platoon moved to Somme and began to dig in.

On the extreme left, 10 Platoon was in no such enviable position. After Sgt Mayson had re-joined, it had become embroiled in fighting through a series of shell holes and ditches, their progress to their initial objective, Somme, held up by heavy fire from the edge of Capricorn Keep (50° 53′ 1.73″ N, 2° 56′ 46.87″ E). Once more, a tank came to the rescue. Despite the heavy MG fire, the tank commander walked in front of his vehicle to guide it into a position where it could knock out the gun, allowing 10 Platoon to storm the position and capture eighteen Germans. Newbold's report allocated 'F16' to the vehicle, but this was once more false. Although it is possible that it was F10, given the map reference, the more likely benefactor was F39, 'Formosa', commanded by 2Lt Charles Strachan. This machine had been allocated to the battalion to Newbold's left, but as he was right on the limit of his tactical bound and F39 is known to have assisted infantry by knocking out an MG in the Capricorn system, this is the machine most likely to have intervened.[24] The enemy were still putting up stiff resistance, especially to their left flank, where the adjoining battalion had not been able to push so far forward.

All the time they had been clearing Capricorn, 10 Platoon had also been under heavy fire from Pond Farm (50° 53′ 7.38″ N, 2° 56′ 49.00″ E) and its surroundings. Although this was outside its tactical area, there was no one else around to deal with the problem, and as it a constituted a considerable hazard to the battalion's left flank, Newbold decided to clear it himself. Faced with such an aggressive action, the enemy immediately surrendered. This was undoubtedly helped along by another solo action from Sgt Mayson, who attacked an MG position and killed all six of its crew. By 11.15 a.m., the platoon had cleared the complete complex and captured 150 prisoners, who had ditched all their equipment and were carrying nothing but their haversacks and gas masks when they surrendered. Before it could move on to its next objective, the platoon was contacted by Capt. Gardner, who ordered it to dig in to the front of Pond Farm and hold this position until further orders. Collecting three stragglers from the Loyals and one from 1/8th King's, Newbold brought the strength of his improvised platoon up to twelve men and two Lewis guns—a modest defensive force, considering the size of the counter-attack it would soon face.

While 10 Platoon had been battling in the shell holes, Ellwood discovered that the barrage had moved too far ahead of his platoon. He therefore ordered the advance to be made in a series of rushes to a group of dugouts on the western flank of Hill 35 (50° 52′ 48.40″ N, 2° 57′ 16.16″ E).

Although the platoon was fired upon from the elevated positions of the enemy trenches to the rear, Ellwood commented that most Germans were in 'an indecent hurry to get away',[25] and the position was quickly cleared. Leaving five men outside, Ellwood took one man and entered the southernmost dugout. (It should be noted that 'dugout' was the term used at the time, 'bunker' or 'pillbox' are a more apt choice of words here, as these massive concrete fortifications were only partially below ground level, as Ellwood's description testifies.) Inside, Ellwood found and captured a German officer, Leutnant Seidlitz of II/454.6 Kompanie. The officer was searched, but apart from an Iron Cross, no item of military interest was discovered. A halting conversation in French between the two officers elicited from the German that 'his Captain had scooted with all papers of importance'. Ellwood's report on the dugouts is highly comprehensive:

> The row of dugouts comprised six concrete dugouts; two of which had evidently been used by officers who were very strong and in good condition; the first one in which I found the officer had had two direct hits on the front but only suffered a chipping. It was built of a very hard quality of concrete at least one yard thick; it had a loophole in the front; the floor was at least six feet below the ground level; the whole dugout was lined by heavy timber; and a pumping set was installed under the floor. The loophole was constructed in such a manner that it was impossible for anyone but the observer to be wounded through it. The next dugout was badly smashed at the back and nothing of importance could be seen in it.
>
> The third dugout was the largest and best fitted of the lot having a roof about eight yards square in area; furnished with table, two chairs and a profusion of empty bottles, cigar boxes *etc.* lying about. Through this rear compartment was a sleeping compartment which had a loophole similar to the first dugout and also a special small chamber at the side with a loophole. The remaining dugouts were more or less rummaged but strongly constructed of concrete. These dugouts were connected by a trench and had a system of trenches behind and to the east of them and the trenches were camouflaged with rabbit wire and foliage, but were badly damaged. Several bomb stores; flare lights and ammunition stores were found and several notice boards stating that the place was the billet for 1 company of infantry.[26]

The dugouts cleared, Ellwood sent all eight prisoners back with just one escort, having no spare personnel to provide Leutnant Seidlitz with his own minder. Leaving another man to 'guard' the dugouts, he took his remaining four men with him to Gallipoli to see if he could find 11 Platoon. Their search unsuccessful, they returned to the dugouts to check if the other two platoons had sent runners, but no news had arrived since 12.30 p.m. It was only later that he discovered that, upon finding nothing at Iberian, 12 Platoon had moved forward to help the Loyals consolidate the Green Line. For the next hour, he and his men collected items from the bunkers and placed them into labelled sandbags for Intelligence to study. Still without news of his platoons, Ellwood went forward again at 1.30 p.m. and found that the battalion was helping to consolidate the Green Line. Upon questioning some kilted soldiers who were moving back through the battalion's area, he made a disconcerting discovery: their battalion was withdrawing away from the enemy's counter-attack. Ellwood then made his way to the left and found that the enemy were also attacking from this flank too; both flanks were now open to counter-attack.

In the wave behind C Company was D to the left and B to the right. D Company only suffered one casualty in the walk to the Black Line, but MG fire claimed another eight almost as soon as it left it. D Company came under heavy enfilading MG fire from the left, some 400 yards after it had passed through 165 Brigade; every officer in D became a casualty in the advance to the Green Line. Assisted by Sergeants Thomas Chapple and James Trebilcock, Sgt Herbert Fearnley took over the company and organised his men to help the Loyals consolidate the Green Line. They found little enemy resistance during the advance, but once the creeping barrage had moved forward, the MG fire became ferocious.

B Company, commanded by Capt. Harold Brocklebank, also had problems with enfilading fire from the left after passing through the Black Line. Shortly before reaching Gallipoli, an enemy aircraft flew low over it, machine-gunning the men. 6 Platoon, under 2Lt Sidney Walker, had its first MG casualty on the Black Line itself, and moved into extended order as it passed through 165 Brigade. Just 200 yards on from the Black Line, they came under enfilading MG fire from the right and took cover, returning fire with their rifles. Although the circumstances of Walker's wounding went un-noted, it's likely that he fell shortly before this point; thirty-four-year-old married Rochdale man Sgt James Cross's report seems to indicate that he took over command of the platoon from here onwards.[27] Cross attacked the strongpoint, captured it, and took five prisoners, the entire action taking just five minutes to complete. Moving on, the platoon had no more opposition until Gallipoli. Here, it was held up by another MG enfilading it from the right. Although unable to locate the hostile MG's position, this was soon put out of action by another unit, and 6 Platoon continued on towards the Green Line. It had not gone far when it was again enfiladed from the right for the third time; this time, the gun seemed to be firing from a small wood. Sgt Cross and 2Lt Alexander of 8 Platoon searched the wood, but finding nothing decided that the hostile gun was probably east of Delva Farm (50° 52′ 41.95″ N, 2° 57′ 41.18″ E). Unable to do anything about this, they pressed on towards the Green Line, the rounds from this gun raining on them for the whole of the journey. The men reached the Green Line level with Kansas Cross at 11.20 a.m., and Cross sent a runner back to battalion HQ to advise of their progress; 6 Platoon helped the Loyals consolidate the position under MG fire from both left and right. These two guns resulted in many more casualties for the battalion, including 2Lt Alexander of B Company, and Second Lieutenants Clement Ford and John McGill of A Company.

Under 2Lt Henry Warbrick, 7 Platoon had also reached the Black Line without casualties and pressed on. The young lieutenant was one of the first to fall in the push towards Gallipoli, wounded by enfilading MG fire. Twenty-five-year-old Sgt George Hewartson took command and moved the platoon on to the Green Line, where it helped the Loyals consolidate until B Company OC Capt. Brocklebank sent it to Gallipoli and Somme to consolidate those positions.

B Company's HQ's report, completed by A Company's A/CSM Sgt Richard Walker, suggests that B Company's platoons kept very close together and at times in the advance to the Green Line, all four platoons collaborated as intermixed units. Near the Green Line, a snipers' post to the left of their line of advance began to cause problems, and Sgt Walker and 2Lt Alexander took five men forward of the Loyals' attacking wave and put the post out of action with rifle grenades.

Alexander's 8 Platoon suffered a few casualties in the move up to the Black Line and then moved into extended order. Twenty-year-old Sgt Horace Dunkerley complained that the men tended to bunch and advance in small columns as they moved towards the Green Line, though this is probably best explained by the appalling ground conditions.[28] British artillery had substantially pummelled the German position, and after the rain of 29 July, the now water-filled shell holes were joined together in many places, adding drowning to the dangers of the battlefield. To compound this, the ground was extremely slippery; clambering around, and in and out of shell holes was slow, exhausting work which delayed the progress of the attackers to the point where they were losing the creeping barrage. These conditions made extended order strenuous to maintain. Like its comrades, 8 Platoon received no artillery fire after the Black Line, though MG fire gradually grew in intensity as the barrage moved too far ahead of the attackers. At one point, a 77-mm battery opened fire from close range and remained in action until the attackers were within 100 yards of it. This was soon overrun, one of five batteries captured by the battalion that day. Sgt Dunkerley noted that once they reached the German positions, the enemy surrendered readily. Dunkerley also discovered, as had Ellwood, that none of the prisoners were wearing equipment, carrying only their rucksacks and gas masks.[29] Just before they reached the Green Line, 2Lt Alexander was wounded by MG fire and Dunkerley took command; the platoon was then sent back to consolidate Gallipoli, where company HQ was situated.

The last unit to leave the starting point was A Company, under Lt Charles Withey, in the seventh wave of the attack: 4 Platoon was positioned on the left, and HQ on the right behind D Company; 3 Platoon on the left; and 2 Platoon to the right, behind B Company. The two left-hand platoons—4 Platoon under twenty-four-year-old 2Lt Clement Ford, and HQ under Sgt Fred Yates—suffered one or two casualties in the walk forward to the Black Line, and for the first 200 to 300 yards after that came under very heavy rifle and MG fire. This soon ceased, and apart from isolated sniping, the remainder of the advance to the Green Line was uneventful.[30] Ford was later killed by MG fire, and platoon command passed into the steady hands of thirty-four-year-old Sgt Arthur Birkett. Before long, both HQ and 4 Platoon were ordered back to Gallipoli to act as carrying parties for the forward troops.

On A Company's right flank, 3 Platoon—commanded by 2Lt Harold Lauder—had a tougher time of it. The ground was so broken after the Black Line, that it was impossible to advance in extended order, so it was forced to move in single file. Unfortunately, these delays resulted in loss of contact with HQ to the left and 2Lt John McGill's 2 Platoon to the right. Particularly heavy MG fire pinned the men down in shell holes, so Lauder ordered them to stay in cover and went forward alone to reconnoitre. Discovering a mixed group of Loyals and King's Own engaging an enemy strongpoint, he returned for his platoon, manoeuvred it forward to the enemy strongpoint's right flank, and brought enfilading fire to bear on the enemy; the Germans surrendered five minutes later. One officer and fifty men were captured and sent back under escort. Both 2 and 3 Platoon made the rest of the advance to the Green Line without further issue and helped the troops there consolidate by digging, under constant MG fire. When McGill was wounded by one of these guns, Cpl George Cox took over; another six men from the platoon were wounded before it was sent back to Gallipoli.

So far, all objectives in 164 Brigade's sector had been taken—the attack was progressing well. The many hours that division had spent in preceding months practising new tactics for overcoming strongpoints and pillboxes had paid off. Now when faced with such an obstacle, the firing slits in these positions were engaged by Lewis guns, rifle grenades, and aimed rifle fire while bombing parties outflanked the positions and neutralised them with grenades.

Rain drizzled on and off, and the very low cloud base hindered aerial observation, so progress updates were slow in coming back to brigade. News of the capture of the Green Line then had to be relayed 6 miles back to the divisional HQ, but it wasn't until 2.30 p.m. that orders were sent for the assaulting battalions of the first wave to move forward to reinforce the Green Line. As had happened so many times before, the difficulties of communication obstructed the full exploitation of any gains made. Cables leading back from the two advanced signal stations in the Blue and Black Line had all been severed in multiple places, and it took runners a minimum of two hours to cover the distance from the Green Line to the old front line where telephone communications to divisional HQ still survived—a length of time that would steadily increase as conditions worsened.[31] In addition, aerial observation proved fruitless due to poor visibility and the not unreasonable disinclination of advanced troops to fire off flares (as this immediately brought down retribution from German artillery and gave their positions away to German contact patrols).[32] But after the planned sorties by the RFC were cancelled due to the poor weather, no one thought to review the situation once the cloud base had lifted; as a result, German ground attack and observation aircraft operated unmolested over the battlefield.

A forward artillery observer sent a message back to 15 Division HQ about copious German troop movements along the Passchendaele Ridge, but the message took nearly an hour and a half to reach its destination. Around 1 p.m. messages of German troops amassing for a counter-attack were received from all along the Front, but as contact had been lost with all the forward observers, the artillery did not know where to fire at.

In the joint battalion HQ of the Loyals and King's Own, both COs decided that they needed a much more detailed idea of the situation at the Green Line and Captains Gardner and Ord (Loyals) were sent to find out. Ord was wounded shortly after leaving the dugout, so Gardner continued alone. The brigade forward station was established at Somme stronghold and news passed back that there was space in the complex for both battalion HQs to move there. At 2 p.m., an intense barrage fell upon the forward positions of 118 Brigade (who held the ground to the left of the 1/4th). Such was the intensity of the counter-attack that 118 Brigade gradually fell back, leaving the 1/4th's flank exposed. At 2.15 p.m., Brig.-Gen. Stockwell ordered a defensive flank to be established along a line from Schuler Farm (50° 53′ 19.07″ N, 2° 57′ 15.45″ E) to Border House (50° 53′ 17.97″ N, 2° 56′ 32.09″ E). Just as this was beginning to take shape, six waves of German infantry, preceded by an accurate barrage of artillery, appeared from over the Zonnebeke Spur. In support, three German aircraft flew low over the 1/4th's positions, machine-gunning and dropping bombs on the defenders.[33]

News of the impending attack was received by battalion HQ at 3 p.m., and Gardner ordered A Company to return back to the Green Line to reinforce the defenders and prepare for counter-attack from both left flanks.[34] The volume of casualties from the units on the Green Line and size of the impending attack made this a necessary decision, but it was also to have major repercussions on the day's success. A Company had been allocated to carrying parties, thus leaving a gaping hole in the supply chain—a situation that became critical a few hours later. At 3.35 p.m., HQ received an urgent plea from Capt. Brocklebank for more ammunition and reinforcements. He also requested help from tanks, but none remained in action by that stage. Ten minutes after receiving this message, the COs of both battalions decided to merge the two battalions into one force, surviving numbers being too few to effectively operate as disparate units.

At 4.35 p.m., Maj.-Gen. Jeudwine ordered 164 Brigade to hold a line from Hill 35 (50° 52′ 48.58″ N, 2° 57′ 22.30″ E) to Somme and through to Border House. But by the time the order was sent, this line was already in German hands. Only about thirty men from the two left-hand battalions of 164 Brigade returned to the Black Line, those holding the line from Somme to Border House having been surrounded and captured after their ammunition had run out. For the men from the King's Own, the battle was reaching a critical stage: all four companies were now helping to stem the enemy counter-attack against the Green Line. The earlier frontal attack had been beaten off with relative success, assisted by the three MGs to the front of the 1/4th's defences; but now the defenders were clearly in imminent danger of being surrounded and cut off.

On the right of the Green Line, Capt. Brocklebank, had been wounded, and as the division to their right withdrew, 2Lt Clement Ford gave the order for his men to fall back, keeping in touch with the battalion to their right as they did so. As he supervised the withdrawal, he was hit and killed. Initially, the men retired to Hill 37, under fire the whole way, and set up a defensive position there. Cpl Cox was wounded on the way back, and 2 Platoon got its third commander for the day, twenty-four-year-old Cpl Phillip Baines. The men held off the enemy from Hill 37 for as long as their ammunition lasted, but then withdrew to Hill 35, collecting as much ammunition as they could from knocked out tanks and the bodies of the dead as they retired. While withdrawing, Sgt Hewartson's platoon encountered a British corporal with a Vickers but no ammunition, and helped him carry the gun back to Hill 35. 6 Platoon, under Sgt James Cross, had dug in close to Gallipoli, and when the division to its right sent a message for help against a counter-attack, Cross gathered together as many men from his platoon as possible along with various stragglers, and with their two Lewis guns successfully covered the retreat of their beleaguered neighbours. For his courage and leadership, Cross was awarded the DCM. The few rounds the defenders had been able to scavenge were not enough, however, and a withdrawal to the Black Line was ordered once all ammunition was expended. On the left the defenders had also been forced to withdraw to avoid being encircled, and their ammunition situation was equally critical; at 4 p.m., they too withdrew to the Black Line, their ammunition completely spent. Although a message that C Company had withdrawn was sent, this didn't actually reach HQ until 8.30 p.m.[35]

As the withdrawal continued, the persistent drizzle morphed into torrential rain, which fell on friend and foe alike. Visibility was extremely poor, but vital time had been bought to boost defences against enemy counter-attack, which had been slowed by the difficulties of fording swollen streams and further still by ever-deepening mud. Men on either side were up to their knees in mud and water. The defending force was a hotchpotch of units from 164 and 165 Brigade, and even kilted soldiers from the division to the left. It wasn't until 6 p.m. that the German counter-attack got to within 300 yards of the Black Line, and a combination of withering MG fire and a heavy and accurate bombardment from British guns broke it, leaving many German casualties in the mud. 2Lt Newbold found that a series of outposts to his immediate front masked the fields of fire of his Lewis guns, so he placed six guns on the roof of the pillbox behind his trench, where they poured lethal fire into the close-packed ranks of the German counter-attack force as soon as they appeared on the ridge of Hill 35.[36] To add to the woes of the enemy, their rifles and light MGs were so jammed with mud that most were completely unserviceable.[37] Then just as today, the British Army was trained in the concept of 'your rifle first, you second', so men who fell would instinctively do their utmost to hold their weapon clear of the slime. There's no reason to suspect that German training was any less thorough, but in these conditions, no amount of training was going to keep the attackers' weapons clear. The defenders were in a much better state, as the ground conditions during their advance had been drier and, more importantly, there had been enough time to clean weapons during consolidation. Newbold had commanded his platoon with skill and courage, and was recommended for—but not awarded—the MC.

Maintaining some advanced outposts, the survivors stood to in their positions along the Black Line, in what was later named the 'Frezenberg Line', awaiting further counter-attacks. At 1.30 a.m., they were relieved with orders to withdraw to the old front line, although 2Lt Gribble and fifteen of his men were unfortunate enough to remain there all night. Battalion HQ pulled back from Pommern Castle and established itself in the dugout in Oxford Trench around 5 a.m., while the combined forces of both battalions manned the section of front line from New John Street (50° 52′ 13.95″ N, 2° 55′ 15.85″ E) to Warwick Farm (50° 51′ 56.19″ N, 2° 55′ 38.76″ E). Throughout the morning, small parties of men made their way back through No Man's Land; of the attacking force, about 150 men returned to the battalion fold. In the late morning, HQ moved once more, this time to No. 30 Dugout in the ruins of Wieltje.

When word reached HQ that the forward outposts had been forced to withdraw to the Frezenberg Line, preparations were immediately begun to try and strengthen the old front line. This was easier said than done, as many of the men were now up to their waists in mud and water and the rain kept falling. For all the good their spades were, they might as well have been trying to shovel soup! For the men in the Frezenberg Line desperately trying to consolidate these positions, it must have been horrendous, yet they succeeded. Around midnight, 2Lt Charles Lingford brought up fifty stragglers collected by the various posts, and these were used to reinforce the meagre garrison. Despite intermittent shelling, the 1/4th suffered no further casualties in this line, and when 9/ Royal Irish Rifles from 108 Brigade took over their positions in the early afternoon of 2 August, the sense of relief was enormous. Company by company, the men marched back to the concentration area in Vlamertinghe, reaching there by 5 p.m. (50° 51′ 1.86″ N, 2° 49′ 34.76″ E). Fate, however, dealt the battalion a severe blow: HQ personnel, including Maj. Robathan and Lt-Col. Hindle of the Loyals, had only just boarded a truck just outside St Jean when a heavy shell landed behind them. Two men were lightly wounded, one of whom was twenty-nine-year-old Pte Charles Golding from Barrow. Another three were more seriously injured, two of whom later died from their wounds. It seems particularly cruel to have survived a battle of this intensity, only to be hit on the way out after the fighting was done. This only goes to show the perpetual perils of mere existence at the Front.

Upon reaching Vlamertinghe, the first thing the men got was a generous rum ration, which mostly went straight to the heads of the haggard and hungry men. Hot baths and clean uniforms followed, and at 8.45 p.m. they boarded a fleet of buses and travelled to No. 3 Area at Watou, arriving at 1 a.m. on 3 August. Even though the camp was a quagmire, the men spent most of the day asleep, their first opportunity to do so since 30 July. The battalion had suffered 212 casualties, with nearly 60 per cent of the attacking force killed, wounded, or missing, sixty of whom either turned out to be killed in action or died of wounds. The men's disillusion must have been palpable; after all, they had come out of the Battle for Pilckem Ridge lightly compared to other battalions in 164 Brigade, which suffered 1,370 casualties—approximately 70 per cent of the strength of each battalion on average.[38]

Of the sixty killed, only six died from their wounds; the others were all classed as killed in action. Of these fifty-four, eight have known graves, while the rest are commemorated on the Menin Gate. It wasn't long before news of the casualties began to appear in the Barrow press, though by 1917, news of the war already received far less coverage than it had in its early stages; Pte John Steel's death would go unrecorded by *The Barrow News*, for instance, even though his minor wounds had been newsworthy just over a year earlier. Unlike in earlier battles, none of those killed were below the age of eighteen, though some like Pte James Speight from Lancaster and Pte Thomas Benson from Barrow were only just eighteen. Many of the casualties were married men with children, and Pte William Bond (170), a thirty-two-year-old drayman from Barrow, had five children, his wife pregnant with a sixth, when he was killed. Thirty-two-year-old father of three from Liverpool Pte Joseph McDonald had enlisted under the Derby Scheme in 1915, but had not been mobilised until 1917 and only joined the 1/4th two weeks before the attack. He had been wounded as his D Company platoon moved forward along the left flank, but was never seen again (officers and men, as usual, were under strict orders not to stop to aid the wounded). In the same draft had been thirty-one-year-old father of two Pte William Prest, born in Kendal. He is one of the eight killed who have a marked grave.

Some of the wounded, such as twenty-three-year-old Pte Frank Evans from Burslem and twenty-five-year-old Cpl John Edgar from Barrow (who had been shot in the chest), were captured when the attackers retired from the Green Line and were treated for their wounds by the Germans. The recovery of any non-walking wounded had been impossible in the fighting withdrawal, as the men had not been able to break contact as they withdrew and every rifle counted. Another captured under similar circumstances was twenty-eight-year-old Capt. Brocklebank. Although the Germans did the best they could for wounded prisoners, not all those captured survived their injuries. Twenty-five-year-old Pte James Cameron from Barrow died from heart failure as a result of his wounds and is buried in Cologne. Some families grieved for the second time in the war; the letter from Infantry Records in Preston to the Lancaster home of the mother of twenty-seven-year-old Cpl John Postlethwaite must have caused tremendous heartache, ten months after the death of her other son with the 1/4th.

Some of wounded had already been hit on more than one occasion. For twenty-four-year-old Dalton soldier Pte George Thompson, who was hit in the hand, this was his third wound; neither would it be his last! This time, the injury to twenty-six-year-old Pte Frank Nolan spelled the end of his soldiering days, as he was medically discharged. Cpl Harold Martin, awarded the DCM for capturing an enemy patrol in 1915, was wounded in the neck and did not return to the battalion, as after his recovery in England he was posted to 2/5th King's Own. Twenty-eight-year-old Pte Charles Higginson from Alderley Edge would not re-join either, as his left leg was amputated when infection set in. Another to get a medical discharge was twenty-year-old Pte Augustus Rodgers from Barrow, blinded in both eyes. Thirty-seven-year-old Pte Arthur Hammond's head wound was minor, but his trench nephritis was so advanced that he was returned to England and after treatment at Englefield Green Red Cross Hospital discharged as medically unfit, his kidneys beyond recovery.

The 1/4th's officers had led from the front, as per British Army tradition, and consequently paid the penalty. C Company probably got off the lightest, with just one officer, twenty-seven-year-old 2Lt Frederick Gilling, wounded upon withdrawal on the morning of 1 August. A Company's twenty-four-year-old 2Lt Clement Ford from Lancaster was killed, and twenty-six-year-old 2Lt John McGill wounded. McGill was born in Liverpool, but had migrated to Canada, enlisted as an ordinary soldier in the 61st Canadian Infantry, and was commissioned into the King's Own. B Company's losses were worse: their company commander was wounded and captured, and twenty-five-year-old 2Lt Sidney Walker, 2Lt Henry Warbrick, and thirty-three-year-old 2Lt James Alexander MC (on attachment from the Fusiliers) all wounded. D Company suffered similarly heavy losses, with four of its officers killed or wounded. The company commander, Capt. William Pattinson, was wounded, as was nineteen-year-old 2Lt Jack Gaulter. This young lieutenant had bumped into a friend from the Fusiliers at the baths in Poperinghe on the 28th and shared their mutual forebodings about the coming attack; incidentally, the two men met again on the hospital train to Boulogne, both having been shot in the leg.[39] The luck of nineteen-year-old 2Lt John Johnstone of D Company, a promising medical student from Barrow, finally had run out; he had been gassed once and wounded twice (once by his own side just a year previously), and had a very narrow escape when a bullet passed through his helmet without harm to himself; yet on this occasion, his body was never found.[40] Also killed from D Company was 2Lt Richard Bradley. Signals officers 2Lt Thomas Middleton MM and 2Lt Percy Taylor attached to 164 TMB also suffered wounds.

Killed or died from wounds in the Battle of Pilckem Ridge 31 July – 2 August 1917

| | | | | | |
|---|---|---|---|---|---|
| L/Cpl Thomas Akister | 200442 | KIA | Pte Thomas Bagot | 241596 | KIA |
| Pte Frank Baines | 202196 | KIA | Pte Thomas William Benson | 202736 | DOW-31/7 |
| Pte William Bevins | 201095 | DOW-17/8 | Pte Albert Billingham | 32887 | KIA |
| Pte William Bond | 24170 | KIA | Pte Leonard Edward Borley | 202175 | KIA |
| 2Lt Richard Bradley | | KIA | Pte Victor Brazil | 201559 | KIA |
| Pte James Cameron | 200485 | DOW-9/8 | Pte Harry Churm | 201457 | KIA |
| Pte Richard Colley | 201525 | KIA | Pte Samuel Corbett | 201155 | KIA |
| Pte Henry Cross | 201789 | KIA | Cpl Harry Duxbury | 23976 | KIA |
| Pte John Edmondson | 33968 | KIA | Pte James Ellis | 202217 | KIA |
| Pte Fred Elston | 201714 | KIA | 2Lt Clement William Ford | | KIA |
| Pte William Gouge | 28103 | KIA | Pte Benjamin Hansom | 28028 | KIA |
| Pte Joseph Harney | 28109 | KIA | Pte John Hart | 201616 | KIA |
| Cpl James Hird | 200170 | KIA | Pte James Hodges | 201205 | KIA |
| Pte Fred Howarth | 22736 | KIA | Pte Albert Hulme | 201620 | KIA |
| 2Lt John Douglas Johnstone | | KIA | L/Cpl Thomas Arthur Lowe | 201731 | KIA |
| Pte Darby Maler | 202084 | KIA | Pte Joseph McDonald | 28115 | KIA |
| Pte John Mitchell | 26131 | KIA | Pte Frank C. Pickthall | 202091 | KIA |
| L/Sgt Henry Hugh Pill | 200583 | KIA | Pte James Pollitt | 201332 | KIA |
| Cpl John E. S. Postlethwaite | 201677 | KIA | Pte William Prest | 26966 | KIA |
| L/Cpl Arthur Edward Rogers | 10861 | KIA | Pte John Henry Rogers | 15204 | KIA |
| L/Cpl Frank Ryder | 202209 | KIA | Pte William Shaw | 22918 | KIA |
| Pte Robinson Shone | 200637 | KIA | Pte James Smith | 202772 | KIA |
| Pte John Joseph Smith | 27305 | KIA | Pte Thomas Smith | 17969 | KIA |
| Pte James Speight | 33065 | KIA | Pte John Steel | 201056 | KIA |

| Pte Sampson Steele | 27044 | KIA | Pte Edward Stewart | 200952 | KIA |
|---|---|---|---|---|---|
| Pte Clarence Swift | 201653 | KIA | Pte John Taylor | 201662 | KIA |
| Pte Charles Henry Turner | 202770 | KIA | Cpl David Vickers | 200690 | KIA |
| Pte Ernest Watson | 202229 | DOW-2/8 | Pte Thomas Henry Wharton | 201308 | DOW-7/8 |
| Pte Thomas Whittle | 201309 | KIA | Pte Stanley John Willis | 202156 | KIA |
| Pte Frederick Henry Worth | 201153 | DOW-10/8 | Pte George Henry Wright | 202157 | KIA |

Reported wounded in the Battle for Pilckem Ridge 31 July – 2 August 1917

| 2Lt James Caldwell Alexander | | WIA | Pte Taylor Binns | 201586 | WIA |
|---|---|---|---|---|---|
| Pte William Bond | 33072 | WIA | Pte Stephen Boundy | 200658 | WIA |
| Pte James Steele Braithwaite | 24467 | WIA | Capt. Harold A. Brocklebank | | WIA/POW |
| Pte Leonard Chorlton | 4914 | WIA | Pte John Clough | 201711 | WIA/POW |
| Cpl George W Cox | 202163 | WIA | Sgt Horace B Dunkerley | 200269 | WIA |
| Pte John Eaton | 200584 | WIA | Cpl John Burnett Edgar | 200367 | WIA/POW |
| Pte Frank Evans | 27567 | WIA/POW | Cpl Thomas Fawcett | 200284 | WIA |
| 2Lt Jack Rudolf Gaulter | | WIA | 2Lt Frederick Cuthbert Gilling | | WIA |
| Pte Charles Victor Golding | 33719 | WIA | Pte Arthur Hammond | 201705 | WIA |
| Sgt Thomas Haskett | 200651 | WIA | Pte Charles Higginson | 200456 | WIA |
| Pte Robert Hodgson | 32488 | WIA | Pte William Longley Holroyd | 201553 | WIA |
| Pte Frederick William Lane | 200501 | WIA/POW | Pte William Arthur Lucas | 202183 | WIA |
| Cpl Harold Martin | 200198 | WIA | 2Lt John Allison McGill | | WIA |
| 2Lt Thomas Harvey Middleton | | WIA | Cpl Joseph Nicholson | 200777 | WIA/POW |
| Pte Frank Harold Nolan | 200782 | WIA | Pte Stanley Russell Parsons | 10822 | WIA |
| 2Lt William Rose Pattinson | | WIA | Pte Augustus Henry Rodgers | 33955 | WIA |
| Pte Frank Roebuck | 21150 | WIA | L/Cpl Samuel Rowe | 23065 | WIA |
| Pte Samuel John Rowe | 200714 | WIA | L/Cpl Robert Schofield | 201386 | WIA |
| Pte Richard Simpson | 200478 | WIA | Pte George Smith | 201743 | WIA |
| 2Lt Percival Charles Taylor | | WIA | Pte George T. Thompson | 200565 | WIA |
| 2Lt Sidney Frederick Walker | | WIA | 2Lt Henry James Warbrick | | WIA |
| Sgt Arthur Goodwin White | 200528 | WIA | L/Cpl Arthur Whittle | 200885 | WIA |
| Pte Joseph Worth | 23178 | WIA | | | |

At Watou the battalion received a special 'Order of the Day' from Maj.-Gen. Jeudwine, in which he commended the men for their achievements.

The attack you made on the 31st is worthy to rank with the great deeds of the British Army in the past, and has added fresh glory to the record of that Army. The courage, determination, and self sacrifice shown by Officers, Warrant Officers, Non Commissioned Officers and men is beyond praise. [...] You have captured every inch of the objectives allotted to you. It is not your fault that you could not hold all you took. You have broken and now hold, in spite of weather and counter-attacks, a line that the enemy has strengthened and consolidated at his leisure for more than two years.[41]

While ultimately the attack had not been a total success, all the objectives had been taken, though not held. Despite all the preparations, the recurring 'Achilles heel' of communications had once more foiled the commanders' ability to react to a changing situation, and the shortage of small arms ammunition had doomed the gains on the battalion's front. Every 'after-action report' states confidently that, had ammunition been available, the Green Line would have been held—although the battalion's own report realistically added that contact with the units to both the right and left would have been necessary to making this feasible, too.[42] The reports overwhelmingly display the men's confidence in their ability to take strongpoints, batteries, and MG positions without losing either impetus or a fervent conviction that the Germans could be beaten.

The battalion won its first VC of the war, awarded to Sgt Tom Mayson, for his series of solo attacks against strongpoints. There was also universal praise for the Lewis guns in both the attacking and withdrawal stages, though concerns about the burden of carrying loaded magazines were voiced. Most reports enthused about the Hales rifle grenades and their use in attacking such positions, though Charles Withey thought them 'useless apart from in isolated circumstances'—a comment so against the grain that Lt-Col. Balfour has penned '||' in the margins and initialled it.[43] The issue of a second water bottle and rations was appreciated by all, though some NCOs thought that the men were carrying too much as it was, and that both holdall and 'housewife' (a sewing kit pronounced 'huzziff') could have been dispensed with. The platoons involved in mopping up were the only platoons who complained about the numbers of grenades carried; Sgt Brown criticised bomb buckets on the grounds that they placed all the weight on one shoulder, and bemoaned the crucial lack of small arms ammunition, advocating that men carry at least 170 rounds in the future—a complaint common to all platoons. Time spent in 'musketry' training had not been wasted, as the intelligent use of rifles in aiming fire during the 'open infantry firefight' of the withdrawal phase was praised by 2Lt Gribble.[44] One successful infantry tactic was 'walking fire', that is suppressing enemy rifle and MG fire by shooting rifles from the hip as one advanced. With a little practice, this could be surprisingly accurate, but as Brig.-Gen. Stockwell pointed out, it was also 'expensive in ammunition'.[45]

Platoon reports show that when they were available, the tanks were highly effective in helping the infantry. It was suggested that tanks in future be adapted to carry up ammunition supplies to forward troops, a suggestion repeated in Brig.-Gen. Stockwell's brigade report.[46] As ground conditions had proved most unsuitable for these machines, this was more a wish than a practical reality, though later in the war attempts were made to implement the idea. The lack of air cover was also a sore point with platoon commanders, who had not appreciated being individually marked out and machine-gunned by the German Air Force.

The British bombardment had been a two-edged sword—so pitted was the ground that the infantry had encountered difficulty in moving forward in an extended line. This inevitably resulted in the infantry falling behind the creeping barrage, with no means to communicate this to the artillery; vexingly, the brigade report describes the German infantry's method of coordinating their barrage by a series of flare signals.[47] Reports also affirmed that enemy wire posed no problems, though it's unclear if the reason for this is a plain lack of wire defences, or that they had been destroyed by the bombardment; the truth is probably somewhere between the two statements. The bombardment of German positions had had mixed results: most concrete dugouts were barely scratched, though the 'will to fight' demonstrated by the men garrisoning some of these positions had clearly been affected. Those positions not made from thick concrete had been smashed beyond all recognition, and even the concrete of Iberian had proved vulnerable to direct hits by heavy artillery. The 'thin' barrages experienced by the men as they advanced towards the Black Line may also be evidence of effective British counter-battery fire and the neutralisation of enemy forward artillery observers by the creeping barrage, though the heavy shelling experienced by the men from the late morning onwards also shows that many enemy batteries were still very much intact.

Sgt Brown thought the preparations for battle had been excellent:

> This is the third battle in which I have participated at Ypres and I wish to say that on no previous occasion had I such clear instructions. The most dense man in the platoon had a perfectly clear idea of what he had to do. The aeroplane photographs were an excellent help and by studying them I was enabled to recognise my objective as soon as I got in the neighbourhood.[48]

On 5 August, brigade gathered at Abele Station and travelled by train and lorry moved to billets in the village of Bonningues-lès-Adres, north-west of St Omer. The accommodation was decent, and the green, rolling hills and wooded valleys a perfect contrast to Flanders. Both the King's Own and Liverpool Irish received a warm welcome from the locals, whose acceptance of foreign troops had not been jaded by frequent billeting. One of the first priorities was to smoothly integrate the influx of reinforcements who had already begun to arrive. A Company was under the command of Lt Charles Withey, who was to be promoted to Captain; in B, 2Lt John Evans replaced Capt. Brocklebank; and in C, Capt. Alfred Procter was in command. The position of OC in D Company was given to twenty-seven-year-old 2Lt Reginald Senton from Ipswich.

Individual platoons were reorganised so that there was a core of experienced men in each platoon—though, if at all possible, men were not moved to a different company. Seventy-one replacements arrived on 4 August, and were allocated platoons on the 6th. The next day, another seventy-seven replacements arrived, and they too were integrated into their new platoons. Although over 150 men were replacing the casualties, the battalion was still considerably under strength. Many of the replacements were actually experienced soldiers who had been wounded and re-posted to the 1/4th upon their recovery, such as twenty-year-old Pte James Reading from Fleetwood, who had been with 8/ King's Own until he was wounded in early 1916. Also on the 7th, the King's Own, Liverpool Irish, and men from 164 TMB were drawn up in the village square and addressed by Maj.-Gen. Jeudwine, who personally delivered his commendations and thanks for their work. The next morning, platoon training began and classes were held on the Lewis gun and bombing techniques, culminating in a battalion parade in the afternoon. Training took place almost every morning, but afternoons and evenings were reserved for sports and entertainments.

On the morning of 16 August, the battalion football team narrowly beat the Fusiliers 1–0 in the first round of the brigade football tournament. Unfortunately, the battalion was knocked out in the semi-finals when 1/5th South Lancashires beat them 3–1. In the afternoon, a keenly contested inter-company sports and gymkhana began, competing for a cup offered by Lt-Col. Balfour. The competition concluded the next day and was won by the battalion transport. That night a concert party was held, organised by 2Lt Robert Mudie, a gifted entertainer and one of twelve officers from the Lancashire Fusiliers attached to the 1/4th in October 1916. Sadly, he returned to his unit shortly after the concert and was as a captain killed in action just over a month later. In the brigade sports, the battalion won the tug-of-war and the races over one and two miles, so there was some consolation for losing the football tournament!

Officers and men also got 'local' leave: forty-eight hours for the officers at the coast and twenty-four hours for the men in Calais. It does not seem much today, but at the time it must have been a welcome break from the daily routine and it was not within the power of the battalion to grant extended home leave to all its personnel. One man, twenty-eight-year-old Pte Thomas Pollitt from Blackpool, overstayed his leave by forty-three hours until he surrendered himself to the military police in Calais and was fined three days' pay—a very lenient punishment considering he was no stranger to the Charge Sheet. He would more than make up for this later when he won the MM. Despite being miles from the Front, there were still casualties during this period. While the battalion was on the range on 17 August, Pte Walker from C Company was accidentally shot and wounded. On the 24th, the battalion also received the news that one of their men had died in hospital from meningitis. Thirty-seven-year-old Pte Albert Bassett was a married man with a young daughter, and had only been with the battalion for ten weeks. On 13 September, another man, thirty-two-year-old Pte Richard Moss from Borwick, also died from illness in hospital at St Omer.

Up until its return to the Front on 14 September, the battalion took part in increasingly complex training on a one-to-one scale layout of the forthcoming attack objectives. Emphasis was placed on attacking pillboxes and defended shell holes, much like the men had done on 31 July. They also trained on German MGs and grenades, as the use of enemy weapons could lend considerable bite to the defence of captured positions. The tactical dispositions the platoons had used with such success on 31 July were honed until all, including the new replacements, could operate fluently; the knowledge that they would have to put these skills into practice again before too long must have produced extra motivation to get it right!

# 8

# 14 September 1917 – 24 September 1917
# The Battle of the Menin Road Ridge

On 14 September, the battalion moved by road to Audruicq, where it boarded a train for Ypres. This time it was accommodated in tents and bivouacs near Goldfish Château, on the Vlamertinghe road west of Ypres (50° 51′ 8.20″ N, 2° 51′ 4.65″ E). Goldfish Château was one of the few large buildings near Ypres not totally destroyed; despite some damage, it outlived the war relatively intact. The grounds surrounding it were, however, anything but safe, and riddled with shell holes. On the 15th, the battalion was carrying out platoon training in the grounds when a squadron of German aircraft flew over and bombed the camp, killing one man and wounding another three from one of the other battalions there. The 1/4th's MO Capt. John Wilson was also slightly wounded, but remained on duty. The next morning brought another attack, and this time the battalion was not so lucky. Three members were killed outright by the bombs: forty-year-old Pte John Powell from Bedminster, thirty-two-year-old Pte Charles Alderson from West Hartlepool, and twenty-one-year-old Pte Charles Green from Lincolnshire. The two older men were both married. In addition, five men were wounded and the unlucky 2Lt Norman Whittaker was hit by a British anti-aircraft bullet when it descended back to earth.

On 17 September, the battalion moved forward to their concentration area. B and D Companies and HQ held one of the old German reserve trenches and A and C Company, were accommodated in part of the old British line. The Front was little changed from when they had left on 1 August, though small gains had been made in one or two places. The battalion would in effect be attacking the same objectives it had captured on 31 July, but had been unable to hold due to casualties and ammunition shortages.[1] On the 18th, officers and NCOs went forward to reconnoitre the front line, and D Company moved forward to relieve the Liverpool Scottish in the 'shell hole' system. (Forward defences for both sides consisted of a chain of fortified positions, linked by a series of shell holes.)

During the night of the 17th and early hours of the 18th, the battalion suffered a number of casualties from shellfire. Forty-one-year-old Cpl William Fletcher from Greenock was terribly wounded and died of his injuries at the RAP late on the night of the 17th. Also killed were Welshman Pte Thomas Evans, resident in Atherton; Pte Henry Hargreaves from Lancaster; Pte Richard Marsden from Preston; Pte Ernest Sellars from Grimsby; and Pte James Wilding from Bolton. Eleven men were wounded. These included twenty-year-old Pte Arthur Durham from Darlington, hit in the hand and face by shrapnel, a Blighty wound that saw him posted to and killed in action with the 1/5th when he returned. At least two other men from the battalion joined him on the hospital ship home. Thirty-four-year-old father of two and hairdresser from Barrow, Pte Robert Holme was wounded in knee and thigh by shrapnel, but would return in 1918. Thirty-three-year-old Blackpool bookie Pte Wilfred

Verdon was hit in the elbow, but when he recovered in April 1918 he was posted to 8/ King's Own and killed with them in September.

The same meticulous planning that had gone into the attack on 31 July was evident in the attack scheduled for 20 September. Assaulting battalions had once more practiced their movements over ground laid out to resemble their objectives, and every man knew his task. The delay between 31 July and September 20 was mainly due to waiting for the weather to improve and the ground to dry out, though bringing supplies and munitions forwards was time-consuming, too. The weather in the first three weeks of September had been mainly fine and sunny and the sea of mud had gradually morphed into a dusty brown desert, though the clouds of dust kicked up by any movement along the roads and trackways brought its own perils in an area still overlooked by enemy observers. Massive efforts had gone on behind the lines to ensure that supplies were delivered to their respective dumps and communications maintained. There was always a shortage of available manpower after an attack, not just because of casualties, but also because infantrymen were more in demand for their combat (rather than porter) skills, so supplies for the immediate aftermath of an attack also needed to be transported beforehand. Eleven days' worth of rations were stockpiled at the battalion HQ in Capricorn Keep, the water alone amounting to 50 tonnes of porterage.[2]

Initially, ground conditions had been so bad that plank roads were 'floated' on top of the mud to provide passage for men, pack animals, and carts. These planks were of elm or beech, and 9 feet long, 1 foot wide, and 2½ inches thick. About four or five were laid lengthways along the road as runners and then covered by others laid crosswise. The top planks were fastened to the runners by spikes, and along each side of the road, half-round pine logs provided a curb which helped keep wheels on track (as mud and water made the surface very slippery). In just one area (held by the I Anzac Corps), 240 tonnes of planks were needed on a daily basis. This work was carried out by the engineers and pioneer battalions of the individual corps, helped by the Labour Corps and British West Indies Regiment, who provided 12,500 and 1,000 men respectively. It wasn't just planks that required moving to the Front: 54,572 tonnes of ammunition were required for this attack, and it was actually brought forward and deposited in the forward dumps in an astounding thirteen days, thanks to both the light railways and horse-drawn transport.[3] One thing that 55 Division really needed before the forthcoming attack was reinforcements. The division had suffered 3,855 casualties on 31 July, and very few replacements had arrived since then. When they did come, they had only been about 1,000 in total for the entire division, and it had been too late to train them for this attack. Consequently, just about every battalion would be vastly under strength on the 20th.[4]

The battalion was to assault what was known as the Keir Sector, probably after Keir Farm (50° 53′ 1.40″ N, 2° 57′ 36.28″ E), under cover of a creeping barrage. Unlike previous attacks, there would be no long, systematic bombardment to prepare the ground for the infantry; instead, there would be an intense twenty-four-hour bombardment immediately beforehand, which Gen. Gough believed would help maintain an element of surprise.[5] To further maintain surprise, troops were ordered that no bayonets were to be fixed until the beginning of the creeping barrage.[6] The final objective was the Green Line of 31 July, but two intermediate objectives were allocated to 164 Brigade, to be assaulted by 1/4th King's Own and to their left 2/5th Lancashire Fusiliers. To the battalion's right would be 1/9th King's for the first part of the attack and 1/6th King's for the second stage, both from 165 Brigade.

The battalion would attack with two companies fronting the assault: D Company to the left and B to the right. Company formation was a first wave comprising two platoons and a second wave of the remaining two, with 70 yards between each wave and 12 yards between each line. These two companies would seize the first objective, known as the 'Red Dotted Line' and running from Schuler Farm (50° 53′ 19.07″ N, 2° 57′ 15.45″ E) through Gallipoli (50° 52′ 54.16″ N, 2° 57′ 26.40″ E) to a position about 200 m east of Iberian (50° 52′ 39.48″ N, 2° 57′ 32.73″ E). The third and fourth waves comprised C Company on the left and A on the right, both using a similar two-platoon frontage. Once they had reached the Red Dotted Line, they would pass through D and B Company and attack the 'Yellow Dotted Line', running from just east of Schuler Farm in the north, southwards and west of Cross Cotts (50° 53′ 11.88″ N, 2° 57′ 30.50″ E), and then curving eastwards half way between Keir Farm and Gallipoli Copse (50° 52′ 55.44″ N, 2° 57′ 52.36″ E).

One platoon of B Company was detailed to drop off in the assault and mop up Aisne Farm (50° 53′ 0.32″ N, 2° 57′ 9.98″ E), leaving a sufficiently strong force behind to garrison it; another platoon was tasked with seizing and garrisoning a strongpoint (at 50° 53′ 1.44″ N, 2° 57′ 22.27″ E). The remainder of B Company was to cooperate with 1/6th King's to capture and garrison another strongpoint (at 50° 52′ 58.23″ N, 2° 57′ 25.14″ E). As it advanced, D Company was to detail one platoon to mop up Loos itself (50° 53′ 6.86″ N, 2° 57′ 14.41″ E) and clear the strongpoints in close proximity to it. Once these tasks were accomplished, both companies were to distribute their defences in depth along the ground between the jumping-off positions and the Red Dotted Line. When the King's Own had achieved these objectives, 1/4th Loyals would pass through and take the Green Line.

After seizure of the Yellow Dotted Line, C and A Company were to distribute their defences, also in depth, between the Yellow and Red Dotted Lines and all four companies were ordered to hold any captured posts 'at all costs'.[7] Detachments of RE and Pioneers would follow closely behind the attacking waves to help consolidate captured positions. The troops were also urged to use captured German MGs to assist their defences, but a section from 164 MG Company was also put under the control of each battalion HQ for deployment as required. The HQs of both 1/4th King's Own and the Loyals were to be positioned in Capricorn Keep (50° 53′ 1.00″ N, 2° 56′ 43.57″ E) for the first stage of the attack, so an advanced HQ was to be set up in a suitable position along the Red Dotted Line. Two divisional aid posts were established in four 16-x-6-foot dugouts at Pond Galleries (50° 53′ 7.38″ N, 2° 56′ 49.00″ E) and Cornhill (50° 53′ 4.47″ N, 2° 56′ 35.27″ E).

Equipment was identical to before, save that this time each man carried a red—rather than white—flare to signal to aircraft. Again, the men were given strict cautioning about souvenir-hunting; still, company commanders were allowed to 'licence' one man from each platoon to collect items to the total bulk of 'one sandbag' for his pals. Each Lewis section was now to carry twenty-five filled magazines for the gun, in addition to any loose ammunition carried—though this was obviously modified to some extent, as several post-battle narratives from D Company mention that an issue of one Lewis magazine to every man in each platoon proved a great success.[8]

As an additional boost to the chances of success, 1/5th King's Own were kept behind as a Special Reserve. They were to move forward from their position in the old German line at 'zero plus ninety minutes', and occupy the area between Aisne Farm and Hindu Cott. (50° 53′ 8.66″ N, 2° 57′ 1.38″ E). Every man was to carry a spade, which would then be collected into a dump at this position for use by those consolidating. The OC of the 1/5th was given considerable independence—he could act as he saw fit in order to carry out his two objectives. These were firstly to drive home the attack on any portion of the Green Line that was proving difficult to seize, and secondly to use his men to immediately handle any German counter-attack that penetrated the front or flanks of the brigade sector.

Although 5.40 a.m. on the 20th had been decided on as zero hour, the date was not set in stone and depended on suitable conditions. As night fell, a gentle drizzle began to descend, turning into steady rain by 11 p.m. Generals Gough and Plumer, the commanders of the Fifth and Second Armies, were concerned, and conferred as to whether or not to call off the attack. After further consultation with meteorologist Lt-Col. E. Gold and a number of divisional commanders as to the suitability of the ground, they were advised that the ground was manageable and that, apart from the risk of thunderstorms, the weather was likely to be fair in the intermediate future.[9]

The battalion moved silently through the rain and into the shell holes that were their jumping-off positions. Those of the left-hand companies were to the north of the road between Wieltje and Kansas Cross; the two right-hand companies to the south of this road and approximately level with Pond Farm, the flank of each leading platoon position marked by a stick bearing a small oblong board giving the number of the platoon, each flank marker joined by tape. Despite the filthy weather and total darkness, the attackers all managed to move into their positions without anyone getting lost, a testament to all the practice in night deployments during recent training. They were now 150 m from the Stützpunkt Line, the nearest German positions upon which the barrage would fall. No doubt these cold, wet, stiff, and muddy men must have heaved a collective sigh of relief when the rain petered out shortly before dawn. The night had been tense, not just because an attack was impending, but also because around midnight, word was passed around in the forward jumping-off positions that an enemy patrol was just to their front. L/Cpl Robert Hinde from 14 Platoon was in the foremost shell hole to the left of the battalion's frontage, and watched the enemy patrol silently, his rifle covering their movements. However, the enemy did not show any signs that they were aware of the battalion's presence, and returned to their own lines.[10] Shortly before zero hour, Sgt William Whiteside, platoon sergeant of 11 Platoon, crept round the shell holes his men were occupying to check they were all awake and ready, no doubt murmuring a few words of encouragement as he did so.[11] Aged only twenty-three, the Ulverston NCO was younger than many of his platoon, and yet, quite apart from flexing disciplinary muscle when required, he was also a 'father' figure to his men. Good sergeants like William Whiteside were the solid foundation that a quality battalion needed.

The intense bombardment of the enemy positions by artillery and the divisional MG companies, had been going on since 3 a.m. on the 19th. At 5.40 a.m. precisely, the leading platoons stood up and quickly moved forward as close as possible behind the barrage and when the first 'lift' occurred five minutes later, they rushed forward to attack. It was just light enough to see about 200 m, or would have been had not a heavy mist arisen just prior to dawn, blanketing the ground—a lack of visibility which C Company CO Capt. Procter believed presented the advance with unexpected difficulties.[12] Across most of the front, the barrage was to lift by 50 yards each time, the one exception being in front of Aisne Farm, B Company's first objective. Here, the barrage lifted 100 yards to allow the attackers to rush around the back and attack from where the defences were at their most vulnerable. Aisne Farm was a series of concrete bunkers linked by fortified shell holes, a formidable obstacle to any advance.

The instant the barrage began the first lift, German artillery began a heavy counter-bombardment, which fell with ferocious accuracy on both jumping-off positions and assembly points to the rear. It was later discovered during the interrogation of prisoners from RR 91 (facing 55 Division's positions) that the tapes had been spotted prior to the assault, alerting them not only to an attack, but also to where the troops would be concentrated, possibly by the very same patrol seen in No Man's Land a few hours earlier.[13] Casualties mounted and the third and fourth waves moved forward to escape this accurate fire. Effective fire on the rear area also forced the Loyals to close up until they made contact with the rear sections of the 1/4th and both units became intermingled in places, the Loyals becoming engaged well before it was anticipated they would.[14]

B Company (the leading company on the right) had mixed fortunes as it advanced. Apart from the heavy artillery fire, enemy MGs around Aisne Farm were particularly active. Although they caused few casualties to 7 and 8 Platoon in the leading wave, who were tasked with dealing with this position, the fire and the ground was badly cut up which had the effect of forcing many of the men too far to the left. Consequently, most of 8 Platoon became mixed up with D Company's platoons to their left. As the remainders of the two platoons neared their objective, they split into sections to converge on it from different angles. Once at Aisne Farm, 2Lt Charles Gribble found that the defenders surrendered immediately, one officer and about twenty men being captured and sent back through British lines. Gribble then garrisoned the position with twenty men, two Lewis guns, and a couple of trench mortars. His platoon sergeant, Henry Bradley, labelled the captured Maxim gun and sent it back to battalion HQ; the men began to dig shallow trenches connecting the series of shell holes to the front (enemy side) and flanks of the bunkers.

B Company's second wave suffered more heavily from the gun in Aisne Farm and others close by it, 2Lt George Taylor's HQ losing its runners and stretcher-bearers to the fire.[15] HQ pushed to the left of Aisne Farm as 7 and 8 Platoon began their assault on it and split into two groups, CSM David Graham taking half towards the right of Schuler Galleries (50° 53′ 12.22″ N, 2° 57′ 10.65″ E), and the Galleries themselves being an objective of the Fusiliers. Taylor led the other half to Loos on the left flank (50° 53′ 6.86″ N, 2° 57′ 14.41″ E) to see if the party attacking there required any assistance, though he was wounded shortly after the platoon divided. Under 2Lt Edgar Veevers, 6 Platoon also had difficulty crossing the churned ground, and lost men to the gun at Aisne Farm as they advanced, though the enfilading MG fire coming from the direction of Gallipoli on their right from the direction was arguably worse. Veevers's objective was a concrete stronghold just under 200 yards in front of Aisne Farm. The British barrage remained on this target for three minutes and as soon as it lifted, 6 Platoon rushed to the objective and captured it. Leaving a small garrison to man the bunker, they advanced to the Red Line, reached it at 6.15 a.m., and began to help consolidate it, spending the rest of the day thus occupied. 5 Platoon had also veered left at the start and although its commander had pulled it back onto course, the men had soon got mixed in with others. The 'bombing section' under L/Cpl A. Johnson was to the extreme right of the advance and Johnson tasked one of his men with keeping in touch with 1/9th King's to their right.[16] He led a section advance on a knocked-out tank which the enemy had fortified. This was possibly F45 'Fiducia', which had ditched and been abandoned just 75 yards from Aisne Farm after an attack on 22 August.[17] During the move forward, some of Johnson's section became separated in the confusion and more were lost to hostile fire. And yet, Johnson led the remainder in a successful assault and captured the objective before joining the rest of the battalion in consolidation.[18]

1. L/Cpl Thomas Hutchinson (centre) enjoys a bottle of beer near Hanwell 1914. (*Andy Moss*)

2. 4th King's Own sergeants at the 1913 camp at Denbigh. William Clark is in the centre of the back row; Lt-Col. W. F. A. Wadham is the seated officer to the left, with Capt. (later Maj.) R. Thompson to the right. (*The Clark Family*)

3. The QM staff at Sevenoaks, December 1914. William Clark stands third from the right. (*The Clark Family*)

4. Suspiciously youthful recruits, Blackpool 1915. Sam Oliver stands second from the right. (*Graham Lindow*)

5. Sap L8 today, taken from just in front of the deep ditch. The building furthest to the left is approximately where point L12 stood. (*Author*)

6. Recruits taking a break at Oswestry, April to June 1916. Arthur Hammond stands on the right at the very back, and in front of him is Saul Cohen with a towel over his shoulder. (*Author*)

7. Park Hall Camp, Oswestry. 4th King's Own trained here in April 1916. (*Author*)

8. Two platoons marching through Oswestry, April to June 1916. Arthur Hammond is on the far right. (*Author*)

9. Recruits and training staff at Oswestry, probably early July 1916. Arthur Hammond is fourth from the left in the first, standing row. (*Author*)

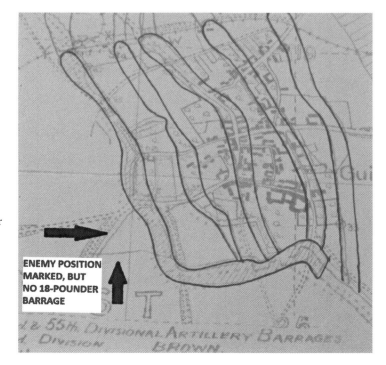

**ENEMY POSITION MARKED, BUT NO 18-POUNDER BARRAGE**

10. The 18-pounder barrage map, showing that the trenches attacked by the 1/4th on 8 August 1916 were not targeted by the barrage. (*Jeudwine Papers, Liverpool Record Office*)

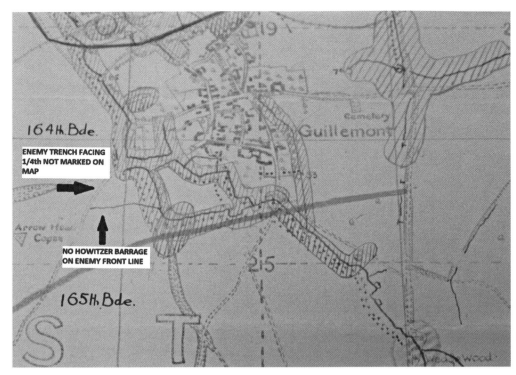

11. The howitzer barrage map for the 8 August 1916. The trench to be attacked is not even marked on this map. (*Jeudwine Papers, Liverpool Record Office*)

12. Guillemont today: the ground that the 1/4th had to cross in the attack on the 8 August 1916, taken from where the German machine-gunner was positioned—107 of the battalion lie there still. (*Author*)

13. Looking towards where the block in the sunken lane at Guillemont was situated. The first enemy line was just over the bank to the right of the lane. (*Author*)

14. Hop Alley, the machine-gunners' view looking towards Ginchy. (*Author*)

15. A view of Hill 35 and Gallipoli from Loos in the Ypres Salient today. (*Author*)

16. The Ypres Salient. Next to Loos the Schuler Galleries ran alongside the track. 2Lt Edwin White was killed just to the right of the poplar tree. Schuler Farm is on the far right of the picture. (*Author*)

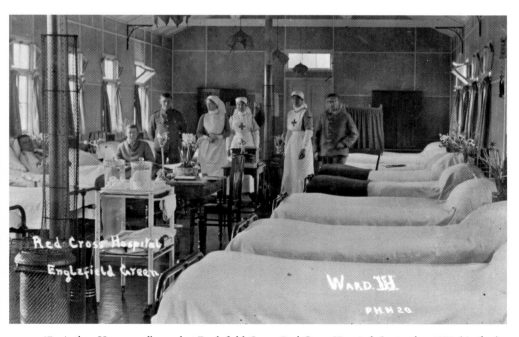

17. Arthur Hammond's ward at Englefield Green Red Cross Hospital, September 1917. (*Author*)

18. The wounded at Englefield Green. Arthur Hammond is seated in the far left, his cap resting precariously on his bandaged head. (*Author*)

19. Givenchy today from near the end of Orchard Road and looking back towards Orchard Keep, where 2Lt Joseph Collin won his VC. (*Author*)

20. An oblique aerial view of the village of Givenchy. The craters are towards the top of the picture. From left to right, they run for about 600 m. (*Jeudwine Papers, Liverpool Record Office*)

21. La Bassée Canal in 1918. Warrington Street ran across the canal via the footbridge behind the lock. (*Jeudwine Papers, Liverpool Record Office*)

22. Givenchy, looking along Cheyne Walk to the left of the canal. Death or Glory Sap was positioned on the canal bank just below '98'; the Tortoise faced it by '97'. (*Jeudwine Papers, Liverpool Record Office*)

23. Pte Joseph Steele, KIA while a POW on 28 April 1918. (*Ivor Holden*)

24. Sgt Tom 'Tickler' Mayson, awarded the VC. (*The Clark Family*)

25. Scant evidence of the bloodshed remains in Givenchy today. This cratered ground next to the 55 Division Memorial is the southern edge of B Sap. (*Author*)

26. RQMS William Clark and the QM Staff after the Armistice. Clark is seated in the centre. (*The Clark Family*)

27. The canal at Givenchy, looking back towards the spot where the 1918 picture of La Bassée Canal was taken. The lock is in the same position as in the 1918 picture. (*Author*)

28. Windy Corner at Givenchy, now a far quieter place than this infamous crossroads was in 1918. (*Author*)

The garrison consolidating the shell holes around Aisne Farm came under sniper fire from the Schuler Galleries, 350 yards to its left, and from the direction of Martha House (50° 53′ 1.96″ N, 2° 57′ 47.80″ E) to its right. The 800-yard range to this last position meant that its fire was more a nuisance than a serious threat, but 2Lt Gribble still warned his men not to expose themselves. Germans hiding in isolated shell holes had been passed over during the advance due to a combination of poor visibility, the high volume of casualties, and disorganisation. These enemy also presented a sniping problem for anyone in the open; although Gribble does not mention sniping from the direction of Sulva (50° 52′ 52.66″ N, 2° 57′ 27.91″ E), Germans in this location almost certainly presented a threat to anyone moving to or from his position.

The *Divisional History* suggests that those platoons designated to mop up around Aisne Farm and then garrison it had swept past in the assault and had inadequately mopped up. This led to serious casualties among the Loyals as they advanced, as close range enfilading rifle and MG fire from Germans who had later emerged from their dugouts scythed them down.[19] Based on the reports from B and A Company, there were certainly isolated cases of encountering Germans who had not been mopped up between zero hour and 7 a.m., but these were minor in nature. It seems more likely that the heavy enfilading MG fire which so affected the Loyals came from Gallipoli and Sulva. According to Capt. John Evans, acting as 2 I/C of the battalion's operation,

> […] our inability to maintain our positions on the Yellow Line was entirely due to the fire from Sulva, which was of so severe a character that our leading lines were wiped out, consequently there could not be the organisation which is of such vital importance in battle.[20]

This fire persisted until about 3 p.m., when the garrison of just seven Germans surrendered to elements of 165 Brigade. After this, the only sniping still bothering the battalion came from the direction of Kansas House (50° 53′ 9.03″ N, 2° 57′ 33.49″ E) and Martha House.

A Company were in the second wave behind B and tasked with taking the Yellow Line. As the men stood up to advance, all four platoons came under heavy MG fire from both flanks. The attack continued and the gun plaguing them on the right flank was soon silenced, though they were still under fire from the left, platoons split up and intermixed. This fire mostly came from the Schuler Galleries, a series of thirteen concrete emplacements linked by tunnels and defended by multiple MGs and wire to its front. As if this outpost wasn't tough enough on its own, it was also protected by the guns of Schuler Farm, Cross Cotts, and a chain of eleven fortified positions in between. A Company CO Capt. Charles Withey quickly rallied his men and moved them onwards. On the right, 1 Platoon had suffered so many casualties from fire on its right flank that it had just two sections remaining, yet it continued towards its objective on the Yellow Line until MG fire from a blockhouse forced the men to ground several hundred yards past Loos. They began to advance upon this, moving from shell hole to shell hole, until twelve heavy shells from a British howitzer battery landed among them. This naturally stopped the advance in its tracks, and the survivors retired 50 yards and waited for the shelling to finish before continuing their advance. Once more they came under heavy MG fire, and were now so weak in numbers that it was difficult to advance any further, the most senior surviving rank in the platoon being L/Cpl John Bussingham.

Also on the right flank of A Company was 2Lt Charles Lingford's 4 Platoon, though unlike 1 Platoon, it had barely been affected by MG fire over the first 100 yards. Upon its approach to Aisne

Farm, it encountered several Germans but these all surrendered readily and were sent back under escort. 4 Platoon finished mopping up this section and then continued to advance in lines of sections, as it was far easier to maintain coherence over the cut-up ground in this formation. Fifty yards further on, it came under heavy MG and rifle fire from a position to its front, and immediately moved into extended order. The enemy fire was so effective, that when the men neared the position it became clear to Lingford that there were too few left to attack it. He therefore pulled the survivors back 50 yards to a position occupied by men from 1/5th King's Own and the Loyals and ordered consolidation to begin. This was just over 50 yards to the rear of the position occupied by Bussingham and the remnants of 1 Platoon, and about 200 yards in front of Loos and Keir Farm. Lingford went forward to confer with Bussingham and ordered him to dig in and consolidate his current position, then returned to his own platoon.

On A Company's left flank, 3 Platoon came under effective fire from the very first. It lost its commander and many men almost immediately, so twenty-nine-year-old Sgt Myers led it on with what now amounted to just half the platoon. To the front of a stronghold, just north of the road and almost in direct line between Kansas House and Keir Farm, he met Capt. Withey, who was organising an assault on the company's final objective on the Yellow Line. Withey took charge of Myers's men and ordered him to return and try to collect the rest of A Company to assist with the attack. This particular stronghold had two MGs and a number of snipers, and was taking a deadly toll of any who showed themselves. Myers managed to collect a few men and led them forward to Withey; this combined force now made a rush at the enemy stronghold, but suffered so many casualties that there were insufficient men left to complete the task. Once more, Myers was sent back to find reinforcements, but only succeeded in collecting two stragglers, which he brought forward to where he had last seen Withey. While he had been away the captain had been killed by a sniper (from this stronghold), and the grand total of six remaining men (including himself) was insufficient to assault this position, so they retreated to another position held by some of 1/5th King's Own and the Loyals and helped them to consolidate.[21] For his exemplary leadership and courage, Harold Myers was awarded the MM.[22]

Some way to the rear and further to the right of Withey's position, Sgt Fred Yates from Lytham had also been a victim of the British howitzer battery and his progress too had been blocked until the barrage ceased. He had managed to rally a dozen men and led his platoon's attack on a strongpoint, which was quickly captured before they advanced to their next objective. Yates took that, then moved forward to join the survivors of his company. Looking around, he must have been shocked to realise that his entire company appeared to consist of just sixteen NCOs and men. As the senior rank, he took command of the much-depleted unit, which had been sheltering in shell holes from MG fire from Martha House that swept the lips of the craters. Fred Yates was awarded the DCM for his leadership of his platoon after his officer had been wounded; his leadership of the entire company for the following days after 2Lt Charles Lingford had been wounded; and for his skilful positioning of his Lewis guns, which later in the day took a heavy toll of German attempts at counter-attack.[23]

No narrative survives to tell the story of 2 Platoon's travails on 20 September 1917, but an annotation on the map accompanying Yates's company report may explain this omission.[24] On it is marked the position where twenty-five-year-old 2Lt Edwin White from Crosby, who—by a process of elimination—must have been the officer in charge of 2 Platoon, was killed, just to the rear of the

Schuler Galleries. Usually, the most senior surviving man would write up a report of the events, and the lack of one such document here suggests that no one from the platoon was alive or unwounded by the end of the day. Another tantalising glimpse into the fate of 2 Platoon can be gleaned from the map accompanying B Company's narrative.[25] On it is a track labelled '2 Platoon', showing that it passed through its apparent objective, Loos, and shortly after which—and not far from the location where 2Lt White was marked killed—the track ends. From the position of his death it is possible to surmise that once the platoon had eventually cleared obstinately defended Loos, they had responded to enemy fire coming from the Schuler Galleries by attacking them, too. White possibly believed that any advance to the Yellow Line by C Company coming up behind him would have been suicidal, given his rear flank was still under enemy control, and tried to tackle it with the meagre forces at his disposal.

On the battalion's left front led D Company, with 14 Platoon to the company's left and 13 Platoon to the right. The leading wave moved ahead far too quickly and was caught by the British barrage, a number of casualties ensuing, including the platoon leader of 14 Platoon, command passing to Sgt Alfred Burton from Dover. The second wave, with 16 Platoon to the left and 15 Platoon to the right, also moved off far too quickly and before very long the carefully planned spacing between platoons had completely disappeared. '[Strained] nerves due to lying for so long in bad weather,' explains Sgt Thomas Barrow of 16 Platoon; 'for many of the men it was the first time in action.'[26] The twenty-one-year-old NCO might have been young, but had enlisted in 1913 and was an experienced soldier. His platoon came under very effective MG fire from the left flank as soon as it advanced; the casualties included both the platoon commander and sergeant. To his right, 15 Platoon did not fare any better, and it too lost its platoon leader. Sgt Frederick Sherley commented, 'the troops appeared tired owing to being exposed too long. Prior to attack some men having no rest—comparatively—for 48 hours previous.'[27]

Things quickly went pear-shaped for 13 (HQ) Platoon, too, under 2Lt James Paterson and accompanied by D Company OC 2Lt Reginald Senton. The ground was a pitted mess almost devoid of feature. As they reached a slight incline, Paterson led them too far to the right, and his platoon got tangled with B Company platoons. To their front was a blockhouse strongpoint (50° 53′ 1.95″ N, 2° 57′ 19.01″ E) being attacked by a small group from 1/9th King's, so they joined the assault and eventually drove the enemy out, capturing two MGs—one of which was put back into service in the defence of these gains. Platoon officers had been ordered to garrison all captured strongpoints and defend them at all costs, and even though this position was right of B Company's tactical bound, Senton remained there and ordered his men to dig a series of shallow trenches around the bunker to connect the shell holes around the side and to the enemy's front, strengthening these with sandbags. Four Lewis positions were fashioned and soon afterwards Lt Clarke from 164 MG Company arrived with several Vickers, which were then stationed around the strongpoint.[28] What Senton didn't know was that he and Paterson were now the only D Company officers left in action, and that HQ was unaware of his presence there. Special emphasis had repeatedly been made beforehand by divisional, brigade, battalion, and company commanders about the vital importance of regular situation updates, and though it's almost inconceivable that Senton did not send a runner back to HQ, none arrived and neither does Paterson's report make any mention of runners.[29]

D Company's objective was to clear the central area of grid square D13 (south of Loos), and a combined force of 14 and 15 Platoon plus some Loyals moved into an attacking position on the right flank of this objective. It was here that Sgt Alfred Burton learned that not only were all the company officers down (he was unaware of 2Lt Senton and 2Lt Paterson in the old battery position), but that the CSM, Robert Thompson from Belfast, had also been killed. Burton took command of the company and gave 14 Platoon to L/Cpl Robert Hinde, a brave and experienced soldier who had earned the MM in July. Burton quickly organised the attack and the objective was taken. Sgt Sherley's 15 Platoon, together with a couple of men from the Loyals, rushed and captured one MG intact, which was labelled and sent back to HQ. Burton organised the consolidation and went forwards to throw out a series of strongpoints which were subsequently held until relief on 24 September.[30] For his coolness and determination, and the example he set in his disregard for his own safety, Alfred Burton was awarded the DCM.[31]

With such confusion due to mixed units, garrisons of captured strongpoints were made up from any men immediately to hand. As Sgt Thomas Barrow led the few survivors from 16 Platoon forward, he met 2Lt Paterson (2Lt Senton had by this time been seriously wounded), and the sergeant and his men were absorbed into the garrison of Paterson's strongpoint. Barrow recounts that out of thirty men now at the location, only sixteen were from the King's Own and the lieutenant put him in charge of these, while a sergeant from another unit was given the remaining men. Barrow also noted that they had been in position there for nearly an hour before any attack was mounted against Gallipoli to their right, and as this position was less than 300 yards from them, fire from there must have presented considerable danger to those consolidating the defences outside the blockhouse.[32] Once Gallipoli had been captured, Paterson ordered his men to try to consolidate their position to the point where they were in touch with the troops manning Loos to their left and Gallipoli to their right—an impressive feat in shovel work, given the distance to Loos was over 150 yards! [33]

C Company were in the second wave on the battalion's left front, and like other units, took fire from both the left and right. Under 2Lt Arthur Latham 11 Platoon moved off in artillery formation, but changed to extended order as soon as the MG fire began to target it. The platoon pushed forward another 100 yards, taking casualties, before being halted by MG fire from a position to their left. The first to be killed was No. 1 in the Lewis gun section; No. 2 collected the gun, and advanced 10 yards further before he too was killed; finally, No. 3 Pte Albert Ashburn picked up the gun, only to find that the rounds that had killed the other gunners had also damaged the gun beyond repair. However, a few yards further on, No. 3 found the bodies of an entire Lewis team complete with gun, which he picked up, tested, and found serviceable. As soon as the barrage lifted, 2Lt Latham and Sgt William Whiteside inclined their platoon to the left and led a successful charge against the gun position, capturing three of the enemy and their MG, which unfortunately was damaged by their grenades; this action earned Whiteside the MM.[34] The platoon realigned themselves by moving about 100 yards to their right and continued their advance towards Loos, Ashburn carrying out 'some very deadly work' with his Lewis against the Germans fleeing their advance, according to his sergent.[35] The MGs in Loos continued to wreak havoc with the platoon, killing three of its four section commanders; only twenty-year-old L/Cpl Herbert Hinchcliffe from Barrow survived the fire.

10 Platoon under 2Lt Charles Newbold got split up shortly after the advance began, as Newbold took most of the platoon to the right. His platoon sergeant, twenty-two-year-old George Huddleston from Millom, noticed that this left a gap to the left and took Pte John Moore and another man over to that side with him. As the three of them advanced, they encountered a few Germans lying in

shell holes, who they dealt with swiftly, and as soon as the barrage lifted from the first stronghold to their front, attacked it, only to find that the enemy had already fled. So far, their attack had been encouraging and the three continued their progress. As Newbold advanced to the right he was wounded and the platoon taken onwards by Cpl Joseph Parker. He discovered that they had moved too far to the right, so changed direction and moved over to the left, only to discover that they had now gone too far in that direction and got mixed with the Fusiliers, one of whose officers ordered 10 Platoon to remain with them.

9 Platoon suffered heavy casualties as it advanced, including the platoon commander and platoon sergeant. HQ had started 30 yards behind 9 Platoon and to the centre of the company's advance; for the first 200 yards, HQ proceeded in section file until heavy MG fire from the front prompted a quick change to extended order. It then followed the path of 9 Platoon, and when he discovered the survivors sheltering in a small trench, L/Sgt John Dickinson took them along with HQ until he met 2Lt Latham and handed 9 Platoon over to him.

The nine concrete blockhouses of Loos were proving a challenging objective to suppress, and attempts were being further exacerbated by a couple of snipers in a pair of concrete dugouts 150 yards beyond Loos and slightly left of the Schuler Galleries. These were swatting down anyone who exposed themselves from cover. Capt. Procter gave 2Lt Latham and part of 11 Platoon the task of ridding the battalion of this impediment, and as they advanced round the south side of Loos covered by fire from the Hales rifle grenades, they were joined by Capt. Baker of the Loyals and a small force of his men. The assault was successful, though at the cost of Capt. Baker. While Latham was clearing these two positions, Loos finally fell to an attack by D Company, assisted by elements from B and C, and the battalion prepared to continue its advance.

Any further movement towards to the Yellow Line was complicated, because the Schuler Galleries were still holding out against the best efforts of the Fusiliers and any troops ahead of Loos would have been engaged by MG fire from two directions (by the enemy to their oblique rear in Schuler Galleries and from the front in Kansas House). With this in mind, the remnants of 9 Platoon were 'loaned' to the Fusiliers for yet another assault against the Schuler Galleries.[36] The 2/5th Fusiliers had suffered heavily from MG fire to their front and flanking fire from their left (emanating from an enemy strongpoint north of the Hanebeck), and were down to 50-per-cent strength by the time they had reached Schuler Galleries. Among the men of 9 Platoon were L/Cpl Frederick Dobbs and his bombing section, who attacked and cleared the right hand dugout of the Galleries, earning Dobbs the MM.[37] The Lancashire Fusiliers were successful in taking the southern section of Schuler Galleries, although the northern section held out against the Liverpool Irish for some time. Once the southern Galleries were taken, Dobbs advanced his section but could not see any troops on his flanks, so returned to Latham and was ordered to help consolidate with the remainder of the battalion.[38]

Shortly after advancing from their last stronghold, Sgt Huddleston and his two men were re-joined by L/Cpl Barnes and some of his section, who had moved to the left after losing sight of 2Lt Newbold, and become separated from Cpl Parker and the rest of the platoon.[39] This group was also joined by twenty-two-year-old Sgt John Pearson, who like Huddleston hailed from Millom. Pearson had lost his platoon officer earlier on in the battle and assumed command of his platoon thereafter. When snipers engaged his men from two shell holes, he made a solo attack on their position, overcame them, then led a section attack against several others. Although wounded, Pearson continued to lead:

he pooled the survivors from his platoon with Huddleston's men, and spurred the combined party on to attack what Pte John Moore understood to be Kansas House.[40] Pearson's composite platoon moved against the objective, cleared part of the enemy stronghold, and got right alongside the first blockhouse of Kansas House when its enemy garrison made a sudden run for the third blockhouse along. Pearson was unable to capitalise on this as the British barrage was still falling on the defences, and he and his men had to pull back. He was awarded the DCM.[41]

Once the barrage had ended, Capt. Procter reorganised his company as much as was possible—minus 9 Platoon, which was no longer under his control—and set about advancing to take the remaining objectives. It became clear to him at this moment that their position formed a pronounced salient and that the fire from Schuler Farm on the left (50° 53′ 19.07″ N, 2° 57′ 15.45″ E) and the ridge joining Hill 35 to Hill 37 on the right (50° 52′ 50.94″ N, 2° 57′ 40.76″ E) was giving his company much grief.[42] It was then that Sgt Huddleston was wounded in the hand and finger and sent back to the RAP. When L/Cpl Herbert Hinchcliffe began to dig in, he looked around and could only count five NCOs and sixteen men, one of whom was the redoubtable Albert Ashburn, whose Lewis continued to give the enemy hell.[43] With his left flank open and Withey's A Company (plus one platoon of 1/5th King's Own and some Loyals) digging in to his right, Procter decided to consolidate where he was (somewhere along the Yellow Line) and lay a protective flank back to the Schuler Galleries. It was now that the Loyals should have moved forwards through the King's Own to take the next series of objectives, but no organised bodies of men appeared at Procter's position. Unbeknown to him, simply too few of them remained to continue the advance by themselves, so the combined forces held the right of the Red Dotted Line.

Officer casualties had been prohibitive, to the extent that three of the four companies were commanded by NCOs at some point during the attack. Sgt Yates took over A Company, Sgt Burton D Company, and CSM David Graham B Company—commanding them until their relief, he too earned the DCM.[44] There was much to do in terms of consolidation, with shell hole defences to be linked to provide a continuous line of resistance; strongholds to be manned; and the remaining serviceable weapons to be cleared of the mud lest they be rendered useless, too. One of CSM Graham's first orders was for half the men to dig in while the other half cleaned their weapons, and once these were all serviceable, the men switched tasks.[45] Capt. Procter, who had assumed command of all forward troops, sent Sgt Myers and the remainder of 3 Platoon to reinforce a small garrison commanded by 2Lt Charles Lingford in a stronghold, some 50 yards to the right of where the platoon had initially dug in.

Communicating progress to the rear was near impossible. Initial mist then smoke obscured all visual communication, and although telephone lines between the three brigade HQs, two artillery groups in the HQ dugout in Wieltje, and division HQ at Canal Bank in Ypres had survived, all cables from advanced HQs back to brigade HQ had been severed. The mud hindered movement across the battlefield and the number of casualties among runners ran high. All messages were copied and carried by two runners moving separately, yet they frequently failed to get through. For Maj.-Gen. Jeudwine at division HQ, the situation around Schuler Farm was sketchy and confused. A message from 38 Division arrived at 11.10 a.m. saying that it had taken Schuler Farm, however, at 2.50 p.m. a contradictory message arrived from a unit of 164 Brigade; it wasn't until 4.25 p.m. that brigade HQ had established for certain that the Germans were still in control of Schuler Farm. In fact, not until 4.20 p.m. on the 21st did it finally fall to the Liverpool Irish.[46] The CO of 1/5th King's Own even lost contact with his own men, and although he'd been able to maintain contact with both the 1/4th and the Loyals, he'd not been able to throw his men into an integral renewed assault on the Green Line as he had planned, causing momentum to falter. His unit had, however, provided vital reinforcements to both the 1/4th and the Fusiliers, helping them seize their objectives on the Red Dotted Line and beyond by midday. Once communications with his battalion were re-established, the 1/5th was concentrated around Loos as a counter-attack force.

At battalion HQ in Capricorn Keep (50° 53′ 1.73″ N, 2° 56′ 46.87″ E), Maj. Percival Robathan was commanding the battalion's attacking forces while Lt-Col. Balfour was back with the B Team. Acting as 2 I/C for the operation was Capt. John Evans, and as the wounded streamed into the RAP close by, he received reports from them indicating that the first objectives had been achieved and onward progress likely.[47] The first signs of concern weren't felt until 9.50 a.m., when a runner arrived with a message dispatched by 2Lt Lingford some thirty minutes earlier, reporting that he was at Keir Farm and delayed by heavy MG and sniper fire, and that reorganisation had been unsatisfactory and casualties heavy.[48] Evans was immediately ordered to make a tour of the line and find out exactly what was happening; accompanied by a runner, he left the dugout.

Capt. Evans's first destination was Aisne Farm, which he reached despite MG fire which targeted his small party from the vicinity of Martha House and sniping from Sulva. Once there, he met 2Lt Gribble, whose garrison had now swelled to about forty men; Evans ordered that the position held at all costs, and moved forwards towards the old gun position held by 2Lt Senton.[49] The captain was fortunate to reach this stronghold alive considering the sniping and his total lack of cover—his runner was shot through the head by a sniper shortly before he reached the position, but he was left unscathed. Senton informed Evans that although he was using his MGs and rifles to try to suppress their fire, these snipers had thus far killed fifteen of his men. The time was about 11.15 a.m., and he had still not reached the front line. Evans was impressed by the courage of the men of MG Company, several of whom he witnessed dash the 400 yards across the open carrying ammunition for the guns from Somme stronghold to Senton's position, at great risk to themselves.[50] From here, he could see some Loyals digging in behind them, with their left near the road, some 450 yards away from him and 250 yards to the rear of Loos (50° 53′ 4.57″ N, 2° 56′ 59.60″ E). As they did so, a company from 1/5th King's Own advanced; all went well until they came to within about 200 yards to the rear of Evans, when heavy rifle and MG fire drove them into cover. Eventually, they reached the Loyals and helped them consolidate. Evans could also see that Loos was now in the possession of the attackers, yet no movement could be seen along the Yellow Line. He sent a runner back to HQ to inform them and he made his way to Loos. Shortly after Capt. Evans left, 2Lt Senton was seriously wounded—probably by one of the snipers—leaving 2Lt Paterson the sole D Company officer.

Upon reaching Loos, Capt. Evans found it garrisoned by about twenty men and a party of RE who were consolidating the position. From there, he went straight to the Schuler Galleries, which were held by forty men, one Lewis, and one Vickers, and spoke to the Fusiliers officer in charge. Confident that their left flank was secure, he headed off to find Procter. While he was at the Galleries, the enemy made a small and very half-hearted attempt at counter-attack advancing from Schuler Farm, but this was easily dealt with by the two guns at the Galleries. It was around 1.30 p.m. when Evans found Procter in a command post (at 50° 53′ 8.29″ N, 2° 57′ 21.34″ E). This position was held by about twenty-five to thirty men and commanded a good field of fire, and after the two captains had discussed the situation, Evans returned to battalion HQ.

Capt. Procter began to fine-tune the defences in readiness for an enemy counter-attack, and after arranging for Loos to be properly garrisoned, put the remainder of B Company onto linking the shell holes between his command post and the Schuler Galleries. Then, C and B Company were arranged into the shell holes to fend off any potential counter-attack, leaving A and D (minus the platoon with 2Lt Paterson) to act as reserves. He also positioned the men from the Loyals such that they were sandwiched between units of 1/4th King's Own, and sent the 1/5th back to the left flank close to Schuler Galleries. A line of Lewis posts was established forwards of the entire brigade frontage, stretching from the Schuler Galleries to Gallipoli and consisting from left to right of Fusiliers, Loyals, 1/4th King's Own, and on the extreme right, Paterson's platoon. All serviceable captured MGs were pressed into service to hold against any enemy counter-attacks. Procter was officially placed in overall command of the battalion's frontage in the early evening, though he had in reality been performing this role for most of the day, having relinquished command of C Company to 2Lt Arthur Latham shortly after Withey had been killed.[51] Any enemy movement observed by the battalion was punished by accurate Lewis, Vickers, and rifle fire; Sgt John Dickinson even reported that Procter used his rifle to successfully snipe a couple of the enemy himself.[52]

Soldiers in battle have a tendency to use 'sniping' to describe any accurate rifle fire they are on the receiving end of; and yet, this is frequently just a random hit. The term seems to have been used by the men of the 1/4th to describe any deliberate and carefully aimed shooting; however, the accuracy of a few enemy riflemen from the locations around Sulva and Martha House suggests that these particular Germans were 'snipers' in the modern-day sense. The casualties suffered by 2Lt Paterson's garrison and those trying to reach the location certainly support this definition of those marksmen in Sulva. Paterson reported that no fewer than sixteen men making for their shelter had been killed by these snipers, two of which were successfully counter-sniped by the defenders. At one time, they had no fewer than thirteen full stretchers awaiting evacuation—two medics attached to HQ, Cpl Christopher Corless and Pte George Helme, did sterling work tending them and organising their removal to safety. Paterson was fulsome in his praise of both, and George Helme was recommended for, though not awarded—the MM. Runners and stretcher-bearers were always uniquely vulnerable, as their duties were mainly conducted out in the open. Pte James Greenhow, who seems to have had fortune on his side during his lengthy career as a runner, was given a MiD for his work in July and September.[53] Earlier in the day, when C Company HQ's L/Sgt Dickinson had sent a message to the officer in charge of the men to his right, the runner had been killed; with men in such short supply, Dickinson decided against risking another's life. His stretcher-bearer, Pte John Wilde from Oldham, had repeatedly jeopardised his own tending the wounded under heavy shell and sniper fire, yet had at all times maintained a cool head and encouraging the men on. He was awarded the MM, but killed trying to save more of his comrades' lives at Gillemont Farm a mere two months later.[54]

Although no German counter-attacks were made on the line the 1/4th held, some ensued against flanking units at 10 a.m., from enemy amassing in the area between Nile and Fokker Farm—the same location as a couple of hours later. The Germans' efforts were nipped in the bud by accurate fire from British artillery and MGs, leaving many dead and wounded. Around 5.30 p.m. on 55 Division's right, a counter-attack was made against Hill 37 by dense waves of German infantry from the direction of Boethoek on the Gravenstafel Ridge. Capt. Procter ordered the Lewis guns to engage these, but as the range was extreme—at 850 yards—the fire only became effective when enfilading from the Vickers and (captured) Maxim guns at Keir Farm and the Schuler Galleries joined in; accurate artillery fire followed, inflicting heavy casualties on the attackers.[55] At about 4 p.m., enemy shell fire started up, bombarding shell hole positions for about an hour; but even though these lacked top cover, they were very difficult for artillery to target accurately, and British casualties were light.

As darkness fell, Capt. Procter ordered 2Lt Latham and Sgt Dickinson to go forward of their defensive line to reconnoitre advanced positions as a buffer against an enemy counter-attack, while other patrols were sent out to determine enemy positions. Latham and Dickinson returned shortly afterwards and Pte Albert Ashburn was put in command of eight other men and took his Lewis to a position 90 yards in front of the battalion's line, which he then held for two nights and a day. When Ashburn was relieved by Sgt William Whiteside and L/Cpl Herbert Hinchcliffe, he went on a search of the trenches looking for more Lewis magazines and found another gun. Even though the butt was broken it worked, so he cleaned it up and added it to the platoon's firepower, giving them a total of five Lewis guns.[56] Sgt Alfred Burton established outposts with D Company, leaving Sgt Sherley in the main line with Cpl Edward Rodgers and two signallers, one of whom was L/Cpl William Bosanko. Though no attacks were made, thirty-four-year-old former teacher Capt. Procter must have felt tense; his men were worn and few in number.

The next morning of the 21st, Germans carrying Red Cross flags were seen on the front slope of the Gravenstafel Ridge. 55 Division held its fire but watched the enemy carefully, as the Germans had in the past used the cover of stretcher-bearers to move MGs. In this instance, it is likely that they were simply looking for the wounded after the abortive counter-attacks of the previous day. Fighting continued to the division's left, as the Liverpool Irish assailed Schuler Farm and the Fusiliers steadily advanced from the Schuler Galleries against Cross Cotts on the Langemark–Zonnebeke Road, as piece by piece the left flank of the Green Line fell into British hands. Despite heavy bombardment during the night, the enemy did not counter-attack, and Procter's men continued to push the advance posts further forward in preparation for another advance by the Fusiliers planned for the night of the 22nd (this attack was ultimately cancelled). Prior to the main attack, the Germans had positioned three *Eingreif* regiments in the area; these were specialists in counter-attack, but had received such a mauling on the first day that they were unable to respond to these later advances. The *Official History* comments on the 459th RR attached to them to make the counter-attack down the Gravenstafel Ridge on the afternoon of the 20th.

[…] every effort made to press the attack failed owing to the terrible artillery barrage and machine gun fire, which tore great gaps in the advancing companies and caused complete disorganisation.[57]

Divisional fire support was indeed a force to be reckoned with.

In response to the attempted enemy counter-attack, more men were sent to forward posts to give early warning in case of attack during the night. Sgt Burton sent Cpl Smith and Privates Holmes and Brockbank to a shell hole some 150 yards ahead of the main line, and put an intermediate post between them held by L/Cpl Robert Hinde and a small party of men, about 80 yards from the main line.[58] That evening, 2Lt Gribble with his mixed force of 8 Platoon and Sgt Henry Bradley's platoon (possibly 5 Platoon) were relieved at Aisne Farm by another unit, and moved forward to Loos. Once there, Gribble was able to take back command of B Company from CSM Graham, and arranged his men in the shell-hole positions to the front of Loos; Bradley and his men were immediately deployed to one of these advanced positions. Cpl Henry Casper reported that his platoon leader, who had been wounded on the first day, had been with them when they left Aisne Farm, but did not go to Loos, the corporal believing that he must have instead gone straight to the RAP. As the senior surviving rank in 8 Platoon, Bradley took command and he and his men were sent back from Loos to collect rations for the battalion; after their return, they were placed in a forward listening post for the night.[59]

At the dawn of 22 September, German artillery began to shell the front line and a small counter-attack developed to their front. British artillery and MGs immediately responded and the counter-attack fizzled out.[60] More shelling occurred during the morning and evening, but no further attempts were made to drive 55 Division back. Despite its intensity, the bombardment was mainly ineffective, as the enemy were still unsure as to the actual whereabouts of British positions. The fortified series of shell holes looked just like all the other thousands of shell holes in the vicinity. In the first couple of hours after daybreak, enemy aircraft busied themselves over the front trying to locate British positions and dropping flares for German artillery. However, as soon as British aircraft appeared over the line in numbers, the enemy left in haste. On this day 2Lt Charles Lingford was seriously wounded and evacuated back to the RAP, and Procter put Sgt Fred Yates in charge of A Company.[61] Just before dawn on the 23rd, another intense bombardment fell on the front line positions, Loos, and the dugout about 150 m east of Aisne Farm—a classic indication of an impending counter-attack. All MGs immediately began to fire at the pre-determined lines of approaches which German infantry would have to take, and the enemy bombardment died down; no counter-attack ensued after all.

During the 23rd, attempts to get food and water to the men at the front met with disaster, for the carrying parties were hit by shell fire. Sgt Sherley, now in an advanced position, sent a man back for water but the runner was wounded before he reached his destination. His men were desperate for water, but Sherley was reluctant to risk any more casualties, so he decided to fetch it himself. As he moved back, a shell burst just behind him and he remembered nothing more until he awoke in the ADS.[62] The next man from the platoon to try was twenty-four-year-old Pte Edward Jackson from Blackburn, who was at last successful! Sadly, this young man's days were numbered. The QM, Lt Phillip Powell, his newly appointed RQMS, William Clark, and their Staff had made every effort to get food and water to the battalion, though ammunition had been their main priority in retrospect of the events of July. Although the enemy had problems registering their artillery onto the men in the shell holes, the well-trodden routes to the front presented no such difficulties, so the supply run was fraught with danger. The QM was awarded the MC for his personal courage in ensuring the supplies reached the men at the front, a service seriously appreciated in the shell holes.[63] (Clark's services at Ypres and Gillemont Farm would also be recognised later.) In his report, L/Sgt Dickinson was full of praise:

> There is one thing I think ought to be mentioned and that is the Quartermaster Sergeant of 'C' Company did very good work as regards getting the food up to the Company. We got plenty to eat and it put a good spirit into the men and gave then courage to take the strain. He had a keen interest in his Company.[64]

Shortly after 5 p.m. began the most violent bombardment yet experienced, lasting for nearly three hours. The whole of the battalion area was targeted this time, and the HQ dugout in Capricorn Keep rocked to the explosions. The Germans built excellent dugouts, but there was one ominous drawback to using captured dugouts—the doorway, which now faced towards any hostile shell fire! For the men in Capricorn Keep, wondering whether the next shell was going to come straight through the door to kill everyone inside must have been nerve-wracking. For the infantrymen sheltering in their shell holes, too, the bombardment must have been unspeakably stressful. It is no surprise to see that 'Casualty Returns' included six with severe shellshock—still, a remarkably low number considering the circumstances. Shell holes gave virtually no shelter from shrapnel, which burst in the air; however, the mud helped negate the effects of HE, for most of the blast and splinters travelled vertically rather than horizontally (as was the case on hard ground). But a near miss could kill from blast alone, and there was the ever present danger of being buried when the mud fell back to earth. When one platoon could not be located, the battalion was relieved at 1.45 a.m. on 24 September by two platoons of 2/6th North Staffs. The weary survivors who marched the 3 miles back through Wieltje and on to St Jean will not have been sorry to be heading west; little did they know, this would actually be the last time they would see the Salient in war.

At St Jean the men boarded the light railway to Vlamertinghe, and continued onwards by bus and train to Area No. 2 at Watou. The cost of the battle had been high—higher even than in July—with 233 casualties from all ranks, seventy-seven of whom were either killed in action or to die later from their wounds. Eleven officers had been killed or wounded, including Maj. Percival Robathan, OC of the battalion in the attack, who suffered from gas poisoning, but had only let himself be evacuated once his men were safely out of the line. Two company commanders were also casualties, A Company Capt. Withey's third 'pip' not even having time to tarnish before he was killed, and D Company's OC, Lt Senton, badly wounded. Twenty per cent of those killed were officers or NCOs, because these men led by example. Both the *War Diary* and *Battalion History* state that 2Lt Charles Lingford died from his wounds.[65] Happily, this was not the case; in fact, post-war the young officer became a surgeon and later a dentist, dying at the age of sixty in 1956. The character of the battalion had undergone a gradual metamorphosis since the early days of 1915, with casualties from Festubert and the Somme speeding the changes. No longer did casualty records show a predominance of men from the Furness Peninsula, for by 1917, the battalion was far more cosmopolitan. A look at the home towns for casualties from this battle shows that men came from fifty-nine different towns (predominantly in Lancashire), and also from as far as Scotland and Cornwall.

When a division went into a large-scale action, many infantrymen were usually killed or wounded, and it fell to one of fourteen Infantry Records Offices to inform the next of kin. All of 55 Division's twelve infantry battalions came under the office in Preston; given that the division's casualties over the past forty-eight hours were just under 2,000, the clerks there were very busy men. Notification was usually given by letter and, not surprisingly during times of great workload, mistakes were made. What is perhaps more surprising is that more were not made, since many records were flawed before they even reached the Records Offices (due to clerical errors made when men enlisted). The King's Own had two men with identical names, who had both enlisted on the same day at the same place and been given regimental numbers one digit apart. In the early days of training, these men had each accidentally assumed the other's number, which led to a great deal of confusion when one was later posted as missing. Similar mistakes led to considerable unnecessary grief.

After Menin Road Ridge, the family of twenty-three-year-old 200802 Pte Albert George Titterington received a letter at their home in Greenodd, informing them of the death of their son.

In fairness, the error was not of the Records Offices' making. The man killed was actually thirty-one-year-old 201821 Pte George Titterington, a married man from Caton who had been with the battalion for less than three weeks before he was killed by gas during the attack. The mistake had come about when a clerk in the battalion transposed two numbers when he completed a casualty report form, in what were probably trying circumstances. On 1 December 1917, another letter was delivered to Greenodd. It simply states,

> In confirmation of my wire this morning, I beg to inform you that a report has been received from the Commanding Officer of the 1/4th Bn, the King's Own R.L.R. stating that your son was not Killed in Action on 20/9/17. The error is very much regretted.[66]

I wonder, how long did the family's joy last before anger at this needless ordeal began? George Titterington's records show that his wife was informed of his death that same day.[67]

After any action, commanders of all units would carry out a detailed analysis; 55 Division's policy of making sure that battalion, brigade, and divisional commanders had access to an analysis which devolved right down to platoon (and frequently section) level was an excellent way of culling the small mistakes before they became problematic on a wider scale. Out of the twenty-six narratives available for this attack, not one reports a shortage of ammunition, so the problems of July's attack must have been resolved. The effectiveness of D Company's policy to give every infantryman a loaded Lewis magazine was commented on favourably by gunners and in the *Company Narrative*.[68] None of the NCOs complained about the load carried by the attacking infantrymen, which suggests that this problem had been ironed out, and the addition of empty sandbags in the personal load was universally praised for assisting quick and effective consolidation.

The artillery and MG barrage support was commended by all. '[It] was magnificent and no soldiers could hope or desire for a better service,' commented Capt. Procter; 'in their response to SOS signals they usually got into action before the signals burned out.'[69] Capt. Evans also vouched that the support from these was so good that battalion would have been able to fight off any counter-attack.[70] The RFC, on the other hand, received mixed reviews. Sgt Fred Yates of A Company reflects,

> The barrage was the best I have seen yet. Aeroplanes were a great success too and were up with us all the time in the most advanced points. I have only one grumble. The enemy aeroplanes are sailing over the lines as soon as day breaks. It is usually several hours after that ours arrive. In every other way aeroplanes excellent.[71]

Capt. Procter was not quite so diplomatic in his appraisal! He sarcastically comments:

> On this occasion the work of our aircraft was splendid. I can only suggest one improvement and that is their alarm clocks be set for two hours earlier. The German planes were always over our position a full hour before our planes put in an appearance. However, when they arrived they did good work.[72]

Other elements of the attack were looked upon with significantly less favour. There was universal criticism of poor 'wave' discipline at the very start of the assault. As previously mentioned, some

NCOs put this down to nerves among men who had never attacked before; others saw the root of the problem the men's exhaustion, having had to lie on cold muddy ground all night. Procter believed the 'wave' formation the best the battalion had ever used, but thought that the distance between waves ought to be stretched to 100 yards, arguing that once the leading wave came up against opposition, the tendency was for the second wave to bunch up behind it, making it nearly impossible for the commander of the second wave to direct his men to crucial points. He also believed that the greater distance would make it easier for parties to mop up isolated shell holes. However, he conceded that this would only work if all the men were 'ideal' soldiers; otherwise, command would be lost for men lagging behind, and insufficient weight gathered for an assault over open ground.[73]

CSM David Graham thought that officers and NCOs would have found it useful when reorganising if the attacking infantrymen had worn distinguishing marks showing whether they were part of the forces tasked with attacking the Black, Yellow and Red Lines, or garrison forces.[74] The signallers themselves came in for praise, though their equipment elicited mixed responses. For example, only one of C Company's signallers survived the advance, and he only carried a small signal lamp which proved inadequate for the task. Although he managed to acquire a shutter later, a Lucas Lamp borrowed from another signaller proved the best option on the day and was recommended for future operations.[75] The battalion signals officer 2Lt Alfred Morton, had personally established a forward command post under heavy fire, and this had allowed Maj. Robathan to maintain communications between himself and the forward companies; for this, as well as his similar work in July, he was awarded the MC.[76]

There were highly contradictory reports about the effectiveness of grenades. A Company criticised the Hales rifle grenades for being useless against the concrete blockhouses, urging that two Mills bombs per man was best for clearing these defences. Yet C Company esteemed them very useful for providing cover for men attacking the concrete blockhouses! Most narratives praised the Hales as good for dealing with snipers, criticising the shorter range of the Mills rifle grenades as being inadequate for this task. Narratives seem to place snipers as one of the greatest problems. According to Capt. Procter,

> [...] the Germans found this [sniping] a far more profitable branch than the machine gun. We undoubtedly suffered more from it than from any other cause. I think that far more range practice should be included in our training—say on a thirty-yard range.[77]

This suggestion was in effect implemented into subsequent training schedules.

Honours were distributed to many of the battalion: both 2Lt George Taylor and 2Lt Arthur Latham were awarded the MC, and the latter promoted shortly thereafter to Captain.[78] Some men, such as Pte Edward Motteram and Sgt George Collins, were recommended for the MM, but did not get the award—though Collins was awarded the Croix de Guerre. Others, like Sgt Ernest Lockey, were successful: he won the MM and in May the following year was commissioned into the regiment. It should not be thought that the decision to award an honour was based on the rank of the nominee; Maj. Robathan, who had acted as battalion commander for both the battles in the Salient despite suffering from mustard gas poisoning, had remained at his post until all his battalion had been relieved and was nominated for a medal—though this was never awarded. It must also be remembered that during the Great War, the only medal that could be awarded posthumously was the Victoria Cross, so many acts of extreme bravery by officers and men went unrewarded if the soldier was killed in the process.

Killed in action or died from wounds at the Battle of the Menin Road Ridge, 20-26 September 1917

| | | | | | |
|---|---|---|---|---|---|
| Pte Albert Victor Ball | 22503 | KIA | Pte David Baxendale | 201708 | KIA |
| Pte William Bielby | 27997 | DOW-21/9 | Pte Leonard Bowker | 201564 | KIA |
| Pte John Brack | 28000 | KIA | Pte William Brooke | 201201 | KIA |
| Pte Richard Brown | 34531 | KIA | Pte Tom Burton | 200593 | KIA |
| Pte Richard Carter | 34608 | KIA | Pte Samuel Carter | 200262 | KIA |
| Pte James Cartwright | 200682 | KIA | L/Cpl Robert Read Clark | 201068 | KIA |
| Pte Ernest Coles | 201597 | KIA | Pte John Cooley MM | 18079 | KIA |
| Pte Alexander Crammon | 28011 | KIA | Sgt James Musgrave Cross | 202738 | KIA |
| Pte Claude Edward Crossley | 202243 | KIA | Pte Alexander Dickinson | 12726 | DOW-8/10 |
| Pte Robert Dickinson | 23727 | KIA | L/Cpl Robert Dobson | 201692 | KIA |
| Pte Hugh Doyle | 28017 | KIA | Pte Peter Duerden | 201770 | KIA |
| Pte Robert Faulkner | 22865 | DOW-4/10 | Pte Herbert Greenhalgh | 202767 | KIA |
| Pte Frederick Griffies | 265686 | DOW-21/9 | Pte Harold Hadfield | 201619 | DOW-21/9 |
| Pte Edwin Hamblett | 201501 | KIA | Pte Gilbert Hardcastle | 32508 | KIA |
| 2Lt Reginald Gordon Hatcher | | KIA | Pte Horace Hayward | 202464 | KIA |
| 2Lt Edward Douglas Howard | | KIA | Pte James Howarth Hudson | 27579 | KIA |
| Pte James Illingworth | 34623 | DOW-24/9 | Pte Thomas James | 200688 | KIA |
| Pte Albert Edward Johnson | 28035 | KIA | Pte Richard Knowles | 240752 | KIA |
| Pte David Leech | 235137 | KIA | Pte John Littleford | 201632 | KIA |
| Pte William Messham | 28116 | DOW-7/10 | Pte Andrew Morrow | 200490 | KIA |
| Pte John Nightingale | 201016 | KIA | Pte John Nutter | 201642 | KIA |
| Pte Joseph O'Brien | 19624 | KIA | Pte John William Oldham | 11870 | DOW-27/9 |
| L/Cpl Albert James Orders | 240813 | KIA | Pte John Owen | 201643 | KIA |
| L/Cpl Joseph Oxley | 200612 | DOW-22/9 | Pte Henry Park | 201507 | KIA |
| Pte Frederick Charles Pearce | 22679 | KIA | Cpl John William Pettitt | 240716 | KIA |
| Pte Charles Stanton Petty | 34589 | KIA | Pte Harry Pickup | 33386 | DOW-22/9 |
| Pte Harry Pownall | 243021 | KIA | Pte John Harold Proctor | 202354 | KIA |
| Sgt Joseph Henry Quayle | 200724 | DOW-24/9 | Cpl David George Rowlandson | 200740 | KIA |
| Pte Herbert William Rudge | 202107 | DOW-22/9 | Pte Edward Salthouse | 201739 | KIA |
| L/Cpl Fred Shepherd | 201018 | KIA | Pte George Alfred Sidebottom | 201530 | KIA |
| Pte Thomas Simpson | 240288 | KIA | Pte Thomas Ingham Spencer | 265498 | KIA |
| Pte George A. Stenhouse | 201244 | KIA | Pte Alfred Thomas Stevens | 201649 | KIA |

| | | | | | | |
|---|---|---|---|---|---|---|
| Pte James Arthur Taylor | 34643 | DOW-23/9 | | A/WO2 James Thistlethwaite | 200019 | KIA |
| Sgt Robert Thompson | 201703 | KIA | | Pte George Titterington | 201821 | KIA |
| Sgt Robert Titterington | 201000 | KIA | | Pte Leonard Truran | 19315 | KIA |
| Pte Frederick Twynham | 9252 | KIA | | Pte Leslie Urwin Tyson | 26651 | KIA |
| Pte Harold Dudley Vity | 201266 | KIA | | 2Lt Edwin Thexton White | | KIA |
| Pte Thomas Whiteside | 201788 | DOW-21/9 | | Capt. Charles Elisha Withey | | KIA |
| Pte James William Young | 201671 | KIA | | | | |

## Known to have been wounded in the Battle of the Menin Road Ridge, 20-26 September 1917

| | | | | | | |
|---|---|---|---|---|---|---|
| L/Cpl George Arthur Allin | 34628 | WIA | | Pte Robert Ashburner | 200771 | WIA |
| Pte William Boydell | 24272 | WIA | | Pte Thomas Brotherton | 34725 | WIA |
| Cpl Thomas Chester | 200239 | WIA | | L/Cpl Adam Clark | 200883 | WIA |
| Pte Arthur Cleminson | 201522 | WIA | | L/Cpl James Coltsman | 200058 | WIA |
| Sgt Horace B. Dunkerley | 200269 | WIA | | Pte William Ellis | 28100 | WIA |
| Pte James Fletcher | 201483 | WIA | | Pte Thomas Norman Gibson | 30030 | WIA |
| Pte Charles Victor Golding | 33719 | WIA | | Pte John Percy Hough | 201722 | WIA |
| Sgt George Huddleston | 200746 | WIA | | L/Cpl Samuel Hughes | 200466 | WIA |
| Cpl Matthew Keelan | 200932 | WIA | | Pte John Law | 200863 | WIA |
| 2Lt Charles George Lingford | | WIA | | Pte William Arthur Lucas | 202183 | WIA |
| Pte Sydney McNa | 202773 | WIA | | 2Lt Charles Hutchinson Newbold | | WIA |
| Pte John Ormandy | 33700 | WIA | | Sgt John Robert Pearson | 200508 | WIA |
| L/Cpl Matthew James Porter | 200595 | WIA | | 2Lt Thomas Henry C. W. Pritchard | | WIA |
| Maj. Percival Edward Robathan | | WIA | | 2Lt Reginald Mayhew Senton | | WIA |
| L/Sgt Frederick Sherley | 202168 | WIA | | L/Cpl Thomas Small | 200841 | WIA |
| 2Lt George Arthur Taylor | | WIA | | 2Lt James Thompson | | WIA |
| Pte Daniel Washington | 23042 | WIA | | Pte John Thomas Watts | 27897 | WIA |

# 9

# 25 September 1917 – 6 December 1917
# Gillemont Farm

Late in the evening of 25 September 1917, 1/4th King's Own was on the move again. The men marched to Hopoutre, boarded a train to Bapaume, and arrived there shortly after midnight. They were accommodated in a camp at Vallulart Wood near Ytres, and spent the day making good kit deficiencies and catching up on the paperwork backlog. The next two days were allocated to training and on Sunday 30th, after morning church parade, football matches were held in the afternoon and early evening. The battalion was now part of the Third Army, in VII Corps under Lt-Gen. Thomas d'Oyly Snow.

On the morning of 2 October, the battalion made the long march to Longavesnes accompanied by the band; they remained there until 11 October. The weather had turned, and the autumnal chill and rains now became a daily feature, all helping to make everyday life that little bit more miserable— though the chalklands of Picardy were a massive improvement over the sloughs of the Salient. Replacements needed to be absorbed into the company and platoon structures and training was carried out assiduously in the knowledge that their time behind the lines would soon end. At 4.30 p.m. on 12 October, the battalion marched to the reserve positions at Ste Emilie, destined to move into the line the next day. The area of line held by 55 Division ran from the trenches (50° 2′ 6.21″ N, 3° 10′ 33.16″ E) opposite Honnecourt Wood in the north to New Post (49° 58′ 57.97″ N, 3° 11′ 36.23″ E) in the south, a stretch of about 8,000 yards—four times that held in the Salient. In addition, rather than a single, unbroken defensive line, it was a series of fortified posts with interconnecting communication trenches.[1] Had the division been up to strength, this length of front would still have stretched its capabilities. The vulnerability of this front was demonstrated on 18 November, when under cover of a heavy bombardment a large German raiding party of over 300 men from 184th Regiment entered the lines in three places.[2] A counter-attack from the support company of the battalion holding the line threw the enemy back out of the trenches with heavy casualties,[3] while the British lost ninety-four men, many of whom were taken prisoner.[4] Despite capturing so many, German reports state that no information was gained that gave any indication of a forthcoming attack.[5]

By 10 p.m. of 13 October, the 1/4th had relieved 1/7th King's in the right of the Epéhy sector. A Company took the left of the line opposite the German position of Gillemont Farm (49° 59′ 25.12″ N, 3° 12′ 1.98″ E), with less than 100 m between the opposing lines in places. On the right, C Company occupied Cat Post (49° 59′ 2.11″ N, 3° 11′ 33.44″ E)—in all about 1,000 yards of trench, quite a stretch for a battalion well below strength. B Company were in support, split between Duncan Post (49° 59′ 12.34″ N, 3° 11′ 21.73″ E), Doleful Post (49° 59′ 28.14″ N, 3° 11′ 20.62″ E), and HQ, with D Company as reserve in Ken Lane (49° 59′ 15.37″ N, 3° 10′ 50.73″ E). As usual, the Germans held the better ground. After the Salient the trenches were an improvement, but new trench boards and revetting were needed; luckily, the sector seemed peaceful, and it wasn't until 16 October that it came under bombardment. German trench mortars targeted the trenches in front of Gillemont Farm with success, though fortunately without casualties. Despite the 17th being reasonably quiet, D Company L/Cpl Adam Clark was wounded in Ken Lane and evacuated home; he was transferred to the Labour Corps after his convalescence. German trench mortars and artillery targeted the trenches opposite Gillemont Farm again the next day, and despite retaliation from 164 TMB, the bombardment continued, destroying all the repair work done after the previous occasion, and causing further damage—though yet again without loss to the battalion. For A Company, which had been on the receiving end of most of this, the battalion's relief by the Loyals at 8 p.m. was welcome.

Back in their billets in Ste Emilie on 19 October, the men began the great clean-up of themselves, their uniforms, and their equipment—not an easy task with the facilities available. The old enemy, the working party, reared its head later that evening, and 200 men were detailed to return to the front to spend the night revetting, cleaning, and draining trenches, undoing all their hard work earlier in the day! The day after saw a football match against 180 Tunnelling Company, RE, which ended in a

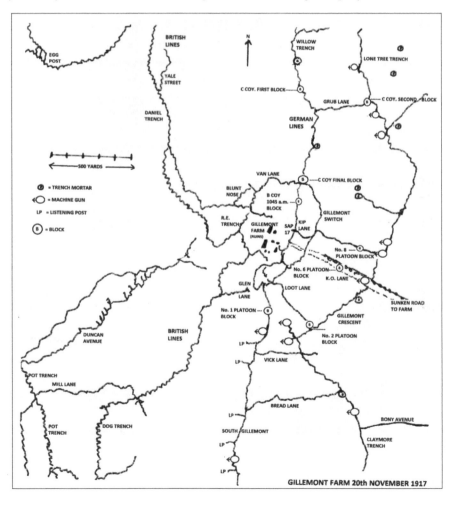

GILLEMONT FARM 20th NOVEMBER 1917

1–1 draw; that evening, 235 men returned to the trenches on a working party, and yet again on the 21st. Despite it being a Sunday, war and toil continued unabated.

22 October saw the battalion back into the same trenches, relieving the Loyals. This time, B Company occupied the Gillemont trenches and A Company Cat Post. C Company took over the role of support and D the reserve in Ken Lane. Unlike their experience in the Salient, moves into these trenches were fairly trouble-and casualty-free as they journeyed up the approach lines in the dark. The 24th and 25th again saw German bombardment of the trenches opposite Gillemont Farm and more activity from enemy MGs. Sentries observed considerable movement behind the German lines and the battalion went onto heightened alert as a result. On the 26th, it was decided that this activity was due to relief of one regiment by another, rather than a proposed attack, and the tension subsided. Even though there was no significant bombardment, the battalion suffered two casualties that day. Cpl William Masters, who had been wounded in mid-July and only returned to the battalion on the day of the Menin Road Ridge, was hit and killed by a burst of MG fire; the thirty-eight-year-old father from Lancaster was buried in Villers Faucon Cemetery. Pte Henry Bolton from B Company was accidentally wounded, though the circumstances of this are lost to posterity. Their last two days of this tour of the trenches were very quiet, and after being relieved by the Fusiliers on the 28th, the battalion moved to support in Lempire. For twenty-four-year-old L/Cpl Joseph Armstrong from Haverigg, this would be his last sight of the trenches, for he was claimed for munitions work by the Hodbarrow Mining Company. After a year in the trenches and the trauma of being buried alive that June by an exploding shell, he was probably heartily pleased to be going back home again.

The last three days of October remained quiet, though working parties of 200 men for the front were needed each night and training continued through the day. There were no working party casualties from enemy action, but on the 29th, Pte Henry Caton managed to shoot himself in the right foot while cleaning his rifle, ending up in 41 Stationary Hospital in Gailly. Surviving battalion records note that he was charged with:

> Conduct to the prejudice of good order and military discipline. Negligently discharged his rifle when cleaning it thereby wounding himself in the right foot.

His court martial took place in January 1918.

Considering that they were back in the line, the month had been quite kind to the battalion, with only one fatality and three wounded (two the results of accidents), and fifteen men in hospital sick. Although fifteen new officers and forty-eight other ranks arrived to replace casualties, battalion strength was still way below establishment. They remained at Longavesnes until 17 November, and spent the time on the range or training for attack. The area to be assaulted was marked out by 'spitlocked' trenches (marked out on ground by tape or by removal of turf) on the slopes between Longavesnes and Villers Faucon,[6] and companies rehearsed their attacks against these, culminating in battalion-sized attacks which were watched by the brigade commander.

Most late afternoons were set aside for sports, and another inter-platoon football tournament was held over five days. On the final night before the return to the Front, the band led by Sgt William Rickwood treated everyone to a concert. For one of the battalion, this marked a kind of farewell, as he was passed along the medical chain and went back to England. Pte Wilfred Goldstan had enlisted in the battalion in 1914, but had not been allowed out to France because of his age, only joining the ranks in January 1917. There had long been concern about his eyesight, and practise on the range had confirmed that there was a definite problem. The hospital in England to have treated him recommended that he be permanently downgraded as 'unfit for musketry or any purely military duties'[7] and he was posted to Heaton Park as a 'general dogsbody'—not at all what he had enlisted for! At 5 p.m. on Saturday 17 November, the battalion began the three-mile march to billets at Ste Emilie, the band playing as it marched with them. At 9 a.m. the next morning, the semi-finals of the inter-platoon football tournament took place, followed by a visit to church. The rest of that day was devoted to preparations for the attack scheduled for the 20 November. Again at 9 a.m. the next morning, the battalion paraded for football to watch the final, won by 13 Platoon, and last preparations were made for the attack, equipment and ammunition issued.

The scheduled attack was supposed to be little more than a diversion to pin down German reserves and prevent them reacting to the main attack further north at Cambrai. The Hindenburg Line, part of which the 1/4th would be assaulting, was a serious adversary to any attacker. Each fire trench was approximately 10 feet wide at the top, 3½ at the bottom, and protected by four rows of wire with forward-projecting triangles at regular intervals. Although the wire was only about waist-high, each belt was about 10 yards deep from front to rear, and where No Man's Land was wide, about 100 yards' deep. Following their practice of 'defence in depth', support lines were similarly defended and adjoining communication trenches wired along their sides. Further behind these, the front was defended by a series of fortified strongpoints, with interlocking arcs of fire, giving in total 6,000 to 8,000 yards of defensive zone behind the front line.[8]

Along VII Corps's 10-mile-long front, an artillery bombardment which included smoke shells was to be fired at zero hour. No preliminary bombardment had been carried out, in order to preserve surprise, and guns would be aimed using 'map-shooting', a technique the Germans had also developed. This depended on the accurate plotting of guns, targets, and a series of bearing pickets determined by trigonometrical survey beforehand. Developments in sound-ranging meant that guns could be calibrated on designated ranges, to determine the individual wear characteristics of each gun with various types of ammunition. Another factor in accurate ranging was the weather, as wind, temperature, and air pressure all played their parts in determining the ballistic trajectories of shells. Accurate information was essential and meteorological telegrams were sent to the gunners on a daily basis.[9] There were a number of German batteries near La Terrière (50° 1′ 55.98″ N, 3° 13′ 46.31″ E) capable of ranging onto both the main attack and the assault by the 1/4th, so it was planned to draw their fire with a 'Chinese Attack' (by the men holding the left sector of 55 Division's line then destroying the German batteries with concentrated counter-battery fire).[10] The dummy attack, which began at 6.30 a.m., was played out from 'Birdcage' (50° 0′ 42.75″ N, 3° 11′ 23.20″ E) and consisted of a wooden tank silhouette and dummy infantrymen placed in irregular ranks and manipulated by a system of wires. This drew considerable MG and artillery fire which would otherwise have fallen on the two attacking forces from 164 Brigade to the south.[11]

Only one brigade could be spared from 55 Division to carry out the attack on 20 November, as the others were needed to hold the elongated front. Two objectives were selected, the 'Knoll' and the German trenches opposite Gillemont Farm. The Liverpool Irish on the left and Fusiliers on the right were to attack the Knoll, while 1,200 m to their south, 1/4th would attack the Gillemont Farm trenches with support from 1/5th King's Own as a counter-attack reserve. As this was merely a diversionary operation to prevent the enemy pulling his reserves northwards, it was decided that it was unnecessary to force through, or to hold on to any gains if the cost became too high; the main objective of the attacks would have been met by tying down German manpower.[12]

The battalion moved to their attack positions at 7 p.m. on the night of the 19th and all were in place by 2.45 a.m. Three companies, each reinforced by a platoon from D Company, would make the assault two minutes after zero hour.[13] On the left, C Company, commanded by Capt. Thomas Blain, would attack from Blunt Nose (49° 59′ 30.61″ N, 3° 11′ 59.35″ E); in the centre, B Company, commanded by Capt. John Evans, was positioned in Stokes Trench (at 49° 59′ 26.41″ N, 3° 11′ 59.09″ E); and A Company to the right, commanded by Capt. Albert Ellwood, was also in Stokes Trench (at 49° 59′ 23.68″ N, 3° 11′ 59.53″ E). The British bombardment from artillery, MGs, and trench mortars began against the two objectives at 6.20 a.m., and two minutes later, the 1/4th advanced close up to the British barrage. The attack immediately hit obstructions, as the German wire was found to be mostly unbroken and the German counter-barrage was already falling on the British front line and its approaches.

The 'Barrage Map' for the attack shows that the wire to the battalion's immediate front was subjected to a two-minute bombardment from 18-pounders, at a rate of fire of four rounds per minute per gun.[14] Although this was to be supplemented by the 6-inch trench mortars, the divisional artillery, who were without their 'heavy' guns, were firing to cover both the attack at Gillemont Farm and at the Knoll; in addition, this initial phase of wire-cutting was distributed along 2,000 yards of frontage and four other areas of trench along which to prevent German movement. Considering the lightweight bombardment and inaccuracy of some of the old 18-pounders, it's hardly surprising that the wire was still mainly intact!

C Company found the wire to its front uncut, which caused delay before squads were redirected further north to gain entry into Gillemont Trench. One squad bombed their way northwards past its junction with Grub Lane (49° 59′ 38.58″ N, 3° 12′ 9.21″ E) and into Willow Trench, forming a temporary block some 60 m along it (at 49° 59′ 40.15″ N, 3° 12′ 7.16″ ). Following close behind them, another squad turned right into Grub Lane and fought its way along until it reached the belt of wire covering Lone Tree Trench, where it too established a block (49° 59′ 39.38″ N, 3° 12′ 16.23″ E). The Germans immediately counter-attacked down Willow Trench from the north and Grub Lane from the east, forcing their way through both blocks. Outnumbered and facing superior firepower, C Company gradually fell back to make a stand at the junction of Gillemont Trench and Van Lane (49° 59′ 35.50″ N, 3° 12′ 8.96″ E), where it built another temporary block. Twenty-one-year-old L/Cpl George Johnson from Bootle organised a bombing party, cleared the trench, then managed to deploy one of the enemy's own *Granatenwerfer* (one of two he captured in the trench), delaying their advance until his ammunition was exhausted. He then destroyed both mortars to deny them to the enemy. For his courage and leadership, he was awarded the DCM; he went on to earn another later.[15] Also awarded a DCM was nineteen-year-old Pte Richard Corbett from Warrington. When his platoon officer and all other NCOs became casualties, he took command, reorganised his platoon, and led it to its objective, destroying a trench mortar position. When he was counter-attacked by superior numbers of enemy, he led his men on a charge against the attackers and blunted their assault. Eventually, they were forced back to the block, but held their position stubbornly until ordered to retire.[16]

Capt. Blain of C Company was wounded at the beginning of the attack, but continued to lead his men. When one of his detachments was in imminent danger of being cut off, he personally led the party to relieve them and kept the enemy at bay with accurate rifle fire. After supervising the withdrawal to another line of defence, loss of blood forced his evacuation off the battlefield. For his gallantry and determination, he was awarded the MC.[17] Command of his company was now taken over by Capt. Evans, OC B Company— the men of both companies were by now intermixed, anyway. Another block was made in Gillemont Switch and held until about noon, when German troops advanced upon it from Gillemont Trench on the right, threatening to cut off the defenders. They retreated to Sap 17 (49° 59′ 26.56″ N, 3° 12′ 9.01″ E), which they blocked and held until the men from the companies to their right had successfully withdrawn.

In the centre, B Company's woes began before it had even left the trenches. The shrapnel from the 18-pounders on the company's left front was actually exploding short, and any movement from its trench before the barrage lifted would have been suicidal. When the left flank did advance, it found the wire uncut. Although the wire further to their right was mostly undamaged, the men could see that there were some fairly wide gaps in it in front of Gillemont Switch. Led by Capt. Evans, they pushed on through them, unmolested as they crossed No Man's Land (for the three German defenders at the eastern end of Sap 17 had been killed by the barrage). Once they had crossed through the wire, resistance against them stiffened and they came under fire from an MG some 200 m to their front (49° 59′ 23.95″ N, 3° 12′ 18.91″ E). Upon reaching the junction of Gillemont Trench and Kip Lane, they again found that the wire was uncut, with 'knife rests' preventing access to the trench. (A 'knife rest' is a free-standing obstacle consisting of two posts lashed into an 'X'-shape, joined by a longer centre post to another X-shaped construction, all liberally festooned with wire.) The officer in charge of 7 Platoon and nearly all his men became casualties at this stage, the few survivors joining the other two platoons. To their right, they spotted some gaps in the wire near K. O. Lane and the survivors of 6 and 8 Platoon affected an entry through these. 6 Platoon pushed forward until they could progress no further, their advance halted by heavy MG fire and repeated counter-attacks. Despite a constant succession of rifle grenades, they succeeded in establishing a block half way along K. O. Lane shortly after 9 a.m. (49° 59′ 23.16″ N, 3° 12′ 13.65″ E). 8 Platoon had split away from 6 Platoon as soon as it penetrated the wire and, once in Gillemont Trench, began to push up Kip Lane until stopped about 50 yards short of Gillemont Crescent. 8 Platoon then built a block (at 49° 59′ 25.28″ N, 3° 12′ 16.93″ E) to hinder any German counter-attacks. It was just twenty-five minutes after zero hour.

The casualty count was significant and some sections, such as L/Sgt George Mason's, were down to a couple of men. Clearing dugouts of enemy had gradually eroded the numbers, until only Mason and one other were left. Placing the private as sentry, Mason took on the remaining dugouts by himself and cleared the final two, killing all the occupants. He too used the enemy's weaponry, turning a captured *Granatenwerfer* against its former owners until ammunition was exhausted. In the late phases of the operation, he collected scattered groups of men and organised them into a final defence of the captured positions, earning himself the MM.[18]

B Company HQ reached Gillemont Switch fifteen minutes after zero hour, Capt. Evans personally accounting for three enemy kills as he led the attack. Here, he met up with Capt. Blain and they exchanged information about their companies' progress. Due to the problems C Company had encountered with uncut wire, some of its men had been absorbed into B Company, and the D Company platoons attached to both C and B had also become intermingled. Unknown to Evans, his right platoons had established contact with A Company, but the runner bringing the news had been hit. Signallers managed to lay telephone cable from B Company's position back to battalion HQ, though communications between individual companies relied on runners. The laying of this cable had come at a cost: Sgt Sam Eagers from Barrow, one of the 1914 'originals', was shot in the head and died instantly.[19] The runners had an equally dangerous job, as Ulverston window cleaner Pte Richard Thistlethwaite discovered. Runners were primarily riflemen, but once he'd helped capture their objective, the twenty-four-year-old then had to relay the news back to battalion HQ, braving shrapnel and MG fire. He made this journey repeatedly, and sooner or later his luck was bound to run out. After a number of trips, he was hit by shrapnel and wounded in the nose and leg. He returned to the battalion upon his recovery and was awarded the MM for his bravery.[20] Another runner was more fortunate: Pte William Hanna from Lostock Hall also made repeated journeys back to battalion HQ, and on his last led back a party of men carrying urgently needed munition supplies; he too was awarded the MM. Both the first name ('Thomas') and regimental number given for this man in the citation documents are incorrect,[21] and were not corrected until he contacted Infantry Records in 1933.[22]

Even though so few men were available, consolidation of Gillemont Trench began under the cover of a Vickers in the ruins of Gillemont Farm, and commanded by one L/Cpl Ruddock (probably Charles Ruddock of 164 MG Company). At 10.45 a.m., the Germans counter-attacked the post in Kip Lane, forcing the defenders back with salvoes of stick grenades. Defenders had little to reply to this onslaught as their supplies of rifle grenades and Mills bombs were soon exhausted. They reluctantly withdrew to Gillemont Switch, and set to work helping the others to consolidate and build another block half way between Sap 17 and Van Lane (49° 59′ 29.79″ N, 3° 12′ 7.26″ E). Upon being appraised of the situation, Lt-Col. Balfour ordered B Company to take the whole of the trench between Sap 17 and its junction with Van Lane and Gillemont Switch, and to join up with A Company to its right; he allocated two platoons from 1/5th King's to reinforce these men. Gillemont Switch was above all to be held, consolidation completed as quickly as possible. Evans decided to consolidate the eastern end of Sap 17 as a strongpoint to provide flank protection in conjunction with C Company. Supplies of rifle grenades and bombs had long run out, the men relying on captured German weapons and ammunition to hold off determined enemy counter-attacks. It was now around noon, and at last a resupply of bombs and small arms ammunition made it through the German barrage to the beleaguered defenders.

On the right, A Company found similar problems with uncut wire of the 'chevaux de frise' variety (similar to knife rests, but with more X-shapes), though they were able to penetrate it with few casualties. Capt. Ellwood was the first man into one trench and quickly disposed of an enemy MG and its crew before they could inflict any harm on his men.[23] Thirteen minutes after zero hour, 2 Platoon reported that they had mopped up their section of Gillemont Switch and were working their way northwards and pushing on along Loot Lane to try to make contact with B Company. 1 Platoon under 2Lt George Raeside was encountering much more resistance from the enemy as they advanced southwards along Gillemont Trench. Thirty-eight-year-old George Raeside had only joined the battalion as a fresh lieutenant on 10 October, but he was not new to soldiering. Prior to his commissioning, he was a CQMS with the Cameron Highlanders; he was a tough and experienced soldier. By 7.10 a.m., his platoon had established a strong block in Gillemont Trench (at 49° 59′ 19.26″ N, 3° 12′ 3.31″ E), the limit of their bound. When the Germans started congregating to rush this block, Raeside tackled them himself, killing five.

Initially, 2 Platoon's progress along Loot Lane had been good, but as the men got closer to Gillemont Trench enemy resistance stiffened, casualties increased, and they began to run short of bombs. The D Company platoon under 2Lt George Ferguson and attached to A Company was positioned at the junction between Loot Lane and Gillemont Trench, and a small bombing squad with lots of bombs was detached from them to help Lt Clark's 2 Platoon. Under this renewed onslaught the enemy fell back, and by 7.45 a.m. 2 Platoon held all of Loot Lane up to its junction with Gillemont Trench (49° 59′ 17.69″ N, 3° 12′ 9.82″ E), where it began construction of a block. The trench here was cut into the chalk, so this was a long and arduous job, especially as the enemy made a series of determined counter-attacks upon the men as they worked. Now that contact had been made with B Company to their left, Capt. Ellwood sent additional men and supplies from 1 Platoon to help hold the block and the immediate area of Gillemont Crescent south of Loot Lane. Meanwhile, the remainder of Clark's platoon fought their way northwards, along Gillemont Crescent.

German resistance in Gillemont Crescent was considerable; every single dugout had to be cleared as 2 Platoon steadily progressed northwards. The enemy repeatedly attacked the holding party to the men's rear, and as their supply of bombs ran out, they were forced back into Loot Lane. Word was sent by runner up to Lt Clark, informing him of the situation, but by the time the news reached him he was already surrounded. Leaving the leading half of his force to hold the front and if possible to try to force their way northwards in the hope of joining up with B Company, Clark led the remainder of his men in an attack back along the trench to try to force the enemy back down Gillemont Crescent past the junction with Loot Lane and secure the rear. Running short of bombs, few of this group survived to fight their way back into Loot Lane. Further reinforcement of the German counter-attack—which used Bony Avenue to enter Gillemont Crescent (at 49° 59′ 8.01″ N, 3° 12′ 17.72″ E)—cut off the front part of Clark's force, and rendered any future hope of re-establishing a block in Gillemont Crescent futile.

With Clark was his orderly, twenty-eight-year-old Pte John Bennett from Barrow. He'd already cleared two dugouts single-handed, killing one officer and several men; when he was wounded, he refused to be evacuated, determined to stay with his lieutenant. More men from 1 Platoon went forward with supplies and Clark hurriedly built a block 30 yards from the end of Loot Lane. It was only at about 9.30 a.m. that the situation to his left became clear to Capt. Ellwood, as news of B Company's failure to force its way into Gillemont Crescent was relayed. He now knew that any men from the lead elements of Clark's platoon still in Gillemont Switch were beyond rescue. Another officer's orderly to stand out that day was twenty-two-year-old Pte John Seed from Preston. He was orderly to one of the company commanders (possibly Ellwood), and on three separate occasions climbed up onto the parapet of the trench they were clearing and poured rapid fire onto the enemy from his exposed position, enabling his comrades to maintain their advance; he was awarded the MM.[24]

Shortly before 10 a.m., an SOS signal rose from A Company's left. Capt. Ellwood learned that B Company had now been forced back to Gillemont Trench, and that C Company had also been forced in until it met B Company, which left his left flank vulnerable, especially if there was further withdrawal there. At 10 a.m., the enemy burst through the block at the end of Loot Lane, and Ellwood decided to withdraw his men to the western end of Loot Lane, as his company's flanks were now 'in the air' and fighting to regain the position was pointless. The western end of Loot Lane was terribly exposed, the trench smashed by shell fire and overlooked by the enemy in Bony Avenue, Claymore Trench, and Bread Lane. Around 10.30 a.m., Lt Clark was killed by a burst of MG fire and one of his men, Pte Thomas Moody, who had earlier taken command of his section after his NCO had become a casualty, braved the bullets to come to his aid. A bullet severed the artery in his left arm, but fortunately Moody's comrades pulled him back out of danger and applied a tourniquet. He survived, but was given a medical discharge in October 1918; he also received a MM.[25] Clark's orderly, Pte Bennett, was unable to do any more for him, but managed to collect Clark's personal effects before retiring to join the survivors; he too earned the MM for his courage.[26]

Soon after Clark was killed a rumour circulated that the forces to A Company's left had withdrawn further and the enemy bombing along Gillemont Switch and Trench were certainly getting closer. German attempts to force the block at the western end of Loot Lane were also increasing in both strength and regularity, but despite this, the men of A Company held their positions.

B Company's situation was also rapidly deteriorating. At 12.30 p.m., an attack against the post in K. O. Lane succeeded in pushing the few survivors back to Gillemont Switch, where they rallied and held off the enemy. By this time, the total strength of B Company, including the two attached platoons from D Company, was down to just three officers, forty men, and three Lewis guns; Capt. Evans now commanded his own and C and D Company. The Vickers in the ruins of Gillemont Farm was no longer in action, so Evans placed two Lewis guns there and sited the third to cover their left flank. (L/Cpl Ruddock had been wounded in the arm by shrapnel and the surviving members of his gun section had withdrawn 80 yards to the old front line and set up position there, though this was unknown to Evans.) These combined forces managed to hold the enemy off with small arms fire, all their bombs long since used up.

At 12.45 p.m., A, C, and D Company used a lull in the fighting to further consolidate damaged positions. A runner came up and told Capt. Evans that reinforcements from two platoons from B Company of 1/5th King's had arrived, and as he went to brief their officer on the situation, the enemy made another resolute counter-attack upon all three company positions from the front and both flanks. Gradually, the combined forces of C and B Company were forced back to Sap 17, inflicting heavy casualties on a determined enemy as they did so. Shortly before this, the Germans had succeeded in driving a wedge between A and B Company, forcing men to retreat across No Man's Land to avoid being surrounded and cut off; with imminent danger of his men being over-run and surrounded, Ellwood ordered the posts to be abandoned and the men to fall back to his position. Before they could carry this order out, the Germans reached the posts in force and a general melee ensued with bitter hand-to-hand combat. The defenders inflicted heavy casualties on the enemy, but given the strength of the German counter-attack, the result was a foregone conclusion: A Company was forced back to its own lines, and many of its wounded captured. Lt Raeside was the last to leave his block, covering the withdrawal of the rest of the company and finally his own men before fighting his way back to friendly lines. For his leadership and courage, he was awarded the MC, as was Capt. Ellwood for his continuous courage and resourcefulness.[27] By 1 p.m., the defenders of Sap 17 were taking heavy casualties in enfilade from bombs and small arms fire, and it was clear that there was only one outcome. The men in Sap 17, the lynchpin of the battalion's defences, held on until all the men to their left had retired; then, covered by the Lewis guns, they made their own retreat back to the British line. For his energy, daring, and wherewithal throughout the day, which had been an inspiration to his men, Capt. Evans also received the MC.[28]

The men had fought like lions. NCOs took over as officers became casualties. Sgt George Maddrell assumed command of his platoon early in the fight, after his officer was hit. He was the first into the trench that was their initial objective, cleared it, and inflicted loss on the enemy. Before he could establish a block, the enemy counter-attacked and Maddrell charged the German bombers alone, accounting for several kills while the rest fled. Despite being severely wounded, he continued to lead until the block was established, earning the MM.[29] When A Company's Sgt Albert Miles saw that a blocking party had almost been annihilated, he organised reinforcements and led them to the rescue. His party also came under heavy fire, sustaining severe casualties, so he too charged the enemy single-handed, killing at least a dozen of them. Although he was recommended for the DCM, he received the MM—though he was commissioned later in the war.[30]

On numerous occasions, the men taking command were privates. One of the signallers, Pte Thomas Menelly, encountered a clearing party who had lost all their NCOs. Taking charge of this disorganised group, he gathered and led them to their objective, accounting for many of the enemy. Later, he also attacked and routed an outpost that was causing problems for his men, acts for which he received the MM.[31] Pte Arthur Knowles also claimed several Germans as they cleared a section of trench, but it was due to his leadership in particular that a block was established in the trench and held against repeated attacks. He stood in front of the block, his rifle and bayonet at the ready, and several times charged and drove off enemy counter-attacks that tried to bomb it. Later in the day, as they were forced to retire to a secondary position, Knowles again stood to the front of the block, though this time he was wounded and then evacuated; his bravery earned him the MM.[32] Pte Thomas Lofthouse from Blackburn cleared one trench, and when the blocking party was attacked by a group of bombers, he and another man staved off the rush. He was wounded and his companion killed in the process, but Lofthouse refused to go back and fought on as the men retired to successive blocks. He was awarded the MM, though sadly, the name of his comrade was not recorded.[33] Twenty-one-year-old Pte John Moore from Newton achieved the same award, after leading a trench-clearing party and personally attacking three small groups of the enemy, killing every single one of them. When the block he was defending came under attack, Moore beat back three determined rushes; he inspired his comrades with his fortitude and determination.[34]

The Lewis and its gunners proved invaluable on 20 November. Blackpool soldier Pte Thomas Pollitt, who had been in trouble some two months earlier for going AWOL for three days in Calais, repaid his lenient sentence with his display of courage. When all the other members of his team had become casualties, he braved the heavy fire to save the gun, under his own initiative set it up in another position, and drove back a strong counter-attack. Later on he took up a fire position in the open, as it gave a much better field of fire and used the gun with great effect to drive off a strong bombing party that was attacking his platoon's block. He earned a MM.[35] Another Lewis-gunner to be similarly rewarded was Pte Thomas Dixon, a former member of the 1/5th. He held his ground against four determined counter-attacks, despite being repeatedly bombarded, and when he was almost surrounded, managed to withdraw with his gun and immediately bring it into action from a secondary position.[36]

In many ways, the problems faced by the 1/4th on the morning of 20 November 1917 were more akin to the early days of the war. Uncut wire, ammunition shortages, and a lack of effective artillery support seemed more early 1915 than late 1917. The attacks by 55 Division were merely a diversion intended to distract, and the available guns were not in a position to influence the outcome much. German counter-attacks could amass in the dead ground to the east of Gillemont Farm, safe from any ground-level observation. Neither does there appear to have been any aircraft allocated to the 1/4th for this operation, so the enemy could efficaciously counter-attack without being targeted by direct shell fire. And even if aeroplanes had been allocated, the visibility was such that they would probably have been ineffective. The short but heavy bombardment decided upon in an effort to preserve surprise had left most of the wire undamaged, although it had caused heavy casualties to the defending Germans.[37] Crucially, what hadn't been neutralised were the German batteries, and it was fire from these that prevented ammunition being resupplied the attackers on the front line.

Neither attack had been unexpected by the Germans.[38] However, the attack on the Knoll by the Liverpool Irish and Fusiliers had run up against greater problems than the 1/4th's—they had been forced back to their own lines as early on as 10 a.m. Brig.-Gen. Stockwell was about to give the order for the 1/4th to retire, but this was countermanded by Gen. Snow, who wanted the 1/4th to hold Gillemont for at least all day. His was a fateful decision, for the Germans in the sector were now able to concentrate all their forces against the 1/4th—a scenario with only one possible outcome. Both attacks had been pushed back from enemy positions, but the overall objective of the attacks, that of pinning down German reinforcements, had been successful. To buy the northern attackers at Cambrai more time, artillery was used to simulate a further attack. At 4.30 p.m., a heavy bombardment of enemy positions by artillery, trench mortars, and MGs caused the defending Germans heavy casualties. At 5 a.m. on the 21st, the enemy positions at Gillemont and the Knoll were bombarded, and again, at 6.30 a.m., a British 'hurricane barrage' complete with smoke shells lifted, as though part of a creeping barrage.[39] There is no doubt that the enemy suffered many casualties in this attack. Twenty-three soldiers of 184th Regiment were captured by the 1/4th at Gillemont and escorted back to British lines. Although the German commander, Kronprinz Rupprecht von Bayern, later claimed that he had not attached any great importance to the attacks on the Knoll and Gillemont, no German guns or infantry were redeployed from the Gillemont sector to Cambrai until much later in the day.[40] The cost to 164 Brigade was dear, with just over 600 casualties. The 1/4th suffered 211 casualties in the action, fifty-four of whom were killed in action or later died from their wounds—a grievous toll considering the 1/4th's casualties in the Salient in July and September.

Killed in action or died from wounds at Gillemont Farm November 1917

| | | | | | |
|---|---|---|---|---|---|
| Pte John Allison | 27992 | KIA | Pte James Henry Barrow | 200985 | KIA |
| Pte Alfred Bennett | 200673 | KIA | Pte William Henry Brown | 34550 | KIA |
| Sgt Frederick Cannon | 200721 | DOW-22/11 | Pte Thomas Chandler | 27226 | KIA |
| Lt Alfred Matthews Clark | | KIA | Pte Ernest Clarke | 201599 | DOW-27/11 |
| Pte Joseph Coates | 34540 | KIA | Pte Robert Lamb Cragg * | 34668 | DOW-27/11 |
| Cpl Herbert Daly | 6028 | KIA | 2Lt Albert John Dartnall | | KIA |
| Pte Thomas Davies | 34669 | KIA | Sgt Samuel Eagers | 200233 | KIA |
| Pte Edward Fairhurst | 201395 | KIA | Pte John Fletcher | 201393 | KIA |
| Pte James Fortune | 201609 | DOW-1/12 | Pte Richard Bowman Foster | 34619 | KIA |
| Pte James Foy * | 28023 | KIA | Pte William Green | 28026 | DOW-23/11 |
| L/Cpl Charles John Gregory | 26887 | KIA | Pte Harold Hacking | 25741 | KIA |
| Pte James Percival Helm | 28032 | KIA | Pte William Crook Hogg | 31618 | KIA |
| Pte Joseph Hoole | 202241 | DOW-23/11 | Cpl Thomas Jackson | 200197 | KIA |

| | | | | | | |
|---|---|---|---|---|---|---|
| Pte William Jameson | 200869 | KIA | | 2Lt Lyndon Rayner Keighley | | DOW-3/12 |
| Pte John Thomas King | 200828 | DOW-21/11 | | Pte Albert Lord | 265141 | KIA |
| Pte William Lowery | 201057 | DOW-26/11 | | L/Cpl Luke Marsden | 201633 | KIA |
| Pte Isaac Moore | 200099 | KIA | | Pte William Moran | 201733 | KIA |
| Pte Walter Nutter | 266036 | KIA | | Pte Cyril Pittaway | 34694 | KIA |
| Pte John W Poucher | 27101 | KIA | | Pte Jonathan Ratcliffe | 16081 | KIA |
| Pte Ernest George Robinson | 200229 | KIA | | L/Cpl John Robinson | 243451 | KIA |
| Pte Frank Rothery | 202108 | DOW-25/11 | | Pte George Rothwell | 34666 | DOW-30/11 |
| 2Lt James Robson Rundle | | KIA | | Pte William Smedley | 201302 | DOW-2/12 |
| 2Lt Robert Smith | | KIA | | Pte Fred Talbot | 201579 | DOW-25/11 |
| Pte James Threlfall | 243067 | KIA | | Pte Thomas M. Timperley | 201580 | KIA |
| Pte John Thomas Watts | 27897 | KIA | | L/Cpl Frederick C Wenham | 201158 | KIA |
| Pte William West | 201764 | KIA | | Pte John Thomas Wilde | 201667 | KIA |
| Pte Henry Wilkins | 201744 | KIA | | Cpl Charles Wilson | 202193 | KIA |

* Pte Robert Lamb Cragg is listed 'KIA' on 27 November by *Soldiers Died*. However, he appears on the battalion's casualty list for 20 November as 'Missing', and his burial place at Le Cateau suggests that he died from wounds and was buried by the Germans. Another soldier buried by the enemy was Pte James Foy, a married father of five from Durham. His identity disc was returned by the Germans via the Red Cross. His burial site was lost and he is commemorated on the Thiepval Memorial.

Known to have been wounded at Gillemont Farm November 1917

| | | | | | | |
|---|---|---|---|---|---|---|
| Pte Ralph Anderton | 202215 | WIA | | Pte Hugh Arrowsmith | 28087 | WIA |
| | | | | Pte Henry Thomas Ashmore | 201429 | WIA |
| Pte Albert E. Ashburn | 200437 | WIA | | | | |
| Pte Henry W Ashworth | 266059 | WIA/POW | | Pte John Astley | 201410 | WIA |
| Pte Joseph Atherton | 200855 | WIA/POW | | Pte Albert Bagshaw | 28088 | WIA |
| Pte John Bailey | 201023 | WIA | | L/Sgt Phillip Baines | 200518 | WIA/POW |
| Pte Frederick Baines | 34711 | WIA/POW | | Pte Harry Bebbington | 19690 | WIA |
| L/Cpl John Frederick Bennett | 201160 | WIA | | Pte Herbert Billington | 34614 | WIA/POW |
| Pte Taylor Binns | 201586 | WIA | | Capt. Thomas Reginald Blain | | WIA |
| | | | | Cpl William Ernest Bosanko | 200172 | WIA |
| Pte Sydney Bloomfield | 200383 | WIA | | | | |
| Pte Harry Bottomley | 20689 | WIA | | Pte Stephen Boundy | 200658 | WIA |
| Sgt Henry Bradley | 200416 | WIA | | Pte Frank Marshall Bridge | 24225 | WIA |
| Pte Ernest Brockbank | 201050 | WIA | | Cpl William Brockbank | 34708 | WIA |
| Pte Edward H. Brocklebank | 200237 | WIA/POW | | Pte George Brown | 27995 | WIA |
| WO2 Robert Butcher | 200372 | WIA | | Pte John Capstick | 200701 | WIA/POW |
| Cpl Henry J. Casper ** | 16272 | WIA | | Pte Percy Chadderton | 28096 | WIA |

| | | |
|---|---|---|
| Pte Joseph Clare | 19447 | WIA |
| Pte Christopher Clarkson | 201524 | WIA/POW |
| Pte Arthur Cleminson | 201522 | WIA |
| Pte Thomas Cookson | 33942 | WIA/POW |
| Pte Hubert Cunningham | 201436 | WIA |
| Pte Thomas Albert Davis | 11186 | WIA/POW |
| Pte John Adam Thwaite Dixon | 34611 | WIA/POW |
| Pte Arthur Downing | 21458 | WIA |
| L/Cpl Guy Eddleston | 200838 | WIA |
| Pte Richard Elboz | 202176 | WIA |
| 2Lt George Field | | WIA/POW |
| Pte Stephen Foster | 200152 | WIA |
| Pte Harold Garside | 26756 | WIA |
| Pte George Golding | 26885 | WIA |
| Pte George Jubilee Gowling | 201560 | WIA |
| Pte Frank Hardman | 201582 | WIA/POW |
| Pte John Reidy Harrison | 201084 | WIA |
| Pte Edwin Hill | 34627 | WIA/POW |
| Pte Robert Holding | 22466 | WIA |
| Pte Benjamin Horn | 28106 | WIA/POW |
| Pte Percy Howarth | 201374 | WIA/POW |
| Pte John Edward Hunt | 27981 | WIA |
| Pte John Edward Jackson | 241597 | WIA |
| A/Cpl Ambrose Kelly | 201116 | WIA |
| Pte Arthur F. Knowles | 201727 | WIA |
| Pte Richard Lawton | 34673 | WIA |
| Pte Frederick Lindsay | 200313 | WIA |
| Pte James Lingard | 241569 | WIA/POW |
| Pte Wilfred Livesey | 15940 | WIA |
| L/Cpl Thomas Lowery | 235054 | WIA/POW |
| 2Lt John Mackay | | WIA |
| Pte Joseph Massey | 27877 | WIA |
| Pte John McLaughlin | 200808 | WIA |
| Cpl Walter Meadowcroft | 201639 | WIA |
| Pte John Monaghan | 16557 | WIA |
| Pte Leonard Mountcastle | 26949 | WIA |
| Pte John William O'Donnell | 242236 | WIA |
| Pte George H Owen | 202320 | WIA |

| | | |
|---|---|---|
| Pte George Arthur H. Clarke | 201601 | WIA |
| Cpl Arthur Clementson | 19484 | WIA |
| Pte Thomas Conroy | 200659 | WIA |
| Pte Stephen Crane | 30139 | WIA |
| Pte Robert S. Cunningham | 34909 | WIA |
| Pte Edward Dickinson | 15609 | WIA/POW |
| Pte Edwin Douglas | 28015 | WIA/POW |
| Pte Robert Eastwood | 26968 | WIA/POW |
| Pte Fred Edmondson | 201218 | WIA |
| Sgt Herbert Fearnley | 201031 | WIA |
| Pte Walter Forbes | 15854 | WIA/POW |
| Pte William Henry Gaffney | 18781 | WIA/POW |
| Pte Wilton Garvey | 201614 | WIA |
| Pte Andrew Goodinson | 22112 | WIA |
| Pte John Halsall | 200977 | WIA |
| Pte Edwin Harker | 28030 | WIA/POW |
| Pte Arthur Hibbert | 2431 | WIA |
| Pte John Hipwell | 27870 | WIA |
| Pte Samuel Holt | 201574 | WIA/POW |
| Pte Jack Howarth | 201760 | WIA/POW |
| Pte Harold Victor Hudson | 201087 | WIA/POW |
| Pte Thomas Swainson Hunter | 26678 | WIA |
| L/Cpl Alfred W. Johnson | 200748 | WIA |
| Pte James Kelly | 201627 | WIA/POW |
| Pte William Lackey | 201220 | WIA/POW |
| Pte John Lees | 25726 | WIA/POW |
| Cpl John W. Lindsey | 12451 | WIA/POW |
| Pte James Lingard | 202778 | WIA |
| Pte Thomas Lofthouse | 200910 | WIA |
| Pte Harry Loydell | 200538 | WIA |
| Sgt George Maddrell | 201076 | WIA |
| Pte James McDonald | 34497 | WIA/POW |
| L/Cpl Albert McWilliams | 17422 | WIA |
| Pte Thomas William Menelly | 201071 | WIA |
| Pte Thomas Moody | 27098 | WIA |
| Pte James Murray | 34839 | WIA |
| Pte Robert Orrell | 15382 | WIA/POW |
| Pte Walter T. Parkinson | 27448 | WIA |

| | | | | | | |
|---|---|---|---|---|---|---|
| Pte William Arthur Peach | 202095 | WIA/POW | Pte Richard S. Penny | 34616 | WIA |
| Pte Frank Redvers Platt | 41548 | WIA | Pte Francis Plimley | 201307 | WIA |
| Pte James Preston | 201336 | WIA | Pte Charles Prince | 202090 | WIA/POW |
| L/Cpl Joseph Slater Purvis | 27346 | WIA | Pte George Radford | 202104 | WIA |
| Pte James Ramsbotham | 200898 | WIA | Pte John Rodgerson | 200789 | WIA |
| Pte Albert Rollinson | 201448 | WIA | Pte James Round | 200813 | WIA |
| L/Cpl Robert Schofield | 201386 | WIA | Pte William Schofield | 34605 | WIA |
| Pte William Scott | 32015 | WIA | L/Cpl John Seed | 200851 | WIA |
| Sgt Thomas Edward Seed | 200829 | WIA | Sgt William Sharp | 200722 | WIA/POW |
| Pte Charles J. Skippon | 202121 | WIA | Pte Horace Skirrow | 201922 | WIA |
| Pte Lewis Charles Snowdon | 202118 | WIA | Pte William G. Steel | 202113 | WIA |
| Pte Charles Stewart | 32661 | WIA | 2Lt Joe Harry Sykes | | WIA |
| Pte Arthur James Taylor | 266038 | WIA/POW | Pte Cecil Elliot Taylor | 202135 | WIA |
| Pte John Thomas Taylor | 201558 | WIA | Pte Arnold Tennant | 201661 | WIA |
| Pte Richard Thistlethwaite | 200632 | WIA | Pte John W. Thomas | 202130 | WIA |
| Pte George Thomas Thompson | 200565 | WIA | Pte Richard Thompson | 242418 | WIA |
| Pte Henry Todman | 201272 | WIA | L/Cpl John Tomlinson | 200794 | WIA |
| Pte John Tongue | 17275 | WIA | Pte William Troughton | 201496 | WIA/POW |
| Cpl Francis Henry Turner | 202170 | WIA/POW | Pte Walter Harry Turner | 26930 | WIA/POW |
| Pte John Walder | 27639 | WIA | Pte James Walmsley | 33245 | WIA |
| Pte Richard Walmsley | 241501 | WIA | Pte John Waltho | 202142 | WIA/POW |
| Pte Frank Ward | 32024 | WIA/POW | Pte Selby Wealleans | 201165 | WIA |
| Pte Pearson Wesencroft | 202152 | WIA | Pte Henry Whieldon | 24096 | WIA |
| L/Cpl Arthur Whittle | 200885 | WIA/POW | Pte Thomas Williams | 202151 | WIA/POW |
| Pte Harrison Williams | 201584 | WIA | Sgt Thomas Wright | 200878 | WIA |

** Cpl Henry J. Casper appears on the King's Own casualty returns for the 20th, but appears to be on attachment from the Loyals, rather than actually belonging to the King's Own.

Once back in their own lines, the men were immediately reorganised and set to clearing the trenches of the dead, the wounded, and the debris from German counter-fire. For battalion stretcher-bearers, their work continued unabated. Twenty-eight-year-old Pte Harry Loydell, originally from Stroud in Gloucestershire, worked for eighteen hours straight, tending the wounded under continuous heavy shell and MG fire. During the battle he went into enemy lines four times to retrieve casualties, and after the withdrawal went forward into No Man's Land on three separate occasions to treat men lying in shell holes. This exceptional bravery was rewarded with the MM.[41] Similarly recognised was Pte Charles Cunningham, who worked throughout the whole action under heavy MG and shell fire, dressing the wounded and carrying them from enemy trenches back through No Man's Land. Though wounded himself by shrapnel in the leg, he refused to be evacuated and continued until the battalion was relieved.[42] Apart from the British bombardment at 4.30 p.m., the front was now quiet. Once the sun went down, patrols went into No Man's Land to look for any wounded and monitor German activity.

The Loyals had relieved the King's Own by 4.30 a.m., and the battalion moved back to dugouts in Ken Lane and Sart Lane (centred around 49° 59′ 23.56″ N, 3° 10′ 51.82″ E). Here they were joined by the portion of the battalion that had been kept in reserve. The remainder of the day was spent recuperating and cleaning kit, the fresher men of the reserve portion going forward to remove the dead from the front line and bring their bodies back to the rear for burial. Out of the battalion's fifty-four dead, only eight would receive a marked burial. At 6 p.m. on the 22 November, the men marched back to St Emilie where they were greeted by the band, and then on to the divisional reserve at Longavesnes, reaching there shortly before 9 p.m.

After bathing and a general maintenance of uniform and equipment the next day, the battalion paraded in fatigue dress in front of Maj.-Gen. Jeudwine, who congratulated them on their performance at Gillemont. Permission to parade in fatigue dress was a kind gesture, and must have originated from Jeudwine himself. The afternoon of Saturday 24 November was devoted to football, the teams much changed since the previous time they had played. After church parade on Sunday 25th (at which the band played), the battalion buried with full military honours 2Lt James Rundle, a married man from Birkenhead who had died from his wounds late on the 20th. From Monday through to Wednesday, the men rotated between training and instruction in the Lewis and rifle grenade in the morning and football in the afternoon. Despite being put on standby with immediate notice to move on Thursday, the situation was relaxed enough for a football match against 164 MG Company to go ahead that afternoon—with a decisive victory to the King's Own, 14–2.

The situation facing 55 Division in the last days of November 1917 was critical. Starved of replacements and long overdue for rest, Maj.-Gen. Jeudwine only had two effective brigades to hold 7 miles of front, which equated to one man every two yards. 164 Brigade could only field 1,400 riflemen in the aftermath of the diversionary attack, some 35 per cent of its establishment strength.[43] The trenches along this now 11,000-12,000-yard front (55 Division also took over the Villers-Guislain section on 28 November)[44] were discontinuous, the wire was in poor repair, and there were insufficient dugouts to protect defenders from an initial bombardment. The division were also chronically short of artillery, with only eight 6-inch howitzers providing the heavy artillery for the entire VII Corps.[45] And in spite of repeated requests, the only additional guns allocated to the division was one battery of 18-pounders.[46] There was increased German movement both in the trenches and behind the lines; artillery was registering targets in the division's area and German air activity was such that no British reconnaissance aircraft could operate, all indications that the Germans were planning a large-scale attack. On 28 November, Jeudwine issued an urgent 'Divisional Warning Order':

> Certain indications during today point to the possibility of enemy making an attack against our front. All troops will be warned to be specially on the alert in the trenches and all posts.[47]

Both Generals Jeudwine and Snow were particularly concerned about the Banteux Ravine, where VII Corps and III Corps's boundary lay, which because of their troop dispositions almost offered the enemy an open door to the rear. Jeudwine had been led to believe that he could rely on a brigade from 12 Division to help defend the Ravine; but when he visited Maj.-Gen. Scott on 29 November, he was turned down. Likewise, 55 Division's CRA, Brig.-Gen. A. M. Perreau, had arranged with III Corps for a barrage by its heavy artillery on obvious German assembly positions to take place at 6.30

a.m. on the 30th, but as reported in the *Official History*, this was cancelled by III Corps on the night of the 29th—another fateful decision.[48]

Maj.-Gen. Jeudwine's papers reveal that there was more to these cancellations than meets the eye. In a letter to Gen. Snow dated 16 November 1926, Jeudwine gave his version of the events.

I do not agree with Knapp's [Brig.-Gen. Kempster Kenmure Knapp] account of what passed between himself and me on the night of the 29th. I have a pretty clear recollection of this conversation and this is what I maintain happened. As soon as Perreau, my C.R.A., told me that the assistance of III Corps, Heavy Artillery had been refused I rang up Burnett-Stuart [Brigadier-General Sir John Theodosius Burnett-Stuart B.G.G.S. VII Corps] and made the strongest representations with regard to the necessity for our having the fire of heavy artillery on our front. He said that the III Corps would not agree, and when I still pressed he asked if I would speak to Knapp about it. Knapp, who was apparently in the room, came to the telephone and I renewed my protests to him. He did not however meet them in at all a sympathetic spirit. He pointed out that there was no certainty that we were going to be attacked and that if the heavy artillery fired and there was no attack it would be a great waste of ammunition. I admit that I was infuriated at this way of looking at it, and I put the opposite case to him, *viz.*, that if on the other hand there *was* an attack and no heavy artillery was brought to bear upon it, there would be a great waste of life and that in my opinion it was better to waste ammunition than to waste lives. I clearly recollect using practically those very words to him.

I have no recollection of Burnett-Stuart saying to me, as Knapp maintains he did, that if I 'considered the matter imperative he would call up the B.G.S., III Corps and reopen the question'. On the contrary, he (Burnett-Stuart) said that he had done everything he could and that if I was not satisfied would I speak to Knapp. The conversation between Knapp and myself then took place which I have given above.[49]

At 5.30 a.m. on the 30th, the men from 165 and 166 Brigade stood to in their trenches while the few guns available to them carried out a short bombardment of the German front line. Patrols sent out overnight had not detected any movement in the German front area and the dark pre-dawn was remarkably quiet, with no movement observed through the thick mist swirling about in No Man's Land. Half an hour later, German guns began to bombard British positions, the barrage gradually increasing in ferocity—gas shells, shrapnel, and HE. Soon all communications to the rear were cut off. The front line came under heavy fire from trench mortars and countless MG positions were blasted to bits or buried by the explosions. A reconnaissance flight by the RFC was unable to detect movement in the valleys because heavy mist had cloaked them and it was still too dark for reasonable observation. At 7.05 a.m., nearly forty minutes before sunrise, the first SOS signals went up, followed within minutes by SOS signals all along 55 Division's front line. A major German attack was underway, preceded by squads armed with light MGs and flame throwers who swept through the gaps between British posts from their flanks and rear.

At 7.30 a.m. the 1/4th were brought to immediate standby, and an hour later marched out of Longavesnes along with the rest of 164 Brigade, bound for Ste Emilie. *En route*, a message arrived from brigade to move a position just to the east of Ste Emilie, and for it to remain under cover south of the road leading to Ronssoy, to provide support for 1/5th King's Own. At 10.30 a.m. the battalion was moved on to Epéhy, which was under fire from German artillery, though casualties from this were light. When Lt-Col. Balfour reported at Epéhy, he was told that the enemy had broken through on the division's left flank and was ordered to hold on at all costs. At noon, the battalion was deployed to the north-east of Epéhy and told to dig in along the spurs 300 yards to the rear of 1/5th King's Own, who were gradually being forced back. Their new line was held by A and B Company, and ran approximately along a curved line from the road between Epéhy and Villers Guislain on the left (50° 0′ 55.59″ N, 3° 7′ 44.72″ E) through to 14 Willows Road in the centre (50° 0′ 57.29″ N, 3° 8′ 43.95″ E). From here it ran to Fallen Tree Road on the right (50° 0′ 44.43″ N, 3° 9′ 10.12″ E), this flank held by C and D Company. HQ moved in with the headquarters of 1/5th King's Own in 14 Willows Road at (50° 0′ 51.14″ N, 3° 8′ 39.67″ E). As soon as the men were in position, they began to consolidate, helped by a section from 422 Field Company RE, which had been detailed to construct wire to the front of its trenches. The battalion Lewis guns were also put forward, giving the best fields of fire over the most conspicuous directions of any enemy advance. D Company on the left and A Company on the right each got two Vickers from a detachment of 164 MG Company commanded by Lt Orme; their positioning on the flanks gave them good fields of fire for enfilading any frontal attack. The situation was still unclear, however, and very little was known about the exact whereabouts of the enemy, especially to their flanks.

Developments on the extreme left flank of the division were indeed most critical, for 1/5th South Lancashires were cut off and attacked by overpowering forces from their rear. Unable to be resupplied with ammunition, this gallant battalion fought on until inundated—not a single man returned. Villers Guislain was lost, but Vaucelette was held by the Loyals, after a magnificent counter-attack of theirs put the German attack towards Heudicourt in check. At 2 p.m., the battalion sent out reconnaissance patrols to try to locate the enemy and it was not too long before they returned with news. One reported Germans on the high ground to their side of the Beet Factory (at 50° 1′ 49.46″ N, 3° 8′ 42.40″ E) and holding the sunken road which ran south-west from it, just under a mile from their positions. Germans were also reported to be holding the continuation of 14 Willows Road, past its junction with Leith Walk and Leith Walk itself. Considerable enemy movement was observed south of Villers Guislain; they seemed to be reorganising and bolstering the forces to the south of the Targelle Valley, just a mile to the front of the battalion's right flank.

Throughout the afternoon on 30 November, reinforcements from various units within the division trickled into the defensive line, and patrols were sent to make contact with brigades to right and left. Capt. Evans was given the task of building a pair of strongpoints on the spurs to the front of Tétard Wood, about half a mile out of Epéhy on the Honnecourt Road. Each strongpoint received a Vickers from 164 MG Company and was garrisoned by an assortment of men from 166 Brigade and from 1/5th South Lancashires who had not been with their battalion when it had been overwhelmed. Evans was also able to ascertain that the Fusiliers were holding Malassise Farm to their right (50° 0′ 3.81″ N, 3° 8′ 49.94″ E), though there was no defensive line between them and Fallen Tree Road, a gap of half a mile. On the left flank, Capt. Alfred Procter had managed to establish contact with the Northumberland Hussars, and ascertain that there was also a gap in the defensive line to their left, though this was soon remedied. 164 MG Company was able to provide an additional eight Vickers, which were placed in a broad arc across the defensive line. Carrying parties were busy all afternoon ferrying ammunition and other stores forward, and the consolidation of the defences progressed well.

What sporadic shell fire there was was not a serious threat; however, one German MG was quickly becoming a nuisance, enfilading 14 Willows Road and hindering HQ or any movement along the road. After dark, A Company advanced to set up an outpost line, its place in the new trenches having been taken by men from 166 Brigade's transport. D Company also moved forward by 300 m until it was in touch with the left flank of 1/5th King's Own, and set up a defensive flank in four outposts there. The night was relatively quiet, though tensions ran high for fear of a night attack; its only real excitement was when a German from 25 IR came to the front line to surrender. Battalion casualties for that day were light compared to recent events, though three men were killed outright by enemy fire: Privates Robert Harris from Earlstown, James Wilson from Wrea Green, and Thomas Rose from Fleetwood. Nineteen-year-old Pte Charles Craggs from Darlington was severely hurt and died from his wounds on 3 December. Two other men also perished as a result of wounds suffered on 30 November, twenty-one-year-old Pte Walter Hunter from Sleaford on 6 December and twenty-eight-year-old Pte Walter Crossland from Preston on 11 January 1918.

Shortly after 5 a.m. on 1 December, a party of seventy men from 1/5th King's Own and twenty from the Liverpool Scottish—who had been surrounded and holding off repeated attacks in Limerick Post (50° 1′ 4.49″ N, 3° 9′ 47.71″ E) since the attack began—managed to fight their way back into British lines, their ammunition exhausted. These men helped boost the defence, enabling closer contact with the Fusiliers on the left flank. (1/5th's *War Diary* gives the total as 120 men, but Capt. Bennett, OC Limerick Post, maintained that the total was ninety, with a seventy-twenty split between the two battalions.)[50] British attempts to recapture Villers Guislain were made in the morning, but they all failed, even though 1 Guards Brigade did recapture Gouzeaucourt. At 1 p.m. a joint attempt to retake the Meath, Kildare, and Limerick Posts was made by 1/5th King's Own, Liverpool Scottish, and two squadrons of 38th Central Indian Horse. This attack was repulsed with heavy casualties due to inadequate artillery support and concentrated MG and rifle fire from Parrs Bank (50° 1′ 2.23″ N, 3° 9′ 25.65″ E) and Kildare Lane (50° 0′ 57.85″ N, 3° 10′ 10.94″ E), assisted by enfilading MG fire from Villers Guislain. From about 4.30 p.m. onwards, abundant artillery fire fell on 1/4th's HQ in 14 Willow Road, and on the front and support lines to the right of the road from Epéhy to Villers Guislain. Three privates from the battalion died: William Brew from Barrow, twenty-year-old Paul Brogan from Blackpool (though born in Stockport), and nineteen-year-old Leo Higgs from Bolton. Seven men were also wounded, one of whom was twenty-two-year-old Pte Joseph Ralph from Millom. The brigade was relieved by 110 Brigade in the early hours of the morning; 7/ Leicestershires had taken over the 1/4th's positions by 1.30 a.m. on 2 December.

The battalion was back in billets in St Emilie by 3.30 a.m. and spent that day resting and cleaning up. The men were still on thirty minutes' notice to move, just in case of another attack and supplies of ammunition, grenades, and a myriad of equipment and disposables needed to be brought up to establishment by the QM and transport. They remained at Ste Emilie right up until 4 p.m. on 4 December, when the battalion was ordered forward to Sandbag Alley to reinforce the reserves of 165 Brigade; all were safely accommodated in dugouts by 8.30 p.m. that evening, and no casualties were sustained during the move. At 5.30 a.m. on the 5th, there was concern of an impending German attack, and C and D Company took up fire positions in Queens Trench while A and B Company remained in Sandbag Alley. All was still quiet at 7.20 a.m., so the men were stood down. After dark, 164 Brigade was relieved by 48 Brigade from 16 Division and marched back to Ste Emilie, arriving in the early hours. The weather was bitterly cold and a hard frost covered everything; billets were in such short supply, so the entire battalion was crowded into one Adrian Hut—an extremely uncomfortable night for all concerned. At 5.30 a.m. the battalion was called out to the Brown Line, the reserve line for 38 Division, as there was concern that the enemy would make another dawn attack. By 10 a.m. they were back in the Ste Emilie billets; their time there was again brief, orders to move were received at 1 p.m. for the division to be relieved. At the transport lines in Villers Faucon, the battalion were greeted by the band, who entertained them while they had afternoon tea. At 5 p.m. they marched off to Longavesnes, where they boarded buses for Peronne.

The German counter-attack of 30 November, and the losses it incurred both among the men and on the ground, came as a shock to a British public regaled with tales of a brilliant victory a mere ten days earlier. Pressed for answers by concerned politicians, Haig requested an immediate report from Gen. Byng; his subsequent criticisms of the performance of the defending troops, who had been led to believe that the defences were in an unbroken line and in good order, was based on the contents of Byng's report. The defences were in fact far from an unbroken, and over much of the sector, the front-line trench was no more than a communication trench connecting outposts. As for the defences, artillery fire during the attack of 20 November had left much of them ruined; little of the wire had survived, and the infantry had neither the manpower nor the resources to do much remedial work. Based on the information given to him by Byng, Haig expressed doubts about the fighting capacity of the troops who had defended the front in the following statement:

> Risks had to be taken in reducing forces at some points in order to be strong at others, but the risk taken at Cambrai was not an undue risk for the enemy should not have succeeded in penetrating any part of our defence.[51]

Gen. Byng, the commander of Third Army, was quick to blame failure on the poor quality of leadership and fighting ability of soldiers in 55, 12, and 20 Division, particularly junior officers and machine-gunners. He further pronounced that no responsibility was attributable to anyone in High Command, and that he and all his subordinate commanders had been happy that there were sufficient troops available to handle any counter-attack.

Byng's insistence that none of his subordinate commanders had been unhappy with the number of troops available to them does not hold up in light of Jeudwine's request for a brigade to cover the Banteux Ravine, made some days before the attack. The findings of a court of enquiry in January 1918 were careful not to criticise High Command, however, and can only be interpreted as a complete and utter whitewash! Maj.-Gen. Jeudwine himself thought the process nothing more than an exercise in self-aggrandisement for Gen. Ivor Maxse, commander of XVIII Corps and member of the Committee of Enquiry. Jeudwine's personal copy of the report was annotated, 'Ivor Maxse again! Personal advertisement.'[52] In summary of his views in a letter to Snow, Jeudwine fumes:

> I have read through the report of the Committee of Enquiry. It is of course Maxse pure and simple, and very poisonous Maxse at that. I find a great many points with which I am in total disagreement: for instance, it is stated near the bottom of Page 5 that there appears to have been a lack of vigilance in the outpost lines. This, as I think you know, I deny altogether. It is further stated here that no SOS signals were sent up. This is of course not the case as you have a copy of a statement from an officer of Artillery in which the reply of the guns to the SOS Signals is referred to. Again, on Page 6, under the heading of 'Warnings from above unheeded', I am as muddled as you are to what is meant by 'Higher Commanders'.

Then at Para. 6 of the note by a member of the Court of Enquiry (same distinguished General again) it is stated that we can 'discover few traces of organised counter-attacks or of methodical resistance'. As you are well aware, the spontaneous counter-attack of the 1/4th Loyal North Lancashires along the Villers Guislain spur stopped for good the enemy's advance in that direction, and pinned him down with the result of making subsequent counter-attacks by the Guards Division possible. But the whole of this memorandum, the anonymity of which is very lightly veiled, is sheer advertisement and hardly worth taking the trouble to contradict.[53]

The mere fact that Haig felt it necessary to order a court of enquiry suggests that he was not totally satisfied with the explanation received from Byng, especially since the fighting qualities of his troops had been called into question. The *Official History*, originally published around twenty years after the events, rightly attributed the blame to Byng and his COS. They should have been aware of the possible dangers of counter-attack through the Banteux Ravine, especially given that Gen. Snow, as one of Byng's corps commanders, had expressed his concerns about this sector to Third Army more than once.[54] Equally, too little artillery had been allocated within the danger area, a problem that could only have been solved at 'Army' level, and yet all requests by Snow for more heavy artillery had been turned down. Much of the criticism aimed at the three divisions was based on the assumption that there must have been a lack of vigilance from the men in the front line because no SOS signals were supposedly sent. Yet officers reported that these signals *were* fired by the men in the forward trenches, and that part of the problem rested with the poor performance of the rifle grenade signal compared to its predecessor, the bulkier but much more visible rocket. Forward artillery observers had been unable to call in a barrage onto the attackers because German artillery fire had cut all telephone lines, but not through any lack of vigilance.[55] The dead ground and weather gave the enemy a strategic advantage, for they could amass safely out of sight of the defenders and put many MGs out of action with a barrage. The surviving gunners were either overwhelmed by attackers descending upon them at short range (sometimes from the rear), or remained at their posts until their ammunition was exhausted. And yet—'Many of the troops had proved unequal to the task', found the court of enquiry; 'the training of junior officers, and NCOs demanded immediate attention.'[56]

It's not unreasonable to comment that many troops that day were inexperienced; casualties prior to their arrival had been so high that there had been little time to train them. However, this was an Army-wide problem not specific to 55 Division. And while frustration that troops were untrained in defensive tactics had some validity, this was also an Army-wide issue; Haig, like most commanders, had his eye on the offence, not defence. Blame clearly rests with Byng as commander of Third Army, whose focus on the main attack on the 20th was such that he failed to take into account events to its flank, an area he had weakened to provide extra impetus to the main push. The most disappointing aspect of this matter is Byng's attempt to deflect culpability away from himself and his staff and onto those unable to defend themselves against this slur.

However, the final word on this stain to 55 Division's reputation should go to the *Official History*.

The 55th Division had no reason to reproach itself. Overwhelmed by numbers and by a vastly superior artillery the troops had shown their quality by standing fast amid their broken defences and resisting as long as resistance was possible.[57]

# 10

# 7 December 1917 – 8 April 1918
# La Bassée Canal

Transferred from the Third to the First Army, for the next week 55 Division moved around France on buses and trains, but most of all on foot. From Peronne on 7 December 1917 it trained to Beaumetz-les-Loges, and from thence onwards by foot to Lattre-St-Quentin on the 8th; Bailleul-aux-Cornailles on the 10th; Eps on the 11th; Crépy on the 12th; and finally Reclinghem in the late afternoon of Thursday 13th. The next two days were spent resting; the men cleaned their equipment and uniforms, and replenishing their kit. They trained right up until the afternoon of Christmas Eve, and even on Christmas Day itself; the brigade commander and CO visited each company at dinner to wish the men a Merry Christmas. The sergeants' mess held their dinner at 5.30 p.m. and as the CO paid them the compliments of the season, snow began to fall. Christmas Day was a busy day for commanding officers; not until the late evening was Lt-Col. Balfour able to sit with the rest of his officers to enjoy his own dinner; the band played as they ate.

Heavy snow on Boxing Day prompted the postponement of an inspection scheduled for the 29th by Gen. Sir Henry Horne, commander of the First Army. The battalion continued to train right up till the afternoon of New Year's Eve. New Year's Day was designated a holiday, but the weather was so poor that the sports that had been planned were not to be. Training resumed the next day amid more snowfalls, and continued unabated until preparations were made to return to the line on 13 February. Like on previous occasions out of the line, the training was focused almost exclusively on attack rather than defence, and there were accidents (though none were fatal). On the morning of Christmas Eve, the infelicitous Pte Samuel Bennett was accidentally wounded by one of his comrades and spent his Christmas in hospital. Each company held platoon competitions, of which the winners then competed for 'Best Platoon' in the battalion: this was won on 30 January by 2Lt Norman Walkden's 7 Platoon, which then went on to win the 'Brigade Platoon Competition' on 5 February—quite an accolade. The following day the battalion was given a demonstration in rapid fire with a SMLE by one L/Cpl Manifold of 46 Division (possibly 240412 George W. Manifold of the Notts and Derby Regiment).

The winter climate inflated sick lists; the men, frequently wet and cold and living in close proximity to each other, suffered a range of pulmonary afflictions. On 16 December, twenty-year-old Pte George Whalley from St Helens died of illness at a CCS at Boisleux-au-Mont. Others were sent home, such as a twenty-three-year-old father of two from Belfast Pte Alexander Smyth of 10 Platoon, who was suffering from severe bronchitis. (Smyth was no stranger to the 'Charge Sheet' and unhappy with his return to England on 25 January, he deserted two weeks later and joined the Navy!)[1] It wasn't just chest infections: trench foot was never far away, and it especially plagued the less experienced soldiers. On 12 January, twenty-six-year-old Pte Henry Shute from Blackpool was invalided home with it and eventually given a medical discharge in September 1918.

Although nine replacement officers and seventy-five men had been allocated to the battalion in December, they ended the year well below establishment. Reinforcements as a whole had been problematic in France, for the Government was deliberately withholding them, to '[...] compel the soldiers to adopt tactics that will reduce the waste of man-power.'[2]

At the beginning of 1918, the Army in France and Flanders were short of 75,000 infantrymen and of labourers behind the lines to keep things operating. The situation had been exacerbated further when Haig was ordered to send five divisions from France to reinforce the Italian Front. Curbing the supply of reinforcements as a way of preventing Haig from 'wasting' them on offensives was a dangerous policy that put the whole outcome of the war in jeopardy.[3] A further forty-two men arrived in January to swell the ranks of the battalion, but changes in Army organisation would soon boost battalion numbers considerably. Shortages of infantrymen prompted the Government to intervene once more. On 14 January, 55 Division received notification from I Corps that the number of infantry battalions in the division was to be reduced from twelve to nine, and a week later the Liverpool Irish, 1/9th King's and 1/5th Loyals all received their orders to join 57 (Second West Lancashire) Division.[4] The Germans and the French had undergone a similar reshuffle earlier on, but these changes had been gradual and compensated for by an increase in firepower to their units concerned with additional MG and artillery resources. There was no such cushion in place to compensate British divisions, robbed of 25 per cent of their strength. Haig protested, citing the damaging effects on troop morale that such changes would cause at a time when he believed the enemy was planning a major offensive—to no avail.[5]

This was the second blow to Haig on the subject of manpower. Earlier in 1917, at a conference to which Haig had not been invited, the Government had agreed on principle with the French to extend the length of line held by the BEF. On the 22 December, Haig had written to the War Cabinet warning that he could not undertake the responsibility of defending the Channel ports if such a proposal went ahead. Thus, at a time of chronic shortages of infantrymen due to a deliberate Government policy of withholding replacements, political interference forced Haig to extend a front with defences in a poor state due to a combination of winter, enemy action and a lack of available labour to repair them. He was also forced to reorganise his divisions, which required considerable internal restructuring of divisional and brigade staffs whose efforts would have been better employed on strengthening the defences.[6]

The first replacement to arrive at the battalion in February was a thirty-five-year-old chip shop worker from Cleckheaton, Pte Harry Wood. He had been with 1/ King's Own and suffered a particularly unfortunate injury some distance behind the lines near Arras in November 1917. He was one of a group of men from 1/ King's Own attached to a salvage party from the New Zealand Engineers Tunnelling Company. His platoon sergeant at the time reported:

The accident occurred about 12.15 p.m. on the 7th Nov 1917. A fire had been lighted in an old shell hole in order to heat some water for the midday meal. At 12 noon the men ceased work and all the men, with the exception of the three injured men, were with me in a neighbouring dugout, when we heard an explosion outside and some shouting. I came up and found the three men whom I had left sitting by the fire wounded and the fire blown out. A fresh hole had been made under the fire and some old German stick bombs were exposed, some of which had exploded.

Wood's platoon leader, 2Lt C. Francis, came to the following conclusion:

> There was nothing to indicate that any bombs were buried there and they must have been at a depth
> of from fifteen to eighteen inches below the surface. According to the rules of the N.Z.E.T. Coy. it
> was quite in order to light a fire.[7]

Wood's close encounter with death left him with severe lacerations above both eyes. On 7 February
the battalion was on the move again, firstly to Ligny-Lès-Aire and on to Busnettes the following day.
On the way to Busnettes, it was joined by substantial reinforcements. One of the battalions disbanded
as a result of the Army reorganisation had been 7/ King's Own, and six officers and 194 men were
posted *en masse* to the 1/4th. Although a good deal better than green recruits, these men still needed
to be assimilated into the battalion, and much training was necessary. All told, this brought the
number of replacements to twelve officers and 245 men for February, however some of the postings
from 7/ King's Own were merely 'paper postings'. One man, thirty-one-year-old Pte Robert Lomax
from Darwin, never actually joined the battalion, though he was officially on their strength. At 4 foot
10 inches, he was the minimum height for a Bantam unit and at Étaples, where they knew only too
well how arduous the life of an infantryman was, he had rightly been classed by a medical board as
'PB'. (Fit only for duties at permanent base) 7/ King's Own had attached him to No. 3 British Hospital
at Le Treport, where he carried out various non-medical duties. One of these was hospital train duty
and he'd even ended up as a patient himself in May 1917, suffering from concussion after misjudging
a jump from a moving car as it arrived at the station. Shortly before 7/ King's Own was disbanded,
he returned to Britain on leave and it was 27 March before the authorities realised that he no longer
had a parent unit and nominally posted him to the 1/4th. Robert Lomax shares the distinction, along
with Walter Farrell, of being the shortest men in the battalion, though the latter was the only man to
actually serve at the front.

On 9 February, the battalion reached billets in Houchin and apart from the ubiquitous football and
tug-of-war competition, the next four days were spent preparing to go into the line. One who didn't
go with them was on the transport section, twenty-two-year-old Pte Arthur Dickinson from Barrow.
On 12 February, he was on picket duty feeding all the horses; the nose bags were positioned behind
the animals and as he went to collect them one of the horses took exception to him and kicked out,
catching Dickinson on the left knee. This injury required two months' treatment in hospital.

Just after midday on 14 February, the battalion moved to support near the Canal d'Aire at Cuinchy.
The trenches were approximately 2 miles south from where the battalion had been in early 1915 and
as at Festubert, were also 'breastworks'. Three years of war had not improved the ground; much of
which was a fetid swamp, and this whole section of the line was universally detested by the troops
who had to man it. Not only were the trenches flimsier than those dug deeper into the ground, but
the line was discontinuous due to the vile conditions.

In late 1917 and early 1918 the British were paying much more attention to defence than ever
before. Haig suspected that the enemy, aware that large numbers of American troops would
overwhelmingly tip the balance in favour of the Allies, may risk all to try to finish the war before
the Americans deployed fully. He believed they would attempt to break through the lines and drive
a wedge between the French and British to seize the Channel ports, leaving the Allies with no choice

but to sue for peace. However, he was also convinced that in attempting this, the German Army would be so weakened that he would be able to deliver a decisive counter-attack on them in Autumn 1918.[8]

Although the campaigns in Verdun, the Somme, and Ypres had seriously weakened the Germans, the situation on the Eastern Front was such that they were able to pull considerable numbers of men to the west to add weight to any offensive—something that would have been unthinkable had Russia still been in the fight. Haig believed that the offensive would breach his front lines, so took a leaf out of the Germans' book.[9] He planned 'defence in depth', leaving the front line relatively weakly manned (not that there were enough men to do much else!) and ordered the construction of a series of strongpoints (keeps or redoubts) to form the second and third line. Wire and other natural obstacles would funnel the attackers into 'zones' where they would be engaged from these keeps. A front defensive line packed with troops was always going to lead to heavy casualties from the initial artillery bombardment, and this strategy would minimise them; moreover, the further the enemy advanced, the less effective his artillery support would become and the more tenuous his logistical lines would be. It was never possible to take this policy to the lengths that the Germans had, for both manpower and preparation time were too little. Technically, the old front line, with its support and reserve positions would become the 'Forward Zone'. Behind this, another line of defences, the 'Battle Zone', would be constructed on what had been the 'Corps Line', and yet another series of defences further back on the 'Army Line', redesignated the 'Rear Zone' or 'Green Line'.[10] Due to shortages of both manpower and time, very little of this work was actually carried out, and whereas the enemy had *Eingreif* divisions, the British could not hold specialised 'counter-attack' forces in reserve. In a conversation with the King on his visit to the Front in late March, Haig informed him that his infantry numbered 100,000 less than a year previously, that he was facing a German Army three times the British strength, and that he expected to defend a front a fifth longer.[11]

The two forward companies occupied part of the 'Village Line', the second line of defence, to the west of Cuinchy. B Company garrisoned the Brewery, just north of the canal bridge and Harley Street, which ran along the line of the current D 166 ('Rue Anatole France'). C, the other forward company, was in Braddell Castle (50° 30′ 48.50″ N, 2° 45′ 1.97″ E), Mountain Keep and the Village Line. Nearly 2 miles to the rear, A and D Company were at Le Preol (Le Préolan on modern maps) (50° 31′ 31.81″ N, 2° 42′ 19.19″ E), and HQ was in a dugout in Glasgow Road (50° 30′ 55.33″ N, 2° 44′ 52.55″ E). The winter had degraded the trenches, so B and C Company worked on replacing sandbags the next day. Meanwhile, A and D continued training at Le Preol under the watchful eyes of their NCOs, and the officers completed their forward reconnaissance of the front line. As far as enemy activity was concerned, 16 and 17 February were quiet according to the War Diary, but at least one man, Pte Fred Tomlinson, was wounded. As might be expected once the men were back in the line, their labours continued with all men either working on improving the trenches, or employed on carrying parties. D Company moved forward from Le Preol into the Village Line next to C Company, leaving only A Company in the rear. The first face-to-face encounter with the enemy actually took place some way behind the lines at 1.30 a.m. on 18 February. Privates Jack Round and Horace Jackson, two runners carrying a message between HQ and A Company, encountered two escaped German prisoners near Westminster Bridge (50° 31′ 32.79″ N, 2° 43′ 46.95″ E). When one of them resisted capture he was shot dead by Jack Round, the other promptly surrendered and was taken to HQ. Once the forward trenches were improved, the men were tasked with strengthening the wiring of the Village Line.

On the morning of 20 February, the battalion relieved 1/4th Loyals in the left sub-sector of the forward trenches, with HQ in Kingsclere (50° 31′ 6.74″ N, 2° 45′ 12.11″ E), B Company in the left front, and A Company in the right front. D Company occupied the left centre and C Company the right centre. Night patrols went forward into No Man's Land, the battalion ethos of dominating this area at night undiminished by three years at the front. Although there was some enemy shelling, particularly on the 23rd, casualties were so far light. Privates Harold Garside and George Slinger were both wounded on the 22nd when Harley Street was shelled, though the German fire had only been aimed by map (poor visibility impeded any direct observation). On the 23rd, the enemy shelled along the Village Line, hitting Braddell Castle, Pont Fixe (50° 31′ 20.25″ N, 2° 44′ 53.20″ E), and Cuinchy Church east of the line (50° 31′ 7.79″ N, 2° 45′ 30.83″ E), but only one soldier, Pte Nicholas Hynes, was wounded.

Unpleasant though the front line was, it presented increased opportunities for the battalion's snipers, who made their presence felt over the coming weeks. The first to open the score was the aptly named Pte James Shute, who on 21 February had got into a position in Warlingham Crater (50° 31′ 39.63″ N, 2° 45′ 52.81″ E) and shot one of the German defenders from there. Warlingham Crater was a double mine crater where the British held the western and the Germans the eastern lip. It was a section of line which included the German-held Ducks Bill, and where both front lines actually met in places—at nowhere along this stretch were the opposing lines more than 15 m apart!

German artillery activity escalated on 24 February, but Cuinchy Church alone was hit (by eighty shells during the day). Harley Street received numerous shrapnel shells, though the men escaped this unscathed. The British replied in kind with artillery and trench mortars on Brickstacks (50° 31′ 1.41″ N, 2° 46′ 0.67″ E) and Canal Bank, and although this tit for tat continued into the night, men

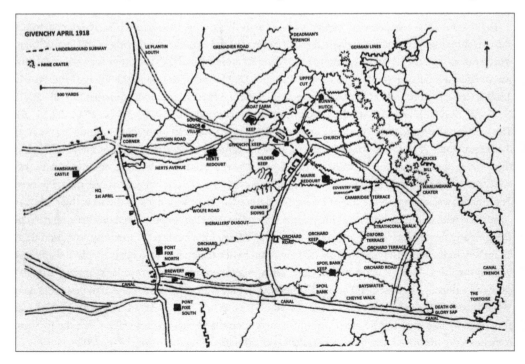

continued to repair the trenches and build wire defences as long as the dark protected them from observation. During the morning stand-to on 25 February, Orchard Road (50° 31′ 26.86″ N, 2° 45′ 43.90″ E), Queen Street (50° 31′ 13.13″ N, 2° 45′ 20.43″ E), and Cuinchy Church were shelled, but once more no casualties resulted.

Again on 26 February, the level of German artillery activity was higher than usual, but this did not deter the battalion's snipers from going about their lethal duties, and Pte Stanley Parsons shot a German who was on the canal bank. The twenty-four-year-old from Manchester had originally been a seventeen-year-old regular with 1/King's Own in 1911, deploying to France with them in August 1914. Wounded in the face in October, he'd been posted home to 3/ King's Own in Plymouth. Less than three weeks later, he deserted, and was caught and sentenced to 112 days' hard labour. Shortly after his release he was in trouble yet again, this time for 'borrowing' a bicycle and given six-months-hard labour. His sentence served, he was posted to 11/ King's Own in France only to be sent home with pleurisy after three months. Upon his recovery he was posted to the 1/4th and shot in the wrist a few weeks later on 31 July 1917. We can only conjecture as to whether it was these bitter experiences which fuelled his proclivity for sniping… Fellow sniper Pte William Pepper also scored a hit that day, killing a German in Warlingham Crater. The German fell forward into the base of the crater and when dark had fallen, the battalion sent a patrol to recover the body for intelligence purposes, which when retrieved was identified as a member of 205 RIR (Reserve Infantry Regiment). At 2.35 a.m. on the 27th, enemy artillery switched their aim to the forward trenches, wounding Privates James Hickey and John Barber. The latter, a former gas metre reader and father of four from Oldham, was at forty-four rather old to be in the front line; in any case, the shrapnel wound to his arm left him unfit for further infantry fighting, so he was transferred to the Labour Corps upon leaving hospital.

By 28 February, German artillery had receded to normal levels, and although Cuinchy was still targeted, the front line escaped notice. In the early hours of the morning, eight patrols went out into No Man's Land, one of which encountered an enemy working party and sent it racing back to German trenches by a fusillade of rifle fire. During the day, sniper Pte Harold Cubin scored a hit on a German who recklessly showed himself above the parapet. On 1 March, work continued strengthening the trenches during the day, but as soon as it was dark enough to slip into No Man's Land unobserved, two reconnaissance patrols crept out. In the early hours, another two, this time fighting patrols of fifteen men and an officer each crept towards enemy trenches. It had long been German practice to man their front line with only a few men as sentries, and these patrols were after prisoners. However, both British patrols were brought to an abrupt halt as they neared the posts selected as their targets, when they discovered that the enemy had laid new and impenetrable belts of wire in front of these. Luckily neither patrol was spotted, and they regained friendly lines without trouble. As far as battle casualties went, February was a good month with just two officers and thirty-five men in hospital as a result of sickness. One of these patients, twenty-seven-year-old married father of two Pte John Fitzpatrick from Manchester, died from pneumonia at No. 1 CCS on the 2 March.

On the morning of 2 March, the battalion was relieved by the Fusiliers and pulled back to the Village Line, where men not on the various carrying parties worked at strengthening the line and adding more wire. The Village Line was key to 55 Division's defences and Maj.-Gen. Jeudwine had designated this as the 'line of resistance to be denied the enemy at all costs'.[12] It ran through Givenchy and south to Cuinchy—hardly a textbook battle zone—being the rear edge of the Forward Zone, but it was the best tactical site for the strongpoints, particularly as both ruined villages contained many intact cellars and fortifiable rubble: this was where 55 Division would make their stand if the enemy attacked. Givenchy itself was also on a slight knoll and provided a useful tactical viewpoint. This was not a continuous line, rather a series of heavily fortified and mutually supportive strongpoints around a battle zone that in many respects resembled Guillemont, site of so much woe for 55 Division on the Somme. Around these strongpoints were thick belts of wire, slanted to funnel attackers into the fields of fire of multiple MGs, situated so as to enfilade the gaps in the wire. In the thick, coarse grass that grew around the strongpoints' older, less visible lurked belts of wire to trap attackers. There seems to be ambiguity as to precisely what is meant by 'Village Line'; sources such as trench maps and the *Divisional History* define it as the line from Festubert through Le Plantin and Windy Corner (50° 31′ 43.55″ N, 2° 44′ 40.06″ E) to Pont Fixe; yet units themselves sometimes referred to the defensive positions within Givenchy as part of it.[13] In reality, the Village Line in the Givenchy locality was a wide belt where the Forward Zone and Battle Zone merged into one deep stretch, a characteristic of huge relevance in the weeks to come. About 1 to 2 miles further to the rear, the Green Line was known as the 'Tuning Fork Line' and ran roughly along the line south from Le Touret to the canal just east of its junction with the Canal Beuvry.

Passive defence was only part of 55 Division's strategy. Each infantry platoon was designated as either a 'garrison' platoon or a 'counter-attack' platoon, and any loss of territory to the enemy would be immediately regained before the foe could consolidate and reinforce. On 4 March, A Company was relieved from their position north of Pont Fixe by A Company of 1/6 King's and moved back to Le Preol. (Pont Fixe was a strongpoint on the north bank and just east of the bridge over the canal connecting the two halves of Cuinchy. Later maps refer to Pont Fixe North or Pont Fixe South, strongpoints to either side of the canal bridge.) This move was actually more dangerous, for the enemy shelled Le Preol with gas during the night, and twenty-year-old Pte Gilbert Wiltshire from Bristol (who had only joined from 7/ King's Own in February) was gassed for the third time in his short military career. Another of his comrades from 7/ King's Own was similarly smitten that night, twenty-three-year-old Pte William Irving from St Helens; but as he was due to go home for leave, Irving did not report sick until he was home, where he was treated for three weeks in the Lord Derby War Hospital in Warrington.[14]

On 5 March, the remainder of the battalion was relieved and as reserve moved back to billets in Hingette. The same out-of-the-line routine followed: cleaning everything and making good any deficiencies. On the 7th and 8th, the men visited the baths in Béthune, though as reserve they needed to wear 'fighting order' in case they were called upon while away from their billets. The quickest routes to various parts of the Village Line were reconnoitred by NCOs and officers in case of emergency deployment. Despite moving onto 'thirty minutes' notice' on the 9th, there was still time for football, the players' weapons and equipment stacked neatly by the side of the game.

There was considerable concern that the expected German offensive could start at any time and on 10 March, the battalion stood to at 4.30 a.m. (the clocks had gone forward just the day before, so this must have felt like the middle of the night). Firing on the range at Oblinghem had been scheduled but was cancelled, as it would have been too far from the Village Line to deploy rapidly if needed. In view of another expected early reveille the next day, lights-out was brought forward to 8.15 p.m. Less than two hours after stand-to on the 11th, the battalion was ordered to the divisional concentration area at Gorre, but released back to Hingette at midday. To the division's left, the sector was held by a division of the Portuguese Army; there were concerns about its ability to hold a German attack, so Maj.-Gen. Jeudwine ordered that officers from the battalion reconnoitre the ground behind the Portuguese area in case they were called to offer support to this division. This pattern was repeated on the 12th, though the battalion was on the move a bare ten minutes after getting the call and dismissed from Gorre by 10 a.m. Instead of returning to Hingette, the battalion was split, with HQ and two companies in Essars and the remaining two companies in Les Choquaux, both locations approximately 2 miles behind the Tuning Fork Line, thus halving the distance to the concentration area. The early morning stand-to continued each day until the battalion returned to the front, as did reconnoitring of the divisional left and rear area of the Portuguese, and its own left flank, for the best defensive positions.

On 17 March, another 4.30 a.m. reveille; then at 7 a.m., a move to the sector immediately north of the canal to relieve 1/5th King's. C Company occupied the left front, D the right, and A the 'Tunnels' in support of both. B Company were back in reserve, divided between Givenchy Keep (50° 31′ 44.89″ N, 2° 45′ 21.18″ E), Mairie Redoubt (50° 31′ 39.69″ N, 2° 45′ 23.27″ E), and Moat Farm Redoubt (50° 31′ 47.73″ N, 2° 45′ 11.72″ E); all three keeps (which we shall subsequently refer to as 'the Keeps') were interconnected by the underground tunnel complex. HQ was in South Moor Villas (50° 31′ 46.66″ N, 2° 45′ 0.67″ E) on Hitchen Road. Visibility throughout the day was excellent, which was problematic, given the enemy had nine observation balloons in the air. Predictably, movement was punished by intermittent shelling. One man, twenty-year-old Pte James Bowfield from Barrow, died from wounds at the CCS at Lapugnoy, however the record of the exact date of his wounding has not survived and it's possible that he may have been a casualty from the gassing at Le Preol on 4 March.

There were casualties in 164 TMB on the 17th, too. Twenty-year-old Lt Stuart Bolton from Alderley Edge was killed by shell fire, and the next day, twenty-two-year-old Pte William Williams from Grange-over-Sands followed; both were buried at Gorre British and Indian Cemetery. The 18th saw increased activity from the German guns and trench mortars, targeting Givenchy Keep, Moat Farm, South Moor Villas, and Herts Redoubt (50° 31′ 42.34″ N, 2° 44′ 58.91″ E), as well as the entire length of the sector's support line. Shell fire decreased on 19 March as rain kept enemy observation to a minimum, but it did not prevent the battalion's snipers claiming another two of the enemy as they dug out their trench at 7 a.m. Throughout the night, German artillery fired sporadically on the communication trenches of King's Road and Wolfe Road, which connected the road from Windy Corner to Pont Fixe with Mairie Redoubt (at 50° 31′ 31.85″ N, 2° 44′ 45.72″ E). Windy Corner lived up to its name: it was on the receiving end of heavy shelling in the morning of the 20th, and twenty-nine-year-old Pte Henry Howarth, a married man from Manchester, was killed.

On the morning of 21 March, Moat Farm, Windy Corner, and HQ were shelled with mustard gas for nearly five hours. Although no casualties ensued, it was an uncomfortable episode thanks to the respirators the men were required to wear. The afternoon was quieter, though shortly after midnight D Company was bombarded for a few hours by 77-mms in retaliation for a British barrage south of the canal. Once daylight broke, the artillery recommenced with HQ, Herts Avenue, and Herts Redoubt all getting attention from 5.9s. The 23rd saw less artillery, though sporadic exchanges continued through the day, with Upper Cut (50° 31′ 54.14″ N, 2° 45′ 26.18″ E), Piccadilly (50° 31′ 48.50″ N, 2° 45′ 30.05″ E), and Gunner Siding (50° 31′ 34.12″ N, 2° 45′ 16.87″ E) all targeted. In return, British artillery concentrated on destroying the enemy wire in front of Mackensen Trench, the enemy front-line trench running south from the Rue d'Ouvert. Not to be outdone by artillery, the battalion's snipers scored another two hits. The 24th saw a slackening of the artillery exchanges until midnight, when British artillery, trench mortars, MGs, and rifle grenades dropped a violent barrage onto the German front line with shrapnel, HE, and thermite shells. Shortly afterwards, 1/5th King's made a very successful raid on Mackensen Trench and the defences behind it, seizing nine prisoners. The 25th was surprisingly subdued considering the night-time activities. Still, twenty-seven-year-old Pte James Edmondson from Ulverston, who'd suffered shell shock in 1916, was lightly wounded again. Less fortunate were Privates James McGuire and Walter Penn, both killed. The battalion's snipers scored again that morning, though the balance for the day rested in favour of the enemy.

The prisoners captured by 1/5th King's talked of an imminent attack and as a result of this information, the Fusiliers were brought forward from reserve to man the Village Line and a company was detached to reinforce the 1/4th at the front. Additional MGs were also brought into the sector, and 27 March began with rumours about an attack, but a long and tense wait in the trenches proved the men wrong. There may not have been an attack, but the snipers were on top form. Pte Shute shot an enemy soldier and L/Cpl John Gardner an officer, though top score for the day went to Stanley Parsons, who hit four Germans. With such a successful sniping team opposite them in the lines, it's surprising that the enemy were not more cautious about exposing themselves or did not deploy counter-snipers, as was common practice. Shortly before 11 p.m., the battalion was relieved by the Fusiliers and moved back into reserve.

HQ and A and B Company occupied the brigade reserve position at Gorre, while C Company moved into the Tuning Fork Line immediately to the north of the canal. D Company went to the Village Line, with two of its platoons in Pont Fixe and two at Windy Corner. In spite of torrential rain, 28 March was spent with all available men strengthening the defences, during which twenty-one-year-old Pte Gilbert Weedon from Dorchester suffered a minor wound to the hand from shrapnel. Although not mentioned in the *War Diary*, there must have been night-time patrols for L/Cpl Tom Crossley was reported missing and subsequently discovered to be a prisoner.[15] (Had he been captured by an enemy raid, the *War Diary* would certainly have mentioned this.) It was still raining on the 29th, but the companies did their best to clean and refit. The garrison of the Village Line was strengthened further when B Company moved from reserve to occupy Windy Corner, allowing the two platoons from D Company to rejoin the others at Pont Fixe. Whenever possible, men were rotated to allow them to bathe at Beuvry, though A Company definitely came out on top as they remained in reserve and spent the 30th on the range at Le Quesnoy—much less tedious than working on the defences!

On 1 April, the battalion moved forward to relieve the Loyals by 11.15 p.m. HQ occupied a dugout in the Village Line (50° 31′ 35.62″ N, 2° 44′ 41.99″ E), with C Company occupying the front left, B the centre, and A the right (D remained in support in the Keeps). The newly christened RAF was maintaining a clear presence with reconnaissance patrols on 2 April; beating back potential German offensives were still at the forefront of the High Command's priorities, and British artillery was engaged in cutting wire for a raid to be undertaken by the Loyals. Three patrols visited No Man's Land during the night, but all was quiet in the enemy line. On the night of 4 April, 2Lt Harry Lyon and 2Lt George Raeside led two successful patrols, penetrating in two places right into the German lines at Canal Trench, just north of the canal itself. The next night, between 8.30 p.m. and midnight, these two officers and 2Lt William Holmes led another four patrols into enemy trenches and found them completely unoccupied from the canal bank to as far north as Warlingham Crater. No casualties were sustained from enemy action, but as Lt Raeside's patrol returned, Pte John Seed lost his footing in the dark as he was dropping back into his own trench and sustained a severely sprained ankle, so swollen it was initially believed to be broken. Shortly after the men had regained safety, British artillery began a bombardment of enemy lines with thermite and gas from Livens projectors. In case of them falling short, the defenders had been pulled back; this indeed turned out to be a sensible precaution, since a patrol on the 7th discovered five unexploded Livens gas projectiles in No Man's Land spread across 200 m of the company frontage. On the 6th, strong patrols from three companies and consisting of six officers and forty-five men entered enemy lines; once more, they found them unoccupied. Such intelligence led to the cancellation of the intended raid by the Loyals. All patrols got back unharmed, but another old hand from 1915 died of his wounds on 6 April: twenty-eight-year-old L/Cpl Henry Towers from Dalton was attached to 164 TMB. On 8 April, HQ moved to a couple of dugouts near Pont Fixe, its old position now employed by the Fusiliers as a support location. The day was unbelievably quiet, not a single shell fell on the battalion's sector. And yet, a storm was brewing.

# 11

# 9 April 1918 – 2 July 1918
# 'They win or die who wear the Rose of Lancashire'

The 1/4th had been stood-to long before the dawn of 9 April 1918. A dense fog compounded the limits of visibility in the dark, and at 4.15 a.m. a heavy bombardment of phosgene shells began to deluge the rear areas, a few HE 4.2-inch and 5.9-inch shells among them. Battery positions, road junctions, the area around canal bridges (but not the bridges themselves), and all HQ positions as far to the rear as Locon were targets, though 55 Division's HQ escaped most of the bombardment. This was because a German map captured in the middle of March had the position of divisional HQ in Locon clearly marked upon it, so a precautionary move to outside of Les Caudrons had been made.[1] Gradually the tempo increased, and shells began to fall on the front line, an attack pattern that repeated that of Operation Michael begun on the Somme on 21 March, the first phase of the *Kaiserschlacht*. Now the 1/4th found itself on the receiving end of the second phase: 'Operation Georgette' would be fought using the same strategy. Elite stormtrooper units would penetrate defences and move as quickly as possible through to attack headquarter positions at the rear. Any strongpoints holding out would be mopped up by following units.

Less than fifteen minutes after the bombardment began, British reserve troops were ordered forward to their battle stations by the codeword 'Bustle'. 166 Brigade had been near Le Preol on the morning of the 8th, but in the afternoon moved north of the canal to Locon in order to relieve the Portuguese on the 9th. This move was partly due to worries about how long the Portuguese would hold, but was also as a result of information from a captured German document, which showed plans to prevent the brigade playing any part in the defence of Givenchy by the use of artillery. As canal crossings were limited, it was prudent to move them north prior to any attack.[2] All reserve positions were planned out in minute detail and moves practised repeatedly, such that all that was needed to put the defensive plans into action was the codeword.

Around 6.30 a.m. the bombardment slackened considerably, and it was thought that it may just have been a large-scale raid against the two Portuguese brigades, but as a precaution 165 Brigade was ordered to make contact with the Portuguese to their left and find out exactly what was happening. At 7.30 a.m. the shelling recommenced, this time on the positions of the 1/4th, *Minenwerfer* effectively obliterating the front line and very heavy artillery fire falling on Oxford Terrace (50° 31′ 31.30″ N, 2° 45′ 40.25″ E) and Bayswater (50° 31′ 23.54″ N, 2° 45′ 33.74″ E). Thirty-five minutes later, HQ near Pont Fixe came under heavy bombardment, leading to serious casualties among runners and pioneers. To the left and as yet unbeknown to 55 Division, the Portuguese had, save for a few isolated strongpoints already fled the field, some reaching the rear areas as early as 7.30 a.m. The Portuguese 3 Brigade which moved forward from reserve actually evacuated the line as soon as men from the front began to pass through them, before they had even seen the enemy. All this was unknown to the British, as the thick fog reduced visibility to 40 yards or less. The regimental record of Bavarian RR 1, which attacked the Portuguese sector, recounts, 'The trench garrisons surrendered after a feeble resistance'.[3] In the sector of the 10th Portuguese Regiment, one strongpoint courageously held out until almost all of its defenders were killed by trench mortar fire, and other isolated pockets fought on until 11 a.m. In fairness, the Portuguese had been in the line for nearly a year, far longer than any British troops would have been expected to endure, and consequently were very tired, many of their ordinary soldiers no doubt wondering what they were doing fighting in somebody else's war! The fog complicated things greatly for the defenders on the left flank; men moving towards them could just as easily be Portuguese as they could be German, and it wasn't until the figures were right on top of them that their nationality was established and appropriate action taken. Appendix G of 164 Brigade's narrative recounts that the defenders at Moat Farm had large numbers of men running towards them out of the mist yelling, 'Portuguese. Beaucoup bombardo', but were unable to engage these until their helmets could be positively identified as German at a range of only 20 yards.[4] The events to the division's left flank, and the gallant defensive actions fought by both 165 and 166 Brigade to plug the gaps were unknown to the 1/4th. They had their own problems.

The enemy's creeping barrage was delivered with textbook precision and in many cases defenders did not see the Germans until they were within 20 yards of their positions. At 9.30 a.m., a runner from Capt. Ellwood at Canal North arrived at the Pont Fixe HQ carrying an SOS message. The message was then immediately passed back to the guns and division by power buzzer and runner (Pte Ernest Redpath). Attackers flooded in at close range; stormtroopers penetrated between the posts, surrounded Moat Farm, and reached Givenchy Church by 10 a.m., where they engaged in a stiff fight with the defenders of the Keeps. On the extreme left flank of 164 Brigade, the enemy had broken through as far as the Village Line at Le Plantin South (50° 31′ 56.90″ N, 2° 44′ 44.16″ E).

The man with the rifle who simply witnessed German after German appear to his front, sides, and sometimes rear did not know it, but the attack against 55 Division was made by nine enemy divisions; three German divisions in the first line of attack (4th Ersatz, 43rd Reserve, and 18th Reserve); two divisions in the second line of attack (44th and 16th Reserve); and a further four divisions in reserve (12th, 48th, 240th, and 216th Reserve). Not only was 55 Division exponentially outnumbered, but many of the troops they faced were the elite of the German Army, specially selected and trained to overwhelm defences. At approximately 9.30 a.m., the enemy penetrated through the fog as far as Windy Corner and occupied a number of the fortified houses there, including the Lancashire Fusiliers' RAP, capturing its MO. This information only reached the Fusiliers when their padre, who had escaped, brought the news down to their HQ near Pont Fixe at 10 a.m. Their CO immediately ordered D Company of 2/5th Fusiliers to form a defensive flank at Windy Corner, then clear the enemy from the position.[5] Some of the attackers had moved straight through the Village Line at this point, though these were few in number, cut off from reinforcement, resupply, or retreat, and easily mopped up later once the fog had cleared.

To begin with, the main effort against the 1/4th was directed against the area between the south of Givenchy and north of the canal, attacking along a front of about 400 m before fanning out to attack the rear. Wave after wave of attackers bombed their way along Orchard Road then stormed Orchard Keep (50° 31′ 28.71″ N, 2° 45′ 29.30″ E), held by twenty-four-year-old 2Lt Joseph Collin and sixteen men of his platoon. After a succession of attacks, only Collin and five of his men remained to fight off the enemy and pressed by close range MG fire and showers of bombs, they slowly withdrew along the keep, fighting all the way. Collin then went onto the offensive, rushed the nearest MG crew emptying his revolver at them before throwing a grenade which damaged the gun, killed four of the crew and wounded another two. When a second MG began to target his men, he took a Lewis gun, placed it in a position high on the parapet, giving him the best field of fire and with total disregard for his own safety, kept the enemy from seizing the keep. But there could only be one outcome in this uneven struggle—he was hit shortly afterwards, falling back into Orchard Keep mortally wounded. For his courage and self-sacrifice, Joseph Collin was awarded the VC.[6] In spite of the death of their leader, the remaining five men kept up this unequal battle, dying one by one. As the Germans rushed into the keep, the defenders' fire finally quenched and there was but one survivor, L/Cpl Joseph Pollitt, who was badly wounded and taken prisoner. The astonishing story of the defence of Orchard Keep doesn't end there, as Pollitt was sent back with just one escort, whom he killed, and then fought his way back through to British lines to report the bravery of his officer. Joseph Pollitt is a perfect illustration of the lottery concerning bravery awards: he too had been closely involved in the fighting when Tom Mayson won his VC in July 1917, and had been nominated unsuccessfully for his own MM at Gillemont Farm. Yet he was fated not to receive so much as a MiD either on this occasion, or for any of his deeds. As Lt-Col. Gardner wrote after the war,

> Lance Corporal Pollitt, as the only survivor of this very gallant band, was an unlucky victim of the fortune of war, in that he received no official recognition of his valuable services on this and other occasions.[7]

The defenders in other posts were equally hard pressed. Cpl Charles Birch, in charge of a section garrisoning a small post under extreme pressure, carried out a fighting withdrawal to a better position. His efforts delayed the enemy enough for troops behind him to organise a counter-attack which beat off the enemy and cleared the trenches of them. For his courage and leadership, Charles Birch was awarded the MM.[8] 2Lt George Ferguson also found his position untenable and withdrew his platoon to an adjacent position which was better placed to hold off the enemy. When he discovered the Germans had occupied a nearby pill box, he organised and led a counter-attack upon it, re-capturing the position, and capturing forty prisoners and three MGs, a deed which earned him the MC.[9] Another platoon leader to earn a MC was 2Lt Irvine Rouse. Despite the uneven odds, he held his position against every assault and accompanied by only one NCO went forward of his position to the wire and captured an enemy officer and eight men. As the enemy tried to work their way around his flank, he carried out a spoiling attack with a group of bombers and then ejected the attackers from a neighbouring strongpoint. His courage and leadership gave his men motivation throughout the day.[10] Sgt Alfred Holmes's platoon came under increasing pressure and he organised a block in the trench which they then held. As soon as was possible, he organised a counter-attack against the enemy who had gained the foothold in his sector, and drove them out, earning the MM for his initiative and skill.[11]

Just 200 m from Orchard Keep was an 18-pounder of A/276 Battery RFA, intended to act as an anti-tank gun and in a camouflaged gun pit rather than a protected position. The crew took shelter as the initial bombardment fell on their position, which was fortunate for them as one of the seats was blown off the gun, both the trail and the breech mechanism damaged. As soon as the bombardment lifted, the gun commander Sgt James Parkinson from Walton-le-Dale re-manned it, and when the enemy was seen advancing through the mist just 200 yards away, they opened fire. The damaged breech needed to be opened with a pickaxe blade after every round, but the gunners still managed to fire 150 rounds of shrapnel before the breech jammed so tightly that not even the pickaxe could free it. All this time they were subjected to bombardment by HE, gas, and MG fire. The gunners took up their rifles and continued to defend their position, the enemy getting to within bombing distance of them on one flank before a group from the 1/4th drove them off.[12] Sgt Parkinson was awarded the DCM for his courageous actions, which had greatly contributed to the defence of Givenchy. A forward section of C/276 Battery RFA, located near Windy Corner, had also been of great use in the defence; although one of the guns was knocked out early in the action, the other was able to provide vital covering fire.

The brigade's MG Battery fought a few epic defensive actions. One gun in Upper Cut (50° 31′ 52.86″ N, 2° 45′ 24.56″ E) fired 7,500 rounds of defensive (as opposed to barrage) fire, and although completely surrounded more than once, successfully held off the enemy. The NCO in charge of this gun actually threw more than 120 grenades during his defence of this position! A gun in Pill Box in Givenchy, was almost captured when the enemy penetrated the rear of the bunker and captured the men there, including a team from another position who were sheltering after their own gun had been destroyed. The NCO in charge of this bunker, upon hearing the enemy in the rear section of his position, drove them out with his revolver, and with the assistance of a Portuguese officer and another man, captured fifteen of the attackers, including two officers. No guns were captured, although a number were destroyed by enemy fire and the Germans eventually overran 'LEP3′ as it was called (50° 31′ 45.90″ N, 2° 44′ 37.78″ E). They left the gun intact, but the defenders were never seen again.[13]

Infantrymen fought with equal determination elsewhere, often taking the initiative for lack of surviving officers or NCOs. One such was Pte John Tyrrell from Blackburn, who took command of a Lewis team and kept up a withering fire against the attackers. Sniper fire accounted for three of his team, but Tyrrell kept his gun in action, despite it jamming four times due to constant use. After he had fired nearly fifty magazines, the barrel mouthpiece burst, finally spelling an end to the weapon. John Tyrrell was awarded the DCM for his pluck and tenacity.[14] When Sgt Harold Morris's men came under fire from an MG, the NCO carried out a single-handed attack on it, killing one gunner and wounding the other. He captured the gun, sent it to HQ for deployment where needed, and continued the fight to protect the company's flank, for which he was awarded the MM.[15] Also defending the left flank was thirty-four-year-old L/Cpl John Kenyon from Blackburn. With an utter disregard for his own safety, he held his position against repeated attacks and made a number of attempts to dislodge the enemy from a nearby strongpoint. He was also instrumental in organising the bombing attacks which finally ejected the enemy from the battalion's trenches, and found time to tend the wounded from his section. He too was awarded the MM, but did not live to collect it himself.[16]

One of the first outposts attacked that morning jutted out into No Man's Land on the northern bank of the canal and was garrisoned by A Company. It was named 'Death or Glory Sap' (50° 31′ 18.69″ N, 2° 45′ 55.83″ E) with just cause. The men from this isolated outpost remained unbeaten throughout the day. It is not recorded who their initial commander was, though 2Lt George Raeside appears the likeliest candidate. When the officer in command was killed, twenty-eight-year-old 2Lt Raymond Dane took over, assisted by twenty-three-year-old 2Lt Benjamin Pemberton, both officers later earning the MC for their conduct in this action. Instrumental in the defence was the platoon sergeant, Arthur Birkett from Bridlington. Already a winner of the MM in July 1917 (he had been nominated for the DCM), Sgt Birkett had enlisted as a regular in 1/ King's Own in 1906, and knew his trade intimately. His steadiness under pressure and skilful fire control cut the enemy down in swathes before they could gain a foothold in the sap, and he personally accounted for at least twenty of them. At one point, the Germans made a determined bombing attack from the rear, but Pemberton, with just one NCO and one man, attacked them so fiercely that they were driven off without loss; thus, these men managed to maintain control of the sap and communications with the rest of the company to the rear. Although their recommendations for the MM do not stipulate the location, it's possible that the two men with whom Pemberton fought were Cpl John Hogg and Pte Jack Round, both of whose recommendations describe an action mirroring that in Pemberton's recommendation. These two runners were also praised for carrying messages back to their company HQ through heavy fire. The defenders were fortunate enough to have a top quality Lewis-gunner with them. L/Cpl William Danson, the commander of one of the guns, had inflicted heavy casualties upon the enemy as they tried to rush the sap. When the NCO in charge of the other gun was wounded, Danson took over that gun too, controlling the fire of both weapons to great effect, for which he was awarded the MM.[17] Around 12.05 p.m., despite harassing fire from an MG positioned at the top of Orchard Road, Birkett led a sortie against the attackers to his front, capturing seventeen Germans and an MG, and ending the attack against his position.[18] His award of the DCM was well-deserved indeed.

In their initial thrust, the Germans had been able to seize parts of Bayswater and Cheyne Walk, though the 1/4th spiritedly held the first 100 yards of Bayswater against the assault from its northern end and from east and west along Cheyne Walk. A Company HQ had been in Spoil Bank (50° 31′ 21.25″ N, 2° 45′ 24.96″ E), but this was seized.

At Windy Corner, battalion sniper L/Cpl George Rothwell from Manchester worked his way along a shallow ditch towards one of the occupied posts, under heavy fire from its occupants the whole time and when he got to within twenty yards, he drove them out with a fusillade of grenades. Returning for more bombs, he collected a group of men and they cleared the enemy from a number of the houses around Windy Corner. Rothwell received the DCM.[19] At 10.30 a.m., the Fusiliers reached the Village Line where D Company had formed a defensive flank around Windy Corner, with one platoon from C Company 2/5th moving forward to support the main line of resistance, where the 1/4th was still fighting to evict the invaders.

The resistance of the 1/4th and the extra men from the Fusiliers sealed the German advance. After this, none of the enemy were able to break through the line from Windy Corner to Pont Fixe, especially as the fog was beginning to lift. The Fusiliers engaged in furious fighting around Windy Corner, with 2Lt Rowland Mowle organising the survivors of his platoon into a bombing squad and clearing one building at a time until a final bayonet charge netted thirty prisoners. With his section commander killed, Pte G. E. Brookes (Albert E. Brookes on his medal index card) took command of his Lewis section and pushed his gun forward to within 10 yards of the enemy, maintaining steady fire until another party of men from the Fusiliers was able to work their way behind the enemy and capture them, for which he was awarded the DCM.[20] Another private from the Fusiliers earned a DCM that morning. Harry Wareing was moving forward with a party of reinforcements when they came under heavy and accurate MG fire. After three failed attempts to get through, he crawled forward and killed the MG crew with a grenade, which enabled another group to work their way around and capture the rest.[21]. By 12.30 p.m., another two platoons from the Fusiliers had arrived at Windy Corner, now secure against further attack. As had been planned and trained for, as soon as territory was lost, the counter-attack units moved against the enemy before they were able to consolidate. Platoons from the 1/4th tackled the southern section of the breakthrough, and the Fusiliers the northern section. By 10.50 a.m., Spoil Bank and its HQ had been re-taken by A Company of the 1/4th, who then bombed its way up Bayswater to completely clear it of enemy and re-take Cheyne Walk past its junction with Bayswater.

The German thrust had broken through along 350 m from the canal northwards, but for once the terrain worked against it. Now that visibility had improved, the MGs of the Village Line, so carefully sited in the weeks leading up to the attack, had an uninterrupted field of fire to their east at the enemy advancing over open ground. The guns of Mairie Redoubt were similarly placed, and despite repeated assaults by the enemy, the redoubt held out intact. The battalion still held the northern part of Gunner Siding closest to Mairie Redoubt and by 10.55 a.m. had bombed the enemy out of Gunner Siding altogether. For any of the attackers still in the open to the west of Oxford Terrace, they were now in a killing ground where MGs enfiladed them from three sides; twenty minutes later, apart from a force still holding Orchard Keep and those in Orchard Road, there were no enemy in this area.

As the fog thinned in the late morning, crumpled heaps of the German dead caught there testified to the effectiveness of the wire defences. Two pockets of Germans had been isolated near the Village Line, one north near Le Plantin South and one south of Givenchy. No longer hidden from British retribution, they were faced with the choice to 'surrender or die', and most chose the former: 641 Germans were captured, including two battalion commanders. Over 100 MGs and even an entire band, complete with all their instruments, fell into British hands. (Many of these instruments found their way into the hands of bandsmen from the British battalions, though I suspect that the Glockenspiels remained redundant!) The Germans had been so confident of an easy victory that these musicians had been sent forward to play their triumphant forces into Béthune.[22] This overconfidence is probably best illustrated by a captured German document which instructed the attacking divisions thus:

In our attack our three regiments will be opposed by at most six companies in front and at most two reserve battalions in Festubert and Givenchy. One battalion in divisional reserve is South of the La Bassée Canal in le Preol. It will be prevented by our powerful artillery fire from taking part in the fight for Festubert and Givenchy. Troops are elements of the 55th Division, which after being engaged on the Somme has suffered heavy losses in Flanders and at Cambrai, and was described by prisoners in March, 1918, as a division fit to hold a quiet sector, that is below the average quality.[23]

In touch with 1/4th Loyals to the left and 2/5th Fusiliers to the right, the battalion could now focus on the remaining enemy to its front. Help was also given by 1 Division, which was to 55 Division's right, south of the canal. Once its commander, Maj.-Gen. E. P. Strickland, realised that the assault was to his north, he deployed 1/ Gloucestershires to the west of Pont Fixe along the south bank of the canal, their weapons adding to the defensive firepower should further breakthrough occur. Some of 1 Division's guns were also pulled from their shelters so they could fire to the north, helping to prevent more Germans moving forward.[24]

At 11.30 a.m., two platoons of the Fusiliers were sent up Wolfe Road and Orchard Road and began to bomb their way along the latter. One of these, under the command of twenty-six-year-old 2Lt John Schofield from Blackburn, met serious resistance from a group of about 100 Germans in a strongpoint. Although he only had nine men under his control, their accurate rifle and Lewis fire drove the enemy down into dugouts. He then personally captured a group of about twenty and with the help of more men cleared the position, killing or capturing the remaining enemy. Schofield sent a runner back to Lt-Col. Brighten to inform him that he was moving forward to re-take the front line and having made his party up to ten, he advanced along Orchard Road. He soon encountered large numbers of enemy in a communication trench to his front and in ditches to both sides and while his men opened rapid fire upon the enemy, he climbed out onto the parapet and forced their surrender, taking officers and 120 men prisoner. Shooting down into the enemy at his side was Welshman Pte C. McGill, who showed as little regard for the danger as his platoon leader, though he survived the engagement and was awarded a DCM for his actions.[25] Very soon after this the second lieutenant was hit by a burst of MG fire and died almost immediately. Schofield was awarded a posthumous VC.[26]

The second Fusilier platoon's commander, 2Lt William Rider, had three bullets pass through his uniform without so much as scratching him, and he calmly encouraged his men on! Finding a large group of the enemy to his front, he led his men around behind the Germans and forced the surrender of several hundred. One of his sections, a bombing party led by L/Cpl Clifford Old (another Welshman), ran straight into a group of Germans with two MGs, who opened up on them at point blank range. Showing no hesitation, the lance corporal rushed straight at them with the bayonet and the entire group promptly raised hands and surrendered. Later in the day, Clifford Old would be the first man back into the crater posts and received the DCM for his courage and inspiration.[27] Rider was awarded the MC.[28]

Orchard Keep continued to hold out against recapture, so the battalion concentrated on isolating it from any hope of reinforcement or resupply. Capt. Evans, despite being wounded early in the day, and Capt. Charles Overton both led forces in parallel attacks to clear Oxford Terrace and Gunner Trench of the enemy; by 3.20 p.m., the enemy was completely expelled from both trenches and all of Bayswater. Between them, these two groups captured three MGs and eighty men, and both officers were awarded bars to their MCs for the action. Foremost in one of Evans's bombing parties was Pte Charles Potterton. This man's courage inspired his comrades to completely drive the enemy out from their foothold in the battalion's trenches.[29] Also pivotal in recapturing the lost territory was Sgt Thomas Rathbone from Manchester. Throughout the fight he had impressed officers and men with his leadership and control of the situation, and when the MGs in Orchard Keep threatened to delay the attack, he personally sniped the hostile machine-gunners and then directed his men to fire on the most suitable targets, providing covering fire for the attackers. Both Potterton and Rathbone earned the MM.[30] Completely cut off, Orchard Keep fell back to the British fifteen minutes later, and by 4 p.m. Oxford Terrace, Cambridge Terrace (the northern continuation of Oxford Terrace), and all of Cheyne Walk were back under the control of the battalion and all of the enemy driven back to his own lines.

The battalion had fought tenaciously against overwhelming odds, and with such aggression that the enemy's will to resist them often melted away. This was frequently the fruit of individual bravery among officers, NCOs, and privates who risked all rather than admit defeat. When 2Lt Harry Lyon led a bombing attack to regain captured trenches, he found that he could not see the situation clearly enough from inside the trench, so climbed onto the parapet in order to guide his men better. Exposed to rifle and MG fire, he continued to direct his men until the enemy began to falter and then led a final charge against them across the open, routing them. His courage earned him a MC, though shortly afterwards, he was wounded. Another to earn the MC was 2Lt Thomas Pritchard, who led a bombing party to oust the enemy from the trenches, inflicting losses and capturing prisoners.[31]

The price paid by the battalion was dear: 166 killed, wounded, or missing. Out of these, sixty-eight were killed or died from their wounds over the coming weeks (among the captured, too). The death toll would have been even higher if it hadn't been for the courage and devotion of the medical staff and stretcher-bearers, such as Pte Frederick Averill. For forty-eight hours he toiled tirelessly, tending and evacuating the wounded. His work on 10 April was under constant heavy artillery, and MG and rifle fire, and as more stretcher-bearers inevitably became casualties themselves, his task accrued in difficulty. Yet he persevered until every wounded man had been evacuated, was awarded the MM.[32] One of the less common recipients of an MC was the American MO, Lt William Henry Jenks of the US Army Medical Corps. The MOs from the other two battalions in the brigade had been captured when the Fusiliers' RAP was overrun, and from that time onwards, William Jenks had been the only doctor. He had tended the wounded from the whole brigade under heavy and continuous bombardment, evacuating them on to the ADS as soon as he could.[33]

The story of a battle quite naturally tends to concentrate on those at the front clutching a rifle, however success also depends very much on those behind them. Key to the successful defence was Lt-Col. George Balfour. His skilful direction of his forces resulted in defeat for the enemy, action recognised by his award of the DSO.[34] His ability to direct the defence depended on him knowing the situation and this was due to the efforts and sacrifices of the signallers and runners. The initial bombardment had destroyed all the signal lines and battalion signals officer 2Lt Thomas Bateson and his men worked all day to repair the lines, frequently finding that shellfire cut a line they'd only just repaired. For their efforts in restoring communications, Bateson was awarded the MC and twenty-six-year-old Cpl Shepherd, a former chauffeur from Thwaites, the MM.[35] George Shepherd also received a payrise, as he was appointed Battalion Signals Sergeant a few days later.[36] Two other signallers were also awarded MMs for their work in the defence of Givenchy. When communications had been lost at 4.30 a.m., Pte George Wakefield donned his gas mask and carrying a reel of cable left the shelter of his dugout, and for the entire day worked under heavy fire, splicing cables repeatedly broken. The constant exposure to risk was not without penalty and he was wounded later in the day. Also working throughout the day on repairs was Cpl Robert Carruthers, though he escaped unwounded.[37]

Two of the battalion attached to brigade HQ were also awarded medals. Capt. Eric Kendall left the relative safety of the HQ dugout to go find a reserve company that had gone astray. This was at the height of the bombardment of HE, gas, and shrapnel, yet despite being wounded, Kendall continued looking until he located the company 1,000 yards from the dugout he'd left. He then directed them to their proper position, where their timely arrival played a significant role in the defence; his conduct earned him the MC. Pte Harold Helme was one of the signallers at the brigade forward exchange and constantly left the safety of the dugout to repair wires broken by the bombardment. His MM was awarded for this and the next six days of courage and devotion to duty, when he maintained communications without thought for his own safety.[38]

While the signallers struggled to mend the cable, the only means of passing on information was by runner, three of whom earned the MM. Twenty-six-year-old L/Cpl George Hewartson from Haverthwaite had been a sergeant until December 1917, when he had reverted to Private at his own request.[39] When the bombardment had been at its most intense, he had taken an important message from his company HQ to battalion HQ and later in the day managed to get in touch with a unit to the flank, enabling a gap in the defences to be bridged at a critical time. Pte Ernest Redpath was a battalion runner and it was he who had braved the intense initial bombardment to carry the SOS message to the nearest gun position and thence onwards to Artillery Group and brigade HQ, ensuring that British guns reacted to the attack. The mist had been too thick for the SOS rockets to be seen, so his actions were vital to the successful defence. Another runner, Pte Thomas Warburton, had repeatedly taken messages from his company HQ to battalion HQ. The communication trenches had been so battered by the bombardment that it was impossible to keep to them, so this gallant man spent the greater part of his journeys in the open, braving heavy artillery and MG fire.[40] These three men were awarded the MM.

The men in the face of the enemy assault needed support from the rear if they were to keep fighting. One to come forward was Sgt Alfred Morris, the battalion's pioneer sergeant. He organised parties of men to carry ammunition forward under heavy shellfire and when the enemy were within 50 yards of battalion HQ, he and his men picked up their rifles to rebuff them, work that earned him the MM. Similarly recognised was a twenty-five-year-old Londoner, Sgt George Watson. He had been captured in a forward position early on in the attack, but escaped and made his way back to support lines, where he reported. He then collected fifty men from various units and, with the help of an officer from another unit, formed them into a successful defensive flank. Later in the day he carried out a forward reconnaissance under heavy MG and rifle fire, showing remarkable coolness in the face of enemy action.[41] Also to win the MM in defence of the support lines was twenty-eight-year-old Sgt Thomas Robinson from Coniston, erroneously called 'John' in his recommendation. After fighting off the enemy, he led a bombing party that ejected them from a communication trench and finally cleared them from the company area.

It's probable that without the assistance of artillery and trench mortars, the enemy would have overrun more of the battalion's positions. L/Cpl William McGill, one of the commanders of a 3-inch Stokes Mortar with the TMB, was another old hand and awarded an MM for his gallantry and devotion to duty. As the enemy advanced, he removed the mortar from its pit, dug it in afresh in a better position, registered it on the advancing Germans, and launched 200 rounds of rapid fire into them, all the while under heavy shell fire and working with only half of his team (the other half made casualties early in the bombardment).[42] In the rear of the support line was an artillery OP and on finding out that this had been occupied by the enemy, 2Lt Lionel Andrews took two men with him and bombed them out, inflicting casualties and making captures. When he discovered that his company HQ had also been taken, he organised another bombing party and cleared the enemy from there too, earning himself the MC.[43] Even one of the battalion cooks won the MM: Pte James Drabble worked tirelessly for three days under heavy shell fire. All the other cooks had become casualties, yet with complete disregard for his own safety, he continued to single-handedly prepare hot meals for the entire battalion—needless to say, the men were appreciative in the extreme.[44]

With such casualties, the battalion was too weak to hold the line with the men remaining and so received reinforcements from other units in the division for the defences in the Keeps. At 4.50 p.m. fifty men and two officers from 1/5th South Lancashires arrived, and ten minutes later a further company from the same battalion under the command of Capt. Hill, which was divided between A and C Company. B Company, down to just seventeen 'other ranks', manned Bayswater alongside A, who also maintained a forward position in Death or Glory Sap. C Company plus a platoon from the Fusiliers manned Oxford Terrace, Mairie Redoubt, Gunner Siding, and Orchard Keep. The men of D Company were spread between Wolfe Road and Cambridge Terrace. The only places of the original front now held by the enemy were Warlingham Crater and a single post in Lower Finchley Road, east of Cambridge Terrace. As night fell, the defenders peered into the darkness, wondering when the enemy was going to renew his attack.

Though not strictly within the scope of this book, it is worth mentioning that the defence against Operation Georgette was fought just as valiantly on 55 Division's left flank, with any ground lost immediately counter-attacked and regained. In places the enemy had got so close to gun batteries that artillery was used on 'open sights' against them, and the gunners were forced to defend themselves with rifle and Lewis more than once. Machine-gunners continued to fire when surrounded, and in one case when the enemy entered the rear of the pill box, the MG continued in action as the rest of the crew fought off the attacks with their revolvers.[45] Practically every man from the division, whatever his customary role, had been put into the line with a rifle. Having come up against an immoveable force at Givenchy, the German pressed their gains on 55 Division's left flank to the morning of 11 August, until the recapture of 'Route A Keep' spelled a temporary end to Georgette.

The night of 9 to 10 August was remarkably peaceful for the 1/4th; a patrol sent out into No Man's Land reported the German front line deserted. The Fusiliers also sent patrols out, and when the craters were reported unmanned by the enemy, they were re-occupied, thus by 12.15 a.m. completely re-establishing the lines held before the attack.

55 Division had suffered heavy casualties on 9 August, but the Germans had endured even more. Caught between the wire or in the open once the fog had lifted, they had been cut down by small arms fire. The divisional artillery, firing on pre-determined SOS and counter-preparation coordinates, had caught the enemy as they amassed in the front line and reserve trenches to follow the first wave across. British prisoners reported after the war that one of the second-line divisions had been virtually annihilated by British fire, this a barrage that also killed twenty-three British prisoners.[46] At least two of those killed by British artillery fire were from the battalion: nineteen-year-old Pte Richard Wormall from Shaw, whose death had been mistakenly reported to his family the week before Christmas of 1916, and thirty-eight-year-old Pte James Maxwell from Widnes. The CWGC has Maxwell's death down as on the 10th, but correspondence from 1919 implies that these men were together, suggesting that James Maxwell was possibly hit on 9 April and died from wounds on 10 April.[47] No figures for German losses at Givenchy for 9 April exist, but between 21 March and

30 April, German casualties were 348,000, and this without including the lightly wounded.[48] What must also be taken into account is the bulk of these were Germany's best troops, specially selected and trained for the *Kaiserschlacht*.

The battalion had made it to the morning of 10 August, but it wasn't in the clear yet. At 9.40 a.m. a German aircraft numbered '18' swooped low over Bayswater and dropped a single bomb. It wounded fourteen men from A Company, who had put up such a valiant defence just twenty-four hours previously. Of those fourteen, three died within three days of the wounds they received. Forty-year-old Pte Thomas Whiting from Pipe-cum-Lyde, passed away at the CCS at Wimereux on 12 August; twenty-four-year-old Pte Stanley Geldart from Barrow at 54 CCS, at Aire, the next day; and twenty-two-year-old Pte Harry Neal from Thorsway Top at Étaples.

The wide distribution of the medical facilities to have treated these three men serves as a reminder of how busy the RAMC was at this time. Although the medics did their best, injuries were often too severe or infection too far-advanced for there to be any tangible hope, and it was often just became a matter of time. Some men lingered for weeks, sometimes even months, to the torment of their loved ones back home. Twenty-three-year-old L/Cpl Frank Knowles from Boothstown was wounded by shrapnel in the thigh, and infection set in where amputation was not possible. On 6 May he finally succumbed, and the military machine went into operation to notify his mother and return his belongings. Sometimes, records contain correspondence from distraught wives and parents wanting to know what had happened to some precious personal item which had not been returned (probably looted by someone from outside the battalion). Often for KIAs, the only items sent back were a cap badge and an ID disc. In fact, the latter happened so frequently that it's reasonable to believe that the battalion actually maintained a spare supply of cap badges and ID discs purely for the purpose of giving relatives a memento when a soldier's body had either been blown to bits or submerged in the mud of the battlefield. In the case of Knowles, the list of returned property on his 'Army Form B 104-126' is reassuringly complete.

2 Identity Discs, Letters—including 7 un-opened, Photographs, Cards, Religious book, Cigarette case, Crucifix, Pocket case, Watch and leather guard, 25 Centime note (defaced), 1 wristwatch and strap.

Also in his record is the letter from his mother, acknowledging the receipt of these items.

Sir,
I thank you so kindly for the belongings of my faithful boy's property. I must say I am bleeding in heart to think he cannot return to me as I am terribly hit by his and my awful loss, busting. If any more value comes through, will you do your utmost to help a poor widow. Mrs Knowles.[49]

It wasn't just German aircraft involved in the ground offensive; the RAF had been active over the enemy trenches opposite the battalion, too. There was still considerable shelling of the British line, and both Pont Fixe and Windy Corner drew the attention of crushing artillery fire, from either 8-inch or even 11-inch howitzers. Troop movement was seen behind the German lines and, concerned this may be the prelude to another attack, the division's artillery and MGs launched fire over the enemy's rear. But no attack was forthcoming, and the artillery duel slacked around 9 p.m.

## Killed in action or died from wounds 9-10 April 1918

| | | | | | |
|---|---|---|---|---|---|
| CSM Robert Adamson | 200024 | KIA-9/4 | Pte Thomas Airey | 240287 | KIA-9/4 |
| Pte Ephraim Aldous | 22696 | KIA-9/4 | Pte Robert Allen | 241617 | KIA-9/4 |
| Pte Moses Andrews | 16929 | KIA-9/4 | Pte Thomas Angove | 201060 | KIA-9/4 |
| Pte John Barry | 26791 | KIA-9/4 | Pte George Beesley | 21569 | KIA-9/4 |
| Pte Henry Beetham | 27697 | KIA-9/4 | L/Cpl John Frederick Bennett | 201160 | KIA-9/4 |
| Pte George Arthur Boulter | 37078 | KIA-9/4 | L/Cpl Harold W. Bransden | 240563 | KIA-9/4 |
| L/Cpl John Bright | 4259 | KIA-9/4 | Pte George Brooks | 37086 | KIA-9/4 |
| L/Cpl John Brown | 200454 | KIA-9/4 | Pte Frank Carson | 200511 | KIA-9/4 |
| Pte Thomas Cheetham | 27641 | KIA-9/4 | Pte George Thomas Clare | 34662 | KIA-9/4 |
| Pte Joseph Collier | 201480 | KIA-9/4 | 2Lt Joseph Henry Collin | | KIA-9/4 |
| 2Lt Richard Court | | KIA-9/4 | Pte James Courtman | 24409 | KIA-9/4 |
| Pte William Croasdale | 201749 | KIA-9/4 | Pte Alfred Dronsfield | 17426 | KIA-9/4 |
| Cpl Joseph Duckworth | 13563 | KIA-9/4 | Pte Alfred Eames | 15153 | KIA-9/4 |
| Pte Joseph Ellis | 26712 | KIA-9/4 | Pte Frederick John Fletcher | 242280 | KIA-9/4 |
| Pte Stanley Geldart | 200567 | DOW-13/4 | Pte William Gordon | 201245 | POW-D-16/4 |
| 2Lt Bert Harold Gough | | KIA-9/4 | Pte John Hargreaves | 201542 | KIA-9/4 |
| L/Sgt Herbert Hinchcliffe | 200749 | DOW-10/4 | Pte Frank Hodge | 28201 | KIA-9/4 |
| Pte Robert Hornby | 37083 | KIA-9/4 | L/Cpl Proctor Howcroft | 201723 | KIA-9/4 |
| L/Cpl Frank Knowles | 26079 | DOW-6/5 | Pte Thomas Lofthouse | 200910 | KIA-9/4 |
| Pte James Maxwell | 202583 | DOW-10/4 | Pte James McAlarney | 200272 | KIA-9/4 |
| Pte Edgar (George?) Mercer | 241664 | KIA-9/4 | L/Sgt William Miller * | 12650 | KIA-9/4 |
| Pte Robert Henry A. Moreton | 33972 | DOW-9/4 | Cpl Harry Neal | 27020 | DOW-13/4 |
| L/Cpl George William Nicholls | 14396 | KIA-9/4 | Pte Arthur Nuttall | 200873 | KIA-9/4 |
| Pte William Porter | 33562 | KIA-9/4 | Cpl Robert Proudfoot | 201164 | KIA-9/4 |
| 2Lt George Forrest Raeside | | KIA-9/4 | Pte Frederick Charles Saggers | 26836 | KIA-9/4 |
| Pte Samuel Scothern | 27037 | KIA-9/4 | Pte Alexander Strick Sharp | 200083 | KIA-9/4 |
| Pte Herbert Simmons | 201577 | DOW-20/4 | Pte Herbert Smith | 38648 | KIA-9/4 |
| L/Cpl Joseph A. C. Stuart | 32607 | KIA-9/4 | Pte James Alexander Surgeoner | 36416 | KIA-9/4 |
| Sgt Samuel Taylor | 13053 | KIA-9/4 | Pte Thomas Hornsby Taylor | 16275 | KIA-9/4 |
| Pte David Arthur Tetley | 38657 | KIA-9/4 | Pte Harry Thompson | 266076 | KIA-9/4 |
| Pte Peter Thompson | 15059 | KIA-9/4 | Pte John Topping | 37120 | DOW-16/4 |
| Pte John Henry Watterson | 200408 | DOW-25/4 | Pte Thomas Charles Whiting | 265968 | KIA-9/4 |
| Pte Ernest Wiles | 202228 | KIA-9/4 | Pte George Wilson | 201025 | KIA-9/4 |
| Pte Richard Wormall | 24306 | KIA-9/4 | Pte James Yates | 14931 | KIA-9/4 |

* L/Sgt William Miller's brother was Pte James Miller, who won a posthumous VC on 30 July 1916 with 7/ King's Own.

Known to have been wounded or captured 9-10 April 1918

| | | | | | |
|---|---|---|---|---|---|
| Pte James Barton | 22279 | POW-9/4 | Pte Albert Thomas Barron | 24849 | POW-9/4 |
| L/Cpl William Baxter | 200217 | POW-9/4 | Pte Frederick Beard | 33465 | WIA-9/4 |
| Cpl Edward Bennett | 201306 | WIA-9/4 | Pte Harry Berry | 30050 | POW-9/4 |
| Cpl Harold Bolton | 22327 | WIA-10/4 | Pte Stephen Boundy | 200658 | WIA-9/4 |
| Sgt Harry Brown | 200530 | WIA-9/4 | Pte Alexander Cartmell | 24395 | WIA-10/4 |
| Pte William Crowther | 200729 | POW-9/4 | Pte James Edward Cuddy | 20614 | WIA-10/4 |
| Pte John Dawson | 265793 | WIA-9/4 | Pte Edward Edwardson | 32591 | WIA-9/4 |
| Capt. John Henry Evans | | WIA-9/4 | Pte Robert Barnes Faith | 28020 | WIA-9/4 |
| L/Cpl John Robert Gardner | 200470 | WIA-9/4 | Pte Joseph Greenhow | 200505 | WIA-9/4 |
| Pte Thomas Hacking | 32622 | POW-9/4 | L/Sgt Amos Goodridge Hall | 24286 | WIA/POW |
| Pte Robert Helme ** | 201115 | POW-9/4 | 2Lt William Holmes | | WIA/POW |
| Pte Percival Lister Hunter | 30129 | POW-9/4 | Pte Thomas Jesson | 22000 | POW-9/4 |
| Capt. Eric Angerstein Kendall | | WIA-9/4 | 2Lt Arthur Selby Latham | | POW-9/4 |
| Pte Frederick Lindsay | 200313 | POW-9/4 | Cpl Osborne Longworth | 200899 | WIA-9/4 |
| Pte Harry Loydell (Laydall) | 200538 | WIA-10/4 | Pte William Arthur Lucas | 202183 | WIA-9/4 |
| Pte William George Lyes | 26517 | WIA-9/4 | 2Lt Harry James Lyon | | WIA-9/4 |
| Pte Atkinson Rothey Mawson | 33584 | WIA-9/4 | 2Lt William McAndrew | | POW-9/4 |
| Pte Albert Scrimshaw Melligan | 33973 | WIA-9/4 | Pte Alexander Minshall | 17136 | WIA-9/4 |
| Pte Bernard Edward Neave | 32949 | POW-9/4 | 2Lt Edwin D. Osgood | | POW-9/4 |
| Pte Walter Pilkington | 33007 | WIA-9/4 | L/Cpl Joseph Pollitt | 24177 | WIA-9/4 |
| Pte Joseph Ralph | 200506 | WIA-9/4 | Pte Robert Ralston ** | 240286 | POW-9/4 |
| Pte George William Robinson | 201785 | WIA-9/4 | L/Cpl George Rothwell | 12073 | WIA-9/4 |
| Pte Frederick William Sarratt | 34614 | WIA-9/4 | Sgt William Shallicker | 202943 | WIA-9/4 |
| Pte John Smith | 200468 | POW-9/4 | L/Cpl Joseph Steele ** | 200738 | POW-9/4 |
| 2Lt Robert Alexander Taylor | | WIA-9/4 | Pte Richard Terry | 203086 | WIA-9/4 |
| 2Lt Tom Chaplin Threadgold | | POW-9/4 | Pte Ernest Ford Topping | 21690 | POW-9/4 |
| Pte John Edward Tyson | 24266 | WIA-9/4 | Pte George Wakefield | 201182 | WIA-9/4 |
| Capt. Sidney Frederick Walker | | WIA-9/4 | Pte Gilbert R. C. Weedon | 202153 | POW-9/4 |
| Pte Henry Whiteside | 22770 | WIA-9/4 | Pte James Wilkinson | 30634 | POW-9/4 |
| Pte Francis Henry Williams | 34707 | WIA-9/4 | Pte Henry Williams | 202212 | WIA-9/4 |
| Pte Jonathan Winder | 200660 | POW-9/4 | Pte John Woodruff | 200847 | POW-9/4 |
| Cpl John Woodward | 22376 | WIA-9/4 | Sgt Wallace Worthington | 22063 | WIA-9/4 |
| Pte Arthur William Yare | 26850 | WIA-9/4 | | | |

** Robert Helme, Robert Ralston, and Joseph Steele were all killed on 28 April 1918.

During the night of 10 to 11 April, reconnaissance patrols into No Man's Land reported no sign of enemy movement at all. Apart from some elongated bursts of MG fire from the north-east, the night was still. This set the precedent for the next day with the exception of Le Plantin, which was shelled violently in the evening, and the relief of D Company in the left sector by C Company from the Keeps was also delayed by shell fire. No mention is made of 'other ranks' in the 'Casualty Returns' in the *War Diary*, but individual service records show that there were some from this shelling. Twenty-five-year-old Pte Richard Thistlethwaite from Ulverston was wounded in the leg by shrapnel, and thirty-two-year-old Pte Arthur Baker from Mill Hill was killed. (Although *Soldiers Died* categorises him as 'KIA', the location of Arthur Baker's grave suggests that he was wounded and possibly died on the journey to hospital in St Omer.) Also wounded was 2Lt Alexander Fyfe.

At 9.30 a.m. on 12 April, the brigade major, Capt. C. L. Chute MC, visited battalion HQ with verbal orders for the relief of the battalion by the Fusiliers, which was carried out one platoon at a time between 1 p.m. and 6.35 p.m. There were also changes to the command structure, as the division was transferred to 1 Corps of the First Army—though this change would have meant nothing below divisional level, or for the ordinary soldier, whose life carried on as before. The Village Line and Pont Fixe were now occupied by A and D Company of 1/5th South Lancashires, and D and B Company of the 1/4th moved to the location of HQ at Fanshawe Castle, between Windy Corner and Pont Fixe (50° 31′ 29.48″ N, 2° 44′ 35.71″ E). C Company remained at Windy Corner for the time being. The Village Line was subjected to bombardment for much of the following day and once it was dark enough to work unseen, the men began to wire their northern flank between Windy Corner and Lone Farm, as a precaution against any breakthrough to their north. In so doing, another of the old hands fell prey to gas shells: Pte John Barrow was wounded for his second time this way, but returned three weeks later. Gas was unpleasant, frightening, and excruciating, but nowhere near as lethal as many today believe it to have been. Soldiers who put on their respirators quickly enough were largely unaffected by it, though concentrated levels of mustard gas did burn unprotected flesh. The respirator itself was an effective piece of equipment, and most of the wounded made a complete recovery within a few weeks, though residual effects might linger throughout their lives. For the Western Front over the entire duration of the war, gas amounted to just 1.2 per cent of the total killed.[50] At 4.45 p.m. on the 14th, C Company was finally relieved by a company of the South Lancashires, and the brigade warned to expect relief by 1 Brigade from the 1 Division over the next few days.

A steady trickle of reinforcements began to arrive from 14 April, with thirteen men joining that day. One of these was twenty-seven-year-old Pte John Byrne from St Helens. He had originally been in 11/ King's Own, but was wounded in a grenade accident in September 1917. He and other bombers were cleaning grenades when a fragment of an accidentally detonated Mills bomb passed straight through his calf muscle. He reported,

On putting one of them together, whilst screwing in the base plug, the pin, which cannot have been pushed home, slipped out at one side and allowed the lever to release the striker. I was going to throw it over the top, but there was a sentry in the way, so I threw it to the far end of the bay, where it struck the traverse and bounced back so we all cleared round the traverse.

His section NCO, L/Cpl Flynn, recounted the incident thus:

I was in charge of a party of men cleaning bombs. They were all experienced bombers, and had been at work for over an hour. No. 22372 Byrne called my attention to a bomb which was smoking in his hand. I called the men to clear out of the bay, and Private Byrne threw the bomb to the other end of the bay before doing so.

Pte E. Harris explained how John Byrne had been wounded:

I ran round the traverse and fell over Pte Haywood, who was working round the corner. Pte Byrne was the last out and did not get round the traverse before the bomb exploded owing to the block caused by the traverse being too narrow and four of us trying to get round at the same time.[51]

14 April also saw the death in action of thirty-one-year-old Capt. Albert Ellwood. A first class officer, Ellwood was also a talented artist who had made a number of officers and men alike the subjects of his sketches. He was irreplaceable to the battalion, and still more to his widow, whom he had married a scant four months previously. Although the circumstances of Ellwood's death were not recorded, shell fire is the most likely cause. By 11.15 p.m. on the 16th, all the 1/4th had been relieved by 1/ Cameron Highlanders and companies proceeded independently to Beuvry, from where they bussed to Marles-les-Mines. Although several 5.9s landed near to the convoy as it was waiting to leave, no casualties occurred. Apart from a rifle inspection upon their arrival on the 17th, the battalion rested in its new billets. The period between 18 and 22 April was just like any other out of the line: saturated with training, including time on the range and route marches. There was opportunity for hot baths, and at least one parade, at Auchel Aerodrome, in which NCOs got the chance to run around shouting at sloppy soldiers! Afterwards, the battalion was inspected by Maj.-Gen. Jeudwine, and although it was anticipated that the French Premier would attend, he failed to show up. In just four days, 287 men and five officers arrived to replace those lost, bringing battalion strength by the end of April up to 335 men and twelve officers. While this may seem positive, the losses for the month amounted to 461, so there was still an overall deficit of 114!

At 6.20 a.m. on 23 April, the battalion moved to Vaudricourt. It was a warm and sunny day, spent resting in the woods. They were bound for the very trenches they had left just a week earlier, but there had been changes while they were away. The enemy had again attacked at Givenchy on the 18th, and although 1 Division had valiantly fought them off, the enemy had succeeded in holding on to the original British line near and including the Givenchy Craters. Suffering 80-per-cent casualties, 1/ Black Watch in Givenchy Keep had been down to one officer and eight men before the assaulting Germans had given up trying to seize it.[52] What the men who'd fought so hard to defend the area on the 9th thought about this has not been recorded, but they could hardly have been happy. Further north, the enemy had also succeeded in capturing Route A Keep, though the task of retaking this would be assigned to the Liverpool Scottish.

The 'B Team' under Capt. William Batchelor departed for Burbure, where they remained while the rest of the battalion manned the front line. At 7.30 p.m., two companies moved off by light railway to relieve the Loyals in the trenches. The remainder and battalion HQ were taken forward by bus an hour later. At 9.30 p.m., as they debussed at Annequin, artillery fire fell around them, causing ten casualties to battalion HQ. Three were killed outright: Pte Thomas McHugh from Whitworth; twenty-one-year-old L/Cpl William Richards from Barrow; and twenty-eight-year-old L/Cpl James Tomlinson from Barrow. Critically wounded was twenty-one-year-old Joseph Whalley, who died two days later. Twenty-four-year-old Pte William Draper was evacuated back to England, but his wounds proved mortal and he died on 15 May. Among those wounded was 2Lt Donald Maclean, fresh to the battalion since nine days earlier.

Once the fighting companies had reached the Front, D Company moved into support, C to the left, B to the centre, and A to the right; all men were in place by 12.30 a.m. of 24 April. During the night, 77-mms fell near to Windy Corner and British artillery carried out sporadic harassment of the craters now in the possession of the enemy. Daylight saw another dull and overcast day, with a lingering mist restricting visibility and there was little enemy activity until mid-afternoon. From shortly after 3 p.m. until the early hours of the morning, German 4.2s targeted Wolfe Road, Givenchy Keep, and Bayswater, and at 5 a.m. on 25 April, heavier 5.9s against Pont Fixe. Part of the threat of German artillery was the improved observation the enemy now had, as possessing the craters gave an elevated view into not just the British front lines, but also the rear areas. Just after dark, at 8.45 p.m. on the 25th, two substantial fighting patrols under Second Lieutenants Joe Sykes and Allen Whitmore slipped out to occupy the old front line from the junctions of Orchard Road (50° 31′ 26.44″ N, 2° 45′ 52.16″ E) and Finchley Road (50° 31′ 33.74″ N, 2° 45′ 51.39″ E). They found the enemy front line exceptionally heavily occupied and both became embroiled in a fierce firefight, resulting in both officers being wounded and the patrols retreating. Later that night at 11.20 p.m., another attempt was made, this time after a preliminary barrage. Unfortunately, the barrage fell onto the old No Man's Land behind their objective, and this patrol also retired after coming up against effective MG fire and sustaining a number of casualties.

The *Divisional History* describes the forthcoming action as taking place on 24th April,[53] but both the *War Diary* and the *Official History* correctly allocate it to 26 April.[54] At 4 a.m., again covered by artillery fire, two platoons from A and D Company rushed the enemy position, but were forced to retire after hand-to-hand encounters. Undaunted, another attempt was made at 2.20 p.m. This time, the 1/4th attacked in conjunction with 2/5th Fusiliers, the King's Own tackling from Warlingham Crater (50° 31′ 39.63″ N, 2° 45′ 52.81″ E) as far north as the craters of E Sap (50° 31′ 46.24″ N, 2° 45′ 42.66″ E), and the Fusiliers from E Sap northwards to K Sap Crater (50°31′ 57.34″ N, 2°45′ 33.64″ E). For this assault an MG barrage boosted the artillery, as two platoons from C and D Company rushed the enemy. The C Company Platoon on the left and led by 2Lt Herbert Hunter, quickly cleared Berkeley Street, (50° 31′ 46.32″ N, 2° 45′ 37.00″ E) E Sap and the front line. To the right, 2Lt William Stewart's D Company platoon were equally successful and rushed from Coventry Sap to take A Sap (50° 31′ 39.59″ N, 2° 45′ 50.43″ E) and the front line, both platoons capturing forty prisoners between them. Stewart's platoon had attacked with such speed that the German garrison had been caught completely by surprise and they did not suffer a single casualty in the initial assault. Foremost in the charge had been one of the older men in the battalion, thirty-eight-year-old Pte Richard Jones, a married man from Manchester. He personally accounted for several of the enemy, and when a hostile MG began to target his comrades, engaged it with rifle fire. He also assisted in the capture of two of the surviving crew, who later gave valuable intelligence when interrogated. For his coolness under fire and continual rallying of his comrades, he was awarded the MM.[55]

To the left of the 1/4th, the Fusiliers had met with much tougher opposition, for the artillery bombardment had missed both K and J Saps, leaving their garrisons unharmed. Although the Fusiliers eventually took their objectives, too many had been wounded for them to hold, a situation which led to the enemy being able to concentrate much greater effort against the 1/4th.

The Germans were not content to let matters lie and made a number of very determined counter-attacks. At E Sap, 2Lt Hunter was killed and command taken over by L/Sgt George Johnson, whose inspirational leadership earned him a bar to his DCM. Five times the enemy forced him out of E Sap and five times he personally led bombing parties to re-take it. The enemy also made repeated determined assaults against A Sap, and although parts of the Sap were taken briefly, Stewart and his men managed to regain them almost as quickly. He was awarded the MC.[56]

Even more impressive was the courage displayed by L/Cpl James Hewitson. During the initial attack he led his section along the enemy-held trench, clearing any enemy he encountered. In one dugout, a group of six Germans refused to surrender and he dispatched them with grenades. As his section reached the final crater objective, he spotted that the enemy were bringing an MG into action against his men, worked his way round the crater, and threw another grenade at the crew, killing five outright and taking the surrender of the sole survivor. Shortly afterwards, an enemy bombing party attacked his Lewis gun team, and he personally routed this group, killing six of them. For this astounding series of actions, he was awarded the VC.[57]

Close to L/Cpl Hewitson was Pte Thomas Cross, whose section commander became a casualty just as they reached their objective. Cross immediately took command of his section and cleared the trench with bombs. Once the objective was secure, he established a forward post and held this against repeated onslaughts, for which he was recommended for the DCM. Although this was not granted, he was awarded the MM for his leadership and courage. Altogether, five men were recommended for the DCM, but received the MM instead; the second was Pte William Morris, who took command of his section when his NCO was wounded and conducted the defence of his advanced sap against vigorous counter-attacks. With just three men, he kept the attackers at bay with salvoes of bombs, inflicting heavy losses upon them, and when almost surrounded, he skillfully withdrew his men without loss.[58] The third man to earn the MM as consolation for a DCM was a twenty-year-old former grocer's assistant from Ulverston, Cpl Fred Jackson. This young NCO led his section with gusto; after clearing the trench of enemy, he mopped up two large dugouts, killing twelve of the garrison, then gained contact with the assaulting party to his left before establishing his section in a captured sap. Armed with rifle fire and bombs, this small party fought off three determined counter-attacks before being forced to withdraw. A few hundred yards to Fred Jackson's right was the fourth MM-winner, Pte Samuel Wolstencroft. After several NCOs had become casualties, he collected together men who had lost their NCOs and set up an advanced post, which they then held against repeated counter-attacks until forced to retire when almost surrounded.[59]

Sgt William Ashton, like his fellow sergeant the formidable Arthur Birkett, was an ex-regular recalled to the colours. Ashton led his section in the attack on the crater sap that was their objective and captured it, causing the enemy heavy losses in both men killed and captured. For several hours they held the position under heavy fire, and when the enemy eventually recaptured it, he led his section in an immediate counter-attack and seized the position back again. In heavy hand-to-hand fighting, the position swapped hands no less than five times, each time Ashton and his men clawed their way back. When eventually they were almost surrounded, he carried out a successful fighting withdrawal back to friendly lines.[60] William Ashton received the MM for his actions, the recommendation for the DCM possibly being overruled as the NCO had not stepped up to take over a higher role in the chain of command during his action.

Around 6 p.m. the Fusiliers were finally driven from their positions and the survivors from C and D Company found themselves encircled on three sides, so carried out a gradual fighting withdrawal, reaching their own lines at 8 p.m. Although these actions had not resulted in the recapture of the ground lost on 18 April, they had caused heavy casualties to the enemy in little more than a strong raid, and congratulatory letters were forthcoming from both brigade and division. Without the action of carrying parties resupplying the forward positions with small arms ammunition and bombs, the two platoons would not have been able to hold on for as long as they did. One of these heroes to receive the MM was Pte William Ward. With great courage and determination, he made no fewer than five journeys carrying bombs to the advanced positions under fire, and on his return trips carrying messages back to company HQs.[61] Compared to the enemy, casualties had been light, with around a dozen men killed or dying from their wounds—considerably less than the number of enemy killed by L/Cpl Hewitson alone. While the fatal casualties may have been few, ninety men were wounded or captured that day; considering only four platoons had been involved in the action, it was a testament to just how ferocious the fighting had been. Casualties would have been worse had it not been for the bravery and sacrifice of the stretcher-bearers. Pte Frederick Lyth(e) was a 'company' stretcher-bearer, and as such had been right up with the assaulting infantry. Exposed to heavy bombing, and rifle and MG fire, he worked tirelessly for twenty-four hours until all the wounded had been evacuated. For much of his work he had been at very close quarters to the enemy, and the MM awarded was extremely well earned.[62]

No attacks followed on 27 April, but the casualties were high when in retaliation the enemy heavily shelled battalion positions in Oxford Keep, Bayswater, Oxford Terrace, and Spoil Bank between 4 and 6 a.m. In all probability this was meant as a 'spoiling barrage' for any intended attack, and the Germans were obviously concerned that there was going to be a repeat of the attacks on the craters. The rest of that day was quiet and gave the battalion an opportunity to reorganise the companies.

Known to have been killed in action or died from wounds caused on 26-27 April 1918

| L/Sgt Charles Edmund Ansell * | 32508 | DOW-27/4 | Pte Richard Bashall | 17240 | DOW-29/4 |
|---|---|---|---|---|---|
| Pte William Bates | 27086 | KIA-26/4 | Pte George Brunt | 28122 | KIA-26/4 |
| Cpl Thomas Crompton | 12554 | KIA-26/4 | L/Cpl John Dickie | 200741 | KIA-26/4 |
| Pte John Edward Everitt | 40898 | KIA-26/4 | Pte Charles Henry French | 41049 | KIA-26/4 |
| | | | Pte Arthur George | | |
| 2Lt Herbert Sidney Hunter | | KIA-26/4 | Northwood | 41061 | KIA-26/4 |
| L/Cpl Robert Porter ** | 34588 | KIA-30/4 | Pte Harold Ramsbottom | 40633 | KIA-26/4 |
| Pte John Slack | 29157 | KIA-26/4 | Pte Sydney Yates | 29141 | KIA-26/4 |
| | | | | | |
| Pte Sam Cornforth | 40966 | KIA-27/4 | Cpl John Hardy | 9508 | KIA-27/4 |
| Pte Alfred James Locker | 40922 | KIA-27/4 | Pte Albert Medhurst | 41055 | KIA-27/4 |
| Pte Herbert Edwin Slaymaker | 265501 | KIA-27/4 | Pte Richard Steele | 26056 | KIA-27/4 |
| Pte Leonard Stevenson | 38646 | KIA-27/4 | | | |

* Charles Ansell was wounded on 26 April 1918, dying of these wounds on the 27th.

** Robert Porter died on the 30th and was buried at Étaples. The site of his burial, coupled with the lack of any other evidence to support it, suggests that *Soldiers Died* erroneously recorded him as 'KIA'. He was most probably wounded in either this action or that of 9-10 April, and died of wounds at one of the base hospitals.

Known to have been wounded on 26 or 27 April 1918

| 2Lt John George Anderson | | WIA-26/4 | Pte Robert Ashburner *** | 200100 | WIA-26/4 |
|---|---|---|---|---|---|
| Pte Charles William Bell | 24380 | WIA-27/4 | Cpl Edward Bennett | 201306 | WIA-26/4 |
| Pte Arthur Cleminson | 201522 | WIA-26/4 | 2Lt George William Ferguson | | WIA-26/4 |
| L/Cpl John Parkinson Moore | 200156 | WIA/POW | Pte Harry Parkington | 21250 | WIA-26/4 |
| Pte Albert James T. Sewart | 22777 | WIA-26/4 | Cpl James Smith | 200713 | WIA-26/4 |
| Pte Albert Stanley **** | 30221 | WIA-26/4 | Pte Ratcliffe Taylor | 21702 | WIA-26/4 |
| Pte Fred Travis | 20991 | WIA-26/4 | Pte John Edward Tyson | 24266 | WIA-26/4 |

*** Robert Ashburner was shot in the face and received a 100-per-cent pension, so was presumably blinded by this wound. He doesn't appear on the list of those from the battalion who underwent reconstructive surgery.
**** Albert Stanley's records don't give the exact date of his injury, but the probability is that he was a casualty from either 26 or 27 April.

28 April is described as a 'quiet day' in the *War Diary*, and although some intermittent shelling of the Village Line was referred to, not mentioned however was the intense trench mortar bombardment that was directed at Death or Glory Sap. A direct hit blew in a portion of the trench, burying four of the garrison. One of the NCOs, Cpl Joseph Mustard, immediately set to work to unearth them and despite mortar rounds landing around him, one of which partially buried him, he continued until he succeeded in rescuing his comrades, an act of coolness and determination for which he was awarded the MM.[63] Although omitted from the monthly 'Casualty Returns', two men were killed, Pte William Logan from Manchester and Pte Samuel Saunt, a thirty-six-year-old married man from Hugglescot. By 9.30 p.m., the battalion were relieved by 1/4th Loyals and retired to the Village Line, with HQ at Fanshawe Castle. B and D Company occupied Canal Bank, with A Company at Pont Fixe and C Company at Windy Corner. There was no rest for the men, as much needed to be done to rebuild and boost the defences and working parties for brigade and battalion were the order for the next couple of days. For the more technical aspects of defensive work, the men, their numbers boosted by the return of the 'B Team' who had arrived from Allouagne, worked under the supervision of the experts from both the RE and the divisional pioneers. Any men not working on these parties were put into one of the numerous carrying parties, delivering stores and munitions to the lines.

The situation behind German lines for members of the battalion captured on 9 April was very poor. Although an accurate figure for those captured on the 9th does not exist, it is possible to estimate this at just under eighty men. Many of these had been wounded before being captured and they were passed along the German medical system. Those not wounded had been kept in a POW cage only 600 yards behind the German front line and were subject to frequent bombardment by British artillery. Of the 2,300 prisoners in the cage at Salomé, some 1,500 were thought to be British. As a result of the nightly shelling, fourteen men from 55 Division were killed and a further eleven wounded. To compound the dangers, the British prisoners had been deprived of their gas masks as soon as they had been captured and the enemy had not seen fit to issue them with a replacement. On 28 April, three men from the battalion, Robert Ralston, Robert Helme, and Joseph Steele were all victims of British fire. These men had been employed on battlefield clearance and also in stretchering off dead bodies to burial sites near the old church in Salomé. When British artillery targeted the general area, the prisoners were herded into the church on Rue Pasteur, where they were abandoned by their captors who all headed for the nearest dugout. Unable to resist the chance of escape, the British captives made a beeline for freedom. Joseph Steele realised he'd forgotten his steel helmet and ran back into the church for it, unfortunately just as a heavy shell scored a direct hit on the building. The twenty-year-old, who had joined the battalion at sixteen in 1914, was killed outright. The story of his death was brought back by his comrades, whose escape was successful, and the treatment of British prisoners investigated later in British Parliamentary Paper No. 19 CD 9106 'The treatment by the Germans of Prisoners of War taken during the Spring Offensives of 1918' (London) 1918.[64] Robert Helme is known to have been the victim of a British air raid, though whether Robert Ralston was killed by shell fire or in the air raid is unknown.

At 11 p.m. on 1 May, the battalion was relieved by 1/7 King's and moved off to Verquigneul as reserve. Relief was always dangerous, as the enemy routinely shelled known routes to and from the front. The presence of the canal made the Givenchy sector riskier, as it reduced the options for transport and produced funnel points that the Germans were only too aware of. During this withdrawal via Canal Bank and Le Preol, twenty-four-year-old Pte Frank Williams from Barrow was badly wounded in the right arm by shrapnel. Unfortunately, this wound was serious enough to require amputation, though the receipt he signed to acknowledge delivery of his Silver War Badge in 1919 shows that he was beginning to cope quite well with writing with his left hand.[65] The battalion reached their billets around 4 a.m. and even though they were in reserve, were still within range of German heavy artillery as they were only 5 miles behind the lines. As they rested through the day of 2 May, a number of gas alerts disturbed their sleep as gas shells from the heavier enemy guns landed in the vicinity at intermittent intervals. During the day seventy-one replacements arrived, which although welcome, did not replace those lost the previous month.

For the CO, adjutant, and the company commanders there was less rest, as they were required to attend a TEWT (Tactical Exercise without Troops) held by Maj.-Gen. Jeudwine at brigade HQ at 5.30 p.m. As had worked so successfully on earlier occasions, there was a codeword to deploy reserve troops to vulnerable positions and 'Bustle' would again bring about this move. This necessarily meant that 3 May was a busy one. Officers and senior NCOs departed to reconnoitre 'Bustle' positions and the best routes there, while the remaining NCOs did their own 'bustling' about, absorbing replacements into the reorganised companies and platoons. Apart from being a sensible precaution anyway, 'Bustle' had been given added impetus by prisoners and deserters who had reported that the enemy were planning an attack for 9 May. There had been a noticeable increase in both air and artillery activity from 2 May and this suggested to the staff that the prisoners may have been correct.[66] Consequently, British artillery fire was stepped up and included the destruction of a large enemy ammunition dump at Salomé on 8 May, with heavy casualties to the troops in the immediate vicinity.

With few working parties needed, training, particularly of Lewis-gunners, continued until 7 May, though a number of men from C and D Company, who had taken part in the attacks on the crater saps on 26 April, were inspected and interviewed by Maj.-Gen. Jeudwine on the 5th. During their stay at Verquigneul, news was passed along of the deaths of a number of men. On 3 May, Pte Albert Fisher from Ulverston died from wounds received some time earlier. On the same day, thirty-one-year-old Pte Ernest May from Birmingham was killed in action. Ernest May had been detached from the battalion in late 1917, posted to division HQ as an observer. He was last seen with one Pte Wallace moving up to the lines and his fate was never determined.[67] On 7 May, Pte Thomas Thompson from Manchester died from his wounds, followed the day after by twenty-seven-year-old 2Lt Arthur Wheatley, a married man from Bradford. Most unusually, the *War Diary* does not mention when Arthur Wheatley was wounded; neither is his arrival with the division, nor his subsequent wounding, recorded in divisional A & Q records, the inescapable conclusion being that he never reached the division and was posted elsewhere when he was mortally wounded. Another man possibly wounded about this time was eighteen-year-old Pte John Calvert from Blackpool. He landed in France in June 1917 and had been about to deploy to the front, when his anxious mother wrote to the Army informing them of her son's real age. 'Army Council Instruction No. 1184' was invoked and the seventeen-year-old pulled back from the Front, though he wasn't returned home. He hadn't been with the battalion long when he was wounded sometime in early May, evacuated back to England, and given a medical discharge in August that year. One who was not enjoying his spell away from the Front was Pte Frederick Tilling. He faced a FGCM on 6 May, for being found asleep at his post, a very serious offence that could lead to the death penalty. Fortunately for him, he received a lesser punishment and eventually rejoined the battalion, only to be wounded later in the war.

In the early hours of 9 May, the battalion relieved 1/5th King's at Givenchy. HQ moved into the same dugout they'd occupied on 1 April, while A Company took the left front, D the centre, and B the right front. C Company remained in a support position in the Keeps. The move into the trenches is described as 'without incident' in the *War Diary*, though the 'Casualty Returns' for May 1918 show that 2Lt Irvine Rouse and seven men were wounded as they moved forward late on 8 May. Until 8 p.m. the only enemy activity had been a few light trench mortar rounds falling around Piccadilly, but this changed when a German observation plane circled low over New Cut (50° 31′ 51.19″ N, 2° 45′ 15.65″ E) and Grenadier Road (50° 31′ 46.74″ N, 2° 44′ 50.04″ E) searching for targets. When white flares were fired from the enemy lines opposite, the aircraft departed, and artillery fire from 5.9s and trench mortars began to fall on both locations. An artillery duel continued until 4 a.m. on the 10th, four men suffering wounds in the exchange of fire.

At 11 a.m. on 10 May, German heavy artillery targeted Givenchy Church (not that any of the building survived, the church left just a bigger mound of mud and rubble than the other ruins) and for three hours 10-cm and 15-cm HE rounds fell around the area. In the early afternoon another low-flying aircraft directed fire onto Gunner Siding and Wolfe Road, thirty-five HE and shrapnel shells hitting these two trenches between 1.45 and 4 p.m. As if this wasn't enough, a trench mortar thought to be sited in Red Dragon Crater (50° 31′ 45.40″ N, 2° 45′ 45.17″ E) fired one round every four minutes onto Piccadilly, King's Road, Moat Farm, or Givenchy Church. This lasted from 4.30 to 8.30 p.m. After darkness fell, this petered out, but the usual harassing fire continued throughout the night. There were bound to be casualties from this amount of shelling, though they were mercifully light, as the heavier rounds—which were capable of destroying dugouts with a direct hit—missed their intended targets. Three men died from the shelling. Nineteen-year-old Pte Harry Daines from Sibil Headingham and thirty-year-old Pte Bertram McVittie from Blackpool and formerly of the 1/5th were both killed outright. Another man from Blackpool, thirty-two-year-old father of three, Pte James Cooper was hit in the chest and died at No. 2 Canadian General Hospital at Le Treport on 16 May. Records survive for four out of the six men wounded that day. Twenty-four-year-old L/Cpl William Jones was wounded in the hand and knee by shrapnel, but returned to the battalion just over two weeks later. (He would rise to Sergeant before he was demobilised.) One of the wounded was another of the old hands who had enlisted on 9 September 1914. Pte John Morgan had been wounded once before, during the attack on Sap L8 in 1915, but this time a serious shrapnel wound to the upper right thigh spelled the end of his military career and the thirty-year-old was medically discharged just after the Armistice. The other two men known to have been wounded were both from Cardiff and had joined the Welsh Regiment only to be amongst a number transferred *en masse* to the 1/4th to replace casualties, part of the batch that arrived on 2 May. Nineteen-year-old Pte Edgar Pinnegar was hit in the right hand by shrapnel and didn't return to the battalion until 7 June. The other Welshman, also aged nineteen, was Pte Thomas Williams, except for him, his five days in the line would be his last, as the wound to his left forearm was serious enough to prevent any more overseas service. On 12 May, two men died from wounds at the CCS at Pernes and it's possible that these were the two 'unknowns' from 10 May, though it's also possible that they may have been casualties from either the 8th or the 9th. Nineteen-year-old Pte Ivor Jones from Devil's Bridge and twenty-four-year-old Pte Herbert Stott MM from Bolton, were both buried at the cemetery next to the CCS.

11 May began quietly enough, no doubt to the relief of the men trying to snatch some rest after the morning stand-to. However, it didn't last and in the afternoon half a dozen 4.2s fell on Givenchy Keep; eight medium-sized trench mortar rounds on The Avenue and The Rookery and another eight on New Cut, near its junction with Cavan Lane (50° 31′ 51.12″ N, 2° 45′ 11.73″ E). The Stokes mortars of the TMB retaliated with fifty rounds to the craters in a frantic half-hour period in the late afternoon. Another German observation aircraft flew low over the lines around 7.20 p.m. but was driven off by anti-aircraft fire from the Vickers and Lewis guns in the trenches. As dusk fell, a heavy mist permeated the area and visibility dropped considerably, though this did not prevent enemy artillery fire from continuing through the night. The same old targets of Windy Corner, Wolfe Road, Grenadier Road, and New Cut received the most attention, though gas shells dropped around the general area intermittently throughout the night. Service records show that on the 11th, twenty-three-year-old Pte William Dent from Ulverston was hit in the chest by shrapnel and evacuated home for treatment, not returning to active service abroad. William Dent was another of the original members, having enlisted in June 1913 and deployed with them in May 1915. Unusually, despite his time at the front, this was his first time in hospital for any reason. Until late March, he had been a lance corporal, but had lost his stripe for having dirty webbing and was probably not sorry to be home once more, especially when he ended up at the Fair View Auxiliary Hospital in Ulverston for

two months. Few soldiers were so lucky, often ending up being treated many miles away from their homes and families.[68]

The morning of Sunday 12 May was very misty again and enemy artillery fire and trench mortars continued to harass for most of the day, only pausing around 3.30 p.m. As the mist cleared, large numbers of German 'sausages' were flown to observe for the artillery. After dark, the bombardment continued until midnight, with ten *Minenwerfer* rounds hitting along King's Road (50° 31′ 43.16″ N, 2° 45′ 28.99″ E) around 9.30 p.m., while eight 4.2s simultaneously fell on Pont Fixe. Around 11 p.m., German 77-mms fired salvoes on South Moor Villas and Windy Corner, eight rounds also landing on the communication trenches between Grenadier Road and Le Plantin. At midnight, the finale consisted of thirty-five 4.2s along the 600m length of the road between Windy Corner and Pont Fixe. There was no let up in the artillery on 13 May either. At 7.45 a.m. nineteen *Minenwerfer* and nine 4.2s fell around Ware Road (50° 31′ 53.67″ N, 2° 45′ 20.82″ E); and in the afternoon, trench mortars targeted King's Road and Piccadilly, while 5.9s concentrated on Wolfe Road.

There were plans for the battalion to the 1/4th's right to make a large raid on enemy positions, so British artillery opened up a preparatory bombardment on the old British (now the German) line, from just north of Finchley Road to just south of Orchard Road. Unfortunately for the men taking part in this raid, their assembly had been spotted and a furious German bombardment was directed onto the Village Line and the Keeps, lasting for over four hours at full intensity and at a reduced rate between 10.30 p.m. until 3 a.m. on the morning of the 14th. It's possible that the enemy believed the 'raid' had been part of a wider attack, as 'spoiling fire' began again in earnest after daylight, despite another low-flying observation aircraft being driven away by MG fire at 7 a.m. From 9.30 a.m. to noon, about 100 5.9s fell along the road from Windy Corner to Pont Fixe, and at 1.30 p.m., one scored a direct hit on an ammunition store at Windy Corner, resulting in a large explosion. Three quarters of an hour later, the Germans sent another reconnaissance plane over Givenchy and shortly afterwards the artillery fire stopped.

That night, artillery targeted Pill Box and also dropped about thirty Blue-X shells on Givenchy. Blue-X was a nasty idea, though not as effective as its designer had hoped. The shells were filled with HE, but also contained in the midst of the explosive charge, a glass bottle full of a solid chemical, diphenylchloroarsine. On detonation, it turned to dust and was spread widely by the explosion. When it was first used in July 1917, diphenylchloroarsine powder was fine enough to penetrate the filters of the respirators, and although not lethal, gave the victim severe sinus pain, caused vomiting and made the victim remove his respirator. When used in conjunction with other lethal chemical agents, it was hoped to cause large numbers of casualties. After its first use, the British introduced an additional layer of filtering material to the canisters which protected the men from Blue-X shells. Despite the vast amount of explosive dropped onto the battalion's positions on 14 May, only two men were killed. Nineteen-year-old Pte Richard Davies from Pontypridd, another of the Welshmen transferred in earlier that month was killed outright, as was Lt Edward Scott-Miller. 2Lt Henry Scaife and eight other ranks were wounded, though the only one for whom records survive is nineteen-year-old Pte Richard Griffiths, who suffered a minor shrapnel wound to his knee. He spent six weeks in hospital before rejoining the battalion, and in spite of his name was not Welsh, but hailed from Manchester.[69]

After a short break, the shell fire began again around 1 a.m. on 15 May, with trench mortars targeting the front line, Givenchy Keep, and Moat Farm. From 3 a.m., 4.2s and 5.9s swept up and down along the Village Line, which continued unabated until 5 a.m. The men did get a break from enemy artillery, but at 10 a.m. about 100 5.9s again swept along the length of the Village Line. All this fire made resupply and any sort of night-time movement in the open extremely hazardous, and although some of the Keeps were connected by underground tunnels, being in the transport section or on any working party was still a risky business. The tunnels went east from Moat Farm and then the subway branched off to Givenchy Keep and on to Mairie Redoubt. The other branch, known as Bunny Hutch Subway, had four entrances close to Bunny Hutch (50° 31′ 49.64″ N, 2° 45′ 21.06″ E) and then continued to an exit at the front line (50° 31′ 50.94″ N, 2° 45′ 31.69″ E). A divisional map has another subway, marked as Coventry West, penned onto it, approximately 300 yards in length, and although only one exit is marked at approximately 50° 31′ 38.87″ N, 2° 45′ 36.00″ E, the eastern end at Coventry Sap almost certainly had an exit, hence the name of the subway.[70]

The remainder of the day is recorded as 'quiet', in the *War Diary*, though around twenty-five 4.2s landed around Givenchy Church and King's Road. At 9.30 p.m. the shelling began again, this time with Blue-X shells; South Moor Villas, Moat Farm, and Herts Redoubt received the initial attention, though New Cut, Grenadier Road, and Le Plantin all received salvoes over a three-hour period. Between 2 and 3 a.m. on the 16th, ten 10-cm shells landed around Fanshawe Castle; and between 4.30 and 7 a.m., twenty-four 15-cm rounds fell in the area between Lambeth Road and the canal. From 10 a.m. until noon, a further fifty-eight of these heavier shells landed at Windy Corner, and thirty-two 77-mms between Givenchy Church and Cheyne Walk. The bombardment from heavy artillery began again in the afternoon with no fewer than seventy-six shells landing at the eastern edge of Windy Corner and Windy Terrace. The heavy fire and poor visibility due to ground mist, which had lingered all day, did not prevent the battalion's snipers from killing three enemy snipers, an outcome which went down well with the entire battalion after all the artillery attention they'd received.

Darkness did not bring an end to the bombardment, with forty 77-mms and ten trench mortar rounds hitting around Givenchy Church between 9.15 and 10.30 p.m., and at 10.30 p.m., fifty gas and HE rounds hitting the Village Line. At 2 a.m. on 17 May, twelve Blue-X shells were fired at Pill Box, near South Moor Villas, and gradually the artillery and trench mortars built up to a crescendo of bombardment across the whole of the front line, not ceasing until 4 a.m. Just under an hour later, the sounds of heavy transport were heard from behind enemy lines and less than an hour after this, increased individual movement by enemy troops was observed in both Grenadier Road and New Rose Trench. Because of the time of day, this movement is unlikely to have been a routine relief and was probably reinforcement in case of a British attack. The rest of the day was remarkably quiet, with almost no shellfire until 8.30 p.m., when 77-mms fired a mixed bombardment of HE and Blue-X at Herts Redoubt and South Moor Villas. At 9 p.m. 1/4th Loyals began to relieve the battalion, which was moving into brigade support—though this relief was not completed until 3 a.m. due to artillery fire, with 120 10-cm rounds landing around Fanshawe Castle in the ten minutes leading up to midnight alone, and Windy Corner receiving occasional Blue-X shells between midnight and 12.45 a.m.

The battalion lost four dead in the shelling of 17 May: 2Lt Adam Thomson; eighteen-year-old Pte Harry Halkon from Garthorpe; nineteen-year-old Pte William Sherlock from Salford; and nineteen-year-old Pte Edward Williamson from Southport. All were noted as 'killed in action'.[71] The shelling, which was far more intense than routinely experienced, wounded five other ranks, but no individual records survive identifying them. The German attack expected on the 9th hadn't materialised, and on the 15th, Maj.-Gen. Jeudwine decided to relax the all-night stand-to which the reserve battalions carried out each night. The *Divisional History* suggests that the attack may have been cancelled because of effective spoiling fire by British artillery.[72] In fact, German accounts suggest that the postponement was actually due to a severe influenza epidemic in this sector, and further demands on German manpower for the next phase of *Kaiserschlacht* (Operation 'Blücher-Yorck' in the Champagne region) undoubtedly reduced their options to replace the sick with men from other areas. The intense artillery fire may possibly have been because the enemy, his forces thus weakened, was concerned that the British would discover this and attack; but it was more likely a strategy to prevent British manpower from being withdrawn from a 'quiet area' to reinforce positions to be attacked in Blücher-Yorck.

Support was not a role the men relished, as they were still close enough to the front to be in danger yet spent much of their time as 'mules' for other units. HQ was yet again at Fanshawe Castle, A Company in Windy Terrace, B in Canal Bank, and C and D at Pont Fixe. During the morning of the 18th, over 150 shells of varying calibres and content were fired into battalion positions, wounding two men; however, the afternoon was quiet. The men were distributed into various working parties, carrying concrete material for bunkers; building wire barricades; clearing ditches; carrying Stokes ammunition; working for the RE; improving dugouts; and extending communication trenches such as Caledonian Road, which ran in a north-easterly direction half way between Givenchy Keep and Moat Farm until it joined Poppy Redoubt (50° 31′ 51.78″ N, 2° 45′ 21.73″ E). Possibly, the safest of the working parties was the one consisting of one officer and sixteen men, which worked in two shifts to pump out the Givenchy tunnels. Though anything but a skive, the shallowness of the water table at Givenchy meant that this task was tantamount to working on the Augean Stables. This pattern of labour virtually repeated itself on the 19th, though for any of the men near Westminster Bridge in the early afternoon, the 250 10-cm shells that fell there in a two-hour period must have been nerve-wracking, and also resulted in another two men wounded.

The battalion was due to move into reserve on the night of the 20th to 21st, so any officers or NCOs who hadn't previously reconnoitred the 'Bustle' positions were sent off to check them out in the afternoon. By 3.25 a.m., the battalion was in its 'Bustle' positions, and when the order to 'stand down' came through at 6.15 a.m., it moved off to billets in Verquigneul. The usual pattern of refitting and cleaning was carried out and the training program instituted.

Reserve was generally safe, though working parties frequently went into the more dangerous areas. The battalion lost one of their men on the 20th, not—as might have been expected—from shell fire, but from illness. Pte John Jones, a twenty-one-year-old from Barrow, had been captured and was a prisoner near Cologne when he died. For other ranks, being a prisoner was no easy life. Food was in short supply and many were put to work close enough to the front to be in danger from Allied artillery fire, and the battalion lost at least three men this way. Many prisoners were put to work in the coal mines, quarries, and factories in Germany, where some, such as Pte James Clegg captured at Guillemont, were injured in accidents. He was working in a coal mine near Munster when a roof fall on Christmas Eve 1916 crushed his leg. The injury turned septic and led to his thigh muscle wasting, for which he was awarded a pension upon his eventual repatriation at the end of the war.[73] There is little doubt that most German medical services near the front line treated British wounded with as much care as their own, but for those prisoners in Germany, neglect and acerbity left a legacy of ill-health evident in numerous pension documents, attributing medical problems to treatment as a POW. When soldiers from the King's Own met some of their freed prisoners after the Armistice, there was widespread anger at the way these had been treated by their captors.[74]

Apart from the occasional working party and a move to the Labour Camp at Drouvin-le-Marais in the afternoon of 23 May, the 1/4th followed reserve routine up until the evening of the 26th, when it began the return journey to the Front. It was to man the same area it had held on 9 April. Unlike the men's previous episode at the Front, their movement into the trenches went off without drama or enemy artillery activity, though during both morning and afternoon fire harassed around the entire sector. After dark, four patrols went out into No Man's Land and each returned intact with nothing untoward to report. For much of the 28th, enemy artillery fire which fell in a haphazard fashion across the sector was more of a nuisance than a serious attempt to obliterate anything. Two men were wounded, as was 2Lt Thomas Pritchard MC, though the lieutenant stayed at his post despite his injury. A patrol from Death or Glory Sap, now very much a mini-Salient after the German advances of 18 April, crept its way out into No Man's Land and observed a German working party. Returning just as stealthily, the patrol then directed Lewis fire against the working party, which rapidly retreated to the Tortoise (50° 31′ 18.02″ N, 2° 46′ 6.24″ E), the German position directly opposite Death or Glory Sap. One of the battalion's snipers in a hide-out in Coventry Crater managed to hit a German, who unwisely raised his head over the parapet in Warlingham Crater, which must have annoyed the enemy as they then brought down artillery fire to destroy a 6-inch trench mortar position in Cheyne Walk, close to Spoil Bank. Enemy artillery fire gradually petered out and ended at 8.15 p.m., the night being quiet for once.

29 May began much like the previous day, with harassing fire from German artillery, though on this day it continued through until 10 p.m. and wounded five men. After dark, a patrol from Death or Glory Sap spotted another German working party about 150-strong, clustered together in a sunken lane (50° 31′ 24.47″ N, 2° 45′ 59.44″ E) less than 200 m to the north-east of the sap. Once more, Lewis gun fire was directed against the party, which dispersed only to reconvene later. This time, the men in Death or Glory Sap's directed artillery fire upon them had the desired effect! (It is still possible to see remnants of this part of the line. Parts of Cheyne Walk, Death or Glory Sap, and the Tortoise endure in a strip of wasteland next to the canal, and in places the original trench line can be discerned. While it is just about possible to penetrate this thick undergrowth in a few spots, the vegetation is so dense that it is hardly worth attempting it … though a winter foray may have more success?)

On the morning of 30 May, the usual harassing fire fell around the battalion's trenches, and it was probably this (rather than the later occasional rounds between Pont Fixe and Windy Corner) that was responsible for the battalion's casualties that day. Thirty-nine-year-old 2Lt Albert Notley from Englefield Green was killed, and eighteen-year-old Pte William Phillips from Shrewsbury badly wounded in the arm and back by shrapnel, and returned to Britain for treatment. According to the 'Casualty Returns', another was wounded, and this was probably thirty-year-old Pte George Parker from Ulverston. Although his service record doesn't have the exact date of his injury, the date of his evacuation back to England would fit in with him being wounded on either 29 or 30 May.

The necessity to stockpile munitions close behind the front line and where they could be rapidly distributed in the event of an attack did make these vulnerable to shell fire. On 31 May, a shell scored a direct hit on one of the grenade dumps and set it ablaze. The bombs immediately began to explode, destroying the shelter the stores were held in. Twenty-seven-year-old Pte Robert Jackson from Lancaster ignored both the hostile bombardment and exploding grenades and tackled the fire, managing to extinguish the flames with buckets of water. His prompt action undoubtedly prevented the fire spreading to the nearby dugouts where other men from the battalion were sheltering, an act which saw the award of the MM for his courage and enterprise.[75]

The battalion was scheduled to be relieved by the Fusiliers and move back into support, but a planned operation for that night turned this into a phased relief. The appearance over two consecutive nights of enemy working parties near the Tortoise had raised Brig.-Gen. Stockwell's curiosity; he decided that the identity of the German regiment involved needed to be ascertained and, if possible, prisoners taken. The right-hand company of the battalion would stay in position while a strong fighting patrol went into No Man's Land with the aim of interdicting the enemy. It made absolute sense for the British line to be held by men from the same battalion as the fighting patrol, as this considerably reduced the chances of friendly fire. At 11.50 p.m. the patrol returned and reported that the enemy working party had not made an appearance and the Fusiliers took over from the right-hand company. By 2.30 a.m. on the 31st the relief had been completed, and the battalion now held the support positions in the Village Line. At Pont Fixe, A Company had two platoons as a permanent garrison, with three platoons of D Company minus one of their Lewis sections with them. B Company occupied Canal Bank and C Company had two platoons at Windy Corner. At Windy Switch, one platoon from D Company plus the additional Lewis section provided the defending force. Working parties laboured throughout the night, be it carting supplies to the men in the front line or providing the muscle power for the RE. During this work, signals officer 2Lt Thomas Bateson was wounded by a gas shell, and a thirty-two-year-old married man from Waterfoot, Pte George Ashworth, was seriously wounded, expiring on the way to the RAP.

1 June was a fairly quiet day as far as enemy artillery activity was concerned, although there was some harassing fire in the morning. Men were required for the usual working parties. Indirect fire from MGs caused a number of casualties among them, with 2Lt Allen Whitmore collecting his second wound in two months and twenty-three-year-old Pte Edward Templeton from Whitehaven sustaining a wound to the head that led to his eventual medical discharge. Nineteen-year-old Pte Gilbert Long from Newport (in Monmouthshire), suffering from the effects from a gas shell, was treated by the Field Ambulance later that night, but soon rejoined the battalion. Just one of the casualties was fatal, nineteen-year-old Pte Percival Doe from Essex. 2 June saw some of the men in the working parties wounded by indirect MG fire, though there were no fatalities. There was partial respite from the fatigue parties, as these were ended at 11 a.m. on 3 June to allow the men to prepare to move back into the front line, relieving the Loyals in the left sector of Givenchy. Despite the break from working parties, there were still casualties from enemy shell fire that day: Capt. Rolland Metcalfe and twenty-four-year-old Pte Stephen Pothecary from Fleetwood were both wounded, the latter with a shrapnel wound to the left arm which required treatment back in England.

The move forward went without a single hitch or casualty. B Company manned the Keeps, with D to the left front, A to the centre and C the right front. 4 June was a quiet day and patrols failed to make contact with the enemy. Once darkness fell, the battalion tasked working parties to labour on the exposed sections of the defences and wiring parties out into No Man's Land to repair and strengthen defences, a pattern repeated most nights the battalion held the front. Behind the front, on the nights of the 4th and the 5th, heavy German bombardments targeted the rear areas in both the Givenchy and Beuvry sections held by 55 Division with mustard and various other types of gas. Constant harassing fire from artillery across the whole of the battalion's sector began on the 5th and Lt Joseph Rudduck was critically wounded, dying shortly after arriving at the RAP. The precautions taken to improve the wire were more than just routine, as German prisoners had indicated that there was yet another offensive planned. Consequently, on 6 June, when it became clear to the battalion that they would be relieved within a couple of days, officers and senior NCOs went to reconnoitre 'Bustle' positions. 7 June saw enemy artillery and MG fire increase markedly, an indication that the prisoners may have been correct, especially as this continued into the 8th. This was far from one-sided, as the division's own artillery fired as many rounds as possible into the enemy's rear areas, where ammunition and men may have been concentrated in readiness for attack.

1/5th King's moved into the forward area to relieve the battalion, and by 2 a.m. on 9 June this was complete. This time, the battalion had been far less fortunate as they retired to the 'Bustle' positions. Enemy artillery including gas, shrapnel, and HE rounds caused a number of casualties, many of whom were serious losses for the battalion. Of the six killed that night, the three Sergeants had all won the MM on 9 April. Twenty-five-year-old Sgt George Watson from London and Sgt Thomas Rathbone from Pendleton died where they were hit. Twenty-eight-year-old Sgt Thomas Robinson died soon after reaching the RAP. Another to die at the RAP was Pte William Lawson from Durham. Both nineteen-year-old Pte Robert Sandlands from Nantwich and twenty-three-year-old Pte Thomas Sharp from Preston were killed outright. All these men are buried at Houchin. Another man from the battalion to die from wounds that night was thirty-four-year-old Cpl John Kenyon MM from Blackburn. Unfortunately, his record does not give the date of his injury, but from the location of his burial at Pernes, it is likely that he was wounded at the same time as Lt Rudduck. A touching letter from his widow survives in his service record, requesting that Fred, their six-year-old son, be allowed to receive his father's MM at the medal presentation parade.[76] There must also have been more men wounded as they moved back from the front, but the only surviving record of a casualty is for 2Lt Benjamin Pemberton MC, making this a very expensive night for the battalion. Once it became clear that the enemy had no dawn attack planned, the 1/4th moved from its 'Bustle' positions at 5.30 a.m. into to the reserve position at Drouvin.

The time until 14 June was occupied with lectures on 'Trench Discipline', 'Mustard Gas', 'Counter-Battery Work'; and training on these various weapons on the range—an activity in which 2Lt Donald Shutt was accidentally wounded, though luckily not seriously. Two men from the battalion are both listed as 'Killed in Action' during this period and their deaths raise a number of questions. The first of these, Pte Sam Wood from Bolton, died on 10 June and is buried at Schoonselhof Cemetery near Antwerp. Both the CWGC and *Soldiers Died* assign him to the 1/4th, though the 'Medal Roll' gives 2/ King's Own as his unit. Although his number is a 2nd Battalion number, they were then in Bulgaria, and it's likely he'd been posted to the 1/4th at an earlier date. Schoonselhof was also behind the German lines, so he must have been a POW at the time of his death. Also buried in German-held territory and listed as 'Killed in Action' on 12 June is Pte Henry Roberts, at Carvin. As both these men were prisoners they either were killed by Allied shellfire after being set to work in a war zone or died from wounds, injury, or disease, and *Soldiers Died* is in error. One man was unlucky enough to be severely injured about as far away from the scene of action as it was possible to get. Pte Lewis Snowdon, a Cornish farmer, had been wounded on the Salient and had a finger amputated as a result. Medically downgraded, he'd been posted to 3/ King's Own that February and was home on leave when, on 12 June, he lifted a saucepan of boiling water off the stove and the handle came off; the water badly scalded his leg and foot.

Late on 14 June, the battalion returned to the front by bus and by the early hours of the 15th were back in the Givenchy sector as support battalion. The men were tasked to the usual working parties, though German artillery was much quieter than when they left. One casualty on the 16th was not due to the enemy. Twenty-year-old Thomas Haworth from Burnley was, as far as I can tell, the only member of the battalion to be shot twice by his own side! The first time was on 21 March that year, when he was in 1/ King's Own. His section NCO, L/Cpl Williams, negligently discharged his rifle while cleaning it in the trenches, hitting Haworth in the thigh. The lance corporal was detained for his negligence and after his recovery, the victim posted to the 1/4th, joining Lt Shutt's 15 Platoon. On 16 June, Haworth was shot again, this time by himself when cleaning his rifle in the cellar of the old divisional canteen at Windy Terrace. His right hand was over the muzzle of his rifle as he reached down to remove the magazine with his left, catching the trigger and sending a round straight through his right hand. Apart from the actual offence of 'negligently wounding himself', he was also guilty of having a live round in the breech when it should have been clear, and of not having applied the safety catch. Shutt spoke up for him at his FGCM, describing him as, 'A very conscientious soldier in all his work'.[77] This obviously swayed the court martial to some extent, for Haworth was sentenced to a remarkably lenient twenty-eight days' Field Punishment No. 1—far less than the six-month detention that most men got for the same offence, which lends weight to the idea that this was a complete accident. On this same day, Pte Wilfred Shipperbottom, a twenty-two-year-old from Bolton captured earlier that year, died from his wounds and was buried in Hamburg. The following day, another of their wounded, nineteen-year-old Pte Eric Friar from St Helens, died from wounds at one of the CCSs near Wimereux.

On 17 June, four platoons moved into the front line to relieve a similar number of platoons from 2/5th Fusiliers. The rest of the battalion moved forward on the 18th and though there were no casualties in this move, the Fusiliers carried out a raid on the German lines and in retaliation, the enemy shelled the front-line trenches, wounding a number of men. One of these was nineteen-year-old Pte Sidney Minter from Nottingham. He was evacuated to the 2nd Canadian Hospital with severe mustard gas burns to his back, and then back to England on the Hospital Ship Newhaven, and played no further part in the war. Another of the casualties was twenty-seven-year-old Pte George Thompson from Dalton, who had enlisted in September 1914 and was wounded for his fifth time. At Gillemont Farm he had been partially buried by a shell which left him bruised and dazed and suffering his third attack of shell shock. Yet this brave young man was back in the trenches five days later and soldiered on until the 18th, when a serious shrapnel wound to the left buttock saw his evacuation back to England. Upon his recovery at the end of August 1918, it was obviously felt that he had done his bit and he was posted to the depot at Heaton Park. Although 19 June was a fairly quiet day with patrols and working parties active after dark, nineteen-year-old Pte Frederick Austin from Rothwell was killed. Another who died on the 19th was a twenty-year-old from Berkshire, Pte Archibald Balding. He had been wounded sometime earlier in the month and died from his wounds at hospital in St Omer.

20 June saw little enemy activity, as C Company were in trouble. Fifty men had gone down with food poisoning—unpleasant enough under any circumstances, but catastrophic in the trenches, and these needed to be evacuated as quickly as possible. One of those affected was nineteen-year-old Pte Samuel Waterfall from Manchester, though he was well enough to rejoin his company after twenty-four hours. As a stop gap, a platoon was brought forward from Herts Redoubt to strengthen the depleted company. Even so, the battalion still sent patrols out into No Man's Land after dark, but they met no enemy opposition whatsoever. The battalion was still receiving a steady trickle of replacements for their casualties and for the first time in ages, the number of replacements actually exceeded the number of casualties for the month, though only by four! Most of the replacements tended to fall into two categories at this time, either fresh young lads recently conscripted and as 'green' as anything, or men transferred *en masse* from the Labour Corps into the infantry. Many of the latter were of an age or medical standard that would have been considered unsuitable for infantry work a year previously, but the demand for manpower was great enough for this to be overlooked. One such was Pte Walter Howkins from Leicester, who claimed to be thirty-two when he enlisted in July 1916, but was actually forty. He had served in the Labour Corps until being wounded in the shin and neck by shrapnel in January 1918, and upon leaving hospital was transferred to the 1/4th. Another from the Labour Corps was a thirty-nine-year-old postman from Thetford, Pte Thomas Beeton. One of the replacement officers who definitely did not fit into the category of 'green' was thirty-year-old Lt Harold Pobgee MC. He had gone to France with 5th Dragoon Guards, transferred to 1/5th King's Own in March 1916, and after winning the MC as their RSM, was commissioned into the 1/4th.

Enemy artillery activity began to pick up again on the 21st and one shell killed or injured ten men from A Company when it struck their post in Grenadier Road (50° 31′ 46.74″ N, 2° 44′ 50.04″ E). While the bombardment was still ongoing, twenty-nine-year-old L/Sgt Sidney Dickinson from Ulverston dug out two of his men who had been buried by the blast, and treated the wounded, organising their evacuation to the RAP. Killed outright were twenty-four-year-old Pte Archibald Vaughan, originally from Runcorn but resident in Barrow, and thirty-eight-year-old Pte Richard Jones MM from Manchester. Thirty-five-year-old Pte Hilton Coupe from Blackburn died the next day, as did twenty-two-year-old Sgt John Banks from Ulverston; twenty-two-year-old Pte William Frith from Croydon; nineteen-year-old Pte Horace Jackson from Greenodd; and twenty-eight-year-old Pte William Rowlands from Manchester. Known to have been wounded but survived were L/Sgt Edward Edwardson from Liverpool, hit in the leg by shell splinters; nineteen-year-old Pte Clarence Townshend from Manchester, wounded so badly in the leg and knee that he was given a medical discharge; and nineteen-year-old Liverpool grocer Pte William Williams, wounded by splinters in the left arm. It's possible that twenty-three-year-old Pte Thomas Eccles MM from Skerton, who died from wounds on 26 June, was an eleventh casualty of that day. L/Sgt Dickinson's prompt and courageous actions saved the lives of two of his comrades and steadied his men, many shaken by their experience. He was awarded the MM for this and though his recommendation is dated the 22nd, it is clear from the *War Diary* that the incident referred to is that of the 21st.[78]

Between 8 a.m. and 9 a.m. of 22 June, enemy artillery bombarded HQ, wounding the assistant adjutant, 2Lt Alfred Thorpe. Once the sun had set, the usual patrols crept into No Man's Land, this time successfully locating an enemy working party in between Northern Craters and New Rose

Trench (approximately 50° 31′ 59.76″ N, 2° 45′ 26.47″ E). The patrol retired as stealthily as it had deployed and a concerted attack with artillery, trench mortars, and rifle grenades was made upon the working party. 23 June was a much quieter day, although during the afternoon, trench mortars fired a few rounds into Givenchy and nineteen-year-old Pte William Chappell from Gloucestershire spent a couple of days in hospital suffering from mustard gas burns. The task given to the enemy working party of the previous night must have been of some importance as it was spotted again that night and once more successfully engaged with artillery. The intermittent artillery fire from enemy guns continued into 24 June, though no casualties resulted from this and with relief impending, officers reconnoitred 'Bustle' positions. The enemy working party did not make an appearance on the 24th, but was back again on the night of the 25th and this time driven off by rifle grenade and Lewis fire. German artillery and trench mortars had targeted the Keeps and choke-points, such as Windy Corner, at intermittent periods over the day, though no casualties had resulted—a situation that was to change for the worse on the next day.

Throughout 26 June, the battalion made repeated requests for retaliation for the accurate artillery and trench mortar fire that was beginning to cause casualties. Nineteen-year-old Pte Harold Southern from Northwich and Pte George Wood from Burslem were both killed outright, and others wounded. There was far less fire on the 27th, as the battalion prepared to handover to 1/7 King's in the early hours of the 28th. Just after 1 a.m. the handover was completed and the men withdrew to the 'Bustle' positions near Le Preol. Once the all clear had been given, most of the battalion moved into the reserve positions at Drouvin. Both A and B Company each had to supply two platoons to garrison the defences at Westminster and Vauxhall Bridges, which would hardly have been a popular task given the attention from German heavy artillery both these locations received. For the rest of the men, hot baths, clean uniforms, and a day's rest awaited them at the camp at Drouvin; they carried out the same old program of training and range firing, remaining there until 3 July. The casualty bill for June was ninety-three men of all ranks, twenty of whom were killed or died from their wounds—a result of enemy action during a period of routine activity. No figures for men reporting sick survive, but the numbers were probably quite low given that the climate was clement.

# 12

# 3 July 1918 – 11 November 1918
# The Last 100 Days

Much has been written about the varying stages of morale of the British Army during the war, but a really accurate and all-encompassing statement on the subject is just not possible. Morale varied not just from unit to unit, but from to individual to individual within them; a man asked how he might feel one day may give a very different response the next. Letters home are never an especially reliable guide to morale, for soldiers rarely speak their true mind back to their loved ones, either understating or overstating their true feelings. Interviews given to eager historians in later life are clouded by time, an awareness of modern attitudes, and feelings of national betrayal in the post-war years. Trench newspapers from the period must be read through the eyes of a soldier, as humorous over- or understatement was and still is a feature of soldiers' magazines; but these are not a reflection of the men's actual morale. Some historians argue that the Battles of the Somme and Passchendaele destroyed optimism and instilled a sense of fatalism among soldiers, and there is probably some currency to this—though this would again vary in degree from unit to unit. In 2003, Gordon Corrigan cites an intelligence report written for the American Expeditionary Force on 28 March 1918, during the grimmest days of *Kaiserschlacht*.

The morale of the British officer and man is just what would be expected of the British soldier. They do not have the attitude of a year ago, but they do show that they are full of fight. One gains the impression that they are out to stay with it to the last regardless of cost.[1]

But what of the 1/4th? A year after the war had ended, Lt-Col. Gardner MC (then still a major), who had been with the battalion throughout its deployment, recalled the period between May and August 1918 thus:

The spirit which now prevailed amongst our troops was restrained optimism. This feeling had an intangible quality, gossamer in texture, more tacit than expressed, but everywhere radiating good cheer, and hope for the near future. The power of the enemy's attack appeared to have been definitely broken, while the time was approaching when our own irresistible advance was to reach a triumphant conclusion.[2]

On 3 July, the battalion moved back into the line without incident, relieving 1/6th King's in the right sub-sector. Just before dawn, the battalion went to stand-to and sent four patrols into No Man's Land. German artillery was quiet, but its snipers were fully alert and one man was wounded on the 4th, a score evened up by the battalion's own snipers the following day. The usual trench maintenance needed to be carried out and for both sides, the dark presented an opportunity to strengthen and wire against future incursions. The enemy sniping team was less active from the 7th onwards, whereas the battalion's snipers claimed two of the enemy that day and another on the 8th. The downturn in enemy sniping was replaced by an increase in artillery fire. On the 7th, there was a direct hit by a 4.2 on the dugout occupied by the signallers from B and D Company in Gunner Siding South (50° 31′ 31.07″ N, 2° 45′ 14.94″ E). There are some discrepancies between the dates given in the battalion's 'Casualty Return', the dates written in service records, and the dates of death as listed by CWGC, but it seems clear that all these refer to this one incident as reported in the *War Diary* for 7 July. The 'Casualty Return' gives a total of eleven men wounded and three killed (all for the 8th). According to CWGC, nineteen-year-old Pte Herbert Knox from Belfast and thirty-five-year-old Pte William Shaw from Huddersfield were reported killed on the 9th. Thirty-year-old Pte George Merritt from Manchester was taken to the West Lancashire Field Hospital, and then on to 4th Canadian CCS at Pernes with a serious thigh wound, where he died on 9 July.[3] Twenty-two-year-old Pte Robert Jones from Wales was badly wounded and his left arm amputated after he was evacuated back to England.[4] Also known to be wounded was Pte Samuel Waterfall, evacuated home with his right elbow shattered and wounds to his right leg and thigh. He was given a medical discharge after a partial amputation to his right leg. Of the other nine wounded, no record survives.

Although enemy sniper activity had reduced over the previous days, it didn't do to let one's guard down, as there was usually at least one on the alert. It was particularly dangerous in the communication trenches running at right angles to the front line, as a sniper in an elevated position on one of the crater lips had a good line of sight along these if anybody forgot to bend low as they walked along them. On 10 July, twenty-two-year-old 2Lt Edgar Veevers, who had been with the battalion a year and was not inexperienced, was killed by a single shot as he moved along Piccadilly. The shot probably came from one of the E Sap Craters (50° 31′ 47.76″ N, 2° 45′ 42.95″ E), for these gave a sniper the perfect angle into Piccadilly at a range of only 200 m. To the accompaniment of high winds, rain, and thunder—which for once was natural and not from artillery fire—the battalion moved back to support on 11 July, its place in the line taken by the Fusiliers. The move was without incident, though shell fire earlier in the day had wounded two men and killed Pte William Chappell, just back from hospital after being gassed on 23 June, outright.

The torrential rain, which continued to fall on 12 July, made movement along communication trenches difficult. Every available man was required for working and carrying parties, never popular at the best of times, but utterly miserable when conditions were like that. The working parties on 13 July and the following few days were mainly engaged in carrying bags of cement and aggregate to enable the RE to build additional dugouts and reinforce existing ones. Although this was hard work, the men could see that they would benefit from their labours. Intermittent shelling of support lines continued and a number of casualties ensued. On the 13th, Pte William Poppelwell from Birkenhead was killed outright and twenty-two-year-old Cpl Edward Greaves from Blackpool died after reaching the RAP. Four men were also wounded; there is no surviving record of their names, but one of them may have been Pte Charles Eastham from Croston, as the twenty-year-old died from his wounds at the CCS at Pernes on 15 July—although it's also possible that he was the man recorded wounded on 14 July. On 15 July, officers and sergeants reconnoitred special 'Bustle' positions in the Beuvry-

Cambrin Line, for abnormally high levels of movement to the German rear areas had been observed over three days, and High Command thought that the enemy may be preparing for an attack. Late on 16 July, 1/7th King's relieved the battalion, which moved into the 'Bustle' positions before marching back to Drouvin Camp at 6.30 a.m. on the 17th.

The day of rest would have been particularly welcome, as it was synonymous with hot baths, clean uniforms, and hot food, even if the following day's training schedule started with a run at 6.15 a.m.! Once evening fell, men were assigned to various working parties and the toil began again. The next morning saw most of the battalion thus occupied, though the RSM took the latest recruits for his own special brand of training! Forty-one men and three officers had already joined the battalion that month as replacements, and another officer and thirty-eight men arrived on the 21st, though not all of these were new recruits. Thirty-year-old CQMS Joseph Northmore had been CQMS at the depot in Oswestry before his posting to France. Pte Thomas Jones, though only twenty, had first gone to France in June 1916 with 11/ King's Own, been wounded and posted to 1/ King's Own, and after recovering from another wound in May 1918, now found himself with the 1/4th. One of the 'green' recruits was Pte Howard Ince—or 'Sidney Ince', or even 'Sidney Howard Ince', depending on which enlistment form one reads. He appears to have been a 'serial' enlister, having enlisted at least twice previously before being found out and discharged as underage. Quite how he got away with lying about his age the third time he enlisted in October 1917, declaring himself eighteen years and one month old, is a mystery. His true age was only disclosed when he re-enlisted post-war. Once conscription was in full swing, false enlistment was virtually impossible, the only explanation being a false registration with parental connivance. Ince's true date of birth was 5 December 1899.

Training and working parties may have taken up much of the men's time, but sport was always played whenever possible. New officers, many of whom now came from the non-horse-owning class, had to be taught to ride, and ball games were always popular. On the morning of 19 July, men were required for a number of working parties; although there were no casualties from enemy action, 2Lt Norman Hutley managed to end up at the RAP with a self-inflicted, but not serious wound. In the afternoon, the battalion held practices for rugby and cricket, two games not universally played by the men, but both of which were well-liked. The battalion had been challenged to a rugby match against 1/3 West Lancashire Field Ambulance and on the 20th, so practice was held to choose the team who would take on the medics. On Sunday 21st, after church parade, the match against the Field Ambulance was held on a rock-hard pitch at Ruitz. Unfortunately, the medics, no strangers to rugby, soundly beat the battalion, whose strength lay with the more traditional soccer. The hard pitch also took its toll in bruises and other injuries and Maj. Gardner's face was badly cut from contact with the ground. The final batch of thirty-eight replacements also arrived that day, led by twenty-nine-year-old 2Lt Harling Richardson DCM. He was actually newly commissioned into the Loyals, but had been posted directly to the 1/4th upon his arrival back in France. His original enlistment had been into 7/ King's Own, and as a corporal he'd won the DCM at La Boiselle in 1916. Monday 22nd was the last day in reserve for the battalion before it moved forward to relieve 1/7th King's in the left sub-sector, without a single casualty.

Despite the miserable weather on 23 July, the battalion had four patrols out in No Man's Land. Yet there was no enemy activity, unlike further north of Givenchy in the neighbouring division's front, where the enemy was far more dynamic and a strong raiding party had penetrated British lines. The days of rain had left all the communication trenches in very poor shape, and as usual this made movement along them by ration and resupply parties arduous and unpleasant. Conditions had not improved on 24 July, but the battalion still sent three patrols out into No Man's Land. Although the *War Diary* reported the day quiet and 'Casualty Return' contains no entries within a five-day window of the 24th, there does appear to have been one man killed. L/Cpl James Lynch from Preston was killed in action and has no known grave, commemorated instead on the Loos Memorial.[5] There was one other death on the 24th: thirty-three-year-old Pte Albert Barron, a married father of two from Blackburn, died from pneumonia while a POW. The weather improved marginally on the 25th, the rain becoming intermittent rather than continuous, but ground conditions were still vile. During the early hours, three patrols were sent out to attack a couple of enemy positions; as these were found to be unoccupied, the patrols returned without gain, though further patrols were sent out just before dawn as part of the routine early-warning procedure. Although the patrols had been fruitless, there were casualties from the intermittent shelling and the battalion lost the services of twenty-three-year-old L/Cpl John Seed, who, badly wounded by shrapnel, was evacuated home to play no further part in the war.

The improvement in the weather had merely been temporary, and on 26 July, as the battalion was relieved by 2/5th Fusiliers, the rain fell in sheets, drenching the men and turning the communication trenches into rivers of mud. It wasn't until 3 a.m. that the last of the battalion reached support lines and the codeword 'Rissoles' was sent to tell brigade that the battalion was in position—not that the men were all in one place anyway, because as soon as platoons reached support they were sent off on numerous working parties. Burdened by heavy loads, these men slipped and slid along yet more communication trenches. It was at times like these that morale must have been at its lowest. The availability of hot baths and clean uniforms the next morning was a great tonic, though in the afternoon more working parties were sent to help the RE and the divisional Tunnelling Company, the absolute antithesis of a tonic and repeated on the 28th and 29th.

The division wished to fool the enemy into thinking that an attack was being prepared and as part of this deception, the RAF deployed a number of aircraft over British lines. Consequently, German artillery fire increased, though casualties from this were light, with just four men suffering wounds between the 28 and 30 July. One was twenty-year-old L/Sgt Harry Smith, a quarryman from Ulverston, whose record merely reports him being 'gassed' on the 29th. There is, however, much more to this story than would appear. An air raid on the Brewery (50° 31′ 22.71″ N, 2° 44′ 51.22″ E) at Pont Fixe resulted in a direct hit on one of the concrete shelters, and one man was trapped in the shelter, pinned down by a fallen concrete beam. Smith risked being crushed by further collapse of the ruined shelter, and despite the asphyxiating fumes from the explosive, he managed to free this man and bring him to the surface. Once back in the fresh air, the courageous NCO collapsed due to the toxic fumes and was later awarded the MM for this rescue.[6]

On 30 July, thirty-nine-year-old Pte John Dalton from Carlisle, attached to the TMB, was wounded in the right hand by shrapnel, though he remained at duty after having his wound dressed. More seriously wounded was nineteen-year-old Pte Hubert Williams from Colwyn Bay, whose multiple shrapnel wounds led to his medical discharge. The last few days of July saw plenty of sunshine and high temperatures, which, although it meant the men were not soaked to the skin the whole time, caused problems of its own, for drinking water was always a rare and valuable commodity in the front line. At 6 p.m. on 30 July, a gradual relief of the Loyals in the right sub-sector began, and was completed without incident shortly after midnight. Five patrols were sent out, returning through the early morning mist around 8 a.m. The clear weather meant that the RAF was also much in evidence on the 31st, but although the enemy were alert, there was little activity from them. British 4.5-inch howitzers concentrated on cutting German wire around the Tortoise during the day, and after dark the battalion sent a number of patrols over to the German lines; these only returned after dawn, one from D Company complete with a single prisoner. One of the patrol commanders, 2Lt Frederick Shuker was wounded, but his men managed to bring him back to friendly lines.

After dark on 1 August, another five patrols went out to reconnoitre enemy outposts. Meanwhile, other men were occupied in putting up yet more wire in front of the battalion's positions or working on improving the shelters in Gunner Siding. When the patrols returned after dawn on the 2nd, they reported that the enemy observation line was unoccupied, a situation that was too opportune not to exploit. After dark, posts were placed forward and consolidated throughout the night. A patrol that had gone out at 5.15 p.m. discovered that there were also a series of shell holes with good dugouts in them, and these too were occupied in the early hours of 3 August, two further patrols being despatched to reconnoitre the German wire and positions further east of these new gains. Numerically, these acquisitions had come at a fairly low cost, with just five men wounded (two on the 2nd, and another three on the 3rd). Tragically for the battalion, one of the wounded from the 2nd was the redoubtable Sgt Arthur Birkett DCM, MM. He had been hit in the left leg, a wound that spelt the end of his active service. One of those wounded on the 3rd was twenty-two-year-old Pte John Allcock, hit in the right knee by shrapnel, also saw his participation in the war concluded by this injury. After being relieved by 1/7th King's, the battalion proceeded to its 'Bustle' positions near Le Preol, German 4.2 artillery rounds falling close to them as they retired.

Once they had been stood down at 5 a.m. on 4 August, the men marched to Drouvin Camp and in the afternoon were given hot baths and clean uniforms. They remained there until 9 August, the time spent on training, sport, and military competitions, such as the brigade 'Concertina Wire Competition', in which 5 Platoon represented the battalion. On the 8th, the battalion cricket competition was won by the signallers and prior to the concert party that evening, His Majesty the King visited and presented L/Cpl Jimmy Hewitson with his VC and Lt William Jenks (USMORC) with his MC. Later the next day, the battalion travelled back up the line by light railway and relieved 1/5th King's who were supporting the right sub-sector. The stormy weather of the previous few days had abated and the air was again extremely hot. With the battalion in dugouts around Pont Fixe there was much to be done, and many working parties were tasked to the RE. The area was constantly shelled by the enemy, though no casualties ensued over the first three days. The battalion's position in support meant that working parties were required both day and night and personnel got little rest. HQ was in a large dugout at Barge House, which for over an hour in the evening of 11 August was subjected to a heavy bombardment. Things quietened down after dark, and despite an enemy air raid on Le Preol, the battalion suffered no casualties. After dark on the 12th, a move forward to relieve 2/5th Fusiliers in the right sub-sector went off without any enemy interference.

During the day of 13 August, British artillery was engaged in wire-cutting to the battalion's front, an activity that always made the enemy nervous and hostile artillery fire predictably likely. A Company in Coventry Sap (50° 31′ 38.90″ N, 2° 45′ 43.02″ E) suffered particularly badly, losing four killed and another eight wounded. The four killed, all privates, were twenty-year-old Robert Faith from Darlington; nineteen-year-old Matthew Loftus from Widnes; twenty-two-year-old Edward Mitchell from Padiham; and eighteen-year-old Fred Shakespeare from West Bromwich. On 14 August, there was little let-up, and the enemy even shelled their own wire. Yet the battalion still sent out a patrol during daylight hours, which penetrated right up to A Sap (50° 31′ 39.59″ N, 2° 45′ 50.43″ E) and found it unoccupied. The patrol commander, 2Lt Clarence Holland, crawled forward to peer over the lip of the crater, and was immediately shot through the head by an enemy sniper who had spotted the patrol. Ignoring the risk to his own life, Cpl Ernest Greenough crawled forward to check his leader for signs of life and, finding none, removed his personal effects before withdrawing the patrol without further loss and bringing back information that was to prove vital for a forthcoming operation, actions which earned him the MM.[7] Casualties from the afternoon bombardment were light, though one of the wounded had only been with the battalion for five weeks. Twenty-one-year-old Pte John Leeming from Manchester was hit in the left shoulder by shrapnel and evacuated home, never to return to France. This was his second time as a casualty, having first been wounded with 1/ King's Own in March 1918.

Casualty figures made a huge leap on 15 August, when in the early morning the enemy bombarded the lines with a mixture of mustard and 'sneezing gas' (Blue-X).[8] 'Casualty Returns' show that a total of fifty-nine men were gassed, though most returned within a few days or weeks.[9] Among those affected were thirty-three-year-old Pte Frederick Beard from Oswaldtwistle (his third wound of the war); thirty-one-year-old Sergeant Richard Cross from Preston; and two nineteen-year-old Privates Richard Griffiths from Manchester and George Tomlinson from Birkenhead. When British artillery stopped targeting the German wire on the 16th, the intensity of enemy artillery fire slackened noticeably. On the same day, some men were placed into quarantine due to a suspected case of cerebro-spinal meningitis—the MO took no chances when it came to an epidemic breaking out, as the battalion had already suffered fatalities from this disease during the war.[10]

The 17th is described as a 'quiet day', though there was patrol activity from both sides. The battalion sent three patrols out to examine the ground around Warlingham Crater and an enemy patrol managed to get close enough to one of the battalion's posts to wound two men with a grenade. In a separate, but un-described incident, twenty-year-old L/Cpl Thomas Else from Bolton was killed. The weather on 18 August was fine and as there was little serious artillery activity, both sides took advantage of this to work on their defences. One night patrol discovered a large enemy working party repairing the damage to their wire and dispersed it with well-aimed fire. The battalion suffered another four gas casualties that day, with twenty-six-year-old Capt. Sidney Walker from Liverpool, 2Lt Norman Smith, and 2Lt L. E. Wharton (on attachment from the Lincolnshire Regiment) all requiring treatment. The final gas casualty, Pte Septimus Derdle from Barrow, had originally enlisted with the battalion in August 1914, but had also served with both 1/5th and 8th Battalion, and this was his fourth wound of the war; he was, however, back with his platoon less than a month later. On the 19th—the final day the battalion spent in the front line before being relieved—British artillery again concentrated on cutting the German wire, with a predictable response from enemy artillery and increased activity from enemy aircraft over the British lines. Fortunately, only one man was wounded by all this unwelcome attention.

The 20th saw the battalion back at Vaudricourt Camp with 2/5th Fusiliers. On the 21st, the officers and NCOs of both battalions were briefed by Brig.-Gen. Stockwell about a forthcoming attack on the Craters; both groups then studied a large-scale model of their objectives. For two men from the battalion, the 21st was also a day of reckoning. Pte Henry Caton, who had been court-martialled in October of 1917 for shooting himself in the foot, and Pte William James were both up before another court martial, this time charged with desertion. Desertion at home was serious enough, but desertion in theatre was going to have only one, ultimate conclusion if they were found guilty. The evidence was clear enough and both men were sentenced to be shot. Luckily for them, this was commuted to five years' imprisonment for Caton and seven years' penal servitude for James. Both must have spent many a sleepless night waiting to hear the final outcome of the Army commander's decision on their sentence.

For the rest of the battalion, the next day was spent on briefings and preparation for the attack, which was scheduled for 24 August. Some replacements arrived on the 22nd, though it's unlikely that they would have been involved in the assault on the Craters, as it was policy to break in new arrivals before using them in any attacks. One was twenty-two-year-old Pte Peter Brannan from Carlisle, who had been with 1/ King's Own, but upon his recovery from wounds was posted to the 1/4th. (Later he would earn the wrath of authority when, as a guard on a working party of German prisoners on 26 July 1919, he allowed two of them to escape, luckily just getting the telling-off of a lifetime as punishment.) Two men from the battalion are recorded to have died on the 23rd. The first, eighteen-year-old Pte George Mansell from Leicester, died from wounds and was buried at Pernes. The second man, twenty-five-year-old Pte Edward Jackson from Blackburn, is shown as killed in action. However, his burial location at Leuze and the fact that battalion records do not show any casualties for that day suggest that he was yet another POW who was killed while working too close to the Front. The 23rd was a very busy day, with all the final arrangements to be made and the battalion taking up its starting positions in the line, while HQ situated itself in Givenchy Tunnel.

For some men, their mission began soon after dark on 23 August, when they crawled forward into No Man's Land. Led by 2Lt Richardson, two platoons began to quietly cut gaps in their own wire and then the enemy's, before laying up silently in their jumping-off positions. By 2.20 a.m., all the men from the two attacking companies (C and D) were in position, a full five hours before the appointed time of attack. The German lines were remarkably quiet through the night, with no sign that they were expecting trouble. Although a few flares had been sent up, the disciplined men from the attacking companies remained motionless, their khaki uniforms blending into the broken earth. For the two supporting companies (A and B), there was a hot breakfast, delivered soundlessly to them in the forward trenches, the men in No Man's Land having earlier been issued sandwiches and chocolate to sustain them during their wait. The battalion's snipers had been deployed to vantage points on the plethora of spoil heaps, and whenever opportunity presented itself, made life uncomfortable for any enemy foolish enough to look over their parapets. Once the attack began, the snipers were to neutralise any enemy who showed themselves. Their vantage points also allowed the snipers to see things the attacking company commanders couldn't, and runners had been allocated to each sniper team to convey information forward if the opportunity arose. There was no preliminary bombardment to alert the enemy, and though the Stokes mortars fired intermittently at the Craters throughout the night and right up to zero hour, this was just routine harassment which further encouraged the enemy not to stick his head out to watch No Man's Land. Shortly after 6 a.m., despite the poor visibility afforded in light rain, an RAF aircraft flew low over the Craters but only drew slight MG fire. The 1/4th were assigned the Craters from Warlingham (50° 31′ 39.63″ N, 2° 45′ 52.81″ E) in the south, to the most northerly of the E Sap Craters (50° 31′ 47.76″ N, 2° 45′ 42.95″ E), a frontal area of roughly 350 m, containing approximately fifteen craters. (So intensive had the mining war been at Givenchy, that even some of the craters had craters!) The Fusiliers were assigned from E Sap to K Sap (50° 31′ 57.34″ N, 2° 45′ 33.64″ E), a similarly sized objective. The Fusiliers were also tasked to carry out subsidiary attacks on New Rose Trench (50° 31′ 55.44″ N, 2° 45′ 30.04″ E) and the old British line.[11]

At 7.20 a.m. signal rockets were fired, and the attackers rose from their positions and rushed the craters. Unbelievably, the enemy didn't fire a single shot for two and a half minutes. Richardson's men had been well to the fore and totally surprised the enemy at their objective, killing or capturing all the defenders in their target crater. The enemy had an MG in the crater, but not the opportunity to bring it into action; indeed, the young officer himself used it to break up a hostile counter-attack just after 8.30 a.m., for which he was awarded the MC.[12] 2Lt Jack Gaulter's platoon captured its objective with few casualties, its commander personally shooting the enemy sentry before he could raise the alarm. Once he was satisfied the objective was secured, Gaulter made a personal reconnaissance of their frontal areas and organised the men to wire and consolidate their gains, earning himself the MC for his courage and leadership.[13] Although he escaped the attack unscathed, he was wounded later in the day. The enemy appeared to have been well and truly caught unawares, and it wasn't until four minutes after zero hour that the first SOS rockets were fired from well behind their lines. The third platoon commander to earn the MC in the attack was twenty-one-year-old 2Lt Frank Place MM from Blackburn. The young subaltern quickly overpowered the garrison at his objective, then later penetrated well forward of the line, reconnoitring the location of a suspected hostile trench mortar emplacement.[14] Both CSMs received the MM for their work: CSM George Holmes and CSM Charles Shearson each proved invaluable to their company commanders in consolidating the gains and organising the defences, their coolness under fire an inspiration to all their subordinates.[15]

Three other senior NCOs in the first wave were also awarded the MM. Twenty-three-year-old Sgt Harry Parnell was at the front of his section in the charge and the first into the crater. Finding five of the enemy there, he killed all of them. Later in the morning, he went forwards under heavy shell fire to rescue a wounded man, whom he brought back to safety. In the work of consolidation and reconnaissance to locate hostile posts and snipers, his energy and initiative set a fine example.[16] His fellow sergeant, Charles Ryder, had also been the first man to enter his objective, capturing one enemy NCO and killing the rest of the garrison. He then helped to clear other craters, consolidating the gains. Sgt Herbert Clegg led his men to his assigned crater and killed or captured all the garrison, controlling his platoon with great skill, as was recognised by his award of the MM.[17] Thirty-one-year-old Pte Cornelius Cafferty, a master window cleaner from Manchester, was orderly to the C Company commander and had been at the front of the attack. As his orderly, he was also the OC's private runner, and on one of these journeys saw that a German machine-gunner had been overlooked and was about to open fire on the attackers from the rear. Cafferty promptly dispatched the gunner and was awarded the MM for his gallantry and initiative.[18] Although he would survive the fighting, fate later dealt Cafferty an extraordinarily cruel hand.

Immediately behind the assaulting platoons were the moppers-up. When Sgt John Dickinson reached his objective, he discovered an enemy MG team just leaving their dugout and with grenade and rifle, killed all six, destroying the MG. L/Sgt George Huddleston had even less opposition at his objective and quickly mopped this up too. Incredibly, the attackers had seized almost all of their primary objectives within ten minutes of the attack beginning, yet German artillery still hadn't reacted to the assault. The enemy in the craters had offered little resistance; most either surrendered or were shot trying to escape. At 7.30 a.m. the British barrage opened up on the German positions beyond the craters, and five minutes later all the far rims of the craters were in battalion hands, and telephone communications established back to battalion HQ. This rapid establishment of communications was largely due to the personal efforts of L/Cpl Frederick Twigg, NCO in command of the company signallers;[19] thanks to him, visual communications had actually been established within five minutes of zero hour, a performance which earned him the MM.[20] German artillery finally woke up to the attack at 7.33 a.m., but the response was feeble and concentrated mainly on Gunner Siding, well away from the attackers and supporting companies.

When consolidation began at 7.43 a.m., reconnaissance patrols went forward to deal with suspected hostile trench mortar positions. The casualties had so far been virtually nil, but now some of the British barrage fell short and the left company lost two men killed and eight wounded, and a similar fate befell the right company. George Huddleston led his section forwards through the barrage to assault his allotted trench mortar position. Once this was dealt with, he personally scoured the enemy lines beyond the craters, killing four of the enemy he found there. Despite suffering a gunshot wound to an arm, he refused to be evacuated and remained at duty until consolidation was well advanced, displaying courage and determination that earned him the DCM.[21] On the left, all the men from L/Cpl John Edwards's section had become casualties of friendly fire, but undaunted he collected other men and carried out his reconnaissance. On the way back, he utilised a captured trench mortar and fired this at enemy positions until all the ammunition was exhausted. Once back at the craters, he took command of another section whose NCO had been killed (Cpl Peter Stanworth, a thirty-year-old married man from Burnley), distinguishing himself with his bravery and leadership; his acts led to him being awarded the DCM.[22] Sgt John Dickinson also went forward and reorganised a party of men who had been struck by the British barrage, bringing them back to help with the consolidation of the captured positions, his courage and leadership earning him the DCM. Another NCO to be awarded the MM was Cpl Arthur Clementson, who led his reconnaissance patrol through the heavy barrage to the area to the front of the craters, bringing back valuable information as to the location of enemy posts and also coming to the attention of his commanders for tending the wounded under shell fire. One thing that makes those acts of bravery recognised on 24 August so special is that just about every man awarded a medal that day had themselves been wounded at least once before. They were no strangers to the pain and dangers likely to result from their actions, yet they still ran these risks to complete their missions or help others.

The attack was also going well for the Fusiliers, and by 8 a.m., all objectives across the whole front had been captured, and an outpost line pushed forward 200 yards to the east of the craters.[23] A key part of consolidation was the positioning of Lewis guns to break up any counter-attacks, and two Lewis-gunners earned the MM for their courage and leadership. Twenty-one-year-old Cpl Percy Vernoun from Bristol led his gun section to the objective so quickly that the enemy were taken completely by surprise and he was the first to establish a Lewis gun on the far lip of the craters. Consolidation was rapidly achieved and his gun continually brought fire to bear on small parties of the enemy seen in the distance. Pte Albert Hargreaves took command of his Lewis section when the NCO in charge was wounded and held the exposed flank position on the extreme right of the attack, his coolness reassuring his team who remained at their posts despite accurate shell fire targeting them.[24] Around 8.34 a.m., a message was received from one of the sniper teams that a party of about forty enemy were massing at the end of the Duck's Bill Extension (50° 31′ 38.22″ N, 2° 46′ 1.84″ E); but when fire was directed onto them, the impending counter-attack simply melted away.

Following closely behind the attackers were men of the Australian Tunnelling Company, who were tasked with checking the dugouts for booby traps. Their searches were soon completed and they reported that all the dugouts were clear, but that one pill box located in Red Dragon Crater (50° 31′ 45.40″ N, 2° 45′ 45.17″ E) had been badly smashed by British artillery. By this time the enemy artillery fire had dwindled away to negligible proportions, probably because the German gunners were unsure of which positions were under British control. By 9.20 a.m. consolidation was mostly completed, and the divisional pioneers were rapidly approaching the craters with communication trenches dug forwards from Wolfe Road and Berkley Street. There was momentary concern when at 9.30 a.m. an SOS rocket was fired from the Fusiliers' position, but this was soon cancelled so had obviously been a mistake. It was only around 9.50 a.m. that German artillery fire began to fall on the craters, mostly around Warlingham Crater to begin with.

Now that British artillery had ceased to fall short, both forward companies sent further reconnaissance patrols out to find the trench mortar positions, only to discover that most had been destroyed by the British bombardment. On the right, Cpl Charles Butt found that the gun had been

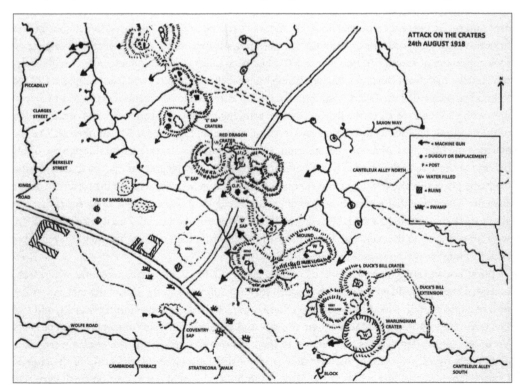

removed, though a rangefinder and plenty of ammunition remained; so, acting on his own initiative, he cleared the trenches and dugouts in the vicinity of his objective killing several of the enemy, for which he was awarded the MM.[25] Enemy artillery began to shell Givenchy with Blue-X shells around 11 a.m., a barrage that lasted for fifteen minutes, and the westerly wind blew the gas towards the craters. Although this had dispersed by 11.45 a.m., from that time onwards much heavier barrages hit the craters themselves. Remarkably, tea and sandwiches were delivered to the men around 12.30 p.m., and an hour later they even got a hot meal. Throughout the morning, carrying parties under twenty-one-year-old Welshman Cpl Alfred Davies (mis-named 'Arthur' in his medal recommendation) braved the shell fire to deliver engineering materials, small arms ammunition, and bombs, but the supply of hot food to the men was a masterstroke! Davies's courage and example inspired the men from the two reserve companies under his command; his MM was well earned, particularly as the ground conditions were so difficult for men bearing such burdens.[26] The snipers also performed well, and there was little enemy sniping apart from opposite Warlingham Crater.

As usual, the battalion's stretcher-bearers risked all to help their comrades, and were in harm's way for considerably longer than many of the attackers. Pte Thomas Cross MM earned a bar to his previous award when for twenty-four hours he worked at collecting and evacuating the wounded, penetrating as far forward as the furthest outpost in his search for casualties. Even though wounded himself, he refused to be evacuated and continued his task until all the wounded had been dealt with. Two other stretcher-bearers, Pte George Mackereth and Pte Ernest Sheppard, were also awarded the MM. Like Cross, both men tended and evacuated the wounded for twenty-four hours, oblivious to their own personal safety and working right up to the furthest outposts in their searches.[27] Not all the men recommended for the MM were awarded the medal; as ever, some recommendations were turned down at brigade or divisional level, sometimes for no greater reason than that a quota had been exceeded. These unlucky men were thirty-two-year-old CQMS Fred Saunders; twenty-three-year-old Pte George Lord from Burnley; L/Cpl Francis Boyle; and thirty-two-year-old Pte William Swarbrick from Bolton.

At 12.25 p.m., the men cheered as an RAF pilot shot down an enemy balloon; however, their joy was short-lived as this brave pilot was himself shot down attacking a second balloon five minutes later.[28] The RAF plane was an S.E.5a from 40 Squadron, though the pilot himself was an American, twenty-four-year-old Lt Louis Bennett Jr from Weston, West Virginia. In just nine days and twenty five sorties, this talented young pilot notched up an astonishing score of three enemy aircraft and nine balloons. The ground fire which brought the S.E.5a down set fire to the aircraft, and although Bennett was pulled out from it alive, the flames and crash mortally injured him and he died soon afterwards.[29] In December 1918, Bennett's mother, no doubt aware that such an invention could have saved her only son, offered a $500 prize to anyone who could invent an effective parachute for pilots.[30]

Casualties had been light, so the battalion had no problems manning the new acquisitions. Nine men had been killed, another two died from wounds, and forty had been wounded—a remarkably low bill for such gains, especially taking into account that nearly 50 per cent of those killed were victims of the British bombardment when some of the guns fired short. Most unusually, only one of those killed was an NCO; yet it is clear from accounts of the attack that officers and NCOs very much led the way. This demonstrates just how surprised and unprepared the enemy was. Although

German casualties had also been light—four officers and thirty other ranks killed, and forty-four men captured—the tactical gains were considerable.[31]

Killed in action or died from wounds on 24 August 1918

| | | | | | |
|---|---|---|---|---|---|
| Pte Edward Anthony Burgess | 40965 | KIA-24/8 | Pte David Holmes | 29340 | DOW-24/8 |
| Pte Arnold Lightbound | 29289 | KIA-24/8 | Pte James Edgar Owen | 41495 | KIA-24/8 |
| Pte Joseph Parker | 201697 | KIA-24/8 | Pte Richard Purchase | 41522 | KIA-24/8 |
| Cpl Peter Stanworth | 202579 | KIA-24/8 | Pte John James Steele | 29338 | KIA-24/8 |
| Pte James Ure | 29127 | KIA-24/8 | Pte John Henry Walton | 42872 | KIA-24/8 |
| Pte Frederick Henry Wilkinson | 41661 | DOW-25/8 | | | |

Known to have been to have been wounded on 24 August 1918

| | | | | | |
|---|---|---|---|---|---|
| Pte Thomas Cross | 238003 | WIA-24/8 | 2Lt Jack Rudolf Gaulter | | WIA-24/8 |
| Sgt George Huddleston | 200746 | WIA-24/8 | Pte James Savage | 201434 | WIA-24/8 |
| Pte Ernest Francis Sheppard | 26920 | WIA-24/8 | 2Lt William McKell Stewart | | WIA-24/8 |
| Pte Percy Troughton | 19503 | WIA-24/8 | Pte Thomas Wood | 29138 | WIA-24/8 |

Despite losing territory, the enemy only attempted two weak counter-attacks. Their artillery fire harassed the communication trenches and support areas with shell fire (though no trench mortars were brought into play), but just five men were wounded during the day. After dark on 25 August, the battalion sent a number of patrols forward to make contact with the enemy, but could find no trace of them. On the 26th, enemy artillery switched to shelling the craters, and another four men were wounded. Thirty-seven-year-old Pte Colin Davies from Birmingham, a draper in civilian life, was hit in the shoulder and foot by shrapnel, his left foot having to be amputated back in England. Twenty-six-year-old Pte George Hume from Newcastle also received multiple shrapnel wounds, and was given a medical discharge and a 20-per-cent pension as a result. The third man known to be wounded that day was twenty-year-old Pte John Steele, a clerk from Manchester, who received shrapnel wounds to both buttocks and was also evacuated home. Reconnaissance patrols sent out to make contact with the enemy had more luck this time, and were able to establish the locations of two enemy posts. German movement along their communication trenches, which had been broken in a number of places by British shell fire, was now much more hazardous, for the battalion held the higher ground overlooking the enemy—an extremely rare scenario on the Western Front. The battalion's snipers were thus able to make any movement along these trenches hurt, and on the 26th, they scored three confirmed hits.

Another five men became casualties on 27 August, four wounded by the enemy and one who managed to hospitalise himself accidentally. Twenty-one-year-old Cpl George Coward from Coniston was a member of battalion transport. He was breaking pieces of wood for the fire, and when he failed to notice that one piece contained a nail and when he broke it over his knee, the nail penetrated his knee joint. Fortunately, the sole witness to this painful injury was Lt Gabriel Ribchester, the transport officer, so the court of enquiry was a very straightforward affair, and no punishment was handed out for this accident. In the evening of the 27th, the battalion was relieved by 1/5th King's in daylight—something which would have been unthinkable before the Craters were seized. Once in the rear area, the battalion was bussed to Drouvin Camp, arriving just after 9 p.m. The death of one man is recorded on 28 August, that of twenty-one-year-old Pte Arnold Whitworth from Littleborough. *Soldiers Died* has him down as 'Killed in Action', but the young soldier almost certainly died of his wounds.[32]

The battalion remained at Drouvin until 2 September, resting, refitting, and training. Various football tournaments were organised, and in the match of 'Sergeants' *versus* 'Officers' on 1 September (won 5–4 by the 'Sergeants'), Maj. Gardner broke a bone in his ankle—though this did not keep him from duty when the battalion went back up the line the following day! A regimental dance on the 29th was a great success, and the divisional theatre gave a performance on the 30th. The tedium of running was additionally alleviated by a divisional paper chase from Vaudricourt Château on the 30th. At Drouvin, one man from A Company was returned to England after reporting sick, diagnosed with Disordered Action of the Heart (DAH).[33] This parting of ways would almost certainly have not upset his officers and NCOs! The hell-raising private, thirty-year-old Harvey Pullen from Swindon, had originally been a driver with the ASC, but they eventually transferred him to the infantry when his conduct became unmanageable. He showed little sign of improvement as part of 55 Division's transport, and after being sentenced to nine months' hard labour for a catalogue of crimes against good order—mostly involving alcohol—he was posted to the 1/4th after serving six months of his sentence. The Glasshouse did not appear to have made much difference, and out of the line he was still a handful; still, his record shows that in the trenches he was a good soldier, and as a runner had braved heavy shell fire on numerous occasions.[34]

In the afternoon of 2 September, the battalion took over the support line from 1/7th King's. Although this was another daytime relief, the handover went smoothly but for one man, twenty-eight-year-old Pte Richard Derham, a married father of one from Skerton, being badly wounded by a shell fragment to the thigh, which led to his medical discharge. As far as enemy activity was concerned, 3 September was a quiet day, though the Village Line was shelled with gas. Over the coming days every single man of the battalion was deployed on working parties, mostly on road-building, the hot and frequently stormy weather adding to their trials. Three men were wounded on the 4th and another on the 6th. However, their labours were soon to cease; before nightfall on the 6th, the battalion relieved the Loyals in the forward positions.

While the battalion had been at Drouvin, events in 55 Division's sector had developed. On 28 August, 166 Brigade had discovered that the Festubert East Keep was unmanned by the enemy and had promptly seized it. Intelligence reports had suggested that the enemy may have been contemplating a withdrawal, and preparations were made to take every advantage of this, which was why the working parties had been making good the roads for horse transport.[35] Numerous fighting patrols from 166 Brigade in the Festubert sector and 165 Brigade at Givenchy moved forward on the night of the 2/3 September, and established a line of posts some 500 yards forward of the craters, further progress being made on subsequent days. While it was apparent that the enemy were not actually in the process of a general retirement, little opposition was put up against these advances. By the morning of the 7th, an outpost had been established as far forward as the southern outskirts of Violaines, though enemy resistance had stiffened noticeably. German intentions were unclear, and although prisoners had talked about a general withdrawal to the Haute Deûle Canal, division were unsure whether or not the enemy's real intentions were to hold a line from La Bassée to Fromelles in strength.[36] The latter option would require a deliberate attack, something that High Command was not prepared to undertake at this stage. There were also further complications for whichever brigade held the right sector, as the division to the south had not been able to progress as far, and the enemy still held Embankment Redoubt (50° 31′ 16.19″ N, 2° 46′ 9.96″ E) on the opposite side of the canal to the Tortoise, and Railway Triangle 400 yards to the east of Embankment Redoubt. Both these positions could enfilade the southern parts of Canteleux Trench north of the canal, the next enemy position that needed to be taken to level the division's front.

Early on 7 September, B and D Company launched a surprise operation against the southern part of Canteleux Trench (50° 31′ 22.41″ N, 2° 47′ 14.52″ E) and seized the outposts there. Fortunately, sappers had followed up the attacking wave and upon searching the enemy dugouts discovered that the shelters were booby-trapped and successfully cleared them. The gains were not held for long, as the enemy counter-attacked with around 200 men at 1.30 p.m. and won back the ground, the battalion being forced back to its previous positions. Overall, the battalion suffered nineteen casualties. One was known to be killed, eleven were wounded, and seven went missing. It later turned out that two men had been killed outright: these were thirty-five-year-old Pte James Orme, a father of two from Leicester, and nineteen-year-old Pte David Simms from Larne. Twenty-one-year-old (785) L/Cpl George Robinson's third wound of the war would also be his last, as the young NCO died from his injuries on 9 September. (Records also show that eighteen-year-old Pte George Parker from Sheffield died on 7 September, however this was from illness and not battle injuries.) The action also cost the battalion one of its best NCOs: twenty-three-year-old Sgt John Pearson DCM was wounded in the left arm, an injury severe enough to warrant a 40-per-cent pension and prevent him from continuing his pre-war occupation as an iron ore miner at Millom. One soldier, Pte John Murray, earned the MM for his courage during the attack.

The evening of 7 September brought heavy thunderstorms which continued into the next day, torrential rain flooding the trenches. Despite this, the battalion made a number of attacks against outposts along Canteleux Trench, capturing a strongpoint at 50° 31′ 32.41″ N, 2° 47′ 8.37″ E; yet, once again a strong enemy counter-attack with superior forces drove the men out. On the 9th, the battalion again attempted to wrest these outposts from the enemy, and after a series of bombing exchanges, minor gains were made around Canteleux Trench. Two men were killed, six wounded, and two missing in the process. Both nineteen-year-old Pte Ian Hargreaves from Staffordshire and twenty-six-year-old Pte Lee Longworth from Swinton were killed outright. One of the missing, nineteen-year-old Pte Frederick Johnston from Belfast, had only been with the battalion for ten days, having transferred from the Leicester Cyclist Regiment. It later transpired that this young man had been taken as a POW, though no evidence survives in his records to show whether he had been wounded, or had just become separated from his section and then captured. Another nineteen-year-old, Pte Gilbert Long, ended up in the CCS for the second time in three months, though this time the shrapnel wound in his left arm was a Blighty one. In the afternoon of 9 September, the battalion was relieved by the Loyals and returned to support, HQ positioning itself in Windy Terrace.

The period in support from 10 to 14 September saw few working parties, mostly because the appalling weather inhibited movement in the extreme. Although there was little shelling, there were still casualties. Two men were reported wounded on the 13th, and records also show that on the 11th, twenty-two-year-old Pte Albert Sidgreaves received shrapnel wounds to the arm which led to his medical discharge.[37] Thirty-year-old Pte John Dalton, attached to the TMB, was wounded with shrapnel to the left arm; he was unlucky enough not to be sent home to have his wound treated, and instead spent eighteen days at the CCS at Wimereux before having to suffer the indignity of a week at the Bull Ring before returning.

The battalion spent five days at Drouvin, in which their timetable pretty much mirrored previous periods of 'rest', with refitting, training and sport all vying for space. One novel experience for two of the companies on 18 September was to be taken by lorry to Aix-Noulette, near Lens, to watch a demonstration of how infantry should work with tanks. The battalion administration also caught up in affairs too petty to be dealt with in the trenches, which reminded the men that they were soldiers, and that the Army required certain 'standards' to be respected. Eighteen-year-old Pte Frederick Dowey from Barrow was awarded ten days' Field Punishment No. 1 for 'Being Dirty on Parade', which could be anything from a tarnished button or dirty boots, to being unshaven or obviously unwashed. Another, probably very young soldier judging by his number, Pte George Manley of C Company, was awarded twenty-three days' Field Punishment No. 1 for an 'Improper Reply to an NCO', a tough punishment for a serious offence. It wasn't just privates who were up before battalion officers on discipline charges; L/Cpl Robert Travis of D Company was reduced to the ranks for 'Neglect of Duty as an NCO' and 'Falling Out of a Working Party Without Permission' while in charge of a ration party. There had obviously been an inspection of the iron rations held by members of C Company, as numbers of men were up before Capt. Overton charged with either 'eating' or 'losing by neglect' these items. (Iron Rations could only be eaten by men when an officer had granted permission.) Whatever the charge, the punishment for these items going missing was the same: Privates Horace Cheney, William Kells, Fred Norbury, William Porter, William Postles, and John Rush would all be keeping the provost sergeant busy, as they were each given five days' Field Punishment No. 1. The only man to be awarded a lighter punishment for lack of iron rations was Pte Alfred Spibey from Golborne, who claimed to have left his at home when he returned from leave. The twenty-one-year-old was fined the equivalent of replacing the rations.

By 10 p.m. on 20 September, the battalion was back in the line near Canteleux. Although not recorded in September's 'Casualty Returns', service records show that the battalion's master-cook, twenty-seven-year-old Sgt Edwin Newton, was badly affected by a gas shell and evacuated back to England for treatment.[38] While the battalion had been on rest, there had been considerable efforts from both 55 and 16 Division to make territorial gains either side of the canal. At first, any gains had been immediately counter-attacked by the enemy, but by the evening of 18 September, Canteleux Trench was firmly held and the German positions along the railway embankment to the south of the canal taken by 16 Division. These gains gave the British a clear observation of any movement between these positions and the La Bassée–Fromelles Line.

21 September saw considerable reorganisation, as the divisional frontage now included the immediate south of the canal. Two out of three battalions in any one brigade would be in the line, each with two companies in the support line and the other two in the outpost line. C and D Company

manned the outposts this time, sending out two daytime and three night patrols. German artillery left the forward companies alone, but HQ again came in for both HE and gas; the only casualty was twenty-five-year-old stretcher-bearer Pte James Kitchin form Dalton, who was evacuated to Wimereux suffering from the effects of gas. Although he was not sent home, this was his last taste of the front line, as he did not return to the battalion until the week before Christmas; this probably didn't upset him, as he'd been in the thick of it since deploying to France in May 1915; he earned a MiD for his brave work on the Somme and in the Salient.[39] As it turned out, the shell fire was the precursor for events of the next day.

22 September began quietly enough, with men working to improve the defences of the outpost line and others gathering salvage in the rear areas. Once again, German artillery left the front line outposts alone and targeted the rear, dropping a number of gas shells into Berkeley Crater where the RAP was situated, and causing the entire medical staff to become casualties and be evacuated (seven men and two officers). The most seriously wounded was twenty-eight-year-old Pte William Bridge from Ellesmere Port. He was too gravely ill to be transferred to England, and was treated at No. 6 CCS. His condition obviously worsened, and—most unusually—a telegram was sent directly to his wife informing her:

> I regret to inform you that 30311 Pte W E Bridge is dangerously ill suffering from wounds at 6th Casualty Clearing Station, France. Regret that permission to visit cannot be granted.[40]

Five days later, another telegraph was sent, this time to Infantry records in Preston, informing them of an improvement in his condition. Sadly, he died from pneumonia on 28 December 1920, and as his wife was awarded a war pension for herself and their young son, a contributing factor in his death must have been pulmonary weakness due to the gassing. (Bridge is not currently commemorated by the CWGC, but an application has been made to rectify this.) Also gassed were the medical officers Lt William Jenks and 2Lt Frederick Waywell, who had been at the RAP. The day did not improve after dark, when three patrols went out forward of the outpost line and one commander, twenty-one-year-old 2Lt Frank Place MC, MM, was killed when his was spotted. His body was brought back by his men and buried at Fouquières Cemetery. Battalions manning the front had been instructed to be active in front of the outpost line in order to help the immediate detection of an enemy withdrawal, a dangerous but necessary policy if any withdrawal was to be exploited. For this same reason, Maj.-Gen. Jeudwine also decided to allow brigade commanders to deploy the whole of the two forward battalions into the outpost line.[41]

23 September was spent strengthening the crater posts and 690 yards of apron wire were put out in front of the battalion's positions. German artillery still concentrated on the rear, practically ignoring the men in the outposts. The battalion also constructed two miniature ranges to allow the men to hone their musketry skills whenever time allowed. Once darkness had fallen, three more patrols moved into No Man's Land to check enemy activity, and that night there were no casualties among them. The 23rd had in fact been a casualty-free day for the battalion, though one of the men wounded at an earlier date, nineteen-year-old Pte George Denton from Rushden, died from his wounds at one of the hospitals (probably Wimereux). In the evening of the 24th, the battalion was relieved by the Fusiliers. But the battalion in question was so short of men that the King's Own had

to lend it B Company—a bitter pill to swallow for the men from that company! Casualties on that day amounted to just one man wounded. Although being support battalion usually entailed massed working parties, there were only a few on the 25th, and most men were able to take advantage of the fine weather to rest. Despite this lack of activity on either side, the battalion still suffered three men wounded, one of whom was possibly Pte Louis Anderson. Although the date of wounding is absent from his service record, it probably occurred on either the 25th or 27th. The twenty-two-year-old from St Helens was hit in the chest and shoulder by shrapnel, evacuated home, and medically discharged with a 40-per-cent pension.[42]

On 27 September, British artillery launched considerable harassing fire on German positions. This provoked the enemy into sending numerous aircraft over the front line, no doubt searching for any sign of an impending attack. Surprisingly, there was little enemy artillery activity against support or outpost lines, though it did wound one man. The lack of enemy artillery fire on the battalion's area was probably down to the attack further north, carried out at 2.55 a.m. by three companies of 1/5th King's. This seized a number of outposts along the La Bassée–Estaires Road, and was subject to considerable enemy artillery retribution right up until 29 September.[43] On the 28th, officers from the battalion carried out a reconnaissance south of the canal prior to moving up to relieve the Loyals that night. The relief went without problems and or casualties of any kind, despite a number of mustard gas shells landing in D Company's area. C and D Company were in support and A and B occupied the outposts, though the battalion's positions were now split as they straddled the canal; this was probably why the battalion still maintained two companies in forward and two companies in support formation.

Intelligence reports suggested that the enemy had made arrangements to withdraw along the whole Fifth Army front, and instructions were issued to 55 Division on 27 September that all divisions of the corps were to simultaneously carry out an advance south of the canal. In preparation for this, artillery would commence harassing fire on the 28th.[44] Though not involved in this attack, which was to be carried out by two companies of the Loyals against the Distillery (50° 31′ 17.21″ N, 2° 47′ 35.26″ E) on the south of the canal, the 1/4th put six daylight patrols out on the 29th and another three out all night. The right front company was relieved by a company of the Loyals just prior to the operation, the two attacking companies going forward at 6.15 a.m. on 30 September. Initially, this attack was very successful, with light casualties and forty-eight prisoners captured from the Distillery. However, 16 Division to the right of the Loyals had not been able to make any headway against determined enemy opposition, and a strong enemy counter-attack at noon drove the Loyals back to their original line. The battalion put daylight patrols out, but these reported little enemy activity subsequent to their counter-attack.

Although the 1/4th carried out no major attacks in September, the month still saw some depletion of the roll. Casualties amounted to fifty-seven killed, wounded, or missing, and a further eighty-nine men were in hospital sick, giving a total of 146 men down. Replacements amounted to a mere thirty-nine; and while many of the sick did indeed rejoin the battalion, a considerable proportion did not, for they were either evacuated back to England or—and in many cases—medically discharged. September also saw men put forward for awards in recognition of their long and loyal service to the battalion; although these were only made public in the 'New Year's Honours List' for 1919, they were published in 'Battalion Orders' on 21 September. Robert Parry was awarded the DCM for his energy and enthusiasm as a CSM and his success as RSM, 'his courage and coolness under fire on many trying occasions having been of great value to the battalion.'[45] Also announced in the same issue of *The London Gazette* was another senior rank to get the DCM: CSM James Cook's courage and devotion to duty had been a great strength for the battalion throughout its time in the Salient. The orderly room sergeant, twenty-four-year-old Samuel Hinds from Ulverston, received a MSM for his efficiency in running it, often under heavy enemy fire, as did band sergeant William Rickwood, who not only led the battalion's band, but also conducted the massed bands of the brigade.[46] The QM's department was not neglected either: in June 1918, William Clark had been awarded the MSM in recognition that, since his appointment as RQMS in 1917, his unfailing energy, enthusiasm, and willingness to sacrifice his personal comfort for that of his men had played an important part in the success of the battalion.[47] Finally, the then QM Lt Phillip Powell was promoted to Captain.

1 October saw the Loyals repeat their attack on the Distillery, and this time they successfully held on to their gains, probably because 16 Division was also able to make advances. A Company then pushed forward on the south bank of the canal to support the Loyals, while on the north bank, B Company sent a series of patrols forward to see if the enemy were still holding the Aubers–Fromelles–La Bassée Line. Information was obtained from a German officer captured early on 2 October that the enemy had begun a withdrawal to the Haute Deûle Canal at 4 a.m. that morning.[48] This news reached the battalion at 10 a.m. and just before noon a patrol from B Company was able to enter the German defensive line, reaching the western outskirts of La Bassée by 1.30 p.m.

There had been plans made within the division some days earlier to capitalise on a general German withdrawal, by the sending out a telegram containing the code name 'Scurry', followed by the divisional objective and the time an advance was to begin. Each unit would then move to predetermined starting positions. To facilitate the advance of an entire brigade, each brigade organised an advanced guard and a main party from each available infantry battalion. In addition, each of the brigade commanders had at their disposal a number of non-infantry units from C Squadron, King Edward's Horse; one section of RE; an investigation party from the Tunnelling Company; an 18-pounder battery; a section of 4.5-inch howitzers; a mobile section of medium trench mortars; a company from the MG Battalion; and a contingent of the Field Ambulance. Behind the lines, the RE and working parties feverishly laboured on improving the roads for the legions of wheeled traffic needed to support such an advance, and surfaced other tracks for pack animals to follow.[49]

No actual 'Scurry' was sent, as the method of German withdrawal did not allow the corps to issue a definite order for an advance at a specific time. Nevertheless, the arrangements for an advance worked perfectly. The intention was to maintain pressure on the retreating enemy, but not to force the engagement of the entire division, as the number of divisions available within the Fifth Army were inadequate for a full-scale offensive. The battalion's advance guard, under the command of Maj. Gardner, was made up of A Company and two platoons from B Company, and would advance to the south of the canal. To the north, the main party under Lt-Col. Balfour consisted of the rest of the battalion, a battery of 18-pounders, two 4.5-inch howitzers, and RE. North of the canal, patrols from the 1/4th pushed northwards up the La Bassée Line, making contact with the Fusiliers who had advanced from Canteleux and Violaines. By 1.30 p.m., an A Company patrol led by 2Lt William Rudall (on attachment from the Lincolnshire Regiment) had pushed southwards along the La Bassée Line to meet patrols from 16 Division, who were working their way northwards along Vert

Alley towards La Bassée. By 2.30 p.m., the whole of the La Bassée Line from the canal to Vert Alley was secured; orders were given to hold it with two platoons, and push the rest forward through La Faubourg to the Canal Basin and into Crassiers.

To the north of the canal, B Company had pushed its patrols as far as 800 yards east of La Bassée. Maj. Gardner, accompanied by the intelligence officer Lt Ernest Tucker and a couple of signallers and runners, moved his command post forwards to the Distillery. There had been no encounters with the enemy and very little shelling, though twenty-six-year-old Sgt Percy Miller from Blackpool was wounded by mustard gas. La Bassée itself was obliterated after years of shelling, and the enemy had blown all the bridges across the canal before retreating. HQ moved to Canteleux, and there were some communications problems between them and the advance guard, mainly because the telephone wire across the canal had been severed when a barge blew up. However, a loop set was established at the Distillery, which managed to keep contact with a similar set in Red Dragon Crater; so, via a convoluted route, communications were maintained. At 5 p.m., patrols north of the canal finally located the enemy some 600 yards to the east of the Canal Basin (50° 31′ 41.95″ N, 2° 49′ 20.82″ E). By 8 p.m., outposts were established along the new line and Gardner's command post moved forward again to a concrete cellar in La Bassée. Although all the bridges had been destroyed, it was just possible to cross the canal on the remains of the partially demolished railway bridge (50°31′ 45.68″ N, 2°48′ 36.21″ E), allowing the major to keep physical contact with his posts to the south of the canal. There had been some hostile MG fire from the position where the patrols had located the enemy, but this solitary gun ceased fire shortly before dusk and soon afterwards a group of about twenty Germans wearing full packs were seen marching towards Salomé. By midnight, a further two outposts were established: one at an old brewery on the Salomé Road (50° 31′ 54.57″ N, 2° 49′ 3.92″ E), and the other south of the canal.

Around midnight, Maj. Gardner sent two patrols out to establish advanced posts, the first to push forwards into Salomé, the other to the south of the canal and roughly level with the northern patrol. Strictly speaking, Maj. Gardner should have only pushed patrols forward to the south of the canal, but as he admitted in his report, he 'misconstructed' [sic] his orders.[50] By 2 a.m. of 3 October, both posts were established and patrols sent out northwards through Salomé to meet the Fusiliers and southwards to make contact with units from 16 Division. Salomé itself was deserted apart from elements of 2/5th Fusiliers, the enemy having retreated east. At 7 a.m. the advance continued, with patrols reaching Canal Angle (50° 31′ 45.46″ N, 2° 51′ 37.80″ E) to the south of Hantay shortly afterwards, and Billy-Berclau just after 10 a.m., where they met up with units of 16 Division. Billy-Berclau was lightly shelled just before 11 a.m., and the men there could see AAA fire and MG tracer arcing upwards from Berclau itself, just over 1,000 yards north-east of them.

Maj. Gardner moved an advanced command post forward to the Canal Basin, though communications were complicated by the need to maintain touch across the canal. It was impossible to put a telephone station at the basin as there was a shortage of wire, so the telephone and Fullerphone were left at the Distillery and the loop set brought forward. The 'loop' or 'spark' set (officially known as the 'Wireless Telegraphy Set Forward Spark 20 Watts B Front and Rear'—hardly a name that rattled off the tongue!) was given enough men to carry the batteries, a reasonably portable short-range Morse transceiver. Visual signals were used to communicate back to the Distillery via an OP in La Bassée and the loop set was able to make contact with the forward brigade loop set, so direct contact could be made with 164 Brigade. MGs and trench mortars were brought forward to the main line of resistance and forward dumps established just behind this. Field kitchens were set up in La Bassée and the men in the forward positions supplied with hot food throughout the day, a process made much easier by the lack of damage to the forward area, which hadn't been subjected to years of concentrated shellfire. At 1 p.m. a post was established in Berclau itself, but after coming into contact with an enemy rearguard also positioned in Berclau, the post was withdrawn. There appeared to be numerous enemy MGs and snipers positioned around the north and north-east of Berclau, so a Lewis post was set up at 50° 31′ 40.04″ N, 2° 52′ 0.58″ E, a position that gave a commanding field of fire should the enemy consider any advance from this direction. At 9 p.m., the sector south of the canal was taken over by 16 Division after it was decided to move the divisional boundaries once more, and the advance guard joined the rest of the battalion in Salomé.

At dawn on 4 October, strong patrols pushed forwards from Hantay, driving the enemy back towards the Haute Deûle Canal in a series of skirmishes. D Company attacked a German position at Prévore Farm and captured it, during which thirty-eight-year-old 2Lt Reginald Robinson from Blackpool and nineteen-year-old Pte William Hickman were both killed. The enemy held the western bank of the canal in strength, with large numbers of MGs protecting their positions. Although all the permanent bridges had been destroyed, a number of temporary bridges were positioned to support the defenders on the western bank. While copious booby traps and mines had been laid by the enemy, many of the latter had not been detonated due to the rapid progress of the advance guard and were defused by the RE. The roads to the west of Salomé had been heavily cratered by the retreating Germans, and the RE and pioneer battalions filled in thirty-two craters and made good 14 miles of road as they followed closely behind the advancing infantry. In just two days, the division advanced 5 miles.[51]

On 5 October, patrols from the battalion continued to pressure enemy defences on the canal but faced stubborn resistance, made worse by the enemy flooding the low ground on the west bank and forcing the battalion to pull its posts back further west to avoid the rising water. Among two men known to be wounded in these exchanges of fire were twenty-five-year-old Sgt George Dockeray from Millom, wounded severely enough in the right arm and leg to warrant his medical discharge; and the highly competent Sgt William Whiteside MM, who got a minor scalp wound which, despite getting him two weeks in hospital at Wimereux, also resulted in another two unpleasant and pointless weeks at the Bull Ring. After dark the battalion was relieved by 1/6th King's and marched back to take up positions as divisional reserve in Givenchy and Pont Fixe. No doubt grateful for the absence of working parties, the battalion bathed, rested, and refitted on the 6th, even though the dugouts were wet and uncomfortable. After bathing first thing in the morning of the 7th, the battalion trained until later in the afternoon whence it was pulled back to billets at Beuvry.

The battalion remained at Beuvry until the morning of 12 October, training for the role of advance guard morning and afternoon, while the evenings were set aside for entertainment. Practice on the ranges was carried out every day and rapid pontoon-bridging too, the battalion not having practised river crossings since the early spring of 1915 in Sevenoaks. On the evening of 9 October, the men were treated to a free cinema show; the next night to a regimental dance; and on the morning of their last day in billets, the first hint from officialdom that the end of the war was in sight. Indeed, the divisional education officer delivered a series of lectures on the scheme for developing the men's education upon the cessation of hostilities. On the same day, news was forwarded to the battalion's orderly office that Pte Arthur Jackson, a nineteen-year-old from Manchester, had died from his wounds at one of the base hospitals in Étaples; there is no record of when he was wounded, but it was probably in one of the platoon actions around the 5th of that month.

At 8.30 a.m. on the 12th, the battalion set off on a series of trains on the light railway, destined for Cambrin. Just over 2 miles from Beuvry, there were two collisions *en route*, fortunately without any injuries. Once safely off the trains, the battalion marched onwards to Marquillies, just over 6 miles away. HQ and A Company remained in Marquillies, while B Company went to Sainghin, C to Le Willy (not marked on modern maps, but at 50° 33′ 34.25″ N, 2° 51′ 8.37″ E), and finally D to an old sugar factory north of Marquillies (50° 33′ 48.66″ N, 2° 51′ 56.51″ E). Once they had relieved 1/10th King's, the men began to establish posts around their new location and spent the next day improving these and setting out large quantities of wire defences. In spite of a great deal of enemy shelling, casualties were light and no one was killed.

On 13 October, a prisoner had given the information that a general withdrawal behind Lille was to take place that night, but when the division sent out patrols, they found that all the German outposts were defended vigorously. Unwilling to force a crossing of the canal against a stout defence unless absolutely necessary, Maj.-Gen. Jeudwine decided that more information was needed and on the night of the 14th, four platoons from 1/5th King's carried out a strong raid against a German position in the railway sidings to the south and south-west of Don. This was highly successful and twenty prisoners were captured; they revealed that a withdrawal was expected daily, but that no notice had been given as to the exact date.[52]

On 14 October, HQ moved to a house near the sugar factory, battalion disposition being two companies in reserve and two in the main line of resistance—the main defensive line should the enemy counter-attack, and not the front line. A miniature range was established and despite wet and windy weather most were able to train, although some men ended up on a working party. There was very little shelling on the 15th, and on the 16th, after training in the morning, the battalion moved to billets in Sainghin. The *War Diary* comments on this being a quiet night with no shelling, but there had been two men killed by shell fire during the day, nineteen-year-old Pte Charles Gorst from Heysham and thirty-three-year-old Pte Walter Thomson from Ulverston. Walter Thomson had been put forward for the MM after Givenchy in April, but the recommendation had been unsuccessful. One of his brothers, Wallace, had been killed with 7/ King's Own in 1916, and their mother had died in January 1918.

While the battalion had been in the Marquillies area, the corps to the right of 55 Division had succeeded in crossing the canal at Pont-à-Vendin and Meurchin, leaving the enemy on the western side of the canal to 55 Division's front, in a pronounced salient. Several attempts were made to push them back over the canal, but these were all met by fierce resistance from German machine-gunners. However, on the afternoon of the 15th, the advance guards of 1/5th King's and 1/4th Loyals had succeeded in pushing all but a few enemy posts to the north-east of Don, back to the east of the canal. That night, 1/5th King's forced a crossing of the canal and occupied Don.

At 9 a.m. on 17 October, the battalion advanced by company through Wavrin and Lattre (now absorbed into Wavrin). There were delays in crossing the canal at 50° 34′ 10.69″ N, 2° 57′ 59.83″ E, where both bridges had been blown up. 422 Field Company RE threw a pontoon bridge across which the battalion used, arriving at Ancoisne at midday. At 2 p.m. the battalion moved off for

Houplines, and at 6.30 p.m. it was ordered to Templemars for the night, where an ecstatic local population greeted them warmly. In one day, the battalion had advanced further than the British had throughout the entire Battle of the Somme.

At 6 a.m. on the 18th, the battalion advanced and moved through the positions held by the Fusiliers, with C and D Company in the outposts and A and B in support. Patrols entered the villages of Sainghin-en-Mélantois and Peronne-en-Mélantois and pushed on towards the La Marque River, where the enemy were holding positions in strength. There was much shellfire, chiefly directed at the forts in Sainghin-en-Mélantois and Peronne-en-Mélantois, but as a patrol from 16 Platoon moved along the road from the first towards the river crossing at the far side of Bas Sainghin, they encountered several MGs defending the fork in the road at 50° 34′ 41.43″ N, 3° 10′ 42.60″ E. Led by Sgt Thomas Barrow, the platoon stormed these positions and seized the village, clearing it of all enemy. In the late afternoon, Barrow used a ladder he found in the village to build an improvised bridge and took his platoon across the river, even though there were still many Germans to his flank. Although he probably didn't know it, the location he chose to cross the river was the southern section of a battlefield of profound significance in English history. Some 704 years earlier, King John's forces had been defeated at the Battle of Bouvines; this had led to English nobles, vexed and humiliated at losing their French lands, forcing John to sign Magna Carta! For his initiative and leadership, Sgt Barrow was awarded the DCM.[53]

A thick mist lay over the lower ground near the river, which blotted out the battalion's advance from German eyes; and later, a clear sky and full moon considerably aided the men's move forwards. Around 10.30 p.m., an 18-pounder battery and MGs fired a barrage at the woods occupied by the enemy, forcing the German rearguard to evacuate Bouvines at 11 p.m. Fifteen minutes later, the battalion occupied the village, much to the joy of the local occupants who were still sheltering in their homes. Only one man, nineteen-year-old Pte Robert Rowlands from Deiniolen, was killed, but there were many more wounded. Nineteen-year-old Pte Alfred Smith from Hereford was shot in the left arm, and Pte Edward Moorhouse received serious shrapnel wounds to the head, forearm, and both feet. So serious were the injuries to the twenty-year-old from Burnley, that a telegram was sent to his mother informing her that her son was dangerously ill. His condition did improve, but upon his discharge he was awarded a 70-per-cent pension for his injuries. The two forward companies (C and D) remained in the village with HQ, while A and B took the lead to push on east. In the early hours, B Company rolled over a German position, capturing three MGs and twenty-three prisoners without loss. By the early morning of 19 October, the two companies were established in an outpost line along the railway, which ran in a north-south direction 1,000 yards to the east of Bouvines. Once the Loyals had passed through them, the men from the outposts withdrew back into Bouvines for some well-deserved rest.

HQ was established in the small chateau (50° 34′ 39.13″ N, 3° 11′ 2.23″ E), much to the delight of all their personnel, and the remainder of the battalion found comfortable billets within the village. The local population were overjoyed at their deliverance, and nothing was too much trouble for them. The inhabitants even helped the RE to build a new bridge across the river, the original having been blown up, and so rapidly did these two groups work together that the new bridge was completed by 11.30 a.m. At 8.30 a.m. on 20 October, the battalion left Bouvines and was at Cysoing by 10 a.m., marching onwards to Creplaine where it halted briefly before moving on to a field on the *Ferme du Baron* just north of Froidmont, to await further orders. When these came in the late afternoon, the next move was actually backwards, with the battalion taking up artillery formation in a field some 800 yards to the north of Esplechin. Shortly afterwards, it was moved forward again to almost exactly where it had just come from! D Company was sent south as support for the left flank of the Fusiliers, who were in a front-line position some 1,500 yards ahead of the support line, and a platoon detached to the north from C Company, to maintain touch with 74 Division who were advancing on 55 Division's left flank. At 6 p.m., HQ was established in a farm in Esplechin and the remaining three platoons of C Company went to join D in the support line on the Fusiliers' left, while A and B Company were to support the right flank of the Fusiliers. Once the companies were settled in, HQ was also moved forward, to the asylum in Froidmont—an institution for the mentally ill run by a monastic order, the Brothers of Charity, who were delighted to see British troops. (No doubt their HQ staff's placement in an insane asylum appealed greatly to the soldiers' sense of humour!) There had been one casualty during the day, when twenty-six-year-old Pte Harold Parker was hit through both thighs by shrapnel, a wound severe enough to lead to him being awarded a 30-per-cent pension.

On the morning of 21 October, the battalion passed through the Fusiliers and continued their advance as lead battalion. It would be a mistake to describe the enemy's defence as feeble; despite the rapidity of the advance, it faced determined resistance. The lead patrols frequently became embroiled in furious fighting and it wasn't until 3.15 p.m. that B Company forced the capture of the high ground on the Froidmont–Tournai Road. At 10.30 p.m., a strong enemy counter-attack lost it this position. On the battalion's right flank the enemy put up considerable resistance in Ere, an MG situated in the church steeple (50° 34′ 55.80″ N, 3° 22′ 1.65″ E) causing particular difficulties. As the troops fought their way into Ere, clearing the buildings of enemy one at a time, it was discovered that the church had been mined; the booby trap was soon defused, however, by the RE. Eventually the enemy, pushed back to a line some 500 yards east of the village, and retaliated by heavily shelling Ere during the day and overnight. At 7 p.m. HQ moved into a chateau near Ere, and men sought shelter from the German bombardment wherever they could. The fire was particularly heavy around all the sunken roads, the enemy no doubt blindly seeking to make chance hits on any troops moving forwards, and supply and ration transport.

Although no one from the battalion was killed outright in this fighting, a number are known to have been wounded. Thirty-one-year-old Pte John Cullum, the manager of a London chocolate factory before the war, was blown through the air by a nearby shell; although the shell fragments caused only minor wounds to his legs, the blast was so violent that internal muscle tears resulted in him having to be operated upon for a hernia three months later. Company runner nineteen-year-old Pte William Walker from Carlisle was wounded by shrapnel in his right thigh and neck, and evacuated home six days later. Another to return home on the same hospital ship as Walker was Cpl Alfred Davies MM, the corporal from transport wounded by shrapnel in the foot and thigh. Also wounded earlier in the day was twenty-one-year-old Pte William Madine from St Bees, shot through the left leg while attacking a German position. Although the wound would have been painful, it was no doubt alleviated to some degree by the knowledge that he was going home and would shortly be sewing the ribbon for the MM onto his tunic for his bravery during the attack.[54] Another two men also awarded the MM that day were thirty-five-year-old Cpl Albert Howarth from Blackburn and Cpl Edward Johnson.

During the morning of 22 October, the battalion moved back into support, its place in the advance taken by 1/5th Loyals. D Company was shelled as it withdrew, and among the casualties was Pte John Mohan from Glossop, hit in the left forearm by shrapnel. This was the third and last time the thirty-one-year-old would be wounded, as he was evacuated back to England three days later. The battalion rested during the day, all the men weary after the spectacular advances of the last twenty days. The enemy, however, was still fighting back fiercely, and German artillery dropped a number of gas shells right into A Company's position at 6 p.m., luckily without causing any further casualties as everyone managed to don their gas masks in time. 23 October saw the battalion holding the Battle Line, and a series of posts were established where any enemy counter-attack which penetrated through the front-line defences could be checked. Rather than having the men outside without shelter, they were billeted in farmhouses as close to the posts as was possible, it then being a simple matter to rush out and man these if the SOS rockets were fired. However, not everyone in the battalion was resting. The battalion held the left flank of 55 Division, and 74 Division to its left had an attack on a sunken road planned for two platoons from B Company and 14/ Black Watch of 229 Brigade. As part of this road was within 55 Division's bounds, one platoon from D Company was to assist in the attack. The road is referred to within grid square N.33.a. in the *War Diary*, but this is clearly a typographical error, as markings on the divisional map show this to be some 7,000 yards behind the lines, and the road in question was probably south-east of Orcq. (Neither can it be in grid square O.33.a. because this was in British hands on 22 October.)[55]

The enemy trenches were well built and strongly wired. As soon as the attackers got to within 100 yards of them, a furore of MG and trench mortar fire brought them to an abrupt halt. D Company's platoon lost its leader and six men within seconds, and the rest of the platoon took what cover they could. 14/ Black Watch met with similar resistance, they too being brought to an abortive standstill some 100 yards from the enemy's trench with thirty-two casualties, eleven of whom died.[56] Three of D Company's casualties were killed: thirty-six-year-old Pte Thomas Collinge from Bentham; twenty-six-year-old Pte Albert Davison from Ulverston; and nineteen-year-old Pte Alfred Timson from Glenfield. Wounded were Pte Wilfred Gunson, a nineteen-year-old from Kirkby-in-Furness, hit in the back by shrapnel; Pte William Lyes, the forty-two-year-old postman from Norfolk, wounded for the second time that year, though this time far more seriously, with a gunshot wound through both thighs; wounded for the second time in two months was nineteen-year-old Pte Thomas Wood from Bury. The platoon was shepherded together by its sergeant, who withdrew the men to a small wood 150 yards to the east of their objective and ordered them to dig in. One of his men, Pte Hugh Shulver, earned the MM.[57]

Commanders began to realise that the recent series of retreats by the Germans had come to an end, and that they intended to defend this current bridgehead to the west of Tournai as vigorously as possible. As it was still not policy to launch an all-out assault against this, Maj.-Gen. Jeudwine decided that the enemy was to be harassed as robustly as possible by artillery, MGs, and trench mortars, while infantry battalions would be given minor objectives to nibble at in the German defences.[58] In case of German counter-attack, some of the division's guns were pulled further back and the main line of resistance was more firmly entrenched by means of a series of outposts similar to those on the Lys front; to this end, the battalion was employed from the early hours of the 24th. Once the CO had supervised the marking out of their locations on the ground, the men began to dig a series of V-shaped trenches, each about 40 yards in length. Although the enemy left these men unmolested, HQ was subject to a mustard gas barrage at 11.30 a.m., though only one man was wounded. The position of HQ had clearly been identified by the enemy, so it was moved to the *Ferme du Baron* later in the afternoon and billets found for the men in the vicinity of Froidmont. It was 2 a.m. on the 25th before they were allowed to finish digging, fifteen of the V trenches completed. Later that morning, D Company was put back on trench digging and the remainder of the battalion moved forward to relieve the Fusiliers in the outpost line. 2Lt Arthur Rigg, formerly a CSM with the battalion and commissioned at the end of May 1918, was wounded in the leg by an MG bullet while he was in the trenches.

Throughout 26 October, the enemy harassed the battalion positions near Ere with a succession of gas shells and 77-mms. The last two men from the battalion to be killed in action were victims of this shelling. These were twenty-eight-year-old L/Cpl Thomas Dunbebin from Runcorn and twenty-two-year-old Sgt George Fletcher from London. Two others of the battalions died that day: Pte William Wilson from Rochdale, from wounds at Estaires (though the date of his wounding is unrecorded), and twenty-two-year-old L/Cpl William Parker, whose death back in England was due to illness. Earlier that morning, an RAF two-seater from C Flight (unfortunately the type of aircraft and squadron number went unrecorded in the *War Diary*) was shot down; it landed almost intact between the lines, and men from A Company braved No Man's Land to retrieve the aircraft, carrying it back behind their own line, where it was collected by an RAF lorry the next day. Around 11 a.m., yet another British plane came down near Pic-au-Vent after an enemy bullet perforated its petrol tank, but both pilot and observer escaped uninjured. Maj. Gardner took command of the battalion on the 26th, as both Lt-Col. Balfour and the IO, Lt Tucker, were admitted to hospital sick.

Both 27 and 28 October were quiet for the battalion (according to the *War Diary*!), with very little enemy activity apart from some gas shells near Pic-au-Vent, Croix-de-Pierre (half way between Pic-au-Vent and Froidmont), and Ere church on the 27th, wounding at least two men. Thirty-five-year-old Pte John Thomas Singleton from Haverigg, whose brother Pearson had been given a medical discharge due to wounds received earlier that year, got a shrapnel wound to the eyelid; as painful as this was, it was minor, and he was back with the battalion three days later. Wounded for the third time was thirty-four-year-old Pte Frederick Beard, who for the second time in two months was gassed. His recovery, however, was delayed by influenza, which he caught three days later, and he was lucky that this combination did not prove fatal. Oddly enough, the *War Diary* does not mention an action against one of the 'minor objectives' suggested by division. When the platoon assaulted this enemy strongpoint, the officer in charge was wounded and the A/CSM, twenty-nine-year-old Albert Hodgson from Blackpool, took command of the platoon. He led it on to the strongpoint, capturing an MG and two prisoners, and was awarded the DCM.[59] At 7.30 p.m. on the 28th, the battalion was relieved by 1/10th King's and marched back to billets at Bourghelles.

The battalion remained in the vicinity of Bourghelles until the early hours of 9 November, carrying out extensive training in open warfare. While there were no battle casualties during this period, several men died from earlier wounds or illness. The first of these was eighteen-year-old Pte Harry Crankshaw from Leicester, who died from his wounds at No. 15 CCS at Don. On 1 November, twenty-six-year-old Pte James Clarke of Mansfield died at home from wounds sustained in France, and L/Cpl Thomas Tomlinson died from illness in a German POW camp. The enemy had held their positions west of Tournai for so long that III Corps was considering forcing the line by a full-blown assault along the length of the Fifth Army's line, and plans were made for 165 and 166 Brigade to force the River Scheldt near Tournai.[60] Yet on the morning of 8 November, it appeared that these outposts west of the river were withdrawing, and two prisoners found by patrols told their captors that the Germans were holding a line east of the Scheldt ('Escaut' in French). In the morning, 1/8th King's crossed the river on the left flank completely unopposed. However, the 1/5th South Lancashires on the right flank had considerably more difficulty due to accurate MG fire, and only succeeded in crossing on the night of the 8/9th.

In the early hours of 9 November, the battalion was ordered to the brigade concentration point at Esplechin. It arrived at 11.30 a.m. and told it was now under the orders of 166 Brigade on the right flank of the advance. At 5.30 a.m. on the 10th, the battalion was ordered to Leuze and set off just over an hour later. Its arrival at 7 p.m. was substantially delayed by numerous craters in the road, which the Germans had mined as they retreated. Once in Leuze, the men were all placed in comfortable billets and made welcome by jubilant locals. The main road from Tournai to Brussels was impassable to all wheeled traffic; only pack horses were able to negotiate it. In a single 13-mile stretch, the RE Field Companies, 107 Tunnelling Company, and pioneers dealt with 500 mines and filled in twenty-two craters.[61]

Rumours may have circulated, but at 10.45 a.m. on 11 November, the battalion was formed up in the town square, along with a squadron from 1st Royal Dragoons, both units ready to continue the advance. On the night of the 10th, 165 and 166 Brigade were given orders for a general assault across the canal and river either side of Ath, to begin on the 11th unless a crossing was forced overnight. No crossing was forced during the night, the bridge barricaded, mined, and held by the enemy. However, at 7 a.m., one daring soul from the Fusiliers managed to establish a Lewis position in a nearby house overlooking the bridge, and the enemy was driven off by its fire. The Fusiliers then crossed the bridge and passed into the town, and mounted troops from Legard's Force (9th Cavalry Brigade) pushed even further eastwards. Battalion commanders from the two brigades were at a conference in Villers-St-Amand discussing the details for the attack, when at 9.05 a.m. a verbal message was passed to the divisional HQ at Barry about a ceasefire, necessitating a hurried phone call to the conference. Various staff officers frantically tried to contact the forward troops, ordering them to hold their positions. Legard's cavalry were 7 miles east of Ath before they were stopped.[62]

Shortly before 11 a.m., Maj. Gardner read out a telegram received from 166 Brigade stating that an armistice would begin at 11 a.m. A bugler from the Dragoons sounded the ceasefire, and the troops gave the royal salute while the band played the national anthems of Britain, France, and Belgium. The battalion then marched off along the main road to Ligne, the streets lined with cheering crowds. After lunch at Ligne, the battalion continued to Villers-St-Amand, where it rejoined 164 Brigade and was given billets. It has to be remembered that this was not a surrender. Neither was it the end of the war, an armistice being no more than a ceasefire. The following weeks were therefore more or less business as usual—fatigue parties, working parties, plenty of training…. Only towards the end of November did the battalion activities take on more of a peace-time character. Neither did this armistice spell the end of the casualty lists.

# Epilogue

The guns may have ceased fire, but the death toll still rose. Nineteen-year-old Pte Samuel Edington from St Helens died from his wounds in an English hospital on 13 November 1918. On 2 March 1919, Pte William Kelly from Ulverston succumbed to his wounds; though it's not known when he was wounded, his injuries had been too serious to risk transporting him home and he died at the hospital in Wimereux. Others died from illness (possibly Spanish Influenza) at home and in France. Pte Edward Atkinson, who died on Boxing Day 1918, is buried at Tournai; Capt. James Fisher died on 23 February 1919 and was buried in Barrow; on 16 April, thirty-three-year-old Pte Albert Rusconi died and was buried in his home town of Burton-on-Trent; on 31 May, nineteen-year-old Pte William Angove died and was buried at Trois Arbres Cemetery in France; and finally, on 21 July, Pte Henry Whieldon from Blackburn, died at home and was buried in Blackburn cemetery.

Lives were cut short in other pitiful ways; the death of father of one, thirty-one-year-old L/Cpl Cornelius Cafferty MM perhaps being the most unusual for an infantryman. This NCO had been evacuated back to England on 12 November 1918, suffering from ICT of his right arm. On 15 January 1919, his condition almost cured, he and two other patients from Nell Lane Military Hospital in Manchester went for a walk. Close to the hospital was the RAF airfield at Alexandra Park, where they arrived at 1.30 p.m. and asked permission to enter the airfield. This was granted, and the three men began talking to one of the mechanics and were told that an aircraft was due to go up on an air test. The Bristol Fighter (F .2b D 2218) required either ballast or a passenger to remain within weight and balance criteria, and it was usual for the mechanic to take the spare seat for the air test; but the three soldiers asked if one of them could go along instead as passenger. The pilot, Capt. Charles Brown, agreed and L/Cpl Cafferty and one of the other patients, CSM W. T. Davidson from 6/ Gordons, tossed a coin to see who would get the flight; Cafferty won the toss. Brown was a very experienced pilot and took off into wind as usual, but according to surprised witnesses, directly after lifting off he made a crosswind turn at low speed and continued to climb. The aircraft almost immediately entered a stall and spun into the ground from 60 feet. The left wing struck first, then the aircraft burst into flames as it turned over. Although the fire took over an hour to extinguish, it was clear from the post-mortem that both men died instantly from broken necks in the impact. Cafferty's widow and son, four-year-old Leo, were presented with his MM at a later date.[1]

Another decorated soldier to have braved battle many times over, only to end his young life after the Armistice, was former regular L/Sgt Albert Howarth MM. The thirty-five-year-old widower from Darwen was the father of a ten-year-old daughter, who lived with his parents while he served. At 10 p.m. on the night of 12 February 1919, the landlady of his French billet ran down to call Cpl Mills, who shared the billet, to tell him that she'd discovered Howarth apparently dead on the floor of his bedroom. The corporal ran up to confirm this and found his sergeant face down on the floor, fully clothed, and without any visible trace of violence about him. He had last been seen alive by a friend at 6.30 p.m. that evening as he was returning to his billet, the friend remarking that the sergeant was sober at the time. Though the post-mortem found evidence of alcohol in his stomach, it adjudged suffocation due to air passages being blocked by vomit, and added that this had been exacerbated by weakness of the left lung and a heart condition—both the result of pleurisy contracted while serving. The post-mortem concluded that these conditions had rendered the sergeant unable to leave his room to call for assistance.[2]

It cannot have been easy to run a battalion after the fighting had finished. Bored and idle soldiers tend to cause trouble, and there was only so much training that could be undergone once the battalion's numbers had dropped. Commanders did their best and education classes were held regularly, as were sporting competitions and social occasions such as dances and concerts. The problem was aggravated by the large number of men who had signed up for the duration of the war thinking that once it was over that they should all go straight home to their families and civilian lives. Some inevitably voted with their feet, and simply failed to return from leave. Demobilisation was not initially carried out on a 'first-in, first-out' basis, and apart from freed POWs who were demobilised almost immediately, preference was given to those men who had been employed in strategic industries, such as coal mining. This, however, caused huge resentment, as this meant that it was often those men who had only been conscripted in the latter part of the war who were demobilised first. The outcry against this soon brought about a change of Government policy.

Long-overdue home leave was given to as many of the men as possible. About sixty-three of these had their return delayed by Spanish Influenza, though none died from this lethal infection. L/Cpl William Postlethwaite (522) from Ulverston, who had been with the battalion since the beginning of the war, found his wife seriously ill when he returned home, and was granted an extension of his leave until she had recovered. Another not to return from leave was Cpl Thomas Rose. Due back on 26 February 1919, he failed to show up and was posted as a 'deserter'; his case is a typical example of how desertion was dealt with immediately after the war. The authorities were none too bothered about chasing after them, and the checks on railway stations, bridges, and public entertainments, routinely carried out by police during wartime, no longer applied (though all the deserters' medals were forfeited, as were those of soldiers convicted of a serious crime). A deserter's main problem was on the job market, as employers invariably asked for discharge papers and expected to see evidence that their potential employees had served their country. But official attitudes softened as the years passed by, and by signing a paper admitting their guilt, many deserters were able to gain a legal discharge from the Army without fear of imprisonment. Cpl Rose's hard-earned medals were subsequently issued to him in 1938.[3]

Had Cpl Rose returned from his leave on time, he would have found a battalion he barely recognised. Its strength had fallen to less than 200 by 24 February 1919, and the battalion was reorganised into two companies—the 'Cadre Company', and the 'Rhine Draft Company'. During this period, men from other units were posted or transferred to the 1/4th and many of the battalion attached to 'POW Companies' to guard German prisoners. One such was twenty-year-old Isaac Williams from Pencoed, who probably didn't relish looking back on his Army service. As a miner, he had been in a reserved occupation, only being called up in mid-1917. He'd been posted to the Welsh Regiment and on 21 April 1918 had been one of a large batch given a compulsory transfer to the 1/4th to replace battle casualties from Givenchy. As a miner, he might have expected a quick demob, but was caught out by the change of policy and posted to No. 24 POW Company. On 19 June 1919, while the lance corporal in charge of the compound guard, a German prisoner escaped, for which he was blamed and put in front of a FGCM. He was sentenced to a crushing forty-two days' Field Punishment No. 2 and demoted to Private.

The 1/4th's discipline does not seem to have suffered too great a dip, though it's fair to say that the numbers of individual soldiers appearing on the charge sheets increased—mostly for fairly minor offences, such as 'overstaying leave' by a day or two, or appearing late for morning parade. Poor behaviour there must have been within all the division, for Maj.-Gen. Jeudwine sent a memo out to all the division about 'incidents of a discreditable character at a dance' on 1 December 1918, and later that month, a letter was sent to all units concerning 'inappropriate behaviour of officers and men in Lille'.[4]

In June, the Cadre Party returned home, reaching Ulverston on Wednesday 11 June. It consisted of only of Lt-Col. Gardner MC, three officers, and twenty-four other ranks, yet was met at the station by the battalion band, various civic dignitaries, and an enthusiastic crowd of locals. After a civic reception the following day, the Cadre Party marched to the Ulverston parish church where the colours were handed over to the rector. Very few men from the Furness district who had been mobilised on 4 August 1914 were still with the battalion when it marched back in 1919. Somewhere between 3,400 and 4,000 men from all over the country had served in its ranks, and although many of those local to the area would attend the 'old comrades' functions for years to come, for those from further afield, this was a luxury few could afford. It might be expected that the last thing the men would want to do was continue to serve in the Army, yet this was exactly what some wanted. Many from the Furness District re-enlisted in the 4th Battalion: whether this was due to financial hardship is hard to determine, but it is possible that these men missed the comradeship of the war years. Some like Cpl John Carrick DCM joined the regulars; he enlisted in 2/ King's Own and was posted to Burma, where he quickly rose to the rank of Sergeant. Tragically, he accidentally drowned on 28 October 1922, and is buried in Rangoon.[5] Quite a few veterans decided that other countries held more future for them and emigrated after the war—mostly to Canada, but some to the USA too.

For many their demobilisation was delayed by hospital treatment. Two men from the battalion were among the earliest patients to receive facial reconstruction surgery. L/Cpl William Wood and Pte Alexander Minshall both suffered serious and disfiguring gunshot wounds to the face, and the pair received treatment at Queen's Hospital in Sidcup from Dr (later Sir) Harold Gillies. Minshall underwent a series of operations conducted by the surgeon Capt. G. H. Lawson Whale, his cheek bone reconstructed using rib cartilage, and areas of his nose and palate reconstructed too. The young soldier was finally discharged on Christmas Eve in 1920.[6] There seems to be a happy ending in this case, as he appears to have got married in 1923, living until March 1963.

Many lives after the war would never be the same. These men had joined up as fit and healthy individuals, but the health of many of them had been ruined by trench conditions, illness, or wounds. Rheumatism and arthritis were common grievances; tuberculosis far from rare, the notes in the service or pension records of those affected attributing it to military service. For Arthur

Hammond, discharged at the end of October 1917 as a result of trench nephritis, persistent ill health and weakness meant his inability to pursue his pre-war profession. The only job which he could physically manage was as a night watchman at a rubber factory in Chorley, on wages that, although topped up by a partial pension, made existence precarious for his family. Life took a turn for the worse when his wife died in 1926, leaving him with two young daughters to bring up on his small wage. Over the next few years, his health and ability to work deteriorated until his death from kidney failure in 1931, and the two girls were farmed out to relatives in different towns. In every photograph taken of him prior to the war, he appears a happy individual; yet his oldest daughter told me shortly before her death in 2004 that she never once saw her father smile.

It wasn't just the physical health of men that suffered. Post-Traumatic Stress Disorder (PTSD) may be a modern terminology and diagnosis, but it's evident that it's not just a modern problem: it quite evidently affected men after both World Wars. One of its darker characteristics is the way it creeps up on a soldier, often many years after the events themselves; and while people in the early twentieth century seem to us far more used to seeing death, they weren't immune to the mental torment associated with combat, and were probably far more reluctant to talk about it than the modern generation. For many old soldiers, night time is 'when the demons walk', but for the unlucky few, they walked all the time. Pte William Meikle was one such tortured soul. His medical discharge came in August 1919, not for wounds to the body, but wounds to the mind; the medal roll notes that his medals were never issued because he became an 'inmate of an insane asylum'. He does not appear to have had any family, since the medals would have been issued to them for safe-keeping had this been the case. The bravest men often paid the highest price in the years after these events. James Hewitson VC (known as 'Jimmy' to his friends and family) returned to Coniston after the war, got married, and continued working as a road mender. Despite being a local hero, Jimmy tried to carry on life as normal, but the display of a German field gun in Coniston was too much to stomach. He and a couple of his contemporaries dragged it down to the shores of Coniston Water, and using the steam yacht *Gondola* as a tug, dragged it into the lake, where it immediately sank from sight! Nightmares haunted this man and began to affect his health so badly that he was admitted to Stone House Hospital in Dartford, where he remained for most of twenty years. He returned home again and went back to his job with the council on the roads, and died on 2 March 1963 from pneumonia following a bout of influenza. 'Passchendaele,' he would call out in a fever during his hospitalisation; 'They're coming to get me'.[7]

In the 1920s and '30s, many of this generation of soldiers felt betrayed by their Government. Instead of 'homes fit for heroes', they got wage cuts, unemployment, and the Great Depression. Twenty-one years after the 'war to end all wars', their sons went off to fight the same foe, followed by conflict in Israel, Korea, Borneo, Malaya, Kenya, Cyprus, and Aden. Perhaps it's just as well that most veterans did not live to see their grandsons fight in the Falklands or in Northern Ireland—the 'war that did not exist', but which resulted in the deaths of 1,337 members of the armed forces and their families. They were thankfully also spared from seeing their great-grandsons off to fight in Iraq and Afghanistan.

During the Great War, 843 of the men who served with the battalion died from enemy action, illness, or accident. Their memory lives on.

# 'The Road to La Bassée'

## by Bernard Newman and Harold Arpthorp, 1934

I went across to France again, and walked about the line,
The trenches have been all filled in—the country's looking fine.
The folks gave me a welcome, and lots to eat and drink,
Saying, 'Allo, Tommee, back again? 'Ow do you do? In ze pink?'
And then I walked about again, and mooched about the line;
You'd never think there'd been a war, the country's looking fine.
But the one thing that amazed me most shocked me, I should say
—There's buses running now from Béthune to La Bassée!
I sat at Shrapnel Corner and I tried to take it in,
It all seemed much too quiet, I missed the war-time din.
I felt inclined to bob down quick—Jerry sniper in that trench!
A minnie coming over! God, what a hellish stench!
Then I pulled myself together, and walked on to La Folette—
And the cows were calmly grazing on the front line parapet.
And the kids were playing marbles by the old Estaminet—
Fancy kiddies playing marbles on the road to La Bassée!
You'd never think there'd been a war, the country's looking fine—
I had a job in places picking out the old front line.
You'd never think there'd been a war—ah, yet you would, I know,
You can't forget those rows of headstones every mile or so.
But down by Tunnel Trench I saw a sight that made me start,
For there, at Tourbieres crossroads—a gaudy ice-cream cart!
It was hot, and I was dusty, but somehow I couldn't stay—
Ices didn't seem quite decent on the road to La Bassée.
Some of the sights seemed more than strange as I kept marching on.
The Somme's a blooming garden, and there are roses in Peronne.
The sight of dear old Arras almost made me give three cheers;
And there's kiddies now in Plugstreet, and mamselles in Armentieres.
But nothing that I saw out there so seemed to beat the band
As those buses running smoothly over what was No Man's Land.
You'd just as soon expect them from the Bank to Mandalay
As to see those buses running from Béthune to La Bassée.

Then I got into a bus myself, and rode for all the way,
Yes, I rode inside a bus from Béthune to La Bassée.
Through Beuvry and through Annequin, and then by Cambrin Tower—
The journey used to take four years, but now it's half an hour.
Four years to half an hour—the best speedup I've met.
Four years? Aye, longer still for some—they haven't got there yet.
Then up came the conductor chap, 'Vos billets s'il vous plait.'
Fancy asking for your tickets on the road to La Bassée.
And I wondered what they'd think of it—those mates of mine who died—
They never got to La Bassée, though God knows how they tried.
I thought back to the moments when their number came around,
And now those buses rattling over sacred, holy ground,
Yes, I wondered what they'd think of it, those mates of mine who died.
Of those buses rattling over the old pave close beside.
'Carry on! That's why we died!' I could almost hear them say,
To keep those buses always running from Béthune to La Bassée!'

# Appendices

## Statistics

The tables below are based on a sample of 1,000 service records from the men who served in the 4th Battalion of the King's Own from August 1914 to 11 November 1918. What is perhaps the most shocking statistic to modern readers is that 67 per cent of these became battle casualties at some time in their service. All units sent in weekly 'Casualty Returns', with numbers killed, wounded, or sick in hospital, and this information was later used to calculate the number of wounded during the war. Official statistics are not accurate for the purpose of studying individuals, however, as they contained only totals, not names—invariably, men wounded on different occasions were counted more than once. A study of Appendix Four will show that a vast number of men were wounded on more than one occasion, but each occasion counted as one man in the official statistics. What is abundantly clear from the figures is that new men were more than three times as likely as their more experienced comrades to become a casualty within the first three months of arriving at the front. Experience counted!

| Hospitalisation causes other than gas or penetrating wounds | |
| --- | --- |
| Scabies | 7.7 % |
| Shell-shock | 4 % |
| Trench foot | 2.5 % |
| Trench Fever | 8 % |
| Trench nephritis | 1.1 % |
| ICT | 4.8 % |
| Percentage of men killed | 24.6 % |
| Percentage battle casualties (killed and wounded) | 67 % |
| Length of the casualties' service in the trenches at the time that they were wounded | |
| 3 months | 51.3 % |
| 4 to 6 months | 16.4 % |
| 7 to 12 months | 15.4 % |
| Over 12 months | 16.9 % |

How was the battalion employed once deployed overseas?
(Calculated based on the *War Diary* from 4 May 1915 to 11 November 1918)

| DAYS' ACTIVITY | 1915 | 1916 | 1917 | 1918 | TOTAL | Total percentage of time spent |
|---|---|---|---|---|---|---|
| TRAVELLING | 8 | 22 | 19 | 8 | 57 | 4 % |
| REST/INTENSIVE TRAINING | 8 | 57 | 95 | 50 | 210 | 16 % |
| RESERVE/SUPPORT | 119 | 164 | 180 | 140 | 603 | 47 % |
| FRONT LINE | 100 | 123 | 71 | 117 | 411 | 32 % |

# Medals and Awards 1914-1918

| | | | | |
|---|---|---|---|---|
| Adamson | R. | CSM | 200024 | DCM, MSM |
| Alexander | J. C. | 2Lt | | MC |
| Andrews | L. R. | 2Lt | | MC |
| Ashburn | A. E. | Pte | 200437 | MM |
| Ashton | W. | Sgt | 3582 | MM |
| Averill | F. | Pte | 26965 | MM |
| Baines | P. | L/Sgt | 200518 | DCM, MiD |
| Balderston | J. | Cpl | 1922 | MM |
| Balfour | G. B. | Lt-Col. | | DSO (Bar), MiD(x3) |
| Barrow | T. | Sgt | 200208 | DCM |
| Bateson | T. S. | 2Lt | | MC |
| Bell | W. | A/CSM | 200086 | MC, DCM, MiD |
| Binns | T. | Pte | 201586 | MM |
| Birkett | A. B. | Sgt | 8931 | DCM, MM |
| Blain | T. R. | Capt. | | MC |
| Bradley | R. | Pte | 201589 | MM |
| Burton | A. J. | Sgt | 202785 | DCM |
| Bussingham | J. | Pte | 202757 | MM |
| Carrick | J. | Cpl | 200476 | DCM |
| Carruthers | R. | Cpl | 200371 | MM |
| Carton | E. J. | Pte | 200222 | MM |
| Chadwick | W. | Sgt | 200120 | MM |
| Chapple | T. J. | Sgt | 200092 | MM |
| Chester | T. | Cpl | 200239 | MM |
| Clark | W. | RQMS | 200540 | MSM |
| Clarke | J. A. T. | Capt. | | CdG |
| Collin | J. H. | 2Lt | | VC |
| Collins | G. E. | Sgt | 8571 | B CdG |
| Cook | J. B. | WO2 | 200065 | DCM |
| Cooley | J. | Pte | 18079 | MM |
| Cooper | C. F. | L/Cpl | 200644 | MM |
| Coward | J. | Sgt | 200252 | MiD |

| Crichton | C. W. | WO2 | 201017 | MM |
|----------|-------|-----|--------|-----|
| Cross | J. M. | Sgt | 202738 | DCM |
| Cross | T. | Pte | 238003 | MM (Bar) |
| Cross | R. | Sgt | 200843 | R CdG |
| Dane | R. S. | 2Lt | | MC |
| Danson | W. | Cpl | 201712 | MM |
| Davies | J. | Pte | 202629 | MM (Bar) |
| Dickinson | J. H. | Sgt | 202739 | DCM, MM |
| Dixon | T. | Cpl | 241420 | MM |
| Dobbs | F. | L/Sgt | 27370 | MM |
| Ellwood | A. | Capt. | | MC |
| Evans | J. H. | Maj. | | MC (Bar) |
| Farish | W. H. | Sgt | 1281 | DCM |
| Fearnley | H. | Sgt | 201031 | MM |
| Ferguson | G. W. | 2Lt | | MC |
| Gardner | R. | Lt-Col. | | MC |
| Gaulter | J. R. | 2Lt | | MC |
| Graham | D. | WO2 | 200680 | DCM |
| Graves | A. E. | Cpl | 200710 | DCM |
| Green | H. | Pte | 24271 | MM |
| Greenough | E. | Cpl | 15227 | MM |
| Hallam | R. C. | 2Lt | | CdG |
| Hanna | W. | Pte | 200880 | MM |
| Hart | H. R. | 2Lt | | MiD |
| Hayhurst | W. | Sgt | 2411 | MiD |
| Helme | H. | Pte | 201418 | MM |
| Hewartson | G. | Cpl | 200434 | MM |
| Hewitson | J. | L/Cpl | 15853 | VC |
| Hewitt | E. H. | Lt | | MiD |
| Hinde | R. F. | Cpl | 201720 | MM |
| Hinds | W. G. | CQMS | 200117 | MM |
| Hinds | S. | Sgt | 200406 | MSM |
| Hodgson | D. | Sgt | 200839 | DCM |
| Holmes | G. | WO2 | 200467 | MM |
| Huddleston | G. | Sgt | 200746 | DCM |
| Huthwaite | H. Y. | Capt. | | MC |
| Jackson | R. J. | Pte | 24201 | MM |
| Jackson | R. N. | Sgt | 200601 | MM, MiD |
| Jackson | F. | L/Sgt | 200162 | MM |
| Jackson | T. | Cpl | 200197 | MM, MiD |
| Johnson | G. | L/Sgt | 200691 | DCM (Bar) |
| Johnson | J. | Pte | 200278 | MM |

| Kendall | E. A. | Capt. | | MC |
|---|---|---|---|---|
| Kitchin | J. A. T. | Pte | 200323 | MiD |
| Knowles | A. F. | Pte | 201727 | MM |
| Latham | A. S. | Capt. | | MC |
| Lockey | E. | 2Lt | 201104 | MM |
| Loydell | H. | Pte | 200538 | MM |
| Lyon | H. | 2Lt | | MC |
| Lyth(e) | J. | Pte | 32922 | MM |
| Mackereth | G. | Pte | 201229 | MM |
| Marsden | L. R. | L/Cpl | 201633 | MM |
| Martin | H. | Cpl | 200198 | DCM |
| Mayson | T. F. | Sgt | 200717 | VC |
| McAlarney | J. | Pte | 200272 | MM |
| McGill | W. | L/Cpl | 200912 | MM |
| McIlheron | T. | CQMS | 200675 | MM |
| Middleton | T. H. | Lt | 2094 | MM (Bar) |
| Miles | A. E. | Sgt | 202159 | MM |
| Miller | P. | Sgt | 200825 | MiD |
| Milton | C. S. | Pte | 200517 | DCM |
| Moody | T. | Pte | 27098 | MM |
| Moore | J. P. | L/Cpl | 200156 | MM |
| Morris | W. | Pte | 12768 | MM |
| Morris | A. E. | Sgt | 200388 | MM |
| Morton | A. E. | Capt. | | MC |
| Murray | J. | Pte | 2905 | MM |
| Myatt | E. | Capt. | | MiD |
| Myers | H. W. | Sgt | 200493 | MM |
| Nicholson | W. | Pte | 200249 | MM |
| Overton | C. L. | Capt. | | MC |
| Owen | J. S. | CSM | 2340 | DCM, MM |
| Parnell | H. | Sgt | 200481 | MM |
| Pearson | J. R. | Sgt | 200508 | DCM |
| Pemberton | B. H. | 2Lt | | MC |
| Percival | H. W. | Sgt | 200550 | MM |
| Place | F. C. | 2Lt | | MC |
| Porter | M. J. | Cpl | 200595 | MM |
| Poskitt | G. E. | Pte | 2512 | MM |
| Powell | P. W. | Capt. | | MC |
| Pritchard | T. H. | 2Lt | | MC |
| Procter | A. P. | Capt. | | MC |
| Raeside | G. F. | 2Lt | | MC |
| Rathbone | T. S. | Sgt | 202784 | MM |

| | | | | |
|---|---|---|---|---|
| Redpath | E. | Pte | 202188 | MM |
| Richardson | H. | 2Lt | | MC |
| Rickwood | W. G. | Sgt | 202192 | MSM |
| Robinson | E. G. | Pte | 200229 | MM |
| Robinson | T. | Sgt | 201123 | MM |
| Rothwell | G. | L/Cpl | 12073 | DCM |
| Round | J. | L/Cpl | 13269 | MM |
| Rouse | I. B. | 2Lt | | MC |
| Shepherd | G. | Sgt | 200484 | MM |
| Sherley | F. A. | Sgt | 202168 | MM |
| Shulver | H. | Pte | 260009 | MM |
| Smith | W. E. | WO2 | 30262 | DCM |
| Smith | H. | Sgt | 200604 | MM |
| Smith | J. W. | Pte | 2433 | MM |
| Stalker | P. | Sgt | 2488 | MM |
| Stott | H. | Pte | 201293 | MM |
| Sugden | J. | Pte | 29121 | MM |
| Swarbrick | W. | Pte | 21056 | MM |
| Taylor | G. A. | 2Lt | | MC |
| Taylor | G. F. | Capt. | | MiD |
| Taylor | R. | Pte | 21702 | MM |
| Taylor | A. V. | L/Cpl | 200999 | MM |
| Thomas | J. W. | Pte | 202130 | MM |
| Towers | H. Q. | L/Cpl | 200736 | MM |
| Vernoun | P. J. | Cpl | 202140 | MM |
| Wadham | W. F. | Lt-Col. | | NVS |
| Wakefield | G. | Pte | 201182 | MM |
| Walker | R. | WO2 | 200554 | BMV |
| Warburton | T. E. | Pte | 201247 | MM |
| Watson | G. H. | Sgt | 202161 | MM |
| Way | J. | Capt. | 1573 | MSM, MiD |
| Whiteside | W. T. | Sgt | 200734 | MM |
| Wilde | J. T. | Pte | 201667 | MM |
| Williams | R. A. | WO2 | 200519 | MC |
| Wolstencroft | S. | Pte | 26990 | MM |
| Wright | A. A. | Capt. | | MC |
| Wright | T. | Sgt | 200878 | MM |

Men known to have been nominated for awards which were not granted 1914-1918

(Medal nominated for to the left, award granted to the right.)

| | | | | |
|---|---|---|---|---|
| Ashton | W. | Sgt | 3582 | DCM, MM |
| Barker | H. E. | Pte | 1236 | MM, Nil |
| Boyle | F. A. | L/Cpl | 35195 | MM, Nil |
| Bradley | R. | Pte | 201589 | DCM, MM |
| Bussingham | J. | Pte | 202757 | DCM, MM |
| Butcher | R. | WO2 | 200372 | MM, Nil |
| Chapple | T. J. | Sgt | 200092 | DCM, MM |
| Collins | G. E. | Sgt | 8571 | MM, B CdG |
| Cooley | J. | Pte | 18079 | DCM, MM |
| Entwistle | T. | Cpl | 201608 | MM, Nil |
| Evans | J. H. | Maj. | | DCM Bar, Nil |
| Fearnley | H. | Sgt | 201031 | DCM, MM |
| Graham | D. | WO2 | 200680 | MM, Nil |
| Hadwin | W. | Pte | 200441 | MM, Nil |
| Hall | F. C. | Pte | 25619 | MM, Nil |
| Helme | G. | Pte | 200805 | MM, Nil |
| Hogg | J. | Cpl | 24198 | MM, Nil |
| Jackson | F. | L/Sgt | 200162 | DCM, MM |
| Joplin | W. S. | Pte | 15099 | MM, Nil |
| Knowles | A. F. | Pte | 201727 | DCM, MM |
| Lord | G. | Pte | 35049 | MM, Nil |
| Miles | A. E. | Sgt | 202159 | DCM, MM |
| Miller | P. | Sgt | 200825 | MM, Nil |
| Morris | W. | Pte | 12768 | DCM, MM |
| Motteram | E. | Pte | 200102 | MM, Nil |
| Newbold | C. H. | 2Lt | | MC, Nil |
| Newton | E. | Sgt | 200446 | MM, Nil |
| Overton | C. L. | Capt. | | MC Bar, Nil |
| Pedder | J. | Pte | 201527 | DCM, Nil |
| Pollitt | J. | L/Cpl | 24177 | MM (x2), Nil |
| Porter | M. J. | Cpl | 200595 | DCM + MM (x2), MM |
| Robathan | P. E. | Maj. | | MC, Nil |
| Saunders | F. W. | CQMS | 200193 | MM, Nil |
| Shepherd | G. | Sgt | 200484 | MM Bar, Nil |
| Taylor | A. V. | L/Cpl | 200999 | DCM, Nil |
| Taylor | W. W. | Pte | 2688 | MM, Nil |
| Thomson | W. | Pte | 201792 | MM, Nil |
| Walker | R. | WO2 | 200554 | MM, Nil |
| Wilde | J. T. | Pte | 201667 | DCM, MM |
| Wolstencroft | S. | Pte | 26990 | DCM, MM |

# Battalion Roll 1914-1918

| | | | | |
|---|---|---|---|---|
| Abbott | Robert | Pte | 3427 | DOW 9/9/16 |
| Abernethy | Walter | Pte | 201085 | WIA |
| Adams | George | L/Cpl | 24054 | |
| Adamson | Robert | CSM | 200024 | DCM, Att. to TMB, KIA 9/4/18 |
| Agar | Thomas Henry | Pte | 201484 | KIA 1/6/17 |
| Ainsworth | Edgar | Pte | 200046 | |
| Airey | James | Pte | 200401 | |
| Airey | John Bradley | Pte | 34512 | |
| Airey | Thomas | Pte | 27989 | |
| Airey | Thomas | Pte | 240287 | Also 1/5th and 2/5th, KIA 9/4/18 |
| Akister | Aaron | A/CSM | 915 | H |
| Akister | Thomas | L/Cpl | 200442 | KIA 31/7/17 |
| Akred | Arthur | Pte | 2783 | WIA (4), DOW 25/12/16 |
| Alderson | Charles George | Pte | 27091 | KIA 16/9/17 |
| Aldous | Ephraim | Pte | 22696 | Ex 7th Bn, KIA 9/4/18 |
| Alexander | James Caldwell | 2Lt | | MC Att. from LF, OC 8 Ptn, WIA |
| Allan | Robert William | Pte | 27990 | |
| Allcock | John | Pte | 20892 | Ex 8th Bn, WIA (2) |
| Allcock | Robert | Pte | 41041 | |
| Allen | Henry | L/Cpl | 266505 | |
| Allen | Percy | Pte | 201688 | KIA 29/9/16 |
| Allen | Robert | Pte | 241617 | Ex 1/5th, KIA 9/4/18 |
| Allen | William | Pte | 200577 | WIA |
| Allen | William Robert | Pte | 200248 | |
| Allin | George Arthur | L/Cpl | 34628 | WIA |
| Allington | Joseph | Pte | 1465 | H |
| Allison | Edwin | Pte | 40953 | |
| Allison | John | Pte | 27992 | KIA 20/11/17 |
| Allsop | Albert Edward | Pte | 40955 | |
| Alston | Thomas | Pte | 34625 | |
| Amos | Thomas | Sgt | 27429 | Ex LF and 7th Bn. POW |
| Anderson | Alexander | Pte | 200968 | |
| Anderson | Charles | Pte | 29164 | Trans. to LC |
| Anderson | John George | 2Lt | | A Coy, WIA |
| Anderson | Louis | Pte | 23028 | Ex 7th Bn, WIA |
| Anderton | Ralph | Pte | 202215 | WIA, Trans. to LC |
| Andrewartha | Loftus | L/Cpl | 200529 | WIA |
| Andrews | Lionel Raymond | 2Lt | | MC |
| Andrews | Moses | Pte | 16929 | Ex 2nd Bn, KIA 9/4/18 |
| Andrews | William | Pte | 40880 | |

| | | | | |
|---|---|---|---|---|
| Angove | Thomas | Pte | 201060 | KIA 9/4/18 |
| Angove | William Wilson | Pte | 38306 | D 31/5/19 |
| Ansell | Charles Edmund | L/Sgt | 32568 | Ex 7th Bn, DOW 27/4/18 |
| Anson | John Charles | Pte | 201351 | KIA 8/8/16 |
| Anthony | Herbert | Pte | 24529 | Ex Notts and Derby, also 1st and 9th Bns. |
| Appleton | Henry | Pte | 22401 | Ex 11th and 1st Bns, WIA |
| Appleyard | Thomas | Pte | 27003 | Ex Lincs and also 1st and 1/5th Bns |
| Armstead | Charles Clifton | Pte | 40882 | |
| Armstrong | Alfred Stanley | Pte | 40881 | |
| Armstrong | Joseph Benson | L/Cpl | 200178 | WIA |
| Armstrong | Oliver | Pte | 24572 | Also 7th Bn |
| Armstrong | Robert Joseph | Pte | 200858 | WIA (2), posted to 1/5th, POW |
| Armstrong | William | L/Cpl | 841 | H |
| Arnold | Albert | Pte | 201142 | WIA, Trans. to RWF |
| Arnott | William George | Pte | 200751 | |
| Arrowsmith | Hugh | Pte | 28087 | WIA, also LF |
| Asbury | William | Pte | 200137 | |
| Ashburn | Albert E. | Pte | 200437 | 11 Ptn, MM, WIA Trans. KLR |
| Ashburner | Robert | Pte | 200771 | WIA (2), trans. to Lincs, POW |
| Ashburner | Thomas | Pte | 200100 | WIA |
| Ashcroft | George | Pte | 3513 | WIA, KIA 3/8/16 |
| Ashcroft | Robert Leslie | Lt | | |
| Ashmore | Henry Thomas | Pte | 201429 | WIA (2) |
| Ashmore | John | Pte | 201312 | WIA |
| Ashton | John Scott | Cpl | 14859 | Also 7th Bn |
| Ashton | Thomas | Pte | 4900 | DOW 26/12/16 |
| Ashton | Thomas | Pte | 200981 | WIA |
| Ashton | William | Sgt | 3582 | MM, WIA |
| Ashworth | Fred | Pte | 201763 | Trans. to LF |
| Ashworth | George | Pte | 201759 | KIA 31/5/18 |
| Ashworth | Henry Whitehead | Pte | 266059 | POW |
| Ashworth | James | Pte | 200735 | KIA 8/8/16 |
| Ashworth | John | Pte | 26745 | Also 7th Bn |
| Ashworth | John Frederick | L/Cpl | 201414 | WIA |
| Ashworth | Joseph | Pte | 201585 | |
| Askew | Edmund Daniels | L/Cpl | 202416 | POW |
| Askew | Herbert | Pte | 201528 | |
| Askew | John | Pte | 201078 | |
| Aspinall | John | Pte | 265237 | WIA |
| Asplin | Ernest Oliver | Pte | 35077 | |
| Astill | William | Pte | 30113 | Also 8th and 1st Bns |
| Astley | John | Pte | 201410 | WIA, POW? |

| | | | | |
|---|---|---|---|---|
| Athersmith | John H. | Pte | 201100 | POW |
| Athersmith | Nelson | Pte | 201099 | KIA 8/8/16 |
| Athersmith | Thomas | Pte | 2053 | WIA |
| Atherton | James Boardman | Pte | 201421 | KIA 8/8/16 |
| Atherton | John | Pte | 3408 | DOW 15/9/16 |
| Atherton | Joseph | Pte | 200855 | WIA, POW |
| Atkin | John Charles | Pte | 41664 | |
| Atkinson | Arthur | Pte | 1975 | DOW 30/8/16 |
| Atkinson | Edward | Pte | 48862 | D 26/12/18 |
| Atkinson | Francis | Sgt | 265012 | |
| Atkinson | Henry Richard | Pte | 2386 | KIA 1/8/16 |
| Atkinson | Isaac | Pte | 200697 | KIA 8/8/16 |
| Atkinson | John | Pte | 2127 | KIA 27/5/15 |
| Atkinson | John J. | Pte | 200737 | WIA |
| Atkinson | Leonard Overell Byng | L/Sgt | 476 | H, D 18/9/14 |
| Atkinson | Thomas | A/Cpl | 200141 | WIA, POW |
| Atkinson | Walter | Pte | 201407 | Att. to TMB, also 7th and 1st Bns |
| Atkinson | Wilfred | Cpl | 1405 | Att. to TMB |
| Austin | Benjamin | Pte | 40884 | Also 2/5th |
| Austin | Frederick Arthur | Pte | 41042 | KIA 19/6/18 |
| Averill | Frederick | Pte | 26965 | Also 11th and 7th Bns, MM |
| Axtell | James William H. | 2Lt | | WIA |
| Backhouse | Herman | Pte | 201848 | WIA, also 2/5th |
| Backhouse | John | Pte | 2392 | WIA, trans. to LNL |
| Bagot | Samuel Charles | Pte | 200462 | |
| Bagot | Thomas | Pte | 241596 | KIA 31/7/17 |
| Bagshaw | Albert | Pte | 28088 | Ex Lanc Fusiliers, WIA, trans. to ASC |
| Bailey | John | Pte | 201023 | |
| Bailey | Percy | Pte | 241100 | Ex 1/5th, WIA |
| Bailey | Walter | Pte | 40885 | |
| Bailey | William Mark | Pte | 41526 | |
| Bailiff | James | L/Cpl | 200819 | Trans. to 1/5th, WIA |
| Bain | George | Pte | 29188 | Also ASC and LC |
| Bainbridge | Frederick | Pte | 1509 | H |
| Bainbridge | | Cpl | | H |
| Baines | Frank | Pte | 202196 | Ex 8th Bn, KIA 31/7/17 |
| Baines | Frederick | Pte | 34711 | POW |
| Baines | Phillip | L/Sgt | 200518 | 2 Ptn, A Coy, MiD, WIA, POW |
| Baines | William James | Pte | 201233 | |
| Baker | Arthur Samuel | Pte | 28164 | Ex 7th Bn, KIA 11/4/18 |
| Baker | Charles William. | Pte | 27124 | Ex Lincs and also 1st Bn |
| Baker | Frederick | Pte | 200171 | WIA |

| Baker | Samuel | Pte | 200524 | |
| Baker | Thomas | Pte | 200908 | WIA |
| Balderson | Thomas | Cpl | 1870 | KIA 27/9/16 |
| Balderston | Joseph | Cpl | 1922 | A Coy, DOW 1/9/16 |
| Balding | Archibald Leonard | Pte | 28186 | DOW 19/4/18 |
| Baldwin | James | Pte | 13615 | Also 9th Bn |
| Balfour | George Boyd | Lt-Col. | | DSO and Bar, MiD (3) |
| Ball | Albert Victor | Pte | 22503 | Ex 11th Bn, KIA 20/9/17 |
| Ball | Arthur | Pte | 29161 | Also LC |
| Ball | Edward | Pte | 40886 | |
| Balm | Thomas | Pte | 201587 | WIA, Also 7th Bn |
| Balshaw | John | Pte | 27529 | Also 8th Bn |
| Bamber | Harold | L/Cpl | 29149 | |
| Bamber | Hugh | Cpl | 201683 | |
| Bamber | James Robinson | Pte | 242700 | WIA (3), posted 1/5th and later 2nd Bn |
| Banks | Ernest Reginald | Pte | 41075 | |
| Banks | John Edward | L/Sgt | 200458 | DOW 22/6/18 |
| Barber | John William | Pte | 201592 | Ex MCR, WIA, trans. to LC |
| Barby | Bernard | Pte | 41532 | |
| Barclay | Stanley | Pte | 42887 | |
| Bargh | George James | Pte | 49363 | |
| Barker | Arthur | Pte | 19513 | Ex 2nd Bn |
| Barker | Charles Wilson | Pte | 200539 | WIA (2) |
| Barker | Harold Edward | Cpl | 1160 | |
| Barker | Horace Edward | Pte | 1236 | DOW 20/6/15 |
| Barker | William | Pte | 2720 | Trans. to LC |
| Barlow | Reginald Joseph | Pte | 41521 | |
| Barnes | George | Pte | 201707 | WIA, Also 1st Bn |
| Barnes | Jesse | Cpl | 29169 | Ex W. Yorks and LC |
| Barnes | Joseph | Pte | 200471 | A Coy, WIA |
| Barnes | Nicholas Edmund | Maj. | | |
| Barnett | Norman | Pte | 200366 | Att. to TMB |
| Barnett | Samuel | Pte | 3651 | DOW 13/5/16 |
| Barr | William | Pte | 27998 | |
| Barrass | Thomas William | Pte | 27993 | Also 1/5th |
| Barratt | Leonard Smedley | Pte | 242361 | |
| Barratt | William | Pte | 42885 | POW |
| Barratt | William Donald | Capt. | | D Coy OC |
| Barron (Baron) | Albert Thomas | Pte | 24849 | POW, D 24/7/18 |
| Barrow | Edward Wilson | Cpl | 200618 | KIA 28/9/16 |
| Barrow | Fred | Pte | 1416 | WIA |
| Barrow | Hadyn | 2Lt | | |

| Barrow | J. V. | Capt. | | |
|--------|-------|-------|---|---|
| Barrow | James Henry | Pte | 200985 | KIA 20/11/17 |
| Barrow | John Edward | Pte | 200799 | WIA (2) |
| Barrow | John Jarvis | Pte | 2509 | KIA 8/6/15 |
| Barrow | Joseph | Pte | 200549 | D Coy, WIA |
| Barrow | Robert George | Pte | 16714 | Ex 2nd and 7th Bns, POW |
| Barrow | Thomas | Sgt | 200208 | D Coy 16 Ptn, DCM |
| Barrow | Thomas S. | Pte | 201169 | Tans to LC |
| Barrow | W. | Pte | 1754 | Trans. to RFC |
| Barrow | William Henry | Pte | 2733 | DOW 5/7/16 |
| Barry | John | L/Cpl | 26791 | Ex KRR and 7th Bn, DOW 9/4/18 |
| Barton | Charles Ernest | Pte | 201565 | POW |
| Barton | Frank | Pte | 40888 | |
| Barton | Henry | Pte | 40960 | |
| Barton | James | Pte | 22279 | POW |
| Bashall | Richard | Pte | 17240 | Ex 2nd Bn, DOW 29/4/18 |
| Bassett | Albert Edmund | Pte | 27999 | D 27/8/17 |
| Bassett | Robert W. | Pte | 2423 | Trans. to Glam. Yeo. |
| Batchelor | Tom | L/Cpl | 20905 | Ex 11th Bn, WIA |
| Batchelor | William Kearns | Capt. | | |
| Bates | Obadiah | Cpl | 200641 | |
| Bates | William | Pte | 27086 | Ex 7th Bn, KIA 26/4/18 |
| Bateson | Thomas Smith | 2Lt | | MC, WIA |
| Battersbey | William | Pte | 51942 | Also LF |
| Batty | Joseph | Pte | 13594 | Also 9th and 7th Bns |
| Baxendale | David | Pte | 201708 | KIA 20/9/17 |
| Baxter | Cecil William | Pte | 40891 | |
| Baxter | Fred | Cpl | 3659 | DOW 8/1/17 |
| Baxter | James Edward | Pte | 28089 | Ex LF, POW |
| Baxter | Thomas | Pte | 1582 | KIA 30/5/15 |
| Baxter | William | L/Cpl | 200217 | POW |
| Bayes | Walter | Pte | 17135 | Also 2nd Bn |
| Bayley | Harold | Pte | 238002 | Ex DLOY, KIA 7/7/17 |
| Bayliff | William | Pte | 3070 | H, D 4/2/15 |
| Bayliffe | Edward W. D. | A/Cpl | 200373 | |
| Baynes | Edwin Arthur | Cpl | 201185 | |
| Baynes | John William | Pte | 1592 | H |
| Beard | Frederick | Pte | 33465 | Ex 8th and 7th Bns, WIA (4) |
| Beard | William | Pte | 3814 | Also 7th Bn |
| Beardsley | Amos | Lt | | MM while in TC |
| Beattie | Robert | Pte | 27637 | Also 1st Bn |
| Beaumont | Jonathan | Pte | 15171 | Also 9th and 7th Bns, DOW 26/7/17 |

| Beazley | Tom Forrest | 2Lt | | WIA |
|---|---|---|---|---|
| Bebbington | Harry | Pte | 19690 | WIA, trans. to LC |
| Bebbington | Leslie | Pte | 200823 | D Coy |
| Beck | Henry | Pte | 200624 | WIA |
| Beckett | Frederick | Pte | 41503 | |
| Beckett | William | Pte | 2905 | KIA 15/6/15 |
| Bee | Richard | Pte | 201508 | WIA |
| Beesley | George | Pte | 21569 | Ex 7th Bn, KIA 9/4/18 |
| Beeson | Robert | Pte | 41558 | |
| Beeston | Bert | Pte | 41524 | |
| Beetham | Henry | Pte | 27697 | Ex 1st and 7th Bns, WIA, D Coy, KIA 9/4/18 |
| Beeton | Thomas James | Pte | 29175 | |
| Bell | Addison | Pte | 2700 | KIA 15/6/15 |
| Bell | Charles William | Pte | 24380 | Ex 7th Bn, WIA |
| Bell | David | Pte | 200732 | WIA |
| Bell | David | Pte | 35259 | Also 2/5th |
| Bell | George | Cpl | 200273 | KIA 8/8/16 |
| Bell | James | Pte | 2284 | H, D 6/10/15 |
| Bell | James | Pte | 200798 | |
| Bell | Robert | Cpl | 200707 | WIA (2), posted 1/5th |
| Bell | Robert | Pte | 49375 | |
| Bell | Tom | Pte | 3019 | KIA 15/6/15 |
| Bell | Walter | Pte | 1715 | KIA 18/8/16 with 8th Bn |
| Bell | William | A/CSM | 200086 | DCM, MC, posted to 1st Bn |
| Bellamy | Alfred | Pte | 200236 | |
| Bellamy | Frank | Pte | 27202 | Also Lincs and 1st and 9th Bns |
| Bellamy | Fred | Pte | 3423 | Att. to TMB, KIA 6/8/16 |
| Bellfield | Joseph | Pte | 24569 | Also 7th and 11th Bns |
| Bellman | William | WO2 | 200378 | Commissioned LC 17/5/18 |
| Bennett | Alfred | Pte | 200673 | KIA 20/11/17 |
| Bennett | Edward | Cpl | 201306 | WIA (3) |
| Bennett | James | Pte | 200513 | |
| Bennett | John | Pte | 2507 | KIA 8/6/15 |
| Bennett | John | Pte | 23900 | Also 7th Bn |
| Bennett | John Frederick | L/Cpl | 201160 | Ex 1/5th, MM, KIA 9/4/18 |
| Bennett | Samuel | Pte | 201257 | Accidentally wounded |
| Bennett | Thomas | Sgt | 1735 | Trans. to MGC |
| Bennett | Thomas James | Pte | 201192 | |
| Bennett | William | Pte | 40964 | |
| Benson | Fred | Pte | 1795 | H |
| Benson | Thomas William | Pte | 202736 | DOW 31/7/17 (CWGC date wrong) |

| Benson | Timothy | Pte | 200774 | D 26/9/17 with 8th Bn |
|---|---|---|---|---|
| Bentley | Richard | Pte | 2437 | H |
| Berry | Edward Clifford | Pte | 265286 | |
| Berry | Fred | Pte | 2624 | WIA |
| Berry | Harry | Pte | 30050 | Ex 8th Bn, POW |
| Bertram | Henry | Pte | 200428 | Att. to TMB and from 7/1/16 to 164 Bde as groom. |
| Berwick | Donald Trevor | Pte | 201709 | WIA |
| Beswick | Thomas | Pte | 202766 | WIA, trans. to MCR |
| Bethune | Robert Thomas | Capt. | | |
| Bett | John | Pte | 1993 | H, D 18/10/14 |
| Bevins | Edward | Pte | 265626 | WIA |
| Bevins | William | Pte | 201095 | DOW 17/8/17 |
| Bewsher | Francis Howard | Pte | 201127 | WIA |
| Bewsher | Thomas E. | Pte | 201140 | WIA |
| Bibby | Albert Edward | Pte | 33961 | Posted 1/5th |
| Bidwell | Harry | Pte | 201591 | WIA |
| Bielby | William | Pte | 27997 | DOW 21/9/17 |
| Biggs | Joseph Bertram | Pte | 202650 | Ex 7th Bn |
| Bigland | George Braddyll | 2Lt | | KIA 15/6/15 |
| Billingham | Albert | Pte | 32887 | Also 6th and 8th Bns, KIA 31/7/17 |
| Billingham | James | Pte | 1584 | H |
| Billington | Albert V. | Pte | 3971 | WIA, trans. to TC |
| Billington | Herbert | Pte | 34614 | POW |
| Billington | John | Pte | 3511 | |
| Binnersley | Henry Charles | Pte | 51737 | Ex KSLI |
| Binnie | Alexander | 2Lt | | |
| Binns | Harold | Cpl | 1303 | Att. to TMB |
| Binns | Taylor | Pte | 201586 | Ex MCR, MM, WIA, trans. to MGC |
| Birch | Charles | Cpl | 32509 | Ex 7th Bn, MM, WIA |
| Birch | Charles Edward | Pte | 2353 | WIA, trans. to MGC |
| Birch | George | Pte | 241221 | Also LC |
| Birch | William | Pte | 200897 | |
| Bird | Frederick | Pte | 1839 | Also 1/5th |
| Birkett | Arthur Bolton | Sgt | 8931 | Ex 1st Bn, DCM, MM, 3 Ptn A Coy, WIA |
| Birkett | Richard | Pte | 200140 | WIA, trans. to RDC and LC |
| Birmingham | Edward | Pte | 2157 | WIA, trans. to AC and then Lincs |
| Bispham | John Tyson | L/Sgt | 1262 | |
| Biss | Louis Alfred | Pte | 29355 | |
| Black | David | Pte | 3621 | WIA, trans. to TC |
| Black | Robert Grieve | Pte | 3746 | |
| Blackburn | Thomas | Pte | 34653 | |

| Blacklock | Richard | Pte | 201774 | 8th Bn, DOW 6/11/18 with N. Staffs |
| Blades | Harry | Pte | 201328 | |
| Blain | Thomas Reginald | Capt. | | OC D Coy, WIA 31/10/17 |
| Blake | James | Pte | 200015 | Trans. to RE |
| Blake | Thomas Patrick | Pte | 200016 | KIA 15/6/15 |
| Blakekley | Herbert | Pte | 201569 | Trans. to LC and then E. Lancs |
| Blakemore | James Lawrence | Pte | 32566 | Also 7th and 8th Bns |
| Blamire | Edward | Pte | 2639 | WIA, also 1/5th |
| Bland | Harry | Pte | 201423 | KIA 11/5/17 |
| Blease | Alfred | Pte | 27781 | Also 11th and 8th Bns |
| Blendall | John | L/Cpl | 2607 | Trans. to ASC and Lincs |
| Blezard | Thomas | Pte | 200627 | DOW 8/8/16 |
| Blimston | Richard | Pte | 3033 | |
| Bloomfield | Sydney | Pte | 200383 | WIA, also 1st Bn |
| Blout | Percy | Pte | 24533 | Also Notts and Derby and 9th and 1/5th Bns |
| Blower | Wilfred | Pte | 40889 | |
| Blundell | Herbert | Pte | 202005 | Also 7th Bn |
| Blundell | Peter John | 2Lt | | |
| Boltar | Arthur | Pte | 28251 | Also ASC and 1st Bn |
| Bolton | Harold | Cpl | 22327 | Ex 11th Bn, WIA (2) |
| Bolton | Henry | Pte | 201588 | B Coy, WIA |
| Bolton | Stuart | Lt | | Att. to 164 TMB, KIA 17/3/18 |
| Bolton | William | Pte | 200986 | |
| Bond | William | Pte | 24170 | KIA 31/7/17 |
| Bond | William | Pte | 33072 | WIA |
| Bonner | Albert Henry | Pte | 28090 | Ex LF |
| Bonnick | James | Sgt | 11289 | Also 1st, 8th, and 7th Bns |
| Bool | George | Pte | 200814 | WIA |
| Boon | William | Pte | 3963 | WIA, trans. to Cheshires |
| Borley | Leonard Edward | Pte | 202175 | KIA 31/7/17 |
| Bosanko | Clarence | Pte | 200574 | Att. to TMB |
| Bosanko | William Ernest | Cpl | 200172 | WIA, commissioned in Border R 12/11/18 |
| Boston | Thomas Patterson | L/Cpl | 27996 | |
| Bottomley | Edward | Pte | 20438 | Also 8th, 1st, and 2/5th Bns |
| Bottomley | Harry | Pte | 20689 | Ex 11th Bn, WIA |
| Boulter | George Arthur | Pte | 37078 | KIA 9/4/18 |
| Boundy | James | Pte | 200280 | |
| Boundy | Stephen | Pte | 200658 | WIA (3), POW |
| Bowes | Thomas | Pte | 201011 | WIA, also 8th Bn |
| Bowfield | James | Pte | 200415 | DOW 17/3/18 |
| Bowker | Leonard | Pte | 201564 | KIA 20/9/17 |

| | | | | |
|---|---|---|---|---|
| Bowling | Joseph | Pte | 201753 | WIA |
| Bowman | George | Pte | 2641 | WIA, trans. to LC |
| Bowman | Leslie Spencer | 2Lt | | WIA, KIA 25/6/17 with RFC |
| Bowron | Thomas | Pte | 3756 | KIA 31/7/16 |
| Boydell | William | Pte | 24272 | WIA, posted 2nd and 9th Bns |
| Boylan | John | Pte | 4578 | WIA, trans. to MGC-RDC-MGC |
| Boyle | Francis Albert | L/Cpl | 35195 | Ex LNL |
| Brack | John | Pte | 28000 | KIA 20/9/17 |
| Brackwell | Ephreim | Pte | 200763 | Trans. to RE Road Construction Coy |
| Bradburn | Albert | Pte | 242215 | |
| Bradley | Henry | Sgt | 200416 | B Coy, WIA (2), POW |
| Bradley | John Henry | Pte | 26067 | Ex 7th Bn, POW |
| Bradley | Richard | 2Lt | | KIA 31/7/17 |
| Bradley | Robert | Pte | 201589 | MM |
| Bradley | William Alfred | Pte | 201547 | KIA 31/1/17 |
| Bradshaw | Harry | Pte | 201248 | |
| Bradshaw | John | Pte | 201505 | |
| Bradshaw | Robert | Pte | 240786 | |
| Brady | Alfred | Pte | 201251 | WIA |
| Brady | James | Pte | 201462 | |
| Braham | Harry | Pte | 244505 | |
| Braithwaite | James Steele | Pte | 24467 | Ex 8th Bn, WIA, posted 2nd and 9th Bns |
| Braithwaite | Joseph | Pte | 3372 | |
| Braithwaite | Thomas | WO2 | 200160 | WIA |
| Braithwaite | William | Pte | 200649 | WIA (2), trans. to LC |
| Braithwaite | William | Pte | 242694 | Posted to 1/5th |
| Brammall | Richard | Pte | 9367 | Ex 2nd, 8th, and 7th Bns, POW |
| Brannan | Peter James | Pte | 21992 | Ex 8th Bn, WIA, POW-esc. Also 1st Bn |
| Bransden | Harold William | L/Cpl | 240563 | Ex 1/5th, KIA 9/4/18 |
| Bray | Lewis | Pte | 19446 | Ex 11th Bn. POW |
| Bray | Robert | Sgt | 200542 | A Coy, WIA |
| Bray | William | A/Cpl | 200570 | WIA (2) |
| Brazier | James George | Pte | 41043 | |
| Brazil | Victor | Pte | 201559 | KIA 31/7/17 |
| Brearley | Squire | Pte | 2804 | |
| Brennan | Patrick | Pte | 202391 | |
| Brew | William Thomas | Pte | 200733 | Att. to TMB, KIA 1/12/17 |
| Brewer | Harry | Pte | 265628 | WIA |
| Brewer | John | Sgt | 2101 | WIA, trans. to LC, DOW 31/7/17 |
| Bridge | Frank Marshall | Pte | 24225 | Also 8th Bn, WIA |
| Bridge | Henry | Pte | 201390 | WIA, also 8th Bn |
| Bridge | William Edwin | Pte | 30311 | Ex 1st Bn 24/9/17. WIA. D 28/12/20 |

| | | | | |
|---|---|---|---|---|
| Brierley | George | L/Cpl | 21270 | Ex 7th Bn |
| Briers | Thomas | Pte | 19939 | |
| Briggs | Fred | Pte | 201005 | KIA 8/8/16 |
| Bright | John | L/Cpl | 4259 | Ex 7th Bn, WIA, KIA 9/4/18 |
| Brinded | Alexander | Pte | 202956 | Commissioned To W. Surreys 2/8/18 |
| Brindley | George | Pte | 201520 | |
| Broadbent | John | Pte | 201831 | |
| Broadbent | Thomas | Pte | 15707 | Also 8th and 7th Bns |
| Brockbank | Ernest | Pte | 201050 | Att. to TMB, POW |
| Brockbank | John Ephraim | L/Sgt | 2239 | KIA 15/6/15 |
| Brockbank | William | Pte | 200254 | H |
| Brockbank | William | Cpl | 34708 | WIA, also 1st Bn |
| Brocklebank | Charles | Pte | 200670 | Trans. to 2nd Bn |
| Brocklebank | Edward Halton | Pte | 200237 | POW |
| Brocklebank | Frederick | Pte | 200509 | |
| Brocklebank | Harold Arthur | Capt. | | MiD, WIA, POW |
| Brocklebank | John Thomas | Pte | 2560 | KIA 15/6/15 |
| Brocklebank | John Thomas | Pte | 1881 | DOW 24/6/15 |
| Brocklebank | William J. | Pte | 2565 | Trans. to MGC |
| Brockman | Albert John | 2Lt | | KIA 8/8/16 |
| Brodrick | Edwin | Pte | 265779 | WIA |
| Brogan | Paul | Pte | 240292 | Ex 2/5th, KIA 1/12/17 |
| Brokenshire | Wilfred | Pte | 265627 | Posted to 8th Bn |
| Brooke | William | Pte | 201201 | KIA 20/9/17 |
| Brookes | Howard | Pte | 27006 | |
| Brooks | Elvy Wilfred | Sgt | 200072 | Seconded to Egba Expedition 5/1/18 |
| Brooks | George | Pte | 37086 | KIA 9/4/18 |
| Brooks | Joseph Armstrong | L/Cpl | 201296 | KIA 8/1/17 |
| Brooks | Josiah William | Pte | 28091 | Ex LF and 8th Bn |
| Brooks | Robert | Pte | 201353 | WIA |
| Brooks | William Alfred | Pte | 29191 | Ex Devons, Royal Berks, and LC |
| Brophy | John | Pte | 48852 | |
| Brotherton | Thomas | Pte | 34705 | WIA |
| Brown | Albert | Pte | 3193 | Real name: Harold Brierley. Drowne 30/7/16 |
| Brown | Alfred Adolf | C/Sgt | 2256 | Commissioned Border Rgt 8/11/15 |
| Brown | Alfred James | Pte | 1637 | H |
| Brown | Charles Edward | Sgt | 10643 | Ex 2nd Bn, 12 Ptn C Coy |
| Brown | Edward | Pte | 28092 | Ex LF, Deserted |
| Brown | Francis | Pte | 3669 | Discharged underage. Re-enlisted into L |
| Brown | George | Pte | 2893 | KIA 28/5/16 |
| Brown | George | Pte | 27995 | WIA |

| Brown | Harry | Sgt | 200530 | Trans. to 405 TMB, WIA |
| Brown | Henry | Pte | 3270 | |
| Brown | Herbert | Pte | 200867 | |
| Brown | Herbert Sidney | Lt | | |
| Brown | John | L/Cpl | 200454 | Ex 8th Bn, KIA 9/4/18 |
| Brown | John | Pte | 40890 | Trans. to Lincs 1920 |
| Brown | Percy | Pte | 40892 | |
| Brown | Richard | Pte | 34531 | KIA 20/9/17 |
| Brown | Stanley Hillard | Pte | 29184 | Ex Devon Rgt and LC |
| Brown | William | Pte | 14175 | Also 9th Bn |
| Brown | William Henry | Pte | 34550 | KIA 20/11/17 |
| Brownlow | James | Pte | 201698 | KIA 10/9/16 |
| Broxholme | William | Pte | 27184 | Ex Lincs and also 1st, 7th, and 9th Bns |
| Brunskill | George W. | Pte | 201573 | WIA, trans. to LC |
| Brunt | George | Pte | 28122 | Ex 7th Bn, KIA 26/4/18 |
| Brunton | R. | L/Sgt | 60 | H |
| Bryan | Sydney William | L/Cpl | 28185 | Ex 7th Bn, WIA |
| Bryson | James | Pte | 35814 | |
| Bullas | George | Pte | 28001 | |
| Bullen | Hugh Thomas | Pte | 28093 | Ex LF |
| Bullivant | Norman | Pte | 200289 | D Coy, WIA, trans. to LC |
| Bullock | John T. | Pte | 4973 | WIA, trans. to LNL |
| Bunford | John | Pte | 200414 | WIA |
| Bunting | W. | Pte | 700 | H |
| Burgess | Edward Anthony | Pte | 40965 | WIA, KIA 24/8/18 |
| Burgess | Frank Alfred | Pte | 10390 | Also 7th Bn |
| Burgess | Harold Butterfield | Pte | 40887 | |
| Burke | James | Pte | 34477 | Also 11th Bn |
| Burley | Edward | Pte | 201710 | WIA |
| Burley | Howard | Pte | 200901 | WIA. Also 8th and 2/5th Bns |
| Burn | Edward Norman | Pte | 2276 | DOW 20/6/15 |
| Burn | Frederick James | Sgt | 1417 | KIA 8/6/15 |
| Burns | Alfred | Pte | 200293 | WIA. Commissioned into LC |
| Burns | Frank | Pte | 2017 | WIA, trans. to KLR |
| Burns | Harold | Cpl | 200294 | |
| Burns | Jack | Pte | 14901 | Also 7th and 8th Bns |
| Burns | James | L/Cpl | 200696 | |
| Burns | James Frederick | Sgt | 200409 | WIA |
| Burns | John Joseph | Pte | 200826 | |
| Burr | David | 2Lt | | |
| Burrow | James | Pte | 17138 | Also 2nd Bn |
| Burrow | John | Pte | 200759 | KIA 8/8/16 |

| | | | | |
|---|---|---|---|---|
| Burton | Alfred J. | Sgt | 202785 | DCM |
| Burton | Myles | Pte | 2701 | B Coy, KIA 14/8/15 |
| Burton | Thomas | L/Cpl | 200276 | Trans. to LC |
| Burton | Tom | Pte | 200593 | KIA 20/9/17 |
| Bury | Reginald George | Pte | 202244 | Trans. to LC |
| Bussingham | John | Pte | 202757 | Ex Lincs, A Coy 1 Ptn, MM, Trans. RF |
| Butcher | Robert | WO2 | 200372 | WIA |
| Butler | Henry | L/Cpl | 14468 | WIA. Also 8th Bn |
| Butler | James Mason | Pte | 240788 | Ex 2/5th |
| Butler | John Albert | Pte | 30469 | Also 1st Bn |
| Butt | Charles | L/Cpl | 40963 | MM |
| Butterworth | Frank | L/Cpl | 201593 | |
| Butterworth | William Joseph | Pte | 20405 | D 26/8/17 |
| Buzzard | Arthur Boughton | Pte | 41512 | |
| Byrne | John | Pte | 22372 | Ex 11th Bn, WIA (accidentally) |
| Byrne | Thomas | WO2 | 240007 | Also 1/5th |
| Caddy | James | Pte | 2088 | H |
| Caddy | John | Capt. | | |
| Caddy | Matthew | L/Sgt | 200124 | KIA 23/12/16 |
| Caddy | Walter | L/Cpl | 14930 | Also 7th Bn |
| Caddy | William | Pte | 200038 | H |
| Cafferty | Cornelius | Pte | 24774 | Ex 7th Bn, C Coy, MM, D 15/1/19 |
| Caine | George William | Pte | 3158 | WIA. Trans. to KLR then LC |
| Caine | Horace Arthur | A/Cpl | 41564 | |
| Caine | John James | Pte | 241909 | Also 2/5th |
| Cairns | Henry | Pte | 201537 | |
| Cairns | Vincent | Pte | 3486 | WIA (2). Trans. MGC |
| Calvert | Henry | Cpl | 200894 | WIA |
| Calvert | John | Pte | 33964 | WIA. Trans. to LC |
| Calvert | William | Pte | 29185 | Also Yorks, Lancs, and LC |
| Cameron | James | Pte | 200485 | POW, DOW 9/8/17 |
| Campbell | John | Pte | 200246 | H |
| Canby | Francis William | A/Sgt | 200298 | POW |
| Canning | Walter | WO2 | 200329 | WIA. Trans. to RE |
| Cannon | Frederick | Sgt | 200721 | A Coy 4 Ptn. DOW 22/11/17 |
| Cannon | John | Pte | 22067 | WIA |
| Capstick | John | Pte | 200701 | WIA, POW |
| Capstick | Thomas | Pte | 9443 | Also 1st Bn |
| Cardwell | George Bowness | Pte | 202417 | |
| Cardwell | John | Pte | 25740 | Ex 8th Bn |
| Cardwell | John | Pte | 201199 | WIA. Trans. to LC |
| Carey | William | Pte | 200526 | |

| | | | | |
|---|---|---|---|---|
| Carey | William Herbert | Pte | 3709 | Also 7th Bn |
| Carleton | Frederick M. | Lt-Col. | | DSO |
| Carr | Thomas | Pte | 28003 | KIA 15/7/17 |
| Carradus | William | Pte | 4401 | DOW 27/9/16 |
| Carrick | John | Cpl | 200476 | DCM, WIA, D 29/10/22 |
| Carruthers | Robert | Cpl | 200371 | MM |
| Carruthers | Thomas | Pte | 49374 | |
| Carson | Frank | Pte | 200511 | KIA 9/4/18 |
| Carter | Arthur Nicholas | Pte | 820 | |
| Carter | Herbert Carlton | Pte | 1561 | H |
| Carter | John | Pte | 242376 | Also 1/5th and 7th Bns |
| Carter | Richard | Pte | 34608 | KIA 20/9/17 |
| Carter | Rupert | Pte | 202745 | Also 9th and 1st Bns |
| Carter | Samuel | Pte | 200262 | KIA 20/9/17 |
| Carthy | Frederick | Pte | 201561 | Also 2/5th |
| Cartlidge | John | A/Cpl | 41504 | |
| Cartmell | Alexander | Pte | 24395 | Ex 7th and 11th Bns, WIA |
| Cartmell | Robert | Pte | 201502 | Also 1st Bn |
| Carton | Edward James | Pte | 200222 | MM. DOW 10/1/17 |
| Cartwright | Edwin J. | Pte | 1855 | WIA. Trans. to Corps of Hussars |
| Cartwright | James | Pte | 200682 | KIA 20/9/17 |
| Casper | Henry J. | Cpl | 16272 | 8 Ptn B Coy. WIA. Trans. RE and LNR |
| Cass | John Barnett | Pte | 34564 | |
| Casson | Fred | Pte | 1689 | WIA |
| Caton | George | Pte | 200957 | KIA 8/8/16 |
| Caton | Henry | Pte | 34650 | D Coy. SI-injury, Deserted |
| Catteral | James | Pte | 24603 | Also 7th Bn |
| Catterall | Edward Garlick | Pte | 202779 | KIA 3/6/17 |
| Chadderton | Harry | Pte | 201600 | |
| Chadderton | Percy | Pte | 28096 | WIA. Trans. LF |
| Chadwick | Arthur | Pte | 1925 | A Coy. KIA 19/7/15 |
| Chadwick | Isiah | Pte | 4381 | WIA. Trans. to ASC |
| Chadwick | John Thomas | Pte | 201156 | |
| Chadwick | Wallace | Sgt | 200120 | MM, WIA |
| Chalcraft | Henry William T. | 2Lt | | |
| Chalkley | Thomas Charles | Pte | 41046 | |
| Champ | James Albert | Cpl | 202216 | |
| Chandler | Reuben | Pte | 200201 | H |
| Chandler | Thomas | Pte | 27226 | Ex 1st Bn-22/9/16. KIA 20/11/17 |
| Chapman | Cyril George | 2Lt | | |
| Chapman | Frederick | Pte | 244507 | |
| Chapman | John William | Pte | 200165 | |

| Chapman | Thomas | Pte | 1731 | Trans. to MGC |
| Chapman | Thomas Albert | Pte | 34675 | Also 2/5th |
| Chapman | William John | Pte | 201157 | WIA. Also 7th Bn |
| Chappell | William | Pte | 28192 | Ex 7th Bn, WIA (2), KIA 11/7/18 |
| Chapple | Richard | Pte | 851 | |
| Chapple | Thomas John | Sgt | 200092 | MM |
| Chapple | William | Pte | 1478 | |
| Charnock | James | Sgt | 1693 | KIA 15/10/15 |
| Charnock | Thomas | Pte | 42894 | |
| Charter | John Thompson | Pte | 200776 | |
| Cheeseman | Thomas Watson | Sgt | 200487 | WIA |
| Cheetham | Thomas | Pte | 27641 | Ex 1st and 7th Bns, WIA, KIA 9/4/18 |
| Cheney | Horace | Pte | 40969 | C Coy |
| Chester | Thomas | Cpl | 200239 | MM, WIA |
| Chesters | Ernest Fielding | Pte | 201550 | To 1/4th 17/12/16. Trans. RE 1/7/17 |
| Chisholm | Thomas Frederick | Pte | 24640 | Also 7th and 1st Bns |
| Chorlton | Leonard | Pte | 4914 | Ex MCR, WIA, trans. to RAMC |
| Christian | Walter Percy | Pte | 200045 | WIA. Trans. RGA |
| Churchman | James | Pte | 201045 | Also 8th Bn |
| Churm | Harry | Pte | 201457 | KIA 31/7/17 |
| Clampitt | Frederick | Sgt | 36511 | WIA |
| Clapham | James | Pte | 26214 | Also 2nd Bn |
| Clare | George Thomas | Pte | 34662 | KIA 9/4/18 |
| Clare | Joseph | Pte | 19447 | WIA. Trans. to LC |
| Clare | William | Pte | 200887 | WIA |
| Clark | Adam | L/Cpl | 200883 | D Coy. WIA (2), trans. to LC |
| Clark | Alfred | Pte | 28005 | |
| Clark | Alfred Matthews | Lt | | WIA. KIA 20/11/17 |
| Clark | Charles | Pte | 35473 | Ex KLR trans. to LC |
| Clark | George | Cpl | 202162 | |
| Clark | Robert Read | L/Cpl | 201068 | KIA 20/9/17 |
| Clark | Samuel Simpson | Pte | 202626 | Also 7th Bn |
| Clark | Sidney | Pte | 244506 | |
| Clark | Thomas | Pte | 201311 | KIA 8/8/16 |
| Clark | Wilfred | Pte | 2316 | KIA 16/6/15 |
| Clark | William | RQMS | 200540 | MSM, WIA |
| Clarke | Barker H. | Sgt | 812 | KIA 15/6/15 |
| Clarke | Ernest | Pte | 201599 | Att. to RE. POW. DOW 27/11/17 |
| Clarke | Ernest | Sgt | 868 | |
| Clarke | George | L/Cpl | 28266 | WIA. Also 11th Bn and ASC |
| Clarke | George Arthur H. | Pte | 201601 | WIA |
| Clarke | Harold | Pte | 201303 | |

| | | | | |
|---|---|---|---|---|
| Clarke | James Augustine T. | Capt. | | WIA |
| Clarke | James William | Pte | 40138 | DOW 1/11/18 |
| Clarke | Jeremiah | Pte | 200131 | WIA (2) |
| Clarke | John Henry | Pte | 4062 | DOW 23/12/16 |
| Clarke | John Henry | Sgt | 200263 | WIA |
| Clarke | John William | Cpl | 19083 | |
| Clarke | Robert | Pte | 201135 | WIA. Also 1st Bn |
| Clarke | Walter | Pte | 48856 | |
| Clarkson | Christopher | Pte | 201524 | POW |
| Clarkson | Edward | Pte | 200955 | WIA. Trans. to Lincs. |
| Clayton | Joseph Bell | Pte | 1453 | A Coy. DOW 22/7/15 |
| Clayton | Samuel | Pte | 37166 | |
| Cleaver | George | Pte | 41530 | |
| Clegg | Abram | Pte | 26104 | Ex 7th Bn |
| Clegg | Edwin | Pte | 201752 | D 24/2/17 |
| Clegg | Herbert | Sgt | 13903 | MM. Also 9th Bn |
| Clegg | James | Pte | 202013 | POW |
| Clegg | Richard | Pte | 200320 | WIA. Trans. to RE Light Rwy Op Coy |
| Clementson | Arthur | Cpl | 19484 | DCM, MM, WIA. Also 8 and 11 Bns |
| Cleminson | Arthur | Pte | 201522 | C Coy. WIA (4). Trans. Notts and Derby |
| Cliffe | Percy | Pte | 202598 | Also 7th Bn |
| Cloudsdale | John | L/Cpl | 1829 | KIA 8/8/16 |
| Cloudsdale | Thomas | Pte | 2469 | KIA 8/8/16 |
| Clough | John | Pte | 201341 | KIA 8/8/16 |
| Clough | John | Pte | 201711 | WIA (2) |
| Clough | Wilson | Pte | 201757 | |
| Clucas | | Pte | H | |
| Coates | Charles | Pte | 34603 | Also 2/5th |
| Coates | Joseph | Pte | 34540 | KIA 20/11/17 |
| Coates | William | Pte | 201364 | Also 1st Bn |
| Coath | William | L/Cpl | 26865 | Also 1st Bn |
| Cobham | William Henry | Pte | 24927 | Also 7th Bn |
| Cocker | Charles Ernest | Pte | 15757 | Also 8th Bn |
| Cockshott | Geoffrey | L/Cpl | 200188 | H |
| Coffey | Thomas | Pte | 40970 | |
| Cohen | Saul | Pte | 30257 | Posted 8th Bn, WIA |
| Colclough | James | Pte | 41545 | |
| Cole | George William | Pte | 22582 | Also 11th and 1/5th Bns, POW |
| Coleman | Henry Oswald | 2Lt | | |
| Coles | Ernest | Pte | 201597 | KIA 20/9/17 |
| Colley | Richard | Pte | 201525 | Att. to TMB. KIA 31/7/17 |
| Collier | Joseph | Pte | 201480 | KIA 9/4/18 |

| Collin | Joseph Henry | 2Lt | | VC. KIA 9/4/18 |
|---|---|---|---|---|
| Collinge | Peter | Pte | 13007 | Also 7th and 11th Bns |
| Collinge | Thomas Edward | Pte | 265522 | KIA 23/10/18 |
| Collins | George Edward | Sgt | 8571 | CdG |
| Collinson | Ernest | Cpl | 1440 | |
| Collinson | Joseph | L/Cpl | 200139 | KIA 14/7/17 |
| Coltsman | James | L/Cpl | 200058 | WIA |
| Colvine | William Sydney | Pte | 28006 | |
| Connaughton | John | L/Cpl | 28007 | |
| Connell | John | Pte | 30064 | Also 8th and 7th Bns |
| Conning | John Henry | Pte | 35212 | Ex KLR. POW |
| Connor | George Edward | Pte | 201358 | |
| Connor | Thomas | Pte | 201380 | WIA, also 1st Bn |
| Conroy | Thomas | Pte | 200659 | WIA, POW |
| Constable | John William | Pte | 40968 | |
| Conway | Edward | Pte | 201794 | |
| Conway | Maurice | Pte | 28008 | POW |
| Cook | James Barry | WO2 | 200065 | DCM |
| Cooke | Arthur | Pte | 38049 | |
| Cooke | William | Pte | 201689 | WIA. Also 1/5th |
| Cooksey | Thomas | Pte | 200043 | H |
| Cookson | Thomas | Pte | 33942 | WIA, POW |
| Cooley | John | Pte | 18079 | Ex 7th and 1st Bns. MM, KIA 20/9/17 |
| Coombe | Joseph | Pte | 1570 | DOW 4/8/16 |
| Cooper | Charles Frost | L/Cpl | 200644 | D Coy. MM |
| Cooper | James | Pte | 242968 | Ex 1/5th Bn, WIA. DOW 16/5/18 |
| Cooper | William Henry | Pte | 41540 | |
| Cope | George | Pte | 201178 | Att. to RE. Also 8th Bn |
| Cope | Henry Richard | Pte | 34593 | Also 1/5th |
| Cope | William | Pte | 41552 | |
| Copland | Edward William M. | Pte | 27223 | Ex Lincs. Also 1st, 7th, and 2/5th Bns |
| Copeland | Henry | Pte | 2847 | Trans. to Monmouths |
| Corbett | Richard | Pte | 23118 | DCM, WIA |
| Corbett | Samuel | Pte | 201155 | KIA 31/7/17 |
| Corless | Christopher D. | Pte | 201673 | WIA. Also 1st and 7th Bns |
| Corless | John Stanley | 2Lt | | |
| Corlett | Thomas Robert | Pte | 3032 | DOW 12/8/16 |
| Cornforth | Sam | Pte | 40966 | KIA 27/4/18 |
| Cornthwaite | Edward | L/Cpl | 2753 | WIA. Trans. to RE as engine driver |
| Cottam | Jesse | Pte | 200913 | WIA. Trans. to LC |
| Cottam | William | Pte | 1895 | KIA 8/8/16 |
| Couldick | William | Pte | 28095 | Ex LF |

| Coulter | Andrew | Pte | 2797 | KIA 8/8/16 |
|---|---|---|---|---|
| Counsell | Harold Herbert | 2Lt | | WIA |
| Coupe | Hilton | Pte | 24924 | DOW 22/6/18 |
| Coupland | James | L/Cpl | 200480 | WIA |
| Coups | Samuel | Pte | 265427 | WIA |
| Court | Richard | 2Lt | | KIA 9/4/18 |
| Court | Robert | 2Lt | | |
| Courtman | James | Pte | 24409 | Ex 1st and 7th Bns. KIA 9/4/18 |
| Courtnell | Henry Grey | L/Cpl | 200187 | WIA. Later to 164 TMB |
| Courtney | Philip Yorke Holman | Pte | 40971 | |
| Coward | George Douglas | Cpl | 200486 | |
| Coward | John | Pte | 200586 | |
| Coward | John William | Pte | 200544 | |
| Coward | Jonathan (John) | Sgt | 200252 | WIA. Att. to E. African Rifles |
| Coward | Joseph | Pte | 201139 | Trans. to Mil Foot Police |
| Coward | Robert Arthur | Pte | 30110 | Posted to 8th Bn |
| Coward | Thomas | Pte | 2244 | WIA |
| Cowburn | James | Pte | 201376 | |
| Cowell | Albert Ernest | A/WO2 | 202423 | Also 7th and 1/5th Bns |
| Cowell | Ernest | Pte | 201091 | WIA |
| Cowell | John | Pte | 200926 | KIA 8/8/16 |
| Cowper | William Burn | Pte | 201103 | KIA 8/8/16 |
| Cox | George W. | Cpl | 202163 | 2 Ptn. A Coy. WIA. Trans. to RAF |
| Crabb | Alexander | Pte | 201363 | KIA 8/8/16 |
| Crabtree | Benjamin | L/Cpl | 1464 | |
| Cragg | Robert Lamb | Pte | 34668 | KIA 27/11/17 (poss a DOW?) |
| Craggs | Charles | Pte | 28009 | DOW 3/12/17 |
| Craig | David Greg | Pte | 2185 | DOW 28/5/15 |
| Craig | James | Pte | 200492 | KIA 8/8/16 |
| Crammon | Alexander | Pte | 28011 | KIA 20/9/17 |
| Crane | Stephen | Pte | 30139 | Ex 8th Bn, WIA |
| Crankshaw | Harry | Pte | 40895 | DOW 28/10/18 |
| Craven | William | L/Cpl | 11859 | Also 2nd Bn |
| Crawshaw | Charles Felix H. | 2Lt | | WIA |
| Crawshaw | Fred | Pte | 200906 | Trans. to LNL and MGC |
| Creighton | William James | Sgt | 200111 | WIA. Trans. to LC |
| Crellin | John Edward | Pte | 28097 | DOW 20/8/17 |
| Crellin | Thomas | Sgt | 200404 | |
| Crichton | Charles W. | WO II | 201017 | MM. Trans. to LC |
| Crilly | Thomas D. R. | 2Lt | | Att. from Lincs |
| Crispe | Benjamin | Pte | 2145 | KIA 8/8/16 |
| Croasdale | William | Pte | 201749 | KIA 9/4/18 |

| | | | | |
|---|---|---|---|---|
| Croasdell | Hubert | Pte | 200620 | |
| Croft | John | Pte | 34641 | |
| Croft | William | Pte | 41660 | |
| Crompton | Thomas | Cpl | 12554 | Ex 7th Bn. KIA 26/4/18 |
| Cross | Henry | Pte | 201789 | KIA 31/7/17 |
| Cross | James Musgrave | Sgt | 202738 | DCM. B Coy 6 Ptn. KIA 20/9/17 |
| Cross | John | Pte | 240403 | Ex MG Coy 1/5th |
| Cross | Richard | Sgt | 200843 | WIA |
| Cross | Thomas | Pte | 238003 | Ex 7th Bn, MM and Bar, WIA (2), trans to RE |
| Crossland | Walter | Pte | 202628 | Ex 7th Bn and LC. DOW 11/1/18 |
| Crossley | Claude Edward | Pte | 202243 | KIA 20/9/17 |
| Crossley | Granville | Pte | 26117 | Also 7th Bn |
| Crossley | James | Lt | | QM |
| Crossley | Tom | L/Cpl | 200149 | WIA, POW |
| Crossling | Arthur James | Pte | 28012 | |
| Crossman | Thomas | Pte | 2262 | KIA 8/6/15 |
| Crosthwaite | John | Pte | 4293 | Also 9th Bn |
| Crowe | William | Pte | 2394 | Trans. to MGC |
| Crowther | William | Pte | 200729 | WIA (2). POW. |
| Cryan | William | Pte | 201357 | WIA. Trans. to LC |
| Cubin | Harold | Pte | 24739 | Also 1st and 7th Bns |
| Cubitt | Jacob | Pte | 2538 | KIA 15/6/15 |
| Cuddy | James Edward | Pte | 20614 | Ex 1st and 7th Bns. WIA (2). Posted 1st Bn |
| Culley | Albert | L/Cpl | 200039 | H |
| Cullum | John | Pte | 203019 | Ex County of London Yeo. WIA |
| Culver | Charles John | L/Cpl | 10839 | Also 1/5th |
| Cumming | John | Pte | 41045 | Also 2/5th |
| Cummings | Harry | Pte | 201344 | |
| Cunningham | Charles | Pte | 28013 | MM. Trans. to LC |
| Cunningham | Hubert | Pte | 201436 | WIA |
| Cunningham | Robert S. | Pte | 34909 | WIA. Trans. to MGC |
| Curran | Joseph | Pte | 265296 | WIA |
| Currie | Harry | Pte | 3128 | KIA 8/8/16 |
| Curtis | James Henry | Pte | 2600 | KIA 1/7/17 |
| Curwen | Ernest | Pte | 2562 | KIA 15/6/15 |
| Curwen | James | Pte | 240992 | |
| Dacre | William G. | Pte | 2135 | WIA. Trans. to MGC |
| Dagger | James Herbert | Pte | 201784 | Also 1st Bn |
| Daines | Harry Bertie | Pte | 40972 | KIA 10/5/18 |
| Dale | John William | Pte | 28165 | Also 7th Bn |
| Dall | Thomas | Pte | 28641 | Also 2/5th and ASC |

| | | | | |
|---|---|---|---|---|
| Dalman | Reginald F. | A/Cpl | 203014 | Ex County of London Yeo. |
| Dalton | John Pickering | Pte | 22158 | Ex 7th Bn, att. to TMB. WIA (2) |
| Daly | Herbert | Cpl | 6028 | KIA 20/11/17 |
| Dane | Raymond Seaton | 2Lt | | Ex Pte, ASC and R. Scots. A Coy. MC |
| Danson | William | Cpl | 201712 | MM, WIA |
| Darby | Stanley | Pte | 3552 | WIA. Trans. to TC, POW |
| Dartnall | Albert John | 2Lt | | KIA 20/11/17 |
| Date | Henry | Pte | 200613 | |
| Date | John | A/Sgt | 2362 | |
| Date | Samuel | Pte | 2801 | KIA 15/6/15 |
| Date | Samuel | L/Cpl | 13019 | Also 7th Bn |
| Davies | Alfred | Cpl | 26114 | Ex 7th Bn. MM, WIA (2) |
| Davies | Alfred Ernest | Pte | 266243 | |
| Davies | Charles | Pte | 4197 | KIA 3/8/16 |
| Davies | Colin | Pte | 29192 | Ex LC. WIA |
| Davies | Edward | Pte | 3572 | Also 7th and 1st Bns |
| Davies | Fred | Pte | 201605 | WIA |
| Davies | John | Pte | 202629 | Ex 7th Bn, WIA |
| Davies | Richard Evan | Pte | 42889 | KIA 14/5/18 |
| Davies | Thomas | Pte | 34669 | DOW 20/11/17 |
| Davies | Thomas William | Pte | 240738 | |
| Davies | William | Pte | 37434 | Probably only home service |
| Davies | William | Pte | 235085 | Also 7th Bn |
| Davis | Edward John | Pte | 200451 | WIA accidentally. Also 8th Bn |
| Davis | Thomas | Pte | 202716 | Ex Royal Warwick. Also 8th Bn |
| Davis | Thomas Albert | Pte | 11186 | Also 1st Bn. WIA, POW |
| Davison | Albert | Pte | 27808 | Ex 11th Bn. KIA 23/10/18 |
| Dawes | Albert James | Cpl | 17900 | Also 1st and 7th Bns |
| Dawson | Frank | Sgt | 12888 | Also 7th Bn. MM, MiD |
| Dawson | Gaskarth | Pte | 201526 | Att. to TMB. Also 1st Bn |
| Dawson | Harold John | Sgt | 200489 | Battalion Tailor |
| Dawson | John | Pte | 265793 | Ex 1/5th. WIA. Posted 1st Bn |
| Dawson | Joseph | Pte | 40956 | |
| Dawson | Moses Jackson | Pte | 201572 | |
| Dawson | Robert | Pte | 200757 | WIA. KIA 2/5/18 with 8th Bn |
| Dawson | William | Cpl | 201712 | |
| Dawson | William George | Pte | 21513 | Also 7th Bn |
| Day | George Herbert | Pte | 266623 | |
| Dean | Fred | Pte | 200770 | A Coy |
| Dean | John | Pte | 29142 | |
| Dean | William | Pte | 4049 | KIA 8/8/16 |
| Delph | Cecil George | Pte | 40973 | Also 2/5th |

| Denham | George William | Pte | 9799 | Also 2nd, 6th, and 7th Bns |
|---|---|---|---|---|
| Denney | Ernest Matthew | Pte | 200580 | |
| Dent | Richard | Pte | 48849 | POW |
| Dent | William Hewitt | Pte | 200211 | WIA |
| Denton | George | Pte | 41047 | DOW 23/9/18 |
| Derbyshire | Harry | Pte | 200866 | Ex LC, KLR. WIA (2) posted 2/5th |
| Derdle | Septimus | Pte | 30118 | Also 1/5th. WIA (3) |
| Derham | Richard | Pte | 34596 | Ex 7th Bn, A Coy. WIA |
| Dewhirst | William | Pte | 201512 | |
| Dewhurst | James E | Pte | 5247 | WIA. Trans. to Lincs |
| Dickie | John | L/Cpl | 200741 | KIA 26/4/18 |
| Dickinson | Alexander | Pte | 12726 | Ex 7th Bn. DOW 8/10/17 |
| Dickinson | Arthur Norman | Pte | 200268 | |
| Dickinson | Edward | Pte | 15609 | Ex 1st and 8th Bns. POW |
| Dickinson | Henry | Sgt | 10190 | Also 2nd and 1st Bns |
| Dickinson | John Henry | Sgt | 202739 | 11 Ptn C Coy. DCM, MM |
| Dickinson | Robert | Pte | 23727 | KIA 20/9/17 |
| Dickinson | Sidney | Sgt | 200301 | MM, WIA |
| Dickinson | Thomas | Sgt | 1406 | |
| Dickson | Andrew | Pte | 29172 | WIA. Also LC |
| Dickson | William | Pte | 28014 | |
| Digby | Henry William | Pte | 30659 | Ex London Rgt. |
| Diggle | Arthur | L/Cpl | 4242 | KIA 11/9/16 |
| Dimond | George Joseph | Pte | 26876 | Also 1st and 7th Bns |
| Dixon | Andrew | Pte | 19293 | Ex 7th Bn. WIA (2), trans. to LC |
| Dixon | Arthur | Pte | 202001 | DOW 26/6/17 |
| Dixon | Ben | Pte | 200692 | KIA 8/8/16 |
| Dixon | Edward Brockbank | Pte | 200291 | Also ASC |
| Dixon | George Walton | Pte | 201124 | |
| Dixon | James | Pte | 201604 | WIA |
| Dixon | James Henry | Pte | 200116 | |
| Dixon | John Adam Thwaite | Pte | 34611 | POW |
| Dixon | Joseph | Pte | 51993 | |
| Dixon | Richard | Pte | 200433 | |
| Dixon | Robert | L/Cpl | 200708 | Att. to TMB. KIA 11/9/16 |
| Dixon | Robert K. | Pte | 200037 | Trans. to RE |
| Dixon | Shepherd | Pte | 1931 | WIA |
| Dixon | Thomas | Cpl | 707 | |
| Dixon | Thomas | Cpl | 241420 | MM. Also 1/5th |
| Dobbs | Frederick | L/Sgt | 27370 | Ex Lincs 9 Ptn. MM, 1st and 8th Bns |
| Dobson | Henry Richard | Pte | 2907 | KIA 10/9/16 |
| Dobson | John | Pte | 202246 | WIA. Also 1st Bn |

| | | | | |
|---|---|---|---|---|
| Dobson | Robert | L/Cpl | 201692 | KIA 20/9/17 |
| Dobson | Robert | Pte | 201997 | Also 1st Bn |
| Dockeray | George | Sgt | 200459 | WIA |
| Dodd | Hugh | Pte | 2379 | |
| Dodd | James | Pte | 2678 | KIA 2/7/15 |
| Dodgson | James | Pte | 200762 | |
| Doe | Percival | Pte | 49974 | KIA 1/6/18 |
| Doe | Robert John | Pte | 37107 | |
| Doidge | William | Pte | 2563 | Trans. to MGC |
| Dolman | Edward Jesse | Pte | 41507 | |
| Donaghy | Owen | Pte | 2367 | Trans. to MGC. Died 27/12/17 |
| Donaghy | Walter | Cpl | 200479 | WIA (2) |
| Donald | Thomas | Pte | 1996 | H |
| Donald | William | Pte | 29174 | Also LC |
| Donian | Martin | Pte | 20698 | Also 7th Bn |
| Donovan | Robert | Pte | 200919 | KIA 8/8/16 |
| Dorman | Arthur D. | Pte | 24525 | Also 7th, 11th, and 1st Bns |
| Douglas | Edwin | Pte | 28015 | POW |
| Douglas | William | L/Cpl | 200438 | KIA 23/12/16 |
| Dowens | George Boston | Pte | 28016 | Also 9th Bn |
| Dowey | Frederick | Pte | 37889 | |
| Dowker | George Henry | Pte | 3633 | WIA. Trans. to N. Staffs and Leics |
| Dowlen | Edward Harry Norris | Cpl | 202164 | |
| Downham | Alfred | Pte | 5011 | WIA. KIA 27/9/16 |
| Downham | James | Pte | 201126 | KIA 8/8/16 |
| Downham | William Albert | Cpl | 1979 | KIA 8/8/16 |
| Downing | Arthur | Pte | 21458 | WIA. Trans. to KLR |
| Downing | Edward | Pte | 201090 | Also 1st Bn |
| Doyle | Hugh | Pte | 28017 | KIA 20/9/17 |
| Doyle | Patrick | Pte | 3724 | |
| Drabble | James | Pte | 6210 | MM. Company Cook. Also 1st Bn |
| Draper | William Penrhyn | Pte | 27821 | Ex 11th Bn. WIA. DOW 15/5/18 |
| Drew | Thomas Edward | Pte | 28018 | WIA. Also 1st Bn |
| Drinkall | Mark | L/Cpl | 2427 | C Coy. WIA |
| Dronsfield | Alfred | Pte | 17426 | KIA 9/4/18 |
| Drury | William Richard V. | Pte | 203037 | |
| Dryden | Kenneth Charles | Pte | 40976 | |
| Duckworth | John | Pte | 4187 | KIA 8/8/16 |
| Duckworth | John | Pte | 35526 | |
| Duckworth | Joseph | Cpl | 13563 | Ex 9th Bn. KIA 9/4/18 |
| Dudding | Robert | Pte | 33434 | Also 9th Bn |
| Duerden | John | Pte | 4200 | Discharged as underage on 7/9/16 |

| | | | | |
|---|---|---|---|---|
| Duerden | Peter | Pte | 201770 | KIA 20/9/17 |
| Dugdale | Douglas J. | 2Lt | | |
| Dugdale | Thomas William | 2Lt | | |
| Duke | John Richardson | Pte | 200516 | WIA |
| Dumbleton | Bertie | Pte | 201552 | |
| Dumphey | Dennis | Cpl | 200344 | |
| Dumphey | Thomas | Cpl | 200948 | WIA. |
| Dunbebin | Thomas | L/Cpl | 24652 | Ex 7th Bn. KIA 26/10/18 |
| Dunkerley | Horace Beresford | Sgt | 200269 | B Coy 8 Ptn. WIA (2) |
| Dunn | Joseph | Pte | 201373 | KIA 8/8/16 |
| Durham | Arthur | Pte | 28019 | |
| Durham | George Henry | Pte | 1853 | KIA 15/6/15 |
| Durkin | Charles | Cpl | 200399 | WIA |
| Durkin | Thomas | Pte | 10959 | Ex 1st and 2nd Bns |
| Durrant | Thomas | Pte | 41076 | |
| Dutton | Donald Swales | L/Cpl | 203018 | Also 2/5th |
| Duxbury | Harry Smith | A/Cpl | 23976 | KIA 31/7/17 |
| Dyson | Harry | Pte | 201603 | |
| Dyson | Joseph | Pte | 2335 | DOW 1/9/16 |
| Eagers | George | Pte | 2035 | WIA accidentally. Trans. to LC |
| Eagers | Samuel | Sgt | 200233 | KIA 20/11/17 |
| Eames | Alfred | Pte | 15153 | Ex 7th Bn. KIA 9/4/18 |
| Earnshaw | Albert | Pte | 34471 | POW |
| Earnshaw | John W. | Pte | 5409 | WIA. Trans. to ASC |
| East | Arthur Wilby | Pte | 27241 | Ex Lincs and 1st and 9th Bns |
| Eastham | Charles Richard | Pte | 200852 | DOW 15/7/18 |
| Eastham | Henry | Pte | 201535 | |
| Eastwood | David Herbert | Cpl | 202214 | WIA |
| Eastwood | Robert | Pte | 26968 | Ex 11 Bn, POW |
| Eastwood | Robert | Pte | 32584 | Also 7th Bn |
| Eatock | William | 2Lt | WIA | |
| Eaton | Ebenezer | Pte | 200617 | WIA |
| Eaton | John | Pte | 200584 | WIA, |
| Eaton | Sidney J. | Pte | 40897 | Records show as '201583'. Trans. to LN |
| Eaves | George | Pte | 201799 | Also 8th Bn |
| Eccles | Thomas | Pte | 241351 | Ex 1/5th and 8th Bns. MM. DOW 26/6/18 |
| Eckford | John Thomas (T. J.?) | Cpl | 200450 | |
| Edgar | John Burnett | Cpl | 200367 | WIA (2). POW |
| Edge | Alfred | Pte | 240741 | WIA. Also 2/5th |
| Edge | John Henry | Dmr | 1407 | |
| Edge | Squire Eaves | Pte | 29152 | |
| Edgeworth | William Stephen | Cpl | 41048 | |

| Edington | Samuel | Pte | 37934 | DOW 13/11/18 |
|---|---|---|---|---|
| Edmondson | Fred | Pte | 201218 | WIA |
| Edmondson | Hugh | Pte | 2391 | WIA. Trans. to LC |
| Edmondson | James | Pte | 200132 | WIA |
| Edmondson | John | Pte | 33968 | KIA 31/7/17 |
| Edmondson | Thomas | Sgt | 2259 | WIA. KIA 21/11/16 |
| Edmondson | Thomas | L/Cpl | 200166 | WIA |
| Edmondson | William | Pte | | H |
| Edwards | George | Pte | 200504 | |
| Edwards | James Howson | Pte | 200427 | WIA (2). Posted 1st Bn |
| Edwards | John | L/Sgt | 23531 | DCM, WIA |
| Edwards | Joseph | Pte | 201554 | |
| Edwards | William | Pte | 29176 | Also LC |
| Edwardson | Edward | Pte | 32591 | Ex 7th Bn, WIA (2) |
| Egan | John | Pte | 14925 | Ex 7th Bn, WIA |
| Elborough | Robert Kelly | Pte | 2210 | H. Discharged underage |
| Elboz | Richard | Pte | 202176 | WIA |
| Elcock | John | Pte | 266232 | WIA. Also 1/5th, 1st Bn and KSLI. |
| Ellam | Tom | Pte | 201110 | WIA |
| Ellen | Albert | Pte | 201151 | |
| Elliott | Clarence | 2Lt | | |
| Ellis | James | Pte | 202217 | Att. to RE. KIA 31/7/17 |
| Ellis | Joseph | Pte | 26712 | Ex LF. WIA. KIA 9/4/18 |
| Ellis | Maurice | Pte | 40977 | |
| Ellis | William | Pte | 28100 | Ex LF, WIA |
| Ellwood | Albert | Capt. | | Ex 1/5th, KIA 14/4/18 |
| Else | Thomas | L/Cpl | 201297 | KIA 17/8/18 |
| Elston | Fred | Pte | 201714 | KIA 31/7/17 |
| Ely | William Wilfred | Pte | 939 | H |
| Entwistle | Tom | Cpl | 201608 | WIA. Att. to RE |
| Erhart | John | Sgt | 35129 | WIA. Also 9th Bn |
| Escolme | William | Pte | 201684 | WIA. Trans. to N. Lancs |
| Eva | Josiah | Pte | 201093 | |
| Evans | Abraham | Pte | 201829 | |
| Evans | Andrew | Pte | 1622 | DOW 18/8/16 |
| Evans | Frank | Pte | 27567 | Ex 8th Bn. WIA, POW |
| Evans | Harry | Pte | 3520 | KIA 26/9/16 |
| Evans | John Henry | Maj. | | OC B Coy. MC and Bar, WIA |
| Evans | J. H. | Pte | 2630 | Trans. to MFP |
| Evans | Richard Everard | Cpl | 25660 | Also 9th Bn |
| Evans | Sydney Frederick | Pte | 1498 | H |
| Evans | Thomas William | Pte | 16911 | Ex 11th and 1st Bns. KIA 18/9/17 |

| Evans | William David | Pte | 200040 | H |
|-------|---------------|-----|--------|---|
| Everitt | John Edward | Pte | 40898 | KIA 26/4/18 |
| Fairhurst | Edward | Pte | 201395 | KIA 20/11/17 |
| Fairhurst | John | Cpl | 13108 | Also 7th Bn |
| Faith | Robert Barnes | Pte | 28020 | WIA. KIA 13/8/18 |
| Fallon | Fred | Sgt | 201610 | |
| Fallows | William | Pte | 200536 | WIA |
| Farish | William Henry | Sgt | 1281 | DCM, WIA |
| Farnen | Robert | Pte | 1940 | |
| Farrell | Walter | Pte | 202645 | Trans. to LC |
| Farren | William | Pte | 34473 | |
| Farrer | Robert | Pte | 202004 | WIA |
| Farrington | Robert | Pte | 201381 | |
| Faulkner | Herbert William | Pte | 40901 | |
| Faulkner | Robert | Pte | 22865 | DOW 4/10/17 |
| Fawcett | John Edward | Pte | 2557 | KIA 15/6/15 |
| Fawcett | Paul Hanson | Pte | 201012 | WIA |
| Fawcett | Samuel | Pte | 18117 | Also 7th and 1st Bns |
| Fawcett | Thomas | Cpl | 200284 | WIA |
| Fearnley | Herbert | Sgt | 201031 | MM. WIA. Trans. to LC |
| Fecitt | Thomas | Pte | 201715 | |
| Fell | George | Cpl | 200461 | |
| Fell | John | Pte | 2405 | WIA (accidentally). Trans. to RE |
| Fell | Nicholas | Pte | 3698 | WIA |
| Fell | Thomas | Pte | 2511 | |
| Fell | William Thomas A. | Pte | 3075 | KIA 11/9/16 |
| Fenton | Abel | Pte | 266049 | |
| Fenton | Robert Edward | Pte | 3269 | WIA. DOW 23/10/16 |
| Fenwick | Frank | Pte | 3388 | WIA. Trans. to KLR |
| Fenwick | George M. | Cpl | 235098 | Commissioned into London Rgt 27/8/1 |
| Ferguson | George William | 2Lt | | D Coy. MC, WIA |
| Ferguson | William | Cpl | 200423 | |
| Ferns | George Hubert | 2Lt | | WIA |
| Field | George | 2Lt | | WIA, POW |
| Fielding | Arthur | A/Cpl | 41501 | |
| Finch | Edward James | Cpl | 13126 | Also 7th Bn |
| Finch | Walter | Pte | 201388 | KIA 23/12/16 |
| Findlay | Samuel Mason | Pte | 34706 | |
| Finlay | John | 2Lt | | |
| Fish | Thomas | Pte | 30132 | Posted 8th Bn |
| Fisher | Albert | Pte | 34687 | DOW 3/5/18 |
| Fisher | Edward | Pte | 1946 | KIA 27/5/15 |

| Fisher | James | Capt. | | D 23/2/19 |
|---|---|---|---|---|
| Fisher | John | Pte | 201445 | DOW 17/2/17 |
| Fisher | John | Capt. | | |
| Fitchie | William | Pte | 202747 | Also 7th Bn |
| Fitters | Harry | Pte | 2198 | WIA. Trans. to Lincs |
| Fittes | Fred | Pte | 200761 | Att. to MGC. DOW 28/9/16 |
| Fitzpatrick | John | Pte | 25322 | Ex 7th Bn D 2/3/18 |
| Fitzsimmons | Thomas | Pte | 201277 | WIA. Also 1/5th and 2nd Bns |
| Fitzsimmons | William | L/Cpl | 201361 | WIA |
| Fitzwilliam | John | Pte | 1567 | KIA 8/6/15 |
| Fleming | Arthur | Cpl | 26754 | Also 7th Bn |
| Fletcher | Frederick John | Pte | 242280 | KIA 9/4/18 |
| Fletcher | George | Sgt | 202165 | MiD. KIA 26/10/18 |
| Fletcher | James | Pte | 201483 | WIA |
| Fletcher | John | Pte | 201393 | WIA. KIA 20/11/17 |
| Fletcher | William Miller | Cpl | 202166 | DOW 17/9/17 |
| Flitcroft | John William | Pte | 201321 | WIA. Also 8th Bn |
| Flynn | William | Pte | 2730 | Also 2nd Bn |
| Foley | Walter Patrick | Pte | 27785 | DOW 24/4/18 with 11th Bn |
| Folley | Joseph James | Pte | 33159 | KIA 15/7/17 |
| Forbes | Walter | Pte | 15854 | Ex 8th and 1/5th Bns. POW |
| Ford | Clement William | 2Lt | | KIA 31/7/17 |
| Ford | Frank | Pte | 23922 | Ex 7th Bn. WIA. Trans. to ASC |
| Ford | Thomas | Pte | 4142 | KIA 8/8/16 |
| Forster | Edward | Pte | 28022 | KIA 10/7/17 |
| Forsyth | George | Pte | 28167 | Also ASC. |
| Fortune | James | Pte | 201609 | DOW 1/12/17 |
| Foster | Herbert | Pte | 201678 | |
| Foster | Richard Bowman | Pte | 34619 | KIA 20/11/17 |
| Foster | Rowland | Pte | 41551 | |
| Foster | Stephen | Pte | 200152 | WIA |
| Foston | Herbert Edward | Pte | 40978 | |
| Fouraker | Leslie Frank | 2Lt | | |
| Fox | Andrew | Pte | 2938 | KIA 15/6/15 |
| Fox | Leonard | Pte | 200333 | POW |
| Fox | Louis | Pte | 14286 | Also 7th Bn |
| Fox | Peter | Pte | 6456 | WIA. Trans. LNR |
| Fox | Thomas | Pte | 241043 | DOW 11/5/17 |
| Foy | James | Pte | 28023 | KIA 20/11/17 |
| France | William | Pte | 1321 | WIA |
| Franks | Albert Edward | Pte | 201154 | Also 7th Bn |
| Frawley | John Henry | Pte | 1863 | KIA 15/6/15 |

| | | | | |
|---|---|---|---|---|
| Frazer | Alexander | Lt | | |
| Frearson | Charles Watson | Pte | 200025 | DOW 8/8/16 |
| Freemantle | William George H. | Pte | 202981 | Ex City of London Yeo. Also 2/5t Bn |
| French | Charles Henry | Pte | 41049 | KIA 26/4/18 |
| Friar | Eric | Pte | 37088 | DOW 17/6/18 |
| Friend | Samuel | Cpl | 875 | |
| Frith | William | Pte | 39663 | DOW 22/6/18 |
| Frodsham | Henry | Pte | 200958 | Posted to 8th Bn. WIA |
| Frodsham | Peter | Pte | 200927 | Att. to RE and TMB. |
| Fryer | Albert | Pte | 201305 | WIA. Att. to RE. Also 1st Bn |
| Fryer | Harry | Pte | 3425 | WIA. KIA 27/9/16 |
| Fullard | Alfred | Pte | 200520 | B Coy, WIA |
| Fullard | Harold | Pte | 3618 | WIA. Trans. to MGC |
| Fullard | William (John) | Pte | 1476 | |
| Fulwood | John | Pte | 12965 | WIA. Also 7th Bn |
| Fury | John | Pte | 3775 | WIA. Trans. to LC |
| Fyfe | Alexander | 2Lt | | OC 6 Ptn, WIA |
| Gaffney | William Henry | Pte | 18781 | Ex 6th Bn, POW |
| Galarneau | William | Cpl | 28102 | Ex LF. Deserted |
| Gale | Albert | Pte | 202754 | Ex Notts and Derby. Also 1st and 9th Bns |
| Gamble | Thomas | Pte | 28024 | POW |
| Gannon | Christopher | Pte | 29158 | |
| Gardener | Herbert | Pte | 201570 | |
| Gardner | John Robert | L/Cpl | 200470 | WIA. KIA 1/9/18 with 8th Bn |
| Gardner | Richard | Pte | 241600 | Also 1/5th |
| Gardner | Robert | Lt. Col. | | Accidentally wounded |
| Gardner | Samuel John | L/Cpl | 200939 | |
| Garner | Harold | Pte | 16240 | Also 9th and 7th Bns |
| Garner | John Thomas | Pte | 27911 | Also 11th and 7th Bns |
| Garner | Leslie | Pte | 41659 | Also LNL |
| Garnett | Albert Hugh | L/Cpl | 1831 | DOW 21/10/15 |
| Garnett | Byram James Henry | 2Lt | | |
| Garnett | John | L/Sgt | 1330 | |
| Garnett | Robert | Pte | 1057 | KIA 15/6/15 |
| Garnett | Thomas | Pte | 200503 | Repeated attachments to ASC Coy |
| Garnett | Walter | Pte | 200030 | |
| Garside | Harold | Pte | 26756 | Ex 7th Bn WIA (2) |
| Garside | Harold | Pte | 201613 | |
| Garstang | Harry | Pte | 3761 | WIA. Trans. to RE |
| Garstang | John | Pte | 27399 | Ex LF and also 7th Bn |
| Garvey | Wilton | Pte | 201614 | WIA |
| Gaskarth | Joseph | Pte | 201029 | WIA. Trans. to ASC Agri. Coy |

| Gaskell | John | Pte | 23637 | Also 1st Bn |
| Gatchell | James Harcourt | Lt | | RAMC. MC. KIA 27/9/17 with R. Sussex |
| Gathercole | James | Sgt | 750 | H |
| Gaulter | Jack Rudolf | 2Lt | 32031 | WIA (2) |
| Gayler | Henry Addis | Pte | 26808 | Also 7th Bn |
| Geldart | John | L/Cpl | 200602 | |
| Geldart | Stanley | Pte | 200567 | DOW 13/4/18 |
| Gendle | Edwin Howaith | Pte | 3786 | |
| Gendle | Harold Pemberthy | WO2 | 2672 | DOW 15/3/16 |
| Gendle | Tom | Pte | 200581 | WIA |
| Gent | Joseph Robert | Pte | 20687 | Alias Robt Cawley. Also 11th and 1st Bns. WIA |
| Gent | Herbert | Pte | 242989 | WIA (accidentally). Also 1/5th |
| Gentles | William Kenneth | Pte | 200821 | KIA 8/8/16 |
| Geraghty | Patrick | Pte | 17150 | also 1st Bn |
| Gibbons | Thomas E. | Pte | 15408 | WIA. Trans. to MGC |
| Gibson | Joseph William | Pte | 2524 | KIA 18/10/16 |
| Gibson | Thomas Norman | Pte | 30030 | Ex 8th Bn WIA (2) |
| Gilbanks | Harold Roger | Pte | 23713 | Also 8th and 9th Bns |
| Gilbert | Charles Henry | Pte | 27335 | Also 1st and 7th Bns |
| Gilbert | Henry William | Pte | 200563 | WIA |
| Gilbert | William | Pte | 201576 | WIA |
| Gildea | Herbert | L/Cpl | 202202 | WIA |
| Giles | Frederick William | Pte | 200543 | |
| Gill | George | Pte | 200548 | D Coy. WIA (2). Att. to TMB, and 177 TC |
| Gill | John Edward | Pte | 1524 | KIA 8/8/16 |
| Gill | John George | Pte | 266454 | |
| Gillbanks | Albert | Cpl | 200376 | WIA |
| Gillenders | Robert | Rev | | Padre |
| Gilling | Frederick Cuthbert | 2Lt | | 12 Ptn C Coy. WIA |
| Glaister | Harry | L/Cpl | 201615 | WIA. Att. to KAR |
| Gleave | Walter Victor | 2Lt | | |
| Glenie | George Richard | 2Lt | | KIA 11/9/16 |
| Glover | Ernest | Pte | 29186 | Also LC |
| Glover | James | Pte | 29183 | Also LC |
| Glover | John | Pte | 200983 | WIA |
| Glover | Walter | Pte | 1636 | KIA 8/8/16 |
| Godel | Clarence William | Pte | 29193 | Ex LC and Jersey Militia |
| Godfrey | Ernest | Pte | 40904 | |
| Godfrey | H. E. | 2Lt | | |
| Golding | Charles Victor | Pte | 33719 | Ex 1/5th. C Coy. WIA (2) |
| Golding | George | Pte | 26885 | WIA |

| Goldsmith | Robert | Pte | 201147 | |
| Goldstan | Wilfred | Pte | 200815 | D Coy. WIA |
| Good | William | Pte | 2517 | Trans. to RE and MGC |
| Gooden | John | Pte | 201303 | WIA |
| Goodinson | Andrew | Pte | 22112 | WIA |
| Goodwin | Charles | Pte | 201467 | |
| Goodwin | George Charles | Pte | 200103 | H |
| Goodwin | Harry | Pte | 201581 | Ex 1/5th. WIA (2) |
| Goodwin | Thomas | Pte | 1934 | Trans. to RE |
| Gordon | William | Pte | 201245 | POW. D 16/4/18 |
| Gore | James Henry | Cpl | 28168 | Also 7th Bn |
| Gornall | George | Pte | 2240 | |
| Gorst | Charles | Pte | 49362 | KIA 16/10/18 |
| Gott | Frederick L. | Sgt | 2026 | D Coy. WIA |
| Gouge | William | Pte | 28103 | KIA 31/7/17 |
| Gough | Bert Harold | 2Lt | | KIA 9/4/18 |
| Gould | Arthur William | Pte | 51141 | WIA, POW |
| Gowling | George Jubilee | Pte | 201560 | WIA |
| Gradwell | Harold | Pte | 240854 | Also 1/5th |
| Grafton | George | Pte | 202741 | Also 1st Bn |
| Graham | David | WO2 | 200680 | DCM. Commissioned 26/6/18 |
| Graham | Fred | Pte | 2943 | WIA. D 4/1/16 |
| Graham | John | Pte | 48859 | |
| Graham | Robert | Cpl | 201612 | |
| Grant | Joseph Ellis | Pte | 41531 | |
| Gravells | Fred Isaac | Pte | 40902 | |
| Graves | Alfred Ernest | Cpl | 200710 | Att. to 179 Tunn Coy. DCM |
| Graveson | George | Pte | 200525 | B Coy. WIA. POW |
| Gray | Edward | Pte | 22457 | Also 11th and 7th Bns |
| Gray | Frederick James | Pte | 34667 | Also 2/5th |
| Gray | George Nichol | 2Lt | | |
| Gray | William | Pte | 200097 | H |
| Grayson | Thomas | Pte | 28025 | Also 9th Bn |
| Greaves | Edward | Cpl | 22054 | Ex 7th Bn. DOW 13/7/18 |
| Greaves | Joseph | Pte | 201563 | |
| Greaves | Joseph | Pte | 202751 | Also 6th Bn. WIA |
| Gredy | Leonard | Pte | 243044 | WIA. Trans. to RWF |
| Green | Charles | Pte | 27246 | Ex 1st Bn. WIA, KIA 16/9/17 |
| Green | Harry | Pte | 24271 | MM. Also 1st Bn |
| Green | James | Pte | 3397 | KIA 18/8/16 with 8th Bn |
| Green | Samuel | A/Cpl | 200370 | |
| Green | William | Pte | 28026 | DOW 23/11/17 |

| Greenhalgh | Benjamin | Pte | 27695 | Also 1st and 1/5th Bns |
| Greenhalgh | Herbert | Pte | 202767 | Ex7th and 8th Bns. KIA 20/9/17 |
| Greenhalgh | James | Pte | 4092 | KIA 8/8/16 |
| Greenhalgh | Peter | Pte | 34655 | |
| Greenhill | Albert | Pte | 41533 | |
| Greenhill | James | Pte | 200665 | WIA (2) Posted 2nd Bn |
| Greenhow | Alfred | Pte | 200020 | |
| Greenhow | Edward | Pte | 2699 | DOW 30/6/15 |
| Greenhow | Harry | Pte | 2698 | WIA (4). Trans. to MGC |
| Greenhow | James | Pte | 200281 | MiD |
| Greenhow | Joseph | Pte | 200505 | WIA |
| Greenough | Ernest | Cpl | 15227 | Ex 7th Bn. MM |
| Greenwood | Joseph Binns | Pte | 13966 | Also 7th and 1st Bns. POW |
| Gregg | Joseph | Pte | 200961 | WIA |
| Gregory | Charles John | L/Cpl | 26887 | KIA 20/11/17 |
| Gregory | Frank | Pte | 34658 | |
| Gregory | Tom | Pte | 201769 | Ex E. Lancs. WIA. Posted 8th Bn |
| Gregson | Harold | Pte | 29156 | |
| Gregson | John | A/C/Sgt | 200942 | WIA |
| Gregson | John | Pte | 24842 | Ex 7th Bn |
| Grenfell | James | Pte | 2290 | H |
| Grenfell | Thomas Henry | Pte | 1414 | |
| Grey | Ernest Albert | Pte | 4930 | WIA. KIA 26/9/16 |
| Gribble | Charles William | 2Lt | | B Coy. OC 5 Ptn |
| Griffies | Frederick | Pte | 265686 | DOW 21/9/17 |
| Griffiths | John | Pte | 4931 | KIA 27/9/16 |
| Griffiths | Richard Lewis | Pte | 29143 | WIA (2) |
| Grigg | Mark | Pte | 2719 | KIA 15/6/15 |
| Grimshaw | John | Pte | 200980 | WIA. Trans. to LC |
| Grimshaw | Richard | L/Cpl | 1519 | |
| Grindal | Joseph | 2Lt | | WIA |
| Grindrod | Charles | Pte | 201912 | WIA |
| Grisedale | Herbert | Pte | 3125 | WIA |
| Grizzall | Arthur | Pte | 41539 | |
| Grosvenor | George | Pte | 200560 | WIA, POW |
| Groves | Albert | Sgt | 241585 | Also 1/5th. |
| Gudgeon | Thomas | Pte | 27451 | Also 1/5th and 7th Bns. |
| Guest | William Frederick | Pte | 41523 | |
| Gunning | Albert | Pte | 200610 | WIA. |
| Gunson | Wilfred Turner | Pte | 49366 | WIA |
| Hackett | Joseph | Pte | 1812 | |
| Hacking | Harold | Pte | 25741 | KIA 20/11/17 |

| Hacking | Thomas | Pte | 32622 | Ex 7th Bn. WIA, POW |
| Hackland | William | Pte | 202750 | Ex 11th Bn. Att. to TMB |
| Hadfield | Harold | Pte | 201619 | DOW 21/9/17 |
| Hadwin | Ernest | Pte | 2604 | KIA 15/6/15 |
| Hadwin | Robert | Pte | 200703 | |
| Hadwin | William | Pte | 200441 | |
| Haffenden | Frank Gordon | Pte | 24281 | Ex 7th Bn. Posted1/5th, WIA |
| Hague | William | Pte | 201416 | WIA |
| Haigh | Allan | Pte | 41435 | |
| Haines | Sidney A. | Pte | 4558 | WIA. Trans. to LC |
| Haley | Abraham | Pte | 29162 | Also LC |
| Haley | William Edward | Pte | 41557 | |
| Halkon | Harry | Pte | 40905 | KIA 17/5/18 |
| Hall | Amos Goodridge | L/Sgt | 24286 | WIA, POW |
| Hall | Edgar | Pte | 3760 | A Coy. KIA 8/8/16 |
| Hall | Ernest Edward | Pte | 28203 | Ex 7th. Posted 1/5th Bn |
| Hall | Frederick Charles | Pte | 25619 | Ex 7th Bn |
| Hall | Gordon Ibbotson | Pte | 25880 | Also 2nd Bn |
| Hall | Henry John | Pte | 28200 | Ex 7th Bn, POW |
| Hall | Joseph Hillyard | Pte | 3049 | KIA 15/6/15 |
| Hallam | Richard Cecil | 2Lt | | WIA |
| Halligan | John | Pte | 200080 | KIA 23/12/16 |
| Hallows | Arthur Douglas | Sgt | 12150 | Ex 7th Bn |
| Halsall | Harold | Pte | 23144 | Ex 7th Bn WIA (2) |
| Halsall | John | Pte | 200977 | WIA. Trans. to LC, SWB |
| Halstead | Tyson | Sgt | 201700 | Also 8th Bn |
| Hamblett | Edwin | Pte | 201501 | KIA 20/9/17 |
| Hamer | John Harris | 2Lt | | |
| Hamer | John William | Pte | 201439 | WIA. Also 2nd Bn |
| Hamilton | Harry | L/Sgt | 10254 | Also 2nd Bn |
| Hammond | Arthur | Pte | 201705 | WIA |
| Hampson | Fred | Pte | 200940 | WIA. Att. TMB |
| Hampson | Thomas | Pte | 16834 | Also 7th Bn |
| Hampson | William | Pte | 201365 | WIA. |
| Hampton | William | Pte | 2401 | H |
| Hand | Ernest Edward | Pte | 40906 | |
| Hanley | Frederick | Pte | 200882 | A Coy. WIA (2) |
| Hanley | Thomas | Sgt | 27441 | Also 7th and 1st Bns |
| Hanna | William | Pte | 200880 | MM. A Coy Runner |
| Hansom | Benjamin | Pte | 28028 | KIA 31/7/17 |
| Hardcastle | Gilbert | Pte | 32508 | Ex LF and 7th Bn. KIA 20/9/17 |
| Harding | James | Pte | 28104 | Ex LF |

| | | | | |
|---|---|---|---|---|
| Hardisty | Leonard | Sgt | 200500 | To W. African Rifles Jan 18 |
| Hardman | Frank | Pte | 201582 | Ex 8th Bn. POW |
| Hardy | Arthur Robbon | Pte | 23188 | |
| Hardy | John | Cpl | 9508 | Ex 2nd, 8th, and 2/5th Bns. KIA 27/4/18 |
| Hargreaves | Albert | Pte | 28686 | MM. Also ASC and 2/5th |
| Hargreaves | Harold | Pte | 24055 | Also 1st Bn |
| Hargreaves | Henry | Pte | 34621 | KIA 18/9/17 |
| Hargreaves | Ian | Pte | 41052 | KIA 9/9/18 |
| Hargreaves | James | Pte | 27799 | Ex 11th Bn |
| Hargreaves | John | Pte | 201542 | KIA 9/4/18 |
| Hargreaves | Robert | Pte | 201718 | |
| Harker | Edwin | Pte | 28030 | POW |
| Harkins | Leonard | Cpl | 200398 | |
| Harney | Joseph | Pte | 28109 | KIA 31/7/17 |
| Harper | John | Pte | 29165 | Also LC |
| Harper | Reginald Arthur | A/WO2 | 10350 | Also 2nd and 8th Bns and LF |
| Harrall | John William | Pte | 200497 | WIA, POW |
| Harris | Ewbank John | Pte | 37215 | |
| Harris | Harold | Pte | 202764 | Also 1st and 7th Bns. Medals Forfeited |
| Harris | John | Pte | 200922 | KIA 16/6/17 with 8th Bn |
| Harris | Joseph | Pte | 200556 | WIA (2) Posted to 8th Bn |
| Harris | Robert Gladstone | Pte | 22642 | Ex 11th and 7th Bns. KIA 30/11/17 |
| Harris | William Henry | Pte | 200175 | |
| Harrison | Edward | Pte | 1289 | |
| Harrison | Frederick Charles | Pte | 240693 | |
| Harrison | Herbert Michael | Pte | 242488 | Also 1/5th |
| Harrison | Isaac Ernest | Pte | 2773 | KIA 15/6/15 |
| Harrison | John Reidy | Pte | 201084 | Also 8th Bn, WIA |
| Harrison | John Thomas | Pte | 28031 | Also 7th Bn |
| Harrison | Joseph | Pte | 201074 | Also 2/5th |
| Harrison | Luke | L/Cpl | 13871 | Also 9th Bn |
| Harrison | William | Pte | 2723 | POW. DOW 7/7/15 |
| Harrison | William | Pte | 16255 | Also 7th, 9th, and 2/5th Bns |
| Harrison | William Schollick | CQMS | 200135 | MiD. Commissioned 28/5/18 |
| Harrop | Frank | Pte | 13498 | Also 7th Bn |
| Hart | Henry Royston | 2Lt | | WIA. |
| Hart | John | Pte | 200800 | Also 1st Bn |
| Hart | John | Pte | 201616 | KIA 31/7/17 |
| Hartley | Fred | Pte | 202221 | Also 1st Bn |
| Hartley | John | Pte | 2689 | KIA 15/6/15 |
| Hartley | Joseph Henry | Pte | 201325 | KIA 8/8/16 |
| Hartley | Roger | Cpl | 200760 | WIA. Att. to div. TC |

| Harvey | Percy | Pte | 265101 | |
| Harwood | Frank | Pte | 263002 | Also 1/5th |
| Harwood | Stanley | Pte | 22798 | Also 7th Bn |
| Haskett | Thomas | Sgt | 200651 | Resident USA. WIA |
| Haslam | Edward | 2Lt | | WIA |
| Haslam | John Edward | L/Cpl | 4195 | WIA. KIA 11/9/16 |
| Hatcher | Reginald Gordon | 2Lt | | DOW 20/9/17 |
| Hatfield | William Frederick | L/Cpl | 19074 | Also 11th Bn |
| Hatton | Harry Ashley | Pte | 201349 | KIA 8/8/16 |
| Hawarden | John | Pte | 201322 | Also 8th Bn |
| Hawkins | Thomas William | Pte | 201772 | |
| Hawksby | Reginald | L/Cpl | 1655 | H |
| Hawley | Septimus | Pte | 23928 | Ex 8th Bn. Trans. to LC |
| Haworth | Albert | L/Sgt | 2512 | Also 2nd Bn |
| Haworth | Thomas | Pte | 33385 | Ex 1st Bn. 15 Ptn D Coy. Accidental wounded + SI-wound. |
| Haworth (Howarth) | George | Pte | 200032 | |
| Hayhurst | Henry William | Pte | 32608 | Ex 7th Bn |
| Hayhurst | William | Sgt | 2411 | MiD. WIA. Trans. to MGC |
| Hayhurst | Wilson | Pte | 3035 | |
| Haylock | Henry George | Pte | 41051 | |
| Haythorn | William Hudson | L/Cpl | 3379 | KIA 8/8/16 |
| Haythornthwaite | Ernest | Pte | 3254 | D Coy. KIA 8/8/16 |
| Hayward | Horace | Pte | 202464 | KIA 20/9/17 |
| Haywood | Horace | Pte | 202464 | |
| Healey | Leonard | Pte | 201630 | Also 8th Bn WIA |
| Heath | George Edward | Pte | 40912 | |
| Heaton | Henry | Pte | 201024 | WIA. Posted to 2/5th then LC and AS◆ |
| Helm | James Percival | Pte | 28032 | KIA 20/11/17 |
| Helme | George | Pte | 200805 | WIA |
| Helme | Harold | Pte | 201418 | MM. Att. to Bde HQ |
| Helme | Robert | Pte | 201115 | Att. to RE. POW, KIA 28/4/18 |
| Hems | James | Pte | 3605 | KIA 3/8/16 |
| Henderson | Robert | Pte | 200418 | WIA. Trans. to LNR |
| Henderson | Thomas | Pte | 200960 | WIA |
| Hensby | Maurice Arthur | Pte | 202179 | WIA |
| Heron | John | L/Cpl | 200463 | |
| Hesketh | Robert Henry | Pte | 201747 | WIA |
| Hesketh | Thomas | Pte | 4936 | KIA 28/9/16 |
| Hewartson | George | Cpl | 200434 | B Coy 7 Ptn. MM |
| Hewitson | James | L/Cpl | 15853 | Ex 7th Bn. VC, WIA (3) |

| Hewitt | Albert E. | Pte | 2356 | Trans. to Lincs |
|---|---|---|---|---|
| Hewitt | Ernest Henry | Lt | | MiD. KIA 15/6/15 |
| Hewitt | John | Pte | 22643 | Ex 11th Bn |
| Heywood | William | Pte | 201617 | |
| Hibbert | Arthur | Pte | 2431 | WIA |
| Hickey | James | Pte | 20060 | WIA |
| Hickman | William James | Pte | 41050 | KIA 4/10/18 with 2/5 |
| Higgins | Charles Thomas | Pte | 28120 | Ex E. Kents and also 7th Bn |
| Higginson | Charles | Pte | 200456 | WIA |
| Higginson | George Leonard | Pte | 266134 | Also 1st Bn |
| Higginson | Reginald Wilfred | 2Lt | | D Coy |
| Higgs | Leo | Pte | 201360 | KIA 1/12/17 |
| High | Henry T. | Pte | 2275 | WIA. Trans. to Monmouths |
| Higson | Peter | Pte | 4093 | A Coy. DOW 16/8/16 |
| Hill | Edward | Pte | 201575 | |
| Hill | Edwin | Pte | 34627 | POW |
| Hill | Herbert Sampson | Pte | 41667 | Deserted 8/4/19 |
| Hill | John James | Pte | 200091 | |
| Hill | John James | Pte | 201719 | Also 2nd Bn |
| Hill | Norman | Cpl | 200640 | KIA 8/8/16 |
| Hill | Robert William | Pte | 203055 | Commissioned 30/4/18 |
| Hillen | Edward | Pte | 2566 | |
| Hillen | John | Pte | 2084 | KIA 10/8/15 |
| Hilton | Clifford | Pte | 37091 | |
| Hilton | George | 2Lt | | KIA 8/8/16 |
| Hinchcliffe | Herbert | L/Sgt | 200749 | C Coy. DOW 10/4/18 |
| Hinde | Robert Francis | Cpl | 201720 | MM. D Coy |
| Hindley | Robert | Pte | 201622 | Also 8th Bn and MCR |
| Hindley | William | Pte | 26706 | Also 7th Bn |
| Hinds | James | Pte | 200287 | Trans. to RE |
| Hinds | Samuel | Sgt | 200406 | MSM. Orderly Room Sgt |
| Hinds | William George | CQMS | 200117 | A Coy. WIA (2), MM |
| Hine | John | Pte | 200163 | A Coy |
| Hingley | Robert H. | Rev. | | Padre |
| Hingley | Thomas | A/Sgt | 33950 | Ex 1/5th. WIA |
| Hinsley | Robert Alfred | Pte | 41550 | |
| Hinson (Henson) | Reginald Charles | Pte | 201721 | |
| Hipwell | John | Pte | 27870 | Ex 11th Bn, WIA |
| Hird | James | Cpl | 200170 | KIA 31/7/17 |
| Hird | Tom | Cpl | 200532 | WIA. POW |
| Hirst | John | Pte | 41655 | |

| | | | | |
|---|---|---|---|---|
| Hiscox | Louis | Pte | 202204 | Ex 11th Bn |
| Hitchen | William | Pte | 201377 | WIA |
| Hodge | Frank | Pte | 28201 | Ex 7th Bn, KIA 9/4/18 |
| Hodges | James | Pte | 201205 | KIA 31/7/17 |
| Hodgkin | Alan | Pte | 41535 | |
| Hodgkinson | Harold Hale | 2Lt | | |
| Hodgson | Albert Edward | Sgt | 200839 | DCM, WIA |
| Hodgson | Albert Edward | Pte | 201704 | |
| Hodgson | Edward | Cpl | 200290 | WIA (2). Posted 1st Bn |
| Hodgson | F. | Pte | 202220 | |
| Hodgson | Herbert | L/Cpl | 16194 | Also 9th and 7th Bns |
| Hodgson | John | Pte | 2752 | KIA 27/9/16 |
| Hodgson | John | Pte | 37928 | |
| Hodgson | John Edward | Pte | 38071 | |
| Hodgson | Robert | Pte | 32488 | WIA. Posted 1/5th |
| Hodgson | Thomas | Pte | 2729 | B Coy. WIA |
| Hodgson | William | Pte | 200716 | WIA (2). POW |
| Hodgson | William | Pte | 17946 | Also 2nd and 7th Bns |
| Hodgson | William | Pte | 201067 | |
| Hodkinson | Harold Hale | 2Lt | | KIA 8/8/16 |
| Hodkinson | William | Pte | 201566 | |
| Hodson | Harry | Pte | 40910 | |
| Hodson | Thomas | Pte | 3314 | KIA 8/8/16 |
| Hogan | James | Pte | 3240 | WIA |
| Hogg | John | Cpl | 24198 | Ex 7th Bn. MM |
| Hogg | William Crook | Pte | 31618 | KIA 20/11/17 |
| Hoggarth | James | Pte | 2485 | WIA. KIA 8/6/15 |
| Hoggarth | Thomas | Pte | 24406 | Ex 7th Bn. WIA |
| Hoggarth | William | Pte | 2755 | WIA |
| Holden | Hubert Edward | Pte | 202988 | Commissioned ASC 7/8/19 |
| Holding | Robert | Pte | 22466 | WIA. Trans. to LNL |
| Holdsworth | Tom | 2Lt | | WIA |
| Holgate | James | Pte | 202774 | WIA (2). KIA 2/9/18 with 1st Bn |
| Holland | Clarence Jennings | 2Lt | | A Coy. KIA 14/8/18 |
| Holland | Richard | Pte | 200619 | |
| Hollingworth | John | Pte | 1550 | WIA. Trans. KLR and Monmouths |
| Hollywood | Thomas | Pte | 200074 | |
| Holman | Albert | Pte | 25593 | WIA. Trans. to TC. POW |
| Holman | Benjamin | L/Cpl | 4194 | |
| Holme | Frederick | L/Cpl | 200379 | WIA (2) |
| Holme | Robert | Pte | 32034 | Ex 1st Bn, WIA (2). Reposted to 1st Bn |
| Holmes | Alfred Glynn | Sgt | 202167 | MM |

| | | | | |
|---|---|---|---|---|
| Holmes | Arthur William | Pte | 28033 | |
| Holmes | David | Pte | 29340 | DOW 24/8/18 |
| Holmes | Frederick Proctor | Pte | 200261 | |
| Holmes | George | L/Cpl | 265270 | WIA. Posted to 8th Bn |
| Holmes | George | WO2 | 200467 | WIA, MM |
| Holmes | James Wilson | Cpl | 200311 | |
| Holmes | Thomas | Pte | 1621 | H |
| Holmes | William | 2Lt | | WIA, POW |
| Holmes | William Myles | Pte | 1864 | DOW 9/6/15 |
| Holroyd | William Longley | Pte | 201553 | WIA. Posted to 9th Bn |
| Holt | Samuel | Pte | 201574 | WIA, POW |
| Holyday | Charles | Pte | 1098 | WIA |
| Hoole | Joseph | Pte | 202241 | DOW 23/11/17 |
| Hooley | William Henry | Pte | 26813 | Also 8th and 7th Bns |
| Hopwood | George | Pte | 13982 | Also 7th Bn |
| Hopwood | James | Pte | 32491 | KIA 18/7/17 |
| Hopwood | James | Cpl | 20759 | Ex 11th Bn WIA |
| Horn | Benjamin | Pte | 28106 | Ex LF, POW |
| Hornby | John | Pte | 201690 | WIA |
| Hornby | Robert | Pte | 37083 | KIA 9/4/18 |
| Hornby | William | Pte | 24602 | Also 7th Bn |
| Horne | Robert | Pte | 1474 | KIA 15/6/15 |
| Horne | Roger Hallewell | WO2 | 495 | WIA. To 12th Bn. Commissioned into RWF |
| Horridge | Frank | Pte | 24019 | Also 1/5th. |
| Horrobin | Herbert | Pte | 201313 | WIA |
| Hosker | John Taylor | Pte | 200167 | |
| Hoskin | Edward John | Pte | 200711 | WIA. Also 8th Bn |
| Hoskin | Joseph | Pte | 2754 | WIA |
| Hosking | George Edward | Cpl | 200226 | A Coy. WIA |
| Hough | John Percy | Pte | 201722 | WIA. Trans. to MFP |
| Hough | Samuel | Pte | 201333 | KIA 27/9/16 |
| Houghton | Randolph | Pte | 4139 | WIA. KIA 27/9/16 |
| Hoult | Albert Edward | Pte | 34571 | POW |
| Hovington | Thomas | Pte | 5609 | WIA. Trans. to LC |
| Howard | Edward Douglas | 2Lt | | KIA 20/9/17 |
| Howard | William | Pte | 41515 | |
| Howarth | Albert | L/Sgt | 2512 | Ex 2nd BN. MM. D 12/2/19 |
| Howarth | Alfred | C/Sgt | 1299 | Commissioned into LF |
| Howarth | Fred | Pte | 22736 | WIA. Ex 8th and 1st Bns. KIA 31/7/17 |
| Howarth | Henry | Pte | 14958 | Ex 7th Bn KIA 20/3/18 |
| Howarth | Henry | Pte | 30218 | WIA (2). Posted 7th. |

| Howarth | Percy | Pte | 201374 | POW |
|---|---|---|---|---|
| Howarth | Thomas | L/Cpl | 202205 | Ex 9th and 1st Bns. WIA (2) |
| Howarth | William | Pte | 21911 | Ex 11th and 1sr Bns. WIA |
| Howarth | William Richard | Pte | 29195 | C Coy. WIA |
| Howarth (Haworth) | Jack | Pte | 201760 | POW |
| Howcroft | Proctor | L/Cpl | 201723 | Att. to MGC. KIA 9/4/18 |
| Howcroft | Thomas | Pte | 200966 | Att. to MGC. KIA 8/8/16 |
| Howie | Robert | Pte | 1669 | H |
| Howkins | Walter Robert | Pte | 29168 | Ex LC. WIA |
| Hubble | Alfred Stanley | Pte | 203010 | Ex County of London Yeo. Also 2/5th |
| Huck | Gerard | Pte | 1779 | DOW 10/3/17 |
| Huck | Thomas Walter (Walker) | Pte | 200108 | KIA 8/8/16 |
| Huddleston | George | Sgt | 200746 | C Coy. DCM. WIA (3) |
| Hudson | Harold Victor | Pte | 201087 | POW |
| Hudson | James Howarth | Pte | 27579 | Ex 8th and 11th BNs. WIA. KIA 20/9/17 |
| Hudson | John | Pte | 28034 | Also 1/5th. Medals Forfeited |
| Huet | Frederick William | Pte | 26450 | Also 9th Bn |
| Hughes | Henry | Sgt | 200216 | H (later to RAF) |
| Hughes | John | Pte | 200546 | |
| Hughes | John Robinson | Pte | 200274 | WIA. KIA 3/5/17 with 1st Bn |
| Hughes | John Thomas | Pte | 10093 | Also 2nd and 7th Bns |
| Hughes | Robert | Pte | 3265 | KIA 8/8/16 |
| Hughes | Robert A. | Pte | 200653 | WIA. Trans. to RE |
| Hughes | Robert Samuel | Pte | 42831 | |
| Hughes | Samuel | L/Cpl | 200466 | WIA, POW |
| Hughes | Thomas Richard | Pte | 42830 | |
| Hull | Frederick | Pte | 37429 | |
| Hulme | Albert | Pte | 201620 | KIA 31/7/17 |
| Hulme | Alfred | Pte | 20056 | Ex 2nd Bn |
| Hulme | Frederick | Pte | 22590 | Also 11th and 8th Bns |
| Hulme | James Edwin | Pte | 202658 | Also 7th Bn |
| Hume | George | Pte | 28294 | Ex ASC and 11th Bn 24/9/17. WIA (2) |
| Humphreys | Edward Newland | Pte | 40908 | |
| Humphreys | Samuel Oliver | Pte | 38092 | Att. to KRRC |
| Hunt | Harry | Pte | 23121 | Ex 7th Bn |
| Hunt | John Edward | Pte | 27981 | WIA. Also 1st and 1/5th Bns |
| Hunter | Herbert Sidney | 2Lt | | KIA 26/4/18 |
| Hunter | Percival Lister | Pte | 30129 | Ex 8th Bn. WIA, POW |
| Hunter | Thomas Swainson | Pte | 26678 | WIA |
| Hunter | Walter | Pte | 27251 | WIA. DOW 6/12/17 |

| | | | | |
|---|---|---|---|---|
| Hunter | William | Pte | 241369 | |
| Huntington | William | Pte | 200663 | |
| Huntington | William | Capt. | | Commissioned from 1/5th 21/9/15 |
| Hurst | Joseph Mason | Pte | 200325 | WIA (2) Trans. to RE |
| Hurst | Wilfred | Pte | 200270 | |
| Hutchinson | Abraham | Pte | 202492 | WIA. Trans. to KLR |
| Hutchinson | Thomas | L/Cpl | 1477 | WIA |
| Huthwaite | Henry Youle | Capt. | | |
| Hutley | Norman Reginald | 2Lt | | |
| Hutton | William | Pte | 3093 | D Coy. DOW 11/10/16 |
| Hynes | Nicolas | Pte | 55074 | WIA. Also S. Lancs and Notts and Derby. |
| Hyslop | Albert Edward | Pte | 13895 | Also 9th and 7th Bns |
| Ibbitson | George | Pte | 202222 | |
| Iddon | Edward | Pte | 200452 | |
| Iddon | John | Pte | 17374 | Also 6th and 1st Bns |
| Iddon | John | Sgt | 10177 | Also 2nd and 7th Bns |
| Ilett | Alfred | Pte | 36537 | |
| Illingworth | James | Pte | 34623 | DOW 24/9/17 |
| Ince | Howard (Sidney Howard) | Pte | 41669 | |
| Ineson | Joseph | Cpl | 200051 | |
| Ingleton | Harold Walter | Cpl | 200747 | H (later 2nd Bn ) |
| Ingram | Charles | Pte | 2456 | WIA. Trans. to MGC |
| Ingram | William | Pte | 13669 | Also 9th and 2/5th Bns |
| Inman | George | Sgt | 200001 | KIA 27/9/18 with 8th Bn |
| Inman | James | Pte | 1893 | H |
| Inman | William Steele | L/Sgt | 1716 | KIA 31/7/16 |
| Ireland | Joseph William | Pte | 200806 | KIA 8/8/16 |
| Ireland | Richard William | Pte | 33236 | Ex 1st Bn |
| Ireland | Sydney | Pte | 3460 | |
| Irving | James | Cpl | 32592 | Ex 7th Bn, POW |
| Irving | William | Pte | 23131 | Ex 7th Bn |
| Irwin | John | Pte | 200219 | WIA |
| Isherwood | Albert | Pte | 201304 | |
| Islip | George A. K. | 2Lt | | |
| Jackson | Albert | L/Sgt | 200804 | WIA |
| Jackson | Arthur | Pte | 29344 | DOW 11/10/18 |
| Jackson | Edgar | Pte | 17968 | Also 1st Bn |
| Jackson | Edward | L/Cpl | 19598 | Ex 7th Bn, POW. KIA 23/8/18 |
| Jackson | Frank | Pte | 913 | |
| Jackson | Fred | L/Sgt | 200162 | MM, WIA (2) |
| Jackson | George | Pte | 41663 | |

| | | | | |
|---|---|---|---|---|
| Jackson | George Frederick | Sgt | 240139 | Provost Sergeant |
| Jackson | Horace | Pte | 201138 | DOW 22/6/18 |
| Jackson | John | L/Cpl | 730 | |
| Jackson | John | 2Lt | | WIA |
| Jackson | John Edward | Pte | 241597 | WIA. Trans. to LC |
| Jackson | John Kerr | Pte | 27516 | Also 8th and 11th Bns |
| Jackson | Joseph Henry | Pte | 200235 | Att. to TMB. POW. D 5/12/17 |
| Jackson | Richard Noble | Sgt | 200601 | MM, MiD |
| Jackson | Robert | Pte | 201077 | KIA 16/6/18 with LC |
| Jackson | Robert James | Pte | 24201 | Ex 7th Bn. MM. WIA. Trans. to LNL |
| Jackson | Thomas | Cpl | 200197 | MM. MiD. KIA 20/11/17 |
| Jackson | Vivian Archer | Capt. | | Att. from York and Lancaster Rgt |
| Jackson | William | Cpl | 200256 | |
| Jackson | William | Pte | 200676 | WIA |
| Jackson | William | Pte | 241813 | Also 2/5th |
| Jackson | William H. | Pte | 1746 | Trans. to LC |
| Jackson | William Stephen | Pte | 3571 | WIA. Trans. to LC |
| Jackson | William W. | L/Cpl | 2558 | Trans. to LC |
| Jacobson | Albert Henry | Pte | 202756 | Ex Lincs. Also 1st Bn |
| James | George | Pte | 200687 | KIA 8/8/16 |
| James | Harry | Pte | 41654 | |
| James | Henry Arthur | Pte | 202239 | |
| James | Horace Henry | Pte | 266092 | |
| James | John | Pte | 200582 | WIA. Trans. to LC |
| James | Thomas | Pte | 200688 | WIA. KIA 20/9/17 |
| James | William | Pte | 23696 | Deserted |
| James | William Thomas | Pte | 200093 | |
| Jameson | William | Pte | 200869 | Att. to RE. KIA 20/11/17 |
| Jamieson | Neil | Pte | 1790 | KIA 8/8/16 |
| Janes | John | Pte | 201009 | |
| Jarman | Thomas Jubal | Pte | 49357 | |
| Jarvis | Joseph | L/Cpl | 4946 | KIA 11/9/16 |
| Jeffery | Fred | L/Cpl | 200731 | WIA. Trans. to LC and Royal Innis Fusiliers |
| Jeffrey | William | Pte | 200029 | WIA |
| Jeffs | William Edward | Pte | 27845 | Also 1st Bn |
| Jenkins | Edward | Pte | 200865 | KIA 25/4/18 with 8th Bn |
| Jenkins | Harold | Pte | 42892 | Trans. to LNL |
| Jenkinson | Robert | Pte | 200151 | Trans. to RE |
| Jenkinson | William | Pte | 201119 | WIA. Trans. to LC |
| Jenks | William Henry | Lt | | USMORC. MC, WIA |
| Jenner | Thomas Cousins | Pte | 200189 | H |

| | | | | |
|---|---|---|---|---|
| Jennings | Herbert Lightbrown | Pte | 40917 | |
| Jervis | John H. | Pte | 3990 | WIA. Trans. to Lincs |
| Jesson | Thomas | Pte | 22000 | Ex 9th Bn and 7th Bns. WIA, POW |
| Jewsbury | Samuel | Pte | 265128 | |
| Johns | Alfred | Pte | 200384 | WIA |
| Johns | John | Pte | 1403 | H |
| Johnson | Albert | Pte | 2140 | WIA |
| Johnson | Albert | Pte | 201141 | |
| Johnson | Albert Edward | Pte | 28035 | WIA. KIA 20/9/17 |
| Johnson | Alfred Paully | Pte | 51943 | WIA |
| Johnson | Alfred W. | L/Cpl | 200748 | WIA. C Coy. Trans. to LC |
| Johnson | Arthur James | Pte | 40916 | |
| Johnson | Christopher | Pte | 2627 | KIA 15/6/15 |
| Johnson | Edward | Cpl | 241319 | MM |
| Johnson | George | L/Sgt | 200691 | A and C Coys. DCM and Bar |
| Johnson | George | Pte | 17256 | Also 2nd Bn |
| Johnson | George Arthur | Pte | 3174 | |
| Johnson | Isaac John | Pte | 201299 | |
| Johnson | James | Pte | 200041 | H |
| Johnson | John | Cpl | 200278 | MM |
| Johnson | Percy | Pte | 3725 | KIA 11/9/16 |
| Johnson | Robert | Pte | 200642 | WIA (2). Posted to 8th Bn |
| Johnson | William Edward | Pte | 2043 | KIA 10/9/16 |
| Johnston | Ernest | Pte | 200180 | |
| Johnston | Frederick | Pte | 41736 | Ex Army Cyclist Corps. POW |
| Johnston | Henry Vincent | 2Lt | | |
| Johnston | John Firth | Pte | 29194 | Ex LC |
| Johnston | William | Cpl | 3050 | WIA. Trans. to LC |
| Johnstone | John Douglas | 2Lt | | WIA. KIA 31/7/17 |
| Jolley | Percy | 2Lt | | KIA 13/7/17 (on detachment) |
| Jones | Alfred James | Pte | 40915 | |
| Jones | Arnold | Cpl | 201562 | |
| Jones | Arthur | Cpl | 23889 | KIA 14/7/17 |
| Jones | Arthur Thomas | Pte | 42832 | |
| Jones | Eli Jasper | Pte | 42835 | 15 Ptn D Coy |
| Jones | Ernest | Pte | 200203 | WIA |
| Jones | Frank | Capt. | | WIA |
| Jones | Frederick E. | Pte | 201571 | WIA |
| Jones | George | Pte | 266191 | Also KSLI |
| Jones | Ivor | Pte | 42834 | DOW 12/5/18 |
| Jones | Jeremiah | Pte | 201411 | |
| Jones | John Ernest | Pte | 200154 | POW. DOW 20/5/18 |

| | | | | |
|---|---|---|---|---|
| Jones | John Francis | Pte | 28111 | Also LF |
| Jones | Joseph Thomas | Pte | 200209 | H |
| Jones | Percy | Pte | 37092 | |
| Jones | Percy | Pte | 29345 | |
| Jones | Richard Lewis | Pte | 235064 | MM. KIA 21/6/18 |
| Jones | Robert Ernest | Pte | 22995 | Ex 7th Bn, WIA |
| Jones | Thomas John | Cpl | 22555 | Ex 11th, WIA (2) |
| Jones | William | Sgt | 200421 | WIA |
| Jones | William Edward | 2Lt | | WIA |
| Jones | William Henry | Cpl | 201624 | |
| Joplin | Walter Shaw | Pte | 15099 | Ex 7th Bn |
| Kay | Albert | Pte | 201422 | WIA. Also 8th Bn |
| Kay | Frank | Pte | 201625 | |
| Kay | Fred | Pte | 40918 | |
| Kay | Frederick Jervis | Pte | 200098 | |
| Kay | John Clayton | CQMS | 66 | B Coy |
| Kay | John Thomas | Pte | 201724 | KIA 14/7/17 |
| Keaton | Edward | Pte | 23748 | WIA. Trans. to RF |
| Keelan | Matthew | Cpl | 200932 | WIA (2) |
| Keighley | Lindon Rayner | 2Lt | | DOW 3/12/17 |
| Keith | Charlie | Pte | 1856 | H. D 21/10/14 |
| Keen | Jacob | Cpl | 1980 | Trans. to E. Lancs and KIA |
| Keller | Ferdinand W. E. | 2Lt | | |
| Kells | William Thomas | Pte | 29346 | C Coy |
| Kelly | Ambrose | Pte | 2364 | KIA 8/8/16 |
| Kelly | Ambrose | A/Cpl | 201116 | WIA. Also 2/5th |
| Kelly | Edward | Pte | 201626 | WIA |
| Kelly | James | Pte | 4154 | WIA. DOW 10/8/16 |
| Kelly | James | Pte | 201627 | Ex 8th BN. WIA, POW |
| Kelly | William | Pte | 27433 | Ex LF and also 7th Bn |
| Kelly | William Edmond | Pte | 200972 | DOW 2/3/19 |
| Kempson | James | Pte | 201726 | WIA |
| Kendall | Eric Angerstein | Capt. | | MC, WIA |
| Kendall | Harry | Pte | 2250 | H. D 9/9/14 |
| Kendall | William | Pte | 201221 | |
| Kendrick | Herbert | Pte | 41543 | Trans. to S. Staffs 1920. |
| Kennedy | Dudley Wolfenden | Pte | 42836 | |
| Kenny | John | Pte | 22489 | Ex 11th BN. POW |
| Kent | Frank | Pte | 41549 | |
| Kent | George Robert | Pte | 26814 | Ex 8th Bn |
| Kenyon | John | Cpl | 24824 | Ex 7th Bn MM. DOW 8/6/18 |
| Kershaw | Charles William. | Pte | 201030 | ex 7th Bn KIA 8/6/17 |

| | | | | |
|---|---|---|---|---|
| Kershaw | Harold Austin | 2Lt | | |
| Kettle | Thomas Charles | Pte | 41511 | |
| Kewley | William | Pte | 1480 | WIA |
| Kibble | Herbert George | Pte | 203111 | Commissioned 26/3/18 |
| Killick | George Henry | Pte | 41508 | |
| Kinder | Harry | Pte | 202350 | |
| King | John Thomas | Pte | 200828 | DOW 21/11/17 |
| Kingswood | George | L/Cpl | 202172 | |
| Kirkby | Benjamin Atkinson | Cpl | 201062 | KIA 8/8/16 |
| Kirkby | William | Sgt | 2314 | WIA |
| Kirkby | William | Sgt | 447 | |
| Kirkham | Charles Frederick | Pte | 201173 | WIA |
| Kirkham | Joseph | Sgt | 2415 | Trans. to MGC. MM |
| Kitchen | Harry Herbert | Cpl | 200267 | WIA. D 20/10/18 with LC |
| Kitchen | John | Pte | 200992 | WIA. Also 7th Bn |
| Kitchin | James Albert | Pte | 200323 | MiD, WIA |
| Knapp | Frederick | Pte | 201706 | POW |
| Kneebone | Ewart | Cpl | 2071 | WIA |
| Knipe | Charles | Pte | 48854 | |
| Knipe | Thomas | Pte | 1454 | WIA |
| Knipe | William | Pte | 2487 | KIA 8/6/15 |
| Knowles | Arthur Frederick | Pte | 201727 | MM, WIA |
| Knowles | Frank | L/Cpl | 26079 | Ex 7th Bn. B Coy. DOW 6/5/18 |
| Knowles | Herbert | Pte | 200753 | |
| Knowles | Richard | Pte | 240752 | KIA 20/9/17 |
| Knox | Herbert | Pte | 32497 | KIA 9/7/18 |
| Lackey | Edward | Pte | 201215 | |
| Lackey | Michael | Pte | 201216 | Also 1/5th |
| Lackey | William | Pte | 201220 | POW |
| Laidlaw | Walter | Pte | 4146 | |
| Lakey | John Forster | Pte | 41658 | |
| Lamb | Benjamin | Pte | 263001 | Ex RDC and 1/5th. WIA. Trans. to LC |
| Lamb | Charles | Pte | 201243 | |
| Lamb | James | Pte | 200672 | WIA |
| Lamb | Richard | Pte | 201695 | WIA |
| Lamb | Thomas | Pte | 49371 | |
| Lamb | William | Pte | 200077 | D Coy. WIA |
| Lambert | George | Pte | 40919 | |
| Lambert | Harry | Pte | 201287 | Also 1st Bn |
| Lambert | John Richard | Pte | 24728 | Also 2nd Bn |
| Lancaster | Arthur | Pte | 3281 | KIA 8/8/16 |
| Lane | Frederick William | Pte | 200501 | WIA, POW |

| Larkin | John Joseph Raymond | 2Lt | | WIA |
|---|---|---|---|---|
| Latham | Arthur Selby | Capt. | | MC. C Coy 11 Ptn. POW |
| Latham | Fred | Sgt | 200113 | |
| Latimer | Robert | Sgt | 200448 | |
| Lauder | Harold Victor Robert T. | 2Lt | | 3 Ptn A Coy |
| Law | James | Pte | 14899 | Also 7th and 8th Bns |
| Law | John | Pte | 200863 | WIA. Posted 1/5th |
| Law | William | Pte | 200956 | |
| Lawrence | Alexander | Pte | 3324 | WIA, Deserted |
| Lawrence | Henry | Pte | 201544 | WIA |
| Lawrence | Percy Josiah | Pte | 41054 | |
| Lawson | Joseph Percy | 2Lt | | KIA 8/8/16 |
| Lawson | William | Pte | 203106 | Ex RFA and 7th Bn DOW 8/6/18 |
| Lawson | William | L/Cpl | 2725 | Trans. to RFC and KLR |
| Lawton | Arthur | Pte | 27409 | Also 7th Bn, WIA |
| Lawton | Richard | Pte | 34673 | Also 11th Bn, POW |
| Lay | John | Pte | 200034 | WIA |
| Lay | Walter | Pte | 41517 | |
| Lea | Fred | Pte | 266042 | Also 8th Bn |
| Leach | William | Pte | 2891 | WIA. Trans. to Essex R |
| Leah | Wilfred Reginald | 2Lt | | KIA 10/9/16 |
| Leake | Herbert | Pte | 3480 | WIA |
| Leather | William | Pte | 4106 | WIA |
| Leck | James Edward | Pte | 3757 | KIA 10/9/16 |
| Leck | Thomas | Pte | 200599 | WIA, POW |
| Lee | Matthew | Pte | 882 | |
| Lee | Thomas | Pte | 201002 | |
| Lee | William | Cpl | 201001 | Att. to ASC |
| Leech | David | Pte | 235137 | KIA 20/9/17 |
| Leeming | John | Pte | 21062 | Ex 1st Bn, WIA (2) |
| Leeming | Robert | Pte | 37085 | |
| Lees | Fred | Pte | 201137 | WIA |
| Lees | John | Pte | 25726 | Ex 8th Bn, POW |
| Lees | Oscar Russell | 2Lt | | |
| Leibrick | Alfred | Sgt | 14194 | Also 7th Bn |
| Lenaughan | Edward | Pte | 4094 | WIA. KIA 10/9/16 |
| Lennon | John | Pte | 35039 | Also 1st Bn |
| Leslie | Bernard Alexander | Lt | | |
| Lever | William | Pte | 4951 | Trans. to KLR |
| Leviston | Arthur | Pte | 2535 | DOW 29/5/15 |
| Leviston | William | Pte | 2620 | B Coy. KIA 15/6/15 |
| Lewis | Albert | Pte | 30219 | WIA. KIA 31/7/17 with 7th Bn |

| | | | | |
|---|---|---|---|---|
| Lewis | Charles Norman | Cpl | 1797 | KIA 8/8/16 |
| Leyshon | Ivor | Pte | 42838 | |
| Liddell | Albert | Pte | 200891 | Also ASC |
| Liddell | George | Pte | 201295 | KIA 29/9/16 |
| Lightbound | Arnold | Pte | 29189 | Ex LC. KIA 24/8/18 |
| Lincey | Charles Edgar | 2Lt | | KIA 31/7/16 |
| Lindsay | Frederick | Pte | 200313 | D Coy. WIA. POW |
| Lindsay | Jacob | Pte | 34930 | Also 8th and 1/5th Bns |
| Lindsay | John Broome | 2Lt | | |
| Lindsey | John W. | Cpl | 12451 | Ex 1st Bn, POW |
| Lingard | James | Cpl | 202778 | Also 1st Bn, WIA |
| Lingard | James | Pte | 241569 | Ex 1/5th. WIA, POW |
| Lingford | Charles George | 2Lt | | WIA |
| Liptrot | William | Pte | 4076 | KIA 8/8/16 |
| Lister | Herbert | Cpl | 32628 | Ex 7th Bn, POW |
| Lister | John William | Pte | 2045 | KIA 8/6/15 |
| Little | Robert Pitcairn | Maj. | | |
| Little | James | L/Cpl | 2658 | DOW 24/12/16 |
| Littleford | John | Pte | 201632 | KIA 20/9/17 |
| Littler | Richard | Pte | 27436 | WIA. Also 7th Bn |
| Livesey | Daniel | Pte | 201316 | |
| Livesey | John | Pte | 200202 | H |
| Livesey | John | Cpl | 11357 | Also 2nd and 1st Bns |
| Livesey | Wilfred | Pte | 15940 | WIA. Also 8th Bn |
| Lloyd | Thomas Edward | Cpl | 1548 | WIA |
| Locker | Alfred James | Pte | 40922 | KIA 27/4/18 |
| Lockey | Ernest | Sgt/2Lt | 201104 | MM. Commissioned 1/4th 28/5/18 |
| Lockhead | John | L/Cpl | 2226 | KIA 8/8/16 |
| Lofthouse | Thomas | Pte | 200910 | Ex 8th Bn MM. WIA. KIA 9/4/18 |
| Loftus | Alfred | L/Cpl | 200846 | KIA 8/8/16 |
| Loftus | John Thomas | Cpl | 19846 | WIA. Trans. to LC |
| Loftus | Matthew | Pte | 42480 | KIA 13/8/18 |
| Logan | James | Pte | 200073 | H |
| Logan | John | Pte | 2598 | KIA 15/6/15 |
| Logan | William | Pte | 29153 | KIA 28/4/18 |
| Lomas | Ralph | Pte | 34698 | |
| Lomax | John | Pte | 22536 | Also 11th and 7th Bns. WIA |
| Lomax | Robert | Pte | 33392 | Ex 7th Bn (paper posting only) |
| Long | Charles Edward | Pte | 200119 | 1/4th to RE then back to 1/4th |
| Long | George | Pte | 200022 | Att. to RE. WIA |
| Long | Gilbert | Pte | 42841 | WIA (2) |
| Long | Thomas | Cpl | 200375 | WIA. KIA 11/3/17 |

| | | | | |
|---|---|---|---|---|
| Long | William | Pte | | |
| Longbottom | Clement | Pte | 12454 | Also 1st Bn. Deserted |
| Longcroft | William Edward Albert | Pte | 202182 | WIA |
| Longmire | William | Pte | 200109 | |
| Longworth | Lee | Pte | 201728 | KIA 9/9/18 |
| Longworth | Osborne | Cpl | 200899 | B Coy. WIA |
| Lonnen | Victor | Pte | 201339 | |
| Lonsdale | Charles | Cpl | 29171 | Also LC |
| Lonsdale | Reginald | Pte | 3453 | WIA. Trans. to Northumberland Fusiliers |
| Looms | John | Pte | 201401 | WIA. Also 8th Bn |
| Loraine | John | Pte | 1852 | KIA 15/6/15 |
| Lord | Albert | Pte | 265141 | KIA 20/11/17 |
| Lord | George | Pte | 35049 | Ex 7th E. Lancs. WIA. |
| Lord | Harrison Heyworth | Pte | 201761 | |
| Lovell | George Vincent | Dmr | 2029 | H. D 30/5/16 |
| Lovell | Robert | Pte | 2767 | KIA 11/9/16 |
| Lovelock | John Charles | Pte | 41534 | |
| Lowden | John Edward | Cpl | 200995 | WIA. Also 2/5th |
| Lowe | Henry | Pte | 201729 | WIA. Also 2nd Bn |
| Lowe | James | Pte | 201730 | |
| Lowe | John Henry | Pte | 37936 | |
| Lowe | Thomas Arthur | L/Cpl | 201731 | B Coy. KIA 31/7/17 |
| Lowe | William | Pte | 201014 | KIA 8/8/16 |
| Lowe | William Sidney | Pte | 15157 | Also 7th and 8th Bns |
| Lowery | Thomas | L/Cpl | 235054 | Ex 1st Bn as '20098'. POW |
| Lowery | William | Pte | 201057 | Att. to MGC. POW. DOW 26/11/17 |
| Lowey | George Herbert | 2Lt | | |
| Lowther | Andrew | Pte | 3617 | WIA. Trans. to LC |
| Lowther | William John | Pte | 2134 | KIA 15/6/15 |
| Lowthian | Alfred | C/Sgt | 30712 | Ex LNL |
| Loydell (Laydall) | Harry | Pte | 200538 | Ex 5th Glosters. MM. WIA |
| Lucas | William Arthur | Pte | 202183 | WIA (3) |
| Lucking | Stanley Charles | Pte | 26258 | Also 2nd Bn |
| Lugard | John Wykeham | 2Lt | | |
| Lundy | Thomas | Pte | 19517 | |
| Lunt | William J. | Pte | 201004 | WIA (2). Posted 7th Bn-13/5/17 Trans to RE |
| Lyes | William George | Pte | 26517 | Ex 9th Bn WIA (3) |
| Lynch | James Clarke | L/Cpl | 36281 | Ex LNL. KIA 24/7/18 |
| Lyon | Harry James | 2Lt | | MC, WIA |
| Lyon | James | Pte | 38808 | |

| Lyth(e) | Frederick William | Pte | 32922 | MM. Also 1st Bn |
| Macdonald | Arthur Leo | Pte | 200609 | KIA 8/8/16 |
| Mackay | John | 2Lt | | WIA |
| Mackereth | George | Pte | 201229 | Also 7th and 8th Bns. MM |
| Mackereth | William Hayton | Cpl | 201242 | Also 8th Bn |
| Mackintosh | Frank | Pte | 202080 | WIA |
| Maclean | Donald | 2Lt | | MC, WIA |
| Maddern | John Richard | Pte | 202081 | |
| Maddrell (Maderell) | George | Sgt | 201076 | MM, WIA |
| Maden | William | Sgt | 200775 | Ex Lancs Fusiliers. WIA |
| Madine | William James | Pte | 23392 | Ex. 12th Bn. MM, WIA |
| Magee | Walter | Pte | 29145 | |
| Magor | Edward J. | Pte | 200650 | WIA Trans. to LC |
| Maguire | Hugh | Pte | 202430 | |
| Mailes | Charles | Pte | 200056 | |
| Maj.or | Edward | Sgt | 200081 | Commissioned to MGC 1917 |
| Makinson | Lewis | Pte | 37472 | |
| Makinson | Thomas | Pte | 4214 | WIA. Trans. to SLR |
| Maler | Darby | Pte | 202084 | KIA 31/7/17 |
| Maliphant | Frederick Emlyn | Pte | 42842 | |
| Malley | Richard | Sgt | 200962 | |
| Mallon | Felix | Pte | 200666 | DOW 16/8/16 with 8th Bn |
| Malone | Joseph | Pte | 201943 | |
| Maloney | Thomas | Pte | 35423 | Ex KLR |
| Manley | George | Pte | 42844 | |
| Mannion | James | Pte | 42845 | WIA |
| Mansell | George William | Pte | 40923 | DOW 23/8/18 |
| Mansfield | Richard | Pte | 1604 | |
| Marland | William | Pte | 200848 | MM. WIA. KIA 9/4/18 with 1/5th |
| Marr | Charles | Pte | 200396 | WIA |
| Marr | George | Pte | 200397 | |
| Marr | Sydney | Pte | 3635 | WIA. Trans. to KLR |
| Marriage | Herbert John | Pte | 202184 | |
| Marriott | James | Pte | 200597 | A Coy. Posted 1/5th |
| Marsden | Hartley | Pte | 3220 | |
| Marsden | Luke | L/Cpl | 201633 | MM. KIA 20/11/17 |
| Marsden | Richard | Pte | 34664 | KIA 18/9/17 |
| Marsh | Walter Edgar | Cpl | 18856 | Also 6th Bn |
| Marsh | William Henry | Pte | 13947 | Also 7th Bn |
| Marshall | James W. | Pte | 1759 | WIA. Trans. to LC |
| Marshall | Thomas | Pte | 42846 | |

| Marshall | William Charles | Sgt | 2164 | Trans. to MGC |
|---|---|---|---|---|
| Martin | Edward | L/Cpl | 200181 | |
| Martin | Harold | Cpl | 200198 | DCM. WIA (2) Posted 2/5th |
| Martin | Thomas | Pte | 200674 | WIA. KIA 8/8/16 |
| Martin | Thomas Henry | Pte | 4190 | |
| Martindale | John | Pte | 200578 | WIA |
| Martindale | Tom | Pte | 3284 | WIA. Trans. to Lincs |
| Martindale | William | Pte | 2161 | H. D 26/9/14 |
| Marwood | Fred | Pte | 41559 | |
| Marwood | Frederick | L/Cpl | 200385 | B Coy. POW |
| Mason | George | Sgt | 200101 | MM Trans. to LC |
| Mason | George Frederick | Pte | 201637 | |
| Mason | Henry | Pte | 1976 | Att. to RE. KIA 31/8/15 |
| Mason | Walter | Pte | 3657 | KIA 8/8/16 |
| Massey | John | Pte | 240419 | |
| Massey | Joseph | Pte | 27877 | Ex Leics R. WIA. Also 11th and 1/5th Bns |
| Masterman | Leonard | Pte | 26082 | Also 7th Bn |
| Masters | William | Cpl | 201732 | D Coy. WIA. KIA 26/10/17 |
| Masterton | Alexander | Pte | 29352 | |
| Mather | Harry | Pte | 29351 | |
| Mather | Joseph | Pte | 4218 | C Coy. KIA 8/8/16 |
| Mather | William | Pte | 26768 | Also 7th Bn |
| Matthews | George | Pte | 202740 | Also 1st Bn |
| Matthews | William | Pte | 3213 | A Coy. DOW 8/8/16 |
| Mawson | Albert | Pte | 201500 | |
| Mawson | Atkinson Rothey | Pte | 33584 | WIA. Posted 1st Bn |
| Mawson | John Mirehouse | Capt. | | |
| Maxwell | James | Pte | 202583 | Ex 7th Bn POW. KIA 10/4/18 |
| May | Ernest | Pte | 29341 | |
| May | Ernest Andrew | Pte | 200413 | KIA 3/5/18 |
| Mayes | Albert | Pte | 29353 | Ex LF. |
| Mayor | John | Pte | 201685 | Att. to RE. |
| Mayor | Thomas Clark | Pte | 29615 | POW. |
| Mayson | Tom Fletcher | Sgt | 200717 | VC. WIA. 10 Ptn C Coy. Trans. to LC. |
| McAlerney (McAlarney) | James | Pte | 200272 | MM. KIA 9/4/18 |
| McAndrew | William | 2Lt | | D Coy. POW. |
| McCall | Walter Bleasdale | 2Lt | | |
| McCallum | Alan Shaw | Pte | 42843 | |
| McCallum | James | Pte | 29343 | |
| McCaul | Thomas | Sgt | 14493 | |
| McClatchey | Henry | Sgt | 4207 | Also 7th Bn |

| | | | | |
|---|---|---|---|---|
| McClinton | Ernest Edward | 2Lt | | |
| McCormick | Thomas | Pte | 200990 | |
| McDonald | Henry | Pte | 2338 | H. D 8/2/15 |
| McDonald | James | Pte | 34497 | POW |
| McDonald | Joseph | Pte | 28115 | D Coy. KIA 31/7/17 |
| McDonald | Robert | Pte | 201097 | WIA. Also 1st Bn |
| McDonald | Thomas Norman | Pte | 37095 | |
| McDowell | Arthur | Pte | 3619 | A Coy. KIA 8/7/16 |
| McDowell | William Henry | Cpl | 1930 | To 164 MGC. WIA. Trans. to RE-3/18. |
| McFarlane | William | Pte | 20201 | Also 2nd Bn |
| McGill | Henry | Pte | 200979 | KIA 4/6/17 |
| McGill | John Allison | 2Lt | | WIA |
| McGill | William | L/Cpl | 200912 | MM. Att. to TMB |
| McGilvray | Henry | Pte | 29350 | |
| McGowan | James Henry | Pte | 4963 | KIA 27/9/16 |
| McGrath | Thomas William | Pte | 241064 | Also 2/5th. |
| McGuinness | Bernard | Sgt | 200853 | WIA. Trans. to LC |
| McGuire | Charles | | 200916 | Deserted. |
| McGuire | Edward | Pte | 202742 | Also 9th BN. |
| McGuire | James Joseph | Pte | 20558 | Ex 1st and 8th Bns. KIA 25/3/18 |
| McGuire | Thomas | Pte | 200240 | H with 1/4th. 1/5th BEF |
| McGuire | Thomas | Pte | 34689 | WIA |
| McHugh | Thomas | Pte | 201263 | KIA 23/4/18 |
| McIlheron | Hugh | Pte | 1310 | |
| McIlheron | Thomas | CQMS | 200675 | MM. Also 2nd Bn |
| McIlveen | Thomas James | Pte | 25576 | Also 8th and 7th Bns |
| McIver | Colin | Sgt | 978 | H |
| McKay | William John | Pte | 3047 | A Coy. KIA 8/8/16 |
| McKenzie | Aubrey | Pte | 30220 | Also 7th Bn. WIA |
| McKenzie (Mackenzie) | Norman Charles | L/Cpl | 2438 | DOW 3/8/16 |
| McKeown | Frank | Pte | 200436 | WIA |
| McKeron | Robert | Pte | 200662 | WIA (6). Posted to 8th Bn |
| McKiernan | James | L/Sgt | 26719 | Ex LF and also 7th Bn |
| McLaughlin | Archie | Pte | 200429 | Also Lincs |
| McLaughlin | Daniel | Pte | 2798 | WIA. Trans. to LC |
| McLaughlin | John | Pte | 200808 | WIA. Posted 8th Bn |
| McLennan | George | Pte | 200348 | |
| McMahon | James | Pte | 201183 | Ex 8th Bn. WIA. DOW 16/6/17 |
| McManus | Frank | Pte | 28400 | Ex 1st Bn, Deserted |
| McMaster | John | Pte | 200652 | WIA |
| McMurray | Frederick | Pte | 201037 | Att. to RE |

| McNa | Sydney | Pte | 202773 | Ex 11th Bn, WIA |
| McNeill | William | Pte | 201782 | POW |
| McQuade | James | Pte | 2452 | D 18/12/15 |
| McQuade | James | Pte | 13039 | Also 7th Bn |
| McVittie | Bertram | Pte | 241572 | Ex 1/5th. KIA 10/5/18 |
| McWilliams | Albert | L/Cpl | 17422 | WIA |
| Meadowcroft | Walter | Cpl | 201639 | WIA |
| Meakin | Lewis William | Pte | 49925 | |
| Medhurst | Albert | Pte | 41055 | KIA 27/4/18 |
| Meikle | William Nathan Muir | Pte | 202725 | WIA |
| Meikleham | John | Pte | 2406 | WIA. Trans. to LC |
| Melligan | Albert Scrimshaw | Pte | 33973 | WIA |
| Melling | George | Pte | 33057 | WIA. Trans. to ASC |
| Mellon (Mellen) | James Harker | L/Sgt | 200585 | KIA 4/6/17 |
| Memory | Kershaw | Pte | 27636 | Ex 1st and 9th Bns. POW |
| Menelly (Meneely) | Thomas William | Pte | 201071 | MM, WIA |
| Menzies | James Ivan | L/Cpl | 200745 | WIA (2). Posted 1st Bn |
| Menzies | Thomas | Pte | 13467 | Also 9 and 2/5th Bns |
| Mercer | Edgar (George) | Pte | 241664 | Ex 1/5th. KIA 9/4/18 |
| Mercer | Robert | Pte | 200963 | WIA |
| Merney | Frank | Pte | 42848 | |
| Merrett | Robert Henry | Pte | 201131 | Also 1/5th |
| Merrills | Wilfred | Pte | 30206 | Also Sherwoods and 7th Bn |
| Merritt | George Arthur | Pte | 265477 | Ex 1st Bn DOW 9/7/18 |
| Messham | William | Pte | 28116 | DOW 7/10/17 |
| Messiter | Herbert | Pte | 23080 | Also 11th Bn |
| Metcalf | Lister (Leicester) | 2Lt | | WIA. KIA 8/8/16 |
| Metcalfe | Albert | Pte | 1958 | Also 7th Bn |
| Metcalfe | Rolland Garratt | Capt. | | WIA (2) |
| Metters | Edward John | Pte | 2657 | KIA 15/6/15 |
| Meyler | Eric Dudley | 2Lt | | |
| Michaels | Harry | Sgt | 10162 | |
| Middlehurst | Charles | Pte | 266107 | |
| Middleton | James | L/Cpl | 265908 | |
| Middleton | Thomas Harvey | Lt | 2094 | MM and Bar. Commissioned into 1/4t 16/9/16. WIA |
| Miles | Albert | Pte | 2447 | Trans. to MGC |
| Miles | Albert Ernest | Sgt | 202159 | MM. 1 Ptn A Coy |
| Miles | John | Sgt | 2946 | KIA 8/8/16 |
| Miles | Jonathan | Pte | 2856 | KIA 3/8/16 |

| Miller | David | Pte | 200562 | WIA |
|---|---|---|---|---|
| Miller | Frederick Harrison | Pte | 242336 | WIA |
| Miller | John | Cpl | 200300 | KIA 8/8/16 |
| Miller | John | Pte | 200888 | |
| Miller | John | Pte | 29173 | Also LC |
| Miller | John Edward | Pte | 201495 | |
| Miller | Percy | Sgt | 200825 | MiD, WIA |
| Miller | William | L/Sgt | 12650 | Ex 7th Bn. WIA. KIA 9/4/18. Brother of J. Miller VC |
| Miller | William | Pte | 13929 | WIA. Also 7th and 8th Bns |
| Millett | Gordon | Pte | 201636 | Ex MCR. Wia. Trans. to ASC |
| Milligan | George | Pte | 211240 | WIA |
| Millington | James | Pte | 201042 | WIA. KIA 23/12/16 |
| Mills | Albert | Pte | 201641 | WIA |
| Mills | David | Pte | 200105 | H |
| Mills | Frederick George | Pte | 202083 | |
| Mills | Jesse | L/Cpl | 11103 | Also 2nd Bn |
| Mills | William | Pte | 41058 | |
| Milton | Charles Spencer | Pte | 200517 | DCM |
| Milton | William Henry | A/CPl | 1203 | KIA 8/6/15 |
| Minshall | Alexander | Pte | 17136 | Ex 2nd Bn. WIA |
| Minter | SidneyEdgar Beresford | Pte | 40926 | B Coy. WIA (4) |
| Mitchell | Edward | Pte | 21730 | Ex 12th Bn. WIA. KIA 13/8/18 |
| Mitchell | James | Pte | 1290 | KIA 15/6/15 |
| Mitchell | James | Pte | 9385 | Also 2nd and 9th Bns |
| Mitchell | John | Pte | 26131 | KIA 31/7/17 |
| Mitchell | Josiah Boase | Pte | 1166 | WIA |
| Mitchell | Stephen | Pte | 26821 | Also 7th Bn |
| Mitchell | Thomas | Pte | 2668 | KIA 15/6/15 |
| Mizon | Harry | Sgt | 14278 | Also 7th Bn |
| Mohan | John | Pte | 23352 | Also 7th and 8th Bns. WIA (3) |
| Mollard | Richard | Cpl | 200258 | WIA. Also 1st Bn |
| Monaghan | John | Pte | 16557 | WIA. Trans. to LC |
| Money | Sidney William | Pte | 28121 | Ex E. Kent and also 7th Bn |
| Monks | Edward Victor | Pte | 201551 | KIA 18/5/17 |
| Monks | Richard | Pte | 200931 | WIA. Also 1st Bn |
| Montgomery | Henry | Sgt | 2585 | Trans. to MGC |
| Montague | Fred | L/Cpl | 1535 | H |
| Moody | Albert Henry Royston | Pte | 42847 | |
| Moody | Thomas | Pte | 27098 | MM. WIA. Also 1st and 7th Bns and Lincs |
| Moorby | Fred | Pte | 2692 | |

| | | | | |
|---|---|---|---|---|
| Moorby | Roland | Pte | 3199 | |
| Moore | Albert | S/Sgt | 9374 | Also 2nd Bn |
| Moore | Benjamin Atkinson | Pte | 1017 | WIA |
| Moore | Harry | L/Cpl | 12970 | Also 7th Bn |
| Moore | Isaac | Pte | 200099 | KIA 20/11/17 |
| Moore | James McGready | Pte | 1531 | |
| Moore | John Parkinson | L/Cpl | 200156 | 10 Ptn C Coy. MM, POW |
| Moore | Samuel | Pte | 32025 | Also 7th Bn |
| Moore | William George | Pte | 41059 | |
| Moorey | Arthur | Pte | 23008 | Also 7th Bn. POW |
| Moorhouse | Edward | Pte | 33475 | Ex 1/5th. WIA (2) |
| Moorhouse | Harry | A/CPl | 202776 | |
| Moorhouse | Lees | A/Sgt | 201634 | |
| Moran | William | Pte | 201733 | KIA 20/11/17 |
| Moreland | Joseph | Pte | 240236 | WIA. Also 8th and 1/5th Bns |
| Moreton | Robert Henry A. | Pte | 33972 | DOW 9/4/18 |
| Morgan | John | Pte | 200499 | WIA (2) |
| Morgan | John Pridy | Sgt | 200614 | WIA |
| Morgan | Sylvester | Pte | 242263 | WIA |
| Morrell | Ralph D'Albin | Capt. | | KIA 8/8/16 |
| Morrey | Harold | Pte | 41547 | |
| Morris | Albert | Pte | 33974 | |
| Morris | Alfred Edward | Sgt | 200388 | MM. Pioneer Sergeant |
| Morris | Archibald S | L/Cpl | 1650 | WIA. Trans. to RE and then LC |
| Morris | Charles | L/Sgt | 3130 | DOW 12/8/16 |
| Morris | David | Pte | 37094 | |
| Morris | Edward | L/Cpl | 884 | |
| Morris | Harold | L/Cpl | 26130 | Ex 7th Bn, MM |
| Morris | William | Pte | 12768 | MM. Also 7th Bn |
| Morrow | Andrew | Pte | 200490 | WIA. KIA 20/9/17 |
| Mortimer | Bryan Briscoe | Pte | 34594 | POW |
| Mortin | Robert | Pte | 243026 | Also 1/5th |
| Morton | Alfred Ellerington | Capt. | | MC Signals Officer |
| Moses | George | Pte | 4055 | KIA 3/8/16 |
| Moss | Richard | Pte | 201219 | D 13/9/17 |
| Motteram | Edward | Pte | 200102 | WIA |
| Mountcastle | Leonard | Pte | 26949 | WIA |
| Mountford | William | Pte | 202082 | |
| Muckalt | Tom | Pte | 2568 | Trans. to Worcs and LC |
| Mudie | Robert Alan | Capt. | | On att. from LF. KIA with LF 20/9/17 |
| Mulholland | David | Cpl | 265018 | H |
| Mullen | John Francis | Cpl | 15577 | Also 8th and 1st Bns |

| Muncaster | Daniel | Pte | 2986 | DOW 11/8/16 |
|---|---|---|---|---|
| Murphy | James | Pte | 200483 | WIA |
| Murphy | John | Pte | 200482 | |
| Murphy | John Percy | Pte | 200812 | WIA |
| Murphy | Peter Joseph | Pte | 201109 | |
| Murphy | Timothy | Cpl | 27381 | Ex E. Lancs and also 7th and 8th Bns |
| Murray | James | Pte | 34836 | Also 1st Bn. WIA |
| Murray | John | Pte | 2905 | WIA. MM. Also 1st and 2nd Bns |
| Murray | Stuart | Pte | 37988 | |
| Murray | William Young | Pte | 24637 | Also 8th Bn |
| Musk | James William | Pte | 244515 | |
| Mustard | Joseph | Cpl | 22392 | MM. Trans. to ASC |
| Myatt | Ernest | Capt. | | |
| Myers | Harold William | Sgt | 200493 | A Coy 3 Ptn. MM |
| Myers | John | Pte | 200064 | H |
| Mylchreest | Wilfred | Pte | 200621 | WIA (2). Trans. to LC and back again |
| Myles | Thomas | Pte | 25739 | Also 8th Bn |
| Nadin | Thomas Clement | A/CPl | 201701 | |
| Nagelkop | Louis | Pte | unknown | Possibly 'J/2637' of 40th RF |
| Neal | Harry | Cpl | 27020 | Ex 7th Bn. DOW 13/4/18 |
| Neal | Percy Harold | Pte | 203072 | Ex Northampt. Yeo. Also 7th Bn |
| Neave | Bernard Edward | Pte | 32949 | Ex 11th Bn POW |
| Needham | Frank | Pte | 202998 | Commissioned RFC 7/3/18 |
| Neill | William Campbell | Capt. | | WIA |
| Nelson | John | Pte | 200881 | KIA 8/8/16 |
| Nelson | Richard | Pte | 34661 | |
| Nelson | Richard Hudson | Pte | 2522 | KIA 9/7/16 |
| Nelson | Robert | Pte | 200460 | Att. to 77th Inf Bde and 9th Bn |
| Nelson | Stanley | Pte | 201291 | |
| Nelson | Stephen | Pte | 200893 | A Coy. WIA |
| Neville | John Francis | Pte | 200394 | |
| New | Thomas Harold | Pte | 200094 | |
| Newberry | Sidney | Pte | 41520 | |
| Newbold | Charles Hutchinson | 2Lt | | 10 Ptn C Coy. WIA |
| Newby | James | Pte | 200044 | H |
| Newby | Joseph Frederick Slater | Pte | 3131 | KIA 11/9/16 |
| Newby | Moses | Pte | 2691 | POW. DOW 2/8/15 |
| Newby | Richard Earnest | Pte | 2407 | Trans. to RE Rwy Op Div |
| Newby | Thomas Henry | L/Cpl | 200719 | WIA. KIA 23/12/16 |
| Newell | Reuben | Pte | 201734 | Also 2nd Bn |
| Newham | Ernest Lascelles | Sgt | 200495 | WIA. Posted KAR in E. Africa |

| Newling | John Frederick | Pte | 202999 | Ex City of London Rgt. WIA. Trans. to TC |
| Newsham | Herbert | Pte | 2129 | Trans. to MGC. WIA |
| Newsham | Randolph | Pte | 2267 | KIA 15/6/15 |
| Newsham | Richard | Pte | 2543 | KIA 15/6/15 |
| Newton | Edwin | Sgt | 200446 | WIA |
| Newton | James Albert | Pte | 32514 | Ex LF and 7th Bn |
| Newton | John Edward | Pte | 265714 | Also 1/5th and 8th Bns |
| Newton | Nicholas James | Pte | 37108 | Also 2/5th |
| Newton | William | Pte | 200541 | C Coy |
| Nicholas | Charles | Cpl | 200338 | Trans. to RE |
| Nicholas | Frank R | Pte | 28125 | WIA. Trans. to LF |
| Nicholas | William | Pte | 200925 | WIA |
| Nicholls | Arthur | Pte | 202087 | |
| Nicholls | Frederick Joseph | Pte | 242331 | Trans. to MCR |
| Nicholls | George William | L/Cpl | 14396 | Ex 7th Bn. KIA 9/4/18 |
| Nichols | William David | Pte | 200159 | H |
| Nicholson | Edward | Pte | 809 | KIA 8/8/16 |
| Nicholson | John James | L/Cpl | 201735 | KIA 9/6/17 |
| Nicholson | Joseph | Cpl | 200777 | Att. to 164 TM Battery. WIA, POW |
| Nicholson | William | Pte | 200249 | MM. Stretcher-bearer. Possibly POW |
| Nicholson | William Henry | Pte | 200655 | KIA 8/8/16 |
| Nicholson | William Norman | Pte | 3690 | DOW 10/8/16 |
| Nield | John | Pte | 27657 | WIA. Also 1st, 1/5th and 9th Bns |
| Nightingale | Harold | Pte | 202777 | WIA |
| Nightingale | John | Pte | 201016 | KIA 20/9/17 |
| Nixon | Walter | Pte | 11903 | Also 9th and 2/5th Bns |
| Noake | Frederick | Pte | 202085 | WIA. Trans. to RFA and RE |
| Nobbs | Sidney | Pte | 41060 | |
| Noble | Joseph | Pte | 14398 | Also 7th Bn |
| Noble | Richard | Pte | 2960 | WIA. KIA 28/9/16 |
| Noble | Thomas Edward | Pte | 2812 | DOW 17/6/16 |
| Nock | Henry | Pte | 201088 | |
| Nolan | Frank Harold | Pte | 200782 | WIA |
| Norbury | Fred | Pte | 244524 | Ex Army Cyclist Corps. C Coy |
| Norris | Hayton | Pte | 200934 | |
| Norris | John Laytham | Pte | 22274 | Ex 7th Bn. WIA |
| Northmore | Joseph Leslie | CQMS | 200754 | |
| Northwood | Arthur George | Pte | 41061 | KIA 26/4/18 |
| Norton | Christopher | Sgt | 240937 | Ex 2/5th |
| Notley | Albert Carr | 2Lt | | KIA 30/5/18 |
| Notman | John | Pte | 244508 | WIA |
| Nott | James | Pte | 200168 | |

| Nottle | James | Pte | 202086 | |
| Nowell | Joshua | Pte | 1173 | D Coy |
| Nunn | James Harold | Pte | 242353 | WIA |
| Nutt | Alfred John Drury | Pte | 41514 | |
| Nuttall | Arthur | Pte | 200873 | KIA 9/4/18 |
| Nutter | John | Pte | 201642 | KIA 20/9/17 |
| Nutter | Walter | Pte | 266036 | KIA 20/11/17 |
| Oatham | George Richard | Pte | 28402 | |
| O'Brien | Daniel | L/Cpl | 202744 | Ex 8th Bn. WIA |
| O'Brien | Joseph | Pte | 19624 | Ex 11th Bn. KIA 20/9/17 |
| O'Connell | Hugh H. | Pte | 27449 | Ex 7th BN |
| O'Donnell | John William | Pte | 242236 | WIA. Also 2/5th |
| Ogden | George David | Pte | 202089 | WIA |
| Ogilvie | Norman | Pte | 200081 | |
| Okell | William | Pte | 38633 | Also 2/5th |
| Oldham | John William | Pte | 11870 | Ex 7th Bn. DOW 27/9/17 |
| Oldham | William | Pte | 201644 | |
| Oliver | Samuel | Pte | 3478 | B Coy. KIA 8/8/16 |
| Oliver | William | Pte | 21983 | Also 11th Bn |
| Ollerton | William | Cpl | 200923 | Trans. to LC |
| O'Neill | Edward | Pte | 15130 | Ex 7th Bn POW |
| O'Neill | William | Pte | 201672 | MiD. KIA 14/7/17 |
| Ord | John Robert | Pte | 26109 | Also 7th Bn |
| Orders | Albert James | L/Cpl | 240813 | KIA 20/9/17 |
| Ormandy | John | Pte | 33700 | Also 1/5th. WIA |
| Orme | James Montague | Pte | 244525 | Ex Leics Cyclist Bn. KIA 7/9/18 |
| Orpwood | Henry Ernest | Pte | 41737 | |
| Orrell | Robert | Pte | 15382 | Ex 1/5th. POW |
| Orritt | Alfred Jon | Pte | 35128 | |
| Ortloff | Ernest | Pte | 201736 | Att. to TMB |
| Orton | William J. | Pte | 4120 | WIA. Trans. to ASC |
| Osgood | Edwin D. | 2Lt | | POW |
| Ottley | Harold | Pte | 1518 | |
| Oversby | Robert | L/Cpl | 2628 | A Coy. KIA 15/6/16 |
| Overton | Charles Lockhart | Capt. | | MC. Recommended for Bar for 9/4/18 |
| Owen | George H. | Pte | 202320 | WIA. Trans. to LC |
| Owen | James Edgar | Pte | 41495 | KIA 24/8/18 |
| Owen | John | Pte | 201643 | KIA 20/9/17 |
| Owen | John S. | CSM | 2340 | DCM. MM. WIA. Trans. to MGC. Rose to RSM |
| Owen | Thomas | Pte | 29180 | Also LC |
| Oxley | Joseph | L/Cpl | 200612 | DOW 22/9/17 |

| Page | Cyril Percy | Pte | 202173 | Att. to TMB |
|------|-------------|-----|--------|-------------|
| Page | Hubert William | CQMS | 496 | KIA 29/5/15 |
| Paine | William H. | Pte | 202094 | WIA. Trans. to LC |
| Palethorpe | Harry Archibald | Pte | 36392 | WIA. Also 2/5th |
| Palmer | Archibald | Pte | 41139 | Also 8th Bn |
| Palmer | Ernest | Pte | 38635 | |
| Palmer | Joseph Tyson | Pte | 200247 | WIA |
| Palmer | Norman | Pte | 1494 | WIA |
| Pankhurst | William Thomas | Pte | 41063 | |
| Park | Albert Barton | 2Lt | | D Coy |
| Park | George Edward | Pte | 2666 | POW. DOW 18/6/15 |
| Park | Henry | Pte | 201507 | KIA 20/9/17 |
| Park | James | Pte | 200871 | Ex 8th Bn. WIA |
| Park | John | Pte | 34615 | |
| Park | William Harold | L/Cpl | 200803 | |
| Parke | William Laurence | Cpl | 201567 | |
| Parker | Francis Arthur | Pte | 200997 | WIA. Trans. to LC |
| Parker | Frederick James | Pte | 33145 | |
| Parker | George Henry | Pte | 200147 | WIA |
| Parker | George Henry Gill | Pte | 41563 | D 7/9/18 |
| Parker | Harold | Pte | 36516 | WIA |
| Parker | Harry | Pte | 3728 | A Coy. KIA 3/8/16 |
| Parker | James | Cpl | 200354 | |
| Parker | James Herbert | Sgt | 32602 | Also 7th Bn |
| Parker | John Edward | Pte | 200386 | WIA |
| Parker | John Robert | Pte | 41671 | |
| Parker | Joseph | Pte | 201697 | Att. to TMB. KIA 24/8/18 |
| Parker | Joseph | Cpl | 12069 | Also 6th and 1st Bns. C Coy |
| Parker | William | L/Cpl | 200049 | WIA. D 26/10/18 |
| Parkington | Harry | Pte | 21250 | Ex 11th Bn WIA (2) |
| Parkinson | Albert | Pte | 202771 | Also 2nd Bn |
| Parkinson | Arthur William | Pte | 4555 | WIA. Trans. to LC Agri. Coy |
| Parkinson | James | Pte | 34670 | Also 1/5th |
| Parkinson | Thomas | Pte | 201098 | WIA |
| Parkinson | Thomas | Pte | 201003 | |
| Parkinson | Walter T. | Pte | 27448 | WIA. Trans. to KLR |
| Parkinson | William Dawson | Pte | 200994 | KIA 4/10/18 with 2/5th |
| Parnell | Harry | Sgt | 200481 | WIA (2). Att. to MGC. MM |
| Parr | William George | Pte | 35424 | Ex KLR |
| Parry | Gwilyn John | Pte | 201371 | |
| Parry | John Simpson | L/Cpl | 200251 | WIA. Also 8th Bn |
| Parry | Joseph | Pte | 201646 | Also 1st Bn |

| | | | | |
|---|---|---|---|---|
| Parry | Robert | WO2 | 202760 | Ex 2nd Bn, DCM |
| Parry | William | Pte | 34587 | |
| Parry | William James | Cpl | 202737 | POW |
| Parsons | John James | Pte | 3470 | WIA. KIA 8/8/16 |
| Parsons | Stanley Russell | Pte | 10822 | Ex 1st Bn WIA (2) |
| Parsons | Thomas Alfred | Pte | 202186 | WIA |
| Partridge | Frederick | Pte | 2413 | Trans. to MGC |
| Partridge | Thomas | Pte | 201075 | |
| Pass | James | Pte | 201432 | |
| Paterson | James Stuart | 2Lt | | D Coy 13 Ptn |
| Paterson | Murdoch Fraser | 2Lt | | |
| Pathecary (Pothecary) | George | L/Cpl | 200822 | H |
| Patience | Kenneth | Pte | 15151 | Also 7th Bn |
| Paton | Patrick | Pte | 14942 | also 7th and 8th Bns |
| Patterson | Mark H. | Pte | 7501 | WIA. Trans. to LC |
| Patterson | Thomas | A/CPl | 201275 | |
| Pattinson | William Rose | Capt. | | Att. from LF. WIA. OC D Coy |
| Paul | George | Pte | 200625 | |
| Payne | Herbert Horace | Pte | 41738 | |
| Peach | William Arthur | Pte | 202095 | POW |
| Peachey | Frank Charles | WO2 | 202942 | Ex County of London Yeo. Commissioned into S. Lancs |
| Peak | Henry | 2Lt | | |
| Peake | John C. | Pte | 200702 | WIA. Trans. to KLR |
| Pearce | Frederick Charles | Pte | 22679 | Ex 1st, 11th, and 2/5th Bns. KIA 20/9/17 |
| Pearce | Horace Harry | Pte | 22678 | Ex 11th Bn. WIA |
| Pearce | Oliver | Pte | 28176 | Also ASC and 7th Bn |
| Pearson | D. G. | 2Lt | | |
| Pearson | Edward | Pte | 2461 | Trans. to LC |
| Pearson | Fred | L/Sgt | 200090 | WIA |
| Pearson | Frederick | Pte | 27490 | Also 8th and 1/5th Bns |
| Pearson | John | 2Lt | | |
| Pearson | John Robert | Sgt | 200508 | DCM. WIA (2) |
| Pearson | William Albert | Pte | 200557 | |
| Pearson | William Gareniares | Capt. | | WIA, POW |
| Pearson | William James | Pte | 2727 | |
| Pedder | Jonathan | Pte | 201527 | Att. to RE |
| Peers | Basil | Capt. | | |
| Peirce | Geoffrey Martin | Pte | 41064 | |
| Pellymounter | Joseph Henry | Sgt | 200023 | H |
| Pemberton | Benjamin Horace | 2Lt | | MC. A Coy. WIA |

| Pemberton | Nathaniel Hilsley | Sgt | 19389 | Also 11th and 8th Bns. 15 Ptn D Coy |
|---|---|---|---|---|
| Penaluna | Richard | Pte | 2969 | KIA 8/8/16 |
| Penn | Walter Norman | Pte | 22677 | Ex 11th and 6th Bns. DOW 25/3/18 |
| Pennington | Norman | Pte | 1437 | |
| Pennington | William | Pte | 201645 | WIA |
| Penny | Albert Edward | Pte | 1529 | H |
| Penny | Richard S. | Pte | 34616 | WIA. Trans. to RE Rwy Op Coy |
| Penny | William | Pte | 3495 | DOW 5/7/16 |
| Pepper | William A. | Pte | 202187 | |
| Percival | Bernard | Cpl | 200551 | Commissioned 25/9/17 |
| Percival | Harry | Pte | 201327 | Also 1st Bn |
| Percival | Hubert William | Sgt | 200550 | MM. WIA |
| Perrin | Arthur James | Pte | 42851 | |
| Perry | John Henry | Pte | 2973 | KIA 1/8/16 |
| Perry | William Thomas | Pte | 40930 | |
| Pettifer | William R. | C/Sgt | 200026 | Commissioned into Border R 31/5/17 |
| Pettitt | John William | Cpl | 240716 | KIA 20/9/17 |
| Petty | Charles Stanton | Pte | 34589 | KIA 20/9/17 |
| Phillip | William | Pte | 1646 | DOW 12/9/16 |
| Phillips | Edward | Pte | 15637 | Also 8th Bn |
| Phillips | Herbert | Pte | 265028 | WIA |
| Phillips | Joseph | Pte | 202761 | WIA. Also 1st and 2nd Bns |
| Phillips | William | Pte | 34579 | Also 2/5th |
| Phillips | William Proctor | Pte | 42852 | Ex Welsh Rgt. WIA |
| Phillipson | Fred | Sgt | 200395 | |
| Phillipson | James | Pte | 235500 | |
| Phillipson | Robert | Cpl | 200671 | |
| Phizacklea | Albert | Pte | 1500 | WIA |
| Phizacklea | Edward | Pte | 2637 | WIA |
| Pickerill | John | Pte | 200534 | |
| Pickering | Tom | Pte | 38639 | |
| Pickin | Robert William | Sgt | 2112 | WIA. Commissioned into RE |
| Pickles | Willie | Pte | 201901 | WIA. Trans. to Lincs |
| Pickthall | Frank | L/Cpl | 200389 | Also 7th and 2/5th Bns. WIA (accidentally) |
| Pickthall | Frank C. | Pte | 202091 | KIA 31/7/17 |
| Pickup | Harry | Pte | 33386 | Ex 8th Bn DOW 22/9/17 |
| Pickup | William | Pte | 202640 | Also 7th Bn |
| Picton | Arthur | Pte | 201548 | |
| Pierson | James | Pte | 202589 | WIA. Also 7th Bn |
| Pilkington | Alfred | Pte | 200924 | WIA. Also 8th Bn |
| Pilkington | Walter | Pte | 33007 | WIA. Posted 1/5th |

| Pill | Albert | Pte | 200635 | WIA. Trans. to LC |
|---|---|---|---|---|
| Pill | Henry Hugh | L/Sgt | 200583 | KIA 31/7/17 |
| Pill | William James | Pte | 2564 | Trans. to and KIA with Middlesex Rgt |
| Pimblett | John | Pte | 38640 | |
| Pimm | Percival Burghope | Pte | 3396 | KIA 27/5/16 |
| Pimm | William Reginald | Pte | 3268 | KIA 25/6/16 |
| Pinnegar | Edgar | Pte | 42853 | C Coy. WIA. |
| Pipe | Richard | Pte | 200752 | WIA. Also 8th Bn |
| Pittaway | Cyril | Pte | 34694 | KIA 20/11/17 |
| Place | Frank Clarke | 2Lt | was G5/4834 | MM. MC. KIA 22/9/18 |
| Plant | William Henry | Pte | 41739 | |
| Platt | Frank Redvers | Pte | 41548 | WIA. Trans. to N. Staffs |
| Plimley | Francis | Pte | 201307 | WIA. Trans. to N. Staffs |
| Plummer | Percy | Pte | 2799 | H |
| Pobgee | Harold Amos | Capt. | 30273 | Ex 5DG and 1/5th. MC. Commissioned 20/6/18 |
| Pollitt | James | Pte | 201332 | WIA. KIA 31/7/17 |
| Pollitt | Joseph | L/Cpl | 24177 | Also 7th and 8th Bns. WIA |
| Pollitt | Thomas | Cpl | 201545 | B Coy. MM. Trans. to LC |
| Popplewell | George | Pte | 42855 | |
| Popplewell | William Henry | Pte | 40931 | KIA 13/7/18 |
| Port | Harry | Pte | 41506 | |
| Porter | Fred | Pte | 201348 | KIA 8/8/16 |
| Porter | James William | Pte | 2263 | WIA |
| Porter | John William | Pte | 201680 | WIA. Also 8th Bn |
| Porter | Matthew James | Cpl | 200595 | MM, WIA |
| Porter | Robert | L/Cpl | 34588 | KIA 30/4/18 |
| Porter | Thomas | A/CPl | 29349 | |
| Porter | William | Pte | 33562 | Ex 7th Bn KIA 9/4/18 |
| Porter | William | Pte | 11285 | Also 2, 7, 8 and 1/5th Bns. C Coy |
| Porter | William | Cpl | 202207 | Att. to RE |
| Poskitt | George Ernest Fisher | Pte | 2512 | MM. DOW 31/7/16 |
| Postles | William Harold | A/CPl | 37715 | Also 1st Bn. C Coy |
| Postlethwaite | Frank | Sgt | 736 | KIA 15/6/15 |
| Postlethwaite | James | Pte | 200606 | WIA |
| Postlethwaite | John Edmund Sedgwick | Cpl | 201677 | KIA 31/7/17 |
| Postlethwaite | Robert Francis | L/Cpl | 201675 | KIA 28/9/16 |
| Postlethwaite | William | Pte | 2597 | KIA 10/5/16 |
| Postlethwaite | William | L/Cpl | 200522 | B Coy |
| Pothecary | George | L/Cpl | 200822 | H |
| Pothecary | Stephen | Pte | 13616 | Ex 9th Bn. WIA |

| | | | | |
|---|---|---|---|---|
| Potter | Joseph Arthur | Pte | 38293 | |
| Potterton | Charles | Pte | 15150 | Ex 7 Bn MM |
| Poucher | John W. | Pte | 27101 | Ex Lincs and 1st Bn. WIA (2), KIA 20/11/17 |
| Powell | John | Pte | 202092 | KIA 16/9/17 |
| Powell | Phillip William | Capt. | | QM, MC |
| Power | David Harry | Pte | 203012 | Commissioned into KSLI 27/8/18 |
| Pownall | Harry | Pte | 243021 | Ex 1/5th. KIA 20/9/17 |
| Prescott | William | Pte | 38636 | |
| Prest | William | Pte | 26966 | KIA 31/7/17 |
| Preston | Daniel | Pte | 200929 | WIA |
| Preston | Ernest | L/Cpl | 200792 | |
| Preston | Ernest J. | Pte | 2051 | Trans. to Royal Fusiliers |
| Preston | James | Pte | 201336 | WIA |
| Preston | John Thomas | Cpl | 200015 | |
| Preston | Thomas | Pte | 2396 | DOW 8/6/15 |
| Price | Charles J. | Pte | 202093 | WIA. Trans. to LC |
| Price | Sidney Nelson | Pte | 40928 | |
| Priestley | Arnold | Pte | 202099 | WIA |
| Priestley | Ben | Pte | 200096 | H with KORL |
| Prince | Charles | Pte | 202090 | POW |
| Prisk | Richard Henry | Pte | 2633 | KIA 15/6/15 |
| Pritchard | James | Pte | 200213 | WIA. Trans. to RE |
| Pritchard | Thomas Henry Charles W. | 2Lt | | MC. WIA (2) OC 6 Ptn 8/1/18 |
| Procter | Alfred Paul | Capt. | | OC C Coy then OC A Coy |
| Procter | Robert | Pte | 201691 | |
| Proctor | John | Pte | 13560 | |
| Proctor | John Harold | Pte | 202354 | KIA 20/9/17 |
| Proudfoot | Robert | Cpl | 201164 | Att. to RE. WIA. KIA 9/4/18 |
| Pryce | Edward | Pte | 243117 | Also 1/5th |
| Puckey | Harold | Pte | 200114 | |
| Pugh | Thomas | Pte | 2707 | |
| Pulfer | William Henry | Pte | 235361 | Also 1st Bn |
| Pullen | Harvey | Pte | 30708 | |
| Pullinger | Leslie | Pte | 38004 | |
| Pumford | Horace | Pte | 41673 | |
| Purcell | Thomas | Pte | 201053 | WIA. Also 8th Bn |
| Purchase | Richard | Pte | 41522 | KIA 24/8/18 |
| Purnell | Gordon James | 2Lt | | |
| Purnell | Roy Lionel | 2Lt | | WIA |
| Purvis | John | L/Cpl | 28378 | Ex ASC. WIA.KIA 12/12/17 with 11th B |

| | | | | |
|---|---|---|---|---|
| Purvis | Joseph Slater | L/Cpl | 27346 | Lincs, 1st, and 8th Bns.WIA (2) KIA 3/5/18 with 1/5th |
| Pye | J. H. | Pte | 202839 | |
| Pyle | Albert Burton | Pte | 202097 | WIA |
| Quayle | Joseph Henry | Sgt | 200724 | DOW 24/9/17 |
| Quigley | Gilbert | Pte | 1749 | WIA |
| Quinn | Hugh H. | Pte | 200444 | Trans. to RE |
| Quinn | Peter | Pte | 200143 | WIA |
| Raby | Thomas | Pte | 20776 | Ex 7th Bn. WIA |
| Radcliffe | Thomas | Pte | 1492 | |
| Radford | George | Pte | 202104 | WIA. Trans. to RDC |
| Raeside | George Forrest | 2Lt | was S/12165 | A Coy. KIA 9/4/18 |
| Rafferty | Robert | Pte | 265492 | WIA |
| Railton | Harry | Pte | 201529 | WIA. Also 7th Bn |
| Rainford | Charles | Pte | 202100 | |
| Ralph | Joseph | Pte | 200506 | WIA (3) |
| Ralston | Robert | Pte | 240286 | Ex 2/5th. POW. KIA 28/4/18 |
| Ramsbotham | James | Pte | 200898 | C Coy. WIA (2). Posted 1st Bn |
| Ramsbottom | Harold | Pte | 40633 | KIA 26/4/18 |
| Ranger | William | Pte | 1710 | WIA. Trans. to RF and then MGC |
| Ratcliffe | Harry | Pte | 202101 | WIA |
| Ratcliffe | Jonathan | Pte | 16081 | Ex 6th, 8th and 11th Bns. KIA 20/11/17 |
| Ratcliffe | Sidney | Pte | 244531 | Ex Leic. Yeo. |
| Ratcliffe | Thomas William | Pte | 40932 | |
| Rathbone | John Charles | Pte | 37387 | Medals Forfeited |
| Rathbone | Thomas Smith | Sgt | 202784 | MM.KIA 9/6/18 |
| Raven | Thomas | Pte | 2264 | KIA 8/8/16 |
| Rawlinson | John Gilbert | Pte | 3705 | WIA |
| Rawnsley | Arthur | Cpl | 2896 | also 1st and 2/5th Bns |
| Rawson | James | Cpl | 265368 | Also 2/5th |
| Rawsthorne | William Henry | Pte | 3655 | KIA 8/8/16 |
| Ray | Frederick Charles | Pte | 14908 | Also 7th Bn |
| Rayment | Henry Robert | L/Sgt | 1442 | DOW 10/11/17 with 9th Bn |
| Raymond | Lewis | Pte | 41668 | |
| Rayner | Thomas | Pte | 201444 | Ex 1st Bn Trans. to RFC |
| Read | Cecil Herbert | Pte | 41744 | |
| Read | Frederick William | Pte | 41067 | |
| Read | George | Pte | 265364 | WIA |
| Reading | James Francis | Pte | 20409 | Ex 8th Bn |
| Reakes | William Henry | Pte | 42856 | |
| Reay | Robert Herbert | Pte | 201781 | Att. to MGC. POW |
| Reay | Thomas Douglas | Pte | 14504 | Ex 9th Bn |

| Record | Horace Adam | Pte | 203005 | Commissioned into RAF 6/6/18 |
|---|---|---|---|---|
| Redcliffe (Reddicliffe) | William | Pte | 200259 | WIA |
| Reddington | Thomas | Pte | 38643 | Also 8th Bn |
| Redman | Francis Arthur | Sgt | 1674 | WIA. DOW 23/10/16 |
| Redman | Samuel Walter | Cpl | 2331 | WIA |
| Redman | Thomas Alfred | Cpl | 2293 | Att. to TMB |
| Redpath | Ernest | Pte | 202188 | MM |
| Redpath | Herbert Gladstone | Pte | 1824 | |
| Reece | William | Pte | 26134 | Also 7th Bn |
| Reed | Ralph Stanley | Pte | 27296 | Ex Lincs and also 1st, 8th, and 7th Bns |
| Reeve | Charles | Pte | 32571 | |
| Reeve | Jack | Pte | 201737 | WIA |
| Reid | Henry | Pte | 2436 | Trans. to MGC. MM |
| Reid | Jack Reginald | Sgt | 1587 | KIA 20/7/15 |
| Relph | Roland Alfred | Pte | 240532 | |
| Remington | Joseph | Pte | 200720 | KIA 8/8/16 |
| Rennison | Thomas | Pte | 3234 | WIA. Trans. to Monmouths |
| Repton | Albert | Pte | 3681 | |
| Retallick | Edgar | Pte | 241765 | Ex 2/5th. WIA |
| Ribchester | Gabriel | 2Lt | | Transport Officer |
| Ribeiro | Joseph Harry | Pte | 202189 | KIA 18/7/17 |
| Richards | John Thomas | Pte | 200715 | |
| Richards | Walter | Pte | 266212 | Ex KSLI and also 2/5th |
| Richards | William Johnson | L/Cpl | 201070 | KIA 23/4/18 |
| Richardson | Albert | Pte | 1467 | H |
| Richardson | Flatcher (Fletcher) | Sgt | 200079 | WIA |
| Richardson | Francis | Sgt | 2310 | Also 8th Bn |
| Richardson | Frank | Sgt | 2113 | |
| Richardson | Harling | 2Lt | | DCM when Cpl with 7th Bn (Att. from LNL) |
| Richardson | John | Pte | 201130 | |
| Richardson | Robert | Pte | 24340 | Ex 7th Bn |
| Richardson | Soloman | Pte | 200547 | WIA |
| Richardson | Stanley | Cpl | 2194 | WIA. KIA 8/8/16 |
| Rickwood | William George | Sgt | 202192 | Ex 2nd Bn MSM. Band Leader |
| Riddle | Charles | Pte | 201786 | WIA |
| Riding | Edison | Pte | 240352 | Also 2/5th and 1/5th |
| Riding | Harold | Pte | 1217 | WIA |
| Ridings | Sidney | A/CPl | 33403 | Ex 8th Bn |
| Ridings | William | Pte | 201318 | WIA |
| Ridley | Edward Walton | Lt | | Vicar of Ireleth. H |

| | | | | |
|---|---|---|---|---|
| Ridley | Thomas Edwin | Pte | 241859 | WIA. Also 2/5th |
| Ridsdale | John Stables | 2Lt | | |
| Rigg | Arthur William | 2Lt | | CSM—commissioned 1918. WIA |
| Rigg | Frank Pearson | Pte | 3792 | D Coy. KIA 8/8/16 |
| Rigg | George | Pte | 1342 | |
| Rigg | Henry | Pte | 200598 | WIA. POW |
| Rigg | Walter | Pte | 37891 | |
| Rigg | William (Wilkinson) | Pte | 200374 | |
| Riley | Fred | Pte | 201647 | Att. to TMB |
| Riley | John | L/Cpl | 2188 | DOW 29/9/16 |
| Riley | John | Pte | 24159 | Also 11th and 1st Bns |
| Riley | John Robert | Pte | 265744 | Also 1st Bn |
| Riley | Robert | Pte | 201230 | H. D 19/2/17 |
| Rimmer | Ernest | Pte | 201038 | POW |
| Rimmer | Harold | Pte | 200904 | WIA |
| Rimmer | William | Pte | 3493 | D Coy. WIA. KIA 11/9/16 |
| Rimmer | William | Pte | 266012 | |
| Rimmer | William | Pte | 42857 | |
| Ritchie | William | Pte | 201089 | |
| Roach | Robert | Pte | 200032 | H |
| Robathan | Percival Edward | Maj. | | |
| Roberts | Albert | Pte | 265827 | Also 7th Bn |
| Roberts | Charles | Pte | 37103 | |
| Roberts | Ernest | Pte | 28152 | Ex LF and 7th Bn |
| Roberts | Francis Alexander | Pte | 41544 | |
| Roberts | Henry | Pte | 34635 | POW. KIA 12/6/18 |
| Roberts | John | Sgt | 1404 | Trans. to RE |
| Roberts | Joseph | Pte | 202743 | Also 7th Bn |
| Roberts | Philip Connolly | Pte | 2163 | KIA 15/6/15 |
| Roberts | William Henry | Pte | 202210 | WIA. Also 1st Bn as '17551' |
| Robertson | Frederick | Sgt | 1506 | WIA |
| Robinson | Albert Victor | Pte | 22365 | Ex 11th Bn, WIA |
| Robinson | Alfred | Pte | 200078 | Trans. to LC |
| Robinson | Ernest George | Pte | 200229 | MM. WIA. KIA 20/11/17 |
| Robinson | George | Sgt | 1577 | KIA 8/8/16 |
| Robinson | George Walton | Pte | 3080 | KIA 3/8/16 |
| Robinson | George William | L/Cpl | 201785 | WIA (2). DOW 9/9/18 |
| Robinson | Harry | Pte | 2393 | Trans. to MGC. Commissioned into KORL |
| Robinson | Henry | Sgt | 200686 | A Coy. WIA |
| Robinson | James Robert | WO2 | 6791 | |
| Robinson | John | L/Cpl | 243451 | Ex 1/5th. KIA 20/11/17 |

| | | | | |
|---|---|---|---|---|
| Robinson | John | Pte | 200443 | A Coy |
| Robinson | John William | Pte | 201682 | WIA |
| Robinson | Joseph H | Pte | 200514 | Trans. to RE |
| Robinson | Michael Victor | Pte | 201516 | Also 8th Bn |
| Robinson | Norman Roper | CSM | 200392 | H |
| Robinson | Reginald Humphreys | 2Lt | | Ex 1/5th. 4/10/18 |
| Robinson | Robert | Sgt | 2159 | KIA 11/9/16 |
| Robinson | Soloman | L/Cpl | 3583 | C Coy. KIA 8/8/16 |
| Robinson | Stephen | Pte | 28217 | Also 7th Bn |
| Robinson | Thomas | Sgt | 201123 | MM. DOW 9/6/18 |
| Robinson | Thomas William | Pte | 41509 | |
| Robinson | Walton | Pte | 3080 | |
| Robinson | Wilfred | Pte | 42859 | WIA |
| Robinson | William | Pte | 200699 | WIA (3) |
| Robinson | William Gordon | Pte | 244532 | |
| Robson | Frank | Pte | 200695 | WIA. Trans. to Royal Scots Fusiliers |
| Robson | Nicholas | A/CSM | 202194 | Also WO2 with 7th Bn as '13151' |
| Rockliff (Rockcliffe) | William | Pte | 201055 | WIA |
| Rodgers | Augustus Henry | Pte | 33955 | WIA |
| Rodgers | Edward | Pte | 200510 | |
| Rodgerson | John | Pte | 200789 | WIA (3). Posted to 1/5th |
| Roebuck | Frank | Pte | 21150 | Ex 11th Bn, WIA (2). Posted 1/5th |
| Rogers | Arthur Edward | L/Cpl | 10861 | Ex 1st and 8th Bns. KIA 31/7/17 |
| Rogers | John Henry | Pte | 15204 | Ex 9th Bn KIA 31/7/17 |
| Rogerson | Fred | Pte | 18007 | Ex 1st Bn DOW 24/5/17 |
| Rollinson | Albert | Pte | 201448 | WIA |
| Romer | Walter | Pte | 21352 | Ex 7th Bn. WIA |
| Ronson | Thomas | Pte | 21657 | Ex 7th Bn |
| Rooke | Frederick | Pte | 41066 | |
| Rorison | Gilbert | A/CPl | 200337 | C Coy. WIA (3) |
| Rose | Bert | Pte | 27156 | Ex Lincs and 1st Bn |
| Rose | Fred | Sgt | 1721 | WIA |
| Rose | Stanley N. | Pte | 202105 | WIA. Trans. to Lincs |
| Rose | Thomas | Pte | 33597 | A Coy. KIA 30/11/17 |
| Rose | Thomas | Cpl | 202753 | Deserted |
| Roskell | John | Pte | 200872 | WIA. Posted 2/5th |
| Rothery | Frank | Pte | 202108 | DOW 25/11/17 |
| Rothwell | George | Pte | 34666 | DOW 30/11/17 |
| Rothwell | George | L/Cpl | 12073 | Ex 7th Bn. DCM, WIA |
| Rothwell | William | Pte | 41505 | |
| Round | Jack (John) | L/Cpl | 13269 | MM |

| Round | James | Pte | 200813 | WIA |
| Rouse | Irvine Burton | 2Lt | | MC, WIA |
| Rowcroft | Robert | L/Cpl | 266477 | |
| Rowe | Andrew | Pte | 200727 | WIA. Trans. to RE |
| Rowe | George Wallace | Pte | 18058 | Also 8th Bn |
| Rowe | Herbert George Thomas | 2Lt | | |
| Rowe | Samuel | L/Cpl | 23065 | Ex 7th Bn. D Coy. WIA. Posted POW |
| Rowe | Samuel John | Pte | 200714 | WIA. Posted 8th Bn |
| Rowell | James | Pte | 3437 | DOW 25/11/16 |
| Rowland | Robert | Pte | 202103 | |
| Rowland | Thomas | Pte | 1341 | Trans. to Middlesex Rgt |
| Rowlands | Robert Thomas | Pte | 37912 | KIA 18/10/18 |
| Rowlands | William Richard | Pte | 201466 | DOW 22/6/18 |
| Rowlandson | David George | Cpl | 200740 | KIA 20/9/17 |
| Rowlandson | William | Pte | 2897 | DOW 2/10/16 |
| Rowse | James Terrell | Pte | 1883 | KIA 15/6/15 |
| Royle | Joseph | Pte | 3207 | WIA. KIA 25/6/16 |
| Ruberston | Charles | Pte | 38304 | |
| Rudall | W. L. | Lt | | Att. from Lincs |
| Rudduck | Joseph John | Lt | | WIA. DOW 5/6/18 |
| Rudge | Herbert William | Pte | 202107 | DOW 22/9/17 |
| Rule | Robert | 2Lt | | |
| Rundle | James Robson | 2Lt | | DOW 20/11/17 |
| Rusconi | Albert | Pte | 202109 | WIA. D 16/4/19 |
| Rush | Felix | Pte | 201066 | WIA |
| Rush | John | Pte | 38642 | C Coy |
| Rushton | Edward | Pte | 200552 | |
| Rushton | William | Pte | 200277 | WIA (2). Also 1/5th and 1st Bns |
| Russell | Cecil Aubrey | 2Lt | | |
| Russell | Gavin Nichol | 2Lt | | |
| Russell | William James | Pte | 28178 | Also ASC and 7th Bn |
| Rust | Charles | Pte | 41068 | |
| Rutherford | A. F. | Maj. | | RAMC |
| Ryan | Joseph | Pte | 9103 | Also 2nd Bn |
| Ryder | Charles | Sgt | 8223 | Ex 1st Bn, MM |
| Ryder | Frank | L/Cpl | 202209 | Ex 2nd and 8th Bns. KIA 31/7/17 |
| Ryland | George Warrior | Pte | 2058 | DOW 16/6/15 |
| Sadler | Herbert | L/Cpl | 200778 | WIA |
| Saggers | Frederick Charles | Pte | 26836 | Ex KRR and 7th Bn. KIA 9/4/18 |
| Salisbury | William Thomas | Pte | 202224 | |
| Salthouse | Edward | Pte | 201739 | KIA 20/9/17 |

| Sanderson | George W. E. | 2Lt | | WIA. |
| Sanderson | Herbert | L/Cpl | 25365 | Ex 1st and 7th Bns. POW |
| Sanderson | John Graham | Pte | 200970 | WIA |
| Sandham | John William | A/CQMS | 1496 | CQMS B Coy |
| Sandham | William | Pte | 200089 | Trans. to LC |
| Sandilands | Joseph | L/Cpl | 2863 | WIA. KIA 8/8/16 |
| Sandlands | Robert | Pte | 42861 | KIA 8/6/18 |
| Sandwell | David | L/Cpl | 200725 | WIA |
| Sankey | Herbert Edward Forshaw | L/Sgt | 200784 | Commissioned into 5th Bn 25/6/18 |
| Sansome | Thomas | Pte | 27964 | Also 1st and 8th Bns |
| Sarratt | Frederick William | Pte | 34614 | WIA |
| Saunders | Alexander | Pte | 200445 | WIA |
| Saunders | Fred Walter | CQMS | 200193 | WIA |
| Saunders | Frederick George | Pte | 200405 | |
| Saunt | Samuel | Pte | 41039 | KIA 28/4/18 |
| Savage | Edward | Cpl | 200279 | WIA |
| Savage | James | Pte | 201434 | WIA |
| Saville | James Henry | Pte | 2015 | KIA 15/6/15 |
| Sayce | Arthur | Sgt | 30246 | Ex Notts and Derby and 7th Bn |
| Scaife | Henry George R. | 2Lt | | Ex Cpl KLR, WIA |
| Scall (Seall) | Edward | Pte | 201511 | WIA |
| Scargill | John Edward | Pte | 202123 | KIA 13/6/17 |
| Schofield | James | Pte | 201359 | KIA 8/8/16 |
| Schofield | James | Pte | 27739 | Also 8th and 7th Bns |
| Schofield | Robert | L/Cpl | 201386 | WIA (3). Posted 2/5th |
| Schofield | William | Pte | 34605 | WIA |
| Schofield | William | Pte | 202234 | |
| Scotchford | Sidney George | Pte | 235111 | Also London Rgt |
| Scothern | Samuel | Pte | 27037 | Ex Lincs, 1st and 7th Bns. KIA 9/4/18 |
| Scott | Frederick Norman | Sgt | 1727 | Commissioned 26/6/17 |
| Scott | Hugh Seymour | 2Lt | | |
| Scott | James | Pte | 29109 | Also 2/5th |
| Scott | James R. | Pte | 27534 | Also 8th Bn |
| Scott | John Thomas | Pte | 200004 | |
| Scott | William | Pte | 32015 | WIA. Trans. to MGC |
| Scott | William James | Pte | 200161 | |
| Scott-Miller | Edward | Lt | | KIA 14/5/18 |
| Scriven | William | Pte | 200892 | |
| Scrogham | Tom | Pte | 201285 | WIA. Also 8th, 1st, and 7th Bns |
| Scrogham | Willie | Pte | 201136 | WIA. Also 1st Bn |
| Scruton | John William | CQMS | 4172 | Also 7th Bn |

| Scullion | John Henry | Pte | 200305 | H |
|---|---|---|---|---|
| Seabridge | Albert | L/Cpl | 26730 | Ex LF. POW |
| Seager | William John | Sgt | 200558 | |
| Seddon | James | L/Cpl | 20275 | Also 2nd Bn |
| Seddon | William | Pte | 26738 | Ex Lanc Fusiliers. POW |
| Seed | John | L/Cpl | 200851 | A Coy. MM, WIA |
| Seed | Thomas Edward | Sgt | 200829 | Ex 2/5th. WIA |
| Segar | Frank | Sgt | 202160 | Commissioned into KORL 25/9/18 |
| Sellars | Ernest | Pte | 202124 | KIA 18/9/17 |
| Senton | Reginald Mayhew | 2Lt | | WIA. OC D Coy 5/8/17 |
| Settle | Cyril | Pte | 4064 | D Coy. KIA 8/8/16 |
| Severs | Charles | C/Sgt | 200244 | |
| Sewart | Albert James Townley | Pte | 22777 | Ex 8th and 1st Bns. WIA (2) |
| Shakespeare | Fred | Pte | 41510 | KIA 13/8/18 |
| Shallicker | William | Sgt | 202943 | Ex MC and Tanks. WIA. Trans. to LC |
| Sharp | Alexander Strick | Pte | 200083 | KIA 9/4/18 |
| Sharp | Thomas | Pte | 201180 | KIA 8/6/18 |
| Sharp | William | Sgt | 200722 | WIA. Possibly POW |
| Sharp | William | Pte | 29163 | |
| Sharpe | William | Pte | 200545 | |
| Sharples | Gilbert | Pte | 27638 | Also 1st Bn |
| Sharples | Norman | Pte | 266296 | Also Border Rgt and 8th Bn |
| Shaw | Arthur | Pte | 202641 | |
| Shaw | Charles | L/Sgt | 200661 | KIA 11/9/16 |
| Shaw | Handel | Pte | 201656 | |
| Shaw | Robert | Pte | 201402 | KIA 8/8/16 |
| Shaw | Thomas | Pte | 24200 | Also 11th Bn |
| Shaw | William | Pte | 22918 | Ex 11th Bn. KIA 31/7/17 |
| Shaw | William | Pte | 12553 | Ex 7th Bn. KIA 9/7/18 |
| Shaw | Willis | 2Lt | | WIA |
| Sheaham | Alexander Thomas | 2Lt | | Att. from LF |
| Shearman | Joseph | Pte | 200818 | |
| Shearson | Charles | WO2 | 8848 | Ex 1st and 7th Bns. MM |
| Shegog | James | Pte | 40936 | |
| Shelley | Henry James | L/Sgt | 202174 | WIA |
| Shelton | Ernest Henry | Pte | 2328 | KIA 15/6/15 |
| Shepherd | Benson | Pte | 2123 | Trans. to RA and ASC |
| Shepherd | Fred | L/Cpl | 201018 | KIA 20/9/17 |
| Shepherd | George | Sgt | 200484 | MM, MiD |
| Shepherd | John Tyson | L/Cpl | 200603 | WIA. KIA 12/4/17 with 1st Bn |
| Shepherd | Thomas | Pte | 201048 | WIA |
| Sheppard | Charles Thomas | Pte | 41750 | |

| | | | | |
|---|---|---|---|---|
| Sheppard | Ernest Francis | Pte | 26920 | MM. Also LNL |
| Sherley (Sherely/ Shirley) | Frederick Albert | Sgt | 202168 | D Coy. MM, WIA, POW |
| Sherlock | William | Pte | 38645 | KIA 17/5/18 |
| Sherman | Albert William | Pte | 29179 | Ex LC |
| Shipperbottom | Wilfred | Pte | 201417 | POW. DOW 16/6/18 |
| Shipton | Ernest Edward | Pte | 2384 | Ex Glosters |
| Shirt | Wright | L/Cpl | 201740 | POW |
| Shone | Robinson | Pte | 200637 | KIA 31/7/17 |
| Shore (Shaw) | James | Pte | 241120 | Also 1/5th |
| Short | Frederick William | Pte | 26919 | Also 1st Bn |
| Short | Norris | Pte | 15447 | Also 8th Bn |
| Shorthouse | George | Pte | 41746 | |
| Shrimpton | Harold | Pte | 200138 | |
| Shuker | Frederick John | 2Lt | | WIA |
| Shulver | Hugh | Pte | 260009 | Also 1/5th. MM |
| Shute | Henry | Pte | 24465 | |
| Shute | James E. | Pte | 201521 | Trans. to LNL |
| Shutt | Arthur | Pte | 241981 | Also 7th Bn |
| Shutt | Donald Béthune | 2Lt | | WIA |
| Shuttleworth | William James | Pte | 200472 | D Coy |
| Siddall | Harold | Pte | 29112 | Also 1/5th |
| Siddall | Harry | Pte | 26138 | Also 7th and 2/5th |
| Sidebottom | George Alfred | Pte | 201530 | KIA 20/9/17 |
| Sidgreaves | Albert | Pte | 41747 | WIA |
| Siggers | Edward | Pte | 36410 | Also 7th Bn |
| Sills | Victor Sarson | Pte | 244526 | |
| Simm | Joseph | Pte | 265201 | Att. to TMB |
| Simm | James | Pte | 201655 | KIA 28/9/16 |
| Simm | John | Pte | 21068 | Ex 11th and 7th Bns |
| Simmons | Herbert | Pte | 201577 | DOW 20/4/18 |
| Simms | David Stanley | Pte | 41751 | Ex MGC. KIA 7/9/18 |
| Simpson | Arthur | Pte | 4319 | KIA 3/6/17 |
| Simpson | Edward | L/Cpl | 200115 | |
| Simpson | George Edward | Sgt | 200308 | WIA |
| Simpson | James Harper | Lt | | OC D Coy 26/4/18 |
| Simpson | James Ian | Capt. | | MC |
| Simpson | Richard | L/Cpl | 200478 | WIA |
| Simpson | Robert | Pte | 201791 | POW |
| Simpson | Samuel Edward D. | Pte | 201129 | WIA |

| Simpson | Thomas | Pte | 240288 | Ex 5th, 2/5th, and 8th Bns. B Coy. KIA 20/9/17 |
|---|---|---|---|---|
| Singleton | Albert | Cpl | 3416 | KIA 8/8/16 |
| Singleton | John | Pte | 201742 | KIA 1/7/17 |
| Singleton | John Robertson | Pte | 1573 | H. D 19/11/14 |
| Singleton | John Thomas | Pte | 200718 | WIA (2) |
| Singleton | Matthew | Pte | 938 | |
| Singleton | Pearson | Cpl | 200176 | WIA |
| Sixsmith | Albert | Pte | 202493 | |
| Skippon | Charles J. | Pte | 202121 | WIA. Trans. to N. Staffs |
| Skirrow | Horace | Pte | 201922 | POW |
| Slack | John | Pte | 29157 | D 26/4/18 |
| Slater | Arthur Robert | Pte | 41753 | |
| Slater | Elvas (Elias) | Pte | 201427 | WIA |
| Slater | Frederick Charles | Capt. | | Att. from LF. WIA |
| Slater | Percy | Pte | 200491 | Trans. to LC |
| Slater | Richard | Cpl | 200455 | WIA |
| Slater | Wilfred | Pte | 201184 | |
| Slattery | Thomas William | Pte | 201657 | |
| Slaymaker | Herbert Edwin | Pte | 265501 | KIA 27/4/18 |
| Slinger | Fred | Pte | 14385 | Trans. to KLR |
| Slinger | George James | Pte | 240530 | Also 1/5 th and 7th. WIA |
| Slinger | Joseph E. | Pte | 23916 | WIA. Trans. to ASC |
| Sloan | John | Pte | 3563 | SAD 16/7/16 |
| Small | Thomas | L/Cpl | 200841 | WIA |
| Small | William | Pte | 1690 | H |
| Smallwood | Frederick | Pte | 38647 | |
| Smallwood | Harold Joseph | Pte | 38653 | Also 8th Bn |
| Smedley | William | Pte | 201302 | DOW 2/12/17 |
| Smith | Albert Edward | A/Cpl | 2327 | |
| Smith | Alfred Edward | Pte | 42860 | WIA |
| Smith | Arthur | L/Cpl | 27946 | Also 11th Bn |
| Smith | Bernard | Pte | 201026 | WIA |
| Smith | Charles | L/Cpl | 27310 | Ex Lincs and 1st Bn |
| Smith | Frederick James | 2Lt | | WIA |
| Smith | George | Pte | 200231 | WIA |
| Smith | George | Pte | 201743 | WIA. Trans. to LC |
| Smith | George William | Pte | 24309 | |
| Smith | Harold Eric | Pte | 41069 | |
| Smith | Harry | Pte | 4978 | DOW 30/9/16 |
| Smith | Harry | Sgt | 200604 | B Coy. MM. WIA (2) |
| Smith | Harry | Pte | 38284 | Ex KLR |

| | | | | |
|---|---|---|---|---|
| Smith | Henry | Pte | 200179 | WIA. Trans. to RE |
| Smith | Herbert | Pte | 38648 | WIA. KIA 9/4/18 |
| Smith | Hubert | Pte | 13383 | Also 9th Bn |
| Smith | James | L/Cpl | 2477 | DOW 6/6/15 |
| Smith | James | Pte | 202772 | WIA. Ex 1st Bn. KIA 31/7/17 |
| Smith | James | Cpl | 200713 | WIA (3) |
| Smith | John | Pte | 200468 | WIA, POW |
| Smith | John | Cpl | 21753 | Ex 8th Bn. WIA |
| Smith | John Joseph | Pte | 27305 | Ex Lincs KIA 31/7/17 |
| Smith | Joseph Downham | Cpl | 1740 | WIA. Trans. to ASC |
| Smith | Joseph Walter | Pte | 2433 | MM |
| Smith | Nehemiah | Pte | 202117 | WIA |
| Smith | Norman | 2Lt | | A Coy, WIA |
| Smith | Percy | L/Cpl | 1616 | KIA 3/8/16 |
| Smith | Richard Feilding | L/Cpl | 27378 | Ex E. Lancs and also 7th Bn |
| Smith | Robert | 2Lt | | KIA 20/11/17 |
| Smith | Robert | 2Lt | | WIA, POW |
| Smith | Robert | Pte | 11878 | Also 9th Bn |
| Smith | Ronald Charles | A/Cpl | 42862 | |
| Smith | Samuel | 2Lt | | |
| Smith | Sidney | A/Sgt | 200555 | |
| Smith | Thomas | Pte | 17969 | KIA 31/7/17 |
| Smith | Thomas | Pte | 200206 | WIA, POW |
| Smith | Thomas | Pte | 41556 | |
| Smith | Thomas | Pte | 265386 | Trans. to LC. D 13/11/18 |
| Smith | William | Pte | 201375 | WIA. KIA 8/8/16 |
| Smith | William | Pte | 200071 | |
| Smith | William | Pte | 200302 | WIA. Posted 8th Bn |
| Smith | William | Pte | 265376 | Also 1/5th |
| Smith | William | Pte | 38651 | |
| Smith | William Edward | WO2 | 30262 | Ex E. Surreys. DCM |
| Smith | William Henry | Pte | 2479 | |
| Smith | Edward | Pte | 200127 | H |
| Smyth | Alexander | Pte | 22390 | Ex 11th and 1st Bns. 10 Ptn. Deserted and joined RN |
| Smyth | Gordon | Pte | 41749 | |
| Snaith | Henry John | Pte | 200411 | KIA 8/8/16 |
| Snowdon | Lewis Charles | Pte | 202118 | WIA |
| Solari | Anthony | Pte | 202126 | KIA 15/6/17 |
| Southam | John William | Pte | 202114 | |
| Southern | Harold | Pte | 42863 | KIA 26/6/18 |
| Southward | George | Pte | 30148 | Ex 8th Bn. WIA |

| | | | | |
|---|---|---|---|---|
| Spafford | Ernest | Pte | 34960 | Also 8th Bn |
| Speakman | John Davies | Pte | 202662 | WIA. Also 7th Bn |
| Spearing | Edward | Lt | | WIA. KIA 11/9/16 |
| Speight | James | Pte | 33065 | KIA 31/7/17 |
| Spencer | Thomas Ingham | Pte | 265498 | KIA 20/9/17 |
| Spibey | Alfred | Pte | 19363 | Ex 7th and 8th Bns. C Coy |
| Spong | James Bernard | A/Cpl | 29118 | |
| Spooner | Arthur | Pte | 10835 | also 2nd and 1st Bns |
| Springthorpe | Levi | Cpl | 200365 | WIA. Trans. to LC |
| Sprout | Henry | Pte | 200698 | WIA. KIA 16/6/15 |
| Sprout | James | Pte | 2947 | DOW 3/7/15 |
| Sprout | William James | Pte | 200681 | KIA 8/8/16 |
| Stables | Thomas | Pte | 1450 | WIA |
| Stacey | Christopher | Pte | 9890 | Also 2nd Bn |
| Stacey | Herbert | Pte | 40937 | |
| Stafford | Walter | Pte | 26778 | Also 7th and 1/5th Bns |
| Staley | Reginald | Pte | 13747 | Also 9th Bn |
| Stalker | Percy | Sgt | 2488 | MM. Commissioned into RFC 25/9/17 |
| Stamfield | Edwin | Pte | 202116 | |
| Stamper | William Stewart | Pte | 200134 | H |
| Stancliffe | Ben | Pte | 28156 | Ex LF and 7th Bn |
| Standrell | William | Pte | 20366 | Also 11th Bn |
| Stanford | Henry Owen | Pte | 41755 | |
| Stanley | Albert | Pte | 30221 | Ex 7th Bn. WIA |
| Stanworth | Peter | Cpl | 202579 | Ex 7th Bn. KIA 24/8/18 |
| Staples | Albert | Pte | 202111 | |
| Stark | Francis | Pte | 1816 | H |
| Statham | John | Cpl | 15516 | Also 7th Bn |
| Staveley | Jeffrey Dinsdale | Pte | 41662 | |
| Staveley | Thomas | Pte | 37104 | |
| Steel | John | Pte | 201056 | WIA. KIA 31/7/17 |
| Steel | Roger Linton | Sgt | 2383 | KIA 31/7/16 |
| Steel | William | Pte | 265771 | WIA |
| Steel | William G. | Pte | 202113 | WIA. Trans. to LC |
| Steele | Fred | Pte | 201658 | WIA |
| Steele | John James | Pte | 29338 | KIA 24/8/18 |
| Steele | John Peatfield | Pte | 42864 | WIA |
| Steele | Joseph | L/Cpl | 200738 | Att. to RE. POW, KIA 28/4/18 |
| Steele | Joseph Westoby | Pte | 42865 | |
| Steele | Richard | Pte | 26056 | Ex 1st and 7th Bns. KIA 27/4/18 |
| Steele | Sampson | Pte | 27044 | Ex Lincs WIA. KIA 31/7/17 |
| Steele | William | Pte | 202122 | WIA |

| | | | | |
|---|---|---|---|---|
| Steenson | William Henry | Pte | 200982 | KIA 8/8/16 |
| Steeple | Stephen | 2Lt | | WIA |
| Steinthall | Robert Ernest | 2Lt | | |
| Stenchion | John | Pte | 232578 | Ex MCR. WIA. Trans. to ASC |
| Stenhouse | George Anthony | Pte | 201244 | KIA 20/9/17 |
| Stephens | William | Pte | 1571 | |
| Stephens | Leonard J. | Pte | 200496 | WIA. Trans. to LC |
| Stephenson | Edward | L/Cpl | 200498 | WIA. Commissioned into Northumberlands |
| Stephenson | Frederick | Pte | 202758 | Ex 1st Bn. POW |
| Stephenson | James | Pte | 201022 | WIA |
| Stephenson | Thomas | Pte | 27390 | Ex E. Lancs and also 7th Bn |
| Stevens | Alfred Thomas | Pte | 201649 | KIA 20/9/17 |
| Stevenson | Harry | Pte | 202125 | WIA. Posted 1/5th Bn |
| Stevenson | Leonard | Pte | 38646 | KIA 27/4/18 |
| Stewart | Charles | Pte | 32661 | WIA |
| Stewart | Edward | Pte | 200952 | KIA 31/7/17 |
| Stewart | James | Pte | 41748 | Also MGC |
| Stewart | John | Pte | 35036 | Also 1st Bn |
| Stewart | William | Cpl | 3271 | KIA 2/8/16 |
| Stewart | William McKell | 2Lt | | D Coy. MC, WIA |
| Stirrup | Robert | Pte | 201406 | WIA. Also 2/5th |
| Stokes | Harry | Pte | 12677 | Also 7th Bn |
| Stokes | Percival Arthur | Pte | 38649 | |
| Stone | Walter | Pte | 200192 | WIA |
| Stops | Clarence Davis | Cpl | 202169 | WIA |
| Storey | Fawcett | Pte | 2528 | Commissioned 25/9/16 |
| Storey | John | Cpl | 32601 | Also 7th Bn |
| Storey | John | Pte | 1865 | Trans. to MGC |
| Stott | Herbert | Pte | 201293 | MM. DOW 12/5/18 |
| Stowe | Frank | Pte | 200706 | A Coy |
| Stretch | James William | Pte | 26729 | Ex LF and 7th Bn |
| Strickland | George | Cpl | 200836 | WIA |
| Strickland | John | Pte | 3456 | KIA 2/8/16 |
| Strode | William John | L/Cpl | 201650 | KIA 28/9/16 |
| Stuart | Joseph Archibald Cooper | L/Cpl | 32607 | Ex 7th Bn. KIA 9/4/18 |
| Sugden | James | Pte | 29121 | |
| Sullivan | Bernard | Pte | 38652 | |
| Sullivan | Thomas | Pte | 28180 | Also 7th Bn |
| Summerson | Wilfred | Pte | 2031 | WIA. Trans. to MGC |
| Sumner | Fred | Pte | 200938 | Trans. to LC |

| | | | | |
|---|---|---|---|---|
| Surgeoner | James Alexander | Pte | 36416 | KIA 9/4/18 |
| Sutherland | Fred Hugh | Pte | 40934 | |
| Sutton | Bertram | Pte | 19385 | |
| Sutton | Richard | Pte | 37123 | |
| Swainson | Joseph Leonard | Lt-Col. | | DSO. DOW 9/8/16 |
| Swainson | Thomas | Pte | 201054 | KIA 8/8/16 |
| Swarbrick | William | Pte | 201694 | KIA 29/9/16 |
| Swarbrick | William | Pte | 21056 | Ex 11th Bn |
| Sweeney | Albert | Sgt | 240477 | WIA. Also 1/5th |
| Swift | Clarence | Pte | 201653 | Att. to MGC. KIA 31/7/17 |
| Swindells | Harry | Pte | 29122 | Also 8th Bn |
| Swindlehurst | Edward | Pte | 200070 | H |
| Swindlehurst | Joseph | Pte | 1873 | KIA 8/6/15 |
| Sykes | David | Pte | 36519 | WIA |
| Sykes | Harry Roberts | 2Lt | | WIA |
| Sykes | Joe Harry | 2Lt | | WIA |
| Sykes | William | Pte | 2066 | KIA 15/6/15 |
| Symons | Herbert Burrow | Pte | 3002 | D Coy. DOW 14/10/16 |
| Tait | Frederick | Pte | 200700 | Trans. to RE |
| Talbot | Douglas | Pte | 34712 | WIA. Also 2/5th |
| Talbot | Fred | Pte | 201579 | DOW 25/11/17 |
| Talbot | George William | Pte | 40939 | |
| Tasker | James | Pte | 48857 | |
| Tatman | Herbert George Thomas | Pte | 41666 | |
| Tattersall | James | L/Cpl | 24992 | Ex 1st Bn. WIA |
| Taylor | Albert Victor | L/Cpl | 200999 | MM. WIA. DOW 16/4/18 with N. Staffs |
| Taylor | Arthur James | Pte | 266038 | POW |
| Taylor | Cecil Elliot | Pte | 202135 | WIA |
| Taylor | Edwin | Pte | 29123 | |
| Taylor | Geoffrey Fell | Capt. | | |
| Taylor | George Arthur | 2Lt | | MC, WIA |
| Taylor | Henry | Pte | 38303 | |
| Taylor | Henry | Pte | 201676 | |
| Taylor | Hugh | Pte | 34686 | |
| Taylor | James | Pte | 201869 | Also 2/5th and 8th Bns |
| Taylor | James | Pte | 202138 | Also 7th Bn |
| Taylor | James Arthur | Pte | 34643 | DOW 23/9/17 |
| Taylor | John | Pte | 201662 | WIA. KIA 31/7/17 |
| Taylor | John | Pte | 200053 | |
| Taylor | John | Pte | 200856 | WIA. Trans. to ASC |
| Taylor | John Thomas | Pte | 201558 | WIA. Also 8th Bn |

| Taylor | Joseph William | Pte | 11865 | Also 2nd Bn |
| Taylor | Leslie Clifford | Sgt | 1439 | B Coy. DOW 2/7/15 |
| Taylor | Nat Humphries | Cpl | 2388 | KIA 15/6/15 |
| Taylor | Percy Charles | 2Lt | | WIA |
| Taylor | Ratcliffe | Pte | 21702 | Ex 11th Bn MM. WIA (2) |
| Taylor | Robert | Pte | 202128 | Also 7th Bn. Possibly POW |
| Taylor | Robert | Pte | 37066 | |
| Taylor | Robert Alexander | 2Lt | | B Coy 5 Ptn. POW |
| Taylor | Samuel | Sgt | 13053 | Ex 7th Bn. KIA 9/4/18 |
| Taylor | Sydney George | Cpl | 29170 | Ex LC. A/CQMS on demob. |
| Taylor | Thomas Hornsby | Pte | 16275 | Ex 9th Bn. WIA. KIA 9/4/18 |
| Taylor | Walter William | Pte | 2688 | WIA |
| Taylor | William | Pte | 38656 | |
| Taylor | William | Pte | 2542 | Trans. to MGC |
| Temple | Ellison | Pte | 18966 | Ex 9th Bn |
| Templeton | Edward | Pte | 30212 | Ex Border Rgt and 7th Bn. WIA 21/9/16 |
| Templeton | William | Pte | 200221 | Att. to 423 Field Coy RE .WIA |
| Tennant | Arnold | Pte | 201661 | WIA |
| Terry | Richard | Pte | 203086 | Ex County of London Yeo. WIA |
| Tetley | David Arthur | Pte | 38657 | KIA 9/4/18 |
| Theobald | James | Pte | 34624 | POW |
| Thistlethwaite | Frederick John | Pte | 201196 | Also 8th Bn |
| Thistlethwaite | James | A/WO2 | 200019 | KIA 20/9/17 |
| Thistlethwaite | Richard | Pte | 200632 | MM. WIA (2). Posted 1st Bn |
| Thistleton | George | Pte | 3355 | |
| Thomas | Alexander | Pte | 244528 | |
| Thomas | Alfred | Pte | 37116 | |
| Thomas | Evan Vincent | Pte | 42866 | WIA |
| Thomas | John Allan | 2Lt | | |
| Thomas | John W | Pte | 202130 | MM, WIA. Trans. to RFA |
| Thomas | Richard | Pte | 202132 | |
| Thomas | Stanley | Pte | 37112 | |
| Thomas | Thomas Henry | Pte | 42867 | |
| Thompson | Frank | Sgt | 200410 | WIA |
| Thompson | George Thomas | Pte | 200565 | WIA (5) |
| Thompson | Harry | Pte | 266076 | KIA 9/4/18 |
| Thompson | James | 2Lt | | WIA |
| Thompson | James | L/Sgt | 21528 | Also 7th Bn |
| Thompson | John | Pte | 201043 | |
| Thompson | John Henry | L/Cpl | 200381 | WIA. |
| Thompson | Peter | Pte | 15059 | Ex 7th Bn KIA 9/4/18 |
| Thompson | Richard | Pte | 242418 | WIA. Also 1/5th Bn |

| | | | | |
|---|---|---|---|---|
| Thompson | Robert | Sgt | 201703 | Ex 8th Huss. A/ CSM D Coy. KIA 20/9/17 |
| Thompson | Robert | Lt-Col. | | WIA |
| Thompson | Robert S. | Pte | 202226 | WIA. Trans. to ASC |
| Thompson | Thomas | Pte | 10259 | Ex 2nd, 1st, and 11th Bns. DOW 7/5/18 |
| Thompson | Thomas Edward | L/Sgt | 200199 | WIA |
| Thompson | Thomas Sidney | Pte | 3248 | |
| Thompson | William | Cpl | 200125 | WIA |
| Thompson | William | Pte | 265932 | Also 7th Bn |
| Thompson | William | Pte | 2813 | Trans. to MGC |
| Thomson | Adam | 2Lt | | KIA 17/5/18 |
| Thomson | John | Pte | 200475 | |
| Thomson | Walter | Pte | 201792 | KIA 16/10/18 |
| Thorley | Frederick Thomas | Pte | 202127 | Also 9th Bn. WIA |
| Thornborough | William Edward | Pte | 265212 | WIA. Also 2/5th |
| Thornley | James | Pte | 266078 | |
| Thornley | John Moulding | A/Cpl | 200879 | WIA |
| Thornton | Ezra Noel | L/Cpl | 200494 | Trans. to ASC |
| Thornton | William | Cpl | 265390 | |
| Thornton | Willie | Pte | 244527 | Ex Army Cyclists Corps |
| Thorpe | Alfred John | 2Lt | | WIA |
| Thorpe | Charles | 2Lt | | |
| Threadgold | Tom Chaplin | 2Lt | | POW |
| Threlfall | James | Pte | 243067 | Ex 1/5th. WIA. KIA 20/11/17 |
| Thwaite | James | Pte | 29124 | Also 1st Bn |
| Tickle | Fred | Pte | 265388 | WIA. Also 1st Bn |
| Tickle | Thomas | A/Cpl | 1470 | |
| Tildesley | Joseph Henry | Pte | 30222 | WIA. Also 7th Bn |
| Tilling | Frederick William | Pte | 40938 | |
| Tillyard | Eustace Mandeville W. | 2Lt | | |
| Timmis | John | Pte | 2585 | Also 1st, 8th, and 7th Bns |
| Timperley | Thomas M. | Pte | 201580 | Ex 1/5th. KIA 20/11/17 |
| Timson | Alfred Wesley | Pte | 40941 | KIA 23/10/18 |
| Tindall | James | Sgt | 1001 | H. D 17/8/14 |
| Tinsley | John | Pte | 200998 | WIA. Also 8th Bn |
| Tinsley | Walter | Pte | 200911 | WIA. Also 1st Bn |
| Titmas | John St Andrew | Capt. | | RAMC |
| Titterington | Albert George | Pte | 200802 | |
| Titterington | George | Pte | 201821 | KIA 20/9/17 |
| Titterington | Robert Edward | Sgt | 201000 | KIA 20/9/17 |
| Todman | Henry | Pte | 201272 | WIA |
| Tollemache | Archibald Harry | Lt | | |

| | | | | |
|---|---|---|---|---|
| Tomlinson | Arthur | Pte | 201006 | |
| Tomlinson | Fred | Pte | 201435 | WIA. Trans. to LNL |
| Tomlinson | George Alfred | Pte | 42868 | WIA |
| Tomlinson | Herbert | Pte | 1683 | H |
| Tomlinson | James | L/Cpl | 200330 | WIA. KIA 23/4/18 |
| Tomlinson | John | L/Cpl | 200794 | WIA |
| Tomlinson | Mark | Pte | 27402 | Ex LF and also 7th Bn |
| Tomlinson | Richard | Pte | 200830 | WIA |
| Tomlinson | Thomas | L/Cpl | 9683 | Ex 2nd Bn. POW. D 1/11/18 |
| Tomlinson | William | Pte | 200537 | WIA, POW |
| Toms | Edgar | Pte | 244529 | |
| Tongue | John | Pte | 17275 | WIA. Also 1st Bn |
| Tooze | Harry | Pte | 200174 | H |
| Topham | George | Lt | | Att. from LF |
| Topham | James | L/Sgt | 9706 | Ex E. Lancs. DCM. C Coy 11 Ptn |
| Topley | Albert | Pte | 202782 | WIA |
| Topping | Ernest Ford | Pte | 21690 | Ex 8th and 7th Bns. POW |
| Topping | John | Pte | 37120 | DOW 16/4/18 |
| Topping | John | Pte | 3387 | |
| Towers | Henry Quayle | L/Cpl | 200736 | MM. Att. to TMB. DOW 6/4/18 |
| Towers | Joseph | Pte | 1555 | WIA. Trans. to LC. SWB |
| Townshend | Clarence N. | Pte | 29125 | WIA |
| Townson | James | Pte | 10479 | Also 2nd Bn |
| Travis | Fred | Pte | 20991 | Ex 11th Bn   3/6/16. WIA (2) |
| Travis | Robert | L/Cpl | 12847 | Also 7th Bn |
| Travis | William | Cpl | 200402 | POW |
| Trayes | William Frank | Pte | 28225 | Also 7th Bn |
| Trebilcock | James | Sgt | 202211 | |
| Trebilcock | Leonard | Pte | 201121 | Trans. to RE |
| Trewern | William George | Pte | 202131 | DOW 30/7/17 |
| Trimble | Joseph | Pte | 38658 | |
| Tromans | Benjamin | Pte | 200905 | Trans. to LC |
| Tromans | John Thomas | Pte | 41757 | |
| Troth | Daniel | Sgt | 200377 | Commissioned 3/7/17 |
| Troughton | Percy | Pte | 19503 | Ex 7th Bn. WIA (2) |
| Troughton | William | Pte | 201496 | POW |
| Truran | Leonard | Pte | 19315 | Ex 11th Bn 31/7/15. KIA 20/9/17 |
| Tubberville | Albert Edward | Pte | 29181 | Also LC |
| Tucker | Ernest Hugh Trimmell | Lt | | Intelligence Officer |
| Tucker | John Ede | Pte | 202227 | WIA. Also 7th Bn |
| Tullick (Tullock) | William J. | Pte | 202139 | WIA |

| Turner | Arthur Henry | Pte | 40940 | POW |
|---|---|---|---|---|
| Turner | Charles Henry | Pte | 202770 | Ex 1st Bn. KIA 31/7/17 |
| Turner | Francis Henry | Cpl | 202170 | POW |
| Turner | Henry Charles | Pte | 28124 | Ex E. Kent and 7th Bn |
| Turner | Norman | Pte | 42888 | |
| Turner | Thomas | Pte | 200786 | WIA. KIA 8/8/16 |
| Turner | Walter Harry | Pte | 26930 | Also 1st and 1/5th. POW |
| Turner | William | Pte | 202133 | |
| Turney | George | Pte | 24433 | Also 1st and 7th Bns |
| Twidale | Ernest William | Pte | 200369 | WIA |
| Twigg | Frederick | L/Cpl | 8310 | MM. Possibly att. from MCR or LNL |
| Twigg | John Leonard | Pte | 1620 | Ex 1/5th. Trans. to RAMC and Gordons |
| Twynham | Frederick | Pte | 9252 | Ex 2nd, 1st, 8th, and 11th Bns. KIA 20/9/17 |
| Tyer | George Frederick | Pte | 1760 | KIA 27/5/15 |
| Tyrrell | John | Pte | 15017 | Also 7th Bn. DCM |
| Tyson | Clarence | L/Cpl | 200791 | WIA. KIA 12/5/17 with 1st Bn |
| Tyson | John | Pte | 1460 | |
| Tyson | John Edward | Pte | 24266 | Ex 7th Bn. WIA (2) |
| Tyson | John J. | Pte | 1827 | Trans. to LC |
| Tyson | John Ormandy | Pte | 1455 | |
| Tyson | Leslie Urwin | Pte | 26651 | KIA 20/9/17 |
| Tyson | Reginald | Pte | 2281 | KIA 2/7/15 |
| Tyson | Thomas | L/Cpl | 200531 | |
| Tyson | William Edward Towers | Pte | 1510 | |
| Ullock | Henry | Sgt | 200028 | |
| Unsworth | William | Pte | 4166 | KIA 8/8/16 |
| Ure | James | Pte | 29127 | KIA 24/8/18 |
| Uren | William | Sgt | 341 | H |
| Usher | Richard | A/CQMS | 2410 | KIA 8/8/16 |
| Vallance | Frank | Pte | 19913 | Also 2/5th and 11th Bns |
| Varcoe | Thomas Cornthwaite | Pte | 3625 | DOW 28/9/16 |
| Vass | Andrew Charles | Pte | 26097 | Ex 8th Bn. POW |
| Vaughan | Archibald | Pte | 26670 | Ex 8th and 1st Bns. KIA 21/6/18 |
| Veevers | Edgar Samuel | 2Lt | | OC 6 Ptn B Coy. KIA 10/7/18 |
| Venables | Arthur | Pte | 2686 | Trans. to MGC |
| Venables | Walter King | Pte | 201536 | |
| Vent | Ernest | Sgt | 200959 | WIA |
| Verdon | Wilfred Melville | Pte | 242405 | WIA. KIA 1/9/18 with 8th Bn |
| Vernoun | Percy James | Cpl | 202140 | MM. Trans. to LNL |
| Vessey | John William | Pte | 40942 | |
| Vicary | Norman C. | Cpl | 25665 | Also 9th Bn |

| Vickers | Albert E. | Pte | 201289 | WIA. Trans. to LC |
| Vickers | David | Cpl | 200690 | KIA 31/7/17 |
| Vickers | Richard | Pte | 201334 | WIA |
| Vincent | James | Pte | 2225 | Att. to TMB. KIA 31/10/15 |
| Vincent | John | 2Lt | | Att. from Lincs |
| Vity | Harold Dudley | Pte | 201226 | KIA 20/9/17 |
| Voyle | Stanley George | Capt. | | WIA |
| Wade | Leonard | Pte | 202146 | Real name: L. Jacobs. KIA 9/6/17 |
| Wadham | Walter Francis Ainslee | Lt-Col. | | Valuable Services Notice |
| Waites | John | Pte | 2662 | |
| Waitson | Frank | Pte | 200345 | WIA. Also 8th Bn |
| Wakefield | George | Pte | 201182 | MM. Trans. to RDC |
| Wakefield | George Henry | Pte | 200521 | WIA |
| Walder | John | Pte | 27639 | Ex 1st Bn. WIA |
| Walkden | Norman | 2Lt | | WIA. 7 Ptn B Coy |
| Walker | Arthur | Pte | 37068 | POW |
| Walker | Frank | Pte | 200631 | |
| Walker | George Henry | Lt | | KIA 15/6/15 |
| Walker | James Whinray | C/Sgt | 107 | |
| Walker | John | Pte | 2845 | KIA 18/8/16 with 8th Bn |
| Walker | John R. | Pte | 24458 | Also 1st and 7th Bns |
| Walker | Milson | Pte | 38554 | |
| Walker | Richard | WO2 | 200554 | Italian Bronze Medal. A/CSM B Coy |
| Walker | Richard | Pte | 240049 | Also 2/5th |
| Walker | Sidney Frederick | Capt. | | B Coy. WIA (4) |
| Walker | Thomas | Pte | 202755 | WIA |
| Walker | Walter J. | Pte | 202149 | WIA. Trans. to LC |
| Walker | William | Pte | 200391 | WIA |
| Walker | William | Pte | 2012 | Trans. to Lincs |
| Walker | William Harrison | Pte | 29129 | Company-Runner. WIA |
| Wall | Thomas | Pte | 2646 | WIA |
| Wallace | Robert | Pte | 1805 | DOW 2/7/15 |
| Wallbank | Thomas | Pte | 201903 | |
| Walmsley | James | Pte | 33245 | WIA |
| Walmsley | John | Pte | 5027 | KIA 28/9/16 |
| Walmsley | Richard | Pte | 241501 | WIA. Also 1/5th and 8th Bns |
| Walmsley | Thomas | Pte | 243070 | Also 1/5th |
| Walpole | Francis Arthur | Pte | 200975 | KIA 8/8/16 |
| Walsh | Edward | Pte | 200121 | A Coy. Posted 1st Bn. WIA |
| Walter | Charles Henry | Pte | 41072 | |
| Walters | Robert Montgomery | Pte | 2378 | KIA 8/8/16 |
| Waltho | John | Pte | 202142 | POW |

| Walton | Alfred | Cpl | 266273 | Also Cheshires |
| Walton | Christopher | Pte | 202148 | Also 8th Bn |
| Walton | John Henry | Pte | 42872 | D Coy. KIA 24/8/18 |
| Warbrick | Henry James | 2Lt | | B Coy 7 Ptn. WIA |
| Warburton | James | Pte | 201367 | WIA. Also 2nd Bn |
| Warburton | Thomas Edward | Pte | 201247 | MM |
| Ward | Frank | Pte | 32024 | Ex 7th Bn POW. |
| Ward | Harry | Pte | 201668 | WIA. Also 8th Bn |
| Ward | John | 2Lt | | DOW 18/12/15 |
| Ward | Thomas | L/Cpl | 1988 | H. D 31/8/14 |
| Ward | William Ernest | Pte | 40950 | MM. Trans. to Leics |
| Wardle | Alfred | Pte | 201379 | WIA |
| Wardle | James | Pte | 200656 | Trans. to MCR |
| Wareing | Robert | Pte | 48853 | |
| Warren | Walter | Pte | 200316 | |
| Warriner | James William | Pte | 29130 | |
| Wash | Edward | Pte | 200121 | Also 1st Bn |
| Washington | Daniel | Pte | 23042 | WIA (2). Posted 9th Bn |
| Wassall | Albert | Pte | 200779 | WIA. Trans. to LC |
| Waterfall | Samuel Birch | Pte | 29131 | WIA |
| Waters | John | Pte | 16860 | Also 2nd Bn |
| Waters | William Ernest | Cpl | 200153 | WIA (2) |
| Watkins | William John | Pte | 202190 | |
| Watkinson | George | Pte | 200566 | WIA. Trans. to ASC |
| Watson | Ernest | Pte | 202229 | DOW 2/8/17 |
| Watson | George Herbert | Sgt | 202161 | MM. KIA 8/6/18 |
| Watson | Graham | Cpl | 24139 | Also 7th and 8th Bns |
| Watson | William | Pte | 2023 | Trans. to MGC |
| Watson | William John | Pte | 1208 | WIA |
| Watterson | John Henry (Andrew) | Pte | 200408 | DOW 25/4/18 |
| Watts | John Thomas | Pte | 27897 | Ex 11th Bn 25/12/16. KIA 20/11/17 |
| Watts | William George | Pte | 26847 | Also 11th and 1/5th Bns. 15 Ptn D Coy |
| Way | Joseph | Capt. | 1573 | Att. from Scots Gds as RSM. Commissioned 28/12/16. MSM, MiD |
| Waywell | Frederick Charles | 2Lt | | WIA |
| Wealleans | Selby | Pte | 201165 | WIA. Att. to RE |
| Wearing | Harold | Pte | 33956 | Ex 1/5th. WIA |
| Weaver | Robert | Pte | 30223 | WIA. Posted 7th Bn then 1/5th |
| Webb | George Maurice | Pte | 26848 | Also 7th Bn |
| Webb | Joseph | Pte | 28182 | Also 7th Bn |
| Webb | Reginald James | Pte | 32978 | Ex RAVC and also 11th Bn |
| Webber | William John B. | Pte | 203094 | Ex County of London Yeo. Also 7th Bn |

| Webster | Frank | Pte | 2903 | WIA. KIA 11/9/16 |
|---|---|---|---|---|
| Webster | John | L/Cpl | 16872 | Also 2nd, 8th, 1st and 1/5th Bns |
| Webster | Thomas Edward | Pte | 14003 | Also 7th Bn |
| Weedon (Weeden) | Gilbert Richard Charles | Pte | 202153 | WIA, POW |
| Weeks | John Henry | L/Cpl | 862 | |
| Welch | John | 2Lt | | WIA |
| Wells | Cyril William | Pte | 200150 | POW |
| Wells | John | Sgt | 167 | D Coy. WIA |
| Wells | Robert | Pte | 37245 | |
| Wenham | Frederick Charles | L/Cpl | 201158 | KIA 20/11/17 |
| Werry | Frederick William | Sgt | 200210 | |
| Wesencroft | Pearson | Pte | 202152 | WIA. Posted 1st Bn |
| West | William | Pte | 201764 | KIA 20/11/17 |
| Westerdale | Thomas Leigh Barlow | Rev | | Padre. Former Pte RAMC |
| Whalley | Albert | Cpl | 12528 | Also 7th Bn |
| Whalley | Cuthbert | Pte | 200607 | MM. WIA (2). KIA 15/5/17 with 8th Bn |
| Whalley | George | Pte | 13006 | Ex 7th Bn. D 16/12/17 |
| Whalley | Joseph | Pte | 34692 | Ex 7th Bn. DOW 25/4/18 |
| Whalley | Joseph | Pte | 13105 | Also 7th Bn |
| Wharton | L. E. | 2Lt | | Att. from Lincs WIA |
| Wharton | Thomas Henry | Pte | 201308 | Att. to RE. DOW 2/8/17 |
| Wheatley | Arthur | 2Lt | | DOW 8/5/18 |
| Whieldon | Henry | Pte | 24096 | Ex 1st and 7th Bns. WIA. D 21/7/19 |
| Whinfield | Myles | Pte | 2849 | Trans. to and DOW with MGC |
| White | Archibald Hudson | Pte | 202145 | |
| White | Arthur Goodwin | Sgt | 200528 | MM. WIA (3) |
| White | Edwin Thexton | 2Lt | | Ex KLR. KIA 20/9/17 |
| White | Leonard Augustus | Pte | 29190 | Also LC |
| White | Sidney | Pte | 40947 | |
| White | Stanley | Pte | 42874 | |
| White | Thomas | Pte | 1776 | H |
| Whitehead | Ernest | Pte | 29187 | Also LC |
| Whitehead | Fred | Pte | 201665 | Ex MCR. Trans. to ASC |
| Whitehead | John William | Pte | 40951 | |
| Whitehead | Thomas Harold Edward | Pte | 201534 | POW |
| Whitehouse | John James | Pte | 38553 | |
| Whiteley | Edward Oldroyd | Pte | 2526 | WIA (2) |
| Whiteman | Richard Arthur | L/Cpl | 200568 | WIA |
| Whiteside | Henry | Pte | 22770 | Ex 7th Bn. WIA (2) |
| Whiteside | Thomas | Pte | 201788 | DOW 21/9/17 |

| | | | | |
|---|---|---|---|---|
| Whiteside | Walter | Pte | 243098 | Also 7th and 1/5th. Medals Forfeited |
| Whiteside | William Thomas | Sgt | 200734 | C Coy. MM. WIA (2) |
| Whiteway | James | Pte | 3640 | KIA 8/8/16 |
| Whiting | Harry | Pte | 201664 | Also 1st Bn |
| Whiting | Thomas Charles | Pte | 265968 | Ex 7th Bn DOW 12/4/18 |
| Whitmore | Allen Gordon | 2Lt | | WIA (2) |
| Whitnear | Harold | L/Cpl | 1485 | Att. 164 MG Coy |
| Whittaker | Norman | 2Lt | | WIA |
| Whittaker | Walter | Pte | 22934 | Also 11th and 8th Bns |
| Whittall | Charles Edward | Pte | 51861 | Also 7th Bn and Cheshires |
| Whittam | Jackson | Pte | 3308 | WIA. Trans. to LC |
| Whittle | Arthur | L/Cpl | 200885 | WIA, POW |
| Whittle | Reuben | Pte | 200874 | WIA |
| Whittle | Thomas | Pte | 201309 | Att. to RE. KIA 31/7/17 |
| Whitwan | Humphrey | Pte | 202155 | |
| Whitworth | Arnold | Pte | 18290 | Ex 1st and 7th Bns. DOW 28/8/18 |
| Whitworth | Thomas | Pte | 21533 | Ex 7th Bn. POW |
| Wicks | George Frederick | Pte | 265032 | |
| Wicks | William | Pte | 200195 | H |
| Wilcock | Dudley James | Pte | 12427 | Also 7th Bn |
| Wilcock | Edmund Andrew | Pte | 201083 | Also 1st Bn |
| Wilcock | Joseph Mark | 2Lt | | WIA |
| Wilcock | Rufus William | Pte | 202150 | WIA |
| Wilcock | Thomas Herbert | Cpl | 200533 | |
| Wild | Edward | Pte | 3334 | WIA |
| Wilde | John Thomas | Pte | 201667 | MM. KIA 20/11/17 |
| Wilding | George | Pte | 201998 | WIA |
| Wilding | James | Pte | 201368 | DOW 18/9/17 |
| Wiles | Ernest | Pte | 202228 | WIA. Att. to TMB. KIA 9/4/18 |
| Wilkins | Samuel | Pte | 27973 | Also 1st Bn |
| Wilkins | Henry | Pte | 201744 | KIA 20/11/17 |
| Wilkinson | Frederick Henry | Pte | 41661 | DOW 25/8/18 |
| Wilkinson | James | Pte | 30634 | Ex KLR and LC. POW |
| Wilkinson | John | Pte | 1599 | H. D 12/1/15 |
| Wilkinson | John | Pte | 1443 | |
| Wilkinson | Miles | Pte | 200207 | |
| Wilkinson | Thomas William | Pte | 201197 | WIA |
| Wilkinson | Tom | Pte | 200036 | WIA. KIA 8/8/16 |
| Wilkinson | William | Pte | 2582 | WIA. Trans. to RE |
| Willett | Richard | 2Lt | | On det. from LF. KIA 31/7/17 with LF |
| Williams | Alfred | Pte | 200183 | |
| Williams | Charles | Pte | 240960 | |

| Williams | Charles John | Pte | 32928 | Also 1st Bn |
| Williams | Edward | 2Lt | | |
| Williams | Francis Henry | Pte | 34707 | WIA (2). Posted 8th Bn |
| Williams | Frank | Pte | 24403 | Ex 7th Bn. WIA |
| Williams | Frederick | Pte | 2069 | KIA 15/6/15 |
| Williams | George | Pte | 40944 | |
| Williams | Gilbert | Cpl | 1311 | |
| Williams | Harrison | Pte | 201584 | WIA |
| Williams | Henry | Pte | 202212 | Ex 7th Bn. WIA (2) |
| Williams | Hubert Lloyd | Pte | 42878 | WIA |
| Williams | Isaac | Pte | 42879 | |
| Williams | John | Sgt | 2575 | KIA 11/9/16 |
| Williams | John | Pte | 51998 | |
| Williams | Richard Almond | WO2 | 200519 | MC. Commissioned 26/6/17 |
| Williams | Robert | Pte | 1809 | WIA |
| Williams | Robert | Pte | 15696 | Also 7th, 8th, and 1/5th Bns |
| Williams | Robert | Pte | 29160 | |
| Williams | Sidney Theophilus | Pte | 203110 | Ex County of London Yeo. |
| Williams | Stephen | Pte | 200555 | KIA 15/6/15 |
| Williams | Thomas | Pte | 200694 | KIA 9/8/16 |
| Williams | Thomas | Pte | 202151 | POW |
| Williams | Thomas Cromwell Stuart | Pte | 42877 | WIA |
| Williams | Thomas John | Pte | 38787 | |
| Williams | William | Pte | 200307 | WIA. Att. to 164 TMB. KIA 18/3/18 |
| Williams | William | Pte | 42875 | |
| Williams | William Arthur | Pte | 29134 | WIA |
| Williams | William Lawrence | Pte | 202376 | Also 7th Bn |
| Williamson | Edward | Pte | 42880 | KIA 17/5/18 |
| Williamson | Edwin | Pte | 201815 | |
| Williamson | Francis H. | Capt. | | Att. from LF. WIA |
| Williamson | John | Pte | 41496 | |
| Williamson | Thomas | Pte | 202230 | Also 8th Bn |
| Williamson | William | Pte | 1479 | WIA |
| Williamson | William | Pte | 24377 | Ex 11th Bn |
| Willis | Ernest | 2Lt | | |
| Willis | John | Pte | 40948 | |
| Willis | Stanley John | Pte | 202156 | KIA 31/7/17 |
| Willshaw | John J. | Pte | 2955 | KIA 15/6/15 |
| Willshaw | Robert Charles | Pte | 201217 | |
| Willson | William | Pte | 41516 | |
| Wilson | Allen Gordon | Pte | 200626 | KIA 28/9/16 |

| | | | | |
|---|---|---|---|---|
| Wilson | Charles | Cpl | 202193 | Ex 6th Bn. KIA 20/11/17 |
| Wilson | George | Pte | 201025 | WIA. KIA 9/4/18 |
| Wilson | George Edward | Pte | 241531 | Also 1/5th and 7th Bns |
| Wilson | Harry | L/Cpl | 200292 | WIA |
| Wilson | J. Harry | Pte | 3604 | DOW 2/6/16 |
| Wilson | James | Pte | 27544 | Ex 7th Bn. KIA 30/11/17 |
| Wilson | James | Pte | 1466 | |
| Wilson | James | Pte | 242053 | Also 2/5th |
| Wilson | James | Sgt | 200453 | Commissioned 5th Bn 1917 |
| Wilson | James Alexander | Sgt | 392 | |
| Wilson | John | L/Cpl | 3003 | WIA. KIA 28/9/16 |
| Wilson | John St George | Capt. | | RAMC, MC, WIA |
| Wilson | Joseph | Pte | 201049 | KIA 8/8/16 |
| Wilson | Joseph Henry | L/Cpl | 200689 | WIA |
| Wilson | Keith | Pte | 42881 | |
| Wilson | Luke | Pte | 40952 | |
| Wilson | Moses Mark | Pte | 32982 | Ex 11th Bn. WIA |
| Wilson | Percy | Pte | 201670 | WIA. Also 1st and 8th Bns |
| Wilson | William Arnold | Pte | 29136 | DOW 26/10/18 |
| Wilson | William Henry | Pte | 200191 | WIA |
| Wiltshire | Gilbert | Pte | 28230 | Ex 7th Bn. WIA |
| Winder | Harry Gordon | Sgt | 200212 | |
| Winder | Jonathan | Pte | 200660 | WIA, POW |
| Winder | Joseph Henry | Pte | 200592 | KIA 21/7/17 |
| Winder | William Henry | WO2 | 118 | WIA |
| Windle | Leonard | Pte | 2128 | Trans. to KLR and then RE |
| Winnicott | Douglas J. | Cpl | 2552 | Commissioned into Notts and Derby 26/1/16 |
| Winstanley | Bernard Richard | Pte | 201533 | WIA |
| Winterton | Henry | Pte | 41040 | Att. to TMB |
| Withey | Charles Elisha | Capt. | | A Coy. WIA. KIA 20/9/17 |
| Wolstencroft | Samuel | Pte | 26990 | Ex 11th Bn. MM |
| Wolstenholme | Thomas | Pte | 201583 | |
| Wood | Edward | Pte | 2153 | Trans. to Middx Rgt and RDC |
| Wood | Ernest Fred | Pte | 202144 | WIA. Also 1st Bn |
| Wood | George Henry | Pte | 40949 | KIA 26/6/18 |
| Wood | Harry | Pte | 30408 | Ex 1st Bn. WIA |
| Wood | Sam | Pte | 11065 | Ex 2nd Bn POW. KIA 10/6/18 |
| Wood | Thomas | Pte | 29138 | WIA (2) |
| Wood | Philip | Pte | 201397 | KIA 8/8/16 |
| Wood | William | L/Cpl | 200795 | WIA |
| Woodburn | Edgar | Pte | 200088 | WIA. KIA 8/8/16 |

| Woodburn | Frederick G. | Pte | 2795 | Trans. to RE |
| Woodburn | William | Pte | 2047 | Trans. to ASC |
| Woodend | William | Pte | 200793 | WIA. Trans. to LC |
| Woodhead | Charles William | Pte | 200241 | D Coy. WIA. Trans. to 21st Manchester |
| Woodhouse | Ernest Melling | Pte | 200523 | C Coy. WIA |
| Woodruff | John | Pte | 200847 | WIA. To 1st Bn. Reposted 1/4th. POW |
| Woods | Albert Edward | Pte | 203099 | Ex City Of London Yeo. Trans. to RFA |
| Woods | David | Pte | 28131 | Ex LF and 7th Bns |
| Woods | George | Pte | 201557 | |
| Woods | John | Pte | 201779 | Trans. to LC |
| Woods | John Hardman | Pte | 241096 | Also 2/5th |
| Woods | Thomas | Pte | 201356 | WIA |
| Woodsworth | Thomas | Pte | 202245 | Also 1st Bn |
| Woodward | Albert W. | Pte | 2357 | Trans. to MGC, RGA, and Essex |
| Woodward | Edward | Pte | 29139 | |
| Woodward | George | Pte | 200420 | |
| Woodward | John | Cpl | 22376 | Ex 11th Bn. WIA |
| Woodward | Richard | L/Cpl | 1462 | B Coy. KIA 17/8/15 |
| Woodward | Thomas Frederick | Pte | 26590 | Also 7th Bn |
| Woodward | William James | Cpl | 202213 | WIA. Also 7th Bn |
| Wooff | Walter | Pte | 1890 | DOW 19/7/16 |
| Woolcock | Charles Gott | Sgt | 200488 | WIA |
| Wooldridge | Richard | Pte | 29140 | |
| Woolley | Claude | Pte | 265951 | Also 7th Bn |
| Wormall | Richard | Pte | 24306 | Ex 8th Bn KIA 9/4/18 |
| Worrall | Fred | Pte | 42886 | POW |
| Worsley | John | Pte | 51186 | POW |
| Worth | Edward | Pte | 200572 | Att. to RE. WIA |
| Worth | Frederick Henry | Pte | 201153 | DOW 10/8/17 |
| Worth | Joseph | Pte | 23178 | WIA (2). Posted 9th Bn |
| Worthington | Percy | Pte | 42883 | |
| Worthington | Wallace | Sgt | 22063 | Ex 7th Bn. POW |
| Wren | John James | Pte | 23917 | Ex 7th Bn. WIA |
| Wrennall | Richard | Pte | 201546 | |
| Wright | Alexander Allen | Capt. | | KIA 8/8/16 |
| Wright | Alfred James | Pte | 200704 | WIA (3) |
| Wright | Edward | Pte | 200464 | WIA |
| Wright | Frank S. | Pte | 3900 | KIA 16/8/16 with 8th Bn |
| Wright | Frederick John | Pte | 202147 | |
| Wright | George Henry | Pte | 202157 | KIA 31/7/17 |
| Wright | Harold John | Pte | 18866 | Also 7th and 1/5th Bns |
| Wright | James | Pte | 200668 | |

| | | | | |
|---|---|---|---|---|
| Wright | John | Pte | 24566 | Ex Notts and Derby and 9th Bn |
| Wright | Reginald George | Pte | 244530 | |
| Wright | Thomas | Sgt | 200878 | MM, WIA |
| Wright | Thomas | Pte | 200507 | WIA |
| Wyld | Benjamin James S. | Pte | 202763 | |
| Wyncoll | Austen Wrench | 2Lt | | |
| Yare | Arthur William | Pte | 26850 | Ex 7th Bn WIA |
| Yarwood | Fred | Pte | 202231 | WIA. Posted 2nd Bn |
| Yates | Fred Stanley | C/Sgt | 12050 | A Coy HQ Ptn. DCM. Also 6th Bn |
| Yates | James | Pte | 14931 | Ex 7th Bn. KIA 9/4/18 |
| Yates | Sydney | Pte | 29141 | KIA 26/4/18 |
| Yates | William | Pte | 29148 | |
| Young | Alfred | L/Cpl | 10058 | Also 8th Bn |
| Young | Cecil Wilbraham | Pte | 265973 | Also 7th Bn |
| Young | James William | Pte | 201671 | WIA. KIA 20/9/17 |
| Young | Robert Allen | Pte | 200575 | WIA (2). Posted 1st Bn |

# Endnotes

## 1. August 1914 – 2 May 1915: Your King and Country Need You

1    Westlake, Ray, *The Territorial Battalions: A Pictorial History 1859-1985* (London: Guild, 1986), pp. 29-31.
2    Simkins, Peter, *Kitchener's Army: The Raising of the New Armies 1914-1916* (Barnsley: Pen & Sword, 2007), pp. 6-9.
3    *Regulations for the Territorial Force and for County Associations* (London: HMSO, 1908), para. 274.
4    Simkins, p. 11.
5    *Ibid.*, p. 42.
6    *The Barrow News*, 10 October 1914.
7    *The Barrow News*, 12 June 1915.
8    *The Barrow News*, 24 October 1914.
9    Wadham, W. F. A., and J. Crossley, *The Fourth Battalion The King's Own (Royal Lancaster) Regiment and the Great War* (London: Crowther and Goodman, 1935), p. 79.
10   *The Barrow News*, 8 August 1914.
11   Simkins, p. 39.
12   *Ibid.*, p. 156.
13   *The Barrow News*, 10 April 1915.
14   *The Barrow News*, 28 August 1915.
15   *The Barrow News*, 23 January 1915.
16   *The Barrow News*, 6 February 1915.
17   Wadham and Crossley, p. 14.

## 2. 3 May 1915 – 20 July 1915: The Apprenticeship

1    Edmonds, Sir James E., *Official History of the Great War, Military Operations in France and Belgium, 1915, Volume 2*, reprint (Uckfield: Naval & Military Press, 2009), p. 33.
2    *Ibid.*, p. 41.
3    Wadham and Crossley, p. 17.
4    Bewsher, Maj. F. W., *The History of the Fifty First Highland Division 1914-1918*, reprint (Uckfield: Naval & Military Press, 2001), p. 14.
5    *Ibid.*, p. 12.
6    *The Barrow News*, 5 June 1915.
7    *The Barrow News*, 5 June 1915.
8    Bewsher, p. 4.
9    *The Barrow News*, 3 July 1915.
10   Bewsher, p. 19.
11   *The Barrow News*, 26 June 1915.
12   *The Barrow News*, 3 July 1915.
13   *The Barrow News*, 3 July 1915.
14   *The Barrow News*, 3 July 1915.
15   *The Barrow News*, 24 July 1915.

16	*The Barrow News*, 26 June 1915.

17	*The Barrow News*, 15 January 1916.

18	*The Barrow News*, 11 September 1915.

19	*The Barrow News*, 3 July 1915.

20	Edmonds, *Official History of the Great War, Military Operations in France and Belgium, 1915, Volume 2*, p. 97.

21	Bewsher, p. 23.

22	Wadham and Crossley, p. 26.

23	Bewsher, p. 26.

24	*Ibid.*, p. 27.

25	Ainslie, Maj. Graham M., *Hand Grenades, A handbook on Rifle and Hand Grenades* (London: Chapman & Hall, 1917), pp. 12-15.

26	*War Diary of 1/4 King's Own (Royal Lancaster) Regiment*, KO-1017/64 (KORRM).

## 3. 27 July 1915 – 2 January 1916: Pastures New

1	*The Barrow News*, 4 September 1915.

2	Bewsher, pp. 33-34.

3	*The Barrow Guardian*, 2 December 1916.

4	*The London Gazette*, 11 March 1916.

5	*Bewsher*, p. 43.

6	*Ibid.*, p. 43.

7	*Ibid.*, p. 37.

8	*Ibid.*, p. 38.

9	Holmes, Richard, *Tommy: The British Soldier on the Western Front* (London: Harper Perennial, 2005), p. 213.

10	Bewsher, p. 38.

11	*Notes for Infantry Officers on Trench Warfare* (Uckfield: Naval & Military Press, 2008), pp. 34-37.

12	*Ibid.*, p. 40.

13	*63rd (RN) Division. Trench Standing Orders*, second ed. (Uckfield: Naval & Military Press, 2004), p. 12.

14	*The Barrow News*, 23 October 1915.

15	Bewsher, p. 39.

16	*Ibid.*, p. 40.

17	*Ibid.*, pp. 40-41.

18	Wadham and Crossley, p. 43.

19	*Ibid.*, p. 44.

20	*The Barrow Guardian*, 25 March 1916.

21	Bewsher, p. 45.

## 4. 3 January 1916 – 20 July 1916: Old Friends, New Places

1	Wadham and Crossley, p. 49.

2	King's Own Royal Regiment Museum (Lancaster), Kolib 0186/02-556 (Archives).

3	Wadham and Crossley, p. 55.

4	*Ibid.*, p. 56.

5	*The London Gazette,* 14 December 1916.

6	*Amos Beardsley*, WO 374/5036 (National Archives).

7	*Gibbons*, Floyd, *The Red Knight of Germany*, 1st ed. (New York: Garden City, 1927), pp. 283-284.

8	Hutton, John, *Kitchener's Men* (Barnsley: Pen & Sword, 2008), p. 231.

9	*Stanley George Voyle*, WO 374/70731 (National Archives).

10	Atenstaedt, R. L., 'Trench fever: the British medical response in the Great War', *Journal of Royal Society of Medicine*, 99 (2006).

11	*Ibid.*

12	*The Barrow News*, 22 July 1916.

## 5. 21 July 1916 – 30 September 1916: Into the Cauldron

1   *The Barrow News*, 12 August 1916.
2   Wadham and Crossley, p. 60.
3   Reid, Walter, *Architect of Victory—Douglas Haig* (Edinburgh: Birlinn, 2006), p. 225.
4   *Ibid.*, pp. 297-298.
5   Miles, Wilfrid, *Official History of the Great War, Military Operations France and Belgium, 1916, Volume 2*, reprint (Uckfield: Naval & Military Press, 2009), p. 166.
6   *Ibid.*, pp. 174-175.
7   *Ibid.*, p. 180.
8   Philpott, William, *Bloody Victory: The Sacrifice on the Somme and the Making of the Twentieth Century* (London: Little, Brown & Co., 2009), p. 108.
9   Holmes, p. 49.
10  Philpott, p. 94.
11  'Objectives of Battle', *Jeudwine Papers*, 356/FIF/2/2/21 (Liverpool Record Office).
12  'Recommendations for Honours and Awards. New Year's List 1917', *Jeudwine Papers*, 356/FIF/6/2/9 (Liverpool Record Office).
13  *The Barrow News*, 18 November 1916.
14  *The Barrow News*, 2 December 1916.
15  *The London Gazette*, 20 October 1916.
16  *The Barrow News*, 9 September 1916.
17  *The Barrow News*, 19 August 1916.
18  *Ibid.*
19  'Map showing positions and objectives of battle', *Jeudwine Papers*, 356/FIF/2/2/21 (Liverpool Record Office).
20  Miles, p. 181.
21  Interview with Andy Moss.
22  *The Barrow News*, 10 February 1917.
23  *The Barrow Guardian*, 23 September 1916.
24  *Ibid.*
25  *The Barrow News*, 23 September 1916.
26  Miles, p. 379.
27  'Recommendations for Honours and Awards', *Jeudwine Papers*, 356/FIF/6/3/1 (Liverpool Record Office).
28  *Ibid.*
29  *Ibid.*
30  Wadham and Crossley, p. 72.
31  'Statement of Casualties 27 July 1916 – 29 September 1916', *Jeudwine Papers*, 356/FIF6/3/1 (Liverpool Record Office).
32  'Conference Agenda', *Jeudwine Papers*, 356/FIF/2/2/21 (Liverpool Record Office).

## 6. 1 October 1916 – 30 June 1916: The Salient

1   Wadham and Crossley, pp. 75-76.
2   *The Barrow News*, 28 October 1916.
3   *The Barrow News*, 4 November 1916.
4   Reid, pp. 297-98.
5   'Operation Order No. 4' (23 December 1916), *War Diary of 1/4 King's Own (Royal Lancaster) Regiment*, KO-1017/64 (KORRM).
6   *William Birch*, WO 363 (National Archives).
7   *Saul Cohen*, WO 363 (National Archives).
8   *The Barrow News*, 6 January 1917.
9   *The Barrow News*, 20 January 1917.
10  *The Barrow News*, 20 January 1917.
11  *The Barrow News*, 23 June 1917.

12 King's Own Royal Regiment Museum (Lancaster), Kolib 0186/02-561 (Archives).
13 'Recommendations for Honours and Awards', *Jeudwine Papers*, 356/FIF/6/3/1 (Liverpool Record Office).
14 *Ibid.*
15 *The Barrow News*, 23 June 1917.
16 *John Richardson Duke*, WO 363 (National Archives).
17 *The Barrow News*, 17 March 1917.
18 *The Barrow News*, April 7 1917.
19 Moss, A., *The King's Own Royal Lancaster Regiment Blog* (www.Korlr.blogspot.co.uk), 3 February 2012.
20 *The Barrow News*, June 16 1917.
21 'Recommendations for Honours and Awards'.
22 *Ibid.*
23 Wadham and Crossley, Appendix E.
24 Edmonds, *Official History of the Great War, Military Operations in France and Belgium, 1915, Volume 2*, p. xvi.

# 7. 1 July 1917 – 13 September 1917: The Battle of Pilckem Ridge

1 Wadham and Crossley, p. 84.
2 *Ibid.*, Appendix C.
3 *John Crellin*, WO 383 (National Archives).
4 'Operational Order No. 44' (copy No. 11).
5 Coop, Rev. J. O., *The Story of the 55th (West Lancashire) Division* (Liverpool: Liverpool Daily Post, 1919), p. 48.
6 Reid, p. 330.
7 *Ibid.*, pp. 372-373.
8 *Ibid.*, p. 354.
9 Edmonds, *Official History of the Great War, Military Operations in France and Belgium, 1915, Volume 2*, p. xvii.
10 Holmes, p. 55.
11 Edmonds, *Official History of the Great War, Military Operations in France and Belgium, 1915, Volume 2*, p. 386.
12 *Ibid.*, pp. 134-135.
13 *Ibid.*, p. 131.
14 'Narratives of 1/4 King's Own Lancashire Regiment', *Jeudwine Papers*, 356/FIF/2/2/30 (Liverpool Record Office).
15 *Ibid.*
16 'Narratives of 164 Bde HQ', *Jeudwine Papers*, 356/FIF/2/2/32 (Liverpool Record Office).
17 Although Albert Ellwood's after-action report lists the platoon order from left to right, it was battalion norm was to order these from right to left, and a look at the platoon objectives against a map clearly shows that the order typed in the report is in error.
18 'Narratives of 1/4 King's Own Lancashire Regiment'.
19 *Ibid.*
20 *Ibid.*
21 *The London Gazette*, 26 January 1918.
22 'Narratives of 1/4 King's Own Lancashire Regiment'.
23 Martin, Rob., '16 Company 31 July 1917. The Tanks at 3rd Ypres. 31st July 191', *Landships* (https://sites.google.com/site/landships/home/narratives/1917).
24 *Ibid.*
25 'Narratives of 1/4 King's Own Lancashire Regiment'.
26 *Ibid.*
27 *Ibid.*
28 *Ibid.*
29 *Ibid.*
30 *Ibid.*
31 Edmonds, *Official History of the Great War, Military Operations in France and Belgium, 1915, Volume 2*, p. 169.
32 *Ibid.*
33 *Ibid.*, pp. 171-172.

34   'Narratives of 1/4 King's Own Lancashire Regiment'.

35   *Ibid.*

36   *Ibid.*

37   Edmonds, *Official History of the Great War, Military Operations in France and Belgium, 1915, Volume 2*, pp. 172-173.

38   *Ibid.*, p. 174.

39   Floyd, Thomas Hope, *At Ypres with Best-Dunkley* (London: John Lane, 1920), pp. 182 and 203.

40   *The Barrow News*, 11 August 1917.

41   Wadham and Crossley, p. 90.

42   'Narratives of 1/4 King's Own Lancashire Regiment'.

43   *Ibid.*

44   *Ibid.*

45   'Report on Operations of 164th Infantry Brigade', *Jeudwine Papers*, 356/FIF/2/2/39 (Liverpool Record Office).

46   *Ibid.*

47   *Ibid.*

48   'Narratives of 1/4 King's Own Lancashire Regiment'.

## 8. 14 September 1917 – 24 September 1917: The Battle of the Menin Road Ridge

1    Coop, p. 55.

2    'Operational Order No. 52.a', *War Diary of 1/4 King's Own (Royal Lancaster) Regiment*.

3    Edmonds, *Official History of the Great War, Military Operations in France and Belgium, 1917, Volume 2*, reprint (Uckfield: Naval & Military Press, 2009), pp. 245-246.

4    *Ibid.*, p. 266.

5    *Ibid.*, p. 248.

6    'Operational Order No. 52.a', *War Diary of 1/4 King's Own (Royal Lancaster) Regiment*, KO-1017/64 (KORRM).

7    *Ibid.*

8    'Narratives of 'D' Company, 1/4th Royal Lancaster Regiment', *Jeudwine Papers*, 356/FIF/2/2/71 (Liverpool Record Office).

9    Edmonds, *Official History of the Great War, Military Operations in France and Belgium, 1917, Volume 2*, p. 251.

10   'Narratives of 'D' Company, 1/4th Royal Lancaster Regiment'.

11   *Ibid.*

12   *Ibid.*

13   Edmonds, *Official History of the Great War, Military Operations in France and Belgium, 1917, Volume 2*, p. 266.

14   Coop, p. 60.

15   'Narratives of 'B' Company, 1/4th Royal Lancaster Regiment', *Jeudwine Papers*, 356/FIF/2/2/69 (Liverpool Record Office).

16   Unfortunately this could be any one of three 'A. Johnsons'.

17   Martin (https://sites.google.com/site/landships).

18   'Narratives of 'B' Company, 1/4th Royal Lancaster Regiment'.

19   Coop, pp. 60-61.

20   'Narratives of 1/4 King's Own Lancashire Regiment'.

21   'Narratives of 'A' Company, 1/4th Royal Lancaster Regiment', *Jeudwine Papers*, 356/FIF/2/2/68 (Liverpool Record Office).

22   *The London Gazette*, 11 January 1918.

23   *The London Gazette*, 6 February 1918.

24   'Narratives of 'A' Company, 1/4th Royal Lancaster Regiment'.

25   'Narratives of 'B' Company, 1/4th Royal Lancaster Regiment'.

26   'Narratives of 'D' Company, 1/4th Royal Lancaster Regiment'.

27   *Ibid.*

28   *Ibid.*

29   *Ibid.*
30   *Ibid.*
31   *The London Gazette*, 6 February 1918.
32   'Narratives of 'D' Company, 1/4th Royal Lancaster Regiment'.
33   'Narratives of 1/4 King's Own Lancashire Regiment'.
34   *The London Gazette*, 11 January 1918.
35   'Narratives of 'C' Company, 1/4th Royal Lancaster Regiment', *Jeudwine Papers*, 356/FIF/2/2/70 (Liverpool Record Office).
36   *Ibid.*
37   *The London Gazette*, 11 January 1918.
38   'Narratives of 'C' Company, 1/4th Royal Lancaster Regiment'.
39   This may have been either George or Joseph Barnes.
40   'Narratives of 'C' Company, 1/4th Royal Lancaster Regiment'.
41   *The London Gazette*, 6 February 1918.
42   'Narratives of 'C' Company, 1/4th Royal Lancaster Regiment'.
43   *Ibid.*
44   *The London Gazette*, 6 February 1918.
45   'Narratives of 'B' Company, 1/4th Royal Lancaster Regiment'.
46   Coop, pp. 62-63.
47   'Narratives of 1/4 King's Own Lancashire Regiment'.
48   *Ibid.*
49   In the various company and battalion written narratives, three different map references are given for the location of the stronghold on the right flank. When these reports are analysed in conjunction with 13 and 16 Platoon narratives, it becomes evident that all three in fact refer to the same location, a position that Paterson denoted as 'Grid D.13.d. 13.58' in 13 Platoon's narrative and encircled on two of the maps.
50   'Narratives of 1/4 King's Own Lancashire Regiment'.
51   'Narratives of 'C' Company, 1/4th Royal Lancaster Regiment'.
52   *Ibid.*
53   '164 Infantry, 1/4 Royal Lancaster Regiment. Immediate Rewards', *Jeudwine Papers*, 356/FIF/6/6/10 (Liverpool Record Office).
54   *The London Gazette*, 11 January 1918.
55   Edmonds, *Official History of the Great War, Military Operations in France and Belgium, 1917, Volume 2*, pp. 275-276.
56   'Narratives of 'C' Company, 1/4th Royal Lancaster Regiment'.
57   Edmonds, *Official History of the Great War, Military Operations in France and Belgium, 1917, Volume 2*, pp. 276-277.
58   'Narratives of 'D' Company, 1/4th Royal Lancaster Regiment'.
59   'Narratives of 'B' Company, 1/4th Royal Lancaster Regiment'.
60   *War Diary of 1/4 King's Own (Royal Lancaster) Regiment*, KO 1017/64 (KORRM).
61.  'Narratives of 'A' Company, 1/4th Royal Lancaster Regiment'.
62   'Narratives of 'D' Company, 1/4th Royal Lancaster Regiment'.
63   *The London Gazette*, 26 November 1917.
64   'Narratives of 'C' Company, 1/4th Royal Lancaster Regiment'.
65   Wadham and Crossley, p. 96.
66   *Albert George Titterington*, WO 363 (National Archives).
67   *George Titterington*, WO 363 (National Archives).
68   'Narratives of 'D' Company, 1/4th Royal Lancaster Regiment'.
69   'Narratives of 'C' Company, 1/4th Royal Lancaster Regiment'.
70   'Narratives of 1/4 King's Own Lancashire Regiment'.
71   'Narratives of 'A' Company, 1/4th Royal Lancaster Regiment'.
72   'Narratives of 'C' Company, 1/4th Royal Lancaster Regiment'.
73   *Ibid.*
74   'Narratives of 'B' Company, 1/4th Royal Lancaster Regiment'.

75　'Narratives of 'C' Company, 1/4th Royal Lancaster Regiment'.
76　'164 Infantry, 1/4 Royal Lancaster Regiment. Immediate Rewards'.
77　'Narratives of 'C' Company, 1/4th Royal Lancaster Regiment'.
78　*The London Gazette*, 26 November 1917.

## 9. 25 September 1917 – 6 December 1917: Gillemont Farm

1　Coop, p. 63.
2　Miles, Wilfrid, *Official History of the Great War, Military Operations France and Belgium, 1917, Volume 3*, reprint (Uckfield: Naval & Military Press, 2009), p. 44.
3　Coop, pp. 65-66.
4　Miles, *Official History of the Great War, Military Operations France and Belgium, 1917, Volume 3*, p. 44.
5　*Ibid.*, p. 48.
6　'9 November 1917', *War Diary of 1/4 King's Own (Royal Lancaster) Regiment*, KO 1017/64 (KORRM).
7　*Wilfred Goldstan*, WO 363 (National Archives).
8　Miles, *Official History of the Great War, Military Operations France and Belgium, 1917, Volume 3*, p. 3.
9　*Ibid.*, pp. 11-12.
10　*Ibid.*, p. 95.
11　Coop, p. 67.
12　*Ibid.*, p. 66.
13　Records do not survive that unequivocally state who commanded the four companies; however, using a combination of medal citations, company reports, and casualty lists, the allocations cited here are 'probably' correct. Evans's medal citation matches B Company's report very well, and although Ellwood was with C Company on the Salient, the actions in his medal citation fit the actions in A Company's report much better (the style of writing in this report and his one from Ypres is also very similar). Blain could be OC 'D', but his citation matches that of 'C' much better. Who OC 'D' was is much harder to say: Lt Clark was the only officer casualty with sufficient seniority to have filled this role, though the narratives in the reports indicate that he was much more likely to have been commander of 2 Platoon, A Company. It seems that OC 'D' for the day might have been given to one of the new second lieutenants, even though none of these had seen more than seven weeks' active service with the battalion.
14　'Barrage map', *Jeudwine Papers*, 356/FIF/3/1/5 (Liverpool Record Office).
15　'164 Infantry, 1/4 Royal Lancaster Regiment. Immediate Rewards'.
16　*Ibid.*
17　*Ibid.*
18　*Ibid.*
19　*The Barrow News*, 15 December 1917.
20　'164 Infantry, 1/4 Royal Lancaster Regiment. Immediate Rewards'.
21　*Ibid.*
22　*William Hanna*, WO 363 (National Archives).
23　'164 Infantry, 1/4 Royal Lancaster Regiment. Immediate Rewards'.
24　*Ibid.*
25　*Ibid.*
26　*Ibid.*
27　*Ibid.*
28　*Ibid.*
29　*Ibid.*
30　*Ibid.*
31　*Ibid.*
32　*Ibid.*
33　*Ibid.*
34　*Ibid.*
35　*Ibid.*

36  *Ibid.*

37  Coop, p. 71.

38  Miles, *Official History of the Great War, Military Operations France and Belgium, 1917, Volume* 3, p. 96.

39  Coop, pp. 70-71.

40  Miles, *Official History of the Great War, Military Operations France and Belgium, 1917, Volume* 3, p. 96.

41  '164 Infantry, 1/4 Royal Lancaster Regiment. Immediate Rewards'.

42  *Ibid.*

43  Miles, *Official History of the Great War, Military Operations France and Belgium, 1917, Volume* 3, p. 172.

44  Annotations to 'Report of Court of Enquiry', *Jeudwine Papers*, 356/FIF/8/2/2 (Liverpool Record Office).

45  Miles, *Official History of the Great War, Military Operations France and Belgium, 1917, Volume* 3, p. 299.

46  *Ibid.*, pp. 166-167.

47  *Ibid.*, p. 373.

48  *Ibid.*, p. 172.

49  'Letter to General Snow', *Jeudwine Papers*, 356 FIF/8/2 (Liverpool Record Office).

50  Hodgkinson, Capt. A., *The King's Own 1/5th Battalion, TF in the European War 1914-1918* (Lancaster: The King's Own Royal Regiment Museum, 2005), p. 73.

51  Miles, *Official History of the Great War, Military Operations France and Belgium, 1917, Volume* 3, pp. 294-95.

52  Annotations to 'Report of Court of Enquiry'.

53  'Letter from General Jeudwine to General Snow', *Jeudwine Papers*, 356/FIF/8/3 (Liverpool Record Office).

54  Miles, *Official History of the Great War, Military Operations France and Belgium, 1917, Volume* 3, pp. 298-99.

55  *Ibid.*, pp. 300-301.

56  *Ibid.*, pp. 300-301.

57  *Ibid.*, pp. 184-185.

## 10. 7 December 1917 – 8 April 1918: La Bassée Canal

1  *Alexander Smyth*, WO 363 (National Archives).

2  Reid, p. 408.

3  Edmonds, *Official History of the Great War, Military Operations in France and Belgium, 1917, Volume 2*, p. 470.

4  Coop, pp. 85-86.

5  Edmonds, *Official History of the Great War, Military Operations in France and Belgium, 1917, Volume 2*, pp. 470-471.

6  *Ibid.*, pp. 472-473.

7  *Harry Wood*, WO 363 (National Archives).

8  Reid, p. 409.

9  *Ibid.*, p. 424.

10  Edmonds, *Official History of the Great War, Military Operations in France and Belgium, 1917, Volume 2*, p. 477.

11  Reid, p. 428.

12  Edmonds, *Official History of the Great War, Military Operations in France and Belgium, 1917, Volume 2*, p. 161.

13  Coop, p. 91.

14  *William Irving*, WO 363 (National Archives).

15  *Tom Crossley*, WO 363 (National Archives).

## 11. 9 April 1918 – 2 July 1918: 'They win or die who wear the Rose of Lancashire'

1  Edmonds, *Official History of the Great War, Military Operations France and Belgium, 1918, Volume 2*, reprint (Uckfield: Naval & Military Press, 2009), p. 164.

2  Coop, pp. 89-90.

3  Edmonds, *Official History of the Great War, Military Operations France and Belgium, 1918, Volume 2*, p. 168.

4  'Narratives of 55 Division', *Jeudwine Papers*, 356/FIF/3/2/1 (Liverpool Record Office).

5  Latter, Maj.-Gen. J. C., *The History of the Lancashire Fusiliers 1914-1918. Volume 1* (Aldershot: Gale & Polden, 1949), p. 328.

6   Wadham and Crossley, Appendix I.

7   *Ibid.*, p. 117.

8   '164 Infantry, 1/4 Royal Lancaster. Immediate Rewards'.

9   *Ibid.*

10  *Ibid.*

11  *Ibid.*

12  'Narratives of 55 Division'.

13  *Ibid.*

14  '164 Infantry, 1/4 Royal Lancaster. Immediate Rewards'.

15  *Ibid.*

16  *Ibid.*

17  *Ibid.*

18  *Ibid.*

19  *Ibid.*

20  *The London Gazette*, 3 September 1918.

21  *Ibid.*

22  Edmonds, *Official History of the Great War, Military Operations France and Belgium, 1918, Volume 2*, p. 174.

23  Coop, p. 108.

24  Edmonds, *Official History of the Great War, Military Operations France and Belgium, 1918, Volume 2*, p. 170.

25  *The London Gazette*, 3 September 1918.

26  Latter, p. 330.

27  *The London Gazette*, 3 September 1918.

28  Latter, pp. 330-331.

29  '164 Infantry, 1/4 Royal Lancaster. Immediate Rewards'.

30  *Ibid.*

31  *Ibid.*

32  *Ibid.*

33  *Ibid.*

34  *Ibid.*

35  *Ibid.*

36  *George Shepherd*, WO 363 (National Archives).

37  '164 Infantry, 1/4 Royal Lancaster. Immediate Rewards'.

38  'Operations at Givenchy. 9 April 1918. Immediate Rewards', *Jeudwine Papers*, 356/FIF/6/6/39 (Liverpool Record Office).

39  *George Hewartson*, WO 363 (National Archives).

40  '164 Infantry, 1/4 Royal Lancaster. Immediate Rewards'.

41  *Ibid.*

42  *Ibid.*

43  *Ibid.*

44  *Ibid.*

45  Coop, p. 100.

46  Edmonds, *Official History of the Great War, Military Operations France and Belgium, 1918, Volume 2*, pp. 175-176.

47  *Richard Wormall*, WO 363 (National Archives).

48  Edmonds, *Official History of the Great War, Military Operations France and Belgium, 1918, Volume 2*, p. 490.

49  *Frank Knowles*, WO 363 (National Archives).

50  Corrigan, Gordon, *Mud, Blood and Poppycock* (London: Cassell, 2004), p. 173.

51  *John Byrne*, WO 363 (National Archives).

52  Edmonds, *Official History of the Great War, Military Operations France and Belgium, 1918, Volume 2*, p. 359.

53  Coop, p. 125.

54  Edmonds, *Official History of the Great War, Military Operations France and Belgium, 1918, Volume 2*, p. 439.

55  '164 Infantry, 1/4 Royal Lancaster. Immediate Rewards'.

56  *Ibid.*
57  Coop, Appendix K.
58  '164 Infantry, 1/4 Royal Lancaster. Immediate Rewards'.
59  *Ibid.*
60  *Ibid.*
61  *Ibid.*
62  *Ibid.*
63  *Ibid.*
64  Interview with Mr Ivor Holden, the great-nephew of Joseph Steele.
65  *Frank Williams*, WO363 (National Archives).
66  Coop, p. 119.
67  Interview with Andy Moss.
68  The 'Casualty Returns' for May 1918 do not show any casualties for this day, but several verifiable omissions and discrepancies as to the severity and date of injuries between this and other records during this period puts the accuracy of this particular month's return into question.
69  The May 'Casualty Returns' give the 15th as the date for these casualties, but both Commonwealth War Graves Commission and other records have the 14th as the date. In view of the difficult environment that battalion administration work was carried out in at this time, it's more likely that the discrepancies of entries for the 14th/15th and also the 16th/17th are errors in May's 'Returns'.
70  'La Bassée Trench Map', *Jeudwine Papers*, 356/FIF/9/2/15 (Liverpool Record Office).
71  The May 'Casualty Returns' offer the 16th as the day these men were killed and state that 2Lt Thomson plus four other ranks were killed in action—clearly incorrect.
72  Coop, pp. 119-120.
73  *James Clegg*, WO 364 (National Archives).
74  Hodgkinson, p. 90.
75  '164 Infantry, 1/4 Royal Lancaster. Immediate Rewards'.
76  *John Kenyon*, WO 363 (National Archives).
77  *Thomas Haworth, Statement of Wounding, 16 June 1918*, WO 363 (National Archives).
78  '164 Infantry, 1/4 Royal Lancaster. Immediate Rewards'.

## 12. 3 July 1918 – 11 November 1918: The Last 100 Days

1  Corrigan, p. 388.
2  Wadham and Crossley, p. 120.
3  His service record gives the date of wounding as the 9th, though it is unlikely that he would have moved as far along the medical chain as Pernes in one day.
4  A scribbled note on the 'Conduct Page' of his service record gives the date of wounding as 8 July, however, as he was evacuated back to England on that day, he was probably a casualty from this shell on the 7th.
5  Although it was possible that James Lynch was actually in a different battalion, three separate sources allot him to the 1/4th. Other surviving sources, such as *Pension* and *Service Records*, have demonstrated that both the *War Diary* and 'Casualty Returns' are incomplete, particularly around this period of 1918.
6  '164 Infantry, 1/4 Royal Lancaster. Immediate Rewards'.
7  *Ibid.*
8  *War Diary of 1/4 King's Own (Royal Lancaster) Regiment.*
9  The end-of-month 'Casualty Returns' give the date as the 16th, though the *War Diary* specifically states the 15th.
10  The *War Diary* intermittently remarks on outbreaks of 'Spotted Fever', which probably refers to the epidemic of cerebro-spinal meningitis, or, and less likely, a tick or louse-borne disease such as typhus.
11  Coop, pp. 124-125.
12  '164 Infantry, 1/4 Royal Lancaster. Immediate Rewards'.
13  *Ibid.*
14  *Ibid.*

15   *Ibid.*

16   *Ibid.*

17   *Ibid.*

18   *Ibid.*

19   *Ibid.*

20   Frederick Twigg does not appear in the King's Own medal rolls and appears to have been on attachment from the Loyal North Lancashires, though it was the King's Own that recommended his award and his actual recommendation document gives his unit as such.

21   '164 Infantry, 1/4 Royal Lancaster. Immediate Rewards'.

22   *Ibid.*

23   Coop, p. 125.

24   '164 Infantry, 1/4 Royal Lancaster. Immediate Rewards'.

25   *Ibid.*

26   *Ibid.*

27   *Ibid.*

28   The time given in the *War Diary* (1.15 p.m.) is at a variance with *The Aerodrome* website, which gives the time of the first balloon's destruction as 12.25 p.m., and the second—which resulted in its being shot down—as 12.30 p.m. It is highly probable that the *War Diary* gives the time that this was reported and not the actual time of the combat. Therefore, the times given in the narrative are those from *The Aerodrome*.

29   'Louis Bennett', *The Aerodrome* (www.theaerodrome.com/aces/usa/bennett1.php).

30   *The New York Times*, 30 December 1918.

31   '55 Division Narrative of Operations. 24 August – 11 November 1918', *Jeudwine Papers*, 356/FIF/3/3/1 (Liverpool Record Office).

32   Battalion 'Casualty Returns' show no one killed after the 24th, and those from the 24th are all accounted for, so he was probably one of the fifty-eight wounded between 23 and 27 August. His burial at Pernes, location of two CCSs, also supports him dying from wounds.

33   DAH is rather a loose diagnosis referring to chest pains, shortness of breath and irregular heartbeat. The causes could be psychological, brought on by combat stress; or physical, for example, over-exertion or heavy drinking.

34   *Harvey Pullen*, WO 363 (National Archives).

35   Coop, pp. 127-128.

36   '55 Division Narrative of Operations. 24 August – 11 November 1918'.

37   It is possible that he was one of those recorded wounded on the 13th, as the 'Casualty Returns' for 1918 have proved wildly inaccurate at times.

38   *Edwin Newton*, WO 363 (National Archives).

39   'Recommendations for honours and awards. King's Birthday List 1917', *Jeudwine Papers*, 353/FIF/6/3/1 (Liverpool Record Office).

40   *William Edwin Bridge*, WO 363 (National Archives).

41   '55 Division Narrative of Operations. 24 August – 11 November 1918'.

42   *Louis Anderson*, WO 363 (National Archives).

43   '55 Division Narrative of Operations. 24 August – 11 November 1918'.

44   *Ibid.*

45   *The London Gazette*, 1 January 1919.

46   'Recommendations for Honour and Awards. New Year's List 1919', *Jeudwine Papers*, 356/FIF/6/5/13 (Liverpool Record Office).

47   *Form W 3121—William Clark*, King's Own Royal Regiment Museum (Lancaster), Kolib 0186/02-551 (Archives).

48   '55 Division Narrative of Operations. 24 August – 11 November 1918'.

49   *Ibid.*

50   'Report by OC Right Advance Guard 164 Infantry Brigade. 2/3 October 1918', *War Diary of 1/4 King's Own (Royal Lancaster) Regiment*, KO 1017/64 (KORRM).

51   '55 Division Narrative of Operations. 24 August – 11 November 1918'.

52   *Ibid.*

53   *The London Gazette*, 11 March 1919.

54  *The London Gazette*, 17 June 1919

55  'Map of Western Front, March-October 1918', *Jeudwine Papers*, 356/FIF/9/1/2 (Liverpool Record Office).

56  Ogilvie, D. D., *Fife and Forfar Yeomanry* (London: John Murray, 1921), p. 138.

57  *The London Gazette*, 17 June 1919.

58  '55 Division Narrative of Operations. 24 August – 11 November 1918'.

59  *The London Gazette*, 30 May 1919.

60  '55 Division Narrative of Operations. 24 August – 11 November 1918'.

61  *Ibid.*

62  *Ibid.*

## Epilogue

1  *Cornelius Cafferty*, WO 363 (National Archives).

2  *Albert Howarth*, WO 363 (National Archives).

3  *Thomas Rose*, WO 363 (National Archives).

4  King's Own Royal Regiment Museum (Lancaster). Kolib 0186/02-352 (Archives)

5  '20th century Roll of Honour', The King's Own Royal Regiment Museum (Lancaster) (http://www.kingsownmuseum.plus.com).

6  *Alexander Minshall*, WO 364 (National Archives).

7  *Cumbria Magazine*, November 2011, pp. 7-10.

# Bibliography

## Published Sources

*1914-15 Star Medal Roll* (Lancaster: King's Own Royal Regiment Museum, 2005)

*63rd (RN) Division. Trench Standing Orders*, second ed. (Uckfield: Naval & Military Press, 2004)

Ainslie, Maj. Graham M., *Hand Grenades, A handbook on Rifle and Hand Grenades* (London: Chapman & Hall, 1917)

Bewsher, Maj. F. W., *The History of the Fifty First Highland Division 1914-1918*, reprint (Uckfield: Naval & Military Press, 2001)

*British War and Allied Victory Medal Roll. Volume 1* (Lancaster: King's Own Royal Regiment Museum, 2006)

*British War and Allied Victory Medal Roll. Volume 2* (Lancaster: King's Own Royal Regiment Museum, 2006)

Coop, Rev. J. O., *The Story of the 55th (West Lancashire) Division* (Liverpool: Liverpool Daily Post, 1919)

Corrigan, Gordon, *Mud, Blood and Poppycock* (London: Cassell, 2004)

Edmonds, Sir James E., *Official History of the Great War, Military Operations in France and Belgium, 1915, Volume 2*, reprint (Uckfield: Naval and Military Press, 2009)

Floyd, Thomas Hope, *At Ypres with Best-Dunkley* (London: John Lane, 1920)

Gibbons, Floyd, *The Red Knight of Germany* (New York: Garden City, 1927)

Hodgkinson, A., *The King's Own 1/5th Battalion, TF in the European War 1914-1918* (Lancaster: The King's Own Royal Regiment Museum, 2005)

Holmes, Richard, *Tommy: The British Soldier on the Western Front* (London: Harper Perennial, 2005)

Hutton, John, *Kitchener's Men* (Barnsley: Pen & Sword, 2008)

Latter, Maj.-Gen. J. C., *The History of the Lancashire Fusiliers 1914-1918. Volume 1* (Aldershot: Gale & Polden, 1949)

Miles, Wilfrid, *Official History of the Great War, Military Operations France and Belgium, 1916, Volume 2*, reprint (Uckfield: Naval & Military Press, 2009)

*Notes for Infantry Officers on Trench Warfare* (Uckfield: Naval & Military Press, 2008)

—*Official History of the Great War, Military Operations France and Belgium, 1918, Volume 2*, reprint (Uckfield: Naval and Military Press, 2009)

—*Official History of the Great War, Military Operations in France and Belgium, 1917, Volume 2*, reprint (Uckfield: Naval and Military Press, 2009)

Ogilvie, D. D., *Fife and Forfar Yeomanry* (London: John Murray, 1921)

Philpott, William, *Bloody Victory: The Sacrifice on the Somme and the Making of the Twentieth Century* (London: Little, Brown & Co., 2009)

*Regulations for the Territorial Force and for County Associations* (London: HMSO, 1908)

Reid, Walter, *Architect of Victory—Douglas Haig* (Edinburgh: Birlinn, 2006)

Simkins, Peter, *Kitchener's Army: The Raising of the New Armies 1914-1916* (Barnsley: Pen & Sword, 2007)

*Soldiers Died in the Great War—The King's Own Royal Lancaster Regiment* (Polstead. J. B., Hayward and Imperial War Museum, 1989)

Wadham, W. F. A., and J. Crossley, *The Fourth Battalion The King's Own (Royal Lancaster) Regiment and the Great War* (London: Crowther and Goodman, 1935)

*War Office, General Staff. Infantry Training (4-Company Organisation)* (London: HMSO, 1914)

Westlake, Ray, *The Territorial Battalions: A Pictorial History 1859-1985* (London: Guild Publishing, 1986)

## Newspapers, Periodicals, and Webpages

Atenstaedt, R. L., 'Trench fever: the British medical response in the Great War', *Journal of Royal Society of Medicine*, 99 (2006)
*Cumbria Magazine*
*Landships* (www.sites.google.com/site/landships)
*Millom Gazette* 1915-1917
*The Aerodrome* (www.theaerodrome.com)
*The Barrow Guardian* 1914-1919
*The Barrow News* 1914-1919
*The King's Own Royal Lancaster Regiment Blog* (www.Korlr.blogspot.co.uk)
*The London Gazette*
*The New York Times*
www.kingsownmuseum.plus.com

## Unpublished Sources

King's Own Royal Regiment Museum, Lancaster (KORRM)
—Archives
—*War Diary of 1/4 King's Own (Royal Lancaster) Regiment*
Liverpool Record Office
—*Jeudwine Papers*
National Archives
—*Medal Index Cards*
—*Officers' Service Records*
—*Pension Records*
—*Service Records*

# Index